SO-AFU-917

PRAISE FOR *GENERATIONS*

"A uniquely organized oral history, *Generations* gives us voices far more gripping, real, and at times simply more unbelievable than any novel's. Many times I came to the close of a vignette and felt somewhat stunned: I wanted to go on, to hear what happened next. This is a book to be shared among all women, and among men, too."

–Betsy Israel, author of *Grown-Up Fast*

"Superbly edited, the book reads as if the women were talking to you. Highly recommended."

—*Library Journal*

"Women listening to women understand why every detail matters. Miedzian and Malinovich recognize, too, that the best of oral histories are mesmerizing not just because they present a panoramic picture of the past made up of individual snapshots but because they reveal how much startling drama each 'ordinary' life encompasses. Readers, I think, will soon start to forget that these narratives were in essence the fascinating gossip of strangers and will recast them gradually in their own memories as the confidences of flesh-and-blood friends."

—Michele Slung, author of *Momilies: As My Mother Used to Say*

"An extraordinary record of the lives of American women over the course of the twentieth century. . . . Essential reading for historians, sociologists, women's studies specialists, and all those who want to understand the recent evolution of the American family and the complex fabric of women's lives."

—Ruth Sidel, author of *Keeping Women and Children Last*

"This outstanding volume gives voice to the generations of American women in all walks of life. Especially important to me are the stories of working women—well-to-~ volunteers and textile mill workers, doctors and secretaries, cabdrivers and tea~ Their matter-of-fact confidence and dignity in their work echoes through the and speaks to us today."

—Karen Nussbaum, Director, Women's Working Departm~

Generations

Generations

*A Century of
Women Speak
About Their
Lives*

Myriam Miedzian and Alisa Malinovich

Delta
Trade Paperbacks

A Delta Book
Published by
Dell Publishing
a division of
Bantam Doubleday Dell Publishing Group, Inc.
1540 Broadway
New York, New York 10036

In some instances, names and details in this book have been changed to ensure privacy.

PHOTO CREDITS: *Page 3:* National Archives. *Page 19, left to right:* Archive Photos; Library of Congress, Marion Post Wolcott; Archive Photos; Photo courtesy of Adele Smith. *Page 67, left to right:* Magnum Photos, Inc. © 1995 Henri Cartier-Bresson; UPI/Corbis-Bettmann; Archive Photos/London Daily Express; Archive Photos. *Page 137, left to right:* Magnum Photos, Inc. © 1993 Eli Reed; Archive Photos/LeGwin; Magnum Photos, Inc. © 1985 Eugene Richards; Magnum Photos, Inc. © 1988 Leonard Freed. *Page 207:* Magnum Photos, Inc. © 1968 Costa Manos. *Page 219, left to right:* Corbis/Bettmann; Photo courtesy of Adele Smith; UPI/Corbis-Bettmann; Archive Photos. *Page 261, left to right:* Archive Photos/Lambert; Photo courtesy of Mary Jane Smith; Photo courtesy of Hettie Jones; Archive Photos. *Page 323, left to right:* Reuters/Lou Damatteis/Archive Photos; Archive Photos; Magnum Photos, Inc. © 1990 Eugene Richards; Magnum Photos, Inc. © 1995 Susan Mieselas. *Page 387:* Photo courtesy of Paul Fusco. *Page 399, left to right:* Archive Photos/Lambert; UPI/Corbis-Bettmann; Photo courtesy of Adele Smith; Archive Photos. *Page 441, left to right:* Archive Photos; Archive Photos/Lambert; Reuters/Corbis-Bettmann; Archive Photos/Express Newspapers. *Page 495, left to right:* UPI/Corbis-Bettmann; Magnum Photos, Inc. © 1984 Eli Reed; Photo courtesy of Matthew Salacuse; The Stock Market, © Michael Keller.

Copyright © 1997 by Myriam Miedzian and Alisa Malinovich

All rights reserved. No part of this book may be reproduced or transmitted in any form or by any means, electronic or mechanical, including photocopying, recording, or by any information storage and retrieval system, without the written permission of the Publisher, except where permitted by law. For information address: The Atlantic Monthly Press, New York, New York.

The trademark Delta® is registered in the U.S. Patent and Trademark Office and in other countries.

ISBN: 0-385-33325-0

Reprinted by arrangement with The Atlantic Monthly Press

Manufactured in the United States of America
Published simultaneously in Canada

November 1998
10 9 8 7 6 5 4 3 2 1
FFG

With gratitude to the women

who made this book possible

by sharing their stories

for Nadia

This book is divided into three main parts: Growing Up, Family, and Work. Each of these sections is in turn divided into three generational periods: The First Generation, women born from 1900 to the early 1930s; The Second Generation, women born from the mid 1930s to the early 1950s; The Third Generation, women born from the mid 1950s to the mid 1970s. Throughout, longer stories are followed by a series of shorter stories grouped around common themes. In addition, the reader will find three life stories, each placed before the book's three main parts.

Contents

FAMILY

Work:
The Third Generation 495

Acknowledgments

Our deepest thanks go to Eric Ashworth who brought us together with our editor, Anton Mueller. Our thanks also go to Neil Olson who succeeded Eric at Donadio and Ashworth, and was always there when we needed help. This book took nearly five years to create. We are grateful to our editor, Anton Mueller, who stood by us as we progressed from casual lunches to frenzied office meetings and around-the-clock phone calls over piles of seemingly endless manuscript which was worked, reworked, and then worked again. And hats off to his assistant, Lissa Smith, whose cheerful disposition and tireless efforts on the part of the manuscript were of immeasurable value. In addition, we would like to express our special thanks to Nadia Malinovich, who read countless interviews as well as large chunks of the edited manuscript and offered useful commentary. We would also like to thank Bonnie Anderson whose suggestions have helped to clarify the structure of the book.

Before we had interviews to edit and edited interviews to choose from, we had the challenge of finding a diverse group of women who were willing and able to tell us their stories. Friends, relatives, acquaintances, and perfect strangers were enormously helpful in assisting us with our search. Because they are so numerous, and in order to protect the anonymity of those interviewees who requested it, we offer a general statement of thanks—without the extra time that so many people took out of their days to look up a number, brainstorm, or make a phone call, we wouldn't have had a book. And to those people who went above and beyond our greatest expectations, making numerous phone calls and doing serious legwork, we are especially grateful.

The rest of our thanks are separate.

Myriam Miedzian

I was very fortunate in finding someone as competent, reliable, and accurate as Robin Vaccai-Yess to transcribe my interviews. During the time that she worked for me, Robin went from being a single woman to a married mother of two. So when, at the end of our project, our editor, Anton Mueller, suggested adding a contemporary high-tech birthing story to contrast with some of the older women's stories, I turned to Robin. Her vitality and sense of humor are obvious in that story as well as in her supermarket story. My thanks also go to Alexandra Wall, who did an excellent job with research and computer work.

I am deeply grateful to my husband, Gary Ferdman, for his unwavering moral support throughout the project and his patience through the final months when everything was put on hold and he often referred to himself as the "book widower." I also want to thank him for reading and commenting on the introduction to the book.

Alisa Malinovich

My first thanks go to my cousin Lynne Maietta, whose early enthusiasm for and willingness to assist me with the project went unmatched. As the interviews piled up, I became eternally grateful to Robin Aabel—mother, llama raiser, and transcriber extraordinaire. Her work was thorough, and I always enjoyed our conversations. Towards the end I appreciated the help of Elissa Descoteau, Claudia Mogel, and Ariana Speyer, who read and commented on large chunks of the manuscript. To Bonnie Anderson, my gratitude for being the first reader of the preface. Finally, I would like to thank my dad and the relatives, friends, and housemates past and present who offered their love and support on what often seemed like an endless journey.

Preface

BY ALISA MALINOVICH

In the summer of 1992, Anton Mueller at Grove/Atlantic met with my mother to suggest an idea for a book proposal he was excited about. He'd been thinking, he explained, about the extraordinary differences between the lives of his grandmother, mother, and sister, and he envisioned a book that would capture—through a collection of narratives—how American women's lives have changed over the past century. Intrigued by the idea but hesitant to undertake a task of such breadth while remaining committed to her work on violence prevention (her first book had been out just over a year and she was busy lecturing and writing on the topic), my mother considered the possibility of my coauthoring the book with her. After all, she thought, it would make perfect sense for a mother and daughter to embark on this project together. I'd bring a different perspective to it, and the youngest women might feel more comfortable with and be able to open up more easily to me.

I remember standing in the kitchen of my mother's apartment, thinking about what an amazing opportunity it would be. Of course, the idea of entering into a long-term project with my mother in the dawn of my twentieth year sent a vague wave of anxiety rippling through my chest. I was on the brink of adulthood, and these years were supposed to be (this part always makes my mother laugh) the time to "individuate." But I am blessed with a mother who, for as long as I can remember, has taken me seriously as a person and as a writer. I believe it is that faith in and respect of me that (despite undeniable moments of panicked claustrophobia) carried our successful partnership through.

The project had immediate appeal and made sense to me: My summer job was that of kindercamp counselor at the Westside YMCA in Manhattan (a place that reflected the world I'd grown up in), and indeed I'd been struck by the enormous changes that had taken place since my own childhood. Working mothers were now the norm, and nannies and fathers were major presences in the drop-off/pick-up scene (though dads were generally seen doing morning drop-offs on their way to work). The landscape felt radically different from the sea of moms I remembered dropping us off and picking us up in the mid to late seventies.

At the same time that I was interested in finding out more about the changes that had taken place in my own world, I was excited about the prospect of interviewing women whose lives and backgrounds were very different from my own. I can remember performing in my summer camp's version of the feminist musical *Free to Be You and Me* as a ten- or eleven-year-old child and hearing my mother complain about the way the mail always came addressed to "Dr. and Mrs." (she'd earned her doctorate years before my father earned his). All my life I'd been surrounded by people who were familiar with feminism, and although I'm sure I also spent time with people who weren't, we never discussed the subject, so that the difference wasn't revealed to me. I'll never forget my surprise when, at the end of an interview, I asked a seventeen-year-old girl in the Bronx what feminism meant to her, and she responded by saying, "Feminist? I think it means you're feminine. Nice, polite, sitting proper. More of a girl than a tomboy." I felt sort of like Dorothy in *The Wizard of Oz*—"Toto, I don't think we're in Kansas anymore."

My mother and I didn't attempt a scientific study or a random sampling of American women, but we were committed to achieving diversity with regard to race and ethnicity, class, and sexual orientation. We wanted to interview women in different parts of the country and in a wide range of professions. We also thought it would be interesting to trace women's experiences in certain careers through the century, and we therefore interviewed doctors, nurses, and lawyers in each generation. At the same time we were not looking for women with any particular experiences. We did not seek out women who had been raped or abused, just as we did not seek out women who had been happily married.

Only toward the very end of the project, in an effort to fill in some historical gaps, did we choose fewer than ten women based on specific stories that we wanted them to tell. Among them were Sybil Jordan Hampton, who told of her experiences as one of the first black students at Little Rock Central High School; Linda Pesso, who spoke about her life as a wartime bride and suburban homemaker in the 1950s; and Robin Vaccai-Yess, who described high-tech birthing in the 1990s.

The agreement from the start was that I would interview the bulk of the younger women, and my mother would do the remainder. I ended up doing between a quarter and a third of the book and—for reasons that made practical sense—we both occasionally crossed over into each other's age group. We interviewed women in the rural and urban Northeast, and although we made separate trips to places that included Colorado and the Washington, D.C., area, we did the major traveling for the book together. Our first big trip was out west, where we both interviewed women in Southern California. My mother continued up north, while I caught a plane back to New England to start my junior year of college.

The following summer we flew to Louisiana, and from there we rented a car, driving north with stops along the way. Being the northerners (and New Yorkers) that we are, we were quite excited to reach the Mississippi border, and we stopped the car on the side of the road to take pictures at the state line. The South was intriguing in many ways, and, despite warnings we'd gotten about southerners being wary of northerners and especially writer-types from New York, we found the southern women we interviewed and the many people who helped us to be across-the-board friendly and open.

The geographic diversity of the women interviewed was amplified by the fact that many women had moved one or several times during their lifetime. A young woman in Michigan (our final destination) described her childhood in New Jersey; an older woman in California described her courtship in Indiana. In addition, we conducted a number of telephone interviews with women in places we did not travel to.

To find the broad range of women we were interested in interviewing, we networked in lots of different ways. I handed out flyers to supermarket cashiers. A friend of mine leafleted the mailboxes of students in her department at college. My mother contacted a friend who runs a marketing research firm and obtained permission to call women who had been in focus groups. To begin finding women down south, we began with three major contacts and watched them grow like the branches of a tree—the head of a nonprofit organization put us in touch with five women on his board, and they in turn provided us with access to countless others; a New York City friend put us in touch with a southern relative of hers who led us to several of his women friends; a young woman who had spent a couple of years as a student in Louisiana gave us the number of a well-connected friend who still lived in the area. Each potential interviewee was a potential resource, and thanks to the combined effort of so many people, we wound up with a diverse group of women who had many stories to tell.

The older women were asked to focus largely on their younger days rather than on their present lives, so that their experiences as young and middle-aged women could be compared with the experiences of young and middle-aged women in later years. We ultimately conceived of the women interviewed as spanning three generations. The first generation, born from 1900 to the early 1930s, was—except for the fact that it often influenced their thinking and altered the course of many of their children's and grandchildren's lives—the least affected by the late twentieth century women's movement. The second generation, born from the mid 1930s to the early 1950s, was old enough to have developed to a significant extent before the movement, but young enough to have their lives affected by it. And the third generation, born from the mid-1950s to the mid-1970s, is essentially post–women's movement. The oldest of them came of age in its heyday.

Of course, in the end, space limitations did not allow for every woman interviewed to appear in the book. It was hard to put fascinating material aside. We can only share our disappointment with the women whose stories do not appear here and offer our assurance that they enriched our understanding. Analysis in the introduction is based on all of the interviews conducted, and in some cases women whose stories do not appear in the body of the book are quoted there.

I learned so much, in so many ways, from the experience of conducting these interviews. It was an exercise in self-restraint to sit with a person for one or two or four hours and listen to her relay experiences and share opinions to which I could not respond. Often I held back the impulse to bounce back with an experience of my own that related to hers or to question an assumption that she made. But in holding back my own responses, I am quite sure that I learned more than I would have from a dialogue of equal length. For the women knew that they were being listened to, not judged, and that it was my intention to hear their experiences and their opinions out, not to respond to or comment on them. In the end I learned a tolerance and surprised myself with the extent to which I could understand where virtually all of the women—some of whom might have been my friends in "real life" and others of whom I would probably never have crossed paths with—were coming from.

There are, of course, those who are unreachable, and when I think of the women I interviewed, I always remember one who turned me away saying, "My life is too horrible to talk about." When we do oral history, we present the stories of those who are willing to tell them, and it seems important to consider the impact that has on who is represented. In the end these women inspired and taught me things. They were open and trusting, and I was amazed at the energy and perseverance that so many of them had in the face of incredible hardship. I can see all of their faces in my mind, and I remember the worlds that they drew me into. There's a sort of magic that happens when you put on the tape recorder and allow someone to talk—their words so often come out like poetry and teach us things that we may already know, but that so often, we forget to remember. I hope that some of that magic is transmitted in the pages to come.

Introduction

BY MYRIAM MIEDZIAN

*A*t the beginning of the twentieth century a woman's life expectancy was fifty-one years. Women did not have the right to vote, and if a married woman worked outside of the home (only five percent did), in many states the law awarded her husband complete control over her salary. Sex and pregnancy were considered so embarrassing that they were rarely talked about and many pregnant women never went out in public after they started to show.

As we approach the twenty-first century, it seems fitting to stop and take note of the extraordinary journey women have traveled over the last hundred years. In recent decades, volumes have been written on women's history, and endless polls, question-naires, and research studies have focused on the contemporary American woman. As a result our knowledge has been greatly enriched. But there are different ways of know-ing. Listening to women tell stories of their own lives, uninterrupted by analysis or comment, of what it was like in 1920, 1950, or 1990 to grow up, to go to school, to fall in love, to work and raise children, permits us to capture the detail, emotions, and com-plexities of life as experienced. The stories compiled here make women's history and the lives of contemporary women come alive in a way that writing about them or com-piling statistics cannot.

Never before in human history has change occurred as rapidly as in this century. The oldest women to tell their stories in the following pages were born at a time when the country was largely rural and agricultural, when electricity was a luxury and mov-ies were silent, and when the desegregation laws of the civil rights movement were still fifty-odd years in the future. To travel twenty miles was a day's journey by horse and buggy. Divorce was scandalous and rare, and many women wore corsets so tight that they sometimes led to fainting spells. Skirts had to cover the ankles, and makeup was worn almost exclusively by prostitutes. Of course, there were always people who broke the rules—for instance, one woman in her eighties tells us that already at the turn of the century her socialist parents and their friends considered marriage bour-geois and simply lived together.

The end of the First World War and the onset of the 1920s brought change on a major scale. Women won the right to vote, and many young women rebelled against

Victorian culture. Flappers scandalized their neighbors by wearing short skirts, bobbing their hair, putting on makeup, and smoking. But the enjoyment of these newfound freedoms was soon dampened by the 1928 stock market crash and the ensuing Great Depression of the 1930s. Now we hear stories of poverty and hardship, and of the hope aroused by Franklin Roosevelt's promises to create jobs for tens of millions of unemployed Americans. The depression is followed by the upheavals and tragic losses of World War II. The war also brings major changes in women's work. In order to replace the men who are off fighting, women in large numbers are recruited for jobs that had previously been closed to them.

As the century progresses, sexual and social mores continue to change, and by the 1940s and '50s a generation of teenage girls is jitterbugging at high school dances and "making out" in the backseats of cars. These young women tend to marry very young and often have children by the time they are twenty. Their daughters' and younger sisters' stories carry us through the social and cultural upheaval of the sixties and seventies —they take us to Woodstock and Haight-Ashbury, to pro–civil rights and anti–Vietnam War demonstrations. Many of them and many of their mothers and older sisters are deeply affected by the women's movement and in large numbers embark on careers and lifestyles undreamt of by the oldest women. The youngest group of women to tell their stories grow up during and after these upheavals. Many of them have divorced parents. Marriage and children are no longer their primary life goals. Becoming a doctor, lawyer, or policewoman is normal, and so is teenage sex.

The century-long life span covered by these stories gives us a sense of how deeply each generation takes for granted the social and cultural environment in which it was raised. In the last thirty years, the rate of social and cultural change has been so dramatic that many women have been caught in between, starting out with one set of attitudes and then shifting to a completely different perspective. Take Jane Foley, born in New Orleans in 1919. Jane talks about how it never occurred to her until the civil rights movement that there was anything wrong with African-Americans having to sit in the back of the bus, or not being allowed to sit at the same lunch counters as white people. She comments, "Years later, you look back and think, 'How can I have just accepted this without question when it's so inhuman, so insulting, and so wrong?' It never occurred to me that there was anything wrong with this! . . . It was the way things were."

Perhaps if I were younger, I would have been perplexed by Foley's blindness, or even suspicious of her sincerity, but I had no trouble relating to what she was saying.

As she spoke, I could see myself back in the early sixties picketing Woolworth's on 109th Street and Broadway in New York City in support of the desegregation of Woolworth's lunch counters in the South. I was picketing against racial injustice, but at the same time I never questioned the fact that I was not allowed to teach at Columbia College solely because I was a woman. I was working on my doctorate in philosophy at the time, and instead of a ten-minute walk to work, I spent close to two hours a day commuting to Brooklyn College, a far less selective and prestigious college than Columbia. How could I with all my philosophical training, with my constant questioning of everything (or so I thought), with my awareness that some of the male graduate students teaching at Columbia were less qualified than I—how could I not have given a thought to this injustice that affected me so deeply. I simply had a different blind spot from Jane Foley's.

Anna Davis also had a blind spot. She tells us that when she first went to work at a printing company in 1966, "a man automatically started with more pay than a woman. We were programmed at that time that that's the way it was. We didn't think about it."

Just as the civil rights movement made Jane Foley and millions of others realize that it was unfair for African-Americans to have to sit at the back of the bus, the women's movement made me and millions of others question what we had taken for granted. "Why wasn't I allowed to teach at Columbia?" I started to wonder. "Why don't women get paid as much as men for equal or harder work," Anna Davis began to ask.

"I don't think any of us could have changed without the women's movement," says Rachel Morgan, who is in her fifties. Like so many women of her generation, Rachel's attitudes toward marriage, family, and work began to change radically after her major life decisions had already been made. She eventually left her very traditional marriage— "I remember marrying him and thinking . . . he needed somebody to take care of him, and I could do that." By the early seventies, tired of being his "satellite," she was working full-time and had a "growing sense of autonomy." Many women, especially those born in the 1930s and '40s, found their lives thus interrupted and were able to begin anew.

The sweeping scope of the book and the dramatic changes it chronicles provide us with a picture of progress that is anything but simple. Because they capture so vividly the conditions and details of daily life, these stories deepen and render more nuanced our understanding of the journey women have taken over the century. When it comes to work, for example, contrasts are sometimes drawn between contemporary women who work and pre-seventies women who did not. In earlier times, women presumably had ample time to spend with their children, and took pleasure in decorating their homes and cooking meals. Our opening story, told by Bernice Stuart Snow, is enough to cure us of any tendencies we might have toward such simplistic notions.

As we hear Bernice describe her mother's life in South Dakota at the beginning of the century, growing food, canning, cooking, cleaning, washing, ironing, sewing clothes and "quilts and quilts and quilts," it becomes clear that except for a small group of wealthy women who had servants, women have always worked, without salary, often from morning to night to maintain their families, which were often very large. It was only during a brief post–World War II period that an extraordinary level of prosperity and new technology—washing machines, dishwashers, vacuum cleaners, canned and frozen foods—gave some working and middle-class homemakers the opportunity for leisure.

Even upper-class American women have often worked as volunteers. By the late nineteenth century many of them were involved in creating and working as volunteers in settlement houses. Eventually, their work became professionalized, and the field of social work came into being. Since then, women have been heavily involved as volunteers in political campaigns, in PTAs, or just in responding to a variety of cultural and humanitarian causes. Suzanne Havercamp, who is in her fifties, describes how when her children were little, she and a few friends got together and started a nursery school from scratch. Suzanne is also typical of many older women in that she worked until she was married and had children, and then continued to work part-time and occasionally full-time outside the home. Some older women with children returned to work after they were widowed or divorced.

Some women, especially working-class and African-American women, have always worked outside the home. Some worked in factories; others did piecework at home. Some served as maids, cooks, or washerwomen for wealthy families. For African-American women, housework was often the only option. But whatever they did, working women were almost invariably relegated to the lowest-paying jobs. Lucille Thornburgh's experience is typical. During the depression, when her father was unable to earn a living, she and her six siblings supported the family. By the time she was twenty years old, Lucille was working a ten-hour day as a spinner in a lint-filled Knoxville textile mill. She tells us that "weaving was the best-paid job, but only men could be weavers."

For older, college-educated women, being relegated to lower-paying jobs took a different form. As late as 1970, women were still either barred from professional schools such as law, medicine, and business or were admitted in very small numbers. Those few exceptional women who went against the tide overcame cultural and academic barriers, and made it in were often treated as second-class citizens. Elana Wiseman, who started medical school in 1961 recalls, "Everybody kept saying, 'You're using up a slot for a man; this is not a profession for women.'" Regardless of talents or interests, teaching, nursing, and social work were considered the proper professions for college-educated women. Miyako Moriki, who is in her fifties, is typical of many older women: "I have a degree from the University of California in teaching," she tells us, "and I was never meant to be a teacher."

But while women were traditionally allowed to become teachers, until the 1940s this was for many a short-lived career. Jean Hughes, who was born in 1923 in Montana, tells us, "My mother had been a schoolteacher, but when she married, that was the end of that. Women were not allowed to teach after they were married." According to a National Education Association survey in 1930, seventy-seven percent of U.S. school districts would not hire married women as teachers, and sixty-three percent fired women if they married. More generally, Bernice Stuart Snow tells us how when she was married, in 1937, she had to give up working—"married women could not work." Bored, with nothing to do, she did eventually get a job—"I didn't tell him I was married."

During the depression, in order to preserve jobs for men, many states passed laws forbidding married women to work. While a 1942 governmental nondiscrimination directive reversed restrictions on the employment of women, enabling them to take over jobs left vacant by men who were drafted to serve in World War II, other discriminatory laws remained in existence. In some states, women were still not allowed to serve on juries. Some limited women's inheritance from a husband without a will to one-third of his property, while granting widowers complete control over a deceased wife's real estate. In some states husbands continued to have control over the earnings of their wives and minor children. It wasn't until 1979 that a Louisiana law giving the husband control over property earned by either spouse was repealed. Janet Riley, a retired law professor from Loyola University in New Orleans, who appears in the Work Section of this book, played an instrumental role in that historic case.

By the early to mid-seventies, enormous changes had started to take place. College women were no longer pressured to become teachers. New doors were opened, and women were encouraged to take themselves seriously professionally. For previous generations, a profession was often viewed as a form of insurance—something to fall back on in case one was widowed or divorced—rather than a goal in itself.

The changes have been remarkable. For example, in 1970, women earned 5.4% of all law degrees and 8.4% of all medical degrees. By 1993, they were earning 42.5% of all law degrees and 37.7% of all medical degrees. How did these changes occur?

The forces that eventually led to this historical transformation are many and complex. Hazel Akeroyd, who worked in a munitions factory making bullets during World War II, tells us that after working in the war effort, "Women were never the same. They had had a taste of independence, freedom, surviving on their own." Indeed, some historians have suggested that World War II work experiences either directly or vicariously played a role in the rebirth of feminism in the 1960s. When Betty Friedan published *The Feminine Mystique* in 1963, she gave a voice to many women of her generation who were beginning to realize that after the war ended, women had been unduly pressured to give up their jobs and the independence that comes with getting one's own paycheck. In order to make room for returning vets, a major cultural campaign had been launched glorifying the role of full-time homemaker and mother. While some enjoyed that role, many others felt stifled by it.

But even before the feminist movement took hold in the late sixties and early seventies, the conformity and traditions of the past decades had begun to come under attack. The sixties brought the civil rights movement, the anti–Vietnam War movement, and more generally the questioning by many of traditional Judeo-Christian values, including those associated with sex. It was in this atmosphere of increased possibilities that many women began to question some of the attitudes and restrictions that continued to limit their freedom.

By the late 1960s, after a forty-year lull, what is often referred to as the second-wave women's rights movement came to the forefront of change. The first-wave movement had started in the mid-1800s with the Seneca Falls, New York, convention in which more than two hundred women and forty men declared, "We hold these truths to be self-evident, that all men and women are created equal." While many of those present feared going as far as actually demanding that women be given the right to vote, Elizabeth Cady Stanton persuaded them to do so. With the strong leadership of women such as Stanton, Susan B. Anthony, Ernestine Rose, and many others, the first-wave movement worked not only for women's right to vote, but also to rescind numerous discriminatory laws and practices. By the beginning of the century they had succeeded in getting many states to pass laws giving women the right to control their earnings and inherited property. Their biggest victory came in 1920, when they succeeded in getting women the right to vote. In 1923, the National Women's Party—originally a women's suffrage organization—introduced an Equal Rights Amendment to the Constitution, which would have banned all discriminatory legislation and practices, but it never passed. At that point, many of the militant feminist organizations disintegrated, and women's rights stagnated.

The second-wave women's movement of the sixties and seventies focused a major part of its energy on winning equal rights for women in education and at the workplace. Its major instrument for change was the 1964 Civil Rights Act, which was originally intended to remedy racial injustice at the workplace. Howard W. Smith, a southern segregationist senator, had added a provision against sex discrimination. He apparently thought that if the bill were saddled with such an unpopular cause as women's rights, it would surely be defeated. But the bill ended up passing, and a new federal agency, the Equal Employment Opportunity Commission (EEOC), was established.

Elizabeth Russell, at the time a high school teacher in the Deep South, tells us that in 1966 when she was passed over in favor of a less qualified man to be departmental supervisor, she went to the EEOC to file a complaint and was told, "We're under court order for integration, but that does not apply to gender." Her experience was typical. The agency's initial focus was almost exclusively on racial discrimination. But soon, newly founded feminist organizations such as the National Organization for Women (NOW) began to exert intense pressure on the EEOC to focus on discrimination against women and also to amend the Civil Rights Act to include educational institutions. They were successful on both counts. They filed hundreds of complaints about sex discrimination in education, and by the early to mid-1970s, professional schools were forced to open their doors to women.

Women now had the option, if they wished, of becoming a doctor instead of a nurse, an attorney instead of a legal secretary. Very quickly the gender makeup of the professional schools began to change. Major victories were also won in the workplace. Common practices such as airlines firing female "hostesses" if they got married or reached the age of thirty-two, and newspaper help-wanted listings being divided into "Male" and "Female" headings were judged to be illegal. Crafts unions such as carpenters and plumbers unions, which previously did not accept women, were now forced to admit them.

Women started to enter professions they had been barred from. Much of the time, they were not exactly warmly welcomed, and in some cases they still aren't. Cynthia Rhodes is in her thirties and for the last eight years has been a project manager supervising the construction of public utilities such as water mains and sewers. She got the job in part because new laws—aimed at undoing past discrimination—required that in New York, any state or federally funded contract give a percentage of work to businesses owned and run by minorities or women. She tells us, "We work for towns, basically, and if it's a town we haven't worked in and I walk into a town meeting, you can feel the tension. I'm introduced as the person you deal with—and the looks! They totally doubt me." But Cynthia goes on to do the job, and invariably she comes to be accepted. Her story captures both the progress that women have made and the prejudices that hinder that progress. Many women still encounter negative attitudes, discrimination, glass ceilings, and lower salaries, but unlike earlier times, they don't accept these as normal.

The contrast between the attitudes and expectations toward work of women who came of age before the seventies and those who came of age after is striking. Take Miyako Moriki and her daughter Kim. Miyako, who got a teaching degree even though she had no desire to teach, never did enter the profession. Instead, she got married at the age of twenty-one, had three children, and has held a variety of jobs including working for the police department and managing a bookstore. She now works part-time in a shopping mall—"I rent strollers, direct traffic, answer the telephone. . . ." Miyako has held many jobs but has not had a career.

Her daughter Kim is an illustrative artist in her thirties who loves her work—"When I'm working, I feel such a rush of ecstasy." She is not in a hurry to get married—"I don't feel marriage is a must because I have my illustration work"—and is uncertain about children.

While the contemporary focus on work is thought to be particularly pronounced among upper-middle-class women, among the young women we interviewed the emphasis seemed to pervade all social classes. Young women of working- and middle-class background, often wary of divorce and irresponsible fathers, put great value on financial independence. Danielle Biasini lives in the Bronx, where she was born in 1975. She says, "My father left when I was one or two. For all I know, he could be dead. I don't think I would just want to stay home with my children; I'm more than that. And I want to be dependent on myself because if my husband ever picks up and leaves, I'll have something to fall back on." Danielle's attitude is a far cry from that of Anna Davis, who was born in 1941 in Poughkeepsie, New York, and has done factory work most of her life. Anna recalls that when she was Danielle's age, "I had that fairy tale idea. I wanted to be married and have four children, stay home and raise my kids." Anna got married when she was eighteen. When her two children were very young, she tells us, "my husband just said one night he didn't want to be married anymore. I raised the kids by myself; I didn't get any help from him—$25 a week."

For someone like Lucille Thornburgh, "the women's movement is the best thing since sliced bread." She explains, "I got so tired of that discrimination—it wasn't only in the unions and the factories, it was everywhere." While her level of enthusiasm is obviously not shared by all, our interviews strongly confirm what polls have shown, that while many women don't like to identify themselves as feminists, a large majority of American women fully accept many of the major goals of the movement such as equal job opportunity and equal pay. The unwillingness to identify oneself as a feminist seems to be related to the fact that the term is associated with what is viewed as extremism—systematic man hating, too much emphasis on lesbianism, a devaluation of femininity and mothering, too much stridency. After expressing a distaste for the movement's stridency, some women would comment that perhaps without it change might not have taken place. Most, even when they were critical, also had something positive to say about it. Carolyn Vance Smith, a professor of English literature, described attending a professional conference in the late 1970s. The women on one of the panels had just come from a NOW conference, and she was appalled to find that "they were all dressed in men's suits, men's ties, and had what we called then butch haircuts. I found that absolutely ridiculous. If they were for women's rights dressed like men, that made no sense to me." But Carolyn then went on to applaud the fact that thanks to the women's movement, outstanding women writers of past centuries are now being read in English literature classes. "When I was an English Lit. major we never heard of people like Mary Wollstonecraft who was writing a vindication of the rights of women in the 1700s." Suzanne Havercamp thought that sexual harassment had gone too far. "This crybaby attitude, it gets to me after awhile. Somebody looks at you cross-eyed, it's now sexual harassment," but then she also said, "Wonderful things have happened because of the women's movement. The aspiration of a woman to the Supreme Court—I mean, wow. Isn't that magnificent!"

While many young women were aware that they owed their newfound rights and opportunities in large part to feminists who had fought for them, a considerable number were uninformed about the changes of the last thirty years or didn't ascribe them to feminism. Some had never heard of feminism (the phrase "women's movement" was a bit more familiar), while others associated it only with the extremism described above. The disparity between identifying as feminist and accepting the major goals of the movement was sometimes startling. Chrissy Robinson, in her twenties, laughed when feminism was mentioned and said, "You mean femi-nazis?" But when asked about the effects of the women's movement, she responded, "I guess it had an effect because now a working woman is highly acceptable. Look at me being a single mother; in the sixties that was unheard of. Now it's acceptable, and I think it's great. I love being able to support myself, getting any job I want if I am qualified." When asked, "So you don't think of all that as feminist?" she responded, "I don't know."

Chrissy feels free to be a single mother; Kim Moriki, the artist illustrator, is not sure she wants to marry; many young women marry at a much later age than their mothers. Feminism has much to do with these new attitudes, but so, too, do the changes that have taken place in women's lives with respect to sexual mores. The two are deeply interrelated. In earlier times, Chrissy as a single mother and "lost woman," would have been socially ostracized to the point that it would have been difficult if not impossible for her to find desirable work. She might not have had any choice but to put her child up for adoption. An unmarried woman in her thirties like Kim might very well have had to pay for her independence and devotion to work by sacrificing her sexuality and leading a celibate life. The difference in the sexual mores of the oldest and youngest women who tell their stories is dramatic.

Most of the older women told us that they were virgins when they married or had had sex only with their future husbands. Until the late sixties, if a young, unmarried woman got pregnant, most often it led either to a "shotgun wedding" or to her being sent away from home until after she gave birth and put the child up for adoption. The shame associated with being unmarried and pregnant was enormous. Bernice Stuart Snow, who was born in 1915, tells us that when a girl got visibly pregnant at her high school, "the school called an assembly. . . . They said that they wanted to correct misinformation going around, and that this student had a nine-pound tumor in her stomach. It wasn't long after that that she disappeared for a while and then came back slim as a rail." Most young women disappeared before their "tumors" became so large.

Getting rid of Victorian hypocrisy, including the denial of equal rights to gay people, the repression of female sexuality, the subjection of young women to profound humiliation if they got pregnant—the young men who got them pregnant suffered no such humiliation—was truly liberating. The introduction of the birth control pill in 1963 was an important factor in making sexual freedom a reality. Christina Martin, born in 1957, remembers in a very positive way going on the birth control pill when she was a freshman in college. "I found [Planned Parenthood] the most amazing place. . . . There was counseling, and you were educated. It wasn't like they just handed that stuff over. Planned Parenthood was a port in every city."

While they would undoubtedly find the traditional restrictions on female sexuality unacceptable, a good number of young women related experiences that suggest that the sexual revolution has been a mixed blessing. Rachel Goldman, born in 1970, says, "I know so many women who have been date raped, so many women who get pressured to have sex by their boyfriends. . . . A lot of times the decision-making process is not about them, it's about pleasing their partner." While many young women seem to enjoy their sex lives, Rachel's comments are echoed by others, like Jillian Schwartz, who tells us, "I've definitely felt with boys that they wanted sex more than I did. I've been in situations where I did not want it, but I was always really afraid to stop them."

The dubious assumption that seems to underlie today's sexual mores is that female and male sexuality are identical. But this is taken to mean not that boys' sexuality is identical to that of girls', but that girls' sexuality is identical to that of boys'. Since most teenage boys seem to want nothing more than to have sex, then the same must be true of teenage girls. But for many of the women whose stories we hear in the following pages, this just doesn't seem to be true.

So while the old rules may have been oppressive, they did provide many young women with a form of protection. Shotgun weddings and sudden disappearances testify to the exceptions, but as a rule nice girls didn't go all the way. It was simply inappropriate for boys to pressure girls beyond petting. The intense fear of pregnancy and the classic dating rituals described by many of the older women created a protective environment. Rene Bailey, who is in her sixties, explains that her parents "had to meet that boy. The boy . . . wasn't allowed no further than the living room. . . . He was sitting there just like a frog sitting on a log. On the weekend, you could go to the movie, and you had to be back home by ten o'clock. The boy felt like, if he didn't want to be run out of the city, he had to have you back by that time because your parents would be sitting there waiting for you." Another factor that makes some of today's young women more vulnerable is the use of alcohol and drugs. While there has always been a lot of drinking—our interviews make it crystal clear how serious a problem alcoholism has been and continues to be for many Americans of all ages—several of the older women's comments suggest that the boys used to drink more than the girls. That no longer seems to be as true.

While the sexual revolution and the new problems it brings are by no means due solely to the second wave of feminism, there is nevertheless a tendency for some who deplore what they see as its excesses to associate them exclusively with feminism. Helen Schiffrin, who is in her eighties, is typical in this respect: "I think the women did it to themselves with this women's lib. I don't like what's going on sexually with these young women today. The men talk about them as if they were a piece of meat. I think women got more respect before."

But if the women's movement is blamed by some older women for what they perceive as excessive sexual freedom, virtually all the women interviewed applauded the many changes brought about by the movement with respect to dealing with rape, wife battering, and sexual harassment. Until the early 1970s, wife battering and sexual harassment were not issues of public concern. They were viewed as private problems that women had to put up with or deal with on their own. "She probably asked for it," was a common attitude and one that was prevalent even in regard to rape. It was also commonly believed that as much as they might protest, deep down women wanted to be raped. I still remember hearing jokes based on the idea that "If you're going to be raped, you might as well relax and enjoy it."

By the mid-1970s a lot of this had changed. Feminists had opened hundreds of rape crisis centers and battered women's shelters. By 1986, they had brought the first sexual harassment case to the Supreme Court, which judged unanimously that the sexual harassment of an employee by her supervisor was a violation of the Civil Rights Act. A number of women we interviewed, like Gina Rotundo, who is in her forties, spoke about the beneficial effects of these changes—"Now the girls don't stand for it. . . . They have organizations for women's rights they can call. I wish I had that support when I was twenty." Some felt that the notion of sexual harassment had gone too far, but still thought it was completely unacceptable for an employer or supervisor to pressure an employee to have sex. And while a number of older women deplored our high divorce rates and thought that many younger couples were unwilling to sacrifice and work to keep their marriages alive, even the most conservative among them believed that if a woman is physically battered by her husband, she is justified in leaving him. This represents quite a change from the days not so long ago when battered wives were advised to grin and bear it. In fact, a number of the stories told here suggest that women's newfound economic independence has permitted many who would have been trapped in earlier times to leave their abusive husbands. Unfortunately, the stories also indicate that wife battering and rape are still prevalent.

Probably more than any other issue, the perceived denigration of mothering by the women's movement and its effect on children concerned many women, including some like Ruth Mandel, who consider themselves feminists. Ruth is in her forties. She is a lesbian and was artificially inseminated by her best friend's husband's sperm and is raising her son with her partner. She explains, "After he was born, all I wanted to do was nurse my baby and hang out with him for a few years. I had friends, they absolutely thought I had lost my mind. . . . They're career mothers, heavy feminists who gotta get to work. I'm very much a part of the feminist movement, but I don't like a lot of the attitudes of the feminist movement towards raising a child."

For some women the emphasis on work at the expense of children was enough to turn them completely against the movement. Elaine Scovill is in her sixties. She says, "I thought it was very wrong to try and make women feel they had to work to be something, because I felt I was something—I was a good mother. My one daughter had a number of problems going through school, and I spent a lot of time with her, and she has commented since, 'I don't know what I would have done, Mother, if you hadn't been there to help me.' If I was working, she would have ended up being a truant. Some of these parents just don't have the time to pay that close attention." Listening to Scovill, I could not help but think of Gina Rotundo (a divorced mother of two children), who worked in the restaurant business and for years came home very late. She says, "They were latchkey children. My daughter was in charge. . . . Jake doesn't like school. . . . He's fifteen, and he still doesn't have good study habits. It's probably my fault for working so much."

Between 1960, and 1994 divorce rates increased by over 100%, and births to single mothers by about 400%, with the largest increases by far taking place between 1960 and 1970, before the women's movement was a major influence.

For those millions of children whose mothers are single or divorced, the common condition—captured in so many of our interviews—of having a mother who works full-time and an absent or minimally involved father, is especially fraught with difficulty. The situation seems to be eased considerably when grandparents or other relatives live nearby, but often in our highly mobile society they do not.

The fact that a majority of women today work outside the home, including mothers of young children, cannot be attributed solely to the women's movement, or to increases in divorce and single mothering. Real salaries have gone down since the 1960s, and even many married women don't have the option of being full-time mothers. In addition, between advertisement-induced consumerism and the high cost of many entertainment and educational products such as computers, stereo equipment, and video games, parents and children today seem to need more money than they did in the past. Our interviews also suggest that parents no longer rely on their teenage children to contribute to household costs. When today's teenager works, it is often for spending money; when children play a major role in helping with housework, parents often pay them for doing so. By contrast, older women spoke of helping with housework without any thought of payment, and when they worked outside the home, it was assumed that their earnings would go mainly to the household.

A recent survey of 250,000 women carried out by the U.S. Department of Labor's Women's Bureau found that "balancing work and family" was the top concern. The stories told here make this concern come alive. Many of the mothers who appear in these pages, single, divorced, or married, lead lives that are nothing short of heroic. Just listening to accounts of their daily lives left me feeling dazed and sometimes incredulous. I raised two daughters while working part-time, with a supportive husband, and I still found it to be by far the most exhausting, demanding period of my life. In fact, the only time in my life that I felt the need, with some regularity, to have a drink before dinner was when my younger daughter (now my coauthor) was two and her sister was six. So how do these women survive? I kept wondering. Year after year, they spend eight hours and more a day or night (quite a few mothers we interviewed work night shifts) working, often an hour or more commuting. Their day begins with getting the children ready for day care or school. After work, they pick up the children, and either make dinner or get fast food. They give baths to younger children, help older ones with homework, deal with temper tantrums and squabbles between siblings, do dishes and laundry. Weekends are spent doing more laundry, housecleaning, shopping, taking the kids to Little League, swimming lessons, or a friend's house.

Many of the working mothers we interviewed rarely get more than five hours of sleep a night. Kim Faggins, a divorced mother of three, had been working an overnight job with mentally handicapped adults and commuting about two hours each way. She tells us, "Sometimes I would get four hours of sleep, sometimes I would get six hours. I would never, ever get eight hours of sleep—never, ever, ever. . . . I was tired all the time." She said, "Sometimes I'd fall asleep driving on the highway, and I'd catch myself." While it is usually more difficult for a single mother to manage, even when both parents are involved, it is often too much when they have demanding work. Elana Wiseman, now in her fifties, married a fellow medical student, and they soon had two children. She explains, "I just got exhausted. . . . I couldn't do the work and take care of the kids and feel like I had any life. . . . I sort of crumped. I think I had an agitated depression. It eventuated in the end of my marriage." She describes her ex-husband as being "very much engaged with the kids and maintaining our household." Some women, like Rosalind Cropper, a New Orleans physician who went off to medical school as a single mother with a nine-month-old baby girl, are endowed with extraordinary levels of energy and require little sleep. They seem to be able to do it all. But then, Rosalind tells us that when she asks her daughter, who is now twenty-two, what she wants to do, she'll say, "'I want to be a mother.' She wants to be able to stay at home with her children. . . . Sometimes . . . she would throw that at my face, that I never had time for her."

Part of the difficulty in the lives of working mothers arises from the fact that while women's lives have undergone enormous changes, society has done very little to accommodate those changes. Just as young girls are now required to fit the mold of standard male sexual behavior, mothers of young children are required to fit into a work schedule that was developed many years ago for men who had wives at home taking care of the children and running the household. Frances Smith Foster, a professor of literature, tells us, "Krishna was born on Christmas break. I was . . . a teaching assistant. I didn't miss a day of work. . . . It was the stupidest thing I ever did in my life, but I was determined that being a female and being pregnant, I wasn't going to give them the opportunity to say you can't do it. . . . I tried everything to have her during the break. I took castor oil—it was terrible." Since men do not get pregnant and do not give birth, instead of being viewed as a normal and accepted part of work life—which needs to be dealt with and planned for in such a way as to minimize problems for employees, colleagues, and coworkers—giving birth and taking time off are viewed as something to feel embarrassed and even guilty about.

If mothers of young children are ever to get off the treadmill of endless exhaustion at work and at home, we will have to begin to create an environment that incorporates the realities of women's lives instead of viewing them as an aberration. More flexible work hours would help enormously. Crystal Romero, a career counselor in her twenties, applauds the fact that at her university four women work half time—"two women share the same job. One comes in from eight to twelve; the other one comes in from twelve to four. They both have young children at home." Some jobs just don't lend themselves to shorter hours, but a vast majority do. Today, part-time work usually means low pay and an absence of benefits. In a family-oriented society, a twenty- or thirty-hour work week for parents of young children would be as acceptable as today's forty-hour week. A certain percentage of families with young children could manage financially with a salary and a half, especially if they were willing to curtail nonessential purchases while raising young children.

Women who can afford to and want to take time out from work to rear their children should not be treated like second-class citizens at the workplace or socially. Nor should they or any women have to live in fear of being left destitute in case of divorce. It is this fear which leads some married women with young children to work outside the home when they could afford not to. We need to make it easier to garnish salaries for child support payments. Perhaps if women (and men) who choose to devote part of their lives to child rearing were treated with respect and admiration, more people might decide to simply take off from work for a certain number of years, and then perhaps work shorter hours until their children are older. Given today's lifespan, even if a woman took a full ten years off from work, she would still be left with thirty to forty work years. If mothering were truly respected, more women might follow the path of women like Nancy Douglas, who is in her sixties and did not work outside the home while raising her four children. Later in life, she became a political consultant. She says, "I just thought it was fabulous being a mother, and I wouldn't have given up the experience for the world. . . . And I also wouldn't give up the life I've led since then. . . . I got to have my cake and eat it, too."

Most likely, a majority of women will not be able to financially afford to stop working, and many will simply not want to stop. It is clear from our interviews that there are enormous differences between people; trying to fit everyone into one mold can only lead to enormous pain. While some women want nothing more than to be with their children full-time after they give birth, others who also love their children can't wait to get back to work. For them, we need high-quality, subsidized day-care centers and after-school programs. Several of the women we interviewed talked about how much more advanced many of the European countries are in this area, as well as in their maternity-leave policies. We Americans have considerable difficulty making the connection between the public and the private; public expenditures that are not directly to one's advantage tend to be viewed with horror. But helping parents to do a good job of raising their children is advantageous not just to the parents but to society at large. It is also cheaper in the long run.

Children placed at a young age in understaffed day-care centers, where overworked women with no knowledge or training in child development work at minimum wage, children who by the age of eight come home from school to empty homes are at a higher risk of angry, antisocial, even violent behavior than children raised with caring attention. Kathleen Ryan is the director of a human services agency. She tells us, "Kids are becoming younger and younger in facilities for treatment. . . . Seven seems to be the age that you get them into the mental health system, and that age is dropping. . . . I don't know if we've made much of a difference in the programs that we've offered. . . . You put a kid away for three years, and they're not rehabilitated." Dealing with children in human service agencies, putting them in juvenile detention centers and later prisons, is costing taxpayers much more than providing high-quality day care, as well as after-school and summer programs.

When it comes to fathers, our interviews again seem to reflect studies done on the subject. A small minority of husbands fully share household and child rearing with their working wives. But in a majority of families, while men help out much more than did their fathers, household and children are still viewed primarily as women's work. This is true even when the wife works as long or longer hours than her husband. Close to fifty percent of divorced fathers do not see their children after about one year and do not provide financial support. How can we imbue boys, from a young age, with a sense of the responsibilities of fatherhood? Some schools are attempting to do this by teaching child-rearing classes, which give young children a realistic sense of the awesome responsibilities of being a good parent and discourage the irresponsible fathering of children. Ideally, we should have such classes in all our schools. A major ad campaign—on the same scale as antismoking ads—aimed at encouraging responsible fathering might be helpful. Perhaps if low-cost marital counseling were readily available for parents of young children wishing to get divorced, it might help cut down on divorce rates and reduce the problem of negligent dads.

Listening to June Wood, a single mother with a full-time job, describe her absolute delight when she found an apartment that had a high-quality day-care center on the premises, made me think that perhaps we would do well to give some serious consideration to the proposals of turn-of-the-century sociologist Charlotte Perkins Gilman. Already in 1898, Gilman understood that running a household, raising children, and working outside the home was just too much. She suggested that household tasks be professionalized. Some young parents, and especially single mothers like June, might welcome the opportunity to live in communities that would provide them with a private apartment or house, a day-care center, and the option of taking evening meals in a common dining room—nutritionally, this would certainly beat the diet of fast food that so many children of working parents seem to grow up on today. Cleaning and laundry services might be added options. A small number of communities of this type already exist; any significant expansion that would include working-class families would probably require government subsidies.

It is unlikely that these or other proposals to improve the quality of life of parents and children will be put into effect as long as we remain a society that defines success and happiness not in terms of human values, but in terms of the accumulation of money and power. Before the advent of the second-wave women's movement, there was a tendency to divide people's lives into the public and the private spheres. The public sphere was the harsh world of men, where love, caring, and respect for other human beings counted for little. In the private sphere the traditional wife was supposed to provide her husband and children with just that love, caring, respect, and affection that were lacking in the public sphere. While women's entering of the public sphere has occasionally brought some humanization to the workplace, by and large, as in the case of sex, women have had to adapt to the male world.

Our best hope for changing our society into a more humane profamily and prochildren one probably grows out of the possibility that an increasing number of men will come to share responsibilities at home. As Amanda Johnson, who is in her forties and a partner in a large western law firm, puts it, "The ideal situation would be for men to take real responsibility for family so that that change in their values would reflect itself in the institutions that they participate in and dominate. I don't think that I would be working sixty-hour weeks if men in any significant number took true responsibility for their families. The work ethic would change. There might even be on-site day care. If you want to make it equal, I would rather men take fathering more seriously than women take mothering more lightly. I would rather see women's choices influence how men think, as opposed to women buying into how men think."

I was born in 1908 and so I was about 12 when women won the right to vote. We still lived in the country and we didn't hear about it right away. We didn't have a telephone. We didn't have a radio. We didn't have electricity. We found out through the newspaper. It would come about 1 o'clock and most of the time it was a day or so late. My mother was real excited about it. She said well at last, at last, now we can vote. My mother voted right up until she died.

—Lucille Thornburgh, born 1908

We in this country are leading the way. The feminist movement has been very important for all women, not just American women. Almost all of the women, especially third world women, that I've encountered and worked with at the university envy American women's freedom and independence. They want to learn how this was forged.

—Beverly Butler Lavergneau, born 1940

I Never Knew
We Were Poor

A LIFE STORY

Bernice Stuart Snow

She is a widow with two children, three grandchildren, and a great-grandchild on the way. She lives in Portland, Oregon, and works part-time

"I was born in Huron, South Dakota, in 1915. My grandfather Stuart was Scotch, and my grandmother was Irish. On my mother's side, I'm French and German. My mother was born in 1896. They didn't even have pavements in the streets at that time. South Dakota hadn't been a state too long. My grandparents were all farmers and homesteaders. My grandmother had twelve children: nine daughters and three sons. There were no contraceptives, and they needed sons to work on the farm. She lost two of her daughters in teenage life, and she lost the last little boy. My mother was the oldest. She and her sister June had to work on the farm as little girls, because they didn't have any boys. It hurt both their health; they were too young to be working out in the fields." (See also p. 238)

*M*y dad left the farm. When I was born, he was a janitor at the high school, and then he became a railroad man up until the thirties, when the railroads went broke. He was a brakeman. To his dying day, if a train would come by, he would light up. After the railroads went bust, in the wintertime he would get a job cutting ice, and in the sum-

3

mer he would deliver it. You had an icebox, and the ice man would come around, and you'd buy ice and put it in the top part of the icebox, and it would keep your food cool. It was delivered only in the summer. From about November to May it is so cold you stored your food in the unheated pantry or root cellar.

My mother was a housewife. When she was seventeen, she and my dad ran away and got married. I'm the oldest of three. I grew up in a town of ten thousand people. Huron was typical, really a lovely town. You could go out at night all by yourself, walk any place. You had your own big garden. Everybody raised their own food.

My folks never owned a home; we always rented. Most people rented houses. The first place we lived in was a one-room house. When I was about eight we moved into a house that had three rooms. In the fall just before the snow, my father would bank up the foundation of the house with cow manure. It would take a week before the odor dissipated, but after the snow came, it kept the house warm. Don't ask me how!

We had electricity. My grandparents still lived on a farm—they didn't have electricity. They made their own soap. They had a great big, round, heavy, cast-iron pot. You would build a fire under it, and they would save up lard from the pigs and put lye in it, and then you cook it and cook it and cook it, and that's how they got their soap.

We bought soap at the store. For shampoo, my mother would take castile soap, add a little water to it, and put it on the stove until it all melted up and got to a certain consistency. You always had a vinegar rinse when you washed your hair to get all the soap out. She also used to give us hot-oil treatments.

On the farms you had to go outside to go to the toilet. We always had an indoor toilet. We had running water but not hot water. Some houses that we lived in, we didn't have a bathroom. When you took a bath, you had to heat the water in a boiler on top of the stove. You had these round galvanized tubs that you filled with water. You sat with your feet hanging over, and then you stood up and rinsed off. Saturday was bath day. Clean the house, and then everybody took a bath.

In one house we lived in when I was about fifteen, the only heat we had was a hard-coal stove in the dining room that you could stoke at night, and when you got up in the morning, there would still be enough fire to keep that room warm. It was in the front of the dining room, so that the living room was heated, too. Everybody always congregated around the stove. And then you also had a wood-burning stove with a reservoir on the end of it to keep water in, in the kitchen. But the bedrooms were always ice cold. Once the temperature was 20 below for six weeks, and we had so much snow that when they cleaned it off the sidewalks, it was twelve feet high. You wore stockings to bed and flannel pajamas. The housewives made quilts and quilts and quilts. You might have six quilts on top of you. And you always slept with your sister or somebody so you could cuddle up. I slept with my sister until I got married. My mother would heat the iron or hot-water bottles to warm the covers before getting into bed. My sister and I once tried sleeping right outside on the porch. I don't know why. We just did. It was not much colder out there than it was upstairs.

In the summer, it gets 110 degrees. In South Dakota, there weren't many trees. There were trees in the yard, and maybe a tree around each house. The wind never stopped blowing, and if you'd go out, your hair would just stand straight up. We used to sleep out in the yard sometimes. Or we'd sleep on the floor downstairs because it would be so hot upstairs you couldn't breathe. You just make do.

My husband said the only time he ever got an orange as a child was in his stocking at Christmas time. But my mother was quite progressive for that time. We bought bananas and oranges and apples. Nothing was expensive. A loaf of bread was ten cents, twelve cents, but it was expensive when you didn't have any money. I was in high school, and I remember coming home from school and there was nothing to eat. My dad went down the street and borrowed a dollar from someone to buy food. It was during the depression, probably about 1930.

Poor as we were, we always had the local paper, *The Huronite,* and my dad subscribed to the *Sioux City Tribune,* which came a day late in the mail. If we didn't read the paper, we didn't know what was happening because we didn't have a radio. But it was in the paper that the banks were all closed, and we went downtown to check it out, and they were closed. Anybody that had any money in the bank never got it back. No government insurance, no nothing. That's before FDIC. There were also the dust storms in the mid-1930s, and the farmers all went broke; they lost their topsoil. There was no work and no money. But everybody helped each other. People shared. If a family was needy, the churches would fix up a basket to take food. My dad always managed.

We were poor, but I never knew that we were poor because everybody was that way. In high school one outfit was all you ever had to wear to school. The way we'd get around it, we'd change clothes. My girlfriend Tucky had a green skirt with a green top, and I just loved it when we could trade clothes.

People didn't change their underwear and their stockings every night, just once a week—after bath on Saturday. You didn't have electrical appliances. The washing machine was a round tub, only a little wider than a barrel. Somebody had to stand there all the time and pull the handle to make the clothes swish around and get washed. All clothes were sorted into piles, and all were washed in the same wash water—whites first, light-colored next, heavy work clothes and darks last. Each load was run through the wringer by hand and into a tub of rinse water and then run through the wringer again, ready for hanging on the clothesline outside.

If you were real persnickety about your clothes—like my mother—you would put the clothes in the boiler, on the stove, in boiling water with Mrs. Stewart's Bluing in the water, to make the white clothes whiter.

My mother did the laundry on Monday morning. It was a pain in the neck. It was so much work, and then, when you got through with the washing on Monday, Tuesday you ironed. You put the iron on the stove and got it hot, and everybody ironed. The men didn't; the women and the girls did.

It took my mother four or five hours to do the washing. Think of my grandmother, who had twelve children. I don't know how they did it. Not only that, but you had to feed those twelve. The women made all the clothes and embroidered them. It was a hard life. And my mother's life was not nearly as hard as her mother's, and her mother's was not as hard as her mother's. It seems like each generation got better and better, easier.

Gardening was a woman's job. I can remember my dad helping to plant and weed. You couldn't go to the grocery store and buy just anything. You'd go to the meat market and get meat, to the grocery store and get sugar, pickles, flour, oatmeal, and such. There were no canned goods. So you had to raise all your own vegetables, and then you had to can them. And canning is the worst. You do it in the hottest time of the year—it would get 110 to 120, and you'd have a stove going in a small kitchen. When I got married, I told my husband, "I'm never going to can." And I never did.

The children worked in those days. Saturday was cleaning day. We girls would have to help. No vacuum cleaner. You had carpet sweepers. You had wood floors with area rugs, and you took them out on the line and you beat them. We had to dust. I did most of the chores because my sister was not very ambitious. She hated to get out of bed.

We didn't have toys, but we had fun. When I was about thirteen or fourteen, we played games outside. You'd have two or three on this side and two or three on the other side of the house, and you'd say, "Annie Annie I Over"—that means you're tossing the ball over the house, and so then they'd catch it and come around and try to hit you with that ball. You played mumblety-peg with pocket knives, and everybody played marbles and hopscotch. I'm talking probably ten, twelve years old. Boys and girls, old and young, played softball. They had adult softball teams that went from town to town. Our towns were about ten miles apart. It was just the men. Housewives didn't have time to do anything but housework.

When we were nine, ten years old, we girls roamed all over the place. We'd go down to the James River and go on picnics. We could go out to the state fair and roam around the grounds and go up in the bleachers. You could go anywhere in town. There were alleys everyplace. At the meat market, they'd bring the cows and calves in and kill them and string them up and then slit them open, and if you could stand it, you'd watch them through the door in the alley.

First grade through high school, we had all these girls we grew up with and were friends with. (In fact, we're still friends; we write, send Christmas cards. I have one or two who are still in South Dakota, and they came out on a bus to see me three years ago. We called it the pajama party. Had a ball. We laughed and laughed and ate.) Somebody in this group of girlfriends was always dreaming up something to do. There were so many places to go.

We had two movie houses in town, and if you could collect twelve Swander's Bakery bread wrappers, you could get in free. So we had Swander's bread, and I went to every movie. You got in for ten cents, twelve cents, fifteen cents. Oh, I loved the movies. I remember one early one with Vera LaPlant—it was a thriller named *The Claw,* and I can see her lying on this bed and this claw coming down at her—one of those scary things. I remember Al Jolson in *Mammy.* When he was saying "Mammy" down on his knees, I looked over at the audience, and everybody was crying. It was a sea of white handkerchiefs—there was no Kleenex in those days—and that made me laugh.

I also remember the one with the chariots—Cecil B. DeMille. I loved the musicals; the women were dressed so beautifully. I loved all their clothes. The newsreels always came on before the movie and lasted about five minutes. We would always be so impatient for them to be over because we came to see the movie.

The church in every small town was the center of social life. The girls went to Sunday school to meet the boys, and the boys went to meet the girls. From the first grade all through high school, I had a yen for this one boy, Robert Swanson, a Swede, blond, curly hair. I went to Christian Endeavor, Sunday evening meeting for teenagers, because Robert would be there.

I gave my Sunday school teacher a hard time. I asked questions. I didn't believe that Jonah was swallowed by the whale. How could that be? Now I'm an agnostic. I feel that there is intelligence, there is something there, but I don't believe in organized religion. The church business turned me off because of a particular incident. Our Sunday school teacher was a college student and we loved her. We called ourselves "Melva's little women." She worked over in the minister's house, helped with the children and the housework, to earn money to go to college. The reverend, I can see him to this day. He raped her, not once but many times. They removed him. His wife was the loveliest person, and he had two children. There was a big scandal about it. But, of course, it wasn't in the paper or anything like that; it was just word of mouth. I never liked ministers from then on. Nothing has changed. It's just the same, only there's more people, and it's out in the open. In fact, in the Catholic church, one of the fathers got a nun pregnant. Everybody in town knew that. He stayed. They hushed it up, but that stuff always gets out.

You got information about sex from your girlfriends. Their mothers didn't tell them, either. I had what was called the curse for three months before my mother knew it. Every summer for about three or four years when we were in our early teens, my sister and I would stay with our aunt Frank in North Platte, Nebraska. We loved Aunt Frank. She wrote to my mother, "Why didn't you tell me that Bernice was menstruating?" My mother wrote back, "I didn't know." Everybody used rags, or an old sheet. It was a mess. I always threw them away. My girlfriend Betty, her mother washed hers. I remember when Kotex came in, it was so wonderful.

And as far as where babies come from, well, you just knew—I don't know how you knew it. But you never got any information from your mother.

I babysat for twenty-five cents an hour. But Mr. Phillips was a salesman, and his wife was having an affair with somebody when he was out on the road. The boyfriend would have to take me home, and I got fifty cents an hour. I suppose you might call that hush money. I must have been twelve years old at that time. One other time, the husband came home when I was taking care of the children, and he put his arm around me and tried to kiss me. I told my mother, and she never allowed me to go over there ever again.

We weren't allowed to wear lipstick until we got to be seventeen or eighteen. People didn't wear makeup. If you did, you weren't a "nice" girl. And as for earrings, they just didn't wear them. You expected it in the gypsies.

My mother was nineteen when I was born. She had 6 younger sisters, and so my aunts were like sisters to me. My grandmother and her younger children had moved out to Portland, Oregon, and my aunt Ethel and my aunt Marge came to visit us. I remember that so well—they came back with real short dresses above their knees, stockings rolled down beneath their knees, and high heels. They had the new hairdo—these big puffs of artificial hair over each ear—like you put great big earmuffs on. They smoked cigarettes, and they were flappers. By that time women weren't wearing long dresses clear to their ankles like the old ladies did; they wore skirts that came down to the middle of their legs. But there were no flappers in our town, and here come Aunt Marge and Aunt Ethel. I've got a wonderful picture of my aunt Marge sitting on this old-looking car smoking a cigarette. You weren't considered a nice girl if you looked like that—there must be something else going on. The town was scandalized, and they loved it. They were in their early twenties. In the flapper age, after World War I, everything changed. People just went wild. We had speakeasies; we called them chicken shacks, and they were outside of the town. They were not in chicken shacks—I don't know why they were called that. A lot of people would go there to drink and dance.

College boys would go after the high school girls. My best girlfriend, Betty, went with Elmer, and after we were out of high school she told me that she started having sex with him at the age of fourteen. Now I absolutely would not get pregnant—that was the greatest fear—and so when I was in high school, I never slept with a guy. But I had plenty of chances. Even when I was working at the Standard Oil, there were two men that had a game going on—they were going to notch the belt with all the girls that worked there. Well, they tried, but they didn't "notch" me, that's for sure. I had sex before I got married, but it was with my husband.

I'm tall and thin, and I was very shy. My sister was little and adorable and cute and sexy and flirted like nobody's business. She started smoking at the age of fourteen. I remember every night after we got through with dinner she'd run across the street to meet with her girlfriends. One night my dad said, "Valeria, tonight you don't need to run across the street and smoke a cigarette with the Joy girls; you can smoke your cigarettes right here at the table with your father." And so she got her cigarettes out and smoked one with my dad.

She told me later she slept with a number of guys. I think she did it to be popular. Maybe it was just heavy petting, not necessarily going all the way. They wanted to please the boys. That's the only reason. They wanted lots of boyfriends and lots of fun. The boys would take them out, take them dancing. Everybody danced. We had dance halls outside of the city, where there was drinking going on, too. And that was part of the scene.

My girlfriend Vera was one of the ones that slept around. Her mother didn't speak good English. And she used to say, "I can't understand—my Vera is so popular, she has so many dates—I can't understand why Bernice doesn't have a lot of dates." Well, I could have told her.

The lawyer's daughter got pregnant. She was going with a college student, a football player. Her stomach got bigger and bigger. Everybody knew that she was pregnant. The school called an assembly, and everybody had to go to it. They said that they wanted to correct misinformation going around, and that this student had a nine-pound tumor in her stomach. It wasn't long after that that she disappeared for a while and then came back slim as a rail. Most generally, if you got pregnant, you left town and stayed away and gave the baby away. Oh, I'm sure there were shotgun weddings, but I didn't know about them. It just seemed like the boys, that's all they lived for, was to have sex with the girls. At that age their hormones are raging. And you really were bombarded if you got started. We had a lot of fun when we went out on dates—we went on picnics and blanket parties. That's where a lot of girls got into trouble. You'd go down the river in a canoe and pitch your blanket under the stars, boys and girls.

We had a big park in town. Thursday night was band concert night. And everybody went. We sat out on a big, beautiful lawn and listened. At the end of the park was the brand new Carnegie library. I just loved that library, and I read every book in it. I'd get three or four books at a time. Everybody read books. No TV. When *Gone with the Wind* came out, I had to be sixteen or seventeen. We got the book at the library finally, and we were all reading it at the same time. My dad always was the last one—he'd be up in the middle of the night when it came his turn.

Our first radio was a real pretty Philco. I was probably fourteen or fifteen. It was a stand-up, flat on the top. My dad listened to opera on Saturday afternoons, and you had to be quiet. The whole family listened to President Roosevelt's radio fireside chats. We all loved Roosevelt. I did not know that he was handicapped until after I was married. It never showed in the newsreels. He always was photographed sitting down, and there was never a word about it in the press. My brother got polio when he was in the service during World War II, and then Roosevelt having polio came up.

As little money as we had, my mother was very culturally minded. They had what was called the Chautauqua. It originated in Chautauqua, New York, and went around to different towns. They would put up a big tent, and they gave concerts, lectures, plays, etc., for both adults and children. They would have week-long classes for children. We'd go and stay all morning.

When John Philip Sousa came to town—he was known as the March King, and his band toured the U.S.—my mother saw that we went to hear him. I got to take two years of piano lessons till they ran out of money. My sister was put on the violin, and my brother took bassoon.

Everybody went to square dances. My parents went dancing with other couples, and I always babysat. People often took their children with them to dances and to parties. It was a real big hall, and everybody had chairs all around, and they'd pile all their coats on the chairs and all the children on the coats. The children would go to sleep, and the parents danced. They'd have a band. I can remember my dad up on the stage calling the square dances. My dad was a beautiful dancer—he just glided. A different kind of dancing than today's bob up and down.

My sister had scarlet fever, and when you got scarlet fever, you were quarantined. They put a big red notice on your door. Nobody could come in your house until you got well and the doctor took the quarantine off. Siblings couldn't leave the house. Sometimes the father would be allowed to stay someplace else; he had to keep working, but, of course, the mother was there. My mother wanted me to get scarlet fever because usually one child would get it and be sick, and then you'd have to go through the same thing with the other one, so she made me sleep with my sister so that I would get it. I never got it. My sister had the whooping cough, and it was the same thing. I never got that either, and it's very infectious.

I was born at home, but by the time my brother was born in 1921, we finally got a hospital in town. That was the same year that we had a new hotel built, the Marvin Hughitt. There was a grand opening, and my father and I went over to go through the hotel, which was a real big event. Anything that happened in the town was a big event. Saturday night everybody sat in their car and watched the people walking up and down the street—all the farmers came to town and did their shopping, and you got to see everybody. You didn't have to have a license to drive. I had a girlfriend, Betty Beddow, her parents owned a grocery store, and she had access to her parents' car, so we girls could sit in the car and watch the boys and the other girls go up and down the street.

People didn't have any money to go in the coffee shop. You'd go into the candy kitchen if you had enough money. When Coke first came out, for ten cents you could get a large glass of fountain Coke. You could have a lemon, cherry, or strawberry Coke, and they had sundaes and malted milks. They had these little round tables with marble tops, and there were chairs that had the wire backs. The Greeks had sort of a monopoly on the restaurants and two grocery stores—like the 7-Eleven today. They had magazines and candy and cigars and cigarettes. There must've been five Greek families, or six, that had those kind of stores. We had a Jewish family, the Axelrods, who had the furniture store, and the Bergs had the most exclusive clothing store.

We had, I think, three black families in town. One of them, I hate to say it, was called Nigger Neely. She was a former slave, and everybody loved her. She lived to be over one hundred years old. Then there was another black family that had little children who went to school with us.

They had a big paddle in elementary school. Once in a while, when a child would get paddled, you could hear it. Children didn't misbehave that much. We respected authority; we were brought up that way. The boys would misbehave more than the girls. It would be some prank of some kind, nothing like today. I loved going to school.

My mother and her sisters all graduated from Huron High School, and so did I. I had three teachers that taught my mother in high school. In South Dakota, school was out in May, because so many of the children came in from farms, and they had to work on the farms. We went to school from nine till four. We really got an education. You had to take two years of a language, either biology or chemistry, mathematics—algebra, and geometry—I took chemistry and biology, two years of Latin. There was no team sports for the girls, not where you would play another school. We had girls' gym, and that's all. The boys had varsity football and basketball. I never did any organized athletics outside of school, nor did the other girls.

When I went to high school, I only had one thing in mind, that I was going to get a job. I would have loved to have gone to college, but I would have had to go to Huron College, and I didn't want to go there. I would have liked to have gone to the university in Vermillion, South Dakota, or some place like that. When my brother came up, by that time, the depression was over, and my folks were able to help him go to college.

I didn't have any money, and I was sick and tired of having one outfit to wear, of having holes in the bottom of my shoes and putting cardboard in them. I had a plan. I took everything I could take in bookkeeping. I took typing and shorthand, and when the teacher gave an assignment to do ten pages of shorthand, I'd always do twenty because I wanted to be good. And I was good. I was the 1933 South Dakota state champion for typing. They came from all over South Dakota to Sioux Falls and took a typing test, and I was the best.

When I graduated in 1933, there weren't that many jobs. Because of a family connection, I got an interview with the head of Standard Oil of Indiana in Huron, the most prestigious office in town. They had an opening in dictaphone—it's a machine with a record on it and earplugs. You listen and you type. Mr. Bailey said, We don't usually hire anybody without a college education. I'm going to give you a three months' try, and then we may give you another three months, and if you're satisfactory in six months, you can be in the stenographic pool. Well, I was prepared and I stayed, and not only that—one of the gals that worked in the stenographic pool was a teacher at Brookings College, and I was promoted over her to legal secretary. I was working at Standard Oil Company when the first dust storm came through. It was noon, and here comes this dust, and it turns dark like night, like you read in the Bible. They had to turn the street lights on in the middle of the day!

In those days, you stayed home till you got married, and that's one of the reasons why girls got married. They wanted to get out of the house. My very best girlfriend, her mother was gone, and growing up she had to live with her stepsister, and she decided to get an apartment of her own. They were just starting to build apartment houses then. She and another girl rented an apartment, which was unheard of. A nice girl didn't live in an apartment. If you did, it must be because you wanted to have boys up there. After that there was an apartment house that went up, and some of the girls at the Standard Oil moved in. So it started to change.

Standard Oil had a big, beautiful brick building. I was there about two years in the stenographic pool, and then I became a secretary in the legal department, and that's when I met my husband. I made eighteen dollars a week. Eighteen dollars was a lot of money. After paying thirty-eight dollars a month to my folks for room and board, needless to say, the rest of my earnings went towards new clothes. I had so many shoes in my closet! I wore high heels one and a half or two inches high; the fashion at that time was suede. I still remember my green suede high heel pumps with fondness.

I met my husband when I was nineteen and got married at twenty-one. Obie was making twelve dollars a week working in a grocery store called the Red Owl. It would be like Piggy Wiggly or Safeway. They gave him his own store to manage in Sioux Falls, which is the biggest city in South Dakota. And he was making thirty-five dollars a week. As soon as he got up to thirty-five dollars, we were going to get married. I don't know whatever possessed me, as I look back. I loved my job, I loved my life, but I was so in love I think if he would have told me to jump off the Brooklyn Bridge, I would have done it. He didn't want a big wedding, and neither did I, because neither family had the money. Obie had to work late on Saturday night, and we got married on Sunday morning; and my sister and his boss stood up with us. Then we went home to tell our folks. My mother cried, and Obie's mother was so glad because somebody was there to take care of her son!

We moved into a one-room apartment in Sioux Falls. There was a law at that time—1937—that married women could not work. There weren't enough jobs to go around. My husband worked eighty hours a week. There I was in Sioux Falls—didn't know anybody. I went to a cooking school, and I learned to crochet, and I learned to knit. I got bored; I had nothing to do—I just had to work. I applied to Iowa National Breeders, a store that sold feed and medicines to farmers for their poultry. I didn't tell him I was married. He hired me as a bookkeeper. He was a very eccentric old man. In the winter time there was nothing to do. I'd read books at work. In the spring he went out to the farms and sexed chickens and that sort of thing, and then I would be in the office and store. I used to be so embarrassed because my husband and I would go to parties, and they were kind of wild parties sometimes, and there would be drinking. And somebody might ask where I was working. "Oh," he says, "she sexes chickens."

Then Obie decided he didn't want to work in the grocery store any longer. And we drove out west to Oregon around 1938–39. But then Obie got homesick, and after about six months we came back, and he got his job back, and I got a job at Barnsoal Oil in the stenographic pool. My oldest daughter, Peggy, was born in Mitchell, South Dakota.

Everybody nursed in those days. We never heard of paper diapers. We washed the gauze diapers in the washing machine. My husband changed diapers—he had seven sisters and was twenty-five years old when his baby sister was born, so he knew all about babies. He gave Peggy a bottle. Oh, he loved her.

I had another daughter, Jane, five years later. Two months after Jane was born, one day she wasn't taking her milk and she couldn't take her water and she hemorrhaged in her diaper, and I called Dr. Lenz and he was gone on vacation, and another doctor took his place. And I told him, "She's filled her diaper with blood. It's just as if a woman were menstruating." "Oh, now, Mrs. Snow, don't be alarmed," he said. "Just send your husband down, and I'll give him a prescription." That's what I did. But it still went on and—a mother's instinct—I knew there was something wrong, so I called him again, and he said, "Well, you just give her that medicine and call me in the morning and I'm sure she's going to be all right." I knew she wasn't all right. I stayed up all night and cleaned house just to have something to do. In the morning I called, and I said, "Doctor, this baby is very ill." "Well, just bring her down about eleven o'clock, and I'll see her." So that's what we did. And when we had got her down to the hospital, she was practically gone. He called in another doctor right away. She had a little polyp in the inside of her bowel, which the bowel had picked up as food, and the little bowel telescoped around the big bowel, and they had to operate. She didn't make it. The hospital said, "Look, we'll not ask you for a dime for this hospitalization."

Today we would have had a huge malpractice suit going, but people didn't do such things then. You just took that it was an error. If my own doctor would have been there, he would have known that I wasn't one of those mothers that worried about every little old thing, and he would have had me bring the baby in. This doctor just thought I was a hysterical woman. It was an error. He never said anything to me afterwards, and I never would have talked to him. Neither would Obie. In those days in our South Dakota culture, everybody was very stoic, and I am to this day. Life was so hard and so grim—we had just come out of the thirties and those terrible dust storms. You practiced stoicism so you could bear the pain. It was a way of life. The farmers never knew if they were going to have a crop or not. They'd plant and it wouldn't rain and they'd lose it, or it would hail and it would take it all.

By the time my son, Eugene, was born, we were living in Syracuse, New York. We moved so much, all around the country. When we got older, my husband and I counted up all the different apartments and houses we lived in—we moved fifty times. It was always because of Obie's work. We made new friends wherever we went. I loved it, never questioned it, kind of like a gypsy. My daughter, Peggy, says she was raised in the backseat of a car, and she really was.

Growing Up

Growing Up:
The First Generation

My mother didn't tell me about sex or babies. I was eighteen years old when my younger brother was born. My mother sewed his whole layette on the sewing machine and she never told me what was going to happen until one day after Mass my father packed us up in the car and said 'We're going to the hospital to see our new baby brother.' Can you imagine that?

—Dorothy Sommer, born 1912

My friends and I have all discussed the fact that we were shortchanged as far as what we were allowed to do. They educated us at the college level and then they said 'now go home and turn on the stove.' How did we get so brainwashed?

I felt vindicated by the women's movement. I always wondered why I had rebelled quietly against my fate.

—Betsy Miller, born 1929

Leave the Door Slightly Ajar

Whitt Davenport

She is a widow, born in 1911. She graduated from Vassar College, married a local boy, and as a result has lived most of her adult life in Stone Ridge, a small town in New York State.

"I grew up in what is called the Delta in Mississippi, up the Mississippi River. It is a very, very rich cotton country. Everything was connected with raising cotton when I was growing up." (See also p. 236)

My mother's family was from England. My grandfather, Aven, was a professor, and he taught Latin and Greek and French. My mother went to the little college in Mississippi where my grandfather taught. She was the only girl in the college and graduated when she was sixteen. She had the highest grades at that point that had ever been made in the college, and three fraternity pins. She finished college, and then she did graduate work at Bryn Mawr. She was after a Ph.D., but instead she met Mr. Whittington and got married, so she never got her degree.

My father was a lawyer, and then he was a congressman for quite a number of years. He had a partner in his office, so the law office was open all the time, and then he had plantations, but we lived in town. He had managers. He went to Washington, D.C., when I was thirteen, and we stayed in Mississippi. He was home a lot more than they are now. There was the long term and the short term in Congress. The short term was only two or three months, and so that wasn't too bad, but the long terms were hard on families.

We all wished Daddy had been home more, but we had a very happy home life. My family was stricter than some, but it never turned me against them—they were silly things. All my friends were driving a car when they were twelve years old, and I couldn't drive till I was thirteen. We didn't have any driver's license in Mississippi at that time, and there wasn't much traffic. It's not like somebody driving today—we probably drove thirty-five miles an hour or something like that. I was not allowed to go out on a school night except for very exceptional things. If we had a real good play that was being put on—well-known actors would come and put on a play, particularly

Shakespeare—I was always allowed to go to something like that. Once, the Chicago Symphony was coming to Greenwood, and I got pneumonia and I couldn't go. I was only about eight or ten years old. It was one of the worst things that happened to me.

My family always welcomed my friends to the house. We went out with a lot of people, and it didn't mean that they were all real beaus—they were just friends. We went to dances all over the Delta within a radius of probably fifty miles, and I was not allowed to go to those without a chaperone. In the car with us, there would usually be two couples. My mother went with us a lot. There were two or three mothers who would do it; they had chairs around the edge of the dance floor. The first time I was allowed to go to an out-of-town dance without a chaperone was when my brother was old enough to go. That was funny because he kept cutting in on me at the dance, and he said, "I didn't really want to dance with you, but I promised Daddy I'd be a good chaperone." He was teasing.

My mother was a wonderful mother and very understanding, and I remember one night I did something she told me positively not to do. We used to have intermissions at dances, and sometimes people had Coca-Cola parties at their house at intermission, and we would go and have some cold drinks and then go back. I was going to a dance that she was not chaperoning, and she said, "I just want you to promise me that you won't go off anywhere at the intermission." Well, I did, and I was so upset I couldn't go to sleep when I got home that night, so I told Mother, and she said, "I'm glad you told me that you knew you were doing something wrong." And that was the end of that.

Most of our dates came to our house. There weren't any places to go out if there wasn't a dance on. A lot of times there would be several boys that would come over to see me at once. My mother was always there, usually upstairs. And then I had very good friends that lived just a block away, and sometimes we'd all walk over to their house and we'd sit in the living room or on the porch and tell stories. Our life was simple in that way. We did not go out to public places.

My mother and father were both very, very interested in education. My mother served on the school board of the public high school I went to and also did things for cultural and civic organizations. Daddy was very proud of her, but I don't think they ever thought of her as having a job.

She taught a grown women's Bible class in our church. She was quite religious. I would have liked to talk to her about religion, but I couldn't because I was sort of falling apart in that field, and I didn't want to hurt her feelings. But she was a scholar. She worked hard on her classes. It was just like being a teacher of Shakespeare for her. When she was finally staying all the time in Washington with Daddy, she was elected president of the Congressional Club, which was a club of all the congressmen and senators' wives. For a little old girl from Mississippi that was pretty good, and Daddy was very proud. I think they had a very happy life.

I went one year to Madeira School in Washington. It was a girls' prep school, and I went there for two reasons: my father just wanted to have me in Washington for one year, and because I would have a better chance of getting into Vassar. Madeira was a very good school scholastically. It was about the strictest school you could imagine, and I was not used to that. My father could have taken me to some of the White House balls, and they would not let me go, not even with my own father! You weren't a young lady until you had finished Madeira. As a little recompense, we were allowed to go to tea with Mrs. Hoover at the end of the year. We didn't think that was the same thing as going to a White House ball, which at the age of seventeen would have been extremely thrilling. The teachers were good there, but we couldn't do anything. We had a limited area where we could walk in the afternoon when our classes were done and before the study periods. And the only place we could go in was an ice cream shop which was near school, so naturally we all went there in the afternoons and got as fat as butterballs.

Vassar seemed quite lenient to me. Every Saturday night they had a dance called a "J." The girls that had dates could go, and if you didn't have a date, you could go and you could cut in. Those Js were fun. All the dances I had ever gone to, it was always the boys that cut in. Then there was the junior prom and senior prom, which were much more elaborate, and you usually asked a boy to come.

Curfew was ten-thirty during the week, and Saturday nights we could stay out until twelve—something like that. I don't think it ever occurred to us to take a boy in our room. There were reception rooms. We could wander around the campus. There was a Shakespeare garden, and there were benches. Sometimes if the weather was good, we'd go out there. If we were lucky, we got taken for dinner. There was a place where we would get something to drink and play bridge, and we did that on dates.

We had something like three weekends off a year. We were supposed to sign out for where we went; I went down to West Point a lot, which was the closest.

This friend of mine and I had two gentlemen that were our beaus—one of them was the man that I married. We decided we wanted to go to Montreal, and we didn't think we could get permits from Vassar to do that. And so we signed out that we were going to Colgate for the weekend, and we went to Montreal. We made the boys stay at a different hotel, but that night we were going to dance somewhere, and so we thought we'd like to have a drink. By this time, we were having drinks—I never had a drink of whiskey until about my junior year. Anyway, my friend made me call downstairs and ask if it was all right if we had two gentlemen come up to our room for a drink. And the man down there said, "I think that's all right if you'll just leave the door slightly ajar." This got to be a saying with us—"You have to leave the door slightly ajar." But we were good; we didn't really do a lot of things we shouldn't have. We shouldn't have gone to Montreal, though. We came back by way of Colgate, and we went around to this boy's fraternity. He had a sign on the door: "If anybody calls for Miss Whittington, or Miss Devine, tell them they're here but out right now." So, we were covering every track. I think that was the only time I did something like that.

During the depression, we never were starving, but we really cut back on things, and I did not think I could stay at Vassar. When I went there, the tuition was a thousand dollars a year, board and tuition. They raised it to twelve hundred, but they said that anybody that was already there who could not afford it could go on for a thousand, and I offered to stay home. I could have gotten a scholarship at Tulane down in New Orleans, but my father said, "You're going to Vassar if it kills me." And so I did. Later on, when things started getting better, he sent Vassar that extra two hundred dollars a year. He just didn't like taking favors. You know what his salary was? Ten thousand dollars a year, and the congressmen cut it back to eight. It also cost a lot less to live, and my father did carry on with his law practice at home. And we just all cut back. I had a very small allowance when I was at Vassar, and I knew better than to ask for any more. The worst part of it was most of the boys that I grew up with, going to school at home, could not get jobs. It was really bad, but when Roosevelt got elected and they started having all those work programs and everything, that was the beginning of everything.

I got married right after I finished college. One of my best friends at Vassar was from Ellenville, and she introduced me to my husband. She tried me out on two other boys first. She was determined she was going to have me living up here. The first one I was not attracted to, and he was not attracted to me at all. When she introduced me to Ken Davenport, I thought, "That's it," and it was. He went to Cornell, but he was through college when I met him. He was making thirty-five dollars a week when we got married.

I told my parents I was going to get married, but Ken did go down to Washington and meet my mother and father and formally asked for my hand. And that was the weekend of Roosevelt's inauguration. We stood in the rain and heard him say, "The only thing we have to fear is fear itself." I actually heard that!

We Respected Our Elders

Laurine Warren

She was born in 1912 and grew up in Mississippi. (See also pp. 52, 63, 225 and 424)

My grandfather was a Confederate soldier. He was born in Jefferson County, Mississippi. His forebears had come to Natchez, Mississippi, from Fort Nashboro, Tennessee, in 1791, and they were awarded a British land grant down in the corner of Jefferson and Franklin County in Mississippi. Shortly after she finished school in the country, my mother asked her father if she could teach the neighbors' children and her own brothers and sisters, and my grandfather said, "I really don't think you ought to start teaching." He thought ladies were supposed to sew a fine seam. But she begged, and so finally he let her teach, and she taught the children in the little schoolhouse that they had. Later, she passed a teacher's examination and did so well that they put her on the board of examiners for teachers in Claiborne County, Mississippi. Later, she taught school in Fayette and went to college, also, to get further education in teaching.

My father saw her name in the paper, and he wrote her a letter, and he asked her if she was the Wales pilgrim that he had known ten years earlier. And she wrote him back and told him yes. So then he wanted to come to see her, and he courted her. The next year he asked her to marry him. I have the letter that he wrote my grandfather asking for my mother's hand and the letter that my grandfather wrote back to him, telling him that he could marry my mother. Days like that, way back, the groom had to always ask for the young lady's hand before they were married. Some do that now, and others don't think about doing things like that.

Helen Schiffrin

She was born in 1915 and has lived most of her life in New York City and Long Island. She is widowed and has three daughters, one of whom, Lois Mayer, was also interviewed.

"Part of my family were born in Europe. My younger sister and I were born here. My father came here first, made a couple of trips, and every time he went back to Poland, he had another baby. We lived in Brooklyn. My father had a butcher store." (See also p. 227)

*W*e were five girls and two boys, and I was next to the youngest. I never knew I was poor until I got older. I wasn't even ten when my mother died. My father died about five years later. There were five of us at home, and my older sisters and my brother took care of us. They went to work and they supported the house. We may not have had very much, but we were a very happy family. One helped the other out. We always had a home together. Our friends came in. My mother had her family in Poland, and she had a brother that she was trying to bring over. It took time to accumulate money, and my mother died before he came over. My father was still alive. My uncle stayed with us for a while, and then he went out on his own, working, trying to have enough money to bring his family over. Well, when my father died, my uncle decided to come back to live with us, and so he lived with us from our teenage years. Many times if I came in at one o'clock or two o'clock, I'd take my shoes off. I didn't want him to know. We were not Cinderellas, but we knew right from wrong. As a rule we respected him. We didn't stay out till five in the morning.

I went to Thomas Jefferson High School in Brooklyn. No guns, hell, no. We didn't have any of that, and even the boys were more respectful. Nobody ever answered a teacher back in those days. You hear stories about kids getting into fights with their teachers and hitting, and we never had that. We respected our elders.

Today you walk on the street, you want to know who's behind you and who's alongside of you. We never worried about that. Even as a teenager, when we girls used to go out or go to a dance, when we came home at twelve, one o'clock, we would separate— we lived in different directions—and walk five blocks home and never give it a thought. I really don't remember murders or rapes. We were never afraid. I would work sometimes evenings until nine o'clock. I never worried about going on the subway or walking from the train home.

The boys weren't rude or fresh. I never heard of date rape. Even those fellows who did have sex with a girl, they didn't brag. They didn't talk about it.

When we were teens, in the summertime, we would go to Coney Island on dates, and we would go on the rides, go to Nathan's. The end of the season, they would have a Mardi Gras there. Parades and tumbling. A lot of noise, a lot of fun, eating on the street and going on the rides.

Another thing we used to do a lot was go to the Jewish shows—they were in Yiddish. I used to love those shows. They had a lot of theaters on the Lower East Side in Manhattan and in Brooklyn. I spoke Yiddish fluently because my parents spoke it at home.

The minute we graduated from high school, we had to get a job. Whatever we earned we put into the household. None of us ever thought twice about it. We knew we had to do it. It's just like when my kids were growing up—they knew they had to go to Hebrew school; there was never a thought that they wouldn't go to college. They just did it.

I worked in a dental office in Queens for a number of years, until I got married when I was twenty-four—to get there I took two subways for a nickel! When I got married, I moved out of the house. One of my cousin's daughters went out on her own in Manhattan. She was the only one. Who did things like that? Her mother was a modern woman, and she went along with it. Oh, everybody thought it was terrible that Mae moved out of her parents' house. She was the first one that I ever heard of moving out.

Dorothy Sommer

She was born in 1912 and lives in New York City. She worked mostly in advertising. In the 1940s she lived in Los Angeles for seven years and was social secretary to film producer Jack Warner. She never married.

"My parents came to this country from Austria-Hungary. They settled in the Midwest and had four children. I was in the middle, which I hated. The middle child never gets any attention." (See also pp. 60, 228, 249 and 422)

*M*y older brother was the apple of my mother's eye. He always got the best part of the roast and the best part of the chicken, which means a lot to children. My younger brother, who was born many years later, was then spoiled all over. My mother favored the boys. You could hear the mothers talking when they were expecting. They always thought it was going to be a boy and hoped it was a boy. There was none of that modern attitude.

My older brother and myself, we were two years apart, and we were brought up very strictly because my parents had strong European standards. My father and mother assimilated into the culture, so with my younger brother they were more lenient.

My mother was extremely critical, very fussy about how we looked. She would inspect us as we went out the door, make sure we had no pins on anywhere. A lot of girls if your hem came down a little bit and you're in a hurry, you stick a little safety pin there that would hitch your hem up and run. . . . Oh, no, you had to go back, and you had to do it again. We wore big sashes behind our dresses and big bows, and my mother always looked to see if the sash was straight, and I disliked that so much. She'd say, "Now, don't let anybody touch it. It's just the way it should be." I'm going out and I'm not supposed to let anybody touch my sash because it wouldn't be as perfect. They inspected you when you got home. "Oh, you got a spot. Did you spill something on that?" You were never allowed to spill a damn thing. Children are children. That was too much. Your socks had to be clean. Everything had to be clean, even the writing had to be no erasures—no, you weren't allowed to cross out or anything. When we learned to write letters, it was a harrowing experience because you threw away paper until you got it absolutely right. Nowadays, I've gotten over a lot of that. My stroke has done that for me because I don't spell very well. I mean I just can't; I have no control.

I was brought up in a convent Catholic school and the sisters were just as bad. You got it from the parents, and then you got it from the sisters. You never escaped. The nuns told us never to wear black patent leather shoes—the boys would be able to see up your skirt if you did. Now, that was really asinine to tell young girls. They would say, "Oh, young ladies don't do that. No, you mustn't do that" "Why?" "Because young ladies don't do that."

Very sad—in those days, they never approached the subject of sex. You learned from your contemporaries. When I first started to menstruate, I was worried something was wrong with me, and I went to my mother. She said, "Now you're going to be a woman and you're preparing to be a mother, and when you get married, this is all part of it." She had pinking shears, and she cut out things from flannel or muslins, or something absorbent, and they were like a pad. And I was shown what to do. We had the elastic belts, and then the safety pins. My mother used to put these pads in the washing machine. It was a very primitive round one with a ringer you put the clothes through. It was considered very modern.

She didn't tell me about babies. I was in the department store with my mother one time, and a friend of hers was walking through, and I said, "What's the matter with Anna?" And my mother said, "Shh," and right away I knew there was something wrong. She never explained that the woman was going to have a baby. I was eighteen years old when my younger brother was born. My mother sewed his whole layette on the sewing machine, and she never told me what was going to happen until one day after mass my father packed us up in the car and said, "We're going to the hospital to see our new baby brother." Can you imagine? The only time that my mother expressed anything is when we were going out on dates. She said to me and my sister, "Now, it's up to the girl to control, and you don't do certain things until you're married; it is a disgrace for a girl to have a baby before she's married; and you have to be careful because there are two terrible diseases, and you can get them." She really built a picture. And it was not that we were morally above everybody. We were scared we were going to be ostracized. We always thought that the boy can really not help it, couldn't be blamed if you allowed him to go beyond where he couldn't control himself.

Abigail Midgeley

She was born in Illinois and was seventy-two when interviewed. She is divorced, has 11 children, and works at the Department of Motor Vehicles. (See also pp. 60, 241 and 256)

I was born in Illinois. My brothers and I were found in an apartment building. There had been reports that babies were crying, and so finally the neighbors called the police, who broke the door down and found the three of us—I was the baby, about five months old; my brothers were a few years older. We were dirty and hungry, and we were all taken to the orphanage in Chicago. I was there from age five months to a year. My father was in prison. My mother was on the street, and that's why we ended up in the orphanage. Each one of us was adopted into different homes. My parents were around fifty when they adopted me. My mother stayed home. My father had his own excavating company.

I met my real mother one time, when I was seventeen, but I never kept in touch with her. She was the direct opposite of the mother that raised me. The mother that raised me was a very Godly woman, soft spoken, clean, just a very nice woman; and my own mother smoked and drank. I never cared to keep in touch with her. So I don't know what ever happened to her. I went to the prison one time to look my father up, around the same time, and I got in the prison, and I got cold feet and left. I don't know what happened to him. One of my brothers tried to find everybody, and he did. He got us together, and then nobody ever kept in touch. We wrote letters for a while, but there was just nothing there, so we lost track.

I had a very good home, although my mother died early for me. My father treated my mother very well. My mother nagged a lot to my dad, but he took it real well. She was very controlling. When we went somewhere, she'd lay out his clothes. He wore what she said. Everything in the house was controlled by her, but I think he liked it that way or he would have said something. She controlled me, also. A lot of my father's work was out of town. He would get a job and be gone for a week or two at a time. So my mother ran everything out of necessity.

We lived in a small town in Illinois. I was raised in the Lutheran church. When I was a kid and an adult came into the room, we stood up, and we didn't sit down until they sat down. We didn't speak until we were spoken to, and that was absolute. You just didn't take over a conversation. You don't have that respect nowadays. When we went to school, we were kids, we thought about kid things. I went to the eleventh grade— and then during the war, there was a bomber factory near my house. A lot of girls from the high school went and worked in the factory, and that was a lot of fun—we begged our parents to quit school so we could work in the factory. We were making bolts for airplanes. We had this big machine we sat at. Then I went back to get my high school diploma. You weren't allowed to date in high school. Well, my folks just didn't allow it. I was busy in high school. I did a lot of public speaking for the Women's Christian Temperance Union.

We did a lot of visiting back and forth with aunts, uncles, grandparents; we always sat and had dinner together. My father opened with a prayer, we ate our meal, he read a chapter of the Bible, he said another prayer, and the meal was over. In the evening my dad would usually read the paper, and my mother would sit knitting or crocheting, and I would be there playing the piano.

I used to go to my grandma's house and wash and comb and braid her long blond hair because she had terrible arthritis. I would make meals for Grandpa, and then I would go out in the barn and help him milk the cows. They lived probably six or seven miles away in the country, but you could bike all over, and there weren't that many cars, and it wasn't dangerous.

I Never Saw My Parents'
Marriage Certificate

Rebecca Rodin

She is a retired high school teacher living in New York City.

"I'm first-generation American. My parents were born in Russia; I was born here in New York in 1913. I have one sister and one half brother—my mother died when I was eleven, and my father remarried. My parents were radicals. My father was a socialist, and later in life, while he never became a party member, he leaned toward communism. That was after the depression when the party influence and the party newspaper were very strong. I became very communist when I was about ten years old. There were several secular Jewish radical organizations, and a number of years I went to the camp which was established by one of them. They conducted everything in Yiddish, and there was a socialist atmosphere. By the time I was fourteen, I went to a communist children's camp by my choice."

We were poor; my father worked in a factory, and his life was very hard. The working hours were very, very long, and it was a long trip to work and back. We lived in a cold-water flat in a rather pleasant working-class neighborhood in Brooklyn. The kitchen was the center of the house. It was what we called a box flat—a big kitchen with a dining area as part of the kitchen and three little boxes around it, two bedrooms and a living or dining room and a bathroom. You had one water faucet and a gas tank. You had to heat the water. The place was heated by a kitchen coal stove—we also cooked on it—and that was the heat for the whole apartment. There was something very cozy about it. After I'd played in the snow, I'd come home and sit near the oven. Mama baked bread once a week, and that was good. In the winter the little rooms around the kitchen were cold all the time. There was no refrigeration except ice and no electricity. We used gas light; we had gas jets—magic lanterns—in the wall. They're kerosene lamps with a mantle that sits over the flame. It makes a rather nice light.

We moved to the Bronx when my mother died, and that apartment had steam heat. There was a very strong workers' co-op movement at the time, and when I was fourteen, we moved to a co-op. A co-op meant you owned the apartment, but you couldn't sell it at a profit; you could only sell it back for what you paid. There was so much idealism attached.

In our group people didn't get married; they lived together. I never saw my parents' marriage certificate. I know my father and stepmother didn't get married. My aunt and uncle didn't get married. Many couples lived together and had children and never married. It was for political reasons, because of their socialist, communist attitudes. "We're against the system, and the system requires that we sanctify the relationship. We can sanctify our own marriages." It was all very ridiculous because they were all so married; they were more married than any couples I've known since. No matter what happened—they would battle, they would hate each other—but the marriages stuck. This was very, very common among small groups of people in places like New York and Chicago.

There was something about revolutionaries and their attitudes towards sex that was very unrealistic. They said things like sex was beautiful, like butterflies flying, but one was embarrassed and didn't talk about it. Underneath it was as repressive as a Victorian household. We did it; we worried about it. Our confusion came from the family, where sex wasn't talked about. More than create guilt, it prevented pleasure and ease. It created ambiguity about what your role should be and prevented women from really enjoying sex.

Guilt about going to bed with someone was not serious. In fact, by a certain age you felt guilty if you didn't, because you had to live up to the ideal that it was perfectly fine for everyone to do exactly what they wanted. But you had a confused feeling about what it should be for you, whether you had a right to choose your partner. Once you were with someone and allowed the foreplay, did you have the right to say good-bye, to say I don't want any more? One of the phrases that was common was "You're a tease." You mustn't be a tease. That's not a nice girl if you make it appear like you're interested, but then you aren't. You were pressured by both the guy and your own ideas about what kind of person you should be. It's strange that that hasn't changed. There was the push to experience and also the fear of experience. And, sure, there was a fear of pregnancy.

When I was very young, I was a Young Pioneer—that was a communist youth group—and we tended to go out in groups. The kissing games started at age fourteen. There were no chaperones. I think that was long past—that was Victorian. I was eighteen the first time I had sex. It was a ridiculous sexual experience, but it happened because I thought I was so old. Life is going to pass me by. I remember a year before, somebody in school implied that she and her boyfriend had had sex but never said it outright. We thought, "Is she lying? Is she bragging? Or is this really true?" I thought she was bragging. I don't think there was any negative stigma attached to it—we were the broad-minded. But there was something about our broad-mindedness that was very much talk. We liked to think about ourselves as being completely tolerant. We saw movies like *Ecstasy*. The talk—What does sex have to do with marriage? Why should you object?—didn't correspond to how people really felt. It was very left-wing ideology.

My parents and their friends also talked about equality between the sexes. But when push came to shove, men were in control of the households. These unmarried families were very conventional, and women stayed at home and took care of the children and did the laundry, the cooking, the washing, the dishes. The men went out to work. He had the money; he controlled it. There were no jobs for women except schoolteachers and secretaries. But the focus for upbringing and education was not marriage and children. It was never brought up that a girl shouldn't have a career. It was, "What are you going to do?" My brother did go to college, but college was not in the agenda for us girls. I reached college age during the depression, and my sister married at eighteen. My family had no money, but many people as poor as we were, particularly Jews, sent their kids—including their daughters—to college.

When I went to high school, I began to have jobs after school. When I was sixteen, I got a job through the guidance office, and I remember feeling very guilty going to the guidance office to ask for a job out of need and then using the money to take music lessons.

For kids like me, it wasn't bad in New York; there was so much theater, and it only cost a dollar. After the theater, if you went to anything, it was the automat. In adolescence it was exciting to go to an event in Manhattan and walk home to the far reaches of the Bronx with three friends. One time I was coming home from something, and friends and I slept all night on benches in front of the lions at the public library and had no fear.

We had a lot of freedom in the city, and it was easy to get around. The streetcars were glamorous and wonderful, completely open in the summer. Some of the cars had one long, wooden bench that went from side to side, the whole width of the car, with no aisle in the middle. There was a running board on the outside, and you hopped on and rode. Macho men—lots of them could be that macho—would stand on the railing on the side and ride that way. It was a nickel to ride on the bus, but the Fifth Avenue bus line was run by a private company, and it was ten cents. I think all the Fifth Avenue buses were double-deckers, and some of them were completely open on top. If it rained you just sat downstairs. Stupid kids would sit there in the wet snow; I remember doing that and having a marvelous time! The subways had wicker seats. When the trains were not crowded, there were often flashers—that was frightening. We were also afraid of groups of young boys who would taunt you verbally. We didn't hear about theft and murder.

I graduated high school in 1931. The depression didn't really hit my family badly until a bit later. At one point I was earning more money on WPA than my father was on PWA. Both of these were work projects created by the Roosevelt administration. My father lost his skilled job, and when the government set up jobs, they were usually manual labor, like ditch digging. His salary was about fifteen dollars a week on jobs like that. On the WPA project I got about twenty-three dollars a week.

I got a full-time job in an office when I was eighteen. My sister was married by then, so I moved in with her, but then I moved a lot. There was more than enough housing at that time, and the landlords were giving concessions—you moved in and had two months rent free, so you lived there until you were thrown out, which could be six months later, and then you started again. People were doubling up to save money. At one point, I had an apartment of my own but no furniture. I had a bed to sleep on and a hot plate. The salaries were so low. My father came to see me and asked for something to eat, and all I had was oatmeal—and he was so upset, but I was young and didn't take it too seriously.

When I was in my mid-twenties, I went to college in the Midwest, stayed there for four years, and graduated in 1941 with a degree in physical education. Before returning to New York, I worked in the Midwest for a few years.

While I lived there, I was raped, but it was my fault, my stupidity. I was hitchhiking at night. I was out somewhere late, and there was no public transportation and I didn't have enough money or even the imagination to think that I could call up a taxi company. This man stopped and picked me up, and we rode for about five minutes, and then he began to make passes, and I said, "No—I'd like to get out please." "What do you think this is?" He was big and strong, and when the guy's about to club you, you don't resist. It didn't have a strong effect on me for very long. It was an ugly experience, and I wanted to put it out of my mind. I blamed myself. It wasn't so much anger as anger at myself. Sure, it wasn't my fault—it was his fault—but it really isn't very sensible to take a ride at night with a man alone. It's not that you know that you're going to be raped; it's that you don't know what will happen. In retrospect, I don't think it was so much naivete as an instinct for taking chances. I wasn't thinking that way at the time, but my tendency is that if the chances are very small, it might not happen this time. So I take a chance.

I Felt Very Sorry for My Mother

Betsy Miller

She lives with her husband in La Jolla, California.

*"I'm fourth-generation Californian in my mother's side, and my father was born in Califor-
nia. I was their only child, born in Oakland in 1929, right before the crash. I majored in political
science at U.C. Berkeley, hoping to go on and do something in that field, but I never did anything. I
got married at the age of twenty-one, before graduating, during the Korean War, and started a
family, and that was it." (See also pp. 52, 258 and 407)*

My mother had been the most talked-about debutante in Berkeley, and my father was
the golden boy. He had been educated in France, went to Lawrenceville Prep School
in New Jersey and to Princeton. He didn't have to do anything. He had a lot of money.
So it was a marriage made in heaven that just fell apart completely.

The family money was lost at the time of the stock market crash, and they never really
recovered. My mother picked up the family and carried on. She worked because someone had to make enough money so we could eat, and she did a wonderful job for a beautiful debutante. She worked down at a department store as an underpaid executive, the
female equivalent of head of department. She was a cultured woman, but she hadn't finished Berkeley. She took a job where she could get it. My grandmother—my father's
mother—lived with us and played the grande dame. She still gave little tea parties with
all the silver and china. She played bridge.

I felt very sorry for my mother. I thought that I needed to take care of her. I did
shopping and cooking and vacuuming. There was none of this mother baking cookies
for me. I became the mother.

My father was a gentleman, a very lovely, sweet, intelligent, wonderful man. He
had been a flier in the First World War. He gave me the most loving background. He
was the person I went to for comfort. I adored him, but he had a very sad life. After
learning that he didn't have any money anymore, he couldn't deal with it. He drank a
lot, and he had jobs, and then he'd lose them. Being an alcoholic, he lost his dominance
in the family. My mother moved out of the bedroom and had her own room and made
him sleep downstairs in another room. He was rejected because he was a failure in life,

she said. I think she simply took the opportunity to do it because she just didn't care for sex. He had a very sorry, sorry demise. He died when I was twenty-three in part from alcoholism.

My mother and her mother had a fight over the fact that she stayed with my father. My grandmother thought that she should leave her husband. There was violence and fights, and my grandmother didn't want me to stay in this atmosphere. I don't think my father physically assaulted my mother, but he could be sort of violent to himself—knocking down doors and things. My mother and grandmother didn't speak until I got married, and I brought them together again.

My grandmother had left her husband. In fact, she'd left two husbands, and so she felt that they were easily discarded rather than staying and putting up and compromising. Her mother—my great-grandmother—had left her husband and was divorced, also. She was a Cornell and grew up in New York society.

I grew up in a very matriarchal society, and I felt that women had a right to express what they needed, to live their lives the way they thought they should, and that one did not have to be caught up in a situation that dragged you down.

My mother didn't like working. She still kept up with all her social friends who met for lunch and played bridge, and she felt ashamed that she was working, but she carried on beautifully. She was a heroine. In my family it was considered proper to go to college, but then you were supposed to get married and raise a family. College was like finishing school—women were sent for the extra years of culture and perhaps to make sure that they were in a social environment where they would find the appropriate husband, of the same social class.

Hazel Akeroyd

She was born in 1911 in South Dakota. (See also p. 420)

*P*regnant women, including my mother, wore tight corsets, and they were not little—they had steel stays in them, and they laced up in the back.

You didn't let anybody know you were pregnant until you just absolutely couldn't keep it in, and then you didn't appear in public. I don't remember my mother going out, not when she was eight or nine months pregnant. You never showed your pregnancy.

Mother told me that she was going to have a baby, but she told me very little about it. Sex and pregnancies were not discussed. They were embarrassing.

She had her babies at home, all except one. You were not aware of it, and you didn't talk about it. When my sister Dorothy was born, the neighbors came over and took my brother and sister and me over to their house to spend the night. I thought it was rather odd—they didn't tell us why we had to go there—and the next day at school recess my brother went home and came back and said, "We've got a new baby sister." Mother stayed in bed three weeks afterward.

Jane Foley

She was born in 1919 in New Orleans, where she lives with her husband. She has thirteen children and is now employed by Catholic Charities working with refugees. (See also pp. 47 and 62)

*I*n 1926 or '27, my mother died. She committed suicide in the Mississippi River, which I didn't find out about until I was thirty-seven years old. This type of thing was never mentioned—it was taboo. We were five children. The oldest was eight, and the baby was just eight months old. I was six. My mother had never recovered from having the baby. She went into a deep depression. My father and the five children then lived with my grandmother and his sister, who was a thirty-year-old schoolteacher. My grandmother and aunt were wonderful and saw to it that we were well taken care of. My aunt had to quit her teaching job because it was too much for her mother to take care of us.

Betty Marin

She was born in San Francisco in 1930, went to the University of California at Berkeley for three semesters, and got married when she was twenty. Her daughter was born two years later. She never finished college and has held mainly part-time jobs, including clerical, secretarial, and sales work. She and her husband live in La Jolla, California. (See also p. 257)

*M*y father was an investment banker, and my mother never worked, ever, ever in her life. She was incredibly attractive and charming and also had a wild temper and was very unhappy, and no one ever really knew why she was so unhappy. She would take to her bed for days at a time and stay in bed all day, and then she'd get up and put on a hostess-type outfit and greet my dad when he came home from work. My mother ended up dying when she was sixty-six of an overdose of sleeping pills. She was about to go to Europe for ten days, and everything was apparently going all right. She had had a problem with sleeping pills off and on all through her life, trying to get prescriptions that she shouldn't really have. We tried to feel that this was an accident—that she had taken some pills and wasn't sleeping and thought she'd take a couple more, and that was the couple more that were too many.

Before my father married my mother he was selling burlap grain bags to the farmers in the San Joaquin Valley. When he met her, it was just this mad falling in love romance, and my mother announced to him that she would absolutely not be married to somebody who sold grain bags. This was not what she had in mind for her life. She suggested that he get into something like becoming a stockbroker, so he went to work for this company in San Francisco. This was just before the 1929 crash, which was not a wonderful time to be starting in the stock market, but this was his absolute calling. He was so successful that by the time I was five, we moved into this house in the Bay Area with a live-in housekeeper.

My mother shopped. She was what I'd call a professional shopper. There were boxes of things when she died that had never even been opened. When they were first married, she had no idea of money, and so they were overdrawn all the time. When she died, she had a huge bank account of like over fifty thousand dollars. My dad would give her presents like money for Christmas, and instead of spending it, she'd put it in an account. That totally surprised us. I think she had this fear of being left without, part of her insecurity feelings.

Towards the end of her life she was in bed more than she was up. She wore those black sleeping shades, and even when I was in grammar school, I used to come home for lunch, and she'd still be in bed; and she'd be sitting up with her Christian Science book (she was a pseudo Christian Scientist, using it when she thought she needed it) and her checkbook and writing, paying bills, and calling stores on the phone and ordering things.

I was brought up to think that you had to please people. So a good part of my life has been spent trying to please people, which fortunately I have now learned I don't have to do. I did all the right things, met my parents' expectations, like getting good grades and being popular. I took the dancing lessons and the piano lessons, and I wore the hair ribbons. At the dinner table if I piped up with something that was controversial to my parents, I was told to be quiet, that children have their place. Neither my brother or I were allowed to voice our opinions. Everything with them was image. From the outside, we looked like the most wonderful family. The father makes all this money, and they live in this gorgeous house, and the mother's so beautiful, and they entertain at these lovely parties—my parents had parties like you would not believe, all the time, parties, parties, parties, parties; my mother arranged flowers, and the house was so gorgeous, and people loved to come to our house for parties—and the children are all so well behaved. And nobody said anything to anybody in this family. You didn't talk about anything bad. Feelings were not discussed. We played this fairy tale game.

I confronted my mother the year before she died and stood up to her for the first time in thirty-six years, and I was so amazed how I won. She was insisting we come for Christmas, and I wanted to stay home with my family. I told her, "I'm sorry—I'm not going to come," and I said, "You can scream and yell and threaten, and I'm not coming." And lo and behold, she backed off and didn't do anything, and I was so overwhelmed—I thought I should have stood up to her twenty years ago. I was glad we kind of got it together the last year of her life. I was able to tell her some of the things that I felt. At least, I'd come to terms with her a little bit. When somebody dies suddenly, if you've got some unfinished business with them, it's hard to deal with and you can't ever finish it.

Helene Weintraub

She is a widow and lives in New York City, where she was born in 1911. She worked in public relations most of her life. Her parents were Russian Jewish immigrants. (See also pp. 52 and 224)

I was my mother's confidante. It was a very, very troubled, tempestuous marriage. My father was constantly in pursuit of some other female. He was also a very volatile personality, strong streak of gambler. From the time I was about ten or younger, I was aware of my father's infidelities and my mother's distress. I remember going to camp when I was ten years old and being worried about what would happen to her while I was away. At one point, my father decided he wanted to leave us and live with or marry his current girlfriend, and he asked me would I understand, and I said I'd never talk to him again if he did this.

My mother was crazy about him, and I'm not sure whether she could ever have brought herself to leave him. But certainly in those days it was far more common that women put up with terrible marriages because they had no means of supporting themselves. They knew perfectly well that they would be penniless if they left. The other thing was that divorce was a *shanda*—something shameful—and their parents expected them to stay in the marriage, no matter what. So I don't think my mother ever thought of divorce, and when my father proposed it, at the time he had met this woman, she was frantic. I never did know the details. I just know that in a relatively short time he and my mother seemed to have reconciled.

Lillian Roth

She was born in 1918 and has always lived in Brooklyn, New York. For most of her life she worked as a legal secretary. (See also p. 437)

We were in a lot of financial trouble during the depression. We moved a lot. In those years, when poor people couldn't pay the rent, they moved somewhere else and got a month's concession. By the time I finished high school, I had been to a dozen schools. We were on relief for a long time.

From the time I was a child I wanted to be a teacher, but there was no thought in my family that they should skimp on other things and send me to college. Even though I was obviously the brightest child in the family, my mother was looking for jobs for me before I finished high school. I remember thinking, "Thank goodness this job fell through, and I can stay in school." Whereas my brother—she would have done anything to push him ahead. But when he was in high school, he was diverted to a vocational school because he wasn't doing well. But this was her pet, the one she loved. She didn't have a great respect for girls because this was the background that she came from. I felt very lucky that I managed to stay in high school until I graduated. Then I immediately went to work and turned whatever I earned every week over to her. I started to go to City College at night, but I found it very hard because I was working and going to school and never having a decent dinner. So after about a year at City, I dropped out. I have to admit that my parents were very poor and uneducated, but I could have gone to City College—there was no tuition. But I had to get a job. That was it.

One of my daughters has a doctorate, the other is an attorney. It never occurred to me that because they were girls, they shouldn't have a good education. I wanted them to have the best.

I didn't go back to school until I was in my mid-fifties. My daughters said to me, "You always wanted to be a teacher, why don't you go on to get a master's degree?" So I did that. I taught for about six years but always as an adjunct.

Everything Was So Segregated

Marguerite Rucker

She is a retired professor of nursing and lives with her husband in New Orleans. She has two daughters, one of whom is a physician.

"I'm African-American, with French and Indian ancestry. I was born in Lake Charles, Louisiana, near the Texas border, in 1926, and I am an only child. My mother was a teacher in a one-room schoolhouse. My father had a market and grocery store. We went to a Baptist and Methodist church, but I attended Catholic school." (See also p. 426)

*B*lacks did not come in contact with a lot of whites in my day, because everything was so segregated. Blacks lived on one side of town, and whites lived on the other. I went to a black school and a black church. My father's business was in a black community. It was very different from what it is now. I appreciate the change.

In Catholic high school, the students were black, but the nuns were white. There were two or three black lay teachers on the faculty. I happened to live next door to the convent, so even though we were not Catholic, my mother sent me there because it was a better school than the public school, and it was very convenient.

The nuns wore the black habit—only the face and hands showed. They had long sleeves and a veil. As a child I used to see them hang these things out on the porch upstairs to dry—they had this long, white underwear, longjohns. Their balcony was on the side of my house, and sometimes I would just look up there, and I'd see the sisters' underwear! It was fascinating to me.

The school was coed. We wore uniforms: navy skirts and white midi blouses with the red tie and the sailor collar. In high school, the uniforms changed to a navy blue jumper and a long-sleeved, white blouse and knee-high socks. No makeup. I can remember wearing lipstick, maybe when I was a junior or senior. You wore it for a special occasion. I'd put a little powder on. I didn't have any of my own, so I'd get into my mother's makeup. She wore eye liner, powder, and rouge.

There were always two or three chaperones for a dance. If you danced with a boy and got too close, somebody gave you the eye, and then if you didn't respond to that, somebody tapped you on your shoulder. It could be a sister or one of the lay teachers, whoever chaperoned the dance. My father used to take me to the door of the party and leave me there, and then he would come back and walk me home. If a young man was with me, then he walked on up ahead, and we followed him, or sometimes he was behind us. My school went only to eleventh grade. The first time I went out with a boy by myself was the junior-senior prom. Before then you saw each other at school, and maybe you wrote notes or something like that.

On my sixteenth birthday I was allowed to have company at my house, and I remember that very, very well. A young man came on a Sunday afternoon, and he met my mother and father, even though they already knew him—we were classmates; they knew his parents. We sat in the living room, and we just talked and giggled and laughed. And then maybe an hour later, my father came to the door and looked at me, and I knew that it was time for him to go. They always teased me about my father. Classmates would ask this young man, "You and Mr. Curtis going to take Marguerite to the dance Friday night?" As I got older, the boys would have their family's car, and then they had to come to the door and take me to the car and open the door. If a young man picked you up and didn't do that, he was not of good breeding, and he was frowned upon. They probably wouldn't let me go out with him again. But I never had anybody who didn't do it. We wore stockings to go out on a date. We dressed like we were going to church. You'd go on a date, and you'd have fun, and a good-night kiss was a big thing. If you got kissed at the door, he had scored!

Now, some girls managed to see fellows in a more intimate relation, because some of them had the misfortune of becoming pregnant. (I never could figure out how they did that.) That was about the worst thing that could happen to a young lady. If you were pregnant, you could not go to school. Premarital sex was just a no-no. Families were very ashamed. We had a neighbor whose daughter became pregnant, and her parents sent her away for about a year. When she came back, she went to school and finished as if it never happened. We found out later that a family member took the baby. When she became an adult, she claimed that child.

One of my cousins got pregnant. She was a senior in high school, and there was this shotgun wedding. It was all hush-hush. I knew that something had gone on—people would whisper. Then when I found out that she was going to have a baby, my mother did talk to me about it. I remember her telling me how disappointed she would be if this happened to me. She said, "I don't know what I would do. I think I would just leave. I don't think that I could handle the embarrassment if you got pregnant." I know that my mother would not have left me, but I always remembered that. I was definitely a virgin when I got married! The worst thing that could happen to me would be to disappoint my mother.

Later, when I was in college in New Orleans during World War II, there were very few men on campus. They had army camps and the navy here in the city, and they would be invited to our dances. That was a lot of pressure on some girls. I never felt pressured. I liked to have a good time, but there was this limit. And it was no ifs, ands, buts about it. There was some petting, but that had to be somebody I knew very, very, very well. They'd call me very stiff.

I finished second in my high school class, and I wanted to go to nursing school. The public health nurse in my hometown had come to my school, and she was my role model. I found out about this new nursing program at Dillard University, a small, black, liberal arts college here in New Orleans. That was in 1943. As far as I know, until then there had been no school of nursing in Louisiana that accepted blacks. Black nurses had been prepared out of state. Dillard offered a five-year collegiate program. You received a bachelor of science degree in nursing.

At Dillard, the nursing faculty was predominantly black. Dillard students only had Flint Goodrich Hospital, which was a small, private, black hospital and could not offer all of the services that the students in a collegiate program were required to have. Flint was good for surgery and outpatient and ob-gyn. For everything else, our dean was able to get an agreement for us to go into Charity Hospital in the black wing. It was completely segregated. You could draw a line down the center of the hospital; there was a colored side, and there was a white side. Charity is an excellent teaching hospital supported by state funds and connected with LSU and Tulane. They allowed us to get pediatric experience there and communicable-disease medicine, eye, ear, nose, and throat. We had to go all the way to Homer Phillips in St. Louis for psychiatric nursing. They would not let us use the psychiatric service at Charity because there was no psychiatric black and white side. I think they just had them separated within the unit.

At the beginning of the third year we began our field experience and went to Charity. Nobody at the hospital—doctors, nurses, secretaries, ward clerk, would call us "Miss." We were called "Nurse," Nurse Hartman, Nurse Davis, Nurse Brown. In those days white people called black people by their first name; they didn't use Miss or Mrs. It was a demeaning thing. I'll never forget Sister Anne, the head nurse in our medical unit. In the morning all of the affiliating students would gather out on the solarium. It was a roll call to find out if you were present, and then you would be assigned to your ward. (Charity Hospital nurses had first preference to everything; this was home to them.) So when Sister called the roll, she went through all of these affiliates, "Miss so-and-so, Miss so-and-so, Miss so-and-so." When she got to the

Dillard affiliates, she started, "Nurse so-and-so, Nurse so-and so, Nurse so-and-so." We didn't believe what we were hearing, but we said, "Here," "Here," "Here." I was just flabbergasted. I had come from a Catholic school, where I had teachers that were nuns that I adored. Well, this went on and on, and one morning she was late getting there, so she was calling the roll, and when she got to the Dillard group, she said, "Miss Davis, Miss Edwards . . ." and then when she realized that she was calling us Miss, she went back to the top of that list and said, "Nurse Davis, Nurse Edwards," etc. So from that day on, we just never answered. We didn't say, "Here." So she didn't know whether we were there or not.

Our dean had talked to us before we went there, and she said, "Ladies, I know you've heard a lot of stories about Charity from the upper classmen, but what you have to remember is that Charity has something that you need. There's some flack that you're going to have to take in order to get what you need. Get it and then walk away from it, and it's yours forever. If you keep that in mind, that will help you to deal with the frustrations that you are going to encounter." So that helped a lot, but it was very, very hard. When the affiliates went to class, the black students sat in the back to the side, and there was a curtain between us and the other students. We could see the speaker, but the white students next to you could not see you.

They would test all the students and post everybody's grades out on the bulletin board in the hall in the hospital. The first semester, they had our names up, and almost always the first eleven or twelve names were Dillard students—there were fourteen of us in my class, and we did better than they did. We were from a college program, and they were right out of high school into nursing, so we had a better background. They could not handle it. You know what they did? They gave us all numbers. From that time on, you had to go and find your number!

One day I was in the labor unit, and the physician wasn't affiliated with LSU or Tulane. Apparently, he was not from this area. My classmate Stella Pecko was assigned to the unit where he was. He came to the door, and he said, "Miss Pecko." So she turned around to go. I was out in the hall, and I heard this head nurse tell Dr. Jacobs, "We don't call them Miss, Doctor." So he looked at her and said, "I call Miss Pecko what I damn please. You can't tell me what to call anybody." So there were some bright lights. It really bothered her—she came out to tell him! If I had not heard that, I would not have believed it. Stella said that's the first time she really felt like a person since she had been there. Those were the kinds of things that we encountered. It was really a pleasure when we were able to go to Homer Phillips in St. Louis, which was a black hospital.

How Could I Have
Just Accepted It

Caroline Hodges

She was born in the Deep South, where she still lives with her husband. They have five children. (See also pp. 54, 246 and 412)

I was born in 1927, the year of a great flood on the Mississippi. I grew up in a small town on a gravel street with board sidewalks. My childhood was a very stable, comfortable, totally segregated, agricultural kind of life, very southern. I was born in the house I lived in until I went off to college. All four of my mother's children were born at home. I went mainly to Catholic parochial schools and a Catholic girls' college. I kind of feel like I'm a product of the *Gone with the Wind* era.

We all lived in close proximity, blacks and whites. The black parochial school was right behind our house, and as a child I would sit on the roof of what started out as the woodshed and ended up as a garage and watch the children play. I grew up firmly believing that we had an equal but separate school system. I understand now, it's not true. I don't know why as a child you can't see the difference between a very large, fairly modern building and a small, not nearly so well kept building.

We always had a black maid. Occasionally, if the maid couldn't stay with me and Mother was going to be gone, I would go to her house and play with Josie. I just envied the maid's daughter so, because she had a little black, iron stove that she could make a little fire in, and I thought that was the most wonderful toy I had ever seen. But otherwise we really didn't play together. That was the way it was. I don't think I was really aware of racial discrimination until I went to college in Texas, and the nuns were rightfully speaking of the injustice of segregation of blacks from whites. The irony of it was that in Texas there existed terrible discrimination between the whites and the Mexicans, but that didn't seem to bother them.

Jane Foley

She was born in New Orleans in 1919 and works for Catholic Charities. (See also pp. 37 and 62)

We used to use the bus and streetcars, and they had wooden boards that said "For colored only." They had little receptacles that would hold the sign in place on the top of a seat. The black people were not allowed to sit in front of wherever that sign was. They could move it, as long as they didn't move it in front of a white person.

They had a fountain for white people, a fountain for black people. Black people were not served in the restaurant, couldn't sit at a counter and get a Coke. There were black public schools, and there were white public schools. Even in church, they had pews at the back of the church, two or three, for colored only.

Years later, you look back and think, "How could I have just accepted this without question when it's so inhuman, so insulting, and so wrong?" It never occurred to me that there was anything wrong with this! I didn't even pay attention. It was the way things were. It makes you understand how people accept things as a way of life, like this is the way it is.

Mining Towns Were
Rough and Ready

Jean Hughes

She is a retired medical technologist and lives with her husband in La Jolla, California. She has four children and three grandchildren.

"I was born in 1923 in Butte, Montana. I have a sister and a brother. My father's family immigrated from Sweden when he was four years old and came to Montana. They were given a land grant, and we had a ranch outside of Butte. When it came time for me to go to school, my parents decided we should go to public schools, so we moved into Butte. My father worked for the highway department in building roads and highways, and he was always employed. We fortunately did not suffer during the depression." (See also pp. 255 and 436)

My mother had been a schoolteacher, but when she married, that was the end of that. Women were not allowed to teach after they were married. I think she accepted it because she enjoyed her family and had clubs she belonged to and always read a lot and was an excellent cook. You look back on your life and on your family, and you wonder what they really thought, but it was never an unhappy home life. Even when I was growing up and going to school, teachers weren't allowed to teach after they were married. That was clear up, I think, until the forties. I guess they thought that it took a job away from someone else, that their husband would have a job and could provide. I had one married teacher, but she was a widow.

My mother was a good musician. We had a grand piano. We had a radio, and I remember very distinctly when Charles Lindbergh landed in Paris. My sister and I were outside playing. My father, my mother, my uncle, my grandmother came out and got us, made us come in and hear about this wonderful event. This man flew a plane nonstop from our country to Europe, and he was the first to do it. It took him about thirty-three hours.

My mother was rather prissy, but in a lot of ways maybe that was nice. I never even knew about gay people until maybe I was in college. And also drugs. I didn't know about marijuana. Proper behavior was to abstain from any sexual activity until you were married. In my mother's eyes you were almost a prostitute if that was your type of activity. She was very strict on that—"That isn't what our family does." But we were allowed to go out on dates, to dances. My mother said, "I trust you." One thing that wasn't allowed—no one could honk the horn in front of the house. They had to come in and be introduced to my parents. My mother would have to know where we were going, what we were going to do.

Butte was very international because it was a mining settlement. People came from everywhere, and it was wonderful because it was small enough to be friends with most people, and you weren't isolated in one nationality. We had a few blacks in high school who were elected to office in our class. In the later years, most people in our community were Democrats; it got so that there wasn't even a Republican on the slate—they could never win. The town at its peak was at most forty thousand. When my father died, there was a great public outpouring from everyone. Even the senator, who we had known in a passing way, wrote to my mother. It was just a nice, warm feeling.

There was an Italian section in Butte called Meaderville, where they had wonderful restaurants that served Italian food, but there were also night clubs and a lot of illegal gambling. Mining towns were rough and ready. I was down there one night when they raided a night club. They would just close up the crap tables and the roulette and roll all the slot machines into the women's restroom—the men wouldn't go into a women's restroom. That was very clever. There was always payola, of course. This was the kind of town I lived in, and I liked it.

Women were respected, and you could walk anywhere. A man might shoot his wife for infidelity, but there was never a rape. And there were bars all over. Somebody wrote their thesis on all the bars in Butte. There was drinking, there was drunkenness, but there was also a respect for a woman. There were women in there that would get just as drunk as the men, but they weren't violated. That was true of all mining camps. There was the red-light district in our town, which rivaled the Barbary Coast because there were so many miners that weren't married. It was a natural thing. The hospital people used to go down and test the prostitutes for gonorrhea and syphilis. Before penicillin, syphilis was a terrible disease. It was terribly hard to cure and the cure was mean, hard on the patient.

My parents wanted me to marry but also to get a college degree. Many of my father's friends would say to him, "Why are you sending your girls to college? You know they'll just get married." And he said, "No, this is what we have in mind for them; if anything happens to their husband or they don't get married, they'll have something better." After a while, I was dissatisfied in college, and I said, "Well, maybe I won't go back." "That's fine," he said. "I bet I could get you a good, hot job in the laundry." So that helped, and I really have always been very appreciative of my parents for having that attitude.

My sister and I went to Montana State School of Mines in Butte. It is now called Montana Tech. The school would not let women graduate at that time, in the forties. Their degrees were in mining, engineering, geology, petroleum engineering, and mineralogy. There was a superstition that women were bad luck in mines. They didn't want any women down a mine, and, of course, you'd have to go down a mine if you were going to get a degree in mining engineering. Also, they had field classes where they'd be camped somewhere, and they felt that there weren't the right facilities for a woman. That was the excuse.

It was a difficult school. I remember the first day of chemistry class. The professor was Dr. Koenig, and everybody was a bit afraid of him. He said, "Look on your right," and you'd look, and then he'd say, "Look on your left," and then he said, "One of those are going to be gone at the mid-term." That was pretty much the attitude, but it didn't hurt me to go there.

I had wanted to take a class in organic chemistry, but it was an upper-division course strictly for boys. So first I had to petition the president of the college. In the interview, he finally believed me that I would not be seeking a degree in mining engineering, so he said, "If the professor lets you in, I give you my permission." He let me in. I told him I was planning to transfer. I was trying to convince him that I didn't want to be a mining engineer.

After two years, I transferred to Montana State University and got a bachelor's degree in bacteriology. World War II was on, and they were training soldiers at the universities. The young men would be there for two or three months, and they took over the dorm. So one year I lived in a private home, and then the last year, '44–'45, the military had left, so we were back in the dorms. Some coeds lived in fraternity houses because the men were all gone to war. There were a few men there that couldn't make the military.

We had to get permission from the dean of admission to be off campus on the weekends. Monday through Thursday nights, we had to be in the dorm about fifteen or twenty minutes after the library closed, usually at ten. We checked in and checked out—we had a book in the entry to the dorm, and you put down your name, the time, where you were going. When you came back, you signed in. On Friday or Saturday night, we had to be back in at one A.M., and Sunday about eleven or twelve.

It was always like, Wouldn't it be fun to come in and sneak back out? And that wasn't unheard of. But mainly you followed the rules because if you were caught, you couldn't go off campus the following weekend. It was a protective thing for women. The fraternity houses, where the males were, had a housemother, but they did not have hours. The men were free.

On a Saturday if we had a lab, we could wear jeans or slacks, but to class even in the coldest of winter you wore a skirt or a dress. That was the dress code, and I'm glad that has changed.

There wasn't a lot of dating, except there were always military groups, and there would be parties for them, or you could go to the student union and drink coffee and Coke and listen to the music. We had jukeboxes, and sometimes we danced. Once this fella came over and asked me to dance, and I stood up, and he said, "Oh, you're too tall," and he walked away. I'm five-eleven, and I felt that a lot.

I was still at the School of Mines when the Japanese bombed Pearl Harbor on December the 7th, 1941. It was a Sunday. Monday morning, the president called an assembly that everyone had to attend. He spoke mainly to the men and said, "I urge you to finish out this year. Don't go and enlist." But the majority enlisted before the end of the year. Now the attitude would certainly be entirely different. Of the fellas who had once been on the Bozeman football team, not one of them came back. One of my roommates had married just before her husband left—he was killed. There was a lot of sorrow.

My grandparents lived in South Pasadena, and I came to California during those summers while I was in college. One summer I worked at Douglas Aircraft in Long Beach, and another I worked for Southern California Gas Company. That's the time that turned the tide for women because they became very essential to our country in defense work. My aunt had been the only woman in the architectural school at Montana State University. She had one semester to finish, and she got married and didn't get her degree (she taught elementary school), which I'm sure she regretted the rest of her life. But during the war she worked in the engineering department at Douglas Aircraft. I worked in their procurement department. They were making C47s and A26s, and I got to go out and see these planes, and it was very exciting for me because I came from a small town. Women were what is now known as liberated because we were doing men's work. "Rosie the Riveter" was real.

John, who became my husband, had gone from school into the service, and so we got married after the war, in September of 1946.

The Path of Femininity

Laurine Warren

She was born in 1912 and grew up in Mississippi, where her family has lived for generations. (See also pp. 25, 63, 225 and 424)

My mother didn't go into the details of sex, but she did tell us that we were going to have a menstrual period. She talked about that at length with us. But as far as sex itself went, my mother said, "There are things that your husband will tell you," and those were the words she used.

Helene Weintraub

She was born in New York City in 1911. (See also pp. 39 and 224)

All my friends had a period of premarital relations with their husbands before they married. All of them were depression babies with long periods of waiting till they were making a living, so there was no question that they would have premarital sex.

We never talked about sex. Certainly, if we had an affair with someone, particularly before we were married, we would have a confidante, and we might even discuss, compare, in terms of his effectiveness as a lover, but not the kind of detailed description of sexual activity that I believe young people indulge in today.

Betsy Miller

She was born in California in 1929 right before the stock market crash.
*   "My mother had been the most talked-about debutante in Berkeley, and my father was the golden boy." (See also pp. 35, 258 and 407)*

*W*hen I was very young, I felt that women were missing out on life. I would help my father build airplanes or boats, and he still flew when he could, and I thought, "A man's world is better than a woman's world." It was exciting, and intellectually they were allowed to go further. I was very good in school and very good in math. In high school there was boys' chemistry and girls' chemistry—for girls who couldn't quite fathom atoms or molecules. I took boys' chemistry. Girls were discouraged from taking math after a certain level.

I was a tomboy. Jeans were very hard to find at that time. I have a picture of myself standing in an army hat with a fishing pole in a pair of jeans catching fish. I've caught the fish and they're on my belt, and I'm five years old. I applied to get a *Saturday Evening Post* route, and they said, "Only boys get to do that." I tried to join the Cub Scouts, and they said, "Only boys get to do that." I just went on butting my head against the brick wall for years. I really wanted to live in this boys' world. I wanted to be a boy.

I was a great runner. I would run all the way to school every day and back, and I bicycled a lot. I was a tall child, so I was stopped in the morning to play basketball with the other boys before school. I was never allowed to play real football, but I played sandlot football and sandlot baseball and sandlot basketball, anything I could. The girls didn't have Little League then. If I had been a boy, I would imagine that someone would have said, "You're very good at running, you could be a triathlon athlete." Also, "You're very good at math."

My mother told me about menstruation in an awkward fashion, sort of mentioning the possibility, and I said, "Well, I refuse to do that. I don't care for that option." I had no idea that she was telling me something that was inevitable. I must have been about eight or nine.

As time went on, I saw the other girls were more oriented towards the female role, so I had to move over. I had to stop playing basketball and football, and I had to be my sex and play my role in society. I started to stop doing those things when I developed breasts. I couldn't get out there in a T-shirt and jeans and look like a little boy anymore. I was a female, and I was destined to marry and have a family. My family was trying to mold me into the proper debutante type, so I worked very hard at being that. I put on my little suit and gloves and hat and went to more of the social things. When we were fourteen years old, we went to lots of charity tea parties and little dances—set social rituals in Piedmont, which was an upper-class suburb.

We did not have a debutante ball in Piedmont. That was done in San Francisco. We were debutantes in our own way—not quite putting this white virgin in this white dress on the dock. When you graduated from high school, there were luncheons and teas organized by the girls with their mothers in charge.

So we were invited to tea parties, and there were fashion shows, and you had to wear your heels and your white gloves and an appropriate little suit and little matching hat. We went and had tea so many times that these friends of mine and I said, let's get our revenge. We planned it for weeks and weeks. We went to my house one afternoon, and we made sandwiches and brownies and brewed the tea and had all sorts of petits fours and we went in the living room with a silver tray I still have. We put on our jeans and our tennis shoes, and we threw the sandwiches and the petits fours at each other, had our cup of tea and sat there with our hands and our feet up over the back of the couch and had a lovely tea party where we didn't have to be polite or sit with our feet on the ground. We were about fifteen by that time. All of us were playing a role. I saw it for what it was, but I knew that was the only way, the only path I had to go.

Our society had various things that started the girls along the path of femininity. You were invited to join these all-girls charitable groups. From the age of twelve, I belonged to a junior branch of the children's hospital and the children's orphanage. These were made into little social groups, and children were elected to them on the basis of popularity. Each Saturday morning this friend and I would get up at six in the morning and take the train out to the children's hospital—we became therapists at the age of thirteen! It was called play therapy. I don't think they would let children do that now. They said the orphaned children will relate to children. We were taught by playing with them to help them. We did that for years, went out there, free of charge, to give our time. In college I still belonged to that group, and we'd go and take the kids out to the movies on Saturdays. We were always involved in the community, and these projects were always girl work.

Caroline Hodges

She was born in 1927 in the Deep South.
"I kind of feel like I'm a product of the Gone with the Wind *era." (See also pp. 46, 246 and 412)*

My mother loved beautiful clothes—she was a wonderful seamstress. I wanted a store-bought dress when I was in grammar school so bad. In high school and college, Mother made my evening dresses. She copied a lot of clothes out of fashion magazines. When

I was a child, we never went to the city where all the big stores were without gloves. You always wore a hat and gloves to church.

When my mother let me shave my legs, that was really important. It was a coming of age. For makeup, we started out with rice powder, at least I did. It's dead white, and I guess it actually is pounded rice. You washed your hair once a week. We used cistern rainwater because it was very soft. We didn't have any hairspray, so I would roll up my hair every night in pin curls with bobby pins. When I was a child, the curlers were made of kid leather, and they had wire in them. You rolled them up and then bent the ends in. But the curl in humid weather would come out very quickly, so sometimes you'd roll your hair up two or three times a day. You could never go to sleep without rolling up your hair. You used lemon juice on it to take the soap out at the end of the shampoo. You couldn't wash your hair if you were menstruating.

When I went to college, you could not get on the bus to go to town without stockings on. Nylons hadn't been invented. There weren't any panty hose. You wore silk stockings. During the war, you couldn't get silk stockings, so you had lisle stockings. They were about as fine as you could get out of primarily cotton fibers. We'd get on the back of the bus and take our stockings off. And, of course, we always wore panty girdles to keep our stockings up. I was always a little chubby, but everybody wore girdles. It wasn't lycra like they have now, but it was elasticized, so it had a lot more in the front to hold your tummy in. Some of the girdles had longer legs, but most of them just came up to where your leg joins onto your body—the way panties used to—and they had supporters, a little loop of elastic, what's on the end of a garter belt. Hot as the devil in the summertime—we didn't have air-conditioning. If you tried to get into a panty girdle on a July day in the South with the humidity and the heat and no air-conditioning, you would have to use talcum powder just to get it up. But we're spending an awful lot of time on underwear. I wish we could get above the waist.

Everybody wore a brassiere whether you needed one or not, and I certainly never did. I always wore a padded bra. That's the only good thing that came out of the women's movement as far as I'm concerned. I burned my bra.

My Parents Were Professional Bridge Players

Jane Winthrop

She lives with her husband in a small town in the Northeast and has two children, one from each of her two earlier marriages.

"I was born in Ohio, in 1931. Mother and Father got divorced when I was thirteen."

My father was a professional bridge player. From day one, I lived with my grand-mother—my father's mother—because my mother and father were traveling all over the world playing bridge professionally. They were life masters. He wrote bridge articles for the *New York Times* under an alias name and was one of the most famous bridge writers in this country.

I didn't see my parents very often. They really weren't too fond of me, but thank goodness for Grandmother. Grandmother was mother. She did everything she pos-sibly could to make my life happy. She raised me and my cousin. I'm very close to my cousin, who's more of a brother to me. His father was remarried, so Grandmother was stuck with two children. And she spoiled us rotten. She was a wonderful person. My grandmother traveled quite a bit, and I'd do a lot of traveling with her. Some-times Grandmother would go to Europe and leave me with the chauffeur and his wife, who babysat me. My parents had a house in Cincinnati, but I never lived there until my grandmother died when I was thirteen. When I went home to their house, my parents would drink all night—they had parties until two or three in the morn-ing—and sleep all day long. Once when I was maybe nine or ten, I slept at their house, and awakened during the night terrified. One of my father's best friends, who was known as a womanizer, was standing over me. I screamed, and he walked away. I don't know if anything happened. It was not healthy.

My grandmother was divorced from my grandfather, who was a famous orthope-dic surgeon in New York City. He married a chorus girl. At that time that was shock-ing. Divorce was a scandal. The family always hated her because she was a chorus girl, but she was a nice person, always so kind to me.

My grandmother had something like ten servants. It was a big house, and we had upstairs maids and downstairs maids and a laundress and at least three gardeners and a chauffeur.

I was so embarrassed sometimes when I had to go to Sunday school at the Baptist church that I made the chauffeur drop me off two blocks before. He promised he'd never tell Grandmother. When he took me to school, that was fine because they were all arriving in these great big, fancy cars, but at Sunday school, we were the richest people there, and I just died. I wanted to become one of their friends, and here I was arriving in this stretch limo.

Grandma died the same time my mother and father got a divorce. At thirteen it was a traumatic experience. After she died, they got rid of me quickly, dumped me in this boarding school in Peekskill, New York. I mean, what were they going to do with me? They drank a lot, they played a lot of bridge, they had very interesting friends—they were so busy doing their thing.

My father remarried and stayed in Cincinnati. My mother moved out to California and eventually remarried a Damon Runyon character. God, he was funny. When I'd go back to San Francisco, I'd live with them. So I traveled back and forth on the train all by myself. We didn't fly—it was a long time ago. I slept on the train, and the porter took care of me, and I loved it. When her husband died, he was cremated, and mother had this wonderful, great big Imari bowl sitting on the piano with his ashes in it. Every night she would sit there and drink with him. It was sad. My mother died of malnutrition; she drank herself to death.

My father was an alcoholic, too. He was a well-traveled, wonderfully attractive guy. He married this woman when I was fourteen. They called me in boarding school and said they got married. She was a social climber, very impressed by Daddy going to country clubs and being in the social register, and she was sort of a mean stepmother, really a dreadful person. She didn't know what to do with me. She was as good if not a better bridge player than my mother. I loved my father even though he was a rotten, rotten father, but he was a charming, handsome man.

I went to boarding school at Saint Mary's, and Episcopal Convent School in Peekskill and I really hated it. My great aunt—my grandmother's sister who lived nearby in Mount Kisco—sort of took over for my grandmother because she knew how much my grandmother loved me. My grandmother's chauffeur/mechanic and his wife who used to babysit for me when Grandmother was away, lived in upstate New York, right down the road. When Grandmother died they came home to New York and Peekskill was only about an hour and a half away from them. If my great aunt couldn't have me, they would take me. I'd spend my summers up here and I landed here be-cause of them. From boarding school in Peekskill, I went to San Francisco and gradu-ated from Bates, another private school.

I probably got upset with my father and my stepmother, whom I hated, so I de-cided to go back to Mother, whom I didn't like much better. I went back there and lived with my grandparents. I loved my grandfather. My grandmother on my father's side and my grandfather on my mother's side were the two stable people in my life. My mother at that point was the buyer at City of Paris, and she lived with her parents. We all lived in this small apartment on Jackson Street in San Francisco.

From the time I was probably six or seven, I was always going to dancing school at this very posh country club we belonged to in Cincinnati. I hated it because I towered over all the boys. I spent half the time in the bathroom. When I went away to school, that stopped the dancing school, except I'd come home at Christmastime and we'd go to these parties.

Ugly duckling went back to Cincinnati to make her debut and was a smash. It was good for the ego. I was a new face even though I'd grown up with these people. I was very popular. Having a debut in Cincinnati was something my stepmother really was pushing at this point. I couldn't care less about the social register and my debut.

I had this nice evening party. It was a step above a tea—the teas were when you really didn't have that much money. You made your debut at the cotillion. You walked down the staircase with an escort, and you wore a white dress, and there was a ball afterwards or a party. In order to be part of it, you had to be in the Junior League. My mother was always Junior League. My grandmother was in the garden club, in the social register—I haven't been in the social register for forty or fifty years now. I came out the year they allowed the first Jewish person ever to come out. Her family had been in Cincinnati probably as long as anyone else, but they were Jewish. It was shocking, a scandal, to have a Jewish girl coming out—there was a lot of talk.

I had the best time at my debut. During the debutante season, you were busy con-stantly going to these balls and parties—you'd have three parties a day. You drank a lot; you smoked. One year I counted I had fifty-six different dates. At this one ball downtown they had real orchids all over. They had big-name bands—Xavier Cugat, Woody Herman—it was absolutely magnificent. When you have your debut, there's a list of bachelors, and you are assigned these dates. You had to have ball gowns or evening dresses. You had to have different clothes for everything you went to.

I went to Western, a small college in Oxford, Ohio, for two years, and then I got married. I married on the rebound, a real creep. He had been after me for years. I loved this other guy very much, and I thought I was going to marry him. I was nineteen or twenty. He was my best beau. I went to this well-chaperoned house party with him— there were twelve of us down in Alexandria, Virginia. A very posh riding place. These friends had a house there. Late one night, I found him under the table with another gal! They were having sex! I was so angry, so hurt, so crushed. I went home and married this jerk. I hated him, hated him since the day I married him, and I think I slept with him once. That was the first time I had sex. It was horrible, dreadful. I don't think I've liked sex since. Maybe I had sex with him more than once, maybe three times. I became pregnant and had a son! So I have a son who is almost forty. I stayed with him maybe four years altogether. And then I divorced him. I was the first person in my group getting divorced. I lived in Cincinnati and worked in this boutique, which paid nothing, and took care of my son.

I never thought I'd have to work. It was expected that you got married and had children, continued the Junior League and garden club bit, belonged to the country club. I never thought about working. So, I met this other man who I fell in love with and married him.

My, How We Danced

Abigail Midgeley

She was born in Illinois and raised by her adoptive parents. She was seventy-two years old when interviewed. (See also pp. 29, 241 and 256)

*W*e had no TV then, didn't even know what it was. We played a lot of games—Chinese checkers, Touring, Old Maid. There were just a few card games that we could play, and the rest were considered sinful. We played croquet. In the summer we would get on our bikes and ride out to the beach, and when you got to the beach, you would throw your bike down on the sand and everybody would race for the pier and everybody tried to be the first one to dive off the pier. You never locked your bike. There wasn't any theft or rape. When I was eight, nine, ten, we girls would go across the bridge into the woods and pick tulips, violets, jack-in-the-pulpits, buttercups, daisies, all the flowers that grew wild, and bring a bouquet to our mothers. You never worried about anybody lurking behind a tree or grabbing you—things like that just didn't happen.

Dorothy Sommer

She was born in 1912 in the Midwest to parents who had immigrated from Austria-Hungary. (See also pp. 27, 228, 249 and 422)

I wasn't allowed to go out until I was almost eighteen years old. Until then you were only able to be with parents' friends' children. They were like a clique—the circle of friends who migrated from Europe. We had birthday parties, picnics, and things like that, and even then, the standards for girls were very high. You had to be home by nine o'clock. My parents—I didn't realize it at that time—but they had a way of checking up on me. One occasion—I was about thirteen, fourteen, and I was allowed to go out to my friend's house because they knew the family and that the family would be there. I was sitting on the porch talking and joking, and, lo and behold, who goes parading past the house but my mother and father. They wanted to be sure that's where I really was.

When I got into senior high school, then the boys would ask me to go out. Well, the talkies had just come out, and the big thing was for the fella to take you to the movies, and then afterwards you went to the ice cream parlor and you had a soda, or a banana split—everybody had their favorites. And that was about it. We didn't really learn about chaperones until we got the dancing part and you would see all the ladies around the ballroom—mostly mothers.

My parents wouldn't allow me to stay in a car. My neighbor up the street—my parents used to say, "My, she's awful. How does her mother let her stay in the car that long?" There was either very heavy petting or something going on; it was mostly done in cars. My father would say, "Bring them in the house." My parents would go to their rooms, but they were listening, and they would have excuses to go down the stairs and go into the kitchen. They allowed a certain amount of petting, but they wouldn't let it get out of control.

In those days we bought sheet music, and we had Victrolas, and we all gathered at each other's houses around the piano. And once my father said, Don't ever come back, that was the end. There was a young man that came to pick me up, but he sat in the car and he tooted his horn, and my father told him to go away. He said, "You think he's going to toot his horn and you're going to run out without our knowing who you are going with?"

There was a boy, he had quite a reputation—in my day they would have called him fast. My father would say, "Well, we don't want you to go out with him." My father was right. One time we had gone to a wedding and the bride came down the aisle and she was all in white, and my mother leaned across to my father and she said, "She has the nerve to be married in white." She was three or four months pregnant, and they all knew it—and the fast boy I wasn't allowed to go with was the father! They used to call them shotgun weddings. His father probably said, "You've got to marry her." My brother was told the same thing: "If you get a girl in trouble, she's your responsibility. You'll have to marry her." The principled parents would have to do the right thing by the girl. There were other parents that would send the boy off to school someplace and have no more contact. They would say, "She was fast, loose with her morals." They would find an excuse.

Lucille Thornburgh

She was born in Tennessee in 1908 and went to work as a teenager at Cherokee Bennett Textile Mill. (See also pp. 64 and 414)

This part of the country is called the Bible Belt, and everybody said that the flappers were going to hell—short skirts and bobbed hair! But girls did it anyway. My sisters and I sure did. We considered the skirts short, and they were just a couple of inches above our knee. My parents didn't mind. We were the most liberal outfit up there in Jefferson County.

All the real nice girls wore pleated skirts, and some of the real flappers just wore a straight skirt. Before that, dresses had to come below the calf of your leg. It was about that time, too, that powder and rouge were introduced, but I don't remember lipstick in the country at all. And there certainly was no such thing as mascara.

My mother said that when she was growing up, nobody wanted to be tanned— they wanted to be real white, so when the girls would be out in the sun in the summer and get tanned, they'd put flour on their face. In those days, it was considered practically being a prostitute to wear makeup. Nice girls didn't.

Jane Foley

"I was born in New Orleans in 1919. I was ten years old when the Great Depression started. My father had a lumber company, and he was able to keep his doors open, so we didn't really feel the pinch. We always had a roof over our heads and food. Some families didn't have food to eat." (See also pp. 37 and 47)

I didn't date until I finished high school. We always went with another couple to chaperoned dances. We belonged to little social sororities, and we would have a dance at a place like the Court of the Two Sisters in the French Quarter. You would ask an escort to the dance, but anybody could dance with you if you wanted to. Somebody would tap the guy on the shoulder, and your current dance partner would just hand you over to the new guy. It was a lot of fun. You got to meet people that way. Going out then was a lot safer and nicer. The young man would come pick you up. There was no honking of horns. If it was the first time, he'd meet your family. They'd be milling around.

If you liked him, maybe you'd invite him to supper, or Sunday dinner. There was a lot more family involvement; we would do things like play cards at home. In grammar school on a Friday afternoon, four of us girls would go home and play bridge. Playing bridge was a good way of meeting people, too. If you met some young man who was nice, you might ask if he played bridge. You'd invite a couple of people. You had more activities at home.

When I was a teenager, nobody in the family ever got a divorce. It was a scandal if there was a divorce in a family. Nowadays I have children, quite a few, who've had divorces. When I married, I married for life, no matter what. That's what we were taught. Now I can see some reasons to separate—if a woman is abused, for instance. It's not easy for two people to live together without disagreeing on certain things. But you can adjust if you have a marriage where the persons respect each other and like each other's company.

When I married at twenty-five, I quit my job two weeks before. That was the mindset back then. You worked up until the time you got married. When people married, they usually had a baby within a year. The birth control that was approved was the rhythm method, which I never perfected because I had thirteen children. I still don't know exactly what the rhythm method is.

Laurine Warren

She was born in 1912 and grew up in Mississippi. (See also pp. 25, 52, 225 and 424)

My, how we danced when I was a teenager. We always had a chaperone, and we might go out of town, but we had good bands. Bud Scott's Band was a black band. It started out as a string band, but then he put in horns and all that stuff. He played beautifully. We bought evening dresses for dancing. We always managed to get dates. We had some name bands come to Fayette. We would just have a wonderful time, and Mother let us stay until the dance was over around two o'clock. She loved dancing herself. She danced as a young girl. We loved to dance so well that if we didn't have the boys, we would gather at someone's house, and we would dance together, the group of girls.

Lucille Thornburgh

She was born in Tennessee in 1908. (See also pp. 62 and 414)

There's some things that you can't legislate. You can't make people stop drinking, so during Prohibition what the people did in Jefferson County and all these other counties around here, they started making moonshine and homebrew. They made corn whiskey in moonshine stills. They had a little pipe for the liquor to run through. They made it out in the field, not in the open field because it was against the law; it was more in the woods. You couldn't make it in the house because you had to have a fire to boil the corn. The way they found the stills was the smoke coming from them. They arrested them once in a while. Not many. They knew everybody was making it. They had a joke here that a man from Knoxville came to our neighborhood and asked where he could buy moonshine, and the man pointed out to him—"Now, you see that house right down the road here?" He said, "That's the only place you can't buy it."

Belle Riding

She lives with her husband in San Diego, where she owns and runs a coffee shop.
"I was born in Indiana in 1928, and my mother died during childbirth." (See also p. 251)

Living on a farm, you didn't have much time to go out and hang around or run around with anybody. In the summertime, we did get to go out once a week to a little town called La Crosse. They'd shut off the street, and everybody would come down for a free movie—they'd have a big movie screen up, just like a drive-in, but it would be in the middle of the street. All the townspeople would bring their chairs, and the kids would get down in front on their blankets and watch the movies, usually a western. They also had an ongoing serial that was just like the soaps are nowadays. Each week you'd have a little section of the movie, like Buck Rogers or something.

We'd be four or five boys, four or five girls, and we'd do things together, but nobody paired off by themselves. My cousin—he was two years older—had a car, and I got it when he joined the Marine Corps. I was the only kid in twelfth grade that had a car, so about ten o'clock, a few of us would sneak out and we'd drive twelve miles to a movie, playing hooky from school. One day we walked out, and there stood the principal in the lobby of the theater. He said, "I knew where I could find you." We all had to stay after school—so, no big deal. They didn't talk about sex. You learned that from the animals. I guess knowing about your period must have come from school, the home-ec course we had. I can remember the teacher—she was also our physical ed teacher—she'd say, "Girls, if you ever get a chance to be raped, don't fight it 'cause it don't happen very often in life." You'd have to see her to figure that out. She was just a little dumpy, short thing and losing all her hair, and I guess men didn't pay much attention to her.

Most of us didn't even consider sex. Except one girl—she was the most popular girl in high school, and when she graduated, she was pregnant. She had a shotgun marriage. The boy and girl's parents expected you to get married unless they were really bad girls and played around with a lot of 'em. Then they wouldn't know who the father was. Evidently, she had figured out that this one guy was the father, and they did get married.

The boys didn't seem to be that interested in sex in those days, and the girls weren't, either. We all had our own shoe skates, and we'd go out twenty miles to the skating rink in three or four carloads, and we'd just have a good time. Or we'd go bowling, horseback riding, hay rides.

Not much drinking, either, and no smoking to speak of. There was maybe two guys in our class when we were seniors who were caught smoking in the library, and they had a fit about that. Things were peaceful in the country.

Lorraine Leroux

She is a retired nurse and lives in Okemus, Michigan. A few years ago she came out as a lesbian in a PBS documentary.

"I was born in St. Paul, Minnesota, in 1920. Of my forty-three-year nursing career, a goodly amount of time was in psychiatric nursing. I retired in 1983."

I had a crush on my gym teacher, and I was upset that she got married, but I didn't know why. This is before I became aware of my own sexual attraction to women. I tried dating, but it wasn't that interesting. I felt a lot more comfortable with my own sex. It was just a warmer group, and we could socialize better.

I would say probably when I was about twenty-two or twenty-three, I started to become aware of being a lesbian. At the time, I was working at Fort Snelling Veteran's

Hospital in the psychiatric unit in Minneapolis. It was during World War II, and I worked with shell-shocked fellas back from the Bataan march. They had horrendous experiences. I set up the two units—one open and one closed ward. I was the only female nurse. There were male attendants.

We were supposed to date the fellows in the open ward and help them get back to "normalcy" as part of their rehab program. We were to go out and go to a movie, and if they wanted to hold hands, then hold hands; if they wanted to go out to a bar, go out to a bar, but nobody should drink beer or any alcoholic beverage. If they wanted to dance, then this was part and parcel of it. About this time, another gal at the hospital and I became lovers. So we would go out together with patients. We were double dating. Isn't that wild? This was one way for us to be acceptable, to be seen as "normal," going out with men. The guys had no idea.

"It takes one to know one," but nobody said the L word. There were a few lesbian nurses at the veteran's hospital, and we did things together like go to the movies or go out to dinner, but we didn't say anything. At this point in time homosexuality was categorized as mental illness. The consequence could very well be incarceration in a state facility. Probably in '51 or '52, I was director of nursing of a large state hospital, and my lover was director of nursing education, and there were a couple of lesbians who were hospitalized there, and we helped these two gals escape. They had gotten permission to be out, and my partner and I picked them up in the car, brought them to our apartment in town, all of this prearranged. We kept them at the apartment for a couple of days and then drove them a hundred miles back to St. Paul, where they lived. I buried that so deeply and for so long I didn't say anything about it until maybe a couple years ago.

Growing Up:
The Second Generation

The Women's movement has influenced my life; I became able to give an opinion. My daugh-
ter once said to me 'you're not a typical Japanese mother.'—because I would say what I thought;
I would give an opinion whereas when I lived at home, growing up, I never had opinions; I
was not allowed to. I had ulcers.

—Barbara Aoki, born 1937

The Women's movement, the 60's saved my life. It was like going from darkness to daylight.
Suddenly there was this book by Betty Friedan and here was Gloria Steinem. Here were all
of these ladies and they were saying all the things that I'd been thinking all these years. It
was like 'oh, thank god,' other people feel and think the same way I do. I had always felt
angry and frustrated at being told women couldn't do this, couldn't do that. It was like there
was this giant awakening. The sexual revolution was part of it; the civil rights movement
was part of it.

—Martha Corson, born 1936

The Jitterbug Was Very Popular

Hannah Mason

She is a sculptor and lives with her husband in Los Angeles. They have a daughter. She was born in a small town in New Jersey in 1933 and moved to the West Coast as a teenager. Her parents were eastern European Jewish immigrants.

I started school when I was five. My school was quite traditional. The teacher read a piece of the Bible every morning, and, of course, we did the flag salute. A Republican Moral Majority person would be very happy with what I had. We wore little dresses and leather shoes exclusively. (Sneakers were for gym.) Up until fourth or fifth grade, the boys wore knickers. I never saw jeans in school until I came to Los Angeles.

The school was in a rather poor but respectable neighborhood where the kids were mixed—there were blacks, Italians, Jews, a couple of Chinese, and whites. Everyone got along pretty well interracially. There was one black kid in my kindergarten and first-grade class, and he used to kiss me all the time, and I didn't like him, and I didn't like being kissed. I would yell at him, or slap at him, or get away or do something. And then he said, "You're only doing that because I'm Negro," and I was absolutely appalled. Like he didn't get that I just didn't like him.

But there were no interracial fights. There was a little black girl named Roberta that I liked very much. I remember going to the candy store across the street from school with her after school and buying her candy. I used to be given money by my parents, and for a penny you could get all this garbage. There were these wax models of little soldiers, little women, little toys, mustaches, red lips. The outside was wax and the inside was some kind of colored syrup, and we used to drink the syrup and chew the wax. The candy stores were very small. I think there was one in every commercial neighborhood. Pop Tate was the owner of the one I went to. He was bald and sort of fat, and he always wore an apron. To me he was a real old man, but he was probably about forty-eight.

The school was only a block from where we lived. I can't recall any fear about kids walking alone. We never heard of kidnappers or molesters. My parents never warned me. Once when I was about twelve years old, I was at the local movie theater, and some man came and sat next to me, and all of a sudden I felt his hand on my thigh, so I got up and I sat somewhere else, and he did not follow me.

I was about eight when I heard the announcements of war starting. I remember Roosevelt's voice on the radio and our family listening, and then the newsreels at the movies showed what was happening. We used to collect scrap metal and stuff for the war effort. I had a little wagon, and I used to go door to door to ask people for old metal, and also to sell defense bonds and stamps.

I would get the bonds from school usually. We had contests—which class could sell the most. I had to collect $18.75 for each bond, and in ten years it was worth $25. People would give me the money, and I would give them a legal bond. If you didn't want to spend a whole $18.75, you could buy $2 worth of stamps and you put them in a special stamp book and then when you got $18.75, you traded it in for a bond.

I went door to door alone in my neighborhood for everything, not only on Halloween. I was a Girl Scout and sold cookies.

There was a time when kids collected playing cards. We used to keep them for the pictures on them—the prized ones for me were the ones with very pretty pictures like houses with a lot of flowers or street scenes—and I would go asking people if they had any old playing-card decks they wanted to discard. When I was into comic books, I would go around and ask people for comic books. I would bother them for anything. No problem. I didn't have a single incident. Nobody was ever even crabby, and kids came to the door almost every day for something!

I had a relative in the Canadian army that I had a crush on. He used to write me V-mail letters—"I'm going to hit a tank just for you" and things like that. He was a really sweet guy. He came and visited us in New Jersey when he was on leave in the United States. He stayed with us for a few days a few times, and then he was sent to Europe. I really was crazy about him. I was somewhere between nine and eleven. Some people corresponded with soldiers that didn't have a lot of family. There were agencies that would give you names and addresses. Sometimes the whole class at school would write letters to soldiers. We used to knit patches for blankets. Then somebody would sew them together, and they would be sent overseas to soldiers. We used to put together tins with cookies and stuff and send them.

When the war ended—that was V-J Day in August 1945—I was in summer camp. It was an unbelievable euphoria. Everyone was going to come home. One of my cousins was killed in the Pacific. Then we found out that my mother's entire family in Europe was killed. They were Holocaust victims.

When I was about thirteen, we used to have parties with boys—this was like predating—and we would play spin the bottle. You got an empty Coke bottle and put it on the ground. Everybody would be sitting in a circle, and the person who was up would spin the bottle and had to kiss the person of the opposite sex closest to where the bottle landed.

I remember having a lot of parties at my house. There was a group of boys and girls that I was part of, and we used to get together mostly at the homes of the girls. Rarely did a boy invite everybody. That would be their bar mitzvah or something—I hung out mostly with Jewish kids because of my parents. My life was not worth anything if I didn't.

If I got together informally with friends, we'd play the phonograph—listened to records and radio, and we used to practice dances; even if there were no boys, the girls would. We didn't have a TV until about 1950, '51, and sometimes we would go bowling, or horseback riding.

I wore lipstick to school starting when I was about thirteen. When I went out, I used to put on eye shadow, eyebrow pencil, mascara, and I had one of those little machines to curl my eyelashes. I wore very sophisticated clothing to go out. I had one really gorgeous black dress that had a fitted waist, a v-neck, and a hood. The inside of the hood was lined with some kind of shiny blue-silver stuff. That was my vamp dress, and I used to wear it if I really wanted to impress somebody. The high heels were very carefully matched. I had suits for going out on dates. They would have a low-cut jacket, and then there'd be a blouse inside with ruffles or frills. I had this one beautiful green suit, and I used to wear red, cobra-skin, platform shoes with it and a red, cobra-skin bag—looked like Christmas incarnate. That was very in when I was around fourteen. You might get a hat with a veil to go with a suit. Sometimes, I would wear one on a date. When I got into that really glamorous style, they didn't go as well.

I was fourteen when I started dating—mostly we used to go places and dance. We almost always went out with several couples. I had this boyfriend who had a friend who had a car, and weekend evenings we would all drive to New York State, where you could drink at age eighteen. We would go to roadhouses. If you were fourteen or fifteen, it was a lot easier to masquerade as eighteen. I used to love whiskey sours when I was fourteen. A lot of places just weren't all that mindful. I don't know whether they paid off the police or what. We would sometimes go to New York City, too, but that was more expensive.

I went steady when I was fourteen for a few months. Going steady meant that if you went with someone else, he would get mad, and you would be upset if he did. He was about two or three years older than me. He was old enough to drive, but he didn't have the money, so he would sometimes just come over and be at my house. He played the french horn, and I loved to play popular music on the piano. We'd go for walks, and occasionally we'd go to see a movie. He played baseball with my brother. He'd have dinner with the family, and sometimes my dad would drive him to the bus stop because he lived in another town—real close. I met him at a party. That's how everybody met everybody. We had lots of parties.

Even though I was going steady, I never had very much sexual activity. I remember one incident where he went from necking to petting—necking was mostly hugging and kissing; petting was below the neck, everything except intercourse—and I got really angry. I was only fourteen, and I found it frightening, and then we broke up. I don't think anybody went much further than necking at age fourteen, fifteen.

I was about sixteen when we moved from New Jersey to Los Angeles. I was in the eleventh grade and went to Fairfax High School. At Fairfax, the kids were a little less respectful of the teachers than at my high school in New Jersey. There was more making snide remarks and sometimes a lack of cooperation. But, in those days, the idea of being a teacher would not terrify anybody. There was no physical violence at any time. We used to smoke in the school bathroom, and at parties we would drink but I never heard of pot.

In high school, you would usually wear a skirt and a sweater or a jumper and lace shoes and socks. At some point saddle shoes came into style. In California, all the boys had Levi's and mostly white T-shirts. People going steady would get the same sweater. This guy I was going out with had gotten us twin sweaters just when I broke up with him. Soon after, he was drafted into the army; it was during the Korean War.

Back east the girls had a prissier, primmer look. In L.A. the clothes colors were brighter. More makeup in L.A., much more. We were all incredibly fixated on our appearances—even in New Jersey, but here it was an even bigger number if that's possible. At Fairfax, there were social clubs that had different color sweaters. They had parties and dances. Two of my girlfriends—one was a distant cousin and one was already in this club—advised me on what kind of haircut to get in order to be accepted. I went to their hairdresser. It was a shorter haircut; it wasn't bad. Then my cousin started telling me things like "Don't speak to that boy anymore—he's really not good enough." In order to get into the club, you had to try to become friendly with somebody who was popular, for no other reason than that they were popular. I found myself unable to do that, and I didn't get in. It wouldn't have worked if I had gotten in, but I was still hurt anyway. I had never before been socially rejected.

Like every school, Fairfax High had dances. We danced everything—the fox-trot, the waltz, the rumba, the samba. The jitterbug was very popular. If it was a prom, you'd dress in a gown. Strapless gowns were very in. There were some with slinky skirts, too. I had a yellow strapless gown with a straight skirt. There were dances that were less formal. You didn't usually go in a skirt and sweater and bobby socks even if they called them sock hops. You dressed more elegantly. You'd wear a cocktail dress. We used to have all the dances in the gym. It would be decorated, and sometimes there'd be a live band, and we usually came in our fathers' cars. But by the time of my senior prom, all my boyfriends had cars, and so did I. There was more prestige connected with cars here than back east. Back east if it was something with wheels and a motor, it was wonderful. Here it was like, What kind of car does he drive? The kids were more materialistic in L.A., and there was much more snobbism having to do with money and looks. Money and looks were tops.

The major high school dating activity in L.A. took place in cars. If you went to a movie or a dance, either before or after, you usually had a hamburger and a malt or something, often at a drive-in. There was one on the corner of Wilshire and Westwood where we used to go. The kitchen and office were in a little building in the middle, and then there were parking places around it in a half circle. You would pull up to a car stand, which had what looked like a country mailbox on a post next to it. It had a door that opened, and inside you would find a menu, a pencil, and a pad. You could mark off what you wanted, and then you put it back in the box. The box traveled on a track—like a little railroad track—that led into the kitchen. Then the carhop would deliver. There were drive-ins where the carhops were on roller skates. I think you could choose if you wanted the window tray inside or outside. There was a different kind of tray for the steering wheel.

A lot of people would use drive-in movie theaters for necking and petting—you didn't have to worry about the police. I only went a few times. Most of them were in the valley. There was a speaker that you'd put inside your car, and you watched the movie through the windshield. They had a little hut where they sold drinks and stuff.

Parking up in the hills was also the thing to do. If you went out on a double date and the two couples knew each other very well, one couple might be making out in the front and the other in the back. The police would patrol, especially the cliff areas overlooking the city like Mulholland Drive. You did worry about them coming by and shining a light into your car. If there was any disrobing going on, you could get in trouble, or if you were actively having sex, that could be a problem.

It was really up to the discretion of the police to give you a bad time or not. I had it happen probably a couple of times. I was embarrassed, but I was never reported—it was just "You better go home" and "You should know better than that!" Or they could be kind of nasty, like "One more step and I'll call your parents." My boyfriend told me about incidents where the police actually raped the girls. I don't think that was super common. He lived in a working class neighborhood not far from South Central L.A.

If there was date rape going on and the police came along, they would stop it. I had some incidents where the guy really tried to overpower me. It happened two or three times while I was at Fairfax High. It never happened in New Jersey, and it never happened in college. The police didn't come along, and I managed not to let it happen. I fought really hard and screamed and yelled and scratched and hit. They would try to get my clothes off and force me. One was a guy who lived next door. He was older and a professional baseball player. My brother fixed me up with him—he thought I'd be thrilled out of my mind to go out with a baseball player. He was very nice looking. I wasn't enthralled, but I thought it was okay, and then he was like that, and I never even said hello to him anymore. Another guy was supposed to be taking me home, but he took me to the ocean instead. That was another popular parking spot besides Mulholland. You parked overlooking the beach on Pacific Coast Highway. This one just started to get very aggressive, but he wasn't as hard to deal with. The hardest to deal with was the baseball player—it was the only time I really was in danger of being raped.

Besides necking and petting, there was probably a lot of intercourse going on in the cars. It was certainly more usual than back east, but for me it was only okay once I was going to get married. Then I felt comfortable more or less, except for the worry of getting pregnant. Getting pregnant was the main deterrent. Some of the older guys used contraceptives, but the younger ones really didn't. They were probably afraid to go into a drugstore and ask for one. Or it could have been their not knowing. I didn't know about diaphragms, but they might have been around. There was the occasional girl who got pregnant in high school. Even in my junior high in New Jersey one girl got pregnant, but it was very rare.

My Mother Was a Housewife

Sharon Goldberg

She was born in 1940 in the Midwest and lives in Southern California with her husband. They have three children. She is an interior designer. (See also p. 448)

*M*y mother was a housewife and really loved taking care of the children. She made a very big business out of making three meals and cleaning. She had no other life. My mother was very bright. She loved books, but she was afraid to leave the confines of her kitchen. Women didn't work. My aunt, my mother's sister, went to law school and graduated and passed the bar. She never practiced.

We had this kitchen with a breakfast room off of it. And here we were, me, my three brothers, and my father. My father would be the first one to sit down and start eating. My mother would dish it all out, and everyone would start, and I would say, "Hey, did anyone think that maybe we could wait until Ma sits down?" and they'd say no, and they wouldn't. By the time she served everyone, they were finished, and my mother would eat afterwards. And I'd say, "What are you, the maid? Why do you do this? This is so awful." She'd say, "What's my choice? It needs to be hot." I said, "Serve it cold." She cared so much that it be hot and wonderful that it never dawned on her she was acting like a servant.

My father was the worst one—he'd say, "Ethel, I want my tea," and she'd get it. I'd say, "What are you getting him the tea for? You eat, and then give him the tea." It was so horrible. I was so embarrassed for my mother. It was her fault. I never really blamed him.

From the beginning when I had children, I would say, "Anybody picks up a fork before I sit down, I'm taking your food away."

Joanne Evans

She was born in 1949 and grew up in a large Catholic family in a rural area in Massachusetts. She now lives in a small northeastern town, where she sells mutual funds for a large brokerage house. She was widowed at a young age and has been in a gay relationship for many years.

*M*y mother's father was pretty wealthy. She could have been a classical violinist; she studied for that. She was supposed to marry a doctor. She would tell me stories, "I had every kind of man in my life I could have married, and somehow I fell in love with your father." And I kept thinking, "Why the hell didn't you marry the doctor?" My mother got married at twenty-six. I don't know why she married this bum. I don't know why she stayed married, because she had opportunities to go back with her family, but if you are Catholic, you stay married.

One day my father came home so drunk he passed out in the bushes. That must have been in '39. He got really bad alcohol, and they had to call a doctor, and he almost died. So my father stopped drinking, but he became very physically abusive. He was always hitting, slapping, beating, and screaming, and then later he became very sexually abusive to my sister and myself. My mother never slept with my father after a while. She told me that having intercourse with a man was like being poked by a pig. Those were the words that she used. And I was maybe eight. That was the only kind of conversation I ever had with my mother about sex.

I slept in the bedroom with my mother, and my father slept with one of my brothers. My sister had her own little bedroom, and my father would go in there every night. She gave up, she submitted. My sister never went to the prom, never had a boyfriend. She always lived with my father; he's in his seventies now. My father's got a lot of charisma. He's a good talker, and he always preaches God, so he's got a real warped way of keeping people in line. My sister idolized him; she really got into Daddy could do no wrong. He preached, and she believed. I don't think their sexual relations continued, but I don't know anymore. None of us can reach her. She is so defensive of her father because it is the only thing she has.

My mother and sister used to fight like crazy over my father because he would buy my sister things—that's how he kept her. I didn't get clothes. I got her hand-me-downs, but if Nancy wanted something, she would get it because she would give something back. We all knew that. I don't know why my mother never got up and said "This is nuts," but she never did. She felt it was important to keep the family together. It is very sad.

For me, it went short of intercourse with my father and not short of intercourse with my brother. I was five maybe, with my father. He used to take us to six o'clock mass in the morning. The man would never sit down in a church, never go past the doorways, because he was guilty as sin. We had a truck. I used to have to sit beside him, so when he moved the stick shift, he could get his hands on my legs. My brother would be sitting right beside me, and everybody would look straight ahead because there wasn't anything you could do about it. He would do whatever he could do, and I would push and shove, and then I would get beaten up. He would tell me to be more like my sister, and I said, "I'll never be like my sister."

My oldest brother was a carbon copy of my father. I was six or seven, so he was sixteen, seventeen. That went on for a very long time. That's the part of me that was angry at my mother, that she didn't save me. She loved her older son quite dearly. She knew that he was abusing me. The women in my family were sacrificed for the males.

One night they had a big fight. It was like an arena in that we stood around watching him beat her. We didn't know what to do. My father was a very strong man, and we were just kids. I was so angry I jumped on my father and told him to stop beating my mother up, and he threw me across the room. He controlled the family by beatings.

Being Catholic and going to confession every week, the priest really knew what my life was about, because I always told him. He would say, "He's your father, and it'll work out," and "Sometimes parents aren't good, but they are still your parents." That's what they preached in those days, so it was difficult to get help. We lived out in the woods. He kept us isolated. My mother was not a stupid lady; she was a very loving mother, as much as she could have been. As bizarre as it sounds, in some form, I think she loved the guy. She didn't want to go back to her family and have to admit to her parents that she was a failure. My grandfather used to tell her that she married a bum, and they would argue about it. Her father was very domineering—do this, do that. He had her whole itinerary for her life set up. People do just the opposite of what their parents want because they feel so repressed.

She left a few times, and we stayed with him. She would get on the bus and go back to her family, but she always came back. I think it had to do with being Catholic. That was her thing, "married for life." I'd say, "But, Ma, he's a maniac." I wanted out. She never divorced the man, never legally separated, even though they never lived together from the time I was thirteen on. He's still alive, but my mother's dead. God has a weird way of doing justice.

My middle brother, Harry, who I love dearly, saved my other brother and I. When he turned eighteen, he said, "This is enough. You are not going to abuse my mother and sister and brother anymore." He told my mother, "I'm taking the kids, and if you want to come with us, I'll support you till we can get things together." He was an electrician, and my mother worked, so we got an apartment, and I went to work that summer. My mom's life got better. We had a nice, clean apartment. My sister stayed with my father; she was not going to leave Daddy.

I loved my mother dearly, and it used to break my heart that she never felt good about herself. But at the same time, I was angry at her because she didn't take us out of there sooner. But she was relatively defenseless. She didn't even know how to drive a car, so she was stuck with all those children.

Anna Davis

She was born in Poughkeepsie, New York, in 1941. She works for the Post Office. (See also pp. 103 and 471)

My parents always had a good marriage. My mother took care of the inside of the house, and my father took care of the outside. He painted and he cut and worked on the cars, and she took care of the house and did the cooking and the shopping. He liked to cook and used to give my mother a break on Sunday. He would tease her and say, "We're going to have a good meal today—I'm cooking." My brothers would do the shoveling, grass cutting, hedge trimming, and the house painting—that was the man's job. I had to do dishes, help my mother with the laundry, change the beds, vacuum, dust, run to the store for the groceries. Those were girls' jobs. I was very careful with my kids growing up. I made them both do everything. I remember my son saying to me, "Doing the dishes, that's a girl's job," and I said, "No, that's your job this week." I made my son do his own room and make his own bed. My brothers never made their own beds. I did.

My mother had the patience of a saint. You knew you went too far when you got her mad. My youngest brother used to really push her, and she'd lose her temper and she'd chase him with a broom, but he was fast, and she couldn't catch him. But there was never any abuse, and my father was always loving. When he'd come home from work, he always had something for me in his pocket—piece of gum, little candy kiss. Saturdays, he'd go get a haircut, and I'd go with him, walk down to the barber shop. I can still remember sitting in the chair, and the old barber would cut my bangs and put the witch hazel on my face like he did my father. He'd lather up my face, and he'd pretend to give me a shave. I was always happy to be with my father. He'd say, "Come on, we're going to go for a walk," and we'd walk down and see the trains or go down to the river and watch the boats. He liked to walk because he drove trucks and got tired of driving. I was very close to my father, and I think the boys were close to my mother. I think that's normal.

Mimi Miller

She lives in Natchez, Mississippi, where she and her husband run the Historic Natchez Foundation.

"I was born in 1945 and grew up in a town of five thousand that was sort of a subdivision of Charlotte, North Carolina. My father and mother and their families had both lived in that area for approximately two hundred years when I was born." (See also pp. 130, 272 and 469)

The African-American woman that reared my brother and me, had she been born today, she probably would have been a nuclear physicist or something like that. Willie came to work for us when I was two years old, and she worked for my family until a few years ago when my mother went into a retirement home—forty-some years, full-time when we were children and part-time as we got older.

I've never understood how southerners who are reared by African-Americans can have any prejudice. Every insult about an African-American I took personally as an insult against her. I think there are a lot of southerners like that. It made me very left-wing, politically. You feel guilty, because you think of all the times you took them away from their own children.

She was well educated; she was smart. If you read a letter she wrote, you would have found it hard to believe that person had been a domestic servant. But she has no bitterness in her heart or sadness that I've ever seen, which I think is remarkable. She is a completely forgiving person, and she had a very tragic life. She's about seventy-seven.

As a child, it never seemed fair to me that Willie's children could not go to the movies I went to, that they could not swim in the swimming pool, and I used to wonder how she explained that to them. That must have been an awfully hard thing for black people to do. To say "You can't do this because you're black" over and over and over again.

Amanda Johnson

She is an attorney, born in the Midwest in 1952. She has remained single and is a law partner in a large western firm. (See also pp. 321, 490 and 493)

My mother graduated from high school in the middle of World War II. She had a scholarship she never took advantage of. Instead, she became a Rosie the Riveter type.

She went to work in the airplane factories for the war effort, and then she and my dad got married when she was eighteen, and her education got put on the back burner. She was a good mom, but she felt stuck and felt that her lack of education and the expectations of everyone, including my father and society in general, limited her options. She felt that she had to stay at home and raise kids, and that's not who she was. I think her life was changed dramatically by the feminist movement. She started going back to school when I was still in high school and my little brother was old enough so she didn't have the child-care problems. Watching my mom go to college when I was in high school was really a cool thing. I was so proud of her, and it opened up her world. Instead of dealing with snot-nose kids, she started dealing with adults and young people and learning new ideas. She went to a local college extension, and then she had a variety of jobs. She worked as a social worker; she taught French on a substitute basis—that was her major.

My parents divorced; they ended a thirty-year marriage. She had her college education by this time, but a lot of her friends ended their marriages after thirty years and found themselves in virtual poverty, totally unprepared for a job market. My mother more than at any other point in her life realized the importance of my having economic security.

My Mother Would Say *Gaman*

Barbara Aoki

She lives in Napa Valley, California, and works as a secretary at a Catholic school. She has two children and was recently widowed.

"I was born in a small town in Northern California in 1937. I lived there until war broke out in 1941, and we were taken to a camp."

I was so young, but I remember on the train to Arizona having to keep the blinds down so that people couldn't see us as we were being transported. I remember being scolded by my mother not to look out the window. The instructions were that the blinds had to be kept pulled, and it was a very long trip from California to Arizona. We were in a camp for the duration of the war.

I started nursery school and went to second grade there, and as a child you think it's fun—you don't know the hardships your parents are going through. I had a lot of friends; we played and we started school. It was hard when I got out because I didn't know nursery rhymes, and I was behind. It was a different culture. In camp we used to go to Japanese school after attending regular kindergarten classes, so I remember words and I can understand a little, but I can't write, read, or speak Japanese. After a while they brought Caucasian teachers in. They were harassed by the outside community for coming to teach, and I imagine it was very hard on them.

During camp my mother worked in the post office. The camp was like a regular town. They had a canteen where they sold drinks and pops and ice cream and stuff like that. We had these rows and rows of barracks that we lived in. They were made of tar paper on the outside and wood and had holes in the floor. The dust would come up through the floor, and everything was always dusty, and it was cold. We had army cots to sleep on. It was just one big room partitioned off with blankets.

We had communal bathrooms, and I can remember watching the older women wash their hair and how black and very shiny it was. They boiled and cooked starch, and after they washed their hair, they ran this starch through it, and it made their hair so shiny. I was peeking through doors and watching these people getting acupressure and acupuncture. They would burn incense, and they would put out the flame, and they would put it on pressure points, so these people were getting these scars all over their arms and legs at these pressure points. I would stand there in the doorway and watch.

People were very organized. The place was clean, and they built a fish pond for fresh fish. The men had clubs, and I remember putting on a skit. They had shows at night at an outdoor theater place; they showed movies, and we'd have to carry buckets of charcoal to keep us warm. They used to do arts and crafts; they were very talented people.

My father had died just before we went into camp. There were three children. My mother remarried in camp, and I have a brother that was born there. We were one of the last families to leave camp because we didn't know where we were going. They burned down our house, and they burned all our possessions, so there was nothing to go back to. We'll never know who did it. Many families had their homes burned while they were gone. So when we came out, we went to a small town in Arizona, and I started third grade. It was transient; we moved a lot, and they did farm work, picking up odd jobs. We children would go out and tie carrots and things like that to help out.

When my mother worked at places where we couldn't go, we stayed home and took care of the younger children. It was dangerous, but there was no choice for my mother. When I was only in the third grade, I was taking care of the baby.

My mother was born in this country. My father, I don't know. She was from a very large family. She was very, very intelligent, and she did go to college for a few years. It's sad because she was ahead of her time—going to college—and she didn't meet anybody. I guess her only choice in marriage was to be married off to a farmer. She never talked about it, but I think it was an arranged marriage. Most of them were. When we were in high school, people would come to the house and say, "I know this young gentleman," and my sister and I would run upstairs, and we wouldn't come down. That's what they would call a "go between." This person would introduce you and would bring you together.

Our parents didn't talk about the camps. I think they were ashamed. People were surviving. It would have been putting energy into something that you couldn't change. When we got out of camp, you couldn't live wherever you wanted to, so we lived in a low-income area. It was Mexican, and they gave us a bad time. My brothers and sisters and I, we'd go to school, and all the way to school the kids would harass us, call us names. They'd pull your hair and hit you, throw rocks at you, spit on you, kick you. I didn't fight back. My brother would fight back, and he would always be in trouble. My mother would say, "*Gaman*"—that's a Japanese word that means you're supposed to just bear it, not complain. She'd come home, and she'd try to soothe and comfort us. A lot of Caucasian kids harassed us, too. I asked my husband if he ever went through this, and he said no. I think it's because we went back to this low-income farming town.

At this one place we had a Caucasian lady across the street who had a daughter my age, and I thought she looked like Margaret O'Brien, the child movie star. She was so cute, and her mother just hated us. But after she found out that her daughter and I were friends, she would let me come over and play. But it took a long time. After a while they figured out we didn't do anything. It wasn't us; it was Japan. We were American citizens, and it was something that we didn't have control over, yet being the same ethnic group, we were blamed. And being children, you don't know why—my mother never really said anything about it or tried to explain. We were supposed to just bear up to this. Be strong.

When we moved out of that town, we drove to California, and we ended up in a town in the San Joaquin Valley, and we worked on the grapes there. Right after that, my mother got this letter from the attorney general, and they paid her off. I think my mother had ten thousand dollars in savings before the war, and they gave her ten cents on the dollar. She signed off. It's like saying, "I'll never contest this again." She thought she had no recourse; she had no papers, nothing to prove that she had these accounts. She said she was taken, it was wrong. But that's the only time I ever heard her say anything. So there probably was anger, but they had these words like gaman, and there's another word—it means make the best of it and move on. That's a carryover from the old generation. I think I've carried on the culture, but I've tried to change it in my children, help them not be quite as silent, as accepting of things that are unfair or unjust, not to be quite the traditional Japanese way.

My stepfather was raised in Japan, so he's more traditional Japanese, whereas my mother had some American culture. When my stepfather said something, you were supposed to say, "*Hi*"—in Japanese that means yes. You're taught to respect the elder's opinion regardless of whether it's right or wrong. You just accept it. My brothers weren't allowed to speak out, either. It was hard going to school and coming home to this rigid way of growing up. We were very quiet in school. You didn't answer questions hardly, or you didn't speak up unless you were very unusual, more outgoing and aggressive.

I think it was very typical. My husband's father was born in Japan, and he was of the old school, too. He wanted something, he asked for it, and that was it. When he said, "Water," you got up and got water. There was no question about it. You may have worked all day, but you still came home and you served and you did everything. That's the way my husband's mother was. When Steve and I got married, she thought that I should wear these somber colors because once you're married, you're supposed to step back and not be in the forefront. You're supposed to be subservient, and she didn't like me wearing red and other bright colors. My husband finally stood up for me.

My mother told us when we were young that if our father was upset with us, she couldn't help. He was very hard on us—right after the war, not having any money, he would take us out to the fields to work before school and in the evenings. You worked cutting grapes, and when it was the season to make raisins, we had to turn the grapes. There were large sheets of paper, and there would be grapes on them; and we had to take another large paper and put it on top of the grapes; and one person stood at each end, and you'd count, and then you'd flip the papers real fast to turn the grapes. We did this after school, until dinner.

After he and my mother started having kids—my mother had six children, three with each husband—my stepfather would always say "my kids," and he'd say to Mom "your kids." We worked hard, and his kids didn't have to go through a lot of what we went through. The second group were spoiled, and after the three of us moved out of the house, he reversed it, and he'd refer to us as his kids, and talking about his own kids, he'd say to Mom, "What happened to your kids?" They had become more westernized. He didn't hold them to the traditions that he held us to. They did a lot of the things we never even got to do. We never went to a football game hardly or participated in after-school things like they did, and they got an allowance every week.

Times had changed, and my parents were making a lot of money; those kids were spoiled, and we couldn't believe what they were getting away with. My mother didn't know what to do with them. When I left home, she would always call me because I had taken care of the house and children while she was working. The youngest really got into trouble. She'd call the police because he'd be out in the car without their permission. He'd be stealing. And then he went on to worse things, so now we don't know where he's at.

When I graduated high school, I stayed home for a little while, and then my friends decided they were going to go to junior college, and my older sister said, "Go, go"— she stayed at home to help work on the ranch. My parents didn't encourage me to go. My stepfather didn't believe in educating women because he felt that you were just going to get married and have children, so it was a waste. He didn't even want us to learn how to drive. He didn't want you to be independent. So we were still stuck at home. It was frustrating. I had ulcers. I must have been fourteen when I first got them, and they didn't know what it was. After I started working, I used to get real bad attacks. I had to go see a specialist, and he sent me to this doctor to talk to me. The doctor said that he had never talked to anybody my age that had ulcers, and he wanted to psycho-analyze me. I didn't continue to go, but I was so torn.

I went to junior college for two years and graduated. My stepfather wouldn't support me, so the dean of girls found me a place to live where I was something called a schoolgirl. I lived in the household and was paid forty dollars a month to take care of their children, to cook and clean. That was very difficult. The first lady I was placed with had four children under four years old. I had to leave after a while because I just didn't have time to do any studying. The dean of girls found me another place to live, with a very wealthy, elderly lady who had married this man. She had this huge, beautiful home, and I lived in the maid's quarters in the basement. I was only expected to vacuum and help cook and clean up, but it was very hard and demeaning. They would ring the bell, and I'd have to run out of the kitchen and do whatever they asked of me—serve them food or get water or do something. I had gotten up for breakfast one morning, and the husband came and put his arms around my shoulder, and I thought, "No, no, no," and I got scared because I knew he was going to try something.

I didn't know what to do. My boyfriend was going to junior college in another town, so I called him and said, "I'm not going to live here," so he came and helped me pack, and I went back home. So at that point I had to quit school because my father got upset that I didn't stay and work. But the dean of girls didn't want me to quit school because I was almost finished; she called me back and found me another place. I stayed with a real nice family—he was the president of one of the banks—and they had three children, and I took care them. They were very nice to me, and I stayed there until I graduated.

I think the other families just expected me to be subservient because I was Japanese. The couple that I didn't stay with, he thought that I knew how to do flower arranging and cook Japanese food. I would always get that when I was growing up and even later at work—"Were you born here?" I'd say, "Yes." "So that's why you speak such good English."

We Were Very Aware
of Being a Minority

Beverly Butler Lavergneau

She was born in 1940. She is African-American and lives in New Paltz, New York, with her husband. She is an administrator at the state university. One of her daughters, Mara Lavergneau, was also interviewed. (See also pp. 102, 109 and 319)

Both of my parents are small-town northeasterners. My dad grew up in Sewickley, outside of Pittsburgh, about eighteen miles south along the Ohio River. A lot of the steel magnates built their homes down there because they were away from all of the pollution that the steel mills created in Pittsburgh, and so many African-American families worked in service or established businesses to service the home owners. My grandfather had a store and made ice cream and potato chips and functioned as kind of a caterer. All of their thirteen children were born there, eight of whom grew to adulthood. My father was the first in his family to go to college. He became a physician.

My mother grew up in Oberlin. My great-grandfather, on her side, was a cook on the oarboats that plied the Great Lakes. My great-grandmother was German Swiss. She and her two brothers had emigrated to the United States with no parents. She was seventeen years old when she met my great-grandfather, and she already had a child. The birth of that child probably severed her ties with her brothers. She and my great-grandfather decided to marry. He moved the family to Oberlin because Oberlin had been known as a town that was very, very supportive of black people, and so she raised all of her ten children there. He basically would come home and make babies and then go back out on the boat. She raised all of them pretty much by herself and was much beloved by all of her children. She was a washer woman. I don't think my grandmother ever lived more than a couple of blocks from her mother.

My grandfather on my mother's side of the family was also from a pretty large family. Their father was a manumitted slave who had been brought by his father to Oberlin. Manumission was the act of the slaveowner choosing to free a slave, and that was fairly common when the slavemaster had fathered a child. Oberlin was notorious because of its connection to the underground railroad through the South, and so his father brought him there from Tennessee. My grandmother scrubbed floors and worked very hard because the college was there, and it was a great incentive. She wanted her kids to go to college.

My mother's older brother was the first to go to Oberlin. Mother was the youngest of three and was very bright and was ready for college by the time she was fifteen. And so she wound up being a townie that went to Oberlin. She became a teacher. She and my father had to keep their marriage a secret so she could continue to work, because married women were not allowed to teach. Later in life, my mother became the first chairperson of the Black Studies Department at the State University at New Paltz. The first time I came up here I went with her to a meeting. The students considered it bourgeois to refer to her as Dr. Butler, so they would call her Butler, and I hated it because I knew what she went through to get that doctorate. I would say to her, "I don't know how you stand it. Don't take that from them." And she would say, "Look, what I want to do is communicate with them, and that really isn't important." I've watched her both in a professional way and, of course, in her role as a mother, and she's always been my hero.

My mother conveyed to each one of us that we could do anything that we wanted to do, and she was always a cheerleader, no matter how busy she was. After my parents' separation and divorce, she went back to school and was working full-time, and yet she was always there. I was ten when they separated and fifteen when they finally divorced. Very few of my friends had parents that were divorced. My father eventually remarried and had three other children, so I have three half siblings. He was very busy when we were small children; he was a general practitioner, and if we saw him even at dinnertime, that was something. As we got a little older, he was studying for the dermatological boards, and I always remember him as a very, very busy person.

I can remember my mother trying to advise me when I was a teenager—because I was a teenager with a mouth—that I was a pretty intelligent person and that guys didn't particularly like very bright girls. Her suggestion at the time was better learn how to camouflage it. She would tell me to modulate my voice. She tried to put some controls on my natural assertiveness, which was termed aggressiveness by one and all. It was not so much trying to control what I did, but just pointing out that you do this and it's not what's accepted and you ought to think about that. We were very much encouraged to speak our minds and talk about issues in the family, but she wanted me to be able to make my way in the world, and her understanding of the world was that I needed to curb myself. It was very definitely her feeling that it was a man's world. Particularly for women who came out of the fifties generation, it probably was not an uncommon thing, that you outsmarted them by hiding your light. She was just offering motherly advice.

Elana Wiseman

She lives in an urban area on the East Coast with her husband and youngest daughter and is a physician in private practice. She has two older children from her first marriage. Her daughter Sharon Wiseman, also a physician, was interviewed as well. (See also pp. 308 and 491)

I was born in New York in 1940, and my parents left six months later to go to the Midwest, where I grew up. When I was in the sixth grade, a kid chased me home from school and called me a dirty Jew all the way home. The teacher made him apologize to me in front of the class, which was very embarrassing because nobody else had to have anybody get up in front of the class and apologize to them. The awareness of being different was fairly profound in a community like that. My father initially didn't get into the Elks Club because he was Jewish. Eventually, he did. Jews couldn't get into the country club. Eventually, they did. Almost none of the Jewish people that I grew up with are living in that community at this point. All of us wanted to get out. We were very aware of being a minority, and it wasn't secure. What I did was withdraw and read a lot. I used to dream about a world that was different. I took my junior and senior years at high school together.

When I was sixteen, I went to Brandeis University. My mother didn't want me to go because I was only sixteen, but she felt safer letting me go to a Jewish school. She didn't know that New York Jews can be as mean as midwestern WASPs. I was really unhappy there. I was ridiculed for being a Jew from a farming state—a hayseed. People would say, "How come you don't have hay in your mouth?" We're viewed as people who are naive, open, and unsophisticated, and I was that. Nobody even knew that my home state existed. A New Yorker's concept of geography ends at the Hudson River. It's almost as if you don't exist because you are not from the island itself or from one of the boroughs, so it was a rather stunning experience. I thought I was going to feel safe because I had gone to Jewish summer camps and felt very safe, and I didn't feel safe there at all. I thought I was going home—my father's family was from New York, but it didn't happen. Then I moved to Cambridge, got an apartment, and enjoyed life a lot.

I felt like I was getting some identity, putting the pieces of this together, beginning to figure out something about who I was.

Mary Wong Leong

She lives in San Francisco, where she was born in 1947, with her husband and two children. She has an elementary school teaching credential but has never used it. Her jobs have included being a secretary, teaching nursery school part-time, and organizing health fairs.

My parents were both born in China. My father immigrated here when he was maybe about thirteen or so, and then he was able to bring my mother over when she was probably in her twenties. They were separated for quite a long time. My parents had eight children: three boys and five girls. I'm right in the middle.

My mother spent most of her time helping my dad run a laundry business. When I was maybe in first grade, we moved to Filmore Street, and we lived right above the laundry. Filmore Street is really gentrified now, and the store where our laundry used to be is a clothes shop. The laundry was huge, and there must have been ten or twelve people working besides my family. We had a live-in cook and overall caretaker who did all the cooking for the employees—they would eat dinner before going home at the end of the day. A lot of times, like on Saturdays, all the kids would be helping out with the laundry, and we would eat lunch and dinner with the employees.

The laundry was on the street floor, and there was another floor, a smaller unit above our unit, where my aunt and uncle lived. They worked in the laundry, too, and they had quite a few children. I think my father was instrumental in bringing a lot of his extended family over from China—cousins and aunties and uncles and my grandmother. I know when my mother came over by boat in the early forties before the war, it was thousands of dollars to get her here. People had to be paid along the way.

When we were really little, my mother would be working in the laundry with us strapped on her back. Or we would be running underfoot. When we were older, we would be playing around in the store. Just kind of being there.

School nights I would go downstairs and yell good night to my parents like ten, ten-thirty. They would still be working. In the morning, when we were older, we'd get ourselves to school—most of the time my parents would still be asleep—and then after school we'd come home and help with deliveries. I remember doing that when I was age eight. My dad had hired drivers who drove our trucks, and we would go along. My sister and I would help load up the trucks, stack all the clean stuff, and we would go to all these different laundries and drop off the clean laundry and carry out all the dirty laundry. Then on Friday nights and Saturdays, we would help sort out the dirty laundry, like shirts would go in one pile, sheets would be bagged differently, socks, just so that they could wash them however they were supposed to, and we would mark the tickets as to what they had in each bundle.

Saturday was a very big busy day. Many times we girls worked till like one and two in the morning sorting a mountain of laundry. The boys didn't have to do that. They became delivery drivers, and when they were done with delivery, they were free. They spent time with their friends, were active in Boy Scouts; they went away on camping trips. They had quite a nice, pampered life doing not nearly as much as the girls had to do. They were paid five dollars a delivery—we were paid twenty-five cents a delivery—because they were the drivers and had more responsibility, and they were older.

My two older brothers were given the traditional role of boys in a Chinese family. They didn't have to do chores. I don't know if they even took out the garbage. We girls did the vacuuming, the dishwashing. My sister would do the food preparation. If there was anything to divide up, the boys were probably the first ones to get their share. They were free to spend their time however they wanted to. The girls never talked about it. It was just accepted that that's how it was and this was our job. To be a good child you obeyed.

We worked hard, but I don't think that was bad for us. We had a very happy childhood. We played a lot. On Sundays the laundry was closed, and the only job we had was to sort out the tickets for the laundry, and that could just take an hour or an hour and a half. On Sundays my father always took my mom to visit her sister, my auntie. Sometimes us kids would tag along and be visiting with our cousins, or sometimes our parents would sleep in on Sunday mornings. We would watch TV. We had a TV when I was probably in kindergarten.

My parents were always working and didn't closely supervise us. Raising a family was just kind of by the way. Also, my mother hardly speaks English. She's led a sheltered life because my father did everything that had to do with the outside world. He was the head of household, ran the business, took care of all the finances—whatever he said was it. It is a problem even today communicating with my mother. There are a lot of words that I can't express to her because I don't know the terms in Chinese. When we were growing up, we talked about the food, the weather, clothes, but nothing very deep and emotional at all. It's traditional not to be very emotional. At this point I realize that I do have emotions and feelings about things, but I'm not able to share it with my mother because I don't have the words. Because she always held everything in, we never heard the words.

When I was in college, my parents sold the laundry and bought a grocery store. They thought it would be less work, but it was not a good move. My father died in 1969 in a grocery holdup. He was beaten, kicked. He was unconscious for about a month before he died. It was very difficult for my mother. She grieved for seven years. She was at a total loss. Her whole world was centered around him. I don't feel I really got over my father's death for at least ten years. The doctors thought he would come out of the coma, but he didn't. I felt like I was somehow responsible. That I didn't pray enough.

His funeral was very old-fashioned. My oldest brother traditionally was supposed to take over the family, but he wasn't at an age and awareness of being able to do that. He was twenty-six. My father was well known in Chinatown with the family associations, so his funeral was huge and unbelievably expensive. All these outside forces were directing us as to what we had to have and do. His coffin cost more than a car. I heard the figure of ten thousand dollars, and this is in '69. We paid traditional mourners to cry. There was a lot of burning of incense, and we had these taffeta blankets, and each of the children would have to go up and cover the body with them. We had to wear these black netted veils and gathered black skirts. I didn't feel I could really mourn; I didn't understand what was happening, what these things meant. I think that was part of why I grieved for so long, too. They never found the people who killed my father.

Maria Rodriguez

She was born in Los Angeles in 1935. She is twice divorced and has a daughter and three grandchildren. She works for the animal rights movement.

"My father was born in Mexico and came here when he was about twelve years old. He was a landscaper. When I was a child, he went back to night school so that he could finish high school. My mother and grandmother were born in New Mexico. My grandfather on my mother's side was a border American Indian." (See also pp. 284 and 476)

*T*his was a traditional Mexican family. My father was the head of the household. If my parents discussed something, my mother would pretty much agree with him. They had a good relationship; they were friends; they did a lot of things together. They had a lot of respect for each other.

Mom was from that generation of women—she used to wait on him. He sat down to the dinner table, and she was always bringing the food to him, and if he needed anything, she'd, of course, jump up and go get it for him. When you were dating somebody and he came to a family gathering, she'd say, "Get him something to eat" or "Do this or do that." You were serving him. That's the role you played. When we'd get together with my sisters and their husbands, she always wanted the men to sit down, and the women were supposed to be serving them.

One time she said to me, "Why don't you get so-and-so a plate," and I said, "Why? Does he have a broken leg?" I just didn't play that game. My sisters usually went along with it. I had one brother-in-law that didn't go along with it. He really objected. Unless the women sat down, he would never sit down. I think my sisters continue the tradition in their homes. They serve their husbands.

We were three girls, one boy, and then three girls. My brother was right in the middle, so not only was he spoiled by the parents, he was also spoiled by the sisters. He always got everything he wanted. It was very loose as far as chores for him. My father would try to get him to help with the lawn, and sometimes he'd do it and sometimes he wouldn't, but he would get paid for doing it. He didn't do housework. The girls did; we didn't get paid.

I went to college for a while, but I didn't graduate. I lost interest because I was going to get married. I don't want to blame anybody, but I didn't have a family that was really supportive, that said, "You will do so much better if you get a college degree." Whatever I did was okay. I was the oldest. I have sisters who have gone to college because they had the benefit of some of the older siblings, and the parents seemed to educate themselves as their children grew.

The older children helped with the housework and helped with the younger ones when my mother went to work. My father being from Mexico was very strict with us. By the time the youngest ones came along, they weren't quite as strict. Life was easier for them. You pave the way.

It Was Like Going from
Darkness to Daylight

Martha Corson

She has published many successful romance novels, short stories, and articles and has worked as a magazine editor. She also devoted seven years to editing and writing for a medical magazine published by the Leprosy Hospital at Carvel, Louisiana. Her work contributed significantly to the improved treatment of that disease. When she was in her thirties she became ill with a life-threatening disease and became deeply involved with the Unity church. Spirituality has been very important to her ever since. She lives in Baton Rouge, Louisiana, where she writes and teaches creative writing. She is divorced.

"I was born in 1936 in El Dorado, Arkansas. My father was the manager of the Arkansas Power and Light Company, and my mother was working there. That's how they met. He was forty, and Mother was thirty. I have a sister four years younger."

They were fanatical housekeepers. Today, one busy woman understands, like other busy women, that you're going to have a little dust, but decent women in south Arkansas did not have dust. If my mother walked into this house today, she would probably faint. Before I had a birthday party—my birthday is July 25—not only every window had to be washed, but the windowsill, too. We didn't clean up for the kids, who couldn't have cared less, but for the parents bringing the children over.

A black woman, Gertrude, worked for us for eight or ten years, and we'd all be working hard, getting the house cleaned. That was the way they determined who was nice folks and who was white trash, basically by how clean your house was and how clean your kids were and which side of the railroad track you lived on. Your husband's salary and status mattered. Once I heard Gertrude talking to one of her ladies, and she said, Mr. Corson is a businessman. He wears a suit and a tie." So she was bragging because my father worked in an office.

I also remember once when Gertrude asked if she could speak to Mr. Corson after lunch, and she was so nervous. She took off her apron and smoothed down her hair, and she went in, and she had this little prepared speech: "Mr. Corson, some of the women in my neighborhood asked me to talk to you. We're wondering if we're ever going to get water into our neighborhood. It's been such a dry summer, and our rain barrels have all dried up, and it's so hard trying to stay clean and trying to keep the children clean." I was thunderstruck. It never occurred to me that Gertrude had to scoop bugs out of a rain barrel to get water to drink, and my father looked like it had just struck him for the first time, too, and he said, "Gertrude, I'm going to get you some water if that's the last thing I ever do." Later, he said, "Right now I think it's a damn shame to be a white man in this society."

Mother went back to work when my father became ill, when I was about fourteen. She had gone to business school, and she'd had a year of college, which was more education than most women from that time and place. She married late and had had quite a few years on her own, so she was used to having her own money, having a career. On the other hand, she had the southern woman's obsession with getting married. To be an old maid was about the worst thing that could happen to you—"She's never married, poor thing."

She had been a very angry and frustrated housewife. She did not like housework. She was crazy about my father, and she certainly loved her children. She was a very conventional woman. She and I had battles all my life because I was a pretty unconventional woman. She enjoyed belonging to the various clubs and organizations in town, but she was happiest when she was working. She was a good legal secretary. She took great pride in her work. But I would have to say my parents were happily married. It didn't affect their marriage.

I remember the summers vividly. My father built us a doll house. I spent a lot of time in that doll house reading. That's where I hid *Forever Amber* from my mother, and that's where I read all the magazines. I remember playing around the sweet gum tree and climbing up in the branches. We just had a lot of fun. He built a two-sided swing with seats, and you could put four kids on either side. And, best of all, he built a merry-go-round with four horses. Later, the merry-go-round got so much wear and tear and it rained so much that the horses' heads rotted. Kids from all over El Dorado would come over because we had a slide, a swing, a playhouse, and we had that merry-go-round. It was just wow!

It was so hot always in the summer, but swimming was a very perilous thing because of polio. Once a single polio case had been diagnosed in town—no more swimming. The community pool was just deemed too dangerous. They thought that it was transmitted through swimming pools. They didn't know what caused it, so there were all these theories. It was terrifying to the adults. It made me aware that life was very perilous at an early age. A Sunday school teacher of mine contracted polio and died within about two or three days, and then later the brother of one of my friends. My mother was herself a polio survivor. When the very first polio vaccine came out, she wrote me and enclosed a check and said, "Go get a shot."

Another way to keep cool was to go to the movies, because that was the only place that was air-conditioned. There were three movie houses in town, but no one wanted their children to go to the Ritz. It was kind of risqué. What was risqué was something called *Ruby* with Jennifer Jones and Charlton Heston. It was a real steamy black-and-white movie. Or *Gilda* with Rita Hayworth—those were movies I wasn't supposed to see but did. *Duel in the Sun,* that was another risqué movie. It was like Sunday school compared to today's movies. The worst thing that happened was a man and a woman went into a bedroom and the door closed. We would sneak in.

The Majestic used to show all the westerns—Roy Rogers and Gene Autry—and I wasn't much into those. Mostly, I liked the Rialto. It was elegant. It had not one but two curved staircases, plush red velvet, thick, thick carpet, and it was cool, so we went to the movies two and three times a week—the girls together. It was thirty-nine cents, and I could make that babysitting.

Air-conditioning and television arrived in Arkansas about the same time. I can remember my mother that summer of 1955 saying, "I think I'm going to buy an air-conditioning unit." I thought, "Oh, that would just be heaven." I can remember after lunch feeling limp; you just had no energy. Perhaps that's where the idea of the southerners being lazy came from. The heat down here was so intense that you learned at an early age not to move too fast, not to talk too fast—just do everything slowly. You didn't get quite so hot.

I'll never forget Dr. Fitch. He put me on my first diet when I was twelve. If he'd just left me alone. The next year I shot up five inches, and my weight didn't change, so all of a sudden I was a tall, willowy girl. But he made me weight conscious for the first time, and I have been all my life. So until my forties it was dieting, lose weight, gain it back, lose weight, gain it back—I was never more than five or ten pounds overweight.

I was tall, and so many of the boys were my height or even less, so when I went out on a date and put on those heels, I was even taller. Sometimes I'd wear flats, but you never felt quite dressed up in flats.

I can remember dabbing a little of my mother's loose face powder because my nose started shining. I was in the eighth grade. I think it was the next year in ninth grade that I started sneaking a little of her lipstick, and I didn't put it on too bright. She and my father both noticed it, and they said, "Are you old enough to wear lipstick?" And I said, "The other girls are"—that was a standard remark—and she said, "Well, don't wear too much." It was just lipstick and loose powder for quite a number of years, and then I discovered eyebrow pencil. I kept using my mother's makeup for the longest time until I started babysitting and had money to buy my own.

Mother told us about menstruation and made sure we were properly equipped with what we needed when that started. I'll give her points for that. For the rest of it, she handed me a little book to read. But then once I was dating, she was totally paranoid. Mother's watchword was "What will people think?" When one of my best friends from college became pregnant, I wanted her to come back to El Dorado. My cousin was a doctor, and he had told me he'd deliver the baby free of charge and find it a good home, and my mother just had a screaming fit. "No, no, no. Not in my backyard"—she urged me not to be friends with her. As it turned out, Janie got married to the father. Believe it or not, they're still married!

Two or three girls got pregnant in high school. In those days, either there was a quick marriage, or they went away and stayed with relatives or at unwed mothers' homes. They gave their babies up for adoption and then came back. Abortion was illegal. Getting pregnant was the worst thing that could happen to a girl. I'm sometimes amazed that my husband and I had sex before we got married.

I think another reason there wasn't much premarital sex in those days was the undergarments. Really, I'm serious. I can't imagine trying to get out of all those undergarments in the backseat of a car. I think they were invented by some mother who was determined to keep her daughter chaste. The worst instrument ever created on the face of the earth had to have been a long-line panty girdle. It was horrible—horrible! They would come down to above the knee and had hooks for your hose. There was even this instrument of torture called a waist cincher. It would pull in your waist fully two inches. Of course, you couldn't breathe, but it was worn primarily to dances—and then they had another instrument of torture called the merry widow, which was part waist cincher, and then it pushed the boobs up. I had a merry widow, I had a waister cincher, and I had panty girdles, and I wore 'em. From about age twelve, as soon as you had boobs, as soon as you went into a brassiere, you'd be wearing all this. It was designed to make you look slimmer and trimmer. To hold in your stomach. It was thought that if you had any flesh jiggling, this was just not ladylike. You didn't want your boobs bouncing, and you didn't want your hips one going up and one going down. It was just part of being a southern lady.

"Nice girls did nothing below the waist"—that was the code in those days. There was the usual pressure, the usual threats—"If you loved me," "If you won't, I'll find somebody who will . . ."—and I'd say, "Take a hike," so they'd take a hike. It never worked too well with me. I can remember how bad I felt the first time I let somebody have a feel below the waist. Oh, I wasn't sure that God wasn't gonna just strike me dead then and there. I grew up with a lot of guilt from the southern Protestant religions.

Later, in the summer of '68, I was back in Arkansas, and I had a new dress that I had bought, and when I sat down, the dress rode up pretty high and I was trying to fight this panty-girdle line, and one of my cousins said, "You need to get some panty hose. They're just wonderful." I was interested in anything where I didn't have to wear a girdle, and I went out and bought a pair of panty hose. They were about three dollars a pair.

My father died my senior year, and so the day after I graduated high school, I went to work as a secretary. We needed the money. It was with an old land lawyer. A lot of land descriptions, northeast fourth of the southwest, eighth of the sixteenth. Every now and then it would be something interesting like somebody adopting a baby or even getting a marriage annulled.

I worked those three months, and then I went to college for a year and a half, and then I dropped out. I wound up working for a couple of years as a secretary, but I was writing all the time while I was in high school. My father had encouraged my writing by giving me a little Royal typewriter. It was my most prized possession.

I was nineteen years old, and I was working for one of my father's friends. He had me backed up to the file case the very first day. My father's friend! He kissed me two or three times, and I was so stunned I didn't know how to react, and I didn't want to lose the job. After two or three weeks of working for him, I told him I didn't think he should kiss me; I didn't like it, but he kept doing it. And Mother said, "Is something wrong? I don't think you like your job very much," and I said, "Well, I don't know if you'll believe me." And after I told her, she said, "I know what you're telling me is true because he tried that same thing on your aunt twenty years ago, and furthermore I've worked for men that acted like that." She said, "You go in there tomorrow, and you tell him to keep his hands to himself or you're quitting the job immediately." I went in and told him that. I told him I'd talked to my mother, and that scared the hell out of him because my mother and his wife were friends—I watched the color literally drain out of that man's face. He never bothered me again.

I dropped out of college partly because of financial reasons and partly because I was sick of school, and overall I kept hearing my father's voice saying, "Oh, there's no need to give a girl an education; they're just going to get married anyway." He used to say, "Send 'em to college for a couple of years to get a little polish and meet the kind of boys you want 'em to marry." I definitely expected to get married, but the idea of having a career just really was not there. I just got lucky and stumbled into one anyway. When I was twenty-two, I saw an article about the School of Professional Writing at the University of Oklahoma. At the time, I was living in El Dorado working as a secretary and dating Charlie at the bank. I really hated my life, and when I read that article, it was like a light went on in my mind, and I started saving money, and six months later I left for the University of Oklahoma to study professional writing. By the time I was twenty-three years old I was making a living writing.

If you got to be twenty years old and you hadn't gotten married, you were beginning to get worried. Twenty-two, you were severely worried. I can tell you exactly when that changed for me. I was twenty-eight years old and had just been to the New York World's Fair. I was an unmarried writer, had just seen my agents and editors in New York City, and was coming back through Arkansas. This was 1965, and Mother said, "A bunch of your friends from high school are all home and having a luncheon." And my first thought was, "Oh, my god, they're all married and I'm not," and sure enough I went, and I really felt like a fifth wheel. They were talking about husbands and babies and when Joey got sick with the croup and this and that, and I'm sitting there bored out of my skull, and finally someone said, "Tell us what you've been doing, Martha Jane." And I said, "Well, I just came back from the New York World's Fair, and I saw my literary agent and my editors," and all of a sudden, I was aware that you could have heard a pin drop. Every woman's head had turned, and they were looking at me, and, I'll never forget, it was Mary Alice who spoke up. She said, "Oh, that sounds so interesting. Did you hear what Martha Jane said? She went to the World's Fair. She's been to New York City." And then they started bombarding me with questions, and I was saying, "Yes, I was in L.A. last year," and "Yeah, I was living in El Paso a couple of years ago, and we used to go down into Mexico," and they were fascinated. I was suddenly the hit of the luncheon, and I hadn't even wanted to go to the luncheon, but they kept saying, "Oh, our lives are just so boring," and that was the first time I ever heard that marriage and babies were boring.

I did get married, however. When I got to Oklahoma University, my husband and I started dating. We dated off and on for six years. Something just always told me not to get married to him. I knew it was going to be my mother's life all over again, just in a little better setting, a college town. I finally convinced myself it would be all right, and it wasn't. I married a man from the same sort of white Protestant background that I came out of, and he was almost thirteen years older. It *was* my mother's life all over again, and I was even angrier and more frustrated than she was to have to put everything on hold. My husband was a full professor at the university. He had incurred all these social debts throughout the years, and as soon as he got married he started paying people back. It seemed like I spent that whole year organizing and cooking for a dinner party. And there were the football games—it was, "Let's have a cocktail party at the house after the game." I was going to all of these faculty organizations—the geology wives, the OU faculty wives—there were teas. He expected me to be into all of this. Only once in the year we were married did I invite my writer and artist friends over. My husband excused himself at ten o'clock and went to bed. He used to call them "your kooky friends."

I was running errands, doing grocery shopping, cooking. I had a lady who came in once a week to do housecleaning, but, of course, I was supposed to keep things just the way his mother had kept things, which was perfectly. My husband thought it was okay if I wrote on the side. That was his phrase. "It's okay if you want to write on the side." He was talking about "Let's have a baby," and I was thinking "Oh, no, no, no."

I have never been so unhappy in all my life. Suddenly, I didn't have friends, I didn't have a life, I didn't have a name any more. I totally lost my identity. They took Corson, my maiden name, away from me. I had written under that name. I got married, and all my creditors immediately wrote back and said if you're married, we must change this account into your husband's name. I got new credit cards with my new last name. I found out once I was divorced that I had lost my whole credit history. All of this was not supposed to bother me, but it bothered me a lot. I think because I had seen my name in print. I had a strong identification.

This was right before feminism exploded. I learned within a year that this was a very traditional marriage. The women's movement, the sixties saved my life. It was like going from darkness to daylight. I was into a real guilt trip that I had walked out on my marriage, and suddenly here was this book by Betty Friedan, and here was Gloria Steinem. Here were all of these ladies, and they were saying the things that I had been thinking all of these years. It was, "Oh, thank God, other people feel and think the same way I do. I had always felt angry and frustrated at being told women couldn't do this, women couldn't do that. Suddenly, it was out in the open, and it was acceptable. It was like there was this giant awakening. The sexual revolution was part of it; the civil rights movement was part of it.

Nice Guys and Not-Nice Guys

Leslie Hampton

She was born in 1940 in Michigan, the youngest of three daughters by eight years.

"My parents were forty-five when I was born. It was not something they planned. They owned a little general store, and after my father died, my mother became the postmaster in this tiny town of four hundred people." (See also pp. 286 and 443)

I went to a very traditional fifties high school in a little town of a couple of thousand just a few miles down the road from where I grew up. The most untraditional thing I remember anybody doing is there was one couple where the guy was real short and the girl was taller than him, and that was considered very brave. Isn't that amazing?

I was 5–8½ when I started high school, and by the time I was a junior, I weighed about 162, which, I believe now, is probably my natural weight. I was sure that I was terribly overweight, and my senior year I went on my first real diet, and I got down to 135 pounds—and I did look good. Most everybody was very concerned about weight. That was a major issue, and for me it has remained a major concern.

The boys were sorted into nice guys and not-nice guys. And a couple of times I dated guys that were in that category of not-nice guys, and they did pressure me. They would do the typical things like moving their hands where their hands weren't supposed to be, or there was talk about trying to having sex and how wonderful it would be. But the nice guys did not pressure me. I was a good girl. There were the good girls and the not-so-good girls. The not-so-good girls might possibly be having sex, but the good girls weren't, or at least nobody knew they were. And if you got pregnant, you were out of school. That was it—there were two or three that dropped out. A very good friend of mine got pregnant toward the end of our senior year. She was not allowed to go on our senior trip because of that. Her boyfriend, of course, did, and I do remember being outraged about that. They got married shortly after, because she was a good girl who made a mistake. Shotgun wedding. About ten, fifteen years ago I started to realize that every time I was with a group of women my age and we started talking, that the majority of them had been pregnant when they got married. My sense now is that by senior year a large percentage of the girls were having sex with somebody they were going steady with, and a lot of them married those guys. This teenage pregnancy is not something new—what's new is not getting married.

Alice Dumont

She was born in 1933 in the Deep South. (See also pp. 271 and 457)

When I was four or five years old, I was molested by a neighbor. He touched me in the genitals. He would put me on his lap, and he would start feeling me. I never forgot him. I never forgot his name. I never forgot the way he looked. His wife and my mother would go off together, and he would always say, "Well, just leave Alice with me, and you go do your shopping or whatever," and then I can remember feeling terrible and knowing it was wrong but not knowing exactly—here was an adult. I would start to cry when my mother wanted to leave me again. "No, no, don't leave me." She never got it.

Beverly Butler Lavergneau

She was born in 1940 and grew up in Pittsburgh. Her daughter Mara also appears in the book. (See also pp. 86, 109 and 319)

We had to walk through major portions of the University of Pittsburgh campus to get home from school. Most days I was with my brother and other kids, but I was much further ahead of them on this particular day. I was maybe eight years old—and this stranger came upon me, and at first he tried to lure me with the offer of money—and I was terrified. I didn't know where the other kids were, and I was very, very frightened, but I didn't quite know what to do. He attempted to enter me, and he had a premature ejaculation—he ejaculated over my clothes. I really didn't understand. Shortly after that, my brother and his friends and the other kids caught up and chased him off, and when we got home, my mother went into hysterics, so it was a horrible experience, but as I look back on it, I consider that I was pretty lucky.

Rachel Morgan

She was born in the Midwest in 1940. Her daughter Lauren Morgan Stern also appears in the book. (See also p. 276)

The subject of sex was never raised in my family. My friends and I had gotten books, we watched TV—we figured it out. We didn't figure it out real well. The conversation all around you was you don't have sex until you're married. We didn't know about contraceptives, and you couldn't just go to the drugstore and buy foam. Condoms were a whole lot harder to get. So this whole fear of becoming pregnant kept a lot of us technical virgins—we did everything but. Heavy petting, yes. Oral sex, we didn't talk about it. I don't think there was a whole lot of it going on, but there was definitely some. Boys understood that we weren't going to be pressured beyond heavy petting. We could definitely be pressured into heavy petting, even though we might not have wanted necessarily to go that far.

Anna Davis

She was born in Poughkeepsie, New York, in 1941. (See also pp. 78 and 471)

When I was a young teenager, if you went bowling, you didn't want to bowl better than the guy because you didn't want to hurt his ego. Today, if I can bowl better than a guy, I'm going to bowl better than the guy, but when I was a young teenager, you didn't excel because you didn't want to damage his ego. They didn't care about ours, but you had to worry about theirs.

Nancy Douglas

She lives with her husband in a large midwestern city and works as a political consultant. She has four children from her first marriage.

"I was born in Salt Lake City, Utah, in 1934. I lived there until 1947, when my family moved to Minneapolis." (See also pp. 270 and 302)

I remember my father coming home from work—the martini, the second martini, Mother cooking in the kitchen, Father commentating, and I would just sit on the stoop of the back staircase and listen. My sister's six years older than I; she was the risk taker in the social world. She had somebody's high school ring, somebody from Ohio she met at a summer job. So, sitting on the stoop outside the kitchen, that's where a lot of my values were formed, to hear them just horrified that this daughter of theirs had a ring from a guy who was from a small town in Ohio. They probably never even met him. They just thought it was tacky for a seventeen-year-old to have a big Ohio high school ring.

I carved a very safe course for my adolescent and high school years. I was very popular. I went out every weekend night with a different boy. That made my mother and father very pleased. To have a steady beau was not acceptable in my parents' world; a young woman should have many beaus so that she had many exposures. I'm sure that fear of sex was latent, but they would not have voiced it. That would not have been proper, and this was a pretty proper household. It was a little bit *Life with Father*. My sister used to always get in heavy kinds of relationships, and she'd be ringed or pinned—being pinned meant you wore a boy's fraternity pin. It was engaged to be engaged. I'd hear my parents rail against this, so I went out and I did the opposite. In retrospect, I think that I missed something in my growing up because the rest of my family were having picnics and doing things, and I was always out on a date.

I often had to impose my own time to be in because my mother and daddy thought I was such a "good girl" that they didn't need to. I rarely crossed the boundaries. Often if I didn't like the boy, I would say, "Oh, I've got to be in by ten or eleven."

I would never have called a boy. I waited for a proper phone call, "Will you go to the theater? Will you go to the movies?" and then he would come to the door, come in, say hi to the parents—"Have a good time." We would go out, and after the movie, you'd go to one of these drive-ins and have a hamburger and fries and a milk shake, and then you'd go home.

Boys used to secure their position. They would say in June, "what are you doing New Year's Eve?" because they wanted to have a legitimate date. I wasn't very picky because I was a nice girl, wouldn't hurt somebody's feelings by saying no. When they kept asking you out, that was always tricky because you wouldn't say, "I don't like you—it's not going to work." You would say, "I'm busy," or "I'm not going to be here." Sometimes you practically locked yourself in your room lest somebody see that you were home.

The super jock, the most attractive boy in the class, never asked me out. I was always asked out safely by the next echelon. I was a good safe choice.

There was a lot of sexual pressure, but I was in a funny spot trying to keep this popular role. I couldn't be out necking in a car with somebody different every night. People to this day remember I was nicknamed "Icey"—I was perceived to be so cold because I wouldn't put out. I was seeing so many people that there was no way I could just flit from one backseat to another. Sexual pressure was primarily necking pressure. It certainly wasn't to-bed pressure. Intercourse was after I was married. And that doesn't mean that we didn't do almost everything, but it was just that prohibition that said that you might get pregnant. To be pregnant out of wedlock was a fate worse than death and kept that whole generation of women virginal. It meant being ostracized from society. The number of sexually active women of my generation even in college, I think, was small. I know people will say that it was greater, but I had pretty wide, broadly based friendship patterns, and I'd say that sexual intercourse was not common.

I didn't like going out every night with somebody different. I did it because it was part of this scenario that said to be popular was a good thing. So I was kind of proud when I heard my daughter say to somebody, "You know, I really don't want to go out with you, I don't want to see that movie, and besides we don't have anything in common." I thought, "Well, way to go," because I was part of the other generation that said, "Oh, yes, I'd love to go, oh, yes."

Rene Bailey

She is a widow who lives in a rural area in Ulster County, New York. She is African-American and has had a long career as a gospel singer and doing shows. For twenty-one years, she was the vocalist of the Peg Leg Bates Country Club. After her husband's death in 1988, she took college classes in order to become a teacher assistant. She now works mainly with mentally handicapped children. She also continues to sing.

"I was born in 1933 in Valdosta, Georgia. My mother and father were gospel singers. I started singing in the church when I was around six years old. After I became a teenager, during the summers, I was on the road with the Gospelite Singers, and we had some of the greatest of singers. I have been gospel singing with Aretha Franklin and her father, Reverend C. M. Franklin, among others."

When I was twelve years old, I became a missy. My period started on me in school. My home-ec teacher, she would tell us girls of becoming a missy; my mom never talked too much to me about it. But, thank God, I got it in school, and my teacher, Mrs. Hadley, gave me a note for my mother and sent one of the girls home with me, and I told my mom. It was on a Friday.

That Sunday my mother with some of her lady friends, and some of the neighbors, had a conference with me. In the living room they came in—"Hi, Mrs. Williams," "Hi"—and my mom called me in. They all tell me, "Now you will get your period every month. Now you have become a young lady. That means you can have a baby. That means you don't play with the little boys anymore. You don't let the little boys feel you or want to feel you or kiss you or anything like that." They had what you would call a church meeting with me that Sunday to let me know the dos and don'ts. I never will forget that. That was a common thing for the ladies to do when a girl in the neighborhood become a young lady.

I knew all the time that you wasn't allowed to do certain things with little boys, because your mother would teach you that. You didn't let a boy feel you or go under your dress. That was a no-no. I also learned that through our teacher, Mrs. Shaw. Yes—I came along in the era where you was taught a little more about sex than it had been in the past.

When I started to see boys, I was sixteen years old. You wasn't allowed to have a boyfriend before you turned sixteen because they just felt like fourteen and fifteen— hey, you had to think about your books. You had to learn.

Growing up, I never believed in having two or three boys hanging around. Just one boy at a time. They had to meet that boy. The boy came to the house, and that boy wasn't allowed no further than the living room. If he wanted a drink of water or whatever, you went to the kitchen and brought him that water. He was sitting there just like a frog sitting on a log. On the weekend, you could go to the movie, and you had to be back home by ten o'clock. The boy felt like, if he didn't want to be run out of the city, he had to have you back by that time because your parents would be sitting there waiting for you. In the summertime, they would be sitting on the porch in the swing or in the rocker. They felt like, "If you are going to stay in my house, you going to go by my rules." In a way, it was good rules, and in a way at times you thought it was the worst rules in the world because it was so strict, but you had rules to go by.

That girl had to be under lock and key. But the boys—well, he's a boy—and that I never really could figure out, never really took to. "So, Dad and Mom, if Charles can do it, why can't I?" "He's a boy, and the boys always have had more leeway than the girls." I really wasn't too happy with that.

As I grew older, I necked and pet, but I didn't come back and tell my mom about it. That was my secret. A respectable young lady didn't do that, as they would put it. But within, I knew what I wanted to do, and I knew how far to go.

I didn't have sex with my high school boyfriend—if you went into the drugstore to get something to protect yourself, half the whole town would have known it before you got it. It was the boy's responsibility for him to inform his father or his oldest brother or whatever, whoever, someone that knew how to go about getting things to protect you. In that era, it was only that the boy could go into the drugstore and ask for a pack of rubbers. My boyfriend was sort of afraid to do that, and I don't know whether he had enough confidence in his father to say, "Dad, I need protection." So it was a good while before I went into the sex bit.

When that happened, I was seventeen or eighteen. I was coming out of high school. I had changed boyfriends at that point because I liked the older-type boy. I didn't feel guilty about having sex because I felt like this a part of life and my parents shouldn't have told me that you are never to have sex until you're married. I think they should have told me how to protect myself. Nature goes on, so I did have sex, but I didn't go back and tell my mom, and I made sure that the boy had protection.

Sometimes me and my best friend would get in the worst argument because she felt like I was a bad person. I'm not a bad person, I say, but you are stupid because you feel like you got to do exactly what your mama say do.

I think that some did wait till they got married to have sex. I just felt like life is to be enjoyed, and you have to put something into life to get something out of it. I never was the one to go from boy to boy to boy. Until when I became around twenty-one, I was going steady with one man, and I went with him until I left Thomasville.

I didn't get married till I was twenty-nine years old simply because I felt like I was doing what I loved to do. Oh, a boy proposed to me. He said, "Will you marry me?" I was around eighteen years old. And I say yes. But one thing he told me, and I say no. He say, "When we get married, I don't want you to sing anymore." That was like telling me to go lay down and die. I wasn't ready to do that, and as he proposed to me, it was broken off at the same time because I felt I was my own woman. Used to be a time that a man would dictate to you what to do, and you felt like you had to do that. But I was coming up in a new generation in which a woman could speak her mind, and you be what you want. Also, I think that strength came from my aunts, Josephine and Eva, on my mother's side. They didn't let their husband just come in and dictate to them what to do. They felt like, "Hey, this is not slavery time, so we're not going to buckle under you." So I say to this boy, "No, I'm sorry." I felt like this made me stronger in my belief, in saying, "Hey, I'm going to go and do what I wants to do when I want to do it. I'm going to sing forever. I'm going to sing till I die. I'm going to sing till I can't sing anymore." The man I married, he was one hundred percent with me in my singing. Yes. That's the reason I didn't get married until I was twenty-nine.

I met my husband about a month after I came to Connecticut. I went down to the store to buy my brother and his family a TV set, and he waited on me. It was the first time he seen me, and he said, "Are you married?" I say, "No, you?" He say, "No," and he said, "But I'm going to marry you." I thought he was nuts. I did. He had to come to the house to set the TV up. He asked me, "Can I call you?" I say, "Yes, you can call me." And so he would call me, and we would talk on the phone, but it was about a month and a half before I went out for dinner with him. He just knew that I was who he wanted, yeah. We met in '62, February, and we got married 5th of July of '63.

Yolanda Casarez

She lives in Los Angeles with her husband and daughter and works in a factory.

   "I was born in El Paso, Texas, in 1950. My parents were also born in El Paso. All of my grandparents were from Mexico. I have a daughter fifteen years old and a twenty-five-year-old son." (See also pp. 305 and 477)

*W*hen I was thirteen. He was an older guy, in his early twenties, and he lived down the street from where I lived. He was standing outside, and I was walking by, coming from a friend's house, and it was already getting a little bit dark, and he came out and he says, "Can I walk with you?" And I just turned around and said, "For what? I don't know you." "Well, I just want to talk to you." So I kept on walking, and he kept walking with me, and he started striking up a conversation, and we were getting close to my house. He told me, "I like you," and he says, "I'd like to get to know you better," and I said, "Look, I'm only thirteen, and I know you're older, so just leave me alone." And then he grabbed me by the arm, and he put his arm forcibly around my neck, and he just dragged me to behind a garage, and he did what he wanted to do. Right after he walked away, my mom drove up. I never told her what happened. I never told anybody. I was scared, and I felt something bad was going to happen if I told. I saw him a few times after that. I would go another way. He would call me. He lived next door to a friend of my mom's, and my mom would say, "Let's go to Gloria's house." "I don't want to go, Mom, I don't want to go."

   It left me really scared. When I started having a boyfriend, he would like try to put his arm around me or something—"Stop it. Don't. Don't touch me," until I was seventeen when I got married, but that was really different.

Beverly Butler Lavergneau

She was born in 1940 and grew up in Pittsburgh. Her daughter Mara also appears in the book. (See also pp. 86, 102 and 319)

My daughters think it's hysterical that I was a virgin until I was almost twenty years old. They can't believe it. The majority of my close friends were probably virgins when they married. A lot of things that I have done with my daughters, I'm sure that my mother would never have allowed. I was in a transition generation.

Abortion has revolutionized so much in terms of the comfort level that young women have about sex. My generation was very much aware of stories of women who were harmed by illegal abortions. Everyone probably knew someone who went through a horror story.

My Parents Dreamed a Big Dream

Sybil Jordan Hampton

She was born September 1, 1944, in Springfield, Missouri.

"I was a child of World War II. My father was part of the black military, which was being trained at Fort Leonard Wood prior to being sent overseas. I was the first child born to my parents' marriage. They were from Little Rock, Arkansas, and I came back to Arkansas with my mother very shortly after I was born because my father was sent to Okinawa. Within the year, my brother was born."

As little children, my brother and I went along to class with our parents. They got their college degrees after we were born. My father left the military and went back to college, and my mother went back after my father finished. He went into the postal service, because, of course, there were no options for him to go on for an MBA, which is what he wanted to do. My mother became a teacher. She even went on to the University of Arkansas and got her master's in teaching there.

I became a teenager in the late fifties, and *Brown vs. Board of Education* was a 1954 event. By 1957 the school integration crisis in Little Rock was well under way. My life was tremendously impacted because I was surrounded by all of the tension and all of the news. The schools in Little Rock were integrated by students' names being put forward. There was interviewing and screening. They came up with a composite of a number of things they were looking for: ability, good grades; there was psychological testing.

People's families were approached and asked whether or not their children could be nominated to go into the screening process. My parents talked with me. They were very aware that there would be some risk, but they also felt that this was something for the betterment of the race and that strong families and strong people really should be involved. It became very controversial. People who didn't want their children to be exposed to this felt uneasy when their friends—it's that whole thing: who's committed and who's not. I don't think I ever felt that people put me down. I didn't feel that kind of pressure, but I knew that there was this other dynamic going on. Not many people were willing for their children to go forward in this process. They were not only afraid of what might happen to their children at school, but they were being intimidated at their places of employment.

My name was put forward in 1958 as one of the students who might go to Central whenever it reopened, and when it did in 1959, I was one of the five students who had been selected. And so I began my tenth-grade year as the only black student in a class of over six hundred at Little Rock Central High School.

After the 1957–58 school year when there was so much media attention and so many stories all around the country and the town about the horrors of what went on in the high school, you can imagine it was somewhat overwhelming to think about going back into the school and having no idea what would happen. But I really was not afraid. My parents were very clear about the fact that the worst enemy that you can have is fear. What you have to do is take every day a step at a time and be very aware of what is happening around you. So I actually began high school with this great sense of "Well, it will be revealed."

My mother was born in 1920, and she was raised as an only child by my grandfather, a single parent who was forty-four when she was born. My grandfather had gone to college at the turn of the century and had not been able to stay for a four-year degree but had taken a program that allowed him to do carpentry and construction. My mother really saw the world through the eyes of her father, and she saw things as being possible and taking risks. He was self-employed, and he owned a business, and she helped him in that business.

My father had grown up in rural Arkansas. He wanted to attend the black high school in Little Rock, which he knew was academically stronger than his rural high school. On his own, he hitchhiked to Little Rock and worked as a servant. He attended night school so that he could get the Dunbar High School diploma because he wanted to go on to college.

And so my parents were people whose lives were testimony to stepping out and doing things that needed to be done. I never had any mixed feelings about participating in the integration. I so completely trusted my parents. I felt very much grounded in their faith. My parents are very strong Christians, very involved in the African Methodist Episcopal church. It just seemed to me that this was another stepping out on faith and doing something difficult that had to be done that would make life better for all of us at some point in the future that I couldn't see.

By the fall of 1959, the city had been so traumatized by all the bad press, that people were quite anxious to have it viewed as a far more civilized place than it had been in the past. I don't remember anyone standing outside the school heckling. That phase had passed, and the good people of the city had really decided that they needed to show their muscle. And I think they did that by planning for the opening of school in the kind of way that it would be as uneventful as possible.

In 1957 they started with nine students, the famous Little Rock Nine. There is a book called *Warriors Don't Cry* that was written by Melba Beals, who was one of the Little Rock Nine. When I read that last year, it was quite revealing for me. I led a six-week discussion on it, and what astonished people was that the experience she had at Little Rock Central did not mirror mine. Since that time some things had changed very dramatically. I wasn't afraid of being attacked in the halls, and I wasn't physically under the kind of duress or stress that book described, time after time after time.

What we lived in 1959 was total isolation. People didn't talk to you. In the three years that I was in the high school the people in my homeroom never spoke to me. The only thing that I ever was asked to do by the people in my homeroom was to take my turn reading the Bible—in those days you could still have Bible readings.

My homeroom teacher spoke to me as infrequently as she needed to, and my classroom teachers certainly spoke to me and encouraged me to participate in class. But in terms of any social interaction with people walking down the hall, talking to people, having a friend emerge in those three years, it didn't happen. What became very clear, in retrospect, is that there was this peer pressure not to "befriend niggers." And so while you might not be in their faces about anything negative, you were also not going to break any of the social codes.

My classroom experiences were very good. I don't think there was a teacher that I was instructed by who particularly wanted me to be in the high school, but those teachers separated out their personal feelings about me and their sense of themselves as professionals. And what I felt was the real blessing, the real benefit that I received in that situation, was that the teachers were first rate, first class, and did an excellent job and therefore did not exclude me from the circle of their influence as teachers.

After you work with a person over a period of time in a class, there is a type of intimacy and warmth—you begin to establish a relationship that moves to different levels when you are a student with a teacher. In this case the relationship always remained the same. It was very clear that my teachers appreciated me as a bright student, as someone who was really very hard working, but their own personal feelings or their own personal pleasure or joy in the fact that I was growing or succeeding, you would never be able to make any statement about what that was.

I never initiated anything towards any of my classmates because it was very clear that that was unacceptable, and it was also very clear to me that it was a place I didn't want to go because I realized that I didn't want to open myself up to any more hurt than I had to. The only student that I ever had any friendly relations with was from France. She came as an exchange student, and so she was not a part of the peer group, and therefore she could extend herself to me and talk to me in the halls or wherever and people would just think of her as being that odd foreign student.

Of course, I interacted with the other black students. We all had lunch together. There were two black students in the eleventh grade, and two of the original Little Rock Nine came back as seniors. We lived our experiences day to day, and that was it. We didn't talk about what it had been like during the 1957–58 school year, which is fascinating for me now, in retrospect.

I also continued to have the same friendships that I had always had in my elementary and junior high school, but when everyone else goes to the same school, you are on the periphery. And then being so very visible in the community by being at Central, my social life was just more limited. My parents were not going to permit me to be out and around the town, never knowing when somebody really idiotic might decide to run me over on the street corner. The students who went to school after the Little Rock Nine were never public figures in the way that the Little Rock Nine were. I wasn't interviewed on TV and my picture was not in the paper, but I was easily identifiable as "one of those niggers that went to Central High School."

By state law you could be excluded from all clubs and activities, and that included honor society—anything that was outside of the traditional educational system. In order to be selected to go to the school, I had of course been an elementary and junior high school leader, and it was very striking to now be prevented by law from participating in any social, extracurricular, or sports activities—band, choir, anything.

You had to go to assemblies—everybody went—but you were always isolated because nobody would sit next to you. In my classes that was not so much the case because the classroom teachers tolerated no funny business. It is very striking that in the classroom I was a full participant; people sat where they needed to sit. There was not this kind of craziness of "I'm not sitting where niggers are" that might go on in the auditorium or in homeroom.

There was still so much concern in 1962 that there might be an incident that the only people who could attend the graduation ceremonies were the immediate family members, which would mean just your parents. I think that some of the people who were then tenth-graders were having different types of relationships with their classmates who were coming into the school new. The black students were getting to know white students. Although it was beginning to change, it had not changed for my class, and the tenor of the times was such that there was still this closed and closely moni-tored graduation. My high school career really began and ended in a very similar fashion.

After high school, I went to a Quaker college instead of Bryn Mawr, where I really wanted to go. My parents were very wise and insisted that I go to a healing place that would provide less academic and other types of challenges. They felt that I was un-aware of how stretched out I was inside, and they were absolutely right. I considered going to a black college. I thought about going to Howard, but my parents thought that there were different kinds of social pressures there, the whole sorority-fraternity thing. My high school experience was more protective than it would have been normally, and that does lead to a certain kind of lack of social maturity. So I ended up going to a small, private, liberal arts, coeducational Quaker institution. My parents felt that it would be the type of environment that was academically rigorous but would also look at larger issues of peace and justice and have people who were really interested in is-sues of the heart.

My parents were not political people. They were very committed and very spiri-tual. They were very much interested in issues of social justice. So much of the civil rights movement came out of churches. It was the church that was the voice of the black community because we really had not for a long time had active roles as full partici-pants in the political life of the community.

I went away to Earlham, and there were three black women out of twelve hundred students. It was just very fascinating to go to the next stage of my life and discover that once again I was truly one of the minorities. But the school was a small, very close com-munity where I felt really very secure. The challenge at Central was to go and keep my wits about me when being excluded; the challenge at Earlham was to go to a very fine liberal arts institution and discover that while I had been an excellent student in high school under very, very difficult circumstances, there were many things that I still had not been exposed to, and this would be an academic struggle. It balanced out and it worked out. But I will certainly say that I was not the best or brightest at Earlham— or so I thought—and yet my life is a testimony to the fact that I was supposed to be there and be the recipient of the fine education that I received there.

A year after leaving Earlham, I went to graduate school at the University of Chi-cago and got a master's in teaching. I did the very thing I thought I was never going to do, follow in my mother's footsteps. I taught for a year and really learned that public school teaching did not, as my principal said, "fit my rhythms." So I had an opportu-nity to move to New York and work at Iona College, where I stayed for fourteen years.

The first time in my life after all the years from Little Rock that I ever took on a formal role that really addressed the whole civil rights thing was in 1993, when I had an opportunity to go to Southwestern University in Texas and work as special assistant to the president on issues of community and diversity. At Iona I initially worked in HEOP, the Higher Education Opportunity Program, where I helped to provide support services and staffing for students who were considered minority disadvantaged. But I really did it from the educator's perspective, developing tutorial programs.

When I went to Southwestern, I worked for the president as his troubleshooter on issues having to do with what kind of advocacy you have for minority students. What do you call the office that would support these students? Is it only for minority students? What do you do to diversify in a town that is thirty miles outside of Austin and people would rather go to UT? How do you recruit more African-American and Latino faculty? I had never in all of those years felt a call, or felt that I was ready to move on to that type of role.

By the time I took the job in Texas, I had come of age, and I felt that I had learned some things and I understood some things and I could really speak to people who were in different camps and had very different perspectives. My life experiences created in me the culture of marginality. I don't fit anyplace neatly anymore, and I have become very comfortable with that. I understand that it offers me a unique opportunity to be of help in the circumstances where you need someone who is neither fish nor fowl. By going back to Texas, I really entered the South again. I had spent almost thirty years living in the Northeast and the upper Midwest since I left for college in 1962.

I felt that the South had changed a lot and that maybe it was a place I could come back to. I am currently president of the Winthrop Rockefeller Foundation in Little Rock, Arkansas. It is a private philanthropy whose primary goal is to improve the quality of life for all Arkansans. I think that my having been in Texas these last three years and having come to grips with some of the issues of life in the South really helped the board to find me an attractive candidate. I feel as if my life has come full circle. All the pieces of what I have done fit.

When my parents talked to me about participating in the integration of Central High School, they were very clear that they could not tell me that there would not be things about this that would be very painful. They said they didn't know what they were and didn't want to raise some unnecessary fears, and they also always wanted me to know that these experiences that I would have if I were selected to go to Central would be the experiences that I would stand on for my future. And that my future was larger than Little Rock. For all the things that were negative, the positive would be that I would be able to live in a very large world. And they were right.

I think that my parents dreamed a big dream. They wanted to make sure that if it was at all possible for their incredible dream to come true, they would have done everything they needed to. They weren't guaranteed a thing. They stepped out on faith.

My parents are today two of the most thrilled human beings on the face of the earth. They are in their seventies and had never expected to have me come home and be with them in these years of their life as a support and now also as a tremendous source of pride and joy. They are two of the people who think that I have one of the best jobs in Arkansas.

It Was 1960

Suzanne Havercamp

She lives with her husband in a small town in upstate New York. They have three adult sons. She has been a schoolteacher and does volunteer work.

"I was born here in 1939, the youngest of four. Mother was a homemaker; Dad was a realtor. Dad was mostly German background, and my mother was of Irish, Scottish, and English descent, and so I'm a mixed bag. I was raised Roman Catholic." (See also pp. 302 and 466)

I went to a Roman Catholic, private girls' school from second grade through senior year in high school. When I graduated, I went on to Dunbarton College at Holy Cross, a lovely all-girls school in Washington, D.C. It closed back in the early seventies, I believe. Those sisters were amazing. They really encouraged us to use the city.

It was 1960. The first time I saw John Kennedy, we went to a rally over to American University, and there was this young Adonis standing up there, and everybody was "Ahhh." And then I belonged to a little singing group octet. We went around to college campuses and hospitals and sang barbershop. The Nixon people heard about us, and so we were traveling with the Nixon campaign around Washington. I met the man and shook his hand, and we had our picture taken. We were not necessarily Republicans. We were just happy little ladies out there having a good time.

We could stay out on school nights. It might have been until seven-thirty, and later on it was until nine unless you had special permission. I don't think we could be out in freshman year. On weekends when you got to be a senior, you could stay out until, I think, midnight, but your dates came in—they signed you out. When they brought you back, they signed you back in. There was a sister there on duty to see that everything was A-okay. If you got so many bad marks against your name, then the next weekend you wouldn't be allowed to go.

It was a wonderful life, and every Catholic school in Washington at the time—I graduated in '61—did principally the same thing, so you didn't feel like an oddball. You resented it to a certain degree, but it was okay. It really wasn't until you got into the sixties a little bit more that attitudes changed. But we were still part of a society where there was a structure and a framework. Most of the girls were engaged by the time they were seniors in college. I never felt pressure to marry from my parents. Everybody in my age group, especially the female part of society, felt great peer pressure, and it wasn't anything that was even discussed. It was more the expectation or the hope maybe of every girl who went to college that by the time they were seniors they might have met the man of their dreams and then they'd be going off and marrying them. That was the next step. When I grew up, you were born, you were educated; after education you were married.

Joanna Rubin

She was born in New York in 1940. She is married, has two adult children, and is a professor of anthropology at an East Coast university.

It was 1962, and I was twenty-two. It was my first year of graduate school. Michael and I studied together. One night we stayed up all night talking, and it was very intense, intellectual. Maybe it was that night, maybe it was some other night, but we became sexually involved. The first or second time I had sex with him, I got pregnant. He didn't ejaculate inside of me—he came out—but I got pregnant. I certainly got birth control right after that, a diaphragm. Before that I hadn't really been seeing anyone; I wasn't particularly promiscuous. I liked Michael as a person, but I was ready to stop seeing him except that I got pregnant.

He knew through the grapevine about this place in Puerto Rico—Dr. Pardo's Clinic—that did abortions. I'm not sure if abortions were illegal at that point in Puerto Rico. They certainly were illegal in this country. Having a safe place alleviated a tremendous amount of anxiety and fear. I was scared until he found that clinic. I was afraid that I might end up having to go to some dirty back room.

I remember having lunch with my father. I wanted to tell him. I remember the intensity of the feelings; I felt alone. I didn't have any support from my parents in general. I had the sense that he knew something was wrong, but he didn't ask, and so I didn't tell him.

I must have borrowed the money to go down there, or Michael may have paid for the plane fare. He didn't have any money, and I didn't have any money. Anyway, I flew to Puerto Rico with him. I was about four to six seeks pregnant. We stayed two or three days. I was fairly confident that this place was okay. Michael knew people who had been there. We stayed in some hotel and took a bus out to the clinic; it was in a free-standing building outside of San Juan. There were other women in the waiting room, but I don't remember seeing any other American women. I remember them putting a mask over my face—they gave me some kind of anesthesia—and telling me to count and then waking up in bed bleeding. There were nurses. It was a real clinic; it wasn't a back room. The place was very clean. I don't know whether it's normal to bleed as much as I bled, but they reassured me and gave me sanitary napkins. I felt very vulnerable and physically weak. I had never felt that way before. I walked out of the clinic not too long after the abortion, and we took the bus back to San Juan. I remember needing to lean on Michael, and I didn't like being dependent. I can picture what I was wearing—a brown and white checked dress, short sleeves, straight skirt, organza, sheer cotton material. It was quite warm there. We went back to the hotel, and I rested.

When I found out I was pregnant, I went to see a doctor, and he had told me to come and see him afterwards. I had a low-grade infection. He was very sweet, supportive, gave me antibiotics. I remember I had an extremely intense dream. I think it was on the way down to Puerto Rico. I remembered it for years. It had something to do with being in a bathtub and bleeding, having a bloody leg. It had to do with wishing that I was pregnant with somebody else's baby. I think if I had had the baby with someone I was in love with, I might have kept it. The dream was a real regret, a sadness. I never at all considered having that baby, and I never regretted having had the abortion. It would have been a total disaster in terms of my education, my relationship with Michael—I was already involved with him longer than I would have been because of the abortion. Although I didn't for a minute think I didn't want the abortion, it was still a very, very heavy experience. It isn't, "Oh, this is a cool, easy decision to make, and there are no consequences."

Hettie Jones

Author, poet, and the mother of two adult daughters, she was recently celebrated in Women of the Beat Generation. *She was born to a Jewish family in Brooklyn in 1934 and now lives in the East Village. (See also p. 316)*

*A*t a certain point—I think it was around 1959 or '60—*Life* magazine published a photo essay about the Beats, showing people in their bohemian pads without the requisite couch and chairs, carpet and avocado refrigerator of the fifties. Everything was sort of makeshift, from the Salvation Army. And my mother just got so upset about that. She despaired over my bohemian lifestyle just as much as she despaired over my interracial marriage and my commitment to it by having children. It made no sense to her that I lived with an old kitchen table that she had given me and a funky wooden coffee table that I'd gotten for a dollar.

The Beats were essentially a spiritual quest. It was the disdain for the trappings of middle-class life and the fact that one could live a wonderful life without it. When my father came to see my first apartment in the Village, he stood at the bottom of five flights of stairs, and he said, "Uh, five flights—why live like this?" Why live in what he thought was a tenement. It wasn't—it was a perfectly nice apartment building in the Village. But to him it was not the American dream; the American dream was to do better than your parents materially. And the dream for women at that time was to marry well, not to go off on your own and live in what they called a one-and-a-half-room apartment in the Village. But I had every reason to live like that.

I grew up in a house in Queens. My father was in business with a brother of his, and they made advertising display cards out of cardboard. He had a loft off of Union Square with printing presses in it. My mother didn't work, although she did lots of volunteer work for the Red Cross and for the Jewish group Hadassah. When she was sixty-five, she took ten years off her age and got a job working in an auto body shop as a bookkeeper, bless her heart. So I think she finally understood a little bit about things. But not really. I think there was a certain amount of pride in later years that my parents took in the fact that I had become a published author, but they didn't see that in order to do what I did afterwards, I simply had to go through that bohemian life that started me off—and I kind of still live like that, too.

It was very exciting to me as a young woman from a lower-middle-class Queens family. I wanted something new in my life. Somehow I had found my way to a women's college in Virginia, of all places, and when I found my way back from Virginia by way of Columbia, and then finally down to the Village, I was ready for something, and I found other people who were also ready for something.

I think we were ready for some kind of protest against the horrors of the cold war, we were ready for an American statement in art, and we were ready to break open the very staid, very repressed atmosphere after the war. Everyone was being very safe, very materialistic. We were living in what was thought of as the affluent society, but those of us who wanted something else had seen that it wasn't really like that. As Allen

Ginsberg's poem says, "I have seen the best minds of my generation starving hysterical naked." We were really ready to protest—oh, how can I describe it—that safe cover. I wanted to invent a new way for a woman to be. After the Second World War women were sent back from the defense plants and sent away from any kind of meaningful role in society—"Leave it to the men." And so the women were told to go home and pet their washing machines.

The Village was altogether different. It didn't have those two-car garages. There were little places where people were doing poetry readings; the coffee shops were waking up after a slumber. There hadn't really been much of a bohemia in the Village since the late thirties because the war interrupted things. So we really felt that we were making it new the way Pound said to do; we were making art new, music new, and poetry new, and everyone was very excited about this.

I found myself set into the middle of people with whom I had an instant affinity, because I didn't have to apologize for what I had always been thinking of, which was an independent woman's life, and a life that would go towards self-expression. A life in which a woman could become something—which actually gave rise to the title of my book: *How I Became Hettie Jones*.

I didn't know what I wanted to become, and I think a lot of the women in the scene didn't know precisely what they wanted to become. They didn't want to be cruel and reject their parents; at least, I didn't. A lot of people didn't want to reject—they just didn't want that same kind of life. I wanted, specifically, to have my own apartment. I wanted to have sex, and I wanted to live as though I were really having sex—not trying to hide it. I wanted to have a career, preferably as an artist—in whatever way I could figure that out. Many of my friends had come from faraway places to come to New York, and they too were looking for a new way. We all arrived here independent of each other and made a life for ourselves.

The streets at night were the streets of the quaint old Village. They smelled like coffee from the coffee shops, and the port of New York was still in operation then, so sometimes you could smell spices being unloaded, and the whole Village smelled like that, and, of course, because it's a port, it alternately smelled to me like spices and the sea and coffee, and it was to me an opening up of the senses.

You know those pocketbooks that women carry now with the little handles? Well, I had been carrying something all my life—that prissy little pocketbook into which you could not fit anything, and you had to have gloves. I didn't want to be a lady, and neither did any of the other women I knew. I remember finding shoulder bags—

and then you had free hands! My first shoulder bag was black, and it had a red inside, and it fit over the shoulder sort of like a quiver that you carry arrows in. It was my proudest possession, and I got it in a leather store in the Village.

The women I knew, including me, had all found the one dance-supply store, on Eighth Street, and we'd buy tights made only in black, for dancers. If you wore those, you could get away without wearing nylon stockings, which ran all over the place, and a garter belt. Tights for women weren't made then. Restraining your body is a way of restraining your mind, as well. The first thing I did when I came to the Village, I took off my girdle, which occasioned my father saying to me that I mustn't wear pants on the Long Island Railroad—obviously, he didn't want anyone to look at my ass.

There was a place we used to go called Jazz on the Wagon. They couldn't get a liquor license. It was in a shed outside a building around Third Street. Sometimes they had jazz, and then occasionally they had poetry readings. This place was so makeshift that the floor slanted. It was there that I first met Jack Kerouac. He was surrounded by people who had just read *On the Road,* and it was very exciting.

The atmosphere was so charged at these places. A lot of the poetry wasn't really any good at all. But a lot of it was engaging, and all of it was by people who were trying to have their voices heard—it wasn't staid. People were trying out all kinds of dirty words just to see if they would get arrested. There weren't, of course, as many women as there ought to have been, but then we were lucky just to have taken off our underwear.

We paid so little for our dwelling places that we could live on very little money, and it was much more possible than now to live a marginal life. Everything, because it was much cheaper, allowed you to make your art in a more committed way.

And don't forget, we used to have wonderful, wild parties where we danced and sang and just let loose and smoked joints, which no one was doing, and drank lots of beer and lost our inhibitions and spoke about things. You didn't hide things the way issues were hidden in fifties society, and that's what appealed to me, the idea of being able to speak my mind and saying whatever I damn pleased. I can grow impassioned about this, I suppose, because it was my youth.

Did You Ever See
Panic in Needle Park?

Rita Curran

She lives in New Orleans and was forty-three years old when interviewed. She started a maid service about five years ago and works along with her employees.

"I grew up in New Orleans. I was raised a Catholic, which I know better now. My dad was Irish, whose grandfather came from Ireland because they ran out of potatoes, and my mom was Italian, whose people came from Sicily, for what reason I don't know. I pretty much guess, like most Italians, they were misbehaving so bad that they had to keep moving. My mom always wanted to pretend she was from northern Italy, but she wasn't; she was from Sicily. Both of them graduated high school, and the old man actually went to Tulane for a while."

My mom and dad were both party animals out of the forties. When they'd go out, the women would wear long, white gloves and long dresses and the guys would wear tuxedos and tails, and they made a big deal out of hanging in dance halls. And they partied—they really partied. When I hear things like Buddy Rich and Duke Ellington and those big-band guys, I have this vision of my parents dancing in the forties with the little short cigarettes that everybody smoked with no filter on them, and a little five-ounce highball glass.

You could say that my parents were alcoholics, but not loser, skid-row alcoholics. Booze is easy to not notice unless you're a low-class alky who's drinkin' wine out of a bottle with cigarette butts in it. But neither one of them got a college degree because of this drinkin'. They didn't get down to the brass tacks when they raised me, either. They would not have been able to ignore a lot of things I was doin' if they hadn't had a drink. When I started cleaning houses is when I came to realize that all families weren't as ridiculous as my family.

He was my mom's second husband, and she was my dad's third wife. They stayed together because of the children in spite of the fact that by the time the fifties were over and they were finished with the dance halls, they really didn't have a lot in common. So I grew up in your typical dysfunctional family and suffered the consequences and had a little party of my own. The sixties were a great time for young women, because we had real freedom to just do any bleedin' thing we wanted. Everybody was already saying we were a disgrace, so they couldn't say anymore, so why not? And the birth control pill was the new thing. It got way out of hand.

I never did well in school. I had dyslexia as a kid, and so by the time I became a teenager I wasn't too well adjusted. Neither was anybody else in those times. It was a good time to be nuts. So we really partied, and we used drugs, and the more adjusted adolescents just experimented and went on to college and became yuppies, and the maladjusted became very addicted. So I became very addicted.

I got thrown out of half the Catholic schools they sent me to—till not too long ago, I would get up and leave a restaurant if a nun came in. The Dominican nuns were overdressed for the weather down here; that was half their problem. I'm real opinionated about nuns. They're running from some terrible circumstances. The Catholic church is a really, really sick thing, very wicked. But at five or six years old, you don't know how to say that, or even think that. They start convincing us at a young age that we have original sin. You never had time to do anything, how could you have original sin? They lock you in the closet, and they tell you you're wicked.

I had been thrown out of their school before I was of the age to be told about sex. I was just too damn tough for them. I have too much of a spirit. I'm gonna tell you, honey, getting over Catholicism required a lot of therapy and a lot of reading. At one point I didn't do anything but read self-help books.

My friend Sandy was a year younger than me, and she was teaching me how to hang out on the streets. Her mom's rule was you had to come home at two o'clock in the morning, and this girl was fourteen, fifteen. My mom's rule was ten o'clock. So we'd be staying at Sandy's house so we could hang out in the street all night long. When my mom realized that Sandy's mom's rules were quite lax, the old man came over and drug me out of there. But it was too late. If you don't have control of a kid early, you can't get control after that kid becomes an adolescent. They tried. They could see that I was fixin' to get in a really miserable lifestyle, and they couldn't stop me.

Did you ever see *Panic in Needle Park* with Al Pacino? Well, that's how it was. A constant effort to stay loaded on expensive narcotics. I was using heroin. It was mostly shoplifting every day and selling what we had stolen or returning it to the store for the amount of purchase—some stores would give a cash refund. And older people would use younger people, especially girls, to go through with their schemes. They would send us to banks with people's checks. We were young and fresh and pink and clean, and we didn't look like they looked, obvious criminals with tattoos.

We'd go straight from the bank to the drug dealer. The whole day was based around that. I was seventeen and living in my mom's house. And stealing their checkbooks, too. And really, really, really, really carrying on. It wasn't the normal lifestyle of the sixties—it was the extreme lifestyle of the sixties, but it wasn't that uncommon. That's why the laws were being changed, because the people who were friends with people in the legislature, all of their kids were getting arrested, and they needed it to be easier to get them out of trouble, so they made marijuana into a misdemeanor. It's the truth. I see things exactly as they are—that's a gift I've always had.

When I was about eighteen, I got raped in City Park. I was heading up to the hamburger place when a guy asked me if I wanted a ride. This was nighttime, and when he parked the car in the park and went to strangling and choking me, I finally was able to unlock the door and get out of the car. I only got a few feet, and then I got caught.

He didn't have nothin', but he was just bigger and stronger than me. White guy. I haven't been raped by a black guy. Down south they always tell you that "the nigger's gonna rape you," and so you're kinda like on guard for the black man. You don't give him the opportunity, cause you've been told that he's gonna do this. But they didn't tell me that the white boys would do that, too, so I kinda wasn't being guarded. I wasn't that far from home. I walked home—I told my mom. She didn't say too much—she didn't know how to be comforting.

The guy who raped me was about twenty-two years old. The police came to my house with pictures about a month later, and I identified him. Several other people identified him—he had really been on a roll. My dad told the cop, "Look, she won't make you a good witness, and I don't want you to subpoena her," and the police never came back. Maybe he thought he was protecting me or protecting himself or whatever. I thought, "Well, according to my dad, it's okay for people to rape me, because he wouldn't let me do nothin' about it." I never talked to him about it.

I was so disassociated with my emotions at that age that I didn't let it break my stride too much. A lot of people like myself have unresolved, ungrieved losses just kinda stored in your soul from the years before we learned how to feel our emotions. And that stuff turns into arthritis, disease of the bones, ulcers. I did a lot of work with this guy with rebirthing and breath work and found out about this. I can't change the past, but now I'm really in touch with my emotions, and if I got something to cry about, let me cry immediately before it turns into diabetes or something.

My mom did bring me to this therapist at some point. I was in therapy at United Way—$2 a session—I kept going until the therapist retired. She was very good. I had a lot of anger at what my mother didn't do, but then I realized that she didn't have terribly clear thinking herself. My mom came up really hard. Her mom had died of natural causes when my mom was only nine years old. Her dad had gotten shot. Well, those Italian guys shot one another on a regular basis. What happened with him was he was such a ladies' man, one lady caught him with another lady and blew him away. My grandpa's name was Two Gun Todaro; he was not a well-behaved man.

Later in life, I got raped by two uniformed cops, on Bourbon Street, at four o'clock in the morning. They were both white. I was out going to collect some money for somebody—we were doing some underhanded stuff, I won't deny it—when two cops said, "Hey, where you going? What are you doin' out here?" And they knew that they had me in a position where they could slap a charge on me, what they call vagrancy by loitering for the sole purpose of prostitution. It never sticks. But it's something that they can charge if an unescorted female is walking up and down Bourbon Street. They can conjure up evidence, what they call constructive truth. You might have been flirtin', dressed kinda trashy—it doesn't mean you were gonna get paid. I couldn't let them charge me with that because I just couldn't let my dad be faced by his cronies down there trying to make my bond—he used to work in the court—getting his daughter the whore out of jail. I just couldn't put him through that. So I went ahead and did them both, which I call rape at badge point. They said, "Get in the car." So I got in the car. They said, "You're under arrest for vagrancy by loitering, sole purpose prostitution." I said, "No, you can't charge me with that." They said, "Well, that's what we're going to charge you with. If you want to, we can make a little deal." Well, it didn't take no Einstein to figure out what the deal was. They both wanted freebies was the phrase they used. So we went and parked the car. They did it in back of the police car. One would stand outside of the car and wait his turn, and do you know the second one tried to hug me? I pushed that animal away from me, and I told him, "This is not romance, you pig, don't hug me—ejaculate and let me out of this car." He must have been out of his frickin' mind. In his mind I don't believe it was rape. He was just bullshitting a girl out of a freebie. What's that thing about perception is reality? They didn't use any condoms. That was before AIDS got real prevalent down here.

My first boyfriend was a guitar player, down on Bourbon Street. I was fifteen, about to be sixteen. He was twenty-seven, one of those old duck-tail–type, beatnik-era guitar players. It was 1966, but the sixties weren't here yet. This town was always about ten years behind. So I was down here with teased hair and the little piccolina pointy-toed shoes everybody wore in the fifties. I broke my heart with the guitar player.

He told me he had a wife and a kid and they were broken up. She was back in Alabama. One day when I got off work, I come over to Bourbon Street to the club, and he explains to me that he had let his wife come back because he couldn't get custody of his son. At fifteen it's easy to go for these kind of stories. So it only lasted about another month after that, and I caused him some misery. I used to hang out at a place named Dixie's Bar and Music, where all the younger people went who thought they were beatniks. We were impersonating the people we saw in the movies. Little boys dressed like James Cagney. Little girls ran around trying to look like the fat blonde, Marilyn Monroe, Sophia Loren, and these people. I went to Dixie's that following New Year's. It was about two months later, and his band was playing in my hangout. I walked right up to his wife's table and told her everything. It was cruel. I just didn't know any better yet. I ruined his New Year's, and I was happy. I was drunk. She didn't really bat an eye—"Thank you" was all she said. She didn't leave him. I'm sure that he had been runnin' around on her a long time. I was learning how to hurt the world back, or whoever in it hurt me. I changed a lot recently—sobriety, therapy. And the clarity of thought that you get about forty.

The next one after the guitar player killed himself. He was more my age, and we went off into a pretty decent romance, but then he cheated on me, too, and that's when I first began to shoot the heroin, and then he began to shoot the heroin, too, and then the heroin just about ruined us both. We broke up, and I moved to Biloxi. He came over to where I was staying and got depressed and shot himself. He had attempted suicide once before I even knew him, so I had that avenue to let myself out of the guilt. He had smoked a little weed that night. Neither one of us were fooling around with heroin anymore. But I was drinking a lot of vodka.

That led into what I call a glacier. It was like I froze emotionally. Ten years after that, I fooled around and broke my heart again. I caught another habit over that. But that one only lasted about three years. By now I was older and smarter, and I didn't go hang in the streets with junkies and chase heroin. I had one or two boyfriends who had a lot of money, and we'd go to doctors, and they would write prescriptions, or I would buy in the street. Diladid and morphine—it's pretty close to heroin. It's a very strong pain medicine, very common in the seventies among drug abusers because when the Vietnam War ended, they had heroin stop coming here.

So I had this rich guy who was ten years older than me buying me drugs, and I had a young, good-looking boyfriend who I was seeing on the side. Then I got stabbed. That experience was a major thing in my getting married. Because Uncle Leo, the man I married, was so good to me, and the boyfriend was so bad.

Some gossip got me stabbed by a guy who thought that I had snitched on him, which I hadn't. So the criminal comes to my house and stabs me seven times, fully intending to kill me. But the knife broke in my shoulder. He had a hand boning knife, which is meant to bend and go around bones, so naturally when he hit a bone, it broke. If he'd have been a marine or somebody who knew how to kill, I would be very dead, but he was just a punk, and he didn't know how to kill me. He was giving it his best, though. He stabbed me in my shoulder, in the back, and a couple of more times. He went to stab me in the breast, but it was real soft tissue, so it just mashed and bruised because now the knife was broken. He's got a juvenile with him, and he's telling the kid, "In the kitchen, you asshole, in the kitchen." He wanted the kid to get him another knife out of the kitchen, but he couldn't find the damn knife. So at this point we get an opportunity to discuss it.

Like all addicts, I was completely out of touch with my emotions, but now this negative vibe came over me—it was fear—I didn't like it a bit. And I started to think about my momma. I realized this man fully intended to kill me, and it was almost Christmas. I became a little angry. I said, "Ed, what's wrong with you? Do you know you're a rude son of a bitch, gonna kill me just before Christmas." And he said, "Man, you went and said that to Hippy Joe about me taking that stereo." I said, "I didn't say it, Ed. That's Bobbie tryin' to run a game on you to get you to give him his stereo back." Well, at that point for a second he believed me, cause he went to help me up. And when I started to come to my feet, he must've stopped believing me, or something snapped in his mind. I don't think he was the sanest person in the world. He reached down and started trying to break my neck. He got me in a headlock, but I was bigger and heavier than him. I had more fuel. He was only angry—I was facing death. And that's when I kinda backed up to the door, and I just kinda drug him along. I got loose and went outside.

I called up the boyfriend, the young, good-looking one, and he was like, "I don't want to get involved." Well, that hurt my feelings a lot. And he suggests to me, "Why don't you call Uncle Leo, the one with the money." "I think I will, you bastard." So I call Uncle Leo. He comes over and takes me down to the hospital, and my back gets sewed up, and then he takes me to the connection, and I get some drugs so I can feel a little better. Then he took me to the barroom to sit down, and that's when I threw up. At that point, I could allow myself to puke—I didn't have to fight anymore, I didn't have to be sewed up, and I was loaded. Then we went out and shot a little pool. Uncle had already asked me to marry him before that, and I didn't want to because I kinda would have liked the younger, good-looking one to steal me away from him, and it didn't work, so I said to myself, "I'll marry this man."

I married strictly for the money and stayed five months. He had just inherited an import business and was in the process of destroying it. They liquidated the business.

He was going to sell flatware, and I said, "I didn't marry no frickin' tinkerer. I married an importer, and if you're gonna go peddle in flatware out of the trunk of your car, get the hell out of here because that ain't the lifestyle that you promised me." And furthermore, he was doing a lot of manipulative, sneaky stuff that was really tickin' me off, and I could see that he wasn't going to fulfill any of the promises he had made, so I ran the bastard out of my house.

Now I make a good living on my own. I started a maid service. It's goin' on five years. It was the best move I ever made. Me and three girls go stampede the houses, and we do about seven to ten of them a day, and by the time I'm finished paying them $5 an hour each, I come out making a pretty nice little chunk of money. And I'm stashing the majority of it to invest in what I don't know. By the time I get the wisdom, I'll have the money. I'm gonna plot a course to financial security in my sixties.

I Was Nineteen, I Was a Hippie

Mimi Miller

She was born in 1945 in North Carolina, and now lives in Natchez, Mississippi. (See also pp. 79, 272 and 469)

*W*omen could only go to the University of North Carolina at Chapel Hill as a junior transfer; originally, it had been all male. So I went to the now University of North Carolina at Greensboro, which was at one time the largest women's college in the world. You could wear pants on campus but not to class or in the dining halls. We were still signing out to leave the campus overnight. Curfew was one o'clock on Saturday nights and ten-thirty or eleven weeknights and twelve on Friday and Sunday, something like that. All these rules were abandoned the year I graduated, in 1967. Oh, I was so jealous. They threw away every rule in the rule book the very year after I finished college. I used to think these regulations were so ridiculous. I still think so, and I think it's much better the way it is today.

Kathleen Ryan

She was born in Poughkeepsie, New York, in 1948. Her father was a cop, and her mother was a homemaker. After working twenty years in direct services with young people, she is now the director of an upstate New York human service agency.

"I was raised Catholic. My mother is Irish, and my dad is German and English. I had a really strict Catholic upbringing." (See also pp. 281, 459 and 479)

I was raped when I was twenty-one. It was at the moratorium on the Vietnam War when they had the big march in Washington. We went down to that, like everybody else, with the knapsacks and the sleeping bags, and we'd spent the whole day at all the rallies and we were coming back, and there was supposed to have been a protest at the Vietnam Embassy, or at one of the embassies, and there was a lot of tear gas. It was burning. We were all running. A car stopped, five guys. I don't feel guilty about it now, but at the time I felt guilty about getting in the car.

The police came—we were very lucky. They had driven us to a wooded area, and it was by knife point. It was very violent. They had dragged my roommate out of the car, and I thought she was dead at that point because I didn't know where she was or what had happened. Out of nowhere, a cop pulled up with a police dog. He had apparently seen the car go in there and thought it was a bunch of kids just partying, but luckily he had come back to check. I often think, "What were they going to do to us? What were they going to do?"

I had been raped by two of the guys, and she had been raped by two, also, so we were naked. It took these cops forever to get a blanket to put on us. I mean, it was like rape after rape after rape—that's what the entire night felt like. We finally got in the police car. These guys were black. Maryland was south enough that they hated blacks, so their response was these niggers, they wanted to string 'em up because black men do not rape white women. They took us to the police station; they got us jail clothing. They took us to the hospital first, and it was very cold, insensitive, demeaning. It was horrible. I had been kicked several times in the ribs, and I was terrified of being examined, and I remember laying on the table. I was so glad to see another woman, the nurse. The cops were men; the doctor was a man. And I said to her, "My ribs, my side, it really, really hurts," and her response was, "You weren't raped there— just lay down." It was an exam to prove that we were raped. We were brought back to the police station, and—this is hard—the questioning—it was the sense that these cops were getting off hearing about it. Asking us details, far more than they needed to ask.

We went back to New York; they reassured us we would have a lawyer. We never heard anything for nine months, and then we got a letter to come to court because they were going to be tried, and then we were told that we didn't need to go—they had dropped the charges. They had plea-bargained the charges down to attempted rape and sexual assault, and I was determined—I'm going down there.

It was a sham. It was family court. They were big guys, but they were like sixteen, fifteen years old, and all this had been prearranged, and they basically got probation. The judge's comment in the courtroom was that ours was a far worse crime. He went on at length about hippies who were this free-love-and-drugs-and-sex generation who desecrated God and country. What it came down to was "Rape's a bad, horrible crime, guys, but these two probably deserved it—but I have to do something to you." If we were just college coeds walking along the street and we were raped, they would have hung them because they were black males in the South, but it was weighed against protesting the government and being hippies, and that was far worse. The guy with the knife who really assaulted us received three years' probation, and the others received one. So, it makes for a very angry woman. I jumped up in the courtroom. They actually brought a deputy over to escort me out. I couldn't believe it. I couldn't believe that we had been raped, and this was all that was going to happen. There was no trial, there was nothing, there wasn't any testimony. It was devastating, really difficult. I drank to block out a lot of things. I spent a lot of years drinking.

Ruth Mandel

She was forty-two years old when interviewed. She lives with her lesbian partner and their son in a small town in the Northeast.

"I'm Jewish. I grew up in a very mixed-white, ethnic, working-class environment in New York City. My father worked at the stockyards, where he unloaded and loaded trucks, and my mother worked as a secretary. I have one sister.

"I've been working at the Social Security Office for the last six years. I'm a clerk. Now I have a job where most days I only work four hours. It's pretty uninteresting work. I spend the rest of the day with my kid and doing what I consider creative stuff. I'm a community activist." (See also p. 306)

I did drugs at the end of high school and in college, too. I was unhappy at home—I was very bored—I needed some adventure. If I had parents with some means, maybe they would have sent me to another country to study. I did pot every day, a lot of psychedelic drugs, some of which I didn't think were a bad experience—but some of the drugs were very bad. I did them for about four years, pretty much every day, and then I stopped.

At the Community College I went to, I really got a political education. There was an SDS chapter; there were Weathermen. In retrospect, they really didn't know who they were talking to, because they would say things like, "We're supposed to give up our privilege." They were talking to working-class kids that didn't have much privilege. So I joined SDS and had a sit-in. There was a communist teacher at my school—his class was one of the only ones I liked. He happened to be a great English teacher, and they wanted to fire him. I got very involved. We took over the administration building and lived at the school for a month. It was a very exciting, great experience for me because it was very social. We blocked ourselves in, and they didn't want to, like, hurt us, so they let us stay there. I remember taking sheets from my mother's house, and we wrote words on them and we hung them out the window, and they were on the news, and my mother's saying, "Those are my sheets!"

The issues were freedom of thought, the Vietnam War. I think the school maybe invested in something, or in some way was tied up with the Vietnam War. There was a lot of pitch harp playing, hanging out, and folk singing, and it was a lovely time. Of course, I failed all my courses that term. I wasn't really interested in studying liberal arts, and I didn't feel career oriented. It was just very boring. It was the school and the movement. I felt like I needed to get out of there and get more of the movement.

In '69 I went to San Francisco for three years, and I lived communally and did all that counterculture stuff. I was nineteen, I was a hippie. That's when I came out as a lesbian. It was different because people were doing their politics to a lifestyle rather than rebelling against the government. Like there were people who grew food, and they would come to San Francisco and sell it to the co-ops. Sometimes we'd do bartering. We were just trying to get away from the way the system works. That was very exciting for me.

I had odd jobs that were very unimportant, like clerical jobs, jobs where hippies were around that I was comfortable with, just ways to make money. What was important was community activity. We were experimenting with living communally, running food co-ops, buying food communally. I worked a lot at food co-ops. People applied for welfare. We were all against the government, so we figured we might as well use it as much as possible. I once took somebody's baby and went down and applied for welfare. Now, in San Francisco there were millions of hippies, so a lot of hippies were working in the welfare offices, and they would give you welfare and food stamps.

We said that we were all dependent upon each other and planning on living together, like a group marriage type of thing. Or we would bring kids and say they were all of our kids, and they would give us food stamps as a group. I also hung around with some Indian people who used to go down in large groups and say they were all family, and they had a very hard time disproving that because they were tribal people. They had to treat them as an alternative family and give them food stamps. So we were kind of taking their model.

I lived in a lot of different places. In one house I lived with about six or seven other people. I had my own room. Sometimes I would share a room with another woman. We would have house meetings if we had problems. There was a constant emphasis on communication and on serving the community—also the larger community of hippies, like making the food co-op work so that we could all get food. There was a lot of antigovernment politics around, a lot of inspiring music. We would always go to concerts for inspiration.

I tried to make a relationship to the land. That was a big emphasis of the movement. I had just come from New York, so I had no relationship with the land. I don't think I particularly prospered in that.

My heterosexuality was a passing phase. I tried, but it wasn't me. I started having relationships with women. I lived for about a year or so in a commune of gay people, men and women. A lot of people from my college in New York City went there, and we wound up all living together. That was kind of nice because we had a history together. We felt safe with each other, but I did a little too much drugs in that house. That commune had group sex a couple of times. Men and women, kind of like everything went. There was definitely a feeling of freedom around sexuality. It didn't really matter who you were with, it was just the feeling like you could do what you wanted to do. The last commune I lived in was lesbian.

I was starting to feel alienated from men. There was a lot of sexism, and it certainly wasn't a big point of the hippie movement to understand sexism. The men would say things like "Oh, you can't do that"—whatever men do, like mechanics. A lot of the men played music, and their emphasis was just on them doing a lot of major things, not the women. I felt like my mind was male dominated and that being around them was very confusing to me in terms of boosting my own self-esteem and knowing what I wanted, knowing that I wasn't thinking what they wanted me to think. I became a separatist for a while. I used to call myself a separatist with a small *s*. I just wanted to put a separation in terms of what was going on in my head. I found it to be very beneficial, and then after a couple of years it was over. There were a lot of women that took it to a very hard extreme. In my family, my mother didn't drive. She was afraid to go places without my father. I have an aunt that can drive, and every time she gets in the car with her husband, she can't drive because he criticizes her. So I was feeling like men knew better, they were smarter. I valued their opinion more than I valued the opinion of women, so I wanted to cut out their opinion for a while so I could just hear the opinions of women and see what I thought about it. So that was really good. I might have to do it again. It might be something that needs to be encouraged every now and then.

I had to deal with men at work, but I didn't live with them and I didn't socialize with them. There was a large lesbian community in San Francisco. You can really live in a community of women if you want to.

Dolores Valenti

She was born in upstate New York in 1950. (See also p. 292)

We stayed home during the first day of the Woodstock festival because when something happens in your backyard—it was sixty miles from our house—you think to yourself, "This isn't going to be anything, right?" At the end of the first day, we heard on the radio that the New York State Thruway was closed all the way to New York City. There were so many cars they wouldn't let anybody else on until these cars got off. So we said, "Man, this must be something—we gotta see it." So we got out the map—we lived in Pennsylvania—and we chose a route. We went north of the festival and came down, so we were able to get the car within about a mile, and we had to abandon it along the road somewhere. We stayed for two days. It was fun! We brought a lot of food and sodas. After we found a place to sit, we realized that there were plenty of thirsty, hungry people running around. So we ended up giving away almost everything that we brought. Nobody was going to starve to death in three days, so no one made a big deal of it.

There was a helicopter that kept circling over and shining its light down on the crowd, and whenever that beam came down, the beam was blue with pot smoke—you could see the haze in the beam. I don't even recall smoking any great deal of pot, but I was stoned. You didn't have to smoke pot; all you had to do was breathe. It was like a sea of people, but it was great. Janis Joplin—one of my favorites—was there. Jefferson Airplane. It was wild. It was sort of like the Boston Tea Party. A group of people trying to give the administration of this country a message. Maybe that wasn't really the intention of the event, but certainly the majority of people who attended were trying to revolutionize our system, even if it was in a small, personal way. The very event itself was testing people's right to certain freedoms. Even if it was for three days out in the middle of nowhere.

Growing Up:
The Third Generation

Growing up, I always got the barbie dolls and my brothers always got the trucks. You don't see any boys on the barbie doll commercials. It's how I was raised so I guess I would continue it. But now that I'm thinking about it, I really don't like that man/woman thing. I think it's society that separates the men and the women. If a girl wants to drive a truck, she can do that, a boy wants to take care of kids, he can do that. So I guess you could say society got me too! I'm thinking about what I just said. I guess it could work out to get the girl a truck.

—Angela Walker, born 1974

My dad's second wife, I think she was a feminist. She kept her last name. I've never really come into contact with it that much. If I'm thinking of it correctly, then I don't consider myself a feminist. I like the southern gentleman opening the door for me and paying for me. The other day I was saying something to my boyfriend about me being a girl and girls should go first and he said "What about this feminist thing, don't y'all want to be treated the same?" and I said, "No I don't, not particularly."

—Maggie Erwin, born 1974

The Real Live Thing

Christina Martin

She was born in the Midwest in 1957, the youngest of four siblings. Her mother is Irish Catholic, and her father was Episcopalian.

"I was brought up Catholic and very staunchly so. When you marry someone non-Catholic, you sign off and say, 'I promise to bring up these children Catholic.' My mother signed those papers. We all went to Catholic school, and she went to church almost every day. It was forced down our throat. My father used to actually laugh when we would go off to church in the morning cause it was like, 'Bye, see ya, sorry you have to go through this.' If he ever had to take us to church, he'd take us to the Big Boy Restaurant, and we'd all pretend like we'd gone to church. He'd be like, 'I showed them a thing or two.'"

We were all star swimmers. When I was four years old, I was in swim meets. I can remember winning, looking over and seeing my mom in the crowd. During the summer we went to a swim and tennis club every day. They would have barbecues on Thursday nights. Growing up in an environment where it felt so beautiful and so picture perfect, I never imagined it would be shattered in any way. This was life, the life you lead. My mother was home all the time, and she was a real housewife, like the real live thing. She didn't actually go to the grocery store; she ordered the groceries on the telephone. I'd hear her say, "five boxes of Popsicles," and so I'd stick stuff in front of her and go, "Mom, don't forget this...." Then they'd come and deliver it. Very bourgeois. She was busy being involved in charity organizations.

My father used to come home from work and go, "Are my slippers there?" Sort of half joking, but we made sure it was done. He'd sit down in the living room, and my mother would put out the hors d'oeuvres and his martini, and we'd all sit around. It was very pretty, very pastel—sixties but tasteful, with my mother's elegant floral-covered furniture and Staffordshire statues.

My father would sit down at the dinner table and say, "I don't like pork chops," and they would have to be taken away. He would never carry anything to the table. My mother had live-in help, even though she wasn't working. The woman was an old German who really couldn't speak English. She had moles with hairs growing out of them.

She had to babysit us a lot. My mother and father were very social. When they left, she would sit down on the couch in the playroom and watch *Lawrence Welk*. It was so depressing. She was mean and nasty and had no compassion and no understanding for kids. My philosophy right now is so focused on my children, and the person I have helping me doesn't clean. I choose the child, and I think my mother was much more choosing the house and the environment.

I remember going around the dinner table with "How was your day?" and "Tell me something you learned." We all had to be practiced in what we said, and it was a time when we learned our manners. It was very much centered around my father, making sure he was comfortable and that we appreciated the lifestyle that we were being given.

My mother and father would have cocktail parties, and it is not like now, where if I had a cocktail party, my kids would be running through the room. You didn't even consider doing that. We were not integrated into their lives. They were more interested in what kind of children we were going to be, what kind of people we were going to grow up and become, as opposed to how they could interact or share themselves with us. My mother was proud, and she was there, but she never talked to us about swimming or became any sort of coach or supporter. At the meets she was dressed perfectly, sitting up in the stands. It was about appearances and about having the star swimmers as her children. That was how she found her identity.

I remember the first time the Beatles were on the *Ed Sullivan Show*. We moved the television into the living room, and the whole family gathered around this small black-and-white television. My father was saying, "Well, I don't really understand what it is about these guys that is so interesting." But it *was* so interesting, so cool. There was an immediate attachment. When headphones came out, I would be sitting somewhere with headphones playing music over and over. My older siblings introduced me to different kinds. I remember going through every Beatles album. When it came out, you had to go get *Rubber Soul*—it was important—and then getting into the *Sgt. Pepper's* stuff—I can just remember the whole transition of it.

I watched so much TV when I was a kid, and my mother just sort of let me. I took the bus to and from school. It was a big social occasion. I have very vivid memories of the bus going down close to the lake. It was beautiful in the winter, icy. Then I'd get home and see if there were any lollipops, Twinkies, or Hohos. Sometimes I'd make instant mashed potatoes, or I'd drink a huge bottle of Coke and eat a big bag of potato chips. I'd sit down and watch *I Love Lucy*, then *Dick Van Dyke*, and I can't even remember what came after that, but then it went into *Bewitched* or *Andy of Mayberry*. I didn't feel that stigma that you shouldn't be watching TV so much.

My father taught me how to play backgammon when I was seven, and that was really a big part of our family life. We played your basic Monopoly, Candy Land. We used to play cards a lot, War, and my brothers used to play poker with my dad. We were big into trading cards. But television was huge. Games were secondary to television, clearly. All the kids would sit down and watch *Mission Impossible* every Sunday night in the playroom. There were several couches, wood paneling, and the washing machine was in there. We had football pictures nailed up on the walls.

My best friend lived next door. In the summer you took advantage of the good weather. We rode our bikes, and eventually we got into skateboarding. We played hopscotch, kickball, hide and go seek, tetherball, and badminton. We had all of this space to just sort of go. There were ravines near our house, and we'd go down there and play adventure. We had this freeness about it all that was really nice, openness and green and trees and flowers.

As I got a little older, things changed in the family dramatically. My father had melanoma cancer, which means it was his entire body, and it was a slow process. I was never really aware of what was going on. My mother did not communicate to me, "Your father has cancer and is dying." I had to figure it out myself by her actions and by her acting afraid of the whole thing.

He was sick for a while, and I was confused. He died when I was twelve, and I was made to feel "just move on." He was fifty years old, and it had never really happened before in the community that we were living in. Nobody really got cancer and died at such a young age. I felt that my friends and my community were looking upon me with such pity, that no one could come forward and say, "I'm so sorry," or "This is what it is," and so I just had to keep going and pretending it was okay.

I remember a few people at my father's funeral coming up to me and saying, "I'm so sorry," but otherwise it was like this formal procedure. "It will just take a minute. And then everything will be back to normal." Which, of course, it never was. And I blame my mother, obviously, but it was the society, too. People did not know how to deal with it, especially in that upper-class community, and it was like we don't know what to say to this woman's poor family that lost their dad. My father died over the summer, and the first day back at school was so bad. It was just like, stay away from her, we don't want to say anything, we might say the wrong thing. And the people who did come up and say stuff, I can remember them.

I got the sense that my mother was really looking for another man, and that that was the way she was going to deal with it. She couldn't possibly be alone, and she couldn't manage alone. She's never had a paid job in her life that I know of. My father had died without leaving a lot of money to her because he was still so young. I felt that she never dealt with my father's death. It was like, How can I recover and get back on my feet and make it look like it is okay?

She remarried a year, maybe two years later, to one of my father's really close friends. By now, they have been married longer than she was married to my father. He was never married and had never had children, so he came into this family pretty clueless about kids and family dynamics, and he tried to be the patriarch. My eldest brother and my sister were already gone. It was miserable.

I remember him insulting the way it had been before, saying stuff about our house or about specific things. My father built a swimming pool in the back before he died because he loved to swim and he had arthritis and that was a way for him to feel better. And he never got to swim in the pool. My stepfather came in and said, "What a stupid thing to have a pool." And I was like, "Wait a second, that was my father, and he lived here," and my mother was standing behind and not coming forth or defending her children.

I just remember losing my temper and losing my cool and being thirteen and thinking, "This is so bad." Being a real wiseass, speaking out and really having a confrontation with him. For a while we just didn't get along at all. Dinner was much more my mother having dinner with her new husband, and her kids were just sitting there. It is still like that. That is the core for her, to have the man with her, and the kids are just extras, especially when they're not his kids.

After my mother got remarried and after it sort of settled in, my life became a lot more free, in that she wasn't paying attention to what I was doing. I hung around with older guys and really became much more of a loose cannon than I probably would have had my father stayed around. Growing up, it was very tight and sheltered, and once he was gone, the top sort of blew off and I was free to do pretty much anything I wanted. My mother was never negligent—she was sending me to an exclusive private school and paying a lot of money—but she was not a mother in the true sense of how I think I am as a mother.

The stuff we did in high school revolved around cars and bars and boys. Basketball games or football games were a place to go and find your friends, hang out and smoke cigarettes underneath the stadium. I'd sneak out of the house at night after my mother was upstairs. We'd drive around and vandalize stuff. We'd throw pumpkins at cars and dent them. It was very much a bar culture. We were either in the parking lot of the bar or in the bar. The drinking age was eighteen, and we were fifteen or sixteen, and we looked old enough, I suppose. Nobody really checked. But I remember actually climbing out the windows when the police raided the bars.

I was arrested when I was sixteen for stealing a sign off the street at like five o'clock in the morning. I had gone to spend the night at a friend's. Her mother was divorced and lived downtown and didn't care what we did. I had to call my mom, and she had to come down and get me from what was then the ghetto. She was mad and imposed all sorts of discipline on me. When it got to the point of no return, she had to step in.

I was actually a virgin when I went to college. The kind of sex that we had in high school was very, I felt, promiscuous, but it wasn't intercourse. It was as close as you could get. It was a time when girls were becoming more promiscuous, and it was sort of a natural progression. Girls were able to do more without being labeled sluts. I don't remember having a lot of guilt about it. It was fun. It was a more toned-down experience where, it sounds dumb, but the boys were gentlemen. The getting-pregnant thing was frightening. There was no torturing you because you didn't do it.

I think I had my first real sex when I was a freshman, and that was with a boy from back home who was wild, much older than I was. When I was in high school, I always wanted to date him and sort of did, but we didn't have sex. There was a little pressure there, but once we got into it, I felt fairly comfortable with it. That was when I went on the pill. I remember going to the Planned Parenthood in the downtown inner city. I found it the most amazing place that I'd ever been. This was probably 1976. It was definitely new, and it was sort of underground.

Having been so repressed about these things in my childhood, it was like, gosh, people would talk to you about it, and they'd give you pills. I stayed on the pill for a good five years or so. I didn't think about health concerns or about it making my body do weird things or anything else. It was nice, and it was real convenient, and it made sex accessible. You didn't even think about condoms. Everybody took the pill. Planned Parenthood was a port in every city. There was counseling, and you were educated. It wasn't like they just handed that stuff over. I actually ended up having two abortions, but I don't know why I wasn't taking the pill. I was older, in my twenties.

I remember smoking pot for the first time—I must have been fifteen or sixteen. Five or six of us girls would get together and smoke pot and get in the car and drive around and be stoned. At that time, when you are just starting to smoke it, it was just so much fun. Everything was transformed into a completely funny situation. And then, of course, it continued into college, and there were more and more drugs. Acid and quaaludes and cocaine, all of them.

Growing up in the late sixties, early seventies, we really felt the civil rights movement. I remember having a curfew imposed upon the whole town when the riots broke out. It was a very segregated city, with a huge black population. The northern suburbs are pretty much exclusively white, and the rest of the city is integrated. We would take our cleaning woman home—she was white, but we would take her into the ghetto—and it was scary, very scary. The riots weren't out in the suburbs where we were living, but there was still a curfew imposed there, and I think that the riots were moving in that direction.

I remember driving around the day before the curfew and seeing roadblocks and people behind them. There were barricades and trash on the street, and the city was being bombed. I remember Kent State being a big thing in the news, and people were killed in Madison, Wisconsin. It was all around us, but we had this safe environment where we were living, so it was a very conflicting thing for us.

People my brother's age and older were going off to the Vietnam War. My father died in 1970, and it was right around that time. I remember this huge tension, because my brother was heir to the throne. He was named after my father, and he was the man in the house—at least until my mother remarried. There was the lottery for who goes off to war, and his number came up, and it was like number two or something really scary. But he was deferred because he went in to have the exam and he had a hearing disability. I just remember the elation and the family being hugely relieved.

Being so young, I didn't really have a clear idea of what you fought a war for, but Vietnam was particularly unclear. It was like, What is going on in such a faraway place?—and all these foreign names coming at you. It was the old-fashioned war reporting—"Live from Phnom Penh," and they'd show the maps on TV and where the troops were moving, and it was just very confusing for me, but also very real because it was happening and it was on the news all the time.

My neighbor and my very best friend's brother went off to war. When I look back on it, the boys were young, but then they seemed older. I wasn't really sure where they were going or what they were going for, except for what vision we had from television, which was explosions. In my community people didn't want to talk about people dying of cancer or going to war. My best friend and I didn't really address it that much. It was like, "Did you get any letters from him?" It was just so far away and so unclear, and it felt, from whatever I had heard about World War II, so different.

I think that that was a truly enlightening thing as a child to understand that we were in a place that wasn't necessarily where we should be. The party line in my community was, "We're fighting communism, and communism is so bad." But I was always more prone to listen to the other side—"We are invading another country—we have no reason to be involved in a civil war in another country."

I remember that song "If You Are Going to San Francisco"—it was like, "Be sure to wear the flower in your hair." The pictures in the magazines and on television of what was going on out there totally fascinated me. I just thought San Francisco possibly could have been the coolest thing in the whole world. It was interesting to see these people with long hair and flowers and to see them feel free about everything. I think that what our generation experienced was the freedom that it evoked.

I was too young to be involved in the protests but old enough to feel the effects. There weren't flower children around where I was. People were wearing whales on their belts, but still I felt it in the outside world, and it was a fascinating pull. Eventually, I ended up going west. The whole idea to me was San Francisco. It was a big deal, going out there, and loving it.

I don't remember the women's movement really until I left home in 1975, feeling like it was a possibility or something that could even be achieved or studied or known about. Women could have a real identity apart from men and suburbia. I started to read more, like *Fear of Flying* and Virginia Woolf. Seeing that the world wasn't as small as I thought it was just gave me huge hope and possibility. The feelings that I had for the sixties and the psychedelic movement, that was so much more clearly something that I wanted. The women's movement was not as clear to me until I broke away from where I was. Growing up, I didn't have any real role models that emanated feminism. It was much more the opposite. Teachers in high school were not encouraging. It was more like, "You are at a finishing school here, sweetheart."

Marriage and family were supposed to be successful and ideal. I would be subservient to a man, and he would make the money and I would raise the kids. I rocked the boat in every category by working and having children and getting divorced eventually. Making money, competing with men, having relationships with men that were much more on a feminist level, I just integrated it into my life and welcomed it and said this is how it is supposed to be.

This American Life

Tiana Dao

She was born in Vietnam in 1977. Her family fled when she was a few months old, traveling through Malaysia and eventually arriving in the United States. They settled in the Deep South.

My dad works at a restaurant, and my mom works at a clothing store. I have six sisters and two brothers. We are Catholic, and we go to church every Sunday. In Vietnam, my mom used to work in a bar, and my dad used to be in the army and then he became a fisherman. We had a small boat back there, but now it's gone.

My mom is still back in Vietnam. She tells me about the past. It is hard work over there. 'You should learn how to do this because we did it when we were kids back there.' I don't want to hear that because we are in America now, and a lot of things are easier. She tells me that when she was eight, she had to cook and she'd go get the wood and make fires, and now it is easy over here and you are lazy, you are not cooking. My dad, he understands us because he finished his high school, and he went to college to learn English. He watches the news and reads the newspaper. He understands what is going around with teenagers.

Mara Lavergneau

She was born on July 31, 1971, in upstate New York and attends Lincoln University, a traditionally all-black college. Her father is a rehabilitation placement counselor, and her mother is a university administrator. Mara's mother, Beverly Lavergneau, also appears in the book. (See also p. 516)

My great-grandfather came from Martinique to Panama, and that's where my grandfather and my father were born. My grandmother's father was Jewish, and her mother was black. On my mother's side of the family, both of her parents' descendants were slaves, and the women got raped by the slave masters. I just found out last weekend that I'm related to William Penn. One of my cousins is doing some research on the family history. We have wedding invitations and other documents. For a black family to be able to go back at least five generations is almost unheard of.

Even though I was the younger child, I had to take on the role of the older child because my sister is disabled. It made it ten times harder for my parents. But everyone came to our house in the summertime. All the kids would be there, and we had the swimming pool and the big yard and porch. My mother works on a college campus, and she would get close to the students and bring them home. When she was working with academic advising and orientation, she would have students in her staff, and she would bring them over for a cookout when the orientation period ended.

They became our extended family. I have a white sister and a Chinese sister. Ten years after graduating they still come home to "Mommy and Daddy's" house in New Paltz. My Chinese sister comes from Taiwan. We had fast-food Chinese tonight, but it's nothing compared to a home-cooked traditional Chinese dinner. I never would have known that if it weren't for her. My white sister, her background is Jewish, and I don't even think some of my black peers at college know what lox and onions and bagels are.

Pixie Haughton

She is a college graduate, shares an apartment with a friend, and works in sales. She was born in the Deep South in 1970. Her mother worked in business, and her father was a lawyer.

"My grandmother is an Indian. I don't know where anyone else is from."

I loved Rose. She looked like an Aunt Jemima lady. She called herself Rose Haughton—my last name. I hated her because she made me do housework. I appreciate it now. I wouldn't know how to do anything if it wasn't for her because we had housekeepers all my life. She was always correcting me, and she made me bake cakes and cook dinner and do things that you need to know how to do.

Rose lived about six miles from us. My mom would go and pick her up about seven-thirty in the morning and then bring her home in the afternoon, about six. On Friday nights she would stay until midnight or one o'clock, however late my parents stayed out. Then she would come over on Saturday nights sometimes. Rose made a lot of red beans and rice, jambalaya and gumbo—McDonald's when Mom and Dad went out. That was always a treat.

Rose came when my baby sister was born. I was seven. She left the day that my sister started school. That was part of the deal. Then she stayed with us in the afternoon until Angie was in about third or fourth grade, but just Monday through Friday, because I was old enough to take care of Angie at night.

We've had housekeepers since then, and it has not been the same at all. She was a mother to me. If I didn't do what she said, I wasn't going to be able to go play. But she would answer my questions when I asked, and if I argued with her, she would listen to why I didn't think she was right. She would say things like "I never thought of that before," or "I never looked at it like that." But she would also tell me, "I'm right. I'm the boss."

We used to have a big, huge, green shag rug. Rose used to make me rake it. It took me so long to understand that you don't rake it toward where you are standing in the middle, you rake so you can get out of it. I can remember telling her, "I'm not doing this. It's your job—you are the maid. Mom pays you." She wouldn't react, and I would get real frustrated, and she'd say, "You are right, I'm the maid, but it is your job today." Now that I am older, I realize that it was good for me. She was very motherly toward me. She was there for so many things in my life.

One morning I woke up convinced I was bleeding to death. I went downstairs and made Rose sit down because there was something we needed to discuss and I wanted her to be calm. I told her I was bleeding to death. She said, "That's terrible. Do you want me to call your mom and bring you to the doctor?" Real calm and cool. She called my mom and said, "Pixie is bleeding to death." She knew exactly what it was, and I remember her saying to my mom, "Yes, I know what to do, you told me." Obviously, they had discussed this before, and my mom had gotten things for me. Rose told me that this made me be able to have children, that I was a woman. She introduced me to maxi-pads.

Rose has a day care now. She is probably sixty-five or seventy, very old, and she is still married to the same man. It is strange when I see her now, I feel very distant. I used to sit on her lap, and now I have to talk to her like an adult. I used to idolize her and put her on such a pedestal. I admired the fact that she went to church and she never preached to me or pushed things on me. She always told me to believe in what I believe in, to understand why, to ask why, and question authority.

I guess it was a strange time in my life when we separated. I was thirteen or fourteen. I wasn't really interested in a relationship with her. She started taking care of younger children every day. She and my mom still see each other, probably once every three or four months. I think they are still close. If I called my mom and asked her what was going on with Rose, she would know. The last time I saw her I was out somewhere—I can't remember where I was, but we were in public. I just talked to her for a minute. We were passing at a fair. There was some reason why we couldn't talk. She likes this one particular cake, and we always bring that to her house at Christmas, but I didn't go this year. Something was going on. I couldn't go.

Jen Rawls

She is a freshman at Barnard College. She was born on Long Island in 1973. "I've been told I'm part German, part Scottish, part everything. I would just say I'm American."

There are five people in my family, and four people are like seeing psychiatrists majorly. They put my brother on Prozac. I don't know what's going on. Everyone seems somewhat stable, but something's askew. And I don't know if it was my father's role or my mother's role or the fact that we were all so close in age. We used to fight all the time. Long car rides were from hell.

My brothers went through their stage where they thought girls were like the worst thing. They'd gang up on me. It was never the right thing I would do. I'd fight with them, and, of course, I'd scream the loudest. Then my dad joined this skating club, and there were ice hockey teams, and my brothers started playing. There was only one other girl playing, and I started to play, too. I enjoyed it a lot, but I guess it was like a displaced sense of enjoyment. Later, my mom was like, "Maybe you were just trying to fit in with them."

My dad would get into taking the boys to ice hockey practice in the morning. He ran my brother's Little League team. They always had the Star Wars figures, and I had dolls. I remember my youngest brother got a Cabbage Patch doll once—maybe he's just more feminine and that's why I get along with him better. I think my parents wanted us all to go to college and do well and be happy, although I can't say that they themselves were.

I can vaguely remember how my parents used to have big screaming fights. There was always a lack of communication that you could sense. They would just end the fight—it would never be resolved. But now they both see shrinks, my mom more willingly than my dad. My dad goes because my mom thought he should. I think he sort of sees what it's doing for him and is trying because of it. But he's still just clueless. You can tell that he's trying to give, but he can't do it.

My father is a nice man, but there's something missing. He was away twenty-four seven, and when he was home he was probably playing golf, watching golf, or talking about golf. He's an investment banker. He went to Europe all the time, really faraway places, everywhere. I'm almost twenty years old, and the conversation at the dinner table is never deeper than golf or the weather or schoolwork, and I think that's pathetic.

My mother started college, but she never finished. She used to be a stewardess, and that's how she met my dad. She feels like her role in life is being a mother. Recently, I've been like, "Mom, you should get a job." She has nothing left to do—all of us are gone.

My brothers are both away at boarding school. I went away for two years, too, but that was an experience and a half, and I ended up leaving in the middle of my second year. I had originally wanted to stay home. My dad came from a really poor family; he got a full scholarship to an Ivy League college, and then he went to business school, and now he thinks that's very important, education and whatever. We've always gone to private school. He's always been like, "I'm making this money, and this is my goal: I send you to school, I give you a good education, and you'll have a good life." He never really considered the emotional side of things.

At boarding school, I didn't do anything except think about weight. I guess weight is always a cover-up for other things. I went away to school weighing 122 pounds, and I thought I was fat then, but I never seriously dieted. I started playing field hockey, and I started getting injured. I would stop playing, but I would eat the same amount. My junior year I weighed about 150 pounds, and I freaked out. For a while all I ate was cereal, water, and grapefruits—I thought grapefruits burned fat. I would eat Special K with water and celery. People were like, "Oh, you look good."

My dad is trying to be like somewhat cool and connected now, but he's so out there. He just turned fifty, and his new thing is like Thursday night he called me up, and he was like, "Oh, um, I'm taking your mother to see the Grateful Dead tomorrow night, do you want to come?" And I was like, "Okay," and so I went with them. My dad's like this anal businessman, wears a suit to work, and it was an experience going to the Grateful Dead together.

Angela Walker

She was born in New York City in 1975. She is African-American and Puerto Rican. (See also p. 196)

I feel my stomach is too big. My friends tell me, "Girl, you don't have no stomach at all." With my friends, weight was never a problem. The real big girls never would say, I want to go on a diet. I never knew anyone who had anorexia or bulimia. But when I ate, I used to throw my food up. I wanted to stay the size I was. After a while I stopped because it was hurting my stomach. Then they told me about the disease at school. I was like, "Oh, my god, maybe that's me." I went to the doctor. They said, "Well, you're not doing it now. Do you ever think about doing it?" I was like, "No." So they told me maybe it was just a little phase or something.

Darleen Robinson Daniels

She is married and works at a child advocacy organization.
    "My birthday is May 16, 1969. I was born and raised in New Orleans, Louisiana. I am African-American and was raised Christian Baptist. God is still very much a part of my life."

*Y*ou felt like you could cut the heat with a knife. The housing development is total brick, and we had only window fans and box fans. They were always broken. We would get so angry at each other and so upset because we were so hot. If you sat still, you were sweating. If you slept, you were sweating. If you talked, you were sweating.

My dad, he had been in the sun all day. He was doing construction. Six o'clock in the morning he was there till dusk, so he didn't want no hot food. When he came home, the first thing he wanted was cold water. "Give me water!" He would sit still for a while, and then he would go and take his bath.

My dad would say, "I want this for dinner," and my mom would make sure it was cooked. My dad was the one who would always take us to the circus and to ice skate shows. He took care of the money for the bills; she made sure they got paid. She would get an amount of money from him to buy whatever we needed. She would be the one to go to school to see if everything was okay. We lived right down the street from the elementary school. Everybody knew my mom, so it wasn't like we could get away with anything.

When Mom was fed up, she gave it to my dad. She was like, "I don't know what to do with these kids, they are not listening." My dad would always say, "Tell them don't go nowhere, I'll be home soon." "Have them right there in the living room" type thing. So we got all scared, and we'd start crying before it even happened. If he whipped one, he whipped all, so we would stand in a line looking at my dad with his belt. And he would start from the youngest and go up to the oldest and just whop us.

If my parents needed to have moments alone or go out to dinner by themselves, we would stay with relatives. We were very well taken care of. My grandmother, my mom's mom, did a lot of it. There wasn't many people that my mom would trust us with. My grandmother would call us up and say, "What do you want to eat today?" and we'd tell her, and she'd have it cooked for us. She was crazy in a loving kind of way and so much fun to be around. She was the family center. Everybody would meet up at her house.

My parents argued about everything a marriage could bring up—family, money, I'm sure sex, but it was not something that I really comprehended at the time. They were trying to make it work because of us children. As we got older, things started getting difficult. The economy was getting really bad, so my dad lost his job. My mom wasn't working because she was a housewife. My parents stuck it out. They did whatever they could to make sure it worked for us. I grew up with kids on drugs, in drugs, all kinds of things, it was always around me from growing up in a housing project. But I never had a problem with people forcing it on me. I think it comes from having the parents that I did. Everybody knew my parents, and they respected them to the utmost.

Celeste Meyers

She was born in the Northeast in 1972, lives with a roommate, and works in publishing. She is Jewish, and her family comes from Eastern Europe.

My aunts and my uncle were all hippies. My dad is totally conservative. He worked for the Department of Agriculture under the Bush administration, taking farms away from family farmers. I think my dad smoked pot in a van once, and I might have been in the van, and he might have gotten in big trouble for that from my mom.

My dad's younger brother was dropping acid and still has flashbacks kind of thing—the whole Vietnam era, which I will never understand. When I went to Washington,

D.C., I saw the memorial, and it confused me a lot. My uncle got out of having to serve in the army because of his drug use.

One family vacation my aunt was sitting rolling these things on her bed, and I said, "What are you doing?" and she answered me, "I'm making cigarettes for your aunt Suzy." At dinner that night we had some guests over, and Aunt Suzy was boasting about how she finally quit smoking. And I said, "Auntie Suzy, you did not quit smoking because Auntie Bea was making you cigarettes today!"

Floy Bossinas

She was born and raised in a Greek immigrant family in Ossining, New York. She is a senior in the dramatic writing program at New York University. "I'm twenty-one. I'm a taurus."

I don't know how I did it or why I did it or how it happened, but from all the other first-generation women, I've gone a different route. I could have gone the route of being very submissive and very typical first-generation. I see that a lot in Italian girls that grew up around my neighborhood and in some Greek girls I know from Astoria. They have this idea of what their role in life is to be. I feel like there was this side of my dad that was just insisting that I get good grades all the time and that I be the best at everything. However much pressure that is, I think it's part of the reason I went the route I went, besides my own personal ambition.

My mother came to the United States when she was eighteen, and the only thing she wanted to do, really, was go to school, because there was a conflict in Greece and she couldn't finish her education. But then she came here, and she had to work to pay the rent, and she never got to go to school, and then she met my dad. They're very Old World. Growing up in the metropolitan area, I was always like, "Oh, I can't be this way."

I can't get over this one incident. I was watching a thriller with my mom, and my brother came in from a soccer game, sits down, and changes the channel. I was like, "Mom, we're watching this," but she just let him do it. That is the epitome of the way my brother was treated.

It was really hard, because my father was like this iron fist. I do have resentment, but I know I'll get over it, because I couldn't ask him to love me more than he does. He is a wonderful person, but there's this selfishness, because he grew up being the oldest boy. In Greece, when baby boys were born, they would throw them up in the air and say, "May you have more and no women!" My dad has just started getting up from the dinner table and getting his own glass of water and cooking for himself and cleaning the dishes. I'd never seen my father clean a dish before. My parents' relationship since the empty nest has begun has changed incredibly for the better.

Growing up, I just remember them fighting. My dad was thirty when he came here. He works for Hudson Wire, and now he's a supervisor, and he's been working in the same place for twenty-seven years. There's this sadness, because they've lived the majority of their lives for us, and I'm torn over how much I should give back. My mother had different odd jobs, and the majority of her jobs, she's been a seamstress. I've lived this American life, and I go back home and it's a smack in the face to see the way they live.

When I go to drop off keys at my mom's job or something, I walk in and it's all these little immigrant Italian and Greek women, and they make six dollars an hour! And then my mom has always, in her quiet way, drilled it into me that you can't depend on a guy, that if you're going to be happy, you've got to—I almost don't know what her dreams were, but I feel like she doesn't want me to live the life she's led. I don't know if it's so much depending on a man as it is not taking your own life into your own hands. She did all she can, and I think she believes that. She knows things now that she couldn't have known earlier. My mother and I, we're on a new level than we were when I was in high school, but it'll never be a friendship one. It can't—we're just from two different mentalities. And as much as my mom wants me to be a strong, independent person, she's lived in a very small, sheltered world her whole life, even though she's crossed the Atlantic.

Would the Mother Please Stand

LaWanda Doss

She was born on May 26, 1969, in Natchez, Mississippi, where she has lived all her life. She is African-American.

"My mother and grandmother both raised me. I am the only child. My grandmother worked at a local contractor's here for thirty-three years. And when she wasn't there, she worked as a house-keeper in different people's homes. My mother is a certified nurse's assistant and does secretarial work, also. I teach nursing. I am Baptist. I pray daily, constantly, about everything."

My father and my mother had been going together for a couple years before she got pregnant. He ended up going to Vietnam right before I was born. When he came back from the war, he did a little for me, but he didn't do much else, and then he just kind of faded away. I saw him once when I was eight years old. It was a Friday evening. He lived, at that time, in Gary, Indiana, and he came home to visit his family in Louisiana, a short drive to Natchez. I was asleep. I was having a migraine, and he told my grand-mother not to wake me up. She said, "No, LaWanda would kill me if I didn't wake her up." I was laying on the couch, and she woke me up, and I remember when I looked over, he was as tall as the door and he was smiling. I was like, "Who is that?" and she told me. I always knew his name, and I had his high school picture.

I went to school that Monday and said, "My daddy came to see me Friday night—he is so tall!" It was a big deal because a lot of our fathers weren't with us. So if one of us heard from our fathers, we would go back to school and tell everybody, "My daddy came." The only way I could think of to describe him was that he was pretty. Where pretty came from I really don't know. I was on cloud nine for ages. When he came, I cried because that was the first time I had seen him, and he stayed maybe two hours, and then when he got ready to go, I cried again. He said he was going to keep in touch with me.

At that time, tape recorders with the pop-up top were the fashion. He sent me a tape recorder for Christmas, and I would take that to school and show everybody. When I talked to him again, I was ten. I called him for that Christmas. He said it was too close to Christmas to send me anything, but he would send me something for New Year's. I haven't gotten it yet, and I'm twenty-five now.

When I was working at the hospital, it just so happened that I met a cousin of my father's. He was working at the same hospital. The last time I asked him about my father he said he thought he was in Texas, but he didn't know for sure. He told me his wife had six or seven children and one on the way, so I do have half brothers and sisters, but I don't know any of them. At one time I wanted to get in touch with my father, but now it doesn't bother me because I can take care of myself and I've got my mother and grandmother. I feel it is his loss, not mine.

When I was very small, my mother wasn't working yet and she kept me during the daytime. All three of us—my grandmother, my mother, and I—were still together then at my grandmother's house. My grandmother adopted me when I got ready to start school. They had passed a new rule here that the children have to be with their parent or their legal guardian, and at that time, my mother had moved to Texas with her husband. They stayed out there maybe a year.

I think I was five when my mother got married. I don't remember when they got married, but I remember her husband because I was about ten or twelve when they got divorced. He was wonderful. He treated me like I was his. He hated to hear my mother say that I was his stepchild. He was like, "I'm the one who helped raise her—that is my child, too." So I still see him every once in a while. He still treats me nice. He was never one to spank or anything like that.

My mother and I always have gotten along like sisters. I can tell her anything. I call my grandmother Mama, and I call my mother by her name. My mother was nineteen when she had me. She wanted to do what she wanted to do, but Mama knew what was best, so they would argue every once in a while.

If I resented my mother going away, I really don't remember. Even when she and her husband lived in Natchez, they lived together and I stayed with my grandmother. Sometimes I would get mad when my mother would get ready to go home with her husband, but later she explained to me that they were having hard times so she really didn't want to take me into their situation. Once she got divorced, she moved back in with my grandmother and me.

When I was in school, they would both try to come to PTA meetings or school programs. They made sure one or the other was there. Sometimes both would come, and somebody would say, "Would the mother please stand," and both of them would stand, and everybody was like, "How did you end up with two?" They were there for everything. They really were. And they still are.

My grandmother normally cooked. She still does. Sunday was a big day. You come home after church and have Sunday dinner. Maybe someone would come home from church with us, or it would just be the three of us. Until Sunday dinner ran out we ate that during the week. I was in the junior choir for ten years, and I was on the junior board, so I would pass out fans or take collection. I had a specific white dress, or black skirt and a white blouse, that I wore depending on the season of the year, white stockings and either black or white shoes. After I was about fourteen or fifteen, Sunday was the day I could put makeup on. When we came home, we'd take off our special clothes, go in the kitchen, fix a plate from the stove. We'd sit at the kitchen table and talk about church service and what we were going to do during the week. The sermon would give you something to think about.

My grandmother made a lot of my clothes when I was growing up. We didn't have a washer and dryer, so on Saturdays if she was working, that was my day to do the wash. We had one of those old-fashioned things that you had to put the water in yourself. I hated it! We rinsed the clothes in the bathtub. You'd get down on your knees and rinse the clothes up and down, then take them outside and hang them on the line.

During the summer, I would run the house. I would dust. My grandmother would normally still cook breakfast before she went to work. If wash needed to be done during the week, I would wash, clean up the house, dust, mop. I would have dinner ready when my grandmother and mother came home so they could eat and relax until the next day.

Every once in a while I would get a spanking. One time it was thundering and lightning on a Saturday morning, but I wanted to look at the *Pink Panther*. My grandmother told me to turn the TV off, but when she went and laid down, I turned it back on. She found out about it, and I got a spanking. Another time I left for Head Start with a yellow pantsuit on. When I came back home, it was dark, dirt brown. I did that two days in a row, and the third day, I got a spanking.

We had a big backyard. When I was little, I would get out in the backyard and play. We would cut the grass, and I would roll all over the yard because our yard is uneven so we have a lot of little hills and valleys. You didn't have to worry about getting run over by a car. My friends would come and visit and play with me. There was only a few of us in the neighborhood, and they really didn't live in the neighborhood, but the grandmother did. So when they came to visit their grandmother, they would come to my house. It was basically just me growing up. I think the reason my mother and I got so close like sisters is she would sit down and play dolls with me. We would color in the coloring book together, play Monopoly. I could always beat her—I think she let me! She was like my playmate because there were no children in the neighborhood.

My first real boyfriend, we broke up a little while after I turned twenty-one. The first time I remember seeing him was at the grocery store. I found out later that he knew my mother. They were in the same church. The first time he actually stopped by the house, he was on his way to work. I was cutting the grass, sweaty, because it is extra hot here. I was like, I look like who knows what, and he stops by!

I would go to church with him sometimes, and I remember we sang a song together in his church. We would go to the movies; he would pay my way. I was like, "I can pay mine," and he was like, "No, I asked you." He opened the doors—everybody would kind of go, "Oooh!" At first it felt strange. I'm not handicapped, I can open the door. But I got used to it after a while, and it was nice. I realized that was just the way he was brought up.

He was the first guy that ever sent me flowers. I was in the house putting something together, and I heard somebody knock at the door and it was him. He gave me this brown paper bag, and he turned around and left. He didn't say anything. When I opened it up, there was a white vase with three white carnations. He had a little nephew that was about five, and one day he parked across the street where I couldn't see the car and sent his nephew across the street with a card and a vase of flowers. He would think of little things and just do them, whatever he thought of. We talked for about two years or a little more. A lot of people call it dating, but we call it "we talked." Anyway, I was in school the whole time, but when I got into the real nursing part of it, that put a real strain on our relationship. I really didn't have time to talk to him. He would call and he wanted to talk and he would ask me a question, and I would answer as short as possible. He would get upset, but he would never tell me. After a while he got to the point where he wouldn't call. We just kind of grew apart. I was going so fast I didn't have time to realize why I hadn't heard from him. We are still good friends.

I haven't had a real relationship that lasted past three months since then. It has been about four years. My best girlfriend and I are real close. And if I find a guy, she finds somebody, too, and then we both break up about the same time. We don't know why we can't find somebody that is really worthwhile. She is a teacher in a junior high school, and I'm teaching nursing at a community college, so we don't know if it is that we are career oriented and the guys can't handle that they may not be or what, but they stick around for a while, and then they are gone.

I would go out with someone who makes less money than me, but it all depends on how they treat me. If you are out to use me, then we are going to have problems. I've encountered that. I feel they are thinking, "She is a nurse, and she can be my meal ticket."

A lot of them are with these little part-time jobs. That is not what I'm here for. I can't afford to take care of somebody else. I have my own bills.

The last guy I was talking to I had known him in high school, and we talked maybe three or four months. He had the nerve to call me cheap—because I didn't buy a pair of hundred-dollar tennis shoes. I said, "Well, last time I checked, you didn't have them either, so you can't call me cheap." It just went on from there, and I was like, "Look, don't call me anymore." I don't know what the whole thing was about.

My mother is the only child, but my grandmother is the baby of seven. So it went from seven to one and one. I would have had a brother and sister, but my mother miscarried once with my little brother, and my sister lived two days. My grandmother and my mother always wanted the best for me. My grandmother got sick right before I finished school, and her whole thing was, "Lord, don't let me die before she can take care of herself." That pulled her through. She was going to live to see me graduate. I was the first one in my family to finish college. That was a big thing. That was something I wanted to do for myself and for the family.

I Remember the Day
My Dad Said He Was Leaving

Cora Sands

She was born and raised in an observant Jewish family in Los Angeles. Her father was a business-man and her mother was a home maker. She was twenty-four years old at the time of the interview. (See also p. 174)

My parents just celebrated their thirty-second anniversary. Point-blank, I wish they would have gotten divorced many years ago. They first separated when I was five. And then they got separated again, and they were going to get divorced when I was twelve. My mom even had the papers drawn up. She and I had moved out, and then I moved back in and I remember my dad set my brother and I down on the couch, I'll never forget this, and he asked us what did we think about my mom sending him the divorce papers. And I wanted to yell out, "Yes, I want you to get a divorce!" but I couldn't, I was quiet, and I never understood how a parent can ask their child, especially when I was only twelve years old, what I thought about it.

My dad was physically violent to my mom, and that affected me greatly. That's why I hated my dad. And I never talked about it. I never mentioned it to anybody until I was eighteen and then to one other person a couple years ago and then to a very good friend. I told her I don't talk about it or don't tell anybody about it because I'm embar-rassed, and she told me, "Why should you be embarrassed when you aren't the one who did it?" And that made me realize that I wasn't the one who did the wrong. And I shouldn't be ashamed.

This happened from when I was like five up through high school. When my brothers lived at home, I remember hearing the arguments and then waiting for the hitting, and as soon as that happened, I would go and run and get my brothers, and they would stop it. To this day, when I hear couples arguing, I always think it's going to turn into violence. I always get a little afraid.

I want to make my life different from what my mother chose. I guess the best thing about me moving out on my own is to prove to myself that if, God forbid, something happens when I do get married, I know that I can survive on my own and won't have to be stuck in a marriage that I'm afraid of leaving.

Maggie Erwin

She is a college senior and was born in New Orleans in 1973. Her mother was a homemaker, and her father was a doctor at the hospital where she was born. Both her parents are Episcopalian.

I remember the day that my dad said he was leaving. It was a Sunday, and I remember going into my older sister's room. When he told her, she started crying so hard. My twin sister and I didn't know what was going on because we were only seven or six. We didn't know anything was bad. I remember going to church with my dad that day—it was just me and him, and that has always been sort of a special day. But after that he left and moved into an apartment, and ever since then we always split up the time. In middle school and high school it was Wednesdays and weekends with my dad and the rest with my mom. My dad has been, in all ways, the financial provider. I don't have that many memories of my mom and dad together. I do remember a dinner where my dad put a gold crawfish in my mom's meal. He gave her a little gift. I don't think it was a bad divorce. They tell us to this day they just had problems that they couldn't work out. I don't think they ever really fought—they just didn't get along. They were married almost twenty years.

Chrissy Robinson

She works as a receptionist, is a single mother, and was born in a small town in the Deep South in 1969.

"My dad was in the navy for a while, and then I don't know what he did. We were dirt poor. We lived in a barn." (See also p. 350)

*W*hen I was real little, my mom got divorced and remarried. I have a half brother and a half sister from my biological father's first marriage, but I didn't meet them until I was sixteen. My sister is exactly eight years older than me, so that would make her thirty-two. My brother is nine years older than me. My biological father, he worked offshore on the oil rigs, and he also hunted. He was an expert marksman.

I can remember meeting my sister for the first time. My mom had told me about my siblings when I was thirteen. I knew that they were there, but I didn't know where they were. I didn't even know how to go about finding them. When I was sixteen, Mom came to me and said, "I saw your brother and sister's mother at the store the other day, and I showed her your picture and she started crying. She said, 'Oh, god, that looks just like Stacey. That looks just like her.'" My sister's mother told Stacey, and Stacey found my mom, and they talked for a long time. She came to our house. I remember opening up the door. It was like looking at a mirror. Even our voices were the same. She is taller than I am; that is the only difference. It was neat. She had a three-year-old, and I spent a lot of time with her. We got to be close.

I got to meet my real dad through all that, too, and my real grandmother, which was kind of unusual. I have no resentment toward my real dad, but unless you call or write him, he won't bother. I don't maintain contact with him a lot. He is a very introverted person, and he spent years in Africa. He loved to hunt. That part of him was neat and interesting. Not the hunting part, but living in Africa. He loved animals, and I have always loved animals. Our temperaments are a lot alike.

Nichelle Ellison

She is a graduate student at a large university on the West Coast. She was born in a small town in Georgia in 1968. She is African-American. (See also pp. 184 and 503)

*T*he neighborhood raised you. If one neighbor saw you doing something wrong, it was not out of the ordinary for him to spank you or tell your mother that he spanked you and why. You knew when you got in trouble, and you knew you were going to get it!

I was born while my mother was in college. She was twenty years old. I think I was born within the same month that her own mother died. She had to quit college and raise me along with her siblings, and her siblings' children later on.

It was usually older relatives and friends that babysat us. My great-aunt raised several generations of children, and she has been the backbone of our family. She was very religious. Right before we would eat dinner at her house everybody would have to say grace and follow it with a Bible verse.

I remember my mother working in a local factory in town. To support us, she eventually became a paralegal. As a child, my day would be to go to school, come home, and wait for my mother to come home. Once she started doing paralegal work, she would take business trips and always bring me back something. On a couple of those trips she took me with her. Now that I think about it, she was tired all the time.

Growing up in my family was pretty hard. I kind of harbored a resentment towards my mother about the cousins she was raising along with me because I felt like they took my mother, part of what could have been all mine, because I was her only child. But they were like my brothers and sisters while growing up.

My mother's expectations for me were higher than they were for the boys. For some reason, she expected the girls to excel more. She wanted all of us to grow up and be good people and lead good lives and be successful. She was very religious. She was just a good woman. She probably didn't want me to go through a lot of stuff that she had gone through, so she stressed education. I had told her that there was this guy on campus who was recruiting for the army, and she just gave me this look. I knew it was the end of that conversation.

My community was basically a community of women, and the way that a lot of the women in my immediate environment were treated has a lot to do with my ambition today. I have an aunt who was physically abused in her household. She was always leaving him, coming to our home, and she was always crying—she was always hurt, and I witnessed it—and I witnessed her being shot by her husband, my uncle-in-law, in front of me, him beating her sometimes. Then, she didn't drive or do anything like that. I remember to see as a child that she was dependent on him, and that was why she was there, and I was determined that was not going to be me.

Lizette Arsuega

She was born in New York City in 1976. Her son is almost five, and she has another child on the way.

"I have eleven brothers and sisters. Three of us are from the same father, and the rest of them are from my stepfather. My mother is Puerto Rican, Cuban, she's mixed. My father's family is from Puerto Rico. When I was little, I was in Catholic church, but now my mother switched into Christian church." (See also p. 367)

I was very young when my parents separated. I see my father every now and then. But I always lived with my mom. I couldn't count on my father. He did support us financially until like ten years ago. He injured himself in his knee—probably it happened at work, but I'm not too sure. When I was younger, he would come by maybe once a month. Sometimes I would go to my grandmother's house, and he would be there. He would take us to Rye Playland. We'll go and buy a whole bunch of candy and cookies, and then we'll come home and be all full and it was time for dinner and we couldn't eat, and my mother would get mad at him.

My mother's on welfare, but she's working into this business of Amway—she's really into this. She doesn't want to let it go. She goes to classes; she goes to meetings like every three or four days. It's basically a job-training program so she can get herself off welfare.

When I was younger, we used to eat dinner together every night. My mother would cook, or if not, her boyfriend or I would cook, or my grandmother would cook. We'd make yellow rice and beans, chicken, pork chops, different things. My grandmother and aunt were living with us, too. My mother was working when I was a baby, and I used to stay with my grandmother. My mother started staying home when I was two years old. Basically, we wouldn't talk about anything at the dinner table because my grandmother would go around smacking us in the mouth if we would talk while we were eating.

My mother was always there when I got home from school. The only drug that anybody in my family does is cigarettes, or on occasion we'll drink, but my mother never does. There was never any physical or sexual abuse. My mother would punish me, like tell me go to my room, or since my closet was open, she'll tell me sit in the closet on top of all the clothes if I didn't want to clean up.

When I was eleven years old, some lady reported my mother, saying the house was messy and that my mother had a lot of problems raising her kids. I think my mother had an argument with the lady, and she was like, "You shouldn't have them kids." They came at two o'clock, three o'clock, I think it was four o'clock in the morning, and my mother answered the door, and she said, "Can I help you?" And all of us were sleeping. The social worker came in through the hallway and from my brother's room she said, "This house is really messy. How can you have your kids in this house if this house is a fire hazard!" They removed us that day. We didn't want to leave. I was crying. We had to stay in one place, a BCW—Bureau of Child Welfare—agency or something, for a couple of hours. I tried to run away and take my brothers and sisters with me. But they caught up with me, and they were like, "You can't go anywhere." So we went into a group home, and some of the kids went into foster care.

The social workers investigated, and they saw it was just a false alarm. From so many kids it wasn't like the house would always be clean, but we would be constantly cleaning it. It wasn't really right of them to take us away because we were going to school, we always had clean clothes, and I felt like we were being taken care of. They just took us because of an argument, and it was somebody else's fault. So we all went back to my mother's house four or five months later. She got a new apartment, and she fixed it up.

Lauren Morgan Stern

Her roots are Irish, Scottish, Russian Jewish, and Swedish. She was born in the Deep South in 1965 and now works in child advocacy with her mother, Rachel Morgan, who also appears in the book. (See also p. 381)

My father was the breadwinner and brought home the paycheck; my mother stayed at home and was the mother. She was president of the PTA in our school for two or three years. She did a volunteer teaching class for accelerated kids in our elementary school. She did a lot of moms' stuff. Then she started getting involved in reading groups and women's groups. I didn't understand it all, and I didn't know exactly what each group was. She started having new friends and her own life. She worked part-time jobs.

They split up maybe mid-seventies—'79 was the year of hell. It was my mother leaving my father but keeping the house. We went through four or six years of custody disputes. It was over and over, and he appealed everything he could appeal to get us. Right after the divorce I became little mom junior, and there was dinner every night with a two-page list of instructions on how to do it, and we would get it started before she came home. When the divorce happened, she had to start working. Her first position was director of a day-care center. She went through a couple of programs and then started a private, nonprofit child advocacy organization.

She was my buddy at an age that was too young. She had a lot of companionship and support, so I won't say she came to me inappropriately, but we had a very unique relationship, and I was happy as a clam. I loved it. It was how I got to where I am without more scars. I did a lot of things that were dishonest, like if she told me not to ride on motorcycles, then I got picked up by one every day at school, but she knew that my friends and I were drinking and smoking pot. She would tell us the things that we could do in her house in order to have us there so that we weren't driving around drunk and stoned. She never let people smoke pot in the house, but I think she let us smoke on the porch. I think it was an "I don't know, I don't see" thing. There was no hard liquor, absolutely, anywhere in her house. They were rules we could go by, and she did make people feel welcome there. I run into these people now and again in different places, and they all say, "How is your mom!?"

We went from just ridiculous, all-American white bread to a pretty typical divorced single-family home. Suddenly, the house was a mess. Frozen pizza entered our lives. On Monday night we started out with a whole chicken, and by Tuesday there were pieces of it that were being made into gravy and poured over rice, and on Wednesday suddenly it was a casserole with chicken and a little bit of squash thrown in. Feminism played a serious part of how my mother changed and why the marriage didn't work.

Jillian Schwartz

She was born in 1973 in a small town in the rural Northeast. Her father was a carpenter.

"I guess I'm Jewish. This has become a big thing for me, especially when I got to college. There was so much emphasis on your roots, and I had no idea where I was from." (See also p. 185)

I grew up differently than a lot of girls. We never had a TV, and my mother wouldn't let me play with Barbie dolls, and I wanted to so badly. She thought they were sexist. My parents were totally fighting all the time. My father was a really bad gambler, so that was a lot of tension. Now he is completely reformed.

My mother was trying to live through me. She wanted me to play the piano. That was her thing, and she would make me practice for hours and just stand there. She had always been very unhappy sitting home as a housewife. When I was sixteen, I was working at this restaurant, and one of the managers left, and I suggested that my mother work there. She totally bloomed. She started taking care of herself and buying clothes.

She met this guy through the restaurant and ended up moving in with him for a couple of months. It was hard. My father was a wreck. He was drinking and crying, and he was just totally depressed. He couldn't handle it at all. I was so mean to him. He would always try to talk to me. I just wanted him to be like a man and be really strong. I feel bad about it now.

My mother's affair with the other man didn't work out, and she came back. It is so amazing that my father would take her back, I guess. It is a magical story. When they found each other again, they just threw all their money into a used bookstore and did really well.

Facades

Jenna Baker

She works at a clothing store and takes courses at a community college. She is of Irish, English, and French origin and was born outside of Chicago. Her mother was seventeen at the time.

"It was kind of rare then, there weren't too many teenage pregnancies in 1974. I don't even know if my father went to the hospital. My grandfather had just left my grandmother. She had all these kids to take care of, and now a grandchild. They were all traumatized by my grandfather leaving, so when I came, I was sort of like a messiah."

The first time my mother ever tried acid I was two years old and we were at the mall in Chicago. She was doing lots of partying—she sold pot for our grocery money. My father had abandoned us. As soon as I was born, he enrolled in the navy and left for Florida. One time, without my father knowing, my mother—this is one cool thing she did—took me on a flight to Florida, and when his boat came back from being out to sea, my mother was standing on the dock waving with this baby in her arms. She was like, "This is your responsibility. You're going to take care of it." So we all lived together for a while in Florida, and they got married. But my father is an alcoholic, and I think he would beat my mother, so I guess she finally got smart and left him. And then she met Robert Baker. The first day I met him he bought me a half gallon of ice cream.

They got married, and we moved to Tennessee. We stayed with his grandparents, and that's when everything got awful. We were out on the porch one day—I don't know where my mother was—and he unzipped my pants and started fondling me. I didn't like it, but I never had a father, so I thought, oh, this must be what fathers do. Then we moved into this old farmhouse, and he would walk around in his underwear. They smoked pot and they grew pot, and I think that's when my nightmares of someone coming to murder me at any moment started. I thought for sure I would die. And then I'd wake up, and I'd think, wow, I'm alive.

After a while we moved out to California. Robert went into the military. We had field day at my house, where everything would get cleaned up. I had to run a mile and a half every day, or I would get the shit beat out of me. I was told if I beat this kid up who was giving me some trouble at school, I would get a jungle gym. But I was too scared; I didn't want to fight him, so I didn't get a jungle gym. Robert would come into my room every night and ask me what had happened during the day, and he would fondle me. He would do oral sex and he would penetrate me with his fingers, and I think he made me do things to him. It was all happening right underneath my mother's nose in a house not much bigger than a typical cottage.

My mother would have black eyes and bloody lips, and he'd rip her hair out of her head and throw her up against walls and punch her. I think once she lost a baby. I would go in and scream, "Get your hands off my mother!" We lived right by the entrance to the base and there were military police there, and I would often get him to stop beating my mother because I would say, "I'm going to go tell the MPs!" and I would run out of the house. And then he would let my mother go so that she could run after me.

I wrote my grandmother letters all the time. I never told her specifically what was going on because, of course, my mother told me not to and I didn't want her to worry. We were being beat all the time and my mother was just accepting it. As far as I'm concerned, a woman has the right to decide if she wants the shit beat out of her, but once you have children you have a responsibility to make sure that they're safe, well cared for, and that they have an opportunity to be educated. My mother was the only hope I had, and she didn't do anything.

It's amazing, most of my friends in elementary school were molested, as well. I can remember at some of the parties someone would bring it up, and out of eight girls, six of them would have been molested. The school I went to was for kids who lived right by the base or on base or in base housing. They're amazing schools. I mean in third grade my science trip was whale watching.

My mother was always the room mother. She'd bring the treats in. She was very into appearances. She made all of my clothes, and every day I would have my hair done, and I always looked like this cute little girl. No one would ever think you take off her shirt and she's got bruises all over her. Facades, I learned a lot about that as a child. I had to lie all the time. If anyone asks why I have a black eye, it's because I fell and hit my head on the banister.

I would look for opportunities to get back at Robert in public situations where I knew he couldn't hit me. One time he was out washing the car. He put the hose down to talk to his friend. I went and turned it off. He picks the hose back up, and he presses it to push the water out, and nothing came out. He's like, "What's goin' on? I know I still had the hose on." I was hiding by the faucet and watching him. He's looking at it and he's hitting it, and I waited until he had it pressed down and he was looking right into the nozzle, and I turned it on full force so it sprayed him right in the face. He chased me and hit me on the side of the head with a water bottle and smacked me a couple of times, but it was worth it. It was hilarious, because he was in front of his macho marine buddy, trying to be cool. He was totally embarrassed. I think my mother was really impressed by that.

Then my grandmother came to visit. Robert stopped molesting me about a month before she came. The whole time she was there I wanted to tell her, "Please rescue me," but I was afraid he would hurt her. And I think he told me, "If you tell, I'll kill you." She left, and he didn't molest me for a long time. And then one night he came into my room, and I moved around and I was like, "Don't, no," and the next morning my mom came home from doing laundry, and I said, "I've got to tell you something." It took me hours to tell her. I wanted to write it, to whisper, to spell it, I wanted to do anything, I just didn't want to come right out and say it.

That Monday morning my mom got us into therapy, and I had the best therapist I could ever hope for. My mom kicked Robert out—we had to go through Base Legal. She didn't want to leave him for financial purposes, though. We moved into nicer housing. He never lived there with us, but it was still base housing. My mother was sleeping with a bunch of different men, and she was smoking pot. But at least she wasn't with Robert. He would still come to our house, but I don't think I ever had to be alone with him again after that.

Then he moved to San Diego and became a drill instructor. I finally had my mother back again. I said to her, "Promise me you'll never get married again." We had a little bit of time to ourselves, and then she starts seeing this other guy, who she's now married to, before the divorce between her and Robert Baker was even final. And I didn't like him—I didn't want any man around, I just wanted to take a short break. I went to visit my grandmother for Christmas break, and I was afraid to go back because I didn't know what this new guy was going to do. We got a lawyer to represent the case and I lived with my grandmother for a while, but eventually I did go back to California.

Halfway through the year my mother's husband told her, "Either your daughter goes, or I'm filing for a divorce." So, of course, my mother said to me, "You've got to go live with your grandmother again." I came back and lived with my grandmother for a while, then I moved to my aunt's house in California. She would say things to me like, "I've got a nail appointment for you today. Do you want to go to school or get your nails done?"

When I was just about to turn sixteen, my aunt couldn't take me anymore, and I couldn't take her, and I couldn't live with my mother. I was going to go live with another aunt and uncle. They were Christian, and they had this huge list of rules that they set out for me when they came to pick me up. By this time I had basically raised myself and my mother. I was certainly not ready to go and live like a normal fifteen year old. So I went to live back with my aunt, and that was just a nightmare—she was on so many drugs. I didn't want to stay there. I wanted to go live with my grandmother again. And that's when everyone decided I was crazy.

One day I was upstairs at my grandmother's doing my hair, getting ready to go to a therapy appointment. She says, "Come down, I've got some friends here I want you to meet." I go downstairs, and there's this woman in the back hallway and a man in the front hallway, and I thought, "How weird." And then my uncle's on the couch, and I'm like, "Hey, why are you here? What's going on?" and he looked at me, and he said, "Well Jenna, I don't really know how to tell you this, but you're going to a home."

I started crying. And then they came and grabbed me. I had no idea what was happening—this was completely out of the blue. They carried me out to this van and put me in the back of it, and all of the handles had electrical tape and you couldn't get out any windows, and I didn't know who these people were, and they drove me to a drug rehab. I was strip-searched. They asked me every drug I had done. There were no drugs in my system for at least a year, but they didn't care. Everyone in there was on medication. I was really scared—I didn't know what this medication was going to do to me. I shake all the time; I've shook all my life, and they thought that I was on drugs because of that. I was pleading with my grandmother, "Please don't leave me here."

I was there for two weeks. You can't be by yourself at any time. You go to different parents' houses who have kids in the program every night, and five girls all sleep there together. They strip you of all personality, all identity, and make you this robot that doesn't do drugs because drugs are bad. They've since been closed down, which is quite a relief because it was disgusting. They would scream insults at you, tell you what a miserable person you are.

I had a dream one night that I woke up and I was at my grandmother's house. I saw my dresser and my mint green wall, and I was like, "Oh, my god, it was just a dream. I never really went to that place!" I was elated, and I went downstairs to get some breakfast, and then I really woke up. I realized, "Oh, my god, this is real." And I just started crying. That was probably my worst experience in there.

A lot of people tried to escape. One day at free time I was planning how I would get out. I was thinking really hard. And then someone came, and they were like, "Jenna, you need to come with me," and I thought, "Oh shit, they saw me plotting—they're going to go put me on medication." But no one grabbed my shoulder—I could walk by myself—and I thought, "This is a trick. They're gonna see if I try to run." They took me to this room, and I went in, and there was my grandmother and my uncle. I just ran to my uncle, and I was like, "This is such a nightmare. You have to get me out." He was like, "Don't worry—it's all over." We got in the car and left.

For about the first two weeks after that I was really glad to be home at Grandma's. Then it hit me what had happened, and I started taking it out on her. She had my uncle come over. He said, I want to talk to you upstairs, and we got up into the room, and he just started picking me up and throwing me and slapping me and punching me. I went to live with my grandmother because it was safe there, no one would beat me up, and then he did that and I didn't want to be there anymore, either. She was behind it. That was the only time she did something like that, and it was awful. She shouldn't have had to go through all that stress, though. I had been with her for about two months, and she said, "You've gotta go—you can't stay here."

So I was sixteen, and I was forced out into the street. I had really nowhere to go. That's when I moved in with my friend Maria Rodriguez. I got a taste of Hispanic culture, a hard-core Mexican family, traditions, etc. And then I left Maria's house and moved in with my friend Teresa and her boyfriend, who lived in her boyfriend's father's basement, and it was just Roach Motel, Cockroach City. Disgusting place—I couldn't eat the food—I lost about thirty pounds in two weeks. This guy Fernando would come over. He was married with two kids, and I soon found out he was a major cocaine distributor. He had a lot of money, and he liked young blonds. He took me out of that place, and I lived in hotels for about a month, shopped all the time. He paid for the hotels, eighty bucks a night easy, on top of room service and whatever movies I wanted to order. My mother had no idea what was going on, and she didn't care. I had started smoking pot again at this point, and I was really into it. Eventually, Fernando and I started sleeping together. He's a very charismatic, handsome man, a good twenty years older than me. Lots of money, fast cars, Jaguars, Mercedes, really nice things, and it was like, whoa.

Then his wife left, so I moved into his house with him and his nephew. I could never walk in front of windows. I had my own gun, and I would take it anywhere I went in the house with me because at any time, someone could come in and try to steal all of his stuff. We had parties there. He was seeing other young girls. A lot of coke was around, obviously. I could never leave the house by myself. I either had to have him or his nephew with me.

Basically, for Fernando the deal was I would look cute; I would be on his side during poker games; when we went to Chicago to get drugs, I would carry them on me. In case we would ever get pulled, I would be the one to go away. It was a pretty tough price to pay, but I had my back up against the wall, I didn't know what else to do. I did coke, not as heavily as you would imagine. Not every day, but at parties and stuff.

After I moved in with Fernando, I would go to school a lot cause he could drop me off and pick me up. I took cabs a lot, too. He never hit me, but he would yell, and it would be terrifying. I had to keep the house clean all the time, spic and span, that was my job. If I wouldn't have a table clean, he would humiliate me in front of people. "Get the fuck over here and clean this up!" People would be like, oh my god! and they would just look at me, this young kid. Girls would come up into the room upstairs so he could weigh out lines for them, and I would be sitting on the bed doing my homework with my revolver next to me. And they would be like, whoa, really freaked out by me because they were just young, white, suburban kids as well, mixed up with this weird guy.

And then I found out that I could go live with Teresa's mother. I left Fernando's, and I wouldn't tell him where I went. Teresa's mother lived in this really shitty neighborhood and is an alcoholic big time, and I didn't like that. I moved in with Teresa's now husband's sister. That's when I started partying with coke more, and I still would see Fernando sometimes. From there I moved in with one friend then another. This was all within less than a year.

And then I went to stay with a friend of our family's, Doug, who was my lawyer when I was twelve. Doug stayed friends with our family, and he felt a lot of sympathy for me. He never had any kids, and he's always seen me as a niece figure or like the daughter he never had. He's a really great guy. He was the only safe man I had met at that point, the first man who didn't want anything sexual from me or want to beat the shit out of me.

I was going to high school, and things were kind of normal for a while. But then Teresa and her boyfriend moved into this place right by Doug's house, and they had a friend who started dealing coke. I basically moved in with them for about a month and a half, and we were doing coke every day, all day, all night. We would start at like six at night and go until six, seven the next morning. My nose only bled a few times, but it was awful, awful, awful, awful. It's just this huge maze: You do coke to want more to do more to want more—I mean, it's not even fun. I stopped hanging out with my friends from school, and they were pretty worried about me. I stopped going to school. Doug didn't know what to do.

I'm surprised I'm alive, and I'm surprised I was never raped. One night it was Teresa and her boyfriend and his friend and his girlfriend and me. They'd all known each other for years, and I was just Teresa's friend. We were all sitting around playing cards as usual, and the men both sat on either side of me and they were looking at me really weird, and I thought, "they're gonna want something in repayment for all this coke—I've gotta get out of here or I'm gonna get raped." So the next day I claimed that I was gonna go do a bunch of laundry, and I took all my clothes and I went back to Doug's house. He was away at the time, and I got in bed for the weekend, and I just let the answering machine pick up all the calls. That was basically all I did to rehabilitate myself, and I didn't go through any weird withdrawals, and I don't crave it now.

Teresa doesn't do any drugs at this point; she's a mother now. Her husband is still addicted to it. I really can't relate to them. They think I'm weird. Any ideas I have about life or my dreams, that's totally foreign to them—they're waiting for the next welfare check. But I'm still friends with Teresa because she needs something outside of that realm. She needs to realize that there is life beyond soap operas, and one day if she ever does decide to leave him, I want to be here to give her resources to utilize. But I won't be hanging out with her and her friends because it's miserable for me.

When I was fifteen, Fernando, the drug dealer, knew a lot of strippers, and from fifteen to seventeen, on and off, I would go in for amateur nights, and I'd always just say I left my ID at home. I never prostituted myself except if you would call the Fernando situation a form of prostitution. But I didn't have to sleep with him—that was a choice that I made. Because I used to use sex in order to get love and affection. A lot of women do.

I think it's a typical pattern for sexually abused women to go into sexual professions. It always left me feeling absolutely degraded. After I turned eighteen, I was working as a waitress in this place called Fantasy Girls, and one night I went through utter turmoil: Should I go in? Should I not go in? I needed money fast. I had started supporting myself and sharing an apartment with some housemates, and I was about to be evicted. Finally, that night I decided, you don't ever have to go back again. I said that to myself: *You don't ever have to go back there again.* If you have to move out onto the street, you'll figure out a way—you don't have to do this anymore. And it was such a weight released off of me, and I've never done it again, and I have no desire to.

I Kept Saying No

Cora Sands

She was raised in an observant Jewish family and was twenty-four years old at the time of the interview. (See also p. 160)

I didn't choose the first time for me to have sex, I didn't choose the place, I didn't choose the person. My boyfriend in my senior year of high school, he was a year older than myself, and he wanted to have sex, and I said no, I kept saying no. I wanted to wait until the right person. There's pressure. He had had sex before with other girls. He said he loved me. I guess I told him I loved him. I didn't love him, I just said it. It wasn't right, and I wanted it to be right.

I was probably fifteen when my brother's friend got accused of raping a girl. He was about seventeen. For some reason, that had an impact on me, and I said, well, I'm going to wait until I'm out of high school. I had a lot of friends in high school who were on the pill, having sex, and I said to myself, I don't want to do that.

Right out of high school I went to Europe. My brother's best friend's father had his own tour group. I had known him since I was in second grade. I was only eighteen at the time, and on the trip he raped me. That was my first time. I'm okay with it right now. It has taken me like six years to get over it.

For a year and a half I didn't tell anybody. I didn't tell my family. I thought I was probably the dirtiest thing on earth. He was somebody I knew. It was almost like he was an uncle, and I trusted him. It was the biggest trust violated. He was married. And instead of me thinking that he did it to me, I thought I had sex with him. I thought, oh gosh, how can I have sex with a married man?

We were in Florence, the group of us, and we went out to this restaurant, and we all had so much wine to drink. We probably had a bottle each. He wasn't drunk, and I was completely drunk, and he knew I was drunk. So I didn't have the capabilities to say something or to push him off. And I remember he locked the door.

I didn't think it was rape because I thought rape is just somebody who throws you down and holds a gun to your head and rips off your clothes. I graduated high school in '87—date rape wasn't really talked about until I got to college. I didn't know that if some guy just takes off your clothes and does all that, that it's rape. I mean, I knew him since I was eight years old.

I talked to this one girl afterwards, and I said, "I think I had sex with him last night." I remember her saying she thought she did, too. But I knew what had happened. And I couldn't look at him the rest of the time. I was so ashamed. When I got back from Europe, I broke up with my boyfriend. I didn't want to be in a relationship for like two years. I didn't have sex with anybody. I wasn't able to concentrate at school.

There's a movie, *The Accused,* with Jodie Foster. I saw it when I was at school, and I started thinking, "That was rape. What happened to me was rape." And then I finally told my family, and they just flipped out. I went to counseling at Santa Monica Hospital. They have one of the best rape programs, and they were very understanding.

A lot of people are very judgmental. With all these things happening, it's made me a lot more understanding of other people. It's made me understand that things happen to people. I'm a lot more patient with people now. At least I hope so.

Nancy Aldridge

She was born in Louisiana in 1969. She works as a receptionist at a small company where she is in training for a higher position.

*W*e were making out really heavily, and I thought it was his fingers, and then I looked on the side of me and both of his hands were there. He had been trying and trying for a long time, and I kept saying, "No, no, no. I'm only sixteen, I'm still a virgin." I guess I went into shock. Everything went blank. I just remember crying and crying and crying and blood. There was blood, a good deal of blood. I went to my best friend, and I told her, and she was like, "Well, let me tell you something. Two days ago I was raped, too." It was her boyfriend's best friend. Both of us ended up going to therapy. At first I thought, oh, I let him go too far—he was getting hot and heavy, and he had no choice. I know better than that now.

I did not tell my mom for about two years. We were fighting. We were yelling and screaming, and she was like, "I don't know what your problem is—what is your problem?" I said, "My problem is I was raped!" It just came out. She was like, "What?" She started freaking out, and I never did tell her who it was, but I think she knows because she put two and two together. I just refused to tell her because she was like, "Press charges!" and I was like, "Mom, it happened two years ago, and he lives across the country now."

Marina Koob

She was born in Kingston, New York, in 1970 and describes herself as a recovering Catholic.

I have had five different abusers at all different stages of my life. The last time was only two years ago, and that was a date rape. It brought up a lot of old stuff that I hadn't dealt with until then. I started having memory flashbacks, and that led me into counseling. I am still in therapy. My parents never took me to counseling. They never talked to me about the incidents of sexual abuse in my childhood. They weren't treated seriously. They weren't treated at all. I told my mother every time something happened to me, and her way of dealing with it was to just get rid of the person who was doing it to me. None of the people that hurt me were ever prosecuted. They were never charged. One of my abusers was my cousin, who was a couple years older than me, and he didn't even get in trouble from his own parents.

I am kind of the odd child in a very large family. I was the one who was left the most. The first six months of my life my mother was ill and couldn't get out of bed, so I didn't have a mother for a while. I was also the only one who had a full-time nanny. I was very close with her. When I started getting older, she went more into housekeeping than child care. My mother ended up firing her, and I didn't understand what was going on, but her husband was molesting myself and my three sisters. The first time I started sleeping over at my nanny's house was probably when I was a baby, but I think the sexual abuse started when I was three. I am really foggy on dates from my childhood. I was out of my body a lot of the time.

There are so many cases of rape that aren't prosecuted, cases of child sexual abuse that aren't reported, let alone prosecuted. God forbid, we listen to a child or what their experience was and believe them. I know that my daughters won't grow up in the world I want them to, but I guess I'll just be there to show them what is wrong and that they need to work to change it, too. If I could, I would want to change every single thing about the way women are viewed. I want my daughter to read fairy tales about princesses who didn't necessarily marry the prince. I want her to realize that she doesn't have to get married, she doesn't have to be with a man. She can, but she can do whatever she wants. There isn't one set way that you end up being happily ever after.

I want the violence against women in the movies, in the media, and basically in every way that you see women, to end. I understand that in some cases date rape is hard to prove, but I would like for every time a woman comes in and says that she was raped that they investigate it and take it to court. I wish that there were some kind of registry or something where the name of any convicted man was entered and you could get a copy of that list and find out. Then you wouldn't have to date him if you didn't want to.

I'm involved with NOW [National Organization for Women], and our next meeting is about gathering information on rapes that haven't been prosecuted in this area or even ones that have been. We are trying to get these women at our next meeting to get this evidence, and then we are going to go to the district attorney, Cavanaugh, who has not had a very good record of prosecuting rapists. Most recently, they didn't prosecute a man who was charged with rape, and he has done it again. Now Cavanaugh is making a big stink about it, but, meanwhile, a woman was raped. He should have done something the first time.

What I think is really sad is that there aren't more clinics or courses or whatever for men who have done this. They need help. Not only do the women need to be in therapy but so do the men, and they should have to be. There is a reason why they are doing it. They are not monsters—they weren't born wanting to rape women. Something happened to them, I think.

Dad, I'm a Lesbian, You Probably Knew

Amy Goldberg

She was born in 1972 and raised in Florida. She was twenty-three years old at the time of the interview.

"My parents got married when they were seniors in college, and I was born a year after they graduated. My dad was an investment banker. My mom was a teacher. She stopped to take care of the kids. My parents got divorced when I was in fourth grade. My mom went into real estate. I'm white and Jewish, and my family comes from that sometimes-Russia-sometimes-Poland part of Eastern Europe. I have a brother who is twenty-one, and my dad got remarried, so I have twin baby sisters. My mom just got married in August, which is very exciting. She'd been living with her boyfriend since I was a junior in high school."

The first words Ellen said to me were, "You have to blot." I was sitting at the kitchen table, drinking water and reading the paper, in the apartment my friend Al shared with two women. He was putting me up for a while because I had just moved to town. Ellen walked in with one of Al's housemates, and they were talking about makeup. I had just started my job at this icky law firm where I have to dress up and be all fancy, and I totally wasn't doing it well. Nobody there would take me aside and explain to me how to do it. So I was like, "Great—makeup—tell me, how do you wear lipstick so that it doesn't come off in ten minutes?"

My friend Al had told me that Ellen was friends with all of these lesbians and that I should get to know them. He said, "She likes tempeh, you like tempeh, you'll become great friends." Tempeh is this soy bean stuff that comes in little packages, and you use it the way other people use meat.

I'm Ellen's first girlfriend. I'm sure she still doesn't think of herself as a lesbian or straight or gay, which confused the hell out of me at first. I was talking about all these gay political actions I did and how I ran this Queer Coffee House at college. She didn't do any of that. I just had a good time with her. I remember wanting to say, "I'm about to have this huge crush on you. Please tell me now if you're straight, and I'll stop." But I didn't get up the guts to do that.

And then we went to a Lesbian Avengers party one night, and we still hadn't touched. Fifty, eighty, one hundred lesbians sitting on a sidewalk because it was the hottest day of the year, so we didn't go in the house. We went home from that party together, and we sat on the couch, and then she said, "So I think you should kiss me," and I was like, thank God, and then a couple of minutes later she was like, "I think you should stay over." I thought we would just sleep there, all clothed, kind of fool around a little and go to sleep. Oh, no, she had other ideas! It was great. I was sure she had had a lot of experience because she seemed to know exactly what she was doing, but she didn't. She had no clue, and I had very little clue, and it was wonderful.

I don't think I could have imagined what sex would be like with a woman until I had it. Coming out as a lesbian had more to do with the realization that my life with a woman makes more sense to me than my life with a man, rather than sex is my life and therefore I'll choose the group with whom sex is better. I haven't had a lot of sex or sexual experiences, and so it hasn't been a central point in my life, and so many other things have been. Sex with my boyfriend was fun, but it wasn't special; it felt good, but it wasn't sacred. There were no fireworks, and I wanted fireworks. I could orgasm with a man or with a woman as long as they were doing the right thing and taking their time, but for me it's just so much more special to make love to a woman.

I had my first real boyfriend in high school, and we fooled around a lot. It was fun—we did the whole "my bra's off and his mom's in the next room" thing. I remember once he was about to come. He was like, "You have to stop right now"—he thought I would be really grossed out by the mess. He ran off to the bathroom. I was in eleventh grade—I should have understood what was going on, but I didn't. I never felt pressured sexually. One time he joked, "Oh, my god, you're going so fast, should I go out and get the condoms?" and I was kind of like, "Yeah," but he didn't, and it was fine that we didn't.

I probably always had crushes on women but didn't know it. There was, of course, the third-grade teacher who was just the greatest and who I wanted to be. She was a Ms., not a Miss or Mrs., and I loved that. And then I read this Ann Landers article by a thirteen-year-old girl who said, "Ann, I have a crush on my best friend. Does this make me a lesbian?" And Ann said, "You're thirteen, you're much too young, you're probably straight, every girl has crushes on her best friend, you'll get over it, you're not a lesbian." I was in second grade, and I panicked. I decided it was wrong for me to be holding hands and kissing my best friend and it might mean I'm a lesbian even though Ann says it probably doesn't. Recently, I was talking to this woman I was dating who had read the response to that same letter. The girl had grown up and written back to

Ann as an adult woman and said, "Ann, you fucked up my life. I am a lesbian. I knew it when I was thirteen—why couldn't you help me deal with it then?"

So anyway, I read that letter and decided that being lesbian was wrong. Then one summer after camp I got this phone call. It was probably a prank call, but I wasn't thinking along those lines. My brother answered the phone, and someone said, "Can I talk to your sister?" so he put me on the phone. The woman said, "Hi, how are you!? Do you remember me—long, dark hair from camp?" and so of course I pulled out my counselor from camp who had long, brown hair. The woman started talking to me, and she was like, "Have you ever thought of being with a girl like with a boy?" The person with long, dark hair from camp was a lesbian so I figured of course she would be talking to me about girls. It got to the point where I was in my mom's bedroom—she was like, "Go somewhere you can be private," and I thought it was my camp counselor so of course I'm going to. Then she basically said, "Pull down your panties and touch yourself." At that point I was like, "No, I'm not comfortable doing that, and I'm going to say good-bye now," and I hung up on her.

I remember thinking for so long that it was the most significant thing that happened to me. It was the big secret I wouldn't tell people until I knew them really well. I called my mom into her room and I told her what had just happened, and she freaked out, and she called my camp, and they probably fired my counselor. What the camp said that really stuck with me for a long time was, "No, we don't have counselors like that. We don't have lesbian or gay counselors." And, in fact, I think probably almost every counselor there was gay—it was an arts camp. The Ann Landers article and then my summer camp saying that they wouldn't have gay people working there, those were my first associations with being gay, and the message was that being gay was bad. It didn't occur to me for the longest time that I could be like that because I was good, not bad.

And then in high school my best friend, Soojin—oh, I still have a crush on her—she and I had a friend named Sean, and the three of us were inseparable. I was at school with the kids of South American dictators and the kids of big drug dealers, too. There are stories about parties where people would take cocaine, spread it around the floor, crawl around and sniff it up. There were gun and drug dealers at my school, but everyone thought that because it was a nice little private school there was none of that going on. I stayed away from all of that, and Sean, Soojin, and I only talked to each other.

Sean decided he was in love with me but mostly because he couldn't date my best friend. She was from a strict Korean family and basically couldn't date anybody. I remember walking down the beach holding her hand, telling her and her telling me how romantic it was. Her hair is beautiful and down to her waist, and it was jet black, and it shone like the sunlight. I had a big crush on her, and I don't think I really knew it. My English teacher might have known it. He basically talked me out of dating Sean. He said, "What do you need him for?"

I remember walking across the quad one day during the first month of my first year at college thinking, "This is such a wonderful and accepting place, and I probably won't come out until I leave." I just had that thought, and then I put it aside. I met this guy, and I started dating him. He'd had two girlfriends before me, and they were both bisexual. He told me one night, "Amy, you're the first straight woman I've dated." I was across the room, and I just kind of laughed. I was like, "I have to go to the bathroom." I couldn't be like, "Well, actually I don't know why I'm dating you because I'm a lesbian."

While I was dating him, I realized that I really couldn't deal with getting married and having kids with a man. If he would say something about having kids, I would just think, "Not with you." He would start talking about forever, and I just couldn't imagine it. It wasn't that I didn't want a future with him, I didn't want a future like he was describing at all. The whole heterosexual fantasy. Get married, be a couple, have kids—he would be a supportive husband and do with the kids as much or more than I would, cook and clean and all that, and I would be able to have my career—he would "permit me" to.

I was in love, but I knew I couldn't be with him in the future. Over the summer I was still dating him technically, and I lived in Washington D.C., and I started having all these crushes on women. I got back to school, and I told my boyfriend that I had to date other people, and we broke up.

And then I had this huge religious crisis, which was all wound up in my coming out as a lesbian. My boyfriend and I had always gone to the campus Hillel together. We got such straight Jewish couple privilege there, and it was wonderful. We were sent to a really amazing professor's house once for Passover, probably because we were a couple and they wanted to encourage that.

And then all of a sudden I stopped going to Hillel. I couldn't deal with Judaism anymore because it's so patriarchal. I couldn't read the Bible and think that it was talking to me. I couldn't deal with the historical inconsistencies with the religion and with what I knew really went on in the world, and I couldn't deal with the male-dominated history and the male-dominated services and the way that the prayers are.

I go to services at a Chavurah now, which is very community oriented. It's very grating to call God him all the time and to refer to God's followers as men, so they change the language of most of the prayers not only in English but also in the Hebrew. And I really like that a lot, and it makes me feel like there's a place for me here to be Jewish. Somebody asked me once, "Why the hell do you have a religion? You don't believe in it—it's total bullshit." I said, "I guess I'm Jewish because for some reason for four thousand years or two thousand years or even one thousand years or whenever it was that someone in my family decided to be Jewish, somebody's managed to be Jewish, and it hasn't been easy." My family left Russia because of the pogroms. I can't just give up being Jewish without a really good reason. And sometimes I really wish I could, because I have huge problems with it, and I feel a lot like I'm fighting with it all the time.

There was this one pivotal weekend in college when it all came out, so to speak. I started by talking to the chaplain of my college. I said, "You're a woman, and you're religious. How do you deal?" And she told me stories for an hour. Then I went to visit Abigail, a very old friend of mine who lives in New York City. She's a ditz, and at lunch one day she was talking about how her ex-boyfriend had two earrings, one in each ear—does this mean that he's bisexual, and wouldn't that be disgusting? And I remember just being like, oh, my god, no, let's kill her now. I remember thinking that I could tell her that somebody she knew since she was five years old and probably likes is queer! But I didn't.

Then I met up with a really cool friend of mine who also lives in New York. The first thing I said to her was, "Oh, my god, you're a real person! All Abigail does is talk about hair and nails—it's horrible." We spent the day at the Museum of Modern Art, and as she was walking me back to the subway, I said, "You should come visit me. Abigail came and visited, and I found her a boyfriend! I can set you up with someone, too." And she was like, "Amy, you should know that I'm a lesbian," and I looked at her, and I said, "Yeah, me, too—we can find you someone." I tried to be totally cool with the fact that I had just come out to the very first person and meant it that time. I was really happy I did that. I felt alive. My mother kept asking me who the new guy in my life was. She was sure I had fallen head over heels in love just from talking to me.

I got really sick of my mom asking me about guys, so I finally told her, "Mom, I'm a lesbian," or I think I said, "I'm queer," and she said, "Don't ever use that word," and I said, "Okay, I'm a dyke," and she's like, "That's worse." It was horrible. The first thing she said was, "So you'll never be attorney general." This was right after Janet Reno got into all that. The message was basically: You're throwing your life away. She called me up one day and just said, "Don't get AIDS," and I said, "What are you talking about?" and she said, "You know, your toys." And I was thinking, "What toys?" And she was like, "You know, your sex toys." And I was just like, "I don't have sex toys." She freaked out. Gay=AIDS. And I was like, "You weren't all that concerned about AIDS when I was dating guys."

I came out to my dad very recently. I wasn't going to. I was really scared that he wouldn't let me see my half sisters. I was also afraid he would take away my tuition money. Then after I finished school, I was applying for some very obviously queer jobs, working for advocacy organizations. And so I told him, "I've got to tell you something, Dad. I'm a lesbian. You probably knew." And he was like, "Yeah, I probably did. Are you happy? Can I still dance at your wedding?" My father turned out to react much more acceptingly to my coming out than my mother did and than I thought he would because he's this crazy conservative Republican, although he's pretty liberal socially. It's really nice. There are still some things he can't deal with—he doesn't want to hear any details about how artificial insemination works!

My mother came to visit me last weekend, and she met my girlfriend. They didn't talk. I had told my mother she was my girlfriend, and she did not invite her anywhere. Once she said, "Well, do you want to invite anyone to dinner?" and I'm like, "Well, what do you mean?" and she said, "Well, I want to meet your friends." But she met Ellen, and she actually told me that we look really good together, which is kind of nice. She talked to all of my other friends a lot more, though. But part of that's because Ellen was terrified to meet my mom because I tell her all these stories about how crazy she is and the whole sex toys thing.

My mother doesn't tell me not to be a lesbian, but she really wishes I would date a man. I was at dinner, and she commented that my housemate Andy, who is a gay man, is gorgeous, and then she just kind of under her breath but not really said, "I don't understand." I looked at her, and I said, "What did you just say? I didn't hear you," and she was like, "Oh, nothing." At least she knows she shouldn't have said that. With time, she'll deal with it. We're pretty close, and she hasn't disowned me, and I haven't disowned her, and things are okay.

I Feel Very Close to Women

Nichelle Ellison

She was born in a small town in Georgia in 1968. (See also pp. 162 and 503)

There was one girlfriend I have been very close to, and I can remember our friendship was very important. We would have an argument, and it would hurt me worse than breaking up with a boyfriend. We're grown and separated—she is married—and we still talk to each other about any and everything.

Marquita Anderson

She was born in New Jersey in 1975 and is now a college student in Lansing, Michigan. She is African-American and was raised Baptist. Her mother was a paralegal, and her father was a longshoreman. They split up when she was four or five. (See also p. 383)

I knew all my life that I was a lesbian, but I thought maybe I could fool myself into being straight. I tried to do the things that I was supposed to do, and it just didn't make me happy. I did it, and I was pretty damn good at it, and my mom was convinced and my boyfriend was convinced, but I wasn't.

I think I was very pressured with men, sitting there making out, and he wanted to have sex but I didn't. In high school, you have everyone around you saying you're heterosexual. It's so easy to buy into it, and I totally did. My first relationship with a guy lasted about a year. I was seventeen. I liked him enough to want to have sex, but I didn't feel like it was for me. I didn't feel heterosexual, and here I was having heterosexual sex. I would not put that damn thing in my mouth. There was no way I was going to do that, and I never have.

In my head, I would always say, "Well, if I was a guy, I would go up to her, and I would say, 'da da da da.' If I was a guy, I'd do such and such and such." And one day, I was just like, I don't have to be a guy to do those things, and I guess that's when it really clicked. Relationships with men were disappointing sexually, emotionally, and in every way. I can't connect with men the way I can connect with a woman. Men don't even know who they are because society has set up and they buy into this idea of what a man is. Not showing much emotion, being an asshole.

My second relationship with a guy, he was your typical sensitive male. He was a nice guy, but he still did fucked-up guy things. He cheated on me. And the guy before that, he would always make me feel insecure about my weight. Like, "Oh, you're getting kind of fat," or "What's wrong with your hair today?" I see that happening so much in heterosexual relationships. I just observe how the woman is so insecure about her own beauty, her own thoughts, her self and becomes dependent on this guy to validate that what she's doing is okay because he criticizes it so much. Her standards of what she is are based on what he thinks she should be.

Jillian Schwartz

She was born in 1973 in upstate New York. Her father was a carpenter. (See also p. 166)

My first sexual experiences were with girls. I had this friend when I was five, and we used to pretend, "You be the boy and I'll be the girl." We would get naked. I would get really excited before I went to her house because I knew eventually it would happen. It would take a long time. We would start playing with Strawberry Shortcake dolls and make them kiss. We would get ourselves sort of worked up, and then by the end we would roll around on the floor together. I remember we would put a sheet between us, and it was kind of arousing. I've shut it out for so long, and then I finally remembered one day that I used to do that. Now I see this girl, and she is really normal. I think if I ever said anything to her like, "Remember this?" she would just freak out. We broke off after elementary school. Now she is just someone I see around town when I go home.

It seems like a lot of girls I've talked to have had similar things. They played that game when they were little. I have one girlfriend that is a lesbian, and most of my girlfriends have had some sort of homosexual encounter or experience. My relationships with women are very important. I feel like it is just much easier. I feel, in a way, if it wasn't for that sexual thing, that I would just be with women all the time.

I have a best friend, a soul mate, and we are just so close. I think we love each other very deeply, and we have this joke about how when we are forty, we are going to live together and just grow old. I was in this really bad relationship, and she was in a really bad relationship, so we kind of bonded out of that and became really close. I've always felt like she is the most beautiful person I know, physically and in every way. We've been in the shower together, but I'm very afraid of anything happening.

The girl I live with, we have had some really beautiful experiences together that I feel I could probably only have with girls. Bonding. We've never kissed or touched each other or anything, but she's gotten in the bathtub with me. She had an experience with a girl. I'm not sure what happened exactly, but she was kind of freaked out. This girl came to visit her that she had been friends with, and they ended up being in bed together sexually. When it comes down to it, I don't know if I could do that at this point in my life. I feel very close to women and I can hug them and I think their bodies are beautiful, but the idea of carrying out the sex part just turns me off immediately.

Jennifer Kramer

She was born in New York City in 1976. (See also p. 204)

Let me tell you something about girls. A lot of girls are very spiteful and deceiving. I've noticed that. Believe you me, I could trust guys a whole lot more. Girls are your friend one day and then leave you the next. I don't need that. I have one girl who is my only true friend. I can make a jerk of myself with her, and she's not going to sit there and ridicule me.

Elizabeth Ives

She was born in 1970 in a small, black, working-class neighborhood in the Northeast. She has just finished art school and lives in a large city. (See also p. 385)

I guess I "came out" two or three years ago. I went away to Africa and did a study abroad. I had an experience with a woman there. We met, and she assumed that I was a lesbian because the friends that I was hanging out with—African-American women who were in another program—were lesbians. We frequented the club scene, and on one particular night a friend of mine said, "I don't even want to deal with this dating thing or this small talk." She went up to this beautiful woman and said, "Do you fuck men or women? I just want to know." And the woman said, "Sometimes men, and sometimes women." My friend said, "Well, we're going to invite you to our house. Come over, we just want to hang out."

We were hanging out a lot. We had this beach party, and that night everybody was getting romantic, traipsing off to their bedrooms hand in hand with people they previously hated. Then it was just her and I. I'm twiddling my thumbs, like, "Well, there is no one else left, it is just you and me." She leaned over and kissed me, and it was a very good kiss. We fooled around a bit, and I think for the most part I was in shock. I was like, "What does this mean?" I really had to figure this out because I was like, "I'm not a lesbian, damnit." It was my own homophobia coming out. But I didn't want to lead her on, so I told her I wasn't a lesbian, and she was like, "After the past hour, now you're telling me you're not lesbian." Obviously, she didn't take me seriously.

The next day I told my friends, and they were like, "We knew all along you were a lesbian." So I'm thinking and I'm realizing that what allowed me to continue that night, while shocked, was because I had always had crushes on women, had always wanted to be physical with women but didn't feel it was an option. In a way, I came out to myself as bisexual. But I didn't want to say anything to anybody because I kept thinking, "Well, maybe it is just this relationship." And I didn't want to be dishonest about it because it seems like bisexuality is the cool thing to do—people go, "I'm bisexual, and I'm so free that I can be bisexual"—and I didn't want to be part of that.

I felt that when you are away from everybody and everything you knew before, you tend to act differently. You experiment, because there is no one to say, "Well, that's not like you at all." I came back to the United States, and I was still very attracted to women, so I figured it was a lasting thing. My friends knew, or if I got involved with a man, I would say to him, "Just to let you know, I'm bisexual." I didn't tell my mother. I had a friend who said, "It's not like you have ever had a conversation about sex with your mother before, so why start now?"

But, unfortunately, I was very excited about the possibility of getting published. A professor of mine who wrote for a gay and lesbian publication was leaving town, and the AIDS Act Up chapter of the city where I went to college was in town doing a bus campaign. They needed somebody to write about it in this paper. And she was like, "Well, you can do it." She told me that I could get one hundred dollars for doing this damn article, and I said, "I'll be there." I was thrilled, and she said, "You realize that you are going to be 'published.'" That's supposed to be an exciting thing. And I was like, "Oh, my god!"

I didn't think "gay and lesbian publication" because it is so much me now. I include my mother in everything, and it didn't occur to me until after I was already on the phone babbling that she was gonna think, "Well, why are you writing for a gay and lesbian publication?" I was just like, "Mom, guess what, I'm going to be published . . . dadada, and the gay and lesbian . . . dadada," and she was like, "*What?*" and then it was just like, "Red alert, Elizabeth."

I always thought to myself that if she ever asked me straight out, thinking that she never would, I would tell the truth. So when she said, "Are you a lesbian?" I was like, "Phew." It never occurred to me that she would ask me if I were bisexual, but she did, and it shocked me, and I said, "Yes" and she was very upset. Ms. Southern Christian Baptist woman, she was very upset.

Her voice got very hoarse, and I thought she was going to cry. I said, "If you're going to cry, I'm hanging up the phone right now and you can call me back if you have any questions." I was sweating bullets. I figured she couldn't really handle this one. She was like, "Why would you want to do that?" and "How did I bring you up wrong?" And I was like, "I don't want to have this discussion, so I'll talk to you later." Got off the phone, and I had told the truth. I think she is in denial. I have no idea what would happen if I got into a serious relationship with a woman. I think she would flip. But she is very resilient. Her daughters are so important to her that I think she would accept it. She always comes back. She always does the right thing.

My Grandmother Raised Me
to Cook and Clean

Abby Soong

She lives in the Northwest with her husband and works for a company that develops games for children and adults. "I like working for them because the games are nonviolent and nonsexist. I paint backgrounds for the games, and I scan them in. I do animations and 3-D modeling. I'm also working on illustrating a children's book.

"I was born in California in 1961. My parents were born in China. They came over here when they were about sixteen. I have two brothers and one sister who is handicapped. I'm the oldest, and I was really lucky because my parents let me go to art school and were supportive. It was very rare for Asian parents to accept that. My friends were pushed into becoming lawyers, doctors, engineers, pharmacists. A lot of our culture is you want to have kids so your kids can be successful. How much money they make shows face and more respect for the family. I would just draw, draw, ever since I was in junior high. I knew I would be an artist. If they wanted to go into art, most people's parents would try to urge them to go into architecture. It sounds very good, 'Oh, my son's an architect, my daughter's an architect.' My parents wanted me to be happy and to make money enough to survive." (See also p. 382)

My grandmother, my father's mother, practically raised me because my mom was too busy having my brothers and sisters. She lived with us. It's traditional that when your parents get old, you're supposed to take them into your home. My grandmother was really proud that all of us went to college, but going to art school she thought was a complete waste of time. She goes, "What are you going to do with your art?" To this day, she still doesn't really understand that I'm making money and I love what I'm doing. She still goes, "When are you going to get a real job?"

She raised me to cook and clean, traditional Chinese, you gotta learn how to be a good wife. She would constantly try to get me to look better, to act like a woman—"Don't speak up, don't make any waves, be nice, do what the man says." When it comes to dating, it's like, no way. There's no kissing, no hugging—the romancing, that's after you get married. My grandmother also thought since I was the oldest, I was the caretaker of my brother and sister. So it's been ingrained in me, I was to be the strong person to hold up and take care of people and never complain.

The traditional mothers, their whole lives were devoted to raising their children. The mothers who were born in the U.S. were not so traditional. They tend to care about themselves more, to spend a little money on themselves and to dress better. My mother always wore hand-me-downs or sewed her own clothes, and my grandmother sewed clothes for her. They didn't believe in buying store-bought clothes—"Oh, it's too much money, it's too much money." It was the same with my friends' mothers. They didn't dress in fashion. They didn't wear any high heels. They never went out.

If you can't get food in Chinatown, go to Safeway but clip out the coupons. If we went on a vacation, we all slept in the station wagon—four kids and Grandma and my parents! I must have been ten or twelve, we went up to Vancouver and back; we only stayed at a motel twice.

I found out later that they hoarded all that money for college. My dad invested in stocks. They're pretty well off, considering that we lived so poorly. They would scrimp and save like twenty or thirty years of their life just so they could send their kids to college.

In my whole life I never heard them say go ahead—like if I wanted a new bike, they would say you have to buy what's cheaper. But when I went to college—books, school, it was like the sky's the limit. Except that I couldn't go away to school. They had to pay for my brothers and my sister to go to college, too. I lived at home and worked part-time, never stayed in a dorm, and so I was really happy when my sister got to go to a special college for the handicapped on the East Coast. I remember the day that she went. I felt I sacrificed for somebody; it was worth it.

I was probably one of three Asians in my class in my grammar school, and I remember being made fun of a lot. It was very painful. One time before I went to Sunday school, my Catholic friends said something about "Hail Mary and Jesus," and I said, "Who's Jesus?" and they started laughing. They said, "You don't know anything because you're Chinese." When everyone played cowboys and Indians, I would always be made the Indian because of my black hair. I'd go, "I'm never a cowboy, I'm never a cowboy, I want to be a cowboy." "No, you can't—you have black hair, you have to be an Indian." So they would braid my hair and shoot me, and I said, "I don't want to die. I don't want to die." "You have to cause you have black hair." Not all of the kids were doing this—just some that I thought were my friends. Later, I didn't experience too much discrimination because more Asians were coming to the area.

I went to Sunday school and to a church community organization. They have a youth program including a Friday night club. I had a really tough time at both. They used to call me Mouse at the Friday night club because I never said anything. When they asked me to read aloud, I would almost pee in my pants. I was scared that somebody might notice me. I was so mad that I couldn't speak up in front of people because my grandmother taught me to be very quiet, nice, polite. You don't want to make waves.

I really grew a lot in church group. It helped me accept being Asian as well as American because most of the kids there are from the same background, where you have very traditional Asian parents, and yet you are American. They helped mesh the two together. They made me feel like it was okay to be both. As I got older, I was a day-camp leader, a camp counselor, a camp director, and then became a department director. I didn't quit until I was about twenty-seven. I wanted to share my growth with kids to help them accept that mix. It's good to be Asian; it's good to be American.

I was taken advantage of a lot. On the bus, men would put their hand on my butt—they would molest me. Somebody would sit next to me and have his hand on my thigh, just rubbing. I was embarrassed, shocked, but I couldn't get out because it would be embarrassing if people saw me stand up and draw attention to myself. It was awful. It happened at least ten times, especially as a teenager. I couldn't bring myself to say, "Hey, get your hand off my butt, get your hand out of my boobs," because I wasn't brought up to speak up. I'm tired of being shy and taking it. I still have a fear of being on crowded buses. I always wonder what I would say now if somebody ever did anything. It hasn't happened lately.

Most of the men were Caucasian or black. One Chinese guy—really pissed me off, too. I used to go to this store in Chinatown after day camp, and I was like in sixth grade, and I asked for some help—I couldn't get the freezer door open. The store owner came up behind me, and he opened the freezer, and he pushed his whole body against me, and I thought, "Oh, my god, he's going to push me in the freezer," but no, he was rubbing himself against me. I was by myself, and I didn't know what to do, so I tried to weasel my way out of it. He had the glass door against me, and I was trapped. I just froze, and I was trying to get out, and I remember I said, "Oh, my god, get me outta here, get me outta here," and I just finally clawed myself out. I was more shocked than anything, and I cried, I felt so ashamed. All the times I've been molested I always felt it was my fault. I thought if I ever told my parents, they would say, "What were you wearing?" Or my grandmother, she would say, "Well, you shouldn't have been wearing pants so tight." To this day my parents don't know.

Later, I found out my friends had these problems, too. I really think that these men pick on Asian girls because they know that we won't say anything. We all felt so angry after we discussed it. Now we're beginning to say we're not going to let this happen anymore. But when you're younger and raised traditionally, it's really tough. You haven't yet discovered that, hey, I can speak up. I have a friend who was raped, and she still hasn't told anybody. I think that they're still doing it now especially with the new immigrants that come over. They're very traditional. It's hard for Asian women to tell anybody, much less the police, because it's very humiliating. I'm really glad that there is a new shelter for Asian women who have been raped and need a place to go.

My maternal grandmother and grandfather hate each other very much. Theirs was an arranged marriage. There's no love between them, and they don't believe in divorce. My grandfather never beat my grandmother, thank God. He does his own thing; she does her thing. It shows in my mom. She's very disaffectionate. I don't know if my mom was hit by my grandmother, I'm not sure. I wouldn't doubt it, though, because I was beaten a lot as a kid, too, by my parents, by my grandmother.

Two years ago I went to therapy because for about twelve years I had these awful, awful nightmares about darkness and lots of blood and ropes and being buried alive and suffocating, and I couldn't figure out why. After a few months of therapy I realized it was a mental block. I just did not want to remember the years that I was beaten. I'm able to talk about it now.

If I was really bad—if I didn't come home for dinner on time, if I talked back to my parents, or if I was very mad, I would throw things, damage the furniture—I remember being tied at my feet and my arms around my back and I was thrown into the closet. I think I was about six or seven years old. The closet was dark, and it was suffocating. I would just scream, scream, scream and say, "Get me outta here" and try to kick the door down, and finally they had to gag me so I couldn't scream. They did that many times. I couldn't eat dinner. I was starving, and they would just leave me in there until I finished screaming.

I was scared of the dark, and they knew it. I thought there were demons, ghosts, in me. I thought there were skeletons in the closet trying to grab at me. My grandmother would always tell me ghost stories about bad children. If you're really bad, the demons will come and take you and never allow you to come back with your family—so I was horrified. After a while they stopped throwing me in the closet—I guess I was about eight—and I remember just being whipped and beaten. I'd rather be beaten than thrown in the closet. My grandmother actually didn't beat me too much. It was mostly my mom and dad. After I got my whipping, I would have to stand there in the corner and watch everybody eat.

I'd sneak out of the house sometimes to play with some friends. One time my mother caught me, and I was so mad—I said I can go to my friend's house any time. They don't start dinner without everyone being there, and everyone was waiting for me. She was furious; she took her fist and went *wham,* and there was blood all over the wall because she hit my nose. A lot of my nightmares have blood in them—the blood would be coming out of the ceiling, and I had to get away from this blood and I couldn't move because my hands and my feet were all tied up. I was struggling on the floor.

My mother never gave me any hugs—she never told me that she loved me—but she would always hug my brothers. My dad was affectionate, gave me hugs, always told me he loved me. So I would talk to my dad. We fought a lot, but we got along.

My brother got beaten the same way, but he didn't get thrown in the closet. I think I was the only one. They never punished my sister. They felt she was punished by being handicapped. They never laid a hand on her. And then my little brother, he always gets away with murder.

It took me a while to tell about this because I love my parents very much. They never hit each other. For a Chinese family, they were very affectionate with each other. They would always cuddle. When they were watching TV, my dad would be kissing my mom. It was great. I knew that they loved each other. I do think that my father was the one who gave her the affection. She would always sit there and go, "Oh, stop it, stop it." I really think it's because my grandmother and grandfather had no love between them. I think my mom got beaten. That's why I'm afraid to have children because I'm afraid of doing the same thing. I see the cycle happening from generation to generation, and I want it to stop here. My dad would occasionally hit my dog, and I just cringed, and I'd go, "No, don't hit animals." They don't know what they're doing. I think it is possible to break cycles.

By my teenage years, something happened where my mom threatened my dad with divorce, and we had no idea where it came from. We all went to family counseling, and my dad and mom have changed greatly. My mom's become more open with me. I initiated it. I wanted to know her. I wanted to know where I came from and how I got these feelings. Some parts she still won't talk about. I started asking her questions, and we stayed up till three in the morning talking about sex. I was sixteen. She said she'd prefer me to wait till I was married, but if I was going to, she said the best thing is for the guy to use a condom. "If he doesn't use a condom, don't do it. But whatever you do, do it discreetly. We don't want our friends or the community to know." My dad sat me down one day. He said, "This may be kind of embarrassing, but I'll say it anyway. Whatever you do, be discreet and don't get pregnant." He got up, and he walked away. You don't do anything that would disgrace your family. I found that to be the same among my friends.

When I was sixteen, seventeen, I had a boyfriend. We waited until our second year before we even talked about sex. Sometimes we'd be really passionate, and then it was, "Oh, no, we should wait," and then one day we just said, "Well, let's talk about this—do we want to have sex? Will we tell our parents?" My parents were open; his parents were not. Would we have to lie all the time? We decided to go ahead with it. I told my mom that we were thinking about having sex. And she was, "Well, don't do it if you haven't done it," and I said, "Well, we're thinking about it, Mom, and if we do it, then I don't want to hide anything from you," and that was my first time I ever really opened up to her. That's when I was starting to come out of myself and not be shy anymore, and I'm still working on it to this day. I got to the point where I would be totally honest, and she would be totally honest with me even if we disagree. I thought that was a very rare thing for me to do, especially with Asian parents who are very traditional.

After they met Stefan, they knew he was a good guy. I thought that I was very lucky to be born in that family with my mom and dad being so open. He stayed over my house a lot of times. My parents didn't like it, but they accepted it because they would rather have me be open and honest. This is America. America thinks differently than China. They're influenced by that. My grandmother totally thought I was a slut. She would not talk to me every time he stayed over. She would just be so mad—"How dare you? How could you?" But I said, "Look, that's the way I want to live my life."

The Last Virgin
on Flatbush Avenue

Jackie Preston

She was born in 1968 in the rural Northeast. She attended public schools.
"My dad's Catholic, and my mom's Episcopalian."

*W*hen you were like ten, in fifth grade, they show you this movie. My mom never really talked to us about it at all. She gave me Judy Blume's book *Are You There God? It's Me, Margaret,* and she thought I'd come to her afterwards with all these questions, but I didn't. We'd never really been open about sex, so I didn't feel comfortable. I just talked to friends at school. I was one of the last of all my friends, so I knew everything by the time I got my period. My friends would all put maxi-pads in their socks, because we didn't have pocketbooks.

When I finally told my mother, I was embarrassed. She called my aunt and said, "Jackie got her friend." That's what she called it—your friend. She ran over to my aunt's house and came home with this big box of pads. That's all I really remember. I doubt my father knew. He would never say a word to me about it.

Colleen McCarthy

She worked as a model for a few years and is now a college student. She was born in the Midwest in 1970, the youngest of eight children in an Irish Catholic family. She attended Catholic schools. (See also p. 522)

*W*e were taught that sex outside of marriage was a sin. They showed us very graphic abortion films, about babies being cut up and being taken out of the mother, to scare us away from having sexual relations. I used to think about sex all the time, and I would think, "Am I really going to wait until I get married?" I was brought up that you don't do anything before you get married, and I thought that everybody did that.

I remember I was really surprised one day because one of the popular girls was really touched—I don't know if touched is the right word, but—by one of these abortion films. She was kind of frightened, and she said, "I'm never going to have sex." That affected her—that worked. I think that in our school there were more girls that wouldn't have sex than there would be in a public school. It was much more accepted and normal to wait. It was more the people that didn't wait that were the outsiders. And then my friend who was so innocent told me that she had sex, and I was so surprised. That was probably just before senior year, but then other friends of mine did it, and I did eventually.

I remember being in psychology class sophomore year of high school and the teacher mentioned that masturbation was a sin, and I turned to one girl and I said, "Oh, wow—I'm a real sinner." Even though I try to ignore my Catholic upbringing, I still have a lot of those things ground into me. The Catholic church is known for making people feel guilty. They're very good at it. I still have it in me that it's a sin.

Angela Walker

She was born in New York City in 1975. She works two jobs and begins college in the fall.

"My father is black, and my mother is mixed, Puerto Rican and black, so I guess I'm in there someplace." (See also p. 151)

When I first started talking to a guy, I was too young. I was like twelve. And I had to sneak it from my mother. Living in the building, I was friends with everybody. My mother let everybody come in and watch TV or just hang in the hallway or whatever. So it was one of my friend's friends, how we met. He was nineteen, but I never knew that because he looked so young. We'll sit in the hallway having a nice conversation. I guess he started it. I didn't know how to talk to a boyfriend.

We'll sit on the bed—if he gets too close, I'm moving over. If we kissed, it was like a tap. I thought he was my boyfriend, but we was friends. We'll go to the movies, he'll take me to eat. When I found out his age, I knew I should have left him alone, but by that time I was liking him too much. Things worked out for a little while. But then when I kissed him, things led one to another. I turned fourteen, decided I wanted to sleep with him. He didn't pressure me into it, but I knew that he wanted to do it, so I more pressured myself. I guess it was all right. People say it hurts the first time, but it didn't really bother me, it was just something that was done.

So many things changed after that. Every time he came by, it was like that was all he wanted to do. At the time he was selling drugs. When I was younger, if a guy was selling drugs, he was just the best. If you wasn't talking to a drug dealer, you just was not down with the crew. At that time, you get all the wrong images.

For a little while, he would call me like everything was fine. But as time went on, calls got shorter. He'll call me this month, he won't call until three months later. And I'm like, What's going on? Then I'm thinking, well, since he was selling drugs, maybe he's in jail. But then he's calling me, "What's up? How ya doin'?" I'm like, if you just came out of jail, you supposed to be kind of mellow or something—you just called me like you was partying. I'm like, "I'm fine. What happened to your calls? I didn't speak to you for three months."

And for a while, I let it go because I was so young and stupid at the time. And then finally I said, I made a big mistake, and I have to cut it out now. So I finally told him, "This is not the way it's gonna be. We have to leave each other alone." I always had older friends, and I told them how he doesn't call me and when he comes over, we sleep together and that's it—he'll go about his business. They said, "He's dogging you—you don't let nobody dog you like that."

I wouldn't tell my mother that I had slept with him so early. But when she found out I was talking to him, she had a fit and told me I will never see him again. She went off. I don't think she even knew then that he was dealing drugs, but she knew his age, and his age just freaked her out. When she found out I was sneaking to see him, she'd let me have it. But after a while she said she didn't want me to sneak off and she didn't want him to do anything to me where I'm scared to tell her, so she kind of let up. She let us see each other and always told me, "If he ever does anything to you, you let me know." She was stuck between a rock and a hard place.

Amy Claire

She was born in the Deep South in 1969. She was a debutante.

The first date I ever went on, we went to freshman Homecoming together. We had parents driving us. I was fourteen years old. It was a nightmare because we had dinner and the waiter spilled spaghetti down my back, right before the dance. I didn't know how to say, "Ouch, my back is burning!" I wasn't that comfortable. I just went "Huh!"

because it was kind of hot, and my date asked me a little bit later, "Did he spill spaghetti on you?" and I said, "Yeah," and the waiter found out, and we ended up getting our dinner for free.

You can drive here when you are fifteen. My grandparents bought me a brand-new car for my birthday. I was spoiled rotten. I went through a stage my freshman and sophomore year where from Friday to Sunday I would drink and drink and drink. I never got a DWI, I never endangered anyone else, but I would drink and drive. One Sunday morning I woke up and looked in the mirror and said to myself, "This is what your dad has done all his life—you know you're gonna do it, too!" and I quit abusing it.

I was friends with a guy named Glenn, and he had a big crush on me. One night I was babysitting, and he asked me where I was gonna be. He drove up and down the street until he found my car, and he showed up with two friends. I said, "What are you doing here? I've been babysitting for this lady for years, and she is gonna think that I have boys over all the time." She always came home early. Anyway, I knew one of the friends Glenn brought over, and I used to always joke and flirt with him. He was my height, and he was no one I would ever be interested in. But he brought along his best friend, Curran. I had never seen Curran until this night.

About two or three weeks later, he called me, and we went out on a date. That was it. I dated Curran for five years. I was sixteen. It was a very serious relationship. We got drunk on senior prom and things like that, but not regularly.

I wouldn't sleep with him because I was raised that you be the big virgin when you are married. We did "everything but"—we were horny little kids. It would always stop at the point of intercourse. There was never pressure. Curran loved me very much, and he was always concerned with what I felt comfortable with. He always respected the fact that I wouldn't want to sleep with him. He would get upset with me, though, when I wouldn't get involved. I can remember him telling me, "You need to pay attention—you're thinking about other things."

He was a virgin, and he thought that that was a big deal when he came to college. He and I argued a lot over it. We both went to our state school. I never really got into the Greek scene. My family was always very much into who's who and being a big socialite. It never has made a difference to me. Curran joined a fraternity, and he met this girl. She had a boyfriend that she had dated for a long time just like he had me, and they did the sleep-together thing and kept their relationships on the side. I found out, and I was devastated. I told him off.

Time went on, and we got back together, and he apologized repeatedly and begged forgiveness, but things were never the same. It was very distant. Then I guess about a year or two later he joined the Marine Corps. While he was in boot camp, Desert Storm started. I was devastated. Even though I knew he wasn't the right person for me, I still loved him. He and I talked a lot about marriage during that time. Absence makes the heart grow fonder. Once, when he came home from the Marine Corps, we had intercourse. I was twenty-two years old. I enjoyed it—I was in love with him, I had missed him so much, and that's what I wanted to do. I knew when I had sex with him that our relationship was over, but I wanted him to be my first. It was important to me. He was such a big part of my life.

Deb Bruckner

She is a college sophomore and was born in Maryland in 1973. Her parents divorced when she was thirteen.

"*I've got a completely Jewish background, Eastern European.*"

My uncle's company built a hotel a few blocks from where my apartment was, and when I got sick or annoyed with my mother, or if I needed to go and have fun, I would get a room there. I could go whenever I wanted to. I would watch HBO and have room service. One night, this guy I vaguely knew was passing through and needed a place to stay. I let him stay there, and we had sex. I was sixteen. I'd kissed people before, but that was the first time I ever did anything more. I always had this idea that the first time I had sex was going to be with someone I really didn't know at all. It was just going to be a one-night stand, and then after that I would wait a long time before having sex with someone that I really cared about and that meant something to me. And that's exactly the way it happened.

I'd never actually met him face-to-face. I just met him the day before we had sex. I only knew him over the phone. I'm on this information service on the computer, and they had this CB thing where you can talk to people all over the country. We just started talking in there, and he gave me his phone number. I thought he was interesting. One of those crazy things. He ended up in an insane asylum after that. He was let off somewhere to get his head together.

It wasn't physically brilliant, but after he left I was like, "God, I should feel guilty about this" and then I was like, "Well, I don't." In this society you're not supposed to have sex with someone you just met, but as far as I was concerned it wasn't anything. I had never seen him before, and I'll probably never see him again. There didn't seem to me to be anything to feel guilty about. I'd done it safely. I was very nervous about getting pregnant or getting sick. He'd been around a little bit, but before we had sex I asked him very thoroughly what his deal was because, you know, the whole AIDS thing.

Rachel Goldman

She was born in New York City in 1970.

"My parents are still married, incredibly enough. They both always worked. They are Jewish, both reform. We weren't very religious growing up, but definitely more so than people I knew." (See also p. 541)

*I*n the beginning, my parents were pretty open. I had all these books with illustrations of people's bodies with correct anatomical parts. They were sixties and seventies folks in that way. I always thought that my mother was the kind of mother that I could go to and say, "Mom, will you take me to the gynecologist." But sure enough, she wasn't at all. A lot of that was her thinking that she was this very liberated person, when really she felt extremely threatened by the idea that I was having sex and was totally closed off to giving me any kind of support. I think that was the first time that I realized that my mother was a person and wasn't my mother only.

When I was younger, I really aspired to thinking of sex as something that was just an act in and of itself. Some people think of it that way, and I think that that's fine, but for me it really isn't. Sex requires a physical intimacy that I personally can't feel comfortable with unless I feel comfortable with that person emotionally, socially, and personally.

There have definitely been times in my life when I felt, "Well, I should be enjoying this and I'm not! What's wrong with me?" Instead of just trying to assess better whether or not I wanted to be having the sex. That really happens to women. I don't have one friend who hasn't had some sexual experience she's totally regretted, and some much worse than others.

It's hard for women to find that line where you're saying, "Okay, I'm listening to myself. I'm listening to what I want." There are so many things that are going against women saying, "I don't want to do this" or "I do want to do this." That's something women struggle with their whole lives. I feel very good about myself now in terms of my sex life and making sure that I'm really there in the decision-making process. I've been very fortunate in a lot of ways. I know so many women who have been date raped, so many women who get pressured to have sex by their boyfriends, and that hurts me so much.

I think that there was a time historically only thirty years ago where women weren't supposed to have sex, and that was difficult, and that brought up a lot of issues about women's roles. Now that we've had our "sexual revolution," women are supposed to want to have sex all the time, and men are supposed to want to have sex all the time, and I don't think that anyone wants to have sex all the time. I think that men are pressured into this role of thinking that they have to want to have sex all the time or they're not manly, and now women have to have sex all the time so they're not frigid, but if they do have sex all the time, then they're sluts. So many women are trying not to be either one of those things that a lot of times the decision-making process is not about them, it's about pleasing their partner or making sure that they're not going to be seen in a way that they wouldn't want to be seen. I think that the sexual revolution will really have happened when men and women can honestly assess what kinds of sex they want to have and how often they want to have it, and I don't think that's happening any time soon. I'll be anxious to see that day.

Pat Jamison

She was born in 1962 and lives in a small town in New England. (See also p. 362)

I didn't go out with a lot of guys. I went out with one guy for like two years, and then I went out with another, and I got pregnant and had an abortion. When I got pregnant, he disappeared. And then I wanted nothing to do with men at all. I never wanted to have another abortion. I never had sex with anyone, not even with my husband until I married him. It was very hard, very scary. I was only sixteen. I never had surgery in my life. I'm at a clinic, and they're telling me, "Okay, we're going to give you needles of valium, and you'll feel this and you'll do that," and I was scared to death. It didn't bother me that I was having an abortion, because what am I going to do with a baby? I wasn't even out of high school. So I've never regretted it. Never. But I did not want it to happen again.

The girl laying in the bed next to me is what convinced me. She said, "Oh, I just can't do this again. They gave me a hard time this time." I said, "What do you mean?"

She said, "Well, this is my third one this year." I said, "This year?" And she said, "Yes, and they told me if I come here again, that they could not do it." And I just looked at her like, you've gone through this pain, this throwing up—the anesthesia wears off, you get sick—and I thought, you've done this three times this year? She was my age, sixteen, seventeen. I had an abortion once, and I will never do it again in my life.

Sarah Wells

She shares an apartment with her best friend in New York City's East Village.

"I'll tell you what I know. I was born in 1972 on kind of like a farm. My parents bought this piece of property, and they hippied out, walked around naked, golden babies, and gardened. We had some goats, we had some chickens, but it wasn't a producing farm. It was in the mountains of California, up north. There was no electricity, no telephone, and the midwife showed up I guess twenty minutes or half an hour before I was born. My mother's first child. It was kinda cool, I guess."

I've been a vegetarian for like ten years now, but when I was with my first boyfriend I started cutting things out of my diet really severely. Cutting meat out was not that severe to me—it made a lot of sense. But when I didn't want to be naked and didn't want to have sex because I was feeling really overweight and gross, it started becoming more of my life. I wasn't going to eat any potato chips, nothing deep fried—I wouldn't eat a french fry if somebody force-fed me. I cut out dairy from my diet. It was for animal benefits, but I used that to some extent as a front. It was really easy for me to let go of it for the cows' sake, and then I wouldn't have to eat pizza or lasagna or think about that.

I'd say to myself, "You can have a piece of toast in the morning, a piece of fruit in the afternoon, and then you can have dinner." I was on like a five-hundred-calorie diet and running eight miles a day and being on the basketball team and burning at least two thousand calories a day, working that night, and then having sex. I'd come home from work and I'd go over to my boyfriend's house, and then I'd drive home at like two in the morning and I'd sit up watching late-night TV doing four hundred sit-ups and then doing push-ups. I dropped weight really fast, and I got annoying encouragement from my mother or friends, "Wow, you look really great!"

I'd try as hard as I could to go to sleep hungry, to the sound of my stomach, and try and convince myself that that sounded really good. But I was not really thin, I was athletic so I was muscular.

The first time I had an orgasm, I will never forget this, I must have been like twelve. I was working out in my room, doing these leg exercises. And it just started feeling really good. I was only going to do one hundred, but I was up to like three hundred and I was still going. I had the most incredible sensation! It was completely confusing to me. I didn't think it was an orgasm, because I wasn't having sex. So every day from then on I was Miss Work-Out Queen.

As far as sex is concerned, I'm not the Multiple Orgasm Queen or anything. It can happen if I put my mind to it and I really want it. Maybe fifty percent of the time I'll give it that much energy, twenty-five percent of the time it'll happen by happenstance, but there are plenty of times where it'll just feel good, it's more of a game, it's not something where I'm striving to have an orgasm. So it has its place in sex, but it also has a very separate place.

I started having sex at a young age because I was totally in love with my first boyfriend, and my parents were like, "If it feels right, it feels right." He was a virgin, too. We were fourteen when we started going out. Time went on, and I turned fifteen. Valentine's Day weekend, his dad was gone, and we went out to dinner and went back to his apartment and had sex for the first time. Totally the best, most love-making thing, and in a big bed, music, lights, candles, it was totally sweet. What a neat first experience—there was not a doubt in my mind. Not one. When I'm dating a guy now, I've got a thousand times more doubts than I did that first time.

My whole sexual understanding and development and curiosity came right hand in hand with that boyfriend for years. And he was a really safe place for me to explore. There wasn't anything that I couldn't do or wouldn't do in his arms. A really comfortable first relationship. He hurt me a lot in the middle of it and towards the end, but as far as sex goes and balance, it was never like I was pressured into anything.

My bedroom was right underneath my parents' bedroom, and my boyfriend and I had some crazy experiences where we were kissing and making out and my parents would start having sex and the roof was going to cave in, and I'm like, "Fuck, I cannot be getting together with my boyfriend while my parents are having sex—this is way too weird!"

My grandmother came out to visit when I was like fifteen, and they'd joke about me dragging my boyfriend into the bedroom, but it really wasn't funny. But I guess it was. If my daughter were seeing some guy and totally in love with him and asked me if he could spend the night, what would I say? I don't know that it would be okay.

My parents were inviting it, because I had an older brother and he had a girlfriend who lived down the street, and her mother had just died. There were all these things going on, and she would spend the night. They'd get up in the morning and walk into the bathroom and take a shower together, and they'd come out and go to school. She was a freshman or a sophomore in high school and he was a junior, and I was eleven or twelve, and it's like, this is normal.

But then when it was my turn, my dad said my brother had some problems—he needed some love, he needed his girlfriend to spend the night. And I was like, "Dad, that's just a lame double standard." My boyfriend lived twenty minutes away by car, and it would be late, so for a little while he would stay the night in the living room, and I was like, "We make out, we do whatever we're going to do, and then at like three or four in the morning he goes to sleep in the living room so he can wake up in the living room. And then when my little brother and sister get up early in the morning, he comes back in bed with me so he can sleep. This is dumb." And my parents were like, "Yeah, it is kind of dumb. I guess we'll just have to accept his sleeping over and staying in your room."

Jennifer Kramer

She was born in New York City in 1976. She is Italian, Irish, and Scottish-American. At the time of the interview, she was two weeks shy of seventeen.

"My parents had to get married because my mother was pregnant with my brother. My mother was nineteen when she had me; my father was twenty. He was working with his father, a car mechanic. Until I was ten, my mother was always there, and when she started working, I missed her so much. But I was happy for her, you know. She got off; she was doing her own little thing. I was like, A+ for you, Ma." (See also p. 186)

*J*ust recently. Last week. Oh, god. I never thought I would, either. I thought I'd be the last virgin on Flatbush Avenue. Oh, my god. It was weird. It really was. I was like, "Ow"—that's all I kept saying—"Ow." I was like, "Okay, are you done now?" And he didn't say nothing. He was like, "What?" I was all embarrassed afterwards. I was like, doo doo doo doo doo. I felt so different afterwards. I was like, uh huh. Mmm hmm. Okay. It was weird. I'm glad I got the first time over with, though. I felt like I wasn't ever gonna do it. I was so nervous, shaking. I don't know what for. He was like, "Why are you so nervous?" I was like, "Cause this is the first time for me! Jesus, what do you think, it's easy to hop into bed? I mean, come on!"

I thought about it for a very long time. Even when we were going, I thought about it. We were going with each other for a year. We've been going out with each other for three months now. I'm glad I waited. Because I felt like it gave me more respect for myself then. Because my friends, they jump right into it. I hate that. I say to myself, Well, how could you do that to yourself? Don't you have any respect for yourself?

A lot of guys around here are very horny. My boyfriend's not. You know what I like about him? He talks to you. He can sit there and chew your ear off. He trusts me. I feel like he opened up to me. It shows he cares about me. And he's been through a lot, too. It's like we just clicked, you know, so it's good.

You Ought to Be
My All and All

A LIFE STORY

Josie Gilchrist Anderson

She is an academic counselor at Copiah-Lincoln Community College in Natchez, Mississippi.

"I was born in Fayette, Mississippi, in 1946, and my mother moved to Natchez when I was four. I am the third of eleven children. Out of eleven, ten of us went to college, and everybody finished high school. I went to Mississippi Valley College, a historically black college. My first experience in a racially mixed class was when I got my master's in guidance and counseling at Wayne State University in Detroit. I taught school fifteen years, and I've been a counselor at a community college for the last ten.

"I'm not divorced, but I've been separated for about twenty years. My twenty-six- and twenty-four-year-old children are from my husband; my eleven year old is not." (See also p. 467)

My mama was the only one around to turn to when we were growing up. My parents separated when I was about five, and my daddy moved to Los Angeles. He never assisted us in any kind of way, so it was a struggle for a long time with my mama trying to work little odd jobs, and her education was only to ninth grade. She was a cook at the restaurant at Stanton Hall—a historic antebellum home—and making thirty-five or forty dollars a week back in '62, '63, '64. It just wasn't enough, so basically we grew up on welfare. My mama felt that education was the key to break that cycle, and in our house nobody dropped out of school.

One of the things she did early in our lives is get a pasteboard box and tear it open, take a magic marker, and write the numbers on the box, using it as a bulletin board—she nailed it on the wall. She'd put the numbers one through a hundred on that box, and then she'd take another box and put the alphabet on it. Before we started going to school, each one of us knew our alphabet and numbers because every night as soon as we were old enough we had to come stand and learn. We had to read the numbers and show her that we knew them out of context. With the alphabet we had to point out this is G or B, and not just say them in order.

Once you started school, then the same thing happened with reading. You were going to read, "See Mary go. Go Mary go." If she had taken you over it several times and you were not catching on, you would no doubt get a whipping and then the next day you tried again. She'd get a switch out of a tree. She hit you on your rear end, on your gluteus maximus. It wasn't light, but then it didn't kill us, either, we didn't bleed. It was enough for us to know she meant business. It worked. I see parents whose kids come home and they say, "Well, I don't want to go to school anymore because those teachers don't like me" or blah blah blah, and they quit, they go to GED. We just couldn't have gone home and told my mama, "Oh, Miss Jones don't like me." My mama would just say, "Well, tough luck. You're not there to like her, either. It's nice to be able to get along with her, but you're there to try to get an education, and so as long as she's not asking you to do anything immoral, you're supposed to do it."

It was a struggle making so little money. She had grown up in Jefferson County picking cotton and stuff. That's why she moved to town, cause she wanted us to have a better life and she felt the only way we could do it was to get an education.

My mama never taught us to hate our daddy. She wouldn't allow us to write him and ask him for anything. She said if he wouldn't do it on his own, then don't ask. If she found out that you asked for something, you were really in trouble. I remember twice he sent us something. One year when I was about ten, he sent us used clothes, boxes of them, from the Salvation Army. My aunt used to work for a white lady, and when she outgrew her stuff, she gave them to my mama for us. A lot of people gave us things, and so we looked good and dressed nice. We lived in a duplex, and our neighbor Mr. Alec was an important part of our lives. All those years, through all of my sisters and brothers, he'd been around and was somebody who'd give you a quarter when the ice cream man came because he knew your mama didn't have it. Mr. Ladd and Miss Bea lived next door and didn't have any children. She worked in the school cafeteria, and at the end of the day she'd bring home her share of the leftover food and give it to my mama to help feed us.

My mother had eight girls and was not squeamish about telling us where babies come from. She was extremely explicit. She would tell us some of the pitfalls. She said I got pregnant when I was sixteen, by your daddy, by listening to him saying if you do this or that, you won't get pregnant, and I ended up pregnant and having to get married. So she would tell us you should wait till you're married. We were struggling as it was. To go out and get pregnant and have a baby, it would just be impossible; she also made you believe that she would literally kill you with her bare hands if you did. She explained exactly what the sex act was. We were not told about any form of birth control because she felt like you need to wait. I had only one sister who got pregnant in high school.

In growing up, I knew segregation was there. We learned early that my mama was having a hard enough struggle trying to provide for us, that to go out and do something that would present other problems for her did not make any sense. So if my mama said because of segregation, whites and blacks could not mix, and you couldn't go in the Main Street park, we just took her word for it and didn't go. I thought it was weird and wondered why. I mean people are people, why can't we go to the park? And she said, "You'd get arrested if you did," and you would. So I just didn't do it.

She told us what to do and what not to do, and none of us were ever in trouble with the law or anything like that. Don't get me wrong, not that we didn't do some of the things she said not to do—like sneaking out to the river where the teenagers were hanging out and that kind of stuff. But stuff we thought could get back to her and might hurt in some way, we didn't do it. It puzzled us about not being able to go to the park, but nevertheless we didn't go. I didn't sit around and think about it.

We had our own friends, and we had big empty lots in our neighborhood where we'd go and play softball. There were fifty-five children in the alley street that I grew up in. My mother had eleven; the lady in the next house had ten. We had a softball lot where we played softball. I was in the band; I was a cheerleader, a majorette. This is who you are. This is your community, and it didn't bother me. I had white children that I talked to every day because we lived within a block of each other, but we didn't play together. We didn't say, "Do you want to go play jump rope or play with our dolls together?"

You grew up in that era where segregation existed, and that was it. My mother always taught us no human being is any better than the other human being—you're as good as anybody else. She taught us not to be mean to anybody else irrespective to what they may have done, and so that for me was not a problem. Maybe occasionally in a store someone may have acted kind of nasty. The salesperson may act as though they don't want to wait on you or they're afraid that they might become black if they touch your black hand. We went to all the regular stores, but in some of those stores, like Kress, I knew that I couldn't sit at the lunch counter. Stores like Sterling sold popcorn and things like that, so you could buy that because it's just a matter of walking up there and purchasing the popcorn and walking out.

We couldn't go and sit down in the restaurants and coffee shops in Natchez, and I didn't go to town a lot. I was about thirteen when my mother would start letting us walk together into town with some of my other sisters and brothers and go to the movies or whatever, and she just gave us instructions on what to do and what not to do. In the movies the white kids sat downstairs on the first floor, and the black kids sat on the balcony. Sometimes we had popcorn fights. We lived through it all. We had Dumas Drug Store downtown on Franklin Street. He was a black pharmacist, and he had a brother who was an M.D. A lot of people called Franklin Street the black street because it was just filled with black businesses.

I was involved with the civil rights movement. That first summer of '64 I participated in the voter registration drive. My friends and I would go along with the people from COFO, or SLCC or NAACP. My mother was involved, too, and we would canvass the neighborhood, going door to door trying to make sure that the people understood their right to vote and that they were registered. We nearly got arrested the summer of '65. We were on our way down to the Macedonian Baptist Church, where they were going to have a rally in the front yard. After I had gone part of the way down the street, this policeman came along and he was saying to us to disperse, and we didn't feel like we needed to because we had the right to assemble and march, and so he kept after us, and we didn't move. He was getting ready to grab me, but Miss Mamie Mazique, who was really involved with the civil rights struggle, grabbed me by the arm and got me out of his reaches. So that was kind of like a close call. But several months later they sent about two busloads of people to Parchman, the state penitentiary, for participating in the marches. They say they gave them Ex-lax and denied them toilets and tissue paper. But I wasn't in that group because college had started at Mississippi Valley. By the time I started college in 1965 and went off to Valley, black had become beautiful, so everything was fine. I never had the problem of not being able to vote because when the Civil Rights Act was passed, it fell about the time that I made eighteen.

I was maybe about sixteen when I started dating the boy I married. We didn't have a car, and he didn't, either, so we just walked to the movies and walked back. My mother thought my husband was the greatest thing this side of heaven. She trusted him, and so I didn't have any problems about wanting to go out with him. We did a little kissing but no deep necking and petting. We were together two years, but since we didn't have cars, there was no place to get into trouble. I mean you could not sit up naked at your mama's house. And then in the movies, maybe a little light kisses—people might see us. He didn't know if I was a male or female and I didn't know if he was when we got married.

The guy I married was three years older than me. He was twenty-one and in the air force. He was stationed in Sacramento, California. I did not like living on the air force base. I didn't get accustomed to my husband. I grew up in a household with eleven children, and there was always someone to talk to, to do something with, and my husband was so quiet and so withdrawn. His grandmother raised him. I think he didn't understand why I felt the need to always have somebody around talking and doing something, and I didn't understand why he always wanted to be by himself. So after about five, six months, I said, "You know what? I've always wanted to go to college; while you are doing this four-year stint in the air force, I'm going to go to school, and when you get out of the air force, I'll be out of college," and so that's what I did. I went to Mississippi Valley college; I got a degree in English. I saw my husband during vacations or when he'd have leave and come home. When he went to Germany for two years, I didn't see him. He asked me to come and and I told him, "I'm almost through with college now, so if I go to Germany, it will interrupt that, so I don't want to go." He accepted it.

I completed my bachelor's degree in November of '68, and I did my student teaching in Oprah Winfrey's hometown, Kosiesko, Mississippi. My husband had gotten out of the air force in February '68 and was going to the University of Detroit. So when I finished college, I went to Detroit and taught junior high English and career education—at that time in Detroit all eighth-graders had to have at least ten weeks of being exposed to various careers, so I did that for about three years. The beginning of my senior year I had gotten pregnant with my oldest daughter (my mother kept her when I went back to college and finished up my student teaching). When I got out of college, I worked a semester, and I got pregnant with my son. I was twenty-one when I had my daughter and twenty-three when I had my son. I didn't know anybody in Detroit, so I watched my students and if the kid seemed to be real nice, I asked them, "Do you think your mother would mind babysitting for me?" And they would ask her, and then the mama would send the phone number.

I had one babysitter, though, that I pulled my children from. My son was going on two, and he wasn't fully potty trained. If he wet himself, her punishment would be to lock him in the bathroom. My daughter was four, and she told me about it. So I asked this woman, and she said yes that she did do that, and I said, "No, you can't do that. You don't know the psychological effect that could have on Marcus, nor do you know whether or not he might turn the hot water on and scald himself, whether or not he might put his face down in the bowl and drown himself. All kinds of things can happen. I don't have a problem with you hitting him on his gluteus maximus if you feel the need. Hitting him in his face, his head, or locking him in a closet or bathroom are no-nos." And she said, "It seems like you don't want the children to mind, so you need to find somebody else to keep them." I told her, gladly, if that was going to be her mode of punishment. The mother of one of my students started keeping the kids, and she was wonderful.

When I was twenty-five, I decided I wanted to get a master's. My daughter was four and my son was two, so I taught school from eight to three every day, and then four nights a week I went down to Wayne State from 4:30 to 9:30. I told my husband, I said, "Now look, I'm going back to school to get my master's. When you were in school, I kept the kids, so now you either need to keep them or give me some money for a babysitter." (I was telling one of my students, I said, "Now, don't let me get you in trouble, honey, but sometimes you have to be firm. You don't go ask him—'I want to go back to school, can you keep the children?' You just say, 'I am going back to school.' That's what I told my husband.") I told him, "I'll try to cook enough for two nights. If you all eat everything up that one night, then it will be your responsibility to get the children fed." And, of course, their favorite place to go was Kentucky Fried. He was a good cook—my husband would help with the housework—so he could cook sometimes himself if he chose to, but he did keep them.

It was hard going back, getting my master's. I had a husband, a good job—I didn't have to put myself through that, but I also realized nothing is promised. In my present job I see a lot of women who have been married twenty, twenty-five years, and sometimes their husbands have died, sometimes they've traded them in for a younger version of a Josie, and just because you're married doesn't mean you'll always be.

I was teaching in Detroit till my daughter was seven and my son was five. I hated the cold weather and the crime, and my husband and I weren't really getting along. I have a great husband, I really do. He was extremely responsible and took good care of us, but I did not feel like he knew how to give of himself. Food, shelter, and clothing, he was eager to provide, but "Come to church with us," or "My school is having the end-of-the-year luncheon, why don't you go with me?" "I'm not going. If you want to go, you go." It was always no to everything.

I think my husband's problem is his mother gave all five of them away. When he was little, his mother used to burn him with cigarettes, and so I can kind of understand. His grandmother raised him, and she tried to provide the best that she could, but as soon as he finished eating, she'd say, "Now go to your room and study." So when we were together, when he came home from work in the evening, he'd go straight to the bedroom, close the door—he had a subscription to about fifteen newspapers—and when he wasn't working, he wanted to read. When he wasn't reading the newspapers, he was reading novels, and if he didn't do that, maybe listening to some quiet music. That's all he wanted to do, and I've always loved going out dancing. I want to be a member of the NAACP. I want to be in a church choir. I want to go see Johnny Taylor or B.B. King, and my husband would say, "Well, make sure the kids got a bath before you go, but I'm not going," and I couldn't draw him out. I didn't know of another woman. There was no other man. I just got tired of being treated like I didn't exist, and I didn't feel like I should have to spend all my young years waiting for somebody to change.

After ten years, I talked to him about it and told him how I felt and what needs I felt weren't being met and asked him to talk to me—"Where do you think this relationship is going? How do you feel about the relationship?" I couldn't get him to talk. He'd listen and he'd say, "Are you through?" And I'd say, "Yes and what do you think about what I've said?" "I don't have anything to say; you've said it all. You're the one who's dissatisfied, you do whatever you want about it," and after three years of trying to talk to him, I decided to leave. I said, "I don't want to lie to you. I don't want to tell you I'm going to the movies when I'm going to meet somebody just to have some kind of ongoing relationship with somebody of the opposite sex. I don't want to live like that. If you're going to be my husband, you ought to be my all and all, and then if you're not and I need a boyfriend, I might as well be single, so I can get a boyfriend in peace without lying to you." So he said, "Do whatever you want to do, but"—this is what he told me before I left—"if I were you, I would take all my good points and put them on this side of the scale and take all my bad points on the other side and kind of weigh them, and perhaps if my good points outweigh my bad points, maybe you ought to stay, and if my bad points outweigh my good points, maybe you ought to go. The decision is yours."

It kills me he's so philosophical. When I made up my mind about three years later, I told him I wanted to go home, and he said, "Well, are you sure?" And I said, "Yes," and he said, "Well, I brought you from home. If you're sure that's what you want to do,

I'll get a U-Haul and take you home." And that's what he did. That was in '75. The children were young, and for the next four years we spent every summer with him in Detroit. We still didn't get along and we were not involved with each other, but it just bothered me that I didn't really know my daddy, and I wanted them to know their daddy and have a relationship with him. Then in '79 he came down here and stayed with us for about a year. We didn't fight or anything, and we didn't get along any better.

My husband always sent the child support money, and when it was time to start school up, he sent back-to-school money. If he did not send the money, he mailed me a credit card and told me how much to spend, and that's how much I spent. Christmas, he always told them, make out a list of what you want. Either go to the stores or look in catalogs, get the prices, put the price opposite of what you want, and mail me the list. They'd mail him the list, he'd total up what they had on the list and send the money order back for what they wanted, and then he always sent them forty dollars every two months for their spending change. So he was one in a million in that way.

He eventually got a job at UCLA, and so he moved to Los Angeles. When our son was fourteen, he said, "Mama, I just can't take your rules and regulations"—I think his biggest problem was he'd want to stay outside at night with other boys in the neighborhood, and I told him no—"and so I want to ask Daddy can I live with him." With my son, you never would have known that he had a mother unless he told you cause his constant talk all his life was his daddy. He just loved his daddy, preferred him to me always. I didn't want to let him go, but my mama and my brothers kept saying, "Well, the boy keeps saying that he is going to get up in the middle of the night one night and hitchhike to where his daddy is, so if his daddy says he can come and he wants to go, he's of an age now, let him go." I told my husband to just tell him to stay home and mind me and do like I say.

The first time he went to live with Daddy he stayed three weeks, and he said, "Mom, can I come home," and I said, "No, you can't. It's the middle of the semester, you started school, and you'll mess up your school record. You have to wait until the semester is over, and if you still want to come home when school is out, then you can." So when school was out, he came home. Well, during the summer he got angry with me again with some of my main rules, and he called his daddy and said, "Can I come back?" And he said yes, so I said, "Jimmy, we can't have this kid pitting us against each other. He can't come to Natchez and get angry with me, go to Los Angeles, get angry about something, and come back to Natchez. He will never finish school, will not have a decent school record by doing that. If you won't say no this time, you have him until he's an adult. You can send him home for Christmas, for holidays." He said okay. So he's been there the last ten years. He's twenty-four now.

He works at a medical center and goes to a community college for physical therapy. I tried to get him to go to college when he first finished high school. He never knew his uncle David, who got killed in Vietnam, but he's always said, "I'm going into the army and be a paratrooper like Uncle David" (we have pictures around the house of Uncle David as a paratrooper). So he went in the army when he first finished high school.

Neither of my children are married, but I do have grandchildren. My son has two children, which I did not know about until recently. December 1991 I went to Los Angeles to the National Vocational Educators Conference, and my husband came downtown to pick me up and take me over to their house. While I was there, a young lady came by, and she said that my son had told her to come by, and she brought the children to meet me. So I found out that I had a six-month-old granddaughter and a one-year-old grandson. It was a shock. I said to my son, "Why didn't you tell me?" He said, "Mama, I did not want to go through the third degree about getting married and about you shouldn't have done this and you shouldn't have done that, and so I figured it was just as easy not to tell you." So I asked my husband why he didn't tell me. "Well, I just found out myself about six months ago. The girl came by to tell me."

They're not living together now. I talked to her recently—I sent the kids some clothes, and so she called me to thank me. He was involved with his children it seems till a short while ago. I don't know if the girl still likes him and gets upset about a new girlfriend and says, "You're not going to see the children." She says she does not feel that he does his fair share for them economically, which I try to talk to him about. I told him, "Your daddy didn't do that to you all. He never missed one payment."

My twenty-six-year-old daughter has a bachelor's degree in mass communications and a master's degree in guidance counseling, and she works as a counselor at a high school in Fort Meyers, Florida. She has an eleven-month-old. When she completed her master's degree, for some unknown reason she got pregnant that year, but she's working. She really doesn't have to do anything in a financial sense for the child because the father does it all.

My sixth-grader is an honor student ever since she's been in school and says she wants to be a pediatrician, and right now she's just going to school being a good student, 4-H, Girl Scouts, junior choir at church. She sees her father from time to time. He lives here in Natchez, but like with my husband, I just think most men, at least all the ones that I seem to have met, don't spend enough quality time with the children.

My daughter said to me when she was home this summer—"You make me so angry. You know Daddy wants you back, and you won't go back." I said, "I'm not sure. Maybe if he lived in Jackson or somewhere close, I'd date him and see." I'm just so scared to give up my good job and my house and go to Los Angeles. I don't like the earthquakes and to get up there, and then we might not get along. It's just hard for me. I tell a lot of my girlfriends that in retrospect I guess I could have stayed with my husband. My mama told me, "Just find somebody else to talk to if the boy's too quiet and won't talk," but I just couldn't. And she didn't mean like a boyfriend. When I was a child, we had a stepfather for a while, but there was not a lot of interacting. You didn't really share or do things together. I think a marriage ought to be where we do things together and with the children. I can't see relationships where it looks like I'm just somebody to go to bed with. I want us to be an intricate part of each other's world. My mama said, "Well, as long as that boy is paying the bills," and I said, "I can work and pay the bills."

The most traumatic thing thus far in my life was the death of my mother. At the time, I did not see how I could live again, eat again, drink again, do anything ever again. I lost twenty-five pounds in three weeks of continuous crying. As distraught as I was, I knew without a shadow of doubt—if I had not known it before then, that clinched it for me—that there has to be a god, someone stronger and greater than us. Religion has really been a source of strength, something to lean on. I have been a Baptist all of my life. In our house if you didn't go to Sunday school or church on Sunday, you could not go any other place, and now that I'm older I'm really glad that was a rule because it gave me an impetus to really be interested in the church all my life. I did the same with my children.

Two years before Mama died, I called the *Natchez Democrat* and asked them if they were going to do any human interest stories for Mother's Day, and they said, "Well, that's a good idea—you got anybody you want to recommend?" And I said, "Yes, my mother," and they said, "Well, tell us a little bit about her," and I did. So they called and she agreed, and they went out to the house. In the hallway, my mama had all eleven of our graduation pictures staggered from the one who finished in '86—and this was 1986 when they did the story—to the one who finished in '61. So they took a picture of her standing in the hallway by the eleven pictures, and the caption under the picture said, "Gertrude Gilchrist's pride and joy, her eleven graduates." When she died the summer of '88, we met the morning after the funeral and agreed that we did not want the pictures separated, so we decided that my brother, the eldest child, who lives in Los Angeles, would be the one to take the eleven pictures and put them in his hallway because that's what she would want.

Family

Family:
The First Generation

I had a wonderful marriage and a very good husband. I may be prejudiced, but I think with women trying to put themselves on equal footing with men, they've lost something. I don't care what anybody says, there is a difference between the sexes and when men felt their wives were their responsibility, women got more love. Both the men and the women did. And also, I don't think there is anything wrong with just bringing up children and running a household. I think that's a job in itself.

—Witt Davenport, born 1911

We hadn't even gotten out of the church yet and Joe said "From now on, you belong to me. You don't talk to anybody unless I tell you to." From then on, it was just one big fight. I should have turned around right then and gone back and said "I want to call this off." I had decided I'd rather get married than go to college. They're not getting married as young nowadays and not messing up their life. Little smarter, I think.

—Belle Riding, born 1928

The Second Marriage Was the Real Marriage, Except We Never Married

Anne Ratner

For the last twenty-five years, she has held classical music concerts in her New York City apartment, with proceeds going to Camphill Village Copake, a community for mentally handicapped adults where one of her granddaughters lives.

"We originated in the Ukraine. I was born there in 1905. I was one when the family immigrated to the U.S. All the rest of the children were born here. There were three girls and twin brothers. My brother Paul was killed in World War II. My mother's family all came here. We imported my grandmother and grandfather and aunt."

I married at twenty—I guess out of defiance. The guy I really wanted to marry didn't marry me, so I married someone else who was a sweet, sweet guy but not very interesting. I knew shortly after our marriage that it was not going to last. He was so dependent on me. He didn't have a job, and he just followed me and worshipped me, and I had work to do. I was playing piano and practicing and teaching. He was not qualified to do very much, and I couldn't abandon him. I felt sorry for him.

I stayed married about three and a half, four years, until he introduced me to his new boss—he got a job finally—who he said was very interesting. So I said bring him home for dinner some night, and that was the end of that.

That was Hyman Ratner. So the second marriage was the real marriage, except we never married. It was 1929. We went to city hall for a marriage certificate, to get married legitimately, and we weren't married because there was something that had to be corrected in the divorce proceeding, and I never bothered. I said the hell with it. We were already living together anyway. Thirty years without being legally married. My parents never knew. Nobody in the family ever knew, and nobody questioned it.

It made no difference. I didn't care. I was sort of offbeat anyway, a rebellious sort, independent. Even when I was in my teens, I met people at the Cafe Royal on Second Avenue and Twelfth Street. All the avant-garde theatrical activity took place there, and all the attitudes were freer there about sex and lifestyles than in the so-called normal population.

The children didn't know we weren't married until they were twenty and eighteen. My husband didn't want to tell the girls when they were little children. I think it was at my insistence at that time that the truth came out.

I taught a little bit between babies, and I didn't play at Carnegie Hall. I never played professionally. We played at private engagements. I did continue to give lessons. When the children were quite little, I guess five and three, something like that, we moved out of the city to Freeport, Long Island. When my daughter Molly was about two years old, she would go to the piano and play every song she heard. She was extremely musical, and I knew there must be something that one could do with children younger than school age. I went to the Child Study Association and asked, and they referred me to a woman who was doing preschool music in groups, teaching children to listen to music, to sing. She had a little percussion orchestra.

I watched her conduct classes with these little, tiny children, and I said this is what I want to do, and before long I was assisting her. And then I went and took some courses in Dalcroze and qualified myself to use that technique in teaching. It's a wonderful method. I started classes out in Freeport with little kids and their parents. After I had done this for a couple of years, there was an opening for a teacher in a new school in Brooklyn. I went in and had an interview and an audition, and I took the job. I kept that job for about eleven years. It was 1935, which made my children five and three. It was three days a week, and I had to commute from Freeport to Brooklyn.

My husband—I suppose in these days he would be called a male chauvinist—had a fit. He did not want me to go to Brooklyn to teach. He didn't think I should have any kind of steady job—stay home, look after the kids, cook, and play music. He hated that I had that job. And we had tiffs over it for eleven years. It didn't break our marriage, but it was not an easy thing to do, very difficult: "Am I not doing enough for you? Aren't you living well enough? What do you need to do this for?" I said, "I'm not doing it for the money. I want the experience of having my own profession, of working at something that I'm enjoying, and I feel I'm doing something worthwhile. "That was no answer for him. He didn't feel that I needed that. He thought he provided me enough of an interesting life not to have to do anything on my own that separated me from my young family. But I got people to look after the children, and I kept on doing it because it was important to me. I was somewhat angry, not enough to break the marriage.

That was not the only component of the marriage. He was very, very bright. He was interested in history and math, literature, he was a tremendous reader. I was too, but not on the same level. I never felt as if I functioned on an intellectual level equal to his. He was a very attractive man. We had a nice, active household—people would come. There were times when I suppose I felt I wasn't entirely getting my due, but I got a lot of satisfaction out of what I was doing in my life, and we would go on trips and have vacations, and I enjoyed him so much that it didn't dominate. Well, I kept doing what I wanted.

Today, a lot of marriages break up because people are not willing to recognize certain differences in their characters and make compromises. I don't think there's enough willingness to put up with the pain and differences in a marriage. You can't have a relationship with a person for a lifetime and be a complete human being yourself without painful things happening. They have to be faced and handled. Today's human beings, I think they are too frivolous about this. Marriages fall apart too easily. It is very sad. It's preposterous.

I don't know how much it has to do with feminism. In terms of relationships, too much emphasis has been put on the fact that women have to assert themselves beyond the point of what's necessary, and the extreme feminists lose perspective. There are sometimes compromises that have to be made either by a woman or a man, which should be respected.

When my husband was thirty-eight—which must have been in 1939—he had a very serious heart attack. They did not have the technology then that they have now, and it interrupted our life entirely. We had nurses in the house, and, of course, I stayed home during that time, and after about six weeks or two months, he recovered enough to start getting around, and so I went back to school to teach.

He had another heart attack after we moved into the city. He needed more attention. He was fragile. After the second heart attack, I retired from the school. I didn't take any other jobs. I just couldn't. He needed me to be around all the time. I didn't do anything with any continuity. I worked with the Red Cross. I worked with music in hospitals for children who couldn't move. He lived till 1960—he was fifty-eight. Within a year after his death, I went to work three days a week. I did music therapy. It was enormously interesting. I developed a wonderful program at the League School. I was about seventy-five when I retired.

I Met My Husband
at the LaGuardia Campaign

Helene Weintraub

She was born in NYC in 1911 and worked in public relations most of her life. (See also pp. 39 and 52)

I met my husband at the LaGuardia campaign; he was a lawyer working for Mayor LaGuardia. I came down to make a proposal about the campaign. I was referred to Lou, who I later learned was in charge of the Department of Crazy Ideas. He said, Well, that was interesting, and he'd let me know if they could use this proposal.

When I was leaving, he said, "Would you like to have a cup of coffee?" And I said, "Sure." So we stopped off at the drugstore downstairs and had a drink. I never expected to hear from him again. About a year later, I got a telephone call. It turned out he was in Washington during the week working for LaGuardia; he just came to New York City on weekends. He called me a couple of times on Saturday night when I couldn't see him.

I decided that since I was never available when he called, he must think that I didn't want to see him, and maybe I better do something to make it clear that I really did. By that time he was working in New York City for a law firm with offices about a block away from my office. So one day I called and told him I wanted to ask his advice on a small legal matter. He said, "Sure. What are you doing for lunch?" That was in '35. We married in '36.

I didn't even feel it appropriate to say, "Since we're so close, why don't we have lunch one day." You didn't make the first move, or if you did, it was extremely devious and disguised, as in my case, where I called for professional advice hoping that he would suggest lunch. Girls who called boys for dates degraded themselves. You didn't do this if you wanted to remain acceptable and retain the image of young womanhood that we were saddled with.

Laurine Warren

She is a retired nurse. She was born in Broken Bow, Oklahoma, in 1912 and grew up in Mississippi.
(See also pp. 25, 52, 63 and 424)

I met my husband when he came up to the hospital in Natchez, Mississippi, to see a patient. He told me later that he was attracted to me when he saw me. I was a little nurse in training. We wore pink dresses with white aprons and caps. I guess he just liked seeing a nurse. Then we went together three years before we married because I wanted to get my registered nurse's degree.

After I finished training he said, "Why don't you come down and just have a room with my mother and dad?" and I said, "Oh, I don't know whether that would be proper or not." He said, "It would be proper with my mother." So I went down there and stayed for three months before we got married in 1935. We were married three years before our first child was born.

My first child was a boy. He went to Tulane medical school and became a doctor of internal medicine. He married and practiced, and they had four children. And one day in the fall he said, "Mama, I don't feel well." He said, "I believe I have cancer of the pancreas." I said, "Oh, no." He said, "Well, I believe this is what I really have." He was forty-six, and that was what he really had. He lived six months, and he was forty-seven when he died. My second son got a Ph.D. in chemical engineering. He is alive and well. He is now fifty-two years old.

My daughter was my youngest child. I wanted a little girl so bad. My obstetrician—he was a general practitioner, actually, and was of the Jewish faith. When I was in training, he was very strict, and he could be right ugly with the nurses sometimes. I thought that was one doctor I never would want for my doctor, but guess what happened. The other doctors had gone to the war. I had to have him. He was wonderful. I loved him. When my little daughter was delivered by him, I said, "Oh, I'm going to give you a kiss," and he said, "Well, let me get my gloves off, and I'm gonna collect." I gave him a big kiss because he had delivered a little girl for me. So this little girl has been a joy to me. She now lives in Tennessee, is married and has a son and a daughter. She has been teaching school for about twenty years.

When our first little boy was two years old, we went out to Duncan Park to live, and my husband was the golf pro there for ten years. He taught and played golf. I always worked as a nurse, except for the ten years that we lived in Duncan Park, and that was a wonderful time that I could stay with my little children.

My husband and I were a great deal like our parents in the discipline. Maybe the children got a little switching or two, but they didn't get a whole lot. We did not have the problems with our children that mothers and fathers have nowadays. There were no drugs, and they weren't at all alcoholics. By high school they may have dropped a can of beer, but they were exceptionally good, studious children, and they were leaders in their school. Now, I think that I am really being honest about this, and this is not just a mother's opinion.

In Duncan Park we had a good playground, and they would go and swing and go down the slides, and I could look out the door and see what they were doing. The boys loved the golf, too. My husband worked out at Armstrong Rubber Company at night, and then I took care of the golf shop so he could get a nap in the morning, and then he would come and work all afternoon in the golf shop. At that time they were working on making shell casings, so he was working for the war. He was old enough and with three children that he did not have to go to the war. We really worked hard, but it paid off. My days and nights just rolled around one after another. It was a very happy period of our lives.

At that time it was hard to find a maid to work for me, and I just did a whole lot of things myself. Then after a while we got a washing machine, and, also, when my little girl was eleven months old, we managed to get a maid, and she worked for us for about fourteen years. We just loved her like a member of the family. She was a black girl. She helped me so much.

My husband and I shared responsibilities more or less. When he had time, he did help out with the children and the house. Now, we had a garden in the backyard, and he would pick those vegetables and cook the butter beans if he were at home—he would cook the midday meal. And my mother lived with us at that time—he watched after her, although I did have a maid for her, too. He did his part. Sometimes I felt like I was doing a little more than he was. He did want me to do a lot, so I did. I think it was good for me in the long run because I was fifty-eight when he died, and I still had years of working. I had handled a lot before, so although I was sad and I missed him, I had no problem dealing with business life and living by myself. It may have done me good to know all of those things.

I would say at times he may have been somewhat overbearing and possessive. I guess it went along with that generation. He didn't seem to be a very jealous sort of person, but he wanted me there. I didn't go out at night or anything like that, but if I went out during the day and stayed a little longer than he thought I was going to, he would be kind of miffed when I got home.

Helen Schiffrin

She was born in New York City in 1915. Her parents were Polish Jewish immigrants. Her daughter, Lois Mayer, was also interviewed. (See also p. 25)

I happened to meet my husband at the Laurels, in the Catskills during Christmas week. He was up there with about eight friends. I went alone because this dentist I worked for would only take a winter vacation, and my friends all took summer vacations. It was the first time I went away. Believe me, I spent my last dime on clothes—a ski suit, ski boots, white snowshoes. They had a store in downtown Manhattan called Russek's— I'm giving my age away—and that's where I bought that ski suit. It was really something. I didn't go skiing, but you wore those outfits. They didn't have skiing. They had tobogganing, and the Laurels was the only place in the mountains that had a beautiful lake that was frozen over. Most people would be on the ice all day long.

There were maybe two or three other hotels that were open for the winter. Concord wasn't around at the time, Grossingers didn't have an ice-skating rink, so most of the young people came to the Laurels. As a matter of fact, I was going to Grossingers, and one of the women in the beauty parlor says to me, "What are you going to Grossingers for? What are you going to meet? A lot of laid-off furriers, this time of year." She says, "Go to the Laurels, that's where they have young people," and that's what I did. And that's where I met my husband. In those days, it was definitely a singles place. And Christmas and New Years' that place really was jumping.

In the evening, of course, they had dancing and shows—they had all the entertainers. New Year's Eve everybody wore a gown. One girl came up without a long dress, and do you know, she did not come down to dinner that night. Most of the people were Jewish. They had the herrings and lox and that type of food, but it wasn't kosher. You were about ten people at a table, so you would get to know people. You would go to the bar, and most fellas in those days were single (years later you had the married men that would come up on their own), so they approached a girl and asked her to dance. That's what they were there for. They'd offer to buy her a drink.

I got up there, and in the morning I went down to breakfast and I noticed that everybody after breakfast was coming down in their outfits carrying their skates, so I went up to my room to change, and I get all dressed up in everything new and I take my skates, and I walked out of my room, and I figured I'd go down to the lake. As I walked out, one of the young men that was in my husband's group—their rooms were right across the hall—walked out, and he started to talk to me, asked me if I was going skating, and he went down with me. We went to the ice—there was a bench there—we sat down, and he was ready to put my skates on, and when my husband skated over, he was the one that did it, and took me out and taught me how to ice-skate. I was very good there for a while. I skated a little bit, and then I caught cold, and I never skated again.

That's how I met him, and I always said, "If I never see him again, it wouldn't matter, but I had the time of my life those ten days." He really wasn't the type I usually go for. I used to like a tall guy—he was short. And I'd never have gotten to know him if I met him in the city, but the ten days that I was with him, he was wonderful. I met him Christmas, and we married the following Thanksgiving and went to the Laurels on our honeymoon.

We all thought we would like to meet somebody nice, someone who could support us, and get married and be on our own. Why not? Most married women didn't work in those days. My husband was working for his father. He got out of law school and went to help his father out and got involved in the plumbing supply business. He took a bankrupt business and just built it up. I worked until I became pregnant. We were naive in those days—we didn't know anything. I got pregnant immediately. That was Joan; everybody was counting on their fingers.

My husband was wonderful. The only arguments he and I had were because he worked so late and so hard. He was always working from the day I married him. It was terrible. He was always, always late for dinner. How many times I got mad when I was in Brooklyn and took that dinner and threw it in the garbage. Look, when you work for yourself, it's not easy, but he was a good father and a good husband. The kids loved him. He would take them ice-skating and sleigh-riding in Bethpage Park.

Dorothy Sommer

She was born in 1912 and lives in New York City. She grew up in the Midwest and went to a convent Catholic school. (See also pp. 27, 60, 249 and 422)

I never got married. I had the chance to marry a lovely man, and I was very much in love with him, but he had two lovely children. And I saw a lot of them, but I said, "I can't. They would resent me; they would hate me." I was afraid of being a stepmother. And then the other time I had the chance to marry, my fiancé wanted children. I couldn't face the responsibility of children. I just couldn't. I was brought up strictly Roman Catholic, and in our faith marriage and sex were for procreation. Otherwise, you observed what they called the rhythm method, which wasn't always that dependable. I never lost my interest in men, but if I was brought down to the wire, I ran. How am I going to say I don't want any children? I hurt myself by not choosing to be happy.

I knew a psychiatrist, and we were talking about those things, and he said to me, "Dorothy, there must be a reason why you fear childbirth." I tried to pin it down one time to a young friend of mine who was married, and she went in the hospital to have her baby. Since she was a very, very good friend, I was with the husband, and I remember the doctor coming out, and I didn't quite understand what they were talking about, but he said, "We have to save the baby." Because the Catholic church says if it came to a decision, you must save the baby and let the mother die.

I was maybe twenty-one, twenty-two, or something like that. I remember the husband of my friend weeping into his hands. "I love my wife; I can always have another child." He was pleading for his wife, and they let her die. That's the Catholic church. I don't go to church. I celebrate Christmas and holidays, but I don't go to mass. It's so much hypocrisy. That's a devastating thing to tell a husband. It's cruel and just devastating for anybody. I was at the age where "there but for the grace of God, go I."

When The First Blade Of Grass Came Up, We Were Thrilled

Linda Pesso

She lives with her husband in Van Nuys, California. She is Jewish and was born in Poland in 1924. When she was five and a half, her father sent for her and her mother, and they arrived in America.

"I was excited to meet my father, but I didn't know what to think when I saw him, because he didn't have a beard! I'd never seen a man without a beard before; every man in Europe had one. And I remember the first day of elementary school, my father took me to class and sat me down next to another little girl. At the end of the day, I got a star for being good. I'd been very quiet because I didn't know a word of English! But I was a quick learner, and I caught on before too long."

I met my husband in February of 1942, and we were married in June of '43. There was no day that he said to me, "Will you marry me?" We were going together for over a year, and after a period of time you just sort of drift into different conversations. We started talking about when we would be married. I was nineteen; Marshall was twenty-one. All of our friends were getting married. It was the norm.

Marshall had volunteered to be in the army, and he was going to signal corps school. The signal corps was attached to the infantry, and he was one of the ten best operators in the army. My mother-in-law had four stars in her window, one for each son that was in the service. The day he graduated from the signal corps was June 25th, and we arranged our wedding for June 26th.

My parents made the wedding, and my in-laws contributed to it, too. It was in a beautiful hall in Brooklyn, where we lived. It was ninety-six degrees and the humidity was about ninety-eight percent. In those days you didn't have air-conditioning. Marshall had to change his collar six times. They had fans. I was hot, but I was too excited about everything to pay attention to the heat. I had a beautiful gown made of Belgian lace. It was floor length and long-sleeved, and the neckline was sort of a criss-cross. It had a six-yard train, and the veil was about eight feet long. They made it up to order for me. In those days people rented gowns. It wasn't customary to purchase them.

My father and mother walked us down the aisle. Marshall gave me a wedding ring during the ceremony. There's a certain prayer that you have to say: "*Ayidat mekadesh es lee,*" and Marshall said he's gonna remember that cause he'll say, "Ayidat mekadesh es lee—son of a gun, you belong to me!"

After the ceremony we had a six-course dinner, and that finished at three o'clock in the morning. I have a copy of the menu. We had fruit cup, fish, chicken, potatoes, vegetable, a salad. We had a big wedding cake with three tiers. We had to serve maybe two hundred people. In those days it was customary when you're sitting at the table that people wanted the groom and bride to kiss each other. People tapped their glasses, and then we had to kiss each other. Marshall and I danced to the first dance, and the song that we picked out was popular at the time, "The Story of a Starry Night," from a Tchaikovsky pathetique. We had a four- or five-piece band. When Marshall and I got up to do the first dance, he said to me, "Linda, drop your hand and pick up your gown to the side." I remember that very distinctly. I lifted my gown on the side, and I remember I felt like I was floating on air.

Three o'clock in the morning we went outside, and Marshall's pockets were full of envelopes because in New York you gave cash usually; you didn't give material gifts. We didn't have a car at the time, and this other couple were driving us home. Lo and behold, we had a flat. There I was in my bridal gown, Marshall in his tuxedo, his pockets stuffed full of money, and we just had to wait until they fixed the flat.

My husband went into the service four weeks later. I stayed mostly with my in-laws. I slept with his pajamas under my pillow. It was very traumatic. He was called into the infantry, ended up being in five major campaigns. It was very dangerous.

I was a bookkeeper and worked for a small company that had retail stores. I was the only girl in the office. I was very busy with my job, and then I took a course in nurse's aid. I didn't want my children to say, "Daddy was in the army—what did you do, Mom?" So I got training, and I worked in the hospital evenings. It was a civilian hospital. It was part of the war effort because they were short of nurses. We took the patients' temperature, and we gave them bedpans. Everybody knew about doing this volunteer work because it was highly publicized. It was through the Red Cross, and I had a blue and white uniform and a hat with a Red Cross symbol. The women were doing a lot of things in those days. I enjoyed what I was doing, and I did that all the time that Marshall was in the service.

I wrote him two letters a day. They were called V-mail, and when you sent V-mail, you had to use a regular form, and then they shrunk it down so it was like a little tiny letter because they didn't have the space to ship all the letters. I used to send him packages once or twice a week, cookies that I would bake. They didn't have the kind of packaging they have today. They had cardboard egg boxes—they were square and had inserts for the eggs, and I used that to put in the cookies.

My sister was a little girl when all this was going on, maybe six or seven. Before the war, Marshall worked for a toy factory. So every time he came to visit me, he used to bring her stacks and stacks of toys, stuffed animals, and other things. She used to say a prayer every time my mother went to the mailbox that there would be a letter from Marshall for me.

One Sunday morning I was at my parent's house, and there was a knock on the door. I went to open it, and there stood somebody in uniform. I saw him, and I thought I would drop dead—I surely thought that was it. My eyes became so big the guy looked at me and he said, "It's all right, lady, don't be frightened." There was a special delivery letter for me from a couple that had gotten one of Marshall's V-mails by mistake, and they wanted me to have it so they sent it special delivery.

Marshall was hurt a lot of times. He had purple hearts, which they gave soldiers who were hurt, and several more medals. He was one of the first soldiers to open up the gates of Buchenwald, one of the concentration camps where they found dead bodies piled up like stacks of wood one on top of the other. He says he still remembers the stench of the dead bodies riding away.

When the Japanese surrendered, Marshall was on a ship going directly to the Pacific to fight the Japanese. They declared victory on the way there, so the ship turned around, came back, and landed in Boston. I remember when he called me up, I was so excited. Do you know the first thing I did? I polished my toenails. I remember that very distinctly.

When he came home, he was a different person. He was afraid to sleep in bed. He wanted to be prepared. He wanted a gun under his pillow, which, of course, he didn't have. So he slept on the floor. I don't think he ever got over the war. He was very traumatized. He was almost killed several times. When he was in Belgium, he was in the snow. He went in right after D day when the American troops invaded Europe. He was in one of the first troops. They were on ships, and they had to wade into shore, and they killed a lot of them on the way. He had a lot of nightmares when he came home. He still talks about it, and we don't watch anything on television that has to do with the war.

It was a very elated feeling when he came home, elated and kind of frightening, because he had gone through so much. People were celebrating in the streets. In Times Square, they were dancing and throwing confetti out the window. Marshall was on furlough for several months before he started working for the same people that I was working for. He didn't have any particular job that he wanted to do, so he worked there helping them out, shipping stuff.

When Marshall first came back, we lived with his parents and my parents. I continued at my job, and after a while Marshall and his brothers decided to open up a factory for ladies' sportswear. Mainly skirts. They found a place in Brooklyn.

One day while I was working, this woman came in and mentioned the fact that her husband-to-be had an apartment in the Bronx. They were getting married, so there was an apartment available. When I heard that, I just jumped at the opportunity because you couldn't get apartments in those days. He had a dog in the apartment, and it was absolutely filthy, but that didn't matter to us. It was a little apartment. It was in a beautiful building in a beautiful neighborhood. We paid the tenant under the table to get the apartment. I think we paid four hundred dollars, which was a large sum at that time. We only paid thirty-eight dollars rent, and we fixed it up like a little dollhouse.

The apartment was around the corner from the Yankee Stadium, and when there was a ball game on, you couldn't even park a car. When they had the World Series, you couldn't even get to the subway. People were sleeping in the streets to get into the Yankee Stadium the following day. We lived there for nine years.

I left my job when I became pregnant with my first child. I had become diabetic five years after we were married. Then the children came two years later. I had two cesarean births. In those days they didn't know too much about diabetic pregnancies. The children would become huge and they would die, so they had to be delivered at eight months. Marshall was in the hospital waiting room. You weren't permitted to have anybody else besides the doctor and nurses in the room.

I was in the hospital for two weeks with both of them. And I had some horrible experiences. When my son was born, I was in insulin shock. After the surgery my stomach blew up so high from the gas that when my aunt Ruthie came in, she thought that I hadn't given birth yet.

At the time there were two types of insulin, long-acting and fast-acting. The long-acting insulin was cloudy, and the fast-acting insulin was clear. After my son was born the nurse came in and was about to inject me with an enormous amount of insulin when I happened to glance and see it was clear. I said, "What are you doing? Don't give me that insulin—that's the wrong insulin!" and she started fighting with me. I was very sick. If I would have taken that injection, I would have died in twenty minutes.

I didn't breast-feed—that wasn't the style in those days, especially since I was diabetic. We had cloth diapers and diaper pins—there was no such thing as disposable diapers. When I became pregnant with my second child, we got an apartment on the sixth floor, which had one bedroom, a living room, and a kitchen. The children slept in the bedroom, and we slept in the living room.

And then we bought a house in Massapequa. We moved there in 1954. Marshall and his brother Sam, who was in the army with him, bought the houses together. They carpooled into work together, and it took them more than an hour and a half. The down payment was several thousand dollars. I think our house at that time was fourteen thousand dollars. We got a veteran's loan at 4½ percent.

Joanne and Ken were two and four years old. There were twelve families—the first contingent that moved into that area. There was a sign that said that this is the site of the Massapequa Jewish Temple, so we knew there would be Jewish people living there.

All of us were in the same situation. We were families with young children. We were really pioneers—they had no mail delivery; the mail had to be picked up at the post office. We had no phones—they weren't in yet. At night it was so strange sleeping in a house that was settling because we were used to being in a building with 108 tenants. We still went back to see the friends we made in the Bronx because it was only an hour away by car. And when our son, Ken, got older, he became a very avid baseball fan, and he said to us, "We lived around the corner from the Yankee Stadium, and you moved!?"

I remember when the first blade of grass came up, we were very thrilled. We had never lived in a house before. We made a lot of friends there, some friends to this very day. We became active in suburban life, and we had a very happy life there for nine years until we moved out to California.

The house is embedded in my memory forever. It was a beautiful brick and field-stone house. It was a split level, and when you walked in, you walked up a few steps to go into the main entrance. It had a thirty-two-foot cathedral ceiling. And Marshall did so much work on that house to improve it. He's always been very handy. We fixed the backyard up so beautifully.

There was a lot of wallpaper to pick out because there were seven rooms. After the paper was up and I walked into the house the first time, I was absolutely astounded because the paper I picked out, I would not live with. I looked at the paper in the book and it looked fine, it blended in, but when you saw it on the wall, all you saw was a wall full of flowers going up and down. It was a busy paper. I couldn't stand it, so I said to Marshall, "I will not live in this house—I cannot stand the paper." So before we moved in he had to get stepladders, and we had to pick out paper which was much simpler, a plain pattern, and since then I have never bought paper with a pattern.

We had parties in our backyards. The kids rode bicycles. They played out in the street. The children on the block were all about the same age, more or less. Their chores were to keep their rooms neat, not to leave their toys laying around. They would help with little things like setting the table.

I was involved with the Diabetes Association; I was a class mother; I was involved in the PTA. I went to meetings once a month, and I was on different committees. We used to participate in any projects that they had, cake sales and things like that. At one of the meetings they gave me a special award.

I was a Girl Scout troop leader. I had a coleader and we're friends to this day even though we live thousands of miles apart. We planned a lot of things for the girls. I had fourteen seven-year-olds—they were Brownies at the time—and I had them until they were ten, when they became junior girl scouts. My coleader and I took them to different places. We once went to a dry cleaning factory. Another time we took them to my house and cooked a lunch. I enjoyed them tremendously.

We had split sessions at the school because there weren't enough schools for the children. So the last session ended at about four. We had our meeting from four-thirty to five-thirty on Thursday afternoons. The girls wore uniforms. My coleader and I were careful not to give our daughters preference, so I took care of her daughter and she took care of my daughter.

I taught them to sew. We made things. For Mother's Day we took empty cans of orange juice and we made paper flowers. We put contact paper around the cans. We made little bunnies out of washcloths and took them to a children's hospital. We used to save all the empty cartons, the empty rolls from paper towels, and we used that for arts and crafts.

I wasn't working, so I had all the time that I wanted to do these different things. I didn't want to just sit home and do nothing. And after a certain number of years, I wanted to go back to work, and I did when we came to California. The children were ten and twelve. I worked part-time. I was home when they came home from school. I was very depressed when we moved out here because I left my friends and family. This took up my time and gave me other things to think about. It was pleasant. When Marshall had the factory, I did his payroll, so I never lost the skills. Except for the fact that when I was in Massapequa we had a manual typewriter and when I came to California for my first interview it was an electric typewriter. I didn't know how to work an electric typewriter. I didn't even know how you turn it on. But I found my way.

A Wonderful Life

Rose Kramer

She was born in 1900 and lives in New York City by herself. (See also p. 427)

I was twenty-three when I was married. My husband was a wonderful person, caring, understanding. He was special. You know the story about the rabbi who is delivering the eulogy and says all these beautiful things about the deceased—the dead man's wife gets up from her pew and goes to see who he is talking about. Not in my case. We were married almost sixty years.

Whitt Davenport

She was born in 1911 in Mississippi but has lived most of her adult life in upstate New York. (See also p. 21)

I would have gotten a job when I graduated from Vassar if I had not gotten married right away. I don't think Ken ever thought about me having a job. It just wasn't the way we grew up. I don't think my parents expected me to have a career, but I remember Daddy always said, "I want you to have a good education so that if you ever need to make your own living, you'll be prepared." What women could do would be to teach. And that was pretty much it unless you had taken a secretarial course, or you were a clerk in a store. Or you could be a nurse. That was another one. That was never my cup of tea.

I went in and signed up as a substitute teacher in English in Kingston, and I thought they would be thrilled to have me with my fine Vassar degree. I never got a call. I didn't have a teacher's certificate. I didn't even know you needed that to teach.

I didn't have any children until I'd been married about three years. I ended up being the librarian over at our Stone Ridge Library. And I did that for thirteen years. I loved it. I started out volunteering—the library was only open two hours a week—and then later on, I was paid. I think it was fifty cents an hour, something like that. That was my only job, but I've done volunteer work all my life. The other thing that my father was adamant about, if you lived in a community that's been nice to you, you've got a duty to do things for the community, and I always liked working on boards and things like that.

I was on the planning and zoning board, the beautification committee. I've also collected for the Red Cross. Another girl and I started a thrift shop for funds for the Junior League projects. I loved selling things. Since then I have been very much interested in several things that were county wide—historical preservation, the philharmonic, and Ulster Performing Arts Center in Kingston. I'm still on that board, and I shouldn't be because I'm too old. I've had my finger in a lot of pies.

Women didn't all work then. And then when you had your children, you were busy with them. Although unlike young ladies today, we had help. From the time I had children we had live-in maids until our youngest was about seven or eight. They were mostly country girls that I kind of trained. The first one I will never forget. She was only thirteen years old, but she was the oldest of a whole bunch of children and she knew more about bringing up children than I did.

I always did the baby's bottles and bathed the baby and dressed them and all that stuff. But if I wanted to go out somewhere in the afternoon, they would take care of the children. I usually did quite a bit of the cooking. I have two daughters and a son.

I had a wonderful marriage and a very good husband. I may be prejudiced, but I think with women trying to put themselves on an equal footing with men, they've lost something. I don't care what anybody says, there's a difference between the sexes, and when men felt their wives were their responsibility, they got a lot more love. Both the men and the women did. And also I don't think there's anything wrong with just bringing up children and running a household. I think that's a job in itself. We always had the house open to the children's friends.

We tried to be around unless we had somebody that we knew was trustworthy taking care of them, particularly when they got to be teenagers. That's much more important than little kids. Any good nurse can take care of children, but a lot of decisions have to be made when they get to be teenagers, and so we made it pretty much a point of always being there when they had friends until they went off to school.

Ken was very much a family man, and he did a lot of things with the children. He used to read to them at night—he did sports. He taught all the children how to ice-skate. After he died, I realized how many things he did around the house that I didn't realize he was doing. He knew where all the electrical things were, fuse boxes. A lot of things like that. He took care of all sorts of things—if we had to have the driveway paved. He loved having ideas about furnishing the house. He was very interested in how things looked. He loved his home.

I think I've had a wonderful life. I've been lucky. I had a wonderful husband, and I've got three good kids, and so far I don't think any of my grandchildren are on drugs or any of those things. Sometimes they lead peculiar lives—one of them is a professional biker. She rides with a group that goes into bicycle races. I think she's about ready to give that up and get a teacher's degree or an MA and teach. The other one is a real red-hot businesswoman—she does marketing and layouts for different companies. And they all take it for granted and their parents take it for granted that they're going to work. Neither one of them is married. I think one is on the verge. I'm not sure what is going on there.

Everybody has their own way of doing things, but I am really opposed to premarital sex. I think it's denigrating the most wonderful relationship that you can have. This business of thinking every time you go on a date that you go to bed, I think it's sad. I'm in the minority, I'm afraid. I hate that word "relationship." I'm having a "relationship" with so-and-so. In my mind that's a dirty word. I like marriage. More than anything, I just feel sorry for the kids. I'm a great believer in love, and I certainly like sex, too, but I think that they should be part of the same thing, not just like a smack on the cheek. Another trend that worries me—so many people are so self-analytical. I think that can be carried to great extremes. It's the "me" era. "Why did I do this?" "Why did I do that?" "Why do I think this?" I think it's overdone. Just get on with it, kids!

Bernice Stuart Snow

She was born in South Dakota in 1915. She is a widow and lives in Portland, Oregon. (See also p. 3)

*M*y children were born at the hospital. In those days, you didn't go to the doctor until you were in about the third or the fourth month. It was way before Lamaze. You didn't do any special exercises. The doctors weren't concerned about drinking or smoking. They kind of warned you about too much weight. Sonograms and amniocentesis didn't exist. If it was going to be a breech, you didn't know it until it came. You didn't know anything.

You didn't get a lot of information about childbirth. My mother and my girlfriends just didn't talk about it. This was in the early forties—you were still a little bit embarrassed about the whole thing because it was connected with sex. I was self-conscious about it. I didn't like looking like I looked at all. You didn't go down to the store and buy maternity clothes. I don't recall that they had maternity dresses—not in Mitchell, South Dakota. Everybody sewed. I made some of my maternity clothes—tank-top hang-downs, no style, no nothing.

I had a Catholic doctor with Peggy, who believed in natural birth. No ether or any-thing. It didn't bother me—I didn't know how painful it was. It's worse than anything you can experience. I felt my first pains during the night, and Obie and I got up at four-thirty in the morning to go to the hospital, and Peggy wasn't born until nine-thirty the next night. I was in labor all that time.

I had another daughter, Jane, five years later, also in South Dakota, and, again, I had a Catholic doctor and no anesthetic. I was in a room with a young Catholic girl—it was a Catholic hospital—who made life so miserable, hollered and screamed and carried on, and the nurses were so mad at her that I made up my mind that I was not going to be like that and I was not going to scream, and I didn't. I didn't utter a sound, and when I got through, my face was completely black and blue from stifling screams. Everybody when they came to see me just couldn't believe it. They thought somebody beat me to a pulp.

When Eugene was born in 1950, times were changed. He was born in Syracuse, New York. I told the doctor about the other two babies, and he said that was absolutely bar-baric. He didn't believe in natural birth and gave me some kind of injection that put you out, but at the same time you were amenable to any sort of instructions that they might give you to push and that sort of thing. I have no recollection of his birth what-soever. It worked for me. In today's world you would have wanted to know all about it. We just didn't do that. We thought doctors were God.

When Peggy was born in 1942, you were in the hospital about ten days, two weeks. That was wonderful. You just loved being in the hospital. With Jane—in 1947—it was ten days. Eugene was born in 1950, and on the third day the doctor circumsized him, and I went home. I think this practice of making women leave the hospital after one or two days is cruel. Women should be able to stay in the hospital at least two or three days. Even longer if they've had a hard birth or if the baby isn't taking the milk like it should. It's just insurance companies and money.

When Peggy was born, my husband just went crazy hanging around the hospital from four-thirty on, all morning long and all afternoon long. About eight o'clock at night she still wasn't born. He left the hospital and went down and got a pint of whis-key, had some, and came back and burst into the delivery room. And the nurse said,

"You can't come in here." And he said, "The hell I can't," and the doctor said, "Let him be." So Obie stood and watched Peggy be born, and that was unheard of at the time. My husband was six-five and probably weighed 250 pounds. The doctor was a big man, too, but he said it was okay. They didn't make Obie wash up or anything. He just stood there and watched—he was okay during the delivery—and when she finally came out, she had a big black head of hair, and I heard him say, "By god, doc, it's a girl."

We never heard of the word "pediatrician." It was just a doctor. You didn't have specialists in those days, not in our hospital, anyway. It was just your regular doctor who delivered the baby and did everything.

Winifred Williams

She lives in High Falls, New York, and was seventy-seven when interviewed. (See also p. 434)

I feel very badly that there's no more romanticism in life. When I think of the way women used to look and act and their demeanor compared to today! Life then was really beautiful. People took time to smell the roses. They don't anymore. It's my place or yours, no romance, no kissing your hair or your neck. That was the most precious thing in life, the thing I miss most of all—my husband touching me and fondling me later in life. Embracing me in the mornings. I mean gentleness. I don't think these people are ever going to experience that. There's no depth of feeling anymore. Maybe I'm wrong. I hope I am.

Men Always Made the Big Decisions

Abigail Midgeley

She was seventy-two years old when interviewed. She lives in an urban area in Ohio and works for the Department of Motor Vehicles. She is once widowed and once divorced and a devout Christian. She has eleven children and thirty-one grandchildren, three greats and another great on the way. (See also pp. 29, 60 and 256)

I got married when I was eighteen, and my husband was a heavy drinker. His drinking was never a big deal to me. I just thought it was something men did, but he died young, as he had liver problems, and then several years later I remarried. He drank but not as much as the first one. You don't know all these habits until you're married, and then it's too late.

I married my second husband in the early fifties. The thing that attracted me to him was he was very witty, very sure of himself. He always seemed to know all the answers. I was very quiet, shy, and when we went somewhere he would carry the whole conversation which was very comfortable for me because I didn't have to say anything. He was in the army and from Chicago, and I used to think to myself, What does he see in me, because I'm just a small town girl. He worked for the State Department of Prisons. After a while, he was raised up to deputy director of his division.

He treated me fine except for not being there half the time. He'd get very mad at me, but I can't say he hit me or cussed me out. He cussed a lot in everyday life, but he never called me names. When he was home, he just ran everything. I didn't mind—I thought it was part of marriage. The way I grew up, the man was the head of the house. Same way voting. I never thought I should vote—that was his job. I'd go to the polls, and I'd have my little paper, and I'd vote for who he said. Men always made the big decisions. Women stayed home and raised the children. That's the way I grew up, and I was content with that. We were married twenty-five years, all told.

When I was forty-seven, my second husband left home to marry his secretary. At the time, I had eight children at home. In those days you didn't have the pill. And we went by rhythm because his background was Catholic. I don't regret it, and it never seemed a burden. One more just always fit in. Those are the happiest times of my life. I had eleven children altogether, but the others were from my first husband, so they were grown.

He came home at noon, and he said, "I won't be back," and that's all he said, and he left. Half of his stuff was gone, anyway. One of my daughters and I were sewing at the kitchen table. She didn't say a word, I didn't say a word, and the silence was deafening. Well, finally we talked about it a little bit. That night when the kids came home, they were all laying on the carpet in the living room, wall-to-wall kids. And I told them that he wouldn't be back. Little by little each one opened up, and they started crying and telling me a lot of things that I didn't know. One example is on Thursday night I'd go to choir practice, and he would abuse the kids while I was gone. He would beat them, and they didn't dare tell me because he threatened them if they did. It was after midnight when we all went to bed. That was just before Christmas. We had no money, no food, presents, nothing. We didn't have any Christmas dinner. We got it from the mission, but we had this artificial tree, and that was already up when he left home. I would find something wrapped in a newspaper under the tree, and the children would give something of their own to another brother and sister. That was our Christmas, but that said a lot to me how much they cared. A bond was knit that Christmas.

My husband had been seeing this other woman. Well, he had been seeing women all along. He would come home from work while we were having our devotions in the living room and go in and shave. But it was always because he was going out with the guys. A lot of nights he didn't come home at all. We got married on a Saturday, and the following Tuesday he was out all night, but he said he was with the guys. That was the pattern all through our marriage, and then it got worse the longer we were married. I didn't say anything. I think back, and I think that I knew, but I wouldn't let myself know. That's the only way I can reason it out. One night a lady called and said she couldn't give me her name, but did I know my husband was running around with another woman? And I remember saying no. The phone call was real shocking, and she told me the woman's name, told me that she worked with my husband, and that at the last Christmas party he bought her a red dress. She knew everything about this woman and told me all about it, and I remember being real upset, very hurt. I confronted him, but he denied it. He would always say he was out with the guys.

He had a pattern. He would be out all night, and then about four o'clock the next afternoon he'd call home as though nothing ever happened, and he'd say, "Whatcha doing?" and I'd say this or that, whatever I was doing, and he'd just have a conversation with me. Looking back, it was like he was feeling the water before coming home, but I can't say we ever discussed those nights. One reason was he would only tell me what he wanted me to know. Anyway, I wasn't going to get the truth, so I blocked a lot of that out.

At dinner I was trying to keep food warm. I'd throw it out eventually. And he'd say, "I forgot." I'd say, "John, how can you forget a wife and eight kids at home? Why don't you call?" If I had a problem during the day with the kids, when he'd come home, I'd tell him what the problem was, but I would end up feeling like I was so stupid to even approach him about it. A lot of things were left unsaid because he made me feel stupid. He had a great way of doing that. I would end up feeling like I bothered him, took his time, how dumb of me to even bring it up.

He complained that I spent too much money on food. One day he came home and said, "There's going to be a woman coming in, and she's going to teach you how to economize on food," and so I said okay. So the day came, this woman came to the door, and she said we're going to talk about economizing on food. So we sat down at the table and exchanged ideas, and when she's getting ready to leave, she said, "I feel like I've learned more from you than you learned from me." He come home that night, and he said, "Did that woman come?" I said, "Yes." He said, "What did she say?" And I said, "She felt like she learned more from me than I learned from her." And the subject was dropped, never brought up again. After he left home, two weeks later, she called on the phone and said, "Would you be interested in helping me teach a home economics class at the college?" and I said, "I can't do it." I said, "My husband left home, and I'm stunned. I can't even think straight." She came to my house, looked in my cupboard and fridge. She couldn't believe we didn't have any food. She said, "You don't have to live like this."

She took me in her car down to social services. This boy that was going to type up my answers for the application was young enough to be one of my sons, and I kept hearing in my mind, "Anybody on welfare is a bum." All I could do was look out the window and cry. I couldn't talk, and so they waited and finally I answered the questions. When I left that day, I had a check for over four hundred dollars and a handful of food stamps.

When I was living with my husband, I never saw his paycheck, but every two weeks he'd say, "Where's your list?" I'd get out my list. For example, one pair of socks, thirty-nine cents; a new light bulb; groceries; and like that. He would go over that with me before he would give me another amount for two weeks, and he'd say, "Now make that do," and I always did. When I left welfare that day with all these food stamps and a check, I said, "Who do I account to?" She said, "You don't account to anybody. That's yours." So I went home and got groceries, loaded the cupboards—it was great. That way I had enough money to pay my rent, because I was really worried. I didn't have a job. How was I going to make the house payment, the car payment? How was I going to live? And I thought, they're really going to take my kids away, but then they didn't. This was two weeks after he left me. The kids say that until then the mission gave us food. I just don't remember. That was a real difficult time.

When I grew up, all the people that were on welfare were bums, according to my parents. And so one day here I am on welfare and food stamps, and so when we'd go grocery shopping, it was real hard to go through those lines. It was very humiliating. Oh, man! My ex-husband gave us no money. He had eight children, but I don't think he cared about any of them. To him they were just a burden. I know they were, or he wouldn't have left home.

The woman he married had a government job, and after I got on Aid to Dependent Children she got into my records and reported me for fraud. We had cemetery lots, and I was supposed to fill out all the property we owned. Well, it was one house, one car, and that's all I filled out. She knew about the cemetery plots, and I never thought of that as property cause you don't live in the cemetery. So we had to be at the Department of Social Services one morning, and it was pouring. No overhang—we just stood in the rain. I reported right away because I couldn't imagine what I did wrong, and I find out it was the cemetery plots. They closed my case. I was cut off completely—all support. She knew this because she worked there. And it was just a hassle for a couple of months, although there was nothing they could do to me. I didn't do anything wrong, but she knew how to play the system to make it uncomfortable for us.

I had never met a woman like her. She would call the house and say, "Is John there?" She'd say, "This is his secretary." He'd been living with her, and he asked me to go with him to her apartment to get his clothes. He was coming back home. So I did, and then the next day she called and said, "Let me talk to John." I said, "I don't think he wants to talk to you." She says, "Put him on the phone." I did. Today if she said that, I'd have an entirely different approach. I didn't know how to deal with her. He says to me, "Tell her I don't want to talk," so I went back to the phone and said, "He doesn't want to talk to you." She said, "Put him on the phone." This is the second time. I said, "John, she wants to talk to you." He said, "What do I say?" I said, "Just tell her, 'I'm home with my wife, leave me alone.'" And he told her that, but she didn't leave him alone, and then the very next night he was with her again.

He only stayed with her a couple years, and then she divorced him. He came back and wanted to come home, and I said, "No, that's okay. I don't need you now." Then he remarried. Now he's remarried again. That's a lot of victims.

When my youngest boy was in school all day, I went to adult ed and got my high school diploma, but I would be home before the kids got home from school, so it worked out fine. I remember the first time the kids were in school all day and I was alone. I should have gone shopping, and I couldn't go. I couldn't go out alone. I'd wait until the kids got home so I could take somebody with me. I had never been alone. There had always been someone with me all those years, so to go out alone, that was really scary to me. When I did start going out alone, I would be just frantic to get home and then one day I thought, "Why am I in such a hurry to get home? There's nobody there." But see, through the years when I did go, I'd hurry to get home because there were kids at home waiting, so I got over that obstacle.

When I was in school, you went to eighth grade, but normally you didn't go into high school because women didn't do much other than stay home and help Mama and then grow up and get married. So I went to the community college for a couple years, and I learned how to type—a couple of my boys were there at the time, and they kind of helped me get started—and took shorthand and some other classes. When I was fifty-two, I got a job with an organization that helps women get off welfare, get into the working world, and earn some money. It was $4.44 an hour, and as my pay increased, they decreased my ADC, and they stuck with me until I was able to take care of the kids myself.

By that time some of them had married and moved on. I ran my own household. I've been doing it ever since. After I went to work everybody pitched in. We did it together. The girls would do laundry and clean. The boys did the yard work, the outside work, the painting. I didn't ask the boys to help with laundry or cooking. I didn't need to—I had enough girls. When I started working full-time, the youngest was like probably thirteen, fourteen, cause it took a couple years at adult ed and a couple years at college.

First, I got a part-time job at the Department of Motor Vehicles, but I needed full-time with all those kids, and so three months later I got a full-time job in the Accounting Department at the DMV. I've been working there ever since. I like my job. I've made a lot of friends. I have no reason to quit.

Women of My Generation
Closed Their Eyes

Cynthia Bowles

She was born in 1935 in the Midwest. (See also p. 259)

We all wanted Prince Charming. We all went to the movies and saw *Gone with the Wind* twenty-five times, so we all wanted to marry Rhett Butler. I have three sisters who have been married and divorced several times, and they can't marry nice, sensible men. They're looking for a Clark Gable, somebody really macho and strong—"Throw me around a little bit." They pick some of the biggest studs you ever saw because a nice, easygoing guy is boring.

Caroline Hodges

She was born in 1927 in the Deep South, where she lives with her husband. She has five adult children and has always been very involved in volunteer work. "Religion is very primary in my life. I go to mass every day." (See also pp. 46, 54 and 412)

Not having a commitment that is "until death do us part" is why marriages don't last. People today, even if they're very much in love, realize when they get married that there's a likelihood they'll divorce. I would hate to think you thought about that during the ceremony! It gets back to the old Protestant work ethic. Marriage is work. Marriages don't just continue because two people love each other, or because they share a home or children or finances. It's hard to live with somebody, even when you love them, and you have to make a lot of adjustments, accept a lot of disappointments. This equality between the sexes tends to make it more difficult. Sometimes one has to dominate, and it was a lot easier for me to be dominated. In fact, I married my husband because I felt he could make good decisions and smooth the path for me, and I didn't feel at all badly about taking advantage of his position in the community. Those giving and taking roles can change and go back and forth, but there are some people who give a lot more than others, and traditionally it's been the woman. If the marriage is important to her, then she is willing to give more to maintain her marriage.

Now, if I were being beaten, then I can understand, you can't live where you're abused physically. Everybody abuses psychologically. I abuse my husband sometimes, and he abuses me, unintentionally very often, but you've just got to swallow a lot and say, Is it gonna be any better separate? I don't see a lot of happy people separate. Most people marry somebody else, and who is to say it's gonna be a lot better the second time? If I could find somebody I thought I'd be a whole lot happier with, or better off with—but with all of Stuart's faults, he's got a lot of good points. You have to believe that marriage is important to maintain. It's just like anything else in life. If you want it to grow and flourish, then you've got to weed and water, and it takes some of that every day. You can't just do it now and then.

I've been married forty-three years, and Catholics do not practice birth control, or at least they didn't then, or they weren't supposed to. Marriage has been good to me. That doesn't mean I'm never lonely or disappointed. I have five children, and I always had a maid. I didn't realize I didn't like children till after they were grown. I hate to play games, I hate to hear spelling. I knew I wasn't enjoying it, but that's just what you did. You're supposed to do what you're supposed to do whether you like it or not. I guess the older they got, the more I enjoyed them, and I like them now best of all.

Sally Evans

She was born in New England in 1920. She lives in Boston and is retired from her job as a lab technician. She has two children and four grandchildren.

I was thirty-two when I got married. It was a late age. I felt very pressured. One time my mother said to one of my sisters, "I don't want any old maids around here." It was an embarrassment to her that I was not married. And when I finally did marry, I didn't marry a man who was right for me.

My husband was a dentist. He was a very bright man but had so many neurotic problems that he was his own worst enemy. He was very rigid, not a fun person. I was married to him for ten years, until he died. I have a son and a daughter, and they were four and six when he died.

I was not physically battered, just emotionally. My husband did a lot of putting me down. He went to bed very early so that in the evenings I had nobody even to talk, to and I remember being on the telephone talking to my brother, and the next day my husband started a whole fuss about why I was on the phone for so long, and I said, "Well, why do you care what I was doing? You were in bed." He had awakened and heard me talking on the phone. He was very jealous. He accused me many times. He used to call me on the phone every day to check on me when I desperately needed a little nap while my baby was sleeping. He was a very sick man, very neurotic. I wanted to break away from him, but I didn't have the courage to because I had two young children. I just stuck with it. I wasn't working from the time my older child was born.

At that time divorce wasn't as acceptable as it is now, but I was not at all concerned about social disapproval. I'm a very practical person, and I just had it in my mind that I couldn't make it on my own. That was the only thing that was upsetting me. I could have dealt with the rest.

My husband made the decisions and was very much in control. I wasn't put off by the fact that he was what I now call very bossy, very domineering. I guess I liked it. It was generally accepted at the time that the man made the important decisions. He was the breadwinner, and if the wife earned any money, it wasn't really very important. I remember there was one young man I went out with a number of times, but he didn't appeal to me because he was sort of docile and sweet. To me this was like he wasn't manly, and so I waited for manly! I have quite different feelings now. I admire my son-in-law, who is very much like this young man that I rejected so many years ago. When I look at my son-in-law, who does everything with his wife, with the children, I think it's great. They're both career people, and they both do all the work that's involved. They're both in it together.

My husband was of very little help around the house. He kept reminding me that he was working all day and he needed his rest. Whatever help he gave was very grudgy. He said that he would be more involved when they were a lot more grown up, but by the time they were four and six he was dead. He liked them and he was proud of them, but he didn't want to get involved in taking care of them. That was my job. He was 44 years old when he had a heart attack and died.

After my husband died, I was lucky. I got some insurance money for myself and my children, plus I had about ten thousand dollars in the bank, which was a lot more than it is now. Because I'm very thrifty and practical, I lived on that money for a few years until they were finally both in school until three. Then I had a job from nine to two, so I was home when they were home. While they were in kindergarten, they only went to school for a couple of hours. And I remember people saying to me, "Well, why don't you get yourself a job?" and I said, "No, it's more important for me to be with my children."

I've never remarried. I did meet a number of men when my children were very young, but I had so many responsibilities, and I felt very guilty because they didn't have a father and I was always working part-time. I felt I couldn't marry anybody who wouldn't become a partner with me in taking care of these children. That was my first priority. I had some poor experiences with men who were resentful because they felt I was paying too much attention to the children. I just gave up on the idea, and by the time my children were older and I was ready, there weren't that many available men. Occasionally, I still meet men even at this advanced age, and I've noticed that I don't really give them a chance. In spite of all the growing up I've done, I'm still a little frightened. I still remember my marriage. So on one level I've gotten over it, but on a deeper level, I really haven't.

Dorothy Sommer

She was born in 1912 and lives in New York City. She worked mostly in advertising and never married. (See also pp. 27, 60, 228 and 422)

I was at a swimming party in Connecticut, and I was about twenty-three years old. I was in the bathhouse, and two ladies were in the adjoining booth, and they were talking about a woman whose husband was two-timing her. And one woman says, "Well, all she has to do is just close her eyes and pretend she doesn't see it." She knew what she was talking about—she wanted to keep her own marriage together, and so she pretended that she didn't see. Women of my generation closed their eyes, turned their faces. You'd never tell from their behavior that they weren't the wonderful married couple that they pretended to be. Close friends might know differently.

I remember one woman, her husband was flirting with me at a party, and we were having a really wonderful time. It was time to leave, and the wife—she's utterly charming, no malice—says, "Thank you, Dorothy, for giving my husband such a good time." And she was really sincere. She knew that he was a ladies' man; he was the kissing-hand type, and if there was a good-looking woman in the room, he would zero right in on her. She must have known all her life she'd have to put up with it, and she just adjusted to it. What she did was she had a good time watching; she knew he would come home. Women were financially dependent. Look at my mother—what would she have done if she had to go out and raise three children? She was a good cook; she could have taken a job as a domestic, as a cook!

When I moved back to New York, I was about thirty-five years old. I had a friend on the West Side who I went to visit. Her eyes were black, and she was so bruised. We were sitting in the living room, and I said, "Ellen, how did that happen to you?" and she said, "Do you want to know?" and I said, "Yes." She said, "Do you see these?" Her bracelets. "They cost me." She stayed with that man because the next day he went to Tiffany and bought her a diamond bracelet. My friend had a so-called wonderful life. They had a house in Florida, and she was down there for six months. She had beautiful furniture, a beautiful apartment, beautiful clothes. There wasn't a thing that man didn't lavish on her, but that's what she endured to have it. He was such a nice man on the surface, and that was the first time that I was aware of wife battering. Then I began to see small signs in other women that they were enduring things.

I Always Had a Wild Temper

Belle Riding

She lives in San Diego with her husband. She owns and runs a coffee shop.

"I was born in Wittick, Indiana, in 1928, and my mother died during childbirth. My grandparents adopted me. From what I gather, my father and my mother didn't want me, and she tried to have an abortion and it didn't work. I guess he was mean to her all the time so that's why my grandparents adopted me when I was born, so he couldn't have me. I think he must have died when I was about seven or something. I only saw him once that I can recall. He came over and brought a basket of fruit." (See also p. 64)

I was raised by my grandmother and grandfather and aunt, who had one son, Bill, who was two years older than me. Her husband had died, so we all lived in the same house. We lived on a farm. We were what the northerners called sharecroppers. You go out and feed the chickens and milk the cows, and all this before you go to school. And a school bus drives a long way to pick you up, about thirty miles, and you go to school, and you come home and you feed the chickens and milk the cows and take care of all the animals. That's the life of a kid on a farm in Indiana in those days.

I considered all the animals my friends, but every year we had to kill a few, for canning and for meat. You had raised it, and then you go out and kill it. I can't eat my friend, so I didn't eat any meat at that time. I didn't mind killing chickens, though. God, I hated 'em. I had to clean up the henhouse every weekend, but I don't think I ate chicken, either. I can still smell those old stinking feathers. Pretty uneventful life. Kids nowadays don't have enough to do, can't keep busy.

I was on the farm till I was fourteen, and then my grandparents died. When the war started in '41, '42, my cousin joined the Marine Corps, and my aunt and I worked in a factory in Wabash, Indiana. All the kids that I knew were doing the same thing.

I figure I was fourteen and a half, fifteen. I worked in the restaurant part of the paper mill, took the lunch wagon around the factory. Later on, I went to work in a factory that made rubber products used on tanks and all kind of army material. I worked on weekends and after school. You were expected to go to school and get an education and be able to work and support yourself.

I finished high school, and I decided I'd rather get married than go to college. They're not getting married as young nowadays and not messing up their life. Little smarter, I think.

I had a scholarship to go to the dental college in Fort Wayne to be a dental assistant, but I didn't use it. That was a stupid decision. When you're seventeen, you kind of think you're tired of school and want to get out and be on your own. When Joe came along, he was just out of the service and lots of fun to be with, always laughing, having a good time, and so we said I do. I had one son when I was eighteen and a half.

Mike was two when we moved to Tucson, Arizona. A year of pure hell. I hate Arizona—there's no trees, no green grass. There's the sun. My cousin lived there and my husband decided we would go live close to them, and we stayed there for a year. Joe would have three jobs at one time. He was a jack of all trades—work in a factory, work in a service station, always working.

Before we left Indiana, I kept on working at the factory, and a lady took care of Mike for me. I didn't work in Arizona. I stayed home, took care of Mike. We decided we'd move to California. We moved to Richmond. I was twenty, twenty-one. I decided I would go to work, and I went to a drive-in. I'd never done restaurant work. The boss hired me. I worked in the Ferris Wheel Drive-In in Berkeley. He said, "I'll teach you how to be a carhop and hang trays. Go out and get the order." I would order like two hamburgers, two milkshakes, and he'd put up four hamburgers and four milkshakes cause he knew I was going to drop one before I got to where I was going. That was part of my training, and then I finally learned to hang the trays on the window without making a mess. You had to hook 'em over the edge of the window and then flip the stand up against the side of the car.

I worked there for three years. It was fun. In the evening all the college kids would come down and meet there—3030 Telegraph. The parking lot was from two streets and they just parked three cars deep, and then somebody in the front row would want out and they'd all have to back up. All easy to get along with, all friends. In those days, the college kids were fun people. They weren't like they got later on; they got weird, you know.

Meanwhile, I got a divorce from my husband. He came home and I wasn't there that one particular time. I was just down to a little restaurant where Gene, my present husband, worked. He was helping out—his friends owned it; it was just a little hamburger place—and I went down there, talking. When I came home, Joe said, "You've been out seeing somebody else." I said, "No, I haven't." "Yes, you have," and he slapped me and busted my lip. And then I just laughed and said, "Well, I haven't been out with anybody, but I'm going out now," and I turned around and left. That was the only time he ever hit me. He moved out and took my new Plymouth and went back to Indiana, and I and Mike stayed here.

Joe and I were just incompatible, I guess. We hadn't even gotten out of the church yet, and he said, "From now on you belong to me. You don't talk to anybody unless I tell you to." From then on, it was just one big fight. I should have turned around right then and gone back and said, "I want to call this off." That was a man's attitude in those days. He'd get mad and say, "You can't go out; you can't go over to your aunt's house; you can't go anyplace without me." This is supposed to be a partnership—not as far as he was concerned. He could do as he pleased, but I couldn't. No sign of that before getting married, just ready and willing to go out and go dancing, and go with other couples, and just have a real good time.

I could go to work if he wanted the money bad enough. I had to help pay the bills. All the money was pooled. Like I say, he was always working, changing jobs. One year he filled out his income tax thing, and I think there was twenty-three jobs on it, and two of them he missed. They looked us up five years later to get the seven dollars tax fom Indiana, and they found us in Richmond. The IRS will find you sooner or later.

By the time we lived in Richmond, he was running around with a guy, and they were going out on dates with other women, but I wasn't supposed to. I wasn't supposed to do anything. I was supposed to work and come home, and maybe he and his buddy would be out with a couple of girls—just friends—yeah, uh huh, yeah, just friends. Okay.

Oh, I fought back. He told me I couldn't do something one time, and I said, yes, I was going to do it, and he stood in front of the car, so I tried to run over him and he jumped on the bumper, missed him. Another time we were out in the woods and he said I couldn't do something, and he turned around and walked away from me. I told him to stop and he didn't stop, so I shot him in the back of the leg. We were out shooting rifles for some reason or other. He kept on walking, and the day he left he still had that lead in the back of his leg. He didn't do anything about it. He was quit fighting at that time. I always had a wild temper. Mellowed out now. I stayed married seven years. Divorce was unheard of in those days. After the war ended, divorces got a lot more common.

After Joe left us, my present husband started babysitting for me. Gene babysat when I was working all night long, and he'd babysit some more, and I'd go out with the girls and we'd go to San Francisco. Yeah, better deal this time. I wasn't married to him. Gene was my boyfriend. We didn't get married till I came down here to San Diego in '55. Meanwhile, he moved to Sacramento to work in a print shop, and my son moved with him. I'd go up on my days off and do the laundry and clean their house, and they lived up there, and they lived up there, and I lived in Berkeley. Gene's quiet, never says he's angry even if he is. So it's just silent with him. Gene don't fight, won't even give you a good argument. It works out better not fighting. That way you don't have to apologize.

Gene felt like a father to Mike. Mike went to school in a little country school. Gene would drop him off on the way to work. I was still carhopping, working nights and sleeping days. Gene would be working days, and Mike would be in school, and they had a house in the country with some friends that lived on the same lot who had a son, so he would just go to their house when the school bus would drop him off. Worked out better that way.

I went to Sacramento for a short time and worked as a carhop up there, and I hated Sacramento. The weather—you're either hot or cold in Sacramento, so we decided to move to San Diego, and we packed up and came down here. Gene was from San Diego.

I worked down at the Zanzibar. They had a bar, a dining room, coffee shop, and a drive-in. Zanzibar went bankrupt eventually, and I started working here in La Jolla at the Coffee Cup in 1956. The people that owned it, there was a man and his daughter, and I was a waitress for them. Then they sold it to an older couple, and I worked for them until she got cancer and they wanted to sell, so in '72 I bought it from them. Six-thirty to two-thirty five days a week; I would go crazy sitting home all day. I've enjoyed it. Same customers all the time. It's just all the working people and the town people. We get very few tourists. Know everybody in this little town and know everybody's business.

That's my life. That's not much of a life. Not much of a life at all, but here I am. Let's see, my son moved to Boise, Idaho. He had bad eyes. He was legally blind. The doctors always said they put too much whatever they put in babies' eyes at that time and they burned 'em. Anyway, he went to a special school, and he wasn't supposed to drive, but he did. He was killed in a motorcycle accident about six years ago. Yup, bound to ride those motorcycles. It wasn't his fault. He was riding real slow, and a truck came out of a Safeway parking lot without stopping, hit him as he was driving in Baker, Oregon, and police from Baker says, "He don't realize how bright the sun can be up here in Oregon at that time of day. That's why the truck driver didn't see him." Uh huh. But life goes on.

This Square That My Kids Thought I Was

Jean Hughes

She was born in 1923 in Butte, Montana, and lives in La Jolla, California. (See also pp. 48 and 436)

In 1968, I went back to work for seventeen years at the University of California at San Diego in the lab at the Student Health Center. I enjoyed working there. I had the option of being off in the summer, which was wonderful because our children were still at home. I enjoyed students. I liked it even in the crazy years when they were streaking; that was really funny.

The job made me be a better mother. Instead of this square that my kids thought I was, I was able to ease up a lot. I was in a different space, as they call it, because it didn't occur to me for a long time that my kids would be experimenting with drugs, but now I know every one of them did.

We had friends whose children became addicted. There were students experimenting with all types of drugs to have highs, and I could never understand that they were talking about how everybody was polluting the world, and yet they were polluting their own bodies with these drugs. One person got too much nitric oxide and had brain damage. Other people went on a high and died. That was a worry for me. Maybe because of my job, another concern was diseases and having children out of wedlock. Whether it was my daughter or my sons, I wanted them to be responsible. I saw a lot of pregnant women in my work. I would say to my children, How would you like to have been a child whose parents had to put you up for adoption? Or how would you like to have an abortion or several abortions? It always puzzled me because these were intelligent women at this university, and yet they would be a victim of this not once but several times. And then I would see the people who had gonorrhea and all the other venereal problems, and I would think back on my days of college. We were free of all that. It was a burden to these students, men and the women, but mostly the women.

There was this peace, love baby, and dropping out. There was a time when our kids were thinking, "What do you need a college education for? Why should I go to school?

Don't listen to anyone over thirty." So we thought, "Gosh, the schools are getting pretty awful doing so many radical things." John graduated from the University of Utah. We thought what a wonderful place that university would be—it would not have these conditions.

Our oldest son went there for two years. He loved it. He was having such a good time. He had a friend that had a plane, and they would fly to Stanford to a game; they'd fly to Colorado. I didn't even know he was doing this. Our second son started up there—he didn't even last the whole year. It was so different from his life in California, and he loved skiing, so he stopped school and went up and got a job on the ski hill. So they had a lot of fun, but they weren't really serious, and so that was a difficult part of the sixties for our family, getting them started in school. My greatest fears were that they wouldn't be able to make a living and that they would not broaden their horizons, get an education, understand, have more than just television.

One of our sons called up one day and said, "Could I come over and speak to you about something?" And I thought that was kind of unusual. He came over and said, "What do you think about me going into the ministry?" And I said, "Stacy, whatever you want to do that would make you happy, you do it. I don't care what it is as long as it's legal." And so that's what he did. Maybe he's our salvation—John and I, we are not members of any church. I don't feel that I'm a heathen, really, but I'm unchurched— that seems to be the politically correct term being used these days.

It took a while for our children to really get with the program, and it was because of the times. We didn't have the tools or the smarts to know how to handle them at that time. In retrospect I would do it differently, but I'm proud of all of them because they're all good citizens and working. Every one has a degree.

Abigail Midgeley

She lives in Ohio, has eleven children and was seventy-two years old when interviewed. (See also pp. 29, 60 and 241)

Those teenage years were a challenge. That's the best way to put it. Well, that was because there was no father in the home and the way he left, the bottom just dropped out of everything.

This was the sixties now, all this free love and drugs. Everything that came our way the kids got into it. It was unreal, and at that time their father lived in a town nearby, and so when the kids wanted to do something and I said no, they'd get mad at me and go to his house, and then he would always say, "Well, I always told you your mother's kind of crazy. She's one of those religious fanatics. So when they'd come home, they'd be twice as cocky, so it was twice as hard.

I raised the children in the church. They left it for a few years, but I've seen them all come back. There were some bad times. There was a lot of hurt, and so they struck out at the ones they cared the most about, and they all hurt each other. They didn't go out deliberately and say, "I'm going to do this cause it'll hurt Mom," but in their blindness, they were striking out.

One of my daughters got pregnant when she was sixteen, and I helped her raise the baby for two years while she finished high school, and then she married and left. Another daughter was picked up one night and raped. One of the boys ran away— troubles in school, at home—and he ran away to go to his older brother in Texas, and we had no idea where he was at first. A lot of bad things happened.

One day I was called to the school. One of my daughters OD'd. I don't remember getting in the car. I don't remember driving there. I just remember leaving the house and running down the hallway at school to the clinic. The first thing I did was start to shake her. "What did you take? What did you take?" Cause they wanted to know what she took so they could give her a shot to counteract it, and she wasn't talking, so I'm yelling, "What did you take? What did you take?" So she says real quiet, "Mom, right now I'm fighting for my sanity." So I just sat quiet, scared to death, but she did come out of it all right.

Betty Marin

She was born in California in 1930, went to UC Berkeley for some three semesters, and got married when she was twenty. (See also p. 37)

My daughter was born in 1952. When she was about seventeen, she got mixed up with the drug scene at her high school. So when she went to college, she stayed for the first quarter or two and then about a week before Christmas, she just up and disappeared, and I was frantic. A week later I got a note from her—she'd gone to Mexico. She lived in Mexico for a while and ended up teaching English to bellboys, busboys, and waiters in Cancun. Then she came back and worked and never lasted very long in jobs.

She met her first husband, and they got married in '77, I guess it was. He was this very likeable kid, but he was big on marijuana, and he not only smoked it, he grew it, and he made a lot of money growing pot, every bit of which went down the drain on more marijuana. I didn't realize until a little bit later how bad this marijuana scene was. They lived up in Oregon, but she came home one time to go to a wedding with us, and she stepped off the plane with this huge suitcase, and I thought, "Oh boy, she's planning to stay a while," and she said, "Mom, I just can't live with him. He's just out of it all the time on pot, and I don't want this to be my life anymore." So we talked it over, and she finally decided to get a divorce.

She went back to college and met this young man that she was crazy about, and when I met him I thought, "Oh, big mistake—he's going to break your heart some day." Well, lo and behold, she found she was pregnant. He came over and said, "You've just got to talk her into an abortion," and I said, "She's not going to have an abortion. She wants that child. If this is your attitude, she doesn't expect one thing from you and you don't have to take any responsibility." He signed her away, and her current husband, the father of the other two, he's legally adopted her. They've been married eight years. My daughter was thirty-two when she graduated from college, and the baby was five months old. We have a picture of her in her cap and gown with this little tiny baby in her arms. I really admired her because she went to classes all the way through this pregnancy, and when she had the baby, finals were starting. She was off four days and went back because she had to finish. I went up to her apartment and babysat like mad with this child, and we'd expel milk so I'd have something in the bottle so she could be at classes.

I didn't have a problem with the fact that she wasn't married. We loved her so much, and we didn't want her to not have this child. For my parents, it would have been a disaster if I had a child out of wedlock. I bent over backwards to not have my daughter be like I was. I encouraged her to give her opinions, to be independent, and in some ways I think I overshot the runway with her.

Betsy Miller

She was born in Oakland in 1928 and lives with her husband in La Jolla, California. (See also pp. 35, 52 and 407)

My daughter is estranged from me right at this point. I miss seeing her, but I hope it's not permanent. She's an artist, and she lives with her husband, and he works in the movies in Los Angeles. We were good friends for years and sent her through three or four different schools. She married this man, was separated from him for a while, and came back to us. Then when she went back to him, she told us that she needed to be separated from us to make her own life. It's sort of the new psychology—I've read some of these books about poisonous parents. Or psychologists that say, well, you just have to make your own way, and family is bad. So we sort of accepted this, and we're sorry, but maybe it'll change sometime in the future. She's an extremely talented and lovely person.

Cynthia Bowles

She was born in the Midwest in 1935. She is a homemaker and lives in Southern California with her husband of forty years. His professional education and work have taken them from the Midwest to the East Coast and then to California, where they have lived for many years. (See also p. 246)

*W*hen I was growing up, there was a train that came and went from town once a day and a bus. There hasn't been any rapid transportation in and out of that town in thirty, forty years. They've torn out the train tracks. Now it's a walking path. The only way you can get there is with your car. The closest airport is about seventy miles away. The town next door, twenty miles away, used to be where you went shopping. They built a shopping center on the edge of town, so instead of having your lovely little shops in town, you've got the shopping center, and then Wal-Mart and Kmart came in. These towns with twenty thousand people used to be the business hub for the community. Now all of Main Street is boarded up. It's very sad, this homogenization.

My grandchildren and children never lived in a small town. My children's graduating class in high school had about 750 students. They do not have a sense of place that I had growing up in a small midwestern town. I always had in the back of my mind, if my world fell apart, I would go back.

Our children kind of consider my hometown as the one constant in their lives because we've lived on the East Coast and the West Coast. I was born and grew up in one house, and it's still in the family. My mother still lives there. I have a sister there. My children would have gotten a real sense of who they are if they had grown up there. I don't think kids get that, and I think that's one of the reasons we have such a problem with peer pressure. When I was growing up, everybody knew who I was. Growing up in a small town, you couldn't get too far out of line without your folks hearing about it. I didn't grow up in a wealthy family. But I never felt like I was poor or deprived. It was just the sense of community and the sense of knowing who you were. I was Mike Andersen's daughter. Everybody knew you. My grandfather lived with us when I was young. Several of my mother's relatives were part of the extended family, and then I had on my father's side other relatives that lived right there in the same town.

In one sense kids have much more freedom in a small town than you'd have here in the city. We lived a block from the school. We would sit with the door open; when we heard the warning bell, we'd run for school. We had a beautiful playground. Now, would you let your six, seven year old go off to a playground alone here in the city? I had a fit when our granddaughter was in kindergarten and I went to pick her up one day and found her sitting all alone in front of the kindergarten bus. I went right to the office and complained and said, "Why is she there? She should have been in the bus." You really have to walk a very thin line with the kids today to not make them total paranoids and yet make sure they're careful about what they do. It's sad.

Family:
The Second Generation

I'm very pro women's movement, but the women's movement in the early 70's did not value women staying home and being full-time mothers and childrearers. I think that was really unfortunate. At that time, you'd go to a party and people would say "What do you do?" and when you'd say "Well, I'm taking care of my kids," their eyes would glaze over. I went to a couple of NOW meetings, and I didn't like the women there. I thought they were trying to throw the baby out with the bathwater. I certainly believed in equal pay, equal opportunity, and equal jobs, but I didn't believe that it wasn't fulfilling to be home rearing children.

—Kate Merrill, born 1945

"I think the women's movement is very good for women. I really do. Because they saying we can do what we wanna do. We don't have to ask nobody permission to do it. Just go out there and do it. I would never take that vow no more letting the man think he'll be head of the household and I'll obey him. I had a relationship for about five years. He asked me to marry him, but I say no. My mother said that everybody should get married at least once in their life, so I did it and that was it.

—Isadora Damon, born 1936

You Never Realize
How Much Work Is Involved

Miyako Moriki

She works fourteen hours a week at a shopping mall in Richmond, California.

"I was going to work here only a year. I've been here almost three years. I rent strollers, direct traffic, answer the telephone, help customers out with complaints. It's kind of fun. I'm a people person, so I see people rather than stay home.

"I was born in 1938. I'm the youngest of four. My father, I think, was sixteen when he immigrated to America, worked, and went back to Japan to get married. It was an arranged marriage. My mother got married and came back with my dad."

Miyako's daughter Kim Moriki also appears in the book.

*Y*ou did well in school, you got married at a certain age, you raised the children. That was the tradition I followed. I think I was nineteen when I met my husband. He was selling Kirby vacuum cleaners. He tried to sell one to my sister, and my sister says, "You got to come and see this guy that's selling vacuum cleaners!" I was twenty-one when I married.

I have a degree from the University of California in teaching, and I was never meant to be a teacher. In our ethnic background, all the women went into nursing and teaching, and all the men went into engineering, technical fields. Our children's generation, they want more, they have more opportunities, they're exposed to more professions. We didn't have that exposure. We didn't have the options because we were severely discriminated against.

My husband brought me home a book called *Jewel in the Desert*, and it's about our relocation camp in Topaz, Utah. I was about two or three when we went there; we lived in army barracks with tar paper. We only had a potbelly heating stove with coal. In the middle of winter, it snowed, and the thing that I remember most was the teenage boys—they put water down to make an ice rink, and my dad used to make us ice-skating blades to attach to our shoes out of wood. In the camp that we were in we lucked out. We had four teachers, and we had a dentist and a doctor.

Before we went to the camps, Dad did gardening for the president of a bank. He had started a small savings account that would have been confiscated by the U.S. government. But this man took my dad's money out of his account and kept it in his name, so that when my dad got back, he had a little nest egg to fall back on. There are people that are good. We have friends that put their nurseries in names of other people that they thought they could trust. Some of them got them back; others didn't. Our parents never talked about the camps. It's in the Japanese culture—to them, it was shameful.

When we got out of relocation camp, they wouldn't even serve us in stores. My mom used to braid our hair. They would cut your hair, take your things away. We were told not to fight back cause it makes it worse. We were always scared. The Japanese custom says you've got to suffer before you can get ahead.

You will do well; you will go to college. This is what has been beaten into our heads since the day we started kindergarten. We were all going to school, keeping our mouth shut. All our energy went to that. Our folks knew the only way to get ahead was by educating ourselves.

If we were included in class functions, social functions, we were always the last ones—the last piece of cake, last in line at the Halloween Parade. All the teachers were white in those days. Probably some teachers had sons or husbands in the armed services during the war, so they didn't like minorities. But there were a lot of teachers that I have never forgotten, that really cared. They knew that the Japanese people on the West Coast that were put in the relocation camp had nothing to do with the war.

We got beat up after school every day by gangs of white people. Especially, it got bad in high school. The blacks were starting to rise, so they sided with the Oriental people. We used to have race riots; you wouldn't believe—we're talking about thirty, forty people on each side. We used to walk three miles to El Cerrito High School and three miles home because we didn't have bus fares. The black football player used to escort my sister and I home. We all lived in the county housing projects in Richmond.

When I was growing up, the blacks had tradition, goals, stability at home. The parents really cared about what their children did. If you did something bad, Mom would say, "Wait till Dad comes home," and you were punished. There was camaraderie, love, helping. The blacks noticed that we were being discriminated against, so we came together for self-protection.

The camp experience made my parents more traditional because there's a safety net in being traditional. My dad spoke English, but my mother didn't. We tried to teach her. She understood, but she didn't speak it enough to get rid of that heavy accent, so it was easier for us to talk to her in Japanese. Part of my mom not speaking better English was our fault; we were impatient.

I don't think my mom was very happy. Traditional Japanese marriages are very strict. She does what she's told, doesn't express opinions. My dad was an alcoholic; being in the relocation camp added to his drinking. He worked seven days a week to survive. We never did without, but I remember him being drunk all the time—minute he hit that door when he came home from work. She was just stuck in a situation she didn't want to be in. She made the best of it, kept the family together with my dad's drinking bouts. It's kind of sad—I didn't realize how bright and strong my mother was until she was in her seventies—until my dad started to fail—because she was raised to be a traditional Japanese wife. I will never, ever recommend anybody in this country to be a traditional Japanese wife.

She tried to instill the Japanese culture in me but yet give me the freedom to be Americanized. But it's very difficult because most of the American culture to the Japanese culture is vulgar. The Japanese custom is tradition—it's set; it's very restrictive. In American culture you go where the wind goes. You go for the opportunities. You go for it. I was the youngest, and I was considered the rebel of the four kids. When I was going to college, my mother thought the way I dressed was outrageous. Like the hippie kids—bright clothes, grew my hair long. I went to parties—that was off limits to us—tried a little drugs, learned to drive at an early age. Traditionally, we were supposed to wait until we were sixteen, seventeen, but I was sneaking out with the car when I was fourteen. Things like that which were unheard of, being from a Japanese background. I'm still very independent, a free thinker.

My mom was a seamstress and worked at home. My dad was a gardener, and they would budget their money to the thinnest. My dad didn't work during the winter cause it rains. He would put away as much as he could while he was working, and to this day we can't figure out how he saved money. We ate a lot of rice.

After my dad got sick and he had to retire, he still saved on social security. When he died, I found eight thousand dollars in his wallet under the mattress. The note in the wallet said it was for my mom when he died, that she would eat. It's a tear jerker.

When we were younger, we used to pick fruit and vegetables during the summer. We would give my folks the money, and they would put it in the bank for college. What little money they had left for education went to my two brothers, who went to college full-time. My folks helped them out, plus they worked part-time, but my sister and I got nothing. Traditionally, in a Japanese family the males are educated and if the girls wanted it, you had to fight for it—there were exceptions—and you did it mostly on your own. I fought for it. No help. They thought you should go to work as a clerk for the state, make good money. The sons get everything—education, marriage first, money. I was working forty hours a week when I got out of high school, going to college part-time, plus helping my folks out financially.

As a really young woman, I really didn't have that many dreams because I had my first child when I was twenty-two, and I had three children two years apart so my whole energy and thoughts were to raise those kids right. That's a tremendous job, and I was lucky to have a husband that made enough money so I could stay home with them.

It was boring because I'm a curious person, but I was fortunate enough to be able to have outlets, take classes, do interesting things with the kids. Right now we're at the point where we're enjoying life 'cause we have no responsibilities of raising the kids. I have a son thirty-two, Kim's thirty and another son twenty-eight. The last one just moved out in July.

I was a traditional mother, housecleaner, housekeeper—I took care of all the finances, did all the yard work, took care of the dogs. He went to work and came back, and he took us on outings. Period. We went to the park and camping. He did play with the kids, but when it came to keeping the living quarters clean, shopping for food, raising the children, I was it, even when I worked full-time. Oh, yeah. It took him this long to figure out that he has to help out.

You never realize how much work is involved until you have children. I was typical, I guess, like any other young lady—you know, all peaches and cream and things are going to work out. You're going to have that dream home. You always think of the good things before you get married, and you never think about the grunt work that goes behind it.

My mother's marriage was traditionally Japanese; mine was more Americanized—night and day. I never really followed the Japanese culture. For me, it was at times a very difficult marriage cause these ideas kind of float in your head—Japanese women are responsible for the children, the house, etc.—and that's what I did. So maybe I was following what my mom was doing cause I did everything. It just dawned on me—I was doing the same thing that my mom was doing. She raised the children, cleaned the house, did the groceries—she did everything but the bills, which I did.

My dad made all the decisions, but my husband and I, we talked about things—that's the difference. At first it was my husband's way, but maybe after the first six years it loosened up as far as decision making, finances, what the kids should do. It just kind of evolved. I refused to do things his way.

I was still going to school after I had my kids. One class here, two classes there. I did my teaching internship one semester. I knew right away I wasn't meant to be a teacher, so I went to work for the police department, graveyard. I did everything, took in juvenile kids, watched female prisoners, twelve to eight at night. This was just before they went to junior high school.

I got off from work at eight, and my husband would help me get the kids off to school. Then I would go to sleep and be up before he went to work the swing shift from four to twelve. We fixed it so we never had a sitter. I slept about six hours, a lot of little naps. The weekends we'd try to clean the place up and spend time with the kids. You take the kids to the park, and while they're playing, you're sleeping. It lasted four years. Then it was time to rest the body a little bit—I did it cause we bought a home and caught up with the bills.

I love my children dearly, but talking to three-feet people all day long just does not do it, and we were strict disciplinarians, too. When you are raising kids, there's so much to do, you don't have time for more than ten work hours a week if you want to do it right. About every three years I would go look for a job that would work around my children's schedule. Until my last kid got out of high school, I was home when they came home from school unless there was something I had to do.

I think it's horrible, women working full-time and having kids. That's why we're in the shape we're in now. They don't need a four-bedroom luxury home, they don't need two new cars every year, they don't need three kids if they want the rest of it, right? It's humanly not possible to raise good kids and have both parents working. Some do it, but I don't know how. I don't think I could do it, and my kids grew up in the age where the city had money. The school would have after-school programs, they would have kickball games, they would have chess tournaments. They don't have that anymore. Nowadays, people have to watch their kids. Some of the kids on the block are even afraid to go to school because of the danger, like guns. It's very bad. Drugs are so predominant with the kids, they would rather have drugs than go out and play. It's not like it used to be.

I stayed home, took more classes, and then my daughter was working at a bookstore and she wanted to go away for the summer. She talked her manager into me working her summer job so she'd have a job when she came back, and when she came back, she didn't want her job, so I was there at the right time. I quit because I didn't like the manager and went to another bookstore, and then Stacey's bookstore asked me to come back as a manager. It was really fun. About five years, and then they lost the lease.

If I were twenty-five years younger, knowing what I know now, I wouldn't get married. I would further my education, probably be in some creative field. I wasn't that eager to have children—too many things I wanted to do. Like Kim, my daughter, she's thirty and she's enjoying life, and she's having a ball. I think if I had a choice, I would've gone the same route. Had a career first.

I think her life has been influenced by our marriage because she saw the rough times. It's for her to find out herself that all marriages aren't the same. I tell her that, because I notice that when she has a long-term relationship, the minute they mention marriage, she cuts it off. I don't know who she talked to, but somebody convinced her that marriage and career and raising children are very difficult. Right now she wants the career, but then every now and then she throws in the biological clock, and I say, "Don't talk to me about the biological clock cause I can't do anything for you, and I'm not going to raise your kids for you, either."

I don't care if she doesn't ever get married. That's the rebel in me. I grew up traditionally, but there's always that one side that says, "Do what's best for you." It took me fifty years to figure that out, but now it's good.

My Generation Was Transitional

Priscilla Lynch

She was born in 1942. She lives with her husband in High Falls, New York, and has two daughters and two grandchildren. She has worked at a variety of jobs, including secretary and office manager.

I wasn't ready at twenty. We started dating, and five years later we got married. I came back from my honeymoon, and I was pregnant. I had my child too quickly. I was twenty-six, and I was used to doing what I wanted to do when I wanted to do it. You don't do that when you have a baby. I went from this very independent person to having a husband, a home, a baby.

At first, being home was terrible, so I worked after my daughter was born, and then I wanted another child. When my second daughter came, I was fine. I was a little more adapted. Pam was almost three when her sister was born, so I quit work because I didn't want my mom to have to watch two children, and my husband's business was taking off. I wasn't that crazy about work. I really wanted to be home with the kids, and I became a real mother and wife.

It was wonderful. I enjoyed it, but married life was difficult, having to make sure dinner was on the table, doing the laundry, cleaning, and I had this little baby. I have one of those husbands, if something lays on the floor, he steps over it. He likes to do the outside, the garden. He's not one to cook and clean. I resented that after a while. I wanted to go to work and get dressed up and be myself again.

He's a very loving man. He's been a wonderful husband, and I don't mean to sound negative. I think it's how he was brought up. He was very spoiled by his mother. Boys were raised as gods; the daughters did all the work. It was common then. I came from that kind of family. Today men pitch in more. I see that with my daughter's husband. He does so much more around the home, and I think it's great. His mother must have made him more responsible. If I had a son, I would raise him that way. My husband doesn't even know where the washing machine is. I've spoiled him. Girls today are smart. The minute they get married, the ground rules are set.

It's changed for younger women because they have to go to work, and maybe it's mothers like myself. I told my daughters, "Don't get into this. It's got to be an equal arrangement." I'm sure the women's movement had something to do with it. I think it's wonderful what girls can do today. That's why I was a little upset when my older daughter got married so young, at twenty-one. But she just fell madly in love. I kind of felt in my heart there's more out there, but now that I see my grandchildren, I love them so much. And she's going to go back to school this fall in the evening, and I'm glad. She wants to be a nurse. And her husband will watch the children, so it's great.

Nancy Douglas

She was born in 1934. She lives in a large midwestern city and works as a political consultant. (See also pp. 103 and 302)

I started my adult life in the pattern of my mother's generation: get married, have a house, have four babies. The feminist movement, because of my age and energy, and maybe my divorce, let me have my cake and eat it. I got to be traditional—cooking and gardening, volunteer leader—and then in mid-adult life the feminist movement came along, and I'm able to read all the material and buy into the tenets.

But I just thought it was fabulous being a mother, and I wouldn't have given up the experience for the world. I loved being the main man to four kids. Given my high energy, and the help of an occasional young woman, it didn't bother me that my husband wasn't very hands-on with the children. I had all or most of the responsibility. I also had all the joy. If you get up with the babies and feed them in the middle of the night, you have the joy of listening to the tugboats out on the lake. So what some people would say is a burden, I'd say, "Wasn't it wonderful."

I didn't play games with the kids, but I read to them voraciously. That was something I always enjoyed, and I liked the sports, so I was the dutiful mother at the swim meets and loved all of that. As a family, we didn't pray together, but practically from the moment the kids could stand we skied together every weekend. We got in the car, packed a backpack full of hard rolls, cheese, candy bars, apples, and we would go to the ski area. We did that every Saturday during the winter.

I wouldn't have given up that life for anything, and I also wouldn't give up the life

I've led since then. After my divorce, I moved from volunteer to paid work, became involved in politics, and married again. My generation was transitional.

Alice Dumont

She was born in 1933 and lives in a large city in the Deep South with her second husband. She loves her job as a nurse in a women's hospital.

"I was married the first time for twenty-four years and this time fourteen years. I have two daughters. From the second marriage I have no children. I was in my forties when I married." (See also pp. 102 and 457)

I was twenty when I married. In those days, if you were not married by the time you were twenty-five, you were an old maid. It was unheard of for a woman to say, "I don't want to get married." They would be ready to put you in a mental institution, especially here in the South.

When my younger daughter started school, I went out and got a job at a hospital. I grew up, and my husband and I grew apart. The only thing that we really had in common was the children. We were very, very different. When I was at work, he resented it, and I wasn't going to give it up. It meant too much to me. He was totally committed to family life, but there was very little sharing of household chores. When I got divorced, I was the one that moved. He would not leave the home. My older daughter, who was in college, said, "Mom, get out of here. Save your life. You're so unhappy." My younger daughter stayed with her daddy. I saw her every week. I worked a lot. She was very angry, resentful that I left. She didn't want to spend the night with me. She would come and see me, or I would see her, and that was it. When she was in college, we went out to dinner one evening, and she told me the words that I wanted to hear. She said, "I'm glad that you're not living together." She understood more why I could not live with him, and she was saying, "It's okay that you did what you did." It was maturation and the fact that she was dealing with him on a one-to-one basis herself every day.

I am now married to an alcoholic. I have asked him to leave, and he has. I filed for a legal separation, and I let him come back.

I could not tolerate physical abuse. My father abused my mother and my family. My mother would leave him because of the abuse, and then we would go back and leave and go back. When you grow up not having a role model as to what is a normal life, the only way you educate yourself is by living, making mistakes, finding out what normal people do, what is the correct behavior. You start out at such a great, great disadvantage choosing a husband if you've had an abusive father. So I didn't do well in the husband department, but I did fantastic in the children department. My children have been blessings from God. They are wonderful—they love me in spite of my mistakes. We have good relationships.

Mimi Miller

She was born in 1945 in North Carolina and now lives in Natchez, Mississippi, where she and her husband run the Historic Natchez Foundation. (See also pp. 79, 130 and 469)

We met at twenty-two and twenty-four and married a year and a half later. We moved to Delaware so that my husband could go to graduate school. I worked part-time doing secretarial work at the University of Delaware, and I was in graduate school part-time.

I had my first child in '71. I brought her home from the hospital and realized that emotionally I was not going to be able to go back to class and stay in the library three hours and take her to a day-care center or a babysitter. So I didn't. Instead, I babysat another child my daughter's age to pick up some money. I don't know that it makes any difference with the children. My inability to leave my children was a part of my personality that I never expected. I don't know where it came from because my mother was not like that. I just had this thing about not wanting to put my children in the care of others where they might be insecure from being left.

A year and a half later I had a second child, and he was born in Mississippi. My husband is an architectural historian, and there was no way around the fact that I had to add to the family income. I've worked part-time—ten or fifteen hours a week— but I was always self-employed until 1989. If a child was sick, I didn't have to go to work. If there was a child's program to go to, I could go. I worked at a travel agency; I did historic preservation, but I always did it at home when my husband was home to keep the children. If I had to go examine and photograph the building, I would do it when he was with the children.

When the children were little and he was working full-time and I was in the house, I did almost all the cooking and all the housework. But he was a very good father and always did his share in taking care of the children, whether it was changing a diaper or washing a load of clothes. Gradually, as the kids got older and I worked more and more, that changed. Ron now does almost all the cooking, all the grocery buying. He doesn't believe in sex roles, and it's not an intellectual choice. It's just the way he is. I expected certain roles to happen. To him if he floated and painted sheetrock, I floated and painted sheetrock.

It is a partnership marriage. And I was conditioned to thinking someone would take care of me. My husband and I have one of the happiest marriages anybody could ever have. Always have. We never quarrel. We just have always been congenial.

Lisa Drake

She was born in 1951, lives in the Deep South, and is a born-again Christian. When she decided to go to college, her husband became highly antagonistic, and they eventually divorced. They were recently remarried.

I got married, I was seventeen. That was the thing to do. Girls were not encouraged to go to college. When I was in high school, I followed the secretarial, business, technology curriculum.

We got married, and I got pregnant right away. It was a terrible time, that first year. It was the wrong thing to do, to have a child without having time to adjust to being married. But we made it. When my son was four weeks old, I went back to work at a plant. My mother kept him. I did not work for many years after my third child was born, mainly because after paying day care for three children, I couldn't really make any money. I loved being a homemaker. I was in the PTA, baked for their little parties, taught some classes at church.

When my children were in high school, I started college, and my husband wasn't opposed to it. He knew that I always wanted to go to college. But my husband did not finish high school, and he's very intimidated about that. I think that it scared him when I started going, that I might outgrow him. The longer I went, the more I was stimulated and really loved it and wanted to get my degree. I had no intention of quitting. But the longer I went, the more it bothered him. He didn't want me to do homework at home. Over the years, I had helped him to try and accomplish what he wanted. Although I didn't always agree with everything. I felt he owed me the same consideration, but he didn't feel that way. Every day I came home and I would have to battle with him, and so finally I asked him to move out.

He was very resentful. He would say things to me, like I was neglecting the family. Even the children were saying things like "You're being very selfish," and "You're only considering yourself." They just didn't seem to see my side of it. I got so emotionally traumatized that I went to my family doctor, who gave me something for my nerves, and then it just escalated to where he recommended that I see a psychologist, which I did do, and I feel that that was a real lifesaver for me.

My home was very organized when I didn't work. I had children who played ball, did swimming, took violin lessons. I kept everybody's schedule and reminded them, kept things going, and when I started going to school and doing things for myself, I was not there to do all that for them, and they were having to learn to be independent, and they didn't like it.

But at the same time, I think the reason that they would say things like that was because it was not pleasant at our house. Their father and I were arguing all the time, and they were just wanting me to go back to the way it was so there would be peace. They knew things were really bad, and nobody wants their parents to separate and divorce. So it was a very horrible time in our lives.

It must have been my second year in college that I got divorced. We were divorced about a year but separated about two years. We have been married again almost a year now. When I asked him to leave, he was happy to do it. He thought, she will never make it without me. But after about a month, he really wanted to come back home. He would come to my place of work, call me in the middle of the night, come by the house when he really shouldn't, and we would get in an argument again. It was terrible. He'd try to talk me into getting back together. But I didn't want to because I felt his attitude was no different. I don't mean it was all his fault. Looking back, I can understand how he felt to some degree, although I still feel that he should've been more supportive, and maybe we could've talked about it and said, "Well, okay, you can go to school, but you maybe need not to do this for a while" or something. We had always had a very good relationship. We always talked things out and were each other's best friend.

When my doctor asked me to go to a psychologist, I said, "No, I could never do that." And it was hard. I went to a psychologist probably six to nine months. Although I had worked for a while before I had started college, I had lost my personal identity, and my life was lived really through my family. I was Matthew's mother, Suzanne's mother, Rick's wife. That was the main thing. When I first went to see the psychologist, I told her that I felt like a fragment—this was after we had separated. She helped me find myself again. She was a real lifesaver. She herself had had a child, been through a divorce, and gone back to school. That really helped me, because she was open and said, "I had this experience, also." So she helped me get my sense of self back and realize that what I wanted was not too much to ask.

She pointed out to me that I really still loved my husband, although I felt like I couldn't live with him. And she told me that we might get back together at some point. I did love him, and I wasn't interested in anyone else, and neither was he. We were divorced a little over a year when we began going out.

He went to a hospital for a couple of weeks when we first separated and went through intensive therapy; it was very traumatic for him. When he came back home, he saw a therapist for a while. He learned a lot. The problem was that I was his whole life, as my family had been to me. He couldn't go through an hour without thinking, what is she doing? That was the focus of his therapy. At first he had to teach himself to think of other things, replacement thinking. They finally told him he needed to get a hobby. And so he did. He bought some antique cars, which he loves. He finally got interested in other things.

For the most part, it's been very good since we remarried. We had very lengthy discussions before we got to the point of saying, yes, we are going to get married again. The last months before I finished school he was very supportive. And even now, since I finished school, I'm very busy. I work full-time as an administrative assistant and also teach accounting classes with the continuing education program at the college.

I started teaching in continuing ed the summer after I graduated, and I just love it. If I could do whatever I wanted to, I would go on and get probably a master's in business education or something like that and come back and teach full-time on a college level. But I have two children in college, so that's not practical, and by the time I get my children out of school, I'll be forty-six. I would have to leave town, too. Surprisingly, my husband is open to that. He knows how important things like that are to me now. Right before school started this fall, he talked about, "Why don't you go ahead and go on to school?" and "You don't really have to work." They have some private schools about eighty-five miles from here, and I could go there two days a week and commute, even though it would be more expensive. We even talked about my going to the state university, just me moving up there and maybe coming home on the weekends. We discussed that last year when my daughter was a senior in high school, and I said, "No, I can't do that. I need to be here this year with her."

He's even talked about the possibility that he could transfer with the company and move somewhere for me to go to school. He works for a chain. It's still kinda on the back burner. But in the meantime, the teaching, the continuing ed classes—I get to do that, and I love it.

I Expanded; He Contracted

Rachel Morgan

She was born in the Midwest in 1942. Her mother's family was fundamentalist Christian from Sweden. Her father's family was Orthodox Jewish from Russia. She was raised in the Protestant church. She has lived in the South for many years. She is divorced and has three children. One of them, Lauren Morgan Stern also appears in the book.

"The agency I run is state based and works on children's issues primarily in health care, childcare, child protection. There's about fourteen of us now—some are part-time. My work has been rooted in my Christian faith—with the problems that we face in this community around children and families, I don't think we could do it if we weren't able to maintain that sense of optimism." (See also p. 103)

After my junior year in high school, my parents sent me off to boarding school. My parents more than encouraged me to go to college. That's just what one did. I was expected to be smart and to get As, but I don't remember being encouraged to prepare for or have a career. It was assumed that I would get married and have children.

I went to an eastern college, and in 1962, after my junior year, I got married to a man from the South and moved there. I finished college here and got a BA in music, because it was what I loved.

I played the piano all my life—still play for my church. When I finished college, I never had any sense of looking forward to a career. My mother wasn't employed. What I wanted to do most was have children, and I did. My first child was born a week before our first anniversary and three months after I graduated from college, and I was absolutely delighted. Between my second and third child I went to work at the half-day nursery school that my son was going to. After the third child, I stopped teaching; I had this wonderful quiet morning at home with my third baby.

We had a fairly traditional relationship. He worked, and I took care of the kids and the house. I was a lot better at taking care of kids than at taking care of the house. To the extent that we fought—it wasn't all that often—it was usually over that. "Couldn't you at least pick up your socks?" I'd say. And he'd say he really would like to pick up his socks, but he was very busy. But he didn't complain about the fact that I didn't, either. I'll definitely give him that. Socks came to exemplify the whole scenario. He was good with the kids—he would stay with them at night if I went to meetings and things like that. He would sometimes say, "I'm gonna take the kids to the zoo."

When we finally divorced, he said to me, "I didn't change; you did." And I said, "That's right." Our relationship couldn't accept the changes in my sense of my own identity. I remember marrying him and thinking that this was good because he was an academic and he was brilliant, and he needed somebody to take care of him, and I could do that. Well, after ten or twelve years I didn't want to be taking care of a husband anymore. It wasn't so much the specifics—like cooking his meals, etc.—which were kind of expected in the traditional role at that time, anyway, but an emotionally taking care of. He could be moody, but I would always be stable and strong and there to cheer him up and urge him on. It was also taking care of the details. He always liked to brag that he didn't know what he earned cause he brought his check home to me and I took care of the money. I would have dinner parties. I would say let's invite so-and-so to go to the movies and make the phone calls. In terms of having friends I would make that happen. I made Christmas happen. Holidays in general.

When he got a post-doctoral fellowship around '69, we moved to Boston for about fifteen months. I had developed this sense that once I got Hannah into nursery school, that I was gonna do something else with my life. Full-time mommying was great, but by now I had a sense of they don't need a full-time mom forever, and I have other things I want to do. I still didn't know what. In Boston most of the wives were working or in graduate school. They were building harpsichords from kits. It was very heady. And so when we came back here, I decided I'd sell real estate, because that was something you could do and make your own schedule. I did that for maybe a year—'70, '71—but I grew to really hate it because of the racism. By then you couldn't blatantly say, "Don't show houses in that neighborhood to black people." But they had these little codes—there was a certain letter on a certain page that meant you could show it to black people. I thought, "I'm not gonna be a part of this." I just quit. So much for real estate. So in '71 or '72 I went to work full-time with the Innovative Education Coalition as a VISTA worker. My husband said that that was fine, as long as it didn't interfere with his life or the life of the family. In other words, if we didn't have to argue about the socks, and dinner was on the table at a regular hour, that was okay. It didn't particularly sit well with me, but I wasn't absolutely õutraged.

The job changed my daily life. I began to have friends and companions that I came to through different interests, that were not professors or their wives. I saw myself in this next stage, where I had a sense of mission and purpose and started having goals, or at the time I called them fantasies—but I've lived them all out—about a career and what I wanted to do. It became very wearing. He was rather resentful of all that, because our lives had always been absolutely connected, and his friends were my friends and his interests were my interests and his politics were my politics. Suddenly, I had this growing sense of autonomy.

How I related to him changed, as opposed to any particular sort of daily occurrence. I may have been gone more at night, at meetings, and I do think he complained about that, but that was kind of a rollover from the volunteer days. It was kind of the same thing. I was getting this little VISTA stipend, and it was a pretty flexible little job. I stopped work when I picked the children up at school. I managed to cook and keep the kids in clean clothes, keep them healthy, do the housework as well as I ever did. So I don't think for him that an ordinary day looked that different. It was real different for me. I didn't go hang out with the other university wives and watch the kids play.

Some people have been wiser, and we obviously should have been and maybe it could have worked. But when we started growing apart, instead of sitting down and saying, "Okay, let's see how we can negotiate this," we just sort of stopped communicating. I expanded; he contracted and tightened up. It was like an equal and opposite reaction. And gradually we grew to thoroughly dislike each other. He would have moods where he wouldn't speak to me for one reason or another for a couple of days, which used to just drive me out of my tree. And it got to the point where I'd say, oh, good, he's not speaking. It was very sad, but it just totally deteriorated.

I left him. At some point I told him that I wanted out, or that I didn't love him, something like that. So then he got scared, and he tried to change. He learned how to use the washing machine, and he even started picking up around the house. He really made this effort, and he insisted that he still loved me. The effect on me was I felt incredibly guilty. Here's this man who's doing this complete about-face and he was going to be perfect, but I hated him for it. It was like, now that I don't love you anymore, you're gonna be perfect, just so that whatever happens will be my fault. It was too late. I figured that he would find someone who would be the wife he needed, who would want to take care of him. And he did. He didn't really want to change. I think he's been very happy.

We had some very stormy years after the divorce. But when the kids started graduating and there were events where it was important to be supportive and together, we did that. And we've behaved well ever since and can even enjoy each other's company at major family kinds of things.

It was important for me to not just be his satellite. And so I'm real grateful for having moved beyond that, and it's real unfortunate that our relationship didn't survive, but I can't say I would have given up the expansion. I don't know how it might have happened differently. I don't mean to put a rosy glow on anything by a long shot, but I had been in this relationship that was grueling. My whole life was expanding—at the same time I was still tethered, so after the trauma of leaving him, getting a house, getting a lawyer, recovering from all that and the children kind of settling down and easing into a routine, I felt a lot better. I remember thinking that it would be nice to find another relationship. When you're in one that's bad, you think, I never want another one again; when you're a free agent, you start looking around. But I really wanted to raise these children by myself. Stepparenting is hard.

At first he was real erratic about child support, but occasionally a check would turn up. He was hurt. He really didn't know how to form his own relationship with the kids, so they didn't see a whole lot of each other. It's not like the kids were totally separate from him. He lived nearby. Then after about three years, he decided he wanted custody, and he took me to court. That was really awful.

Seth by that time was fifteen or sixteen and said that he would just as soon be with his dad, so we gave that, and Seth's been fine. He lost custody of the girls, but the judge said that he should have regular visitation, which was fine with me. I had never stood in his way. It was just he didn't quite know how to pull that off. The judge said at the end that he could have the kids every other weekend and two months, or six weeks, in the summertime. So we walked out of the courtroom, and he came over to me, and he said, "We're going to have to talk about this summertime business. I'm going out of town this summer." And I remember tears started rolling down my face, and I said, "What were you gonna do if you got custody?" He just walked away. He was easing his pain, or trying to regain his power—I have no idea. I said, "Take your six weeks whenever you want, just let them know. It doesn't have to be in the summer—whatever suits your schedule." It was such a mind boggler that he wanted full custody of these kids, but he couldn't take them.

Being a single parent didn't seem to me inordinately rigorous. When the kids were teenagers, there were some times that were difficult. I remember thinking how much harder that would be if I also had a husband around. You'd have to negotiate how to handle certain situations as opposed to figuring it out in your head. I haven't the faintest idea how we did it financially. For a while I was just making a stipend, and he was giving me a check now and then. We had to cut out piano lessons and a few things like that, and we certainly didn't buy clothes much, but we certainly never lacked for anything.

We Split Up

Kate Merrill

She lives in Southern California with her husband and has three children from her first marriage. She is a registered nurse and runs a clinic at a large urban hospital. She was born in Indiana in 1945 and grew up there. (See also p. 458)

*M*y mother was killed in a car accident when I was thirty. She was fifty-nine. I was in the car. We were hit by a drunk driver the day after Christmas. It was a kid who had too much beer; he passed on a hill and hit us head on. It was a pivotal marker point in my life. I had always believed up until then if anything bad happened to you, you had to somehow be contributory toward it. I know now that you can drive thirty-five miles an hour in your own lane in your own car a half a mile from your home and get killed. It was terrible, earthshaking. My daughter, who was seven, woke up one night crying, and she said, "If this can happen to your mother, it can happen to my mother, and I'm only seven, and I don't know what I'd do." That was devastating.

My first marriage was probably already on the skids, but it disintegrated because my husband was unavailable to me during my grieving period. I woke up one day and said, hey, I'm thirty-two years old, and I got a lot of life ahead of me—this is two years after my mother died—and I don't want to spend the rest of my life with somebody who's not there for me. I think he feels these things, but he was never allowed any way of expressing them. Death was terribly frightening for him, and he just didn't know how to be there emotionally. He didn't go to my mother's funeral. She died in Indiana, and he said, "Well, I think I should probably stay here with the children."

I was married for twelve years before I divorced, and I married my present husband in 1980. He has three children. Between the two of us we have six. It was hard for me to get divorced. My grandparents had been married sixty-eight years. Nobody in my family had ever been divorced. My fantasy was I would have my fiftieth wedding anniversary, as well. I am now married to somebody who is totally there for me, supportive in every way. It's worked out for the best.

I was married the first time when I was twenty in 1966. I would not recommend getting married at twenty to anyone. My daughter is twenty-five and in veterinary school. She's really a woman of the nineties—extremely independent and self-sufficient, much more adventuresome than I was. I admire her a lot.

My divorce agreement was affected in a negative way by postfeminist changes. He was from a wealthy family, but in California in the late seventies everything was divided in half. I was young, and I was deemed capable of working, so I was not given the house. I was allowed to live in the house for five years with the children, and then at the end of five years I had to either sell and give my husband half the money, or I could buy him out at the current market value. In another time I would have gotten the house to raise the children in. Things would have been a bit easier, but on the other hand I did work. I managed to buy him out. He paid me child support. I always took the children over to their grandparents when they were small, and I still speak to his mother. She really understood why I didn't stay with her son. I think she would have divorced her husband if it had been thirty years later. He's very much like his father.

The children were two and six and eight when we split up. My husband married the nursery-school teacher who taught my youngest child. My son said, "You can't marry her, she lives at the school." Little kids think that's the teacher, so she must live there. You assume that children know what's going on—when he was about six, one day I said to him, "Well, when I was married to your father," and he looked at me and he said, "You were married to Dad? Like Jennifer's married to Dad?" and I said, "Yeah." He said, "I had no idea," and I said, "Well, who did you think Dad was?" and he said, "I thought Dad was sort of like Uncle Larry," who's my brother. He'd seen his father come to the house to pick the kids up. He assumed that his father was sort of the same relationship as his uncle! He didn't have a concept of a father or a family, and I think that's very sad. Rob, my current husband, was very much of a father to them when they were young. They introduce him as their father. They call both dads Dad. Rob is very athletic and was always the one playing ball with the boys and coached their teams. He went to every single soccer and baseball game they ever played, and their father would never show up.

Kathleen Ryan

She was born in Poughkeepsie, New York, in 1948 and is the director of a human services agency. (See also pp. 130, 459 and 479)

I didn't have a clue. I found out about the affair a week before Christmas. I can't even begin to tell you what I felt. He was not a womanizer; this was a good marriage. My friends that have been married for twenty-two years, the fear of God struck them, like, "God, if this can happen to you, can it happen to us?"

What I loved most about Harry was that he had tremendous respect for women; he was not chauvinistic in any way. He agreed to go to couple's therapy all through January. He said he was committed to the relationship, and he had stopped seeing her. Well, he never stopped seeing her, and he wasn't committed to the relationship, and he walked out on February 1st. Completely. I begged him to stay, and he was gone in an hour with no explanation to the kids, no contact with them. It's been devastating.

This was not a marriage made in hell or on the rocks. You don't make a decision when you're forty-two and forty-four to have another child if the marriage is going down. Kaitlin wasn't an accident. We wanted another child. She's three now, and Kelly's sixteen.

Luckily, I've had a lot of support from family and friends and therapist, but it's awful. The feeling of rejection and abandonment, the betrayal. I would've understood a young girl—it's like, no, she's my age. She left her marriage of twenty years. Her relationship with her husband was very similar to mine with my husband. She has four children. They're all teenagers. They do not speak to her. My daughter does not speak to her father. There are six children involved that are devastated. I stopped trying to figure him out. I feel like he went off the deep end. Maybe a two-year-old baby is a little more stress and pressure than you think at forty-four. And maybe the grass looks greener somehow.

He called our sixteen year old, Kelly, five or six days after he left and moved in with this woman, and she said, "I don't want to talk to him." Well, he took that like gospel truth, and he never made any attempt for four months. He would pick the little one up—he doesn't ask about Kelly. It's like he's guilty, and the only thing that I can figure out is that he can't lie to Kelly. I mean he could go to you and say I was this, I was that, I was the other thing, but Kelly lived in the house with us, so there's not any story to tell about Mom. He's become mean and nasty, and he's not a mean, nasty man, and he was never a neglectful father.

He does provide child support, actually more than he would have to in court, but certainly no emotional support. He doesn't have a clue as to what the kids are doing—he doesn't even ask. Kelly's hurt, she's devastated, she's angry, and her thing is that she doesn't care whatever he was feeling, it was just not the way to do it. She's a very strong, independent young woman.

He moved around the corner with this other woman, and the town is small. It means every time I went to the supermarket I had to ride around the parking lot to make sure they weren't there. I couldn't take the kids. Emotionally, I couldn't handle it. All of a sudden what you shared with someone for twenty-two years; you're the only one doing it. He would pick the baby up after work, so now I was running home to town, getting the baby, bringing her home to Kelly, getting back to work.

It's a new start. I feel in one sense energized back to what I felt like when I was in college, that as a woman, I can do anything that I put my mind to doing. I don't know that I ever really lost that. I dulled it over the years, maybe. I just have this strength, I think, drawn from other women—that's what I'm most impressed by. Some women have had much more horrendous things happen to them, in terms of being left with four kids and no money and ending up on welfare and still surviving, so I'm really into women have tremendous survival spirit, and I can do it. Women are willing to reach out to help other women, whether it's emotionally or physically. I don't know what I would have done without the women friends, the colleagues I have.

I'm not sure that men have that. I think if they did they wouldn't do what my husband did. That's really a key to a lot of it. We tend to talk things out. If I look at my husband, there's a lot going on inside that never got dealt with, so it comes out in another way. In a way, he's an acting-out adolescent right now. In watching him, in watching my brother-in-law, my brothers, I don't think they have that network of emotional support with other men. They don't reach out to other men, and yet they've got feelings.

One of the things that my daughter felt very good about as a child was that we were one of the only couples together. All of her friends' parents had been divorced and were remarried. After my husband left and she went to her friends for support, she came in one day, and she said, "You aren't going to believe this—all my friends, Mom, you know why their parents were divorced? Because their fathers had affairs." They would just say their parents were divorced, but now they started talking. It's just striking the number of marriages that are ending over an affair. The women I know weren't willing to put up with this—I wasn't. My first reaction was, "That's it, you're gone. You can't betray me in this way." I walked out of the house and actually spent a night at my friend's when I found out. We had twenty-two years. I felt that it was worth taking a look at what happened— you don't throw it out the window—but my initial reaction was, "Pack your bags. I'm not doing this, uh uh."

Maria Rodriguez

She was born in Los Angeles in 1935 and raised in a traditional Mexican family. (See also pp. 91 and 476)

For my mother the natural thing was, you find a husband, you have a big Catholic wedding and have children, and you live happily ever after. That's the way it was supposed to be. It was not that way for me.

I was married in my early twenties. When my daughter was born, he became jealous. He didn't want me devoting any of my time to anything or anybody besides him, and he started to get violent. The second time that he displayed any kind of violence, I left. He tried pushing me around, and I fell against the bassinet that the baby was in, and that scared me. I had been married almost three years when I had the baby. Until then, he had never been violent, but he used to drink. I don't know if I didn't want to see it, but he was obviously an alcoholic.

I moved out and stayed for a few months with my parents and got a job, got my own place, and I raised my daughter. My parents were very helpful. The shift that my mother was working allowed her to watch the baby while I was at work. I never had any child support, so it would have been very difficult without her help. At one point I took a second job. My father was a very generous person. If my daughter needed anything, he was always there.

I remarried briefly when my daughter was young. When we were dating, we were having a good time and he was fun and he was good to my daughter, but he was also very jealous, and I knew that before we got married. He was never violent, but we'd have arguments, and I just really got tired of it. I remember one family gathering in particular. My uncle asked me to dance, and my husband was so angry. He went into the bedroom, and I went in there to talk to him. He didn't want me to go back in to the party. I sat in this bedroom with him most of the evening, and it was horrible. At every event we went to, we had arguments. It was jealousy.

We were married about three years, maybe. I don't think I'm cut out for marriage. I'm quite happy with my life.

Isadora Damon

She was born in 1936, is African-American, and lives in the Bedford-Stuyvesant area of Brooklyn. She does housework.

"I always wanted to be a nurse. I was brought up in Virginia. My father died when I was about nine. Being I was the oldest, my mother let me go to school some days, and some days I stay home to help her with the other children." (See also p. 477)

I was married when I was eighteen. I came to New York when I was twenty-three because there wasn't no work, and it was segregated in the South. We couldn't go into white restaurants or bathrooms or sit in the front of the buses. I have one daughter. She's thirty-three, works for the Board of Ed, and she's getting married Valentine's Day.

I would never take that vow no more, letting the man think he'll be the head of the household and I'll obey him. I live by myself and always gonna be like that. I love the way I'm living. I really, really do. My aunt, my sister, and three of my nieces live in my building, visit a lot.

I had another relationship for about five years. He asked me to marry him, but I say no. My mother said that everybody should get married at least once in their life, so I did it, and that was it.

I didn't want to get tied up into that anymore. Like when I go home today, if I don't want to do nothing, I don't have nothing to do because this is my place, right? Now with a husband you gotta be doing things—cook, clean—and I don't feel like it anymore.

I have this friend, she works part-time, she have two kids, and when he comes home, he wants his dinner—everything gotta be just right for him, yes. All husbands not alike. Compared to years ago, it is an improvement. I have this friend if she get home first, she does what gotta be did; if he get home first, he does what have to be did. That's much better instead of putting everything on one person.

I Had Sex, Therefore
I Must Be in Love

Leslie Hampton

She is divorced, has three sons, and lives in Michigan, where she works for the Department of Mental Health.

"I was born in 1940 in Michigan. I was the third of three daughters and named after my father. I graduated from high school and went to airline school in Minneapolis and went to work for Northwest Airlines for a couple of years, came back and went to college for about two terms, and then got married at twenty and divorced about five years later. I have three children, two as a result of that marriage." (See also pp. 101 and 443)

My husband was the first man I ever had sex with, and that's why I married. I'd had sex, therefore I must be in love. I was nineteen when I met him and twenty when I got married. Several days before, I knew I was doing something truly stupid, but everybody has wedding jitters, so you're not really sure. But by the time the wedding was over, I knew this was a terrible mistake. I did not love this man. I didn't really even like him very much, and he did not like me very much, either, and we were together about four years. He was extremely good-looking, and it was very flattering because I did not consider myself to be very attractive. You didn't use the term *hippie* then, maybe *beat* would have been the right word for him. He worked very seldom and played the guitar. He was very smart, witty, and charismatic, and he was interested in me. It was like, whoa! He was about six years older than I, so he was also a little more mature, a man of the world. I found all those things very appealing. They're all very shallow. You have to have at least one adult in a marriage, and both of us were very immature, so it was doomed from the start.

We were married in November, and my son was born the following September, and then the second one was born seventeen months after that. When I was six or seven months pregnant for my first child, my husband held me down and raped me. He did one of those "you're my wife and I'm your husband and you have to," and held my hands down and had sex with me. At the time I thought it was awful, but I didn't think of it in terms of rape until many years after, when people started talking about those things.

I was fairly happy about the first pregnancy, although I had not intended to get pregnant that quickly. I was extremely upset when I was pregnant the second time because the marriage was not going well, and I did not want another child. I did want him after he was born.

When I was pregnant for that baby, my husband worked a whole year, and I did not, but most of the time I was working as a secretary. We moved eight times in the five years we were married. He was always off looking for jobs and never finding them. He was an alcoholic. He died of alcoholism at fifty-six. He was a very active, good father. He took care of the boys, fed them, bathed them, changed them except for their really dirty diapers—if they had a bowel movement, he didn't do that. Even his changing a wet diaper was extraordinary because a lot of men did not do that. But after we separated, they rarely saw him.

He didn't want the divorce. He threatened me that he would fight it and he would take the children away from me. He did that for about a year. But as soon as the divorce was final, he moved out of state, and they were lucky if they saw him once a year. I think that he loved them very much, but it takes a lot of work, a lot of commitment, to keep that kind of partial involvement with children, the every-other-weekend thing. I don't think he had it in him to make that kind of a continuing solid commitment to anything. I don't think he was a terrible person other than he just didn't live up to his responsibilities. He did a lot of damage to his sons. They grew up thinking he did not love them, and if love is measured by actions, he didn't. Part of it was his lifestyle. He was drinking a lot.

They were three and five when we separated. Gosh, it was not a lot of fun. It was difficult not having somebody else to deal with things, to share things with. I never had enough money. It was very difficult to keep the electricity on, to make sure there was enough food on the table and that they had clothes to wear. I was in Michigan at that point living in a trailer park. I found a babysitter that was right there in the trailer park, which really made life much easier. We would get up around six or so, have breakfast, get dressed, and they could go down to the babysitter's. I would be off to work. I certainly didn't live a monastic life—I had times when I went out and did things, too. A lot of things I probably shouldn't have done.

Oh, I had a little spell of what probably would be termed promiscuity. I came out of that marriage with very low self-esteem. He and I really did a job on each other as far as saying demeaning things. I didn't go into it with a lot of self-confidence, and I came out convinced that I was pretty worthless. I was not a good wife. I was not good in bed. I was not good for much, and so I set out to prove that maybe I was not quite as bad in bed as he thought I was. It was 1965 when we separated. I wasn't being a proper mother—mothers did not do that.

My fatigue level was terrible. I probably slept about six hours. On the weekends I would sleep. I was probably being very neglectful because I would sleep even when the kids were awake. They were never outside running around, but I could sleep through anything in those days.

I never remarried. I met a guy who played in a piano bar near where I worked. He was in his senior year of college. We were both twenty-eight, and he was married, and I had an affair with him. I would love to say it was a grand romance, but it wasn't; it was purely sexual and didn't last that long. By the time I realized I was pregnant by him, he was graduating and moving out of town. I really didn't see any reason to tell him. It certainly was not going to be a child he would want to be involved with. Other than screwing around a little bit, I think he had a fairly stable marriage. He had a year-and-a-half-old little girl.

When I first realized I was pregnant, I was sure that I would give this baby up. Abortion was not really an option because this was 1968, so it would have had to be an illegal abortion. I set out to keep my pregnancy a secret. None of my family lived here in town. I didn't gain a lot of weight and I'm tall, and, conveniently, that was the year tent dresses were in style.

I didn't tell them, but the women I worked with knew I was pregnant. They never said a word. My boss never realized it. I never had any doctor's care, but I was very healthy, and my other two pregnancies and births were very, very easy. The first one I was in labor five hours; the second one was born an hour and a half after I started having pains. I never realized how many terrible things can happen in childbirth, and so I put off doing anything. I planned to have the baby at home. I could not think of anything other to do. I couldn't go to the hospital because I was still obsessed with keeping it a secret. I was very embarrassed that this had happened to me.

The baby was born around seven o'clock in the morning, and labor was only about an hour and a half. I do remember the last couple of pains thinking, "Oh, my god, what have I done? I'm going to die here alone and nobody'll know." I was in a bedroom in the back. The two other boys were out in the front room. They were five and seven years old; they were sleeping. I had read someplace about how you were supposed to do this: The placenta is delivered, and then about four or five inches from the baby's stomach you tie two threads so you don't have bleeding from the umbilical cord, and then you cut in between them. I did that, and then I washed him up, and I took the rest of that yucky stuff and wrapped it all up and put it in the regular garbage. I was in such denial that I didn't have anything at the house, so I had to take the little baby and my two little boys and go to the store and get some diapers and some formula for him.

They didn't know I was pregnant, so when this baby appeared, my story was that I was taking care of this baby for somebody. If he had been born when my sons were awake, I don't know what in the world I would have done. I had not thought it through. Probably just made them play up in the front and told them some story about doing something in the back. I don't know.

The next day I went into the Salvation Army and talked to the man who was in charge in this area. I will never forget that man; he was so kind, it still brings tears to my eyes. At that time they had a home for unwed mothers in Detroit, and he called the woman down there and said I have this young woman in my office with a child born out of wedlock and I need to know what to do to help her. He got some advice from her and called the local Catholic social services, and they took over. I went in to see them. They sent me to the doctor, and luckily there was nothing wrong with either of us. They put the baby in a foster home for a month, then I did a little counseling with one of the social workers at this Catholic Youth Services agency. I had called in sick with the flu and took a week off work. After several counseling sessions, the counselor said, "Do you want to see the baby again?" and I did, and that was the end of this adoption. Here was this adorable little child—I was not going to adopt him out.

One of my biggest concerns, along with the social thing of having this child and not being married, was the fear that my ex-husband would find out and might be able to use it to take my two other children away. I did talk to a lawyer, who advised me that it would not be able to be used against me as long as I had not been having sex in front of the kids or that kind of thing. I took the baby home, and I had to break the news to everybody.

I remember telling my sons that I had had this baby, that they had a new brother, and my oldest son, who was seven at the time, had often said, "Can we have another child," and I had always said, "No, because I'm not married," and his reaction was, "Wow, you did it and you're not married!" I've never forgotten that. To him that was great. They were very good. They loved him until he got big enough to get into all their stuff, and then it was sort of typical. The mundane concerns were I had to get him on my insurance at work. There was still a concern at that point of would the company fire me because this had happened.

My oldest sister was very supportive. I called her first—boy, those were hard phone calls to make. My other sister, who's eight years older than me, her reaction was, "How could you do this to our mother? You're such a selfish bitch." Those were her exact words. And my mother reacted like I was an eighteen-year-old, that this was a shameful thing, and how could she hold her head up, but she eventually got over it. I just went on as if life were normal and went out there to visit her and make her hold that baby, and after a few visits he won her over, and he was probably one of her favorite grandchildren. My father was not alive.

The babysitter at the trailer park who took care of the other boys took care of him and became his second mom so much so that by the time he was two, I had to find another babysitter because she was into competing with me for who was really mom of this baby.

I'm not so sure that it was totally the right thing to do for Barry. It was the right thing to do for me. I would not have been able to live with giving up that child. I would have felt too guilty, too irresponsible. I've often wondered, maybe his life would have been worse, but there's always the chance that some nice couple would have adopted him. He would have been a prime adoptable child, a healthy little white male that could have had a mom and a dad and a life in the suburbs.

He's very smart, very talented. He plays the piano. It's really funny, his dad played the piano by ear, and he inherited that. From the time he was little my mother had an organ in her house, and he was the only grandchild that was allowed to play it. He started trying to make little tunes. After I decided to keep him, I did try to find the father, but I couldn't. I named him after his father. He's never seen him, and I only recently told my son that he had a half sister, which blew his mind. I just never had really thought about telling him that.

I think not having a father has been somewhat of a problem. It is harder as a mother to discipline them because there comes a time when you're no longer bigger and stronger than they are, and it's much more difficult to enforce things, to make things stick, not that they should be beaten. My middle son says, "There was nobody around to kick our butts." I grew up without a father myself, and I know that it is a hole in your life. I feel sorry that he didn't get that and that the other two boys didn't, either, but that's the way it played out.

Maybe This Is Really What I Am?

Joan Herbert

She is a physician practicing internal medicine and lives in an urban area in one of the mountain states with her three children, an eleven-year-old son and eight-year-old twin daughters. She was recently divorced. She was born in 1952 to a Catholic family and is one of five children.

I thought for years that we had a wonderful marriage, but after falling in love with a woman, I just couldn't stay. I ended up getting divorced. It was something I absolutely was not prepared for, and I've done a lot of therapy because this came out of left field. When I grew up, I was totally heterosexually oriented, and it wasn't until I met this woman that I looked at life any differently, and it kind of snuck up on me, being attracted to her.

There are men that I'm attracted to, too, but right now it's more the emotional relationship I can have with women that is not available with men that attracts me. I was married to a man who has a very highly developed feminine side, who is this modern-generation type of person, and I think that's why it lasted as long as it did. But the bottom line is I still can't have the kind of relationship with him that I could with another woman. Somehow it's not enough, and it was meeting this other woman and having this connection that I had never had before that just touched my soul. It was a person who could understand me in a way that he never could. And not that he didn't try. He tried very hard, and when all of this was happening, I talked to him about it, and we tried really hard, but somehow once I saw what I could get somewhere else, I was not okay staying married. He is a very controlling, bright, articulate person. I got tired of that. I wanted a more nurturing kind of relationship. I haven't had a relationship with the woman I fell in love with—she doesn't want it. A lot of the attraction has calmed down, and we are good friends. I've had some dating relationships with other women, but I don't have any significant involvement at present.

My children kind of know. Jonathan has a lot of trouble with all these gay women. He's very anti-gay at this point, and that makes it a little tough. He feels that with us getting divorced, he was gypped out of the American dream, that he deserves to have a mom. When we split up, I moved out of our house, and for a year I rented an apartment. During that period, the children spent more time with Peter than they did with me. He's a wonderful father. It really was a very difficult time for all of us. My son was more aligned with his dad, and he had trouble with everything that was going on. There was one time after I moved out when Jonathan said that he wanted me to be like Mrs. Ladera across the street—"I want you to be home making cookies. I do not want you at work. I want you driving a carpool." He can laugh about it, but he does feel like he was entitled to that male privilege, that he doesn't get it all and that's not quite fair. He felt that way even before we were divorced, but it's more intense now.

The suburb I live in is very fifties-ish. People get divorced, but it's not as rampant as in other parts of town. Their friends' parents are together, and so it's very hard for them dealing with the fact that their parents are not married anymore. There are different stages. Jonathan had a horrible year last year and is much better this year. Kathleen's had more trouble this year, and she's back seeing a therapist in the last few weeks. Rebecca's a more quiet kid who just internalizes it, and she's pretty much okay right now. The girls are more accepting, but they're younger, and they don't really know what all that involves, and it's risky. I think about what their friends' parents will say when and if they find out and what will happen to those kids. Society is not very kind. It's a complicated life.

Dolores Valenti

She was born in Port Jervis, New York, in 1950 and raised in an Italian Catholic family. She now lives in Woodstock with her partner and does landscaping. (See also p. 135)

I was married when I was sixteen and he was nineteen, and divorced when I was twenty-four. My husband and I had great adventures together. It was fun, like finding a friend. He did as much housecleaning as I did. We split everything pretty much down the middle. Trying to find friends was difficult because a lot of married couples that we knew, the men did not want their wives acting like me. Nineteen sixty-nine was the Woodstock festival, and there were a lot of people trying to make changes, everybody was discussing freedom, but as far as the role of women was concerned, the general hippie couple that you saw was the man and his old lady. Most women were baking bran and raisin brownies and seeing how many kids they could have. So there wasn't any real progress there.

In 1969, my husband and I went into the swimming pool construction business. My father was a builder, so I was on the job with him from the time I was eight years old, and I really knew it inside out and backwards. I was young. I weighed about 110 pounds, and I was blond. Even though I'm the one signing the paycheck at the end of the week, they didn't want to take instructions from a woman. I had one guy tell me flatly that he did not take orders from a woman.

I had a man driving a cement truck who was a teamster in Long Island. He brought the cement to the job—we had women working for us—and he wouldn't dump the cement because there was a woman operating a piece of equipment. We had to threaten him with calling his boss.

Frequently, we would have three to five jobs going and sometimes in different counties. As these jobs were set up, either my husband or I would be the one running it. I ran this one job from the beginning and was there every day working with concrete and shovels, telling the crew what to do. One night the owner called up and wanted some information about the progress of the job. I started to answer him, and he said, "Oh, no, no, no, I don't want to talk to you. Have your husband call me when he gets home." Like he would have dismissed anybody's wife who had been sitting home all day watching soap operas.

My husband called when he got home, and he said, "If you want to know anything, ask Dolores. She's running your job." The man finally talked to me because he didn't have any choice. My husband got annoyed with people when they exhibited that kind of behavior, but I didn't want him going around all the time having to stick up for me, so I tried to handle as much of it as I could on my own.

I'm the one that decided to leave the marriage, and it was pretty much because it was taking too much energy. Every time I was out there in the world doing something, people could ignore me and choose to believe that it was my husband that was doing it. I'm not fragile enough that one incident put me over the edge. It was hundreds of them. In a marriage at that time it was much more difficult for me to make an impact than it was as a single person. If I came in here as a single woman painter and painted your wall, I came, I did it, I was in charge. If I was married and my husband and I were painters, people thought he was the boss. It's not like this is the only reason, and our choice not to be married I'm sure had something to do with how young we were when we got married and the fact that one wonders what life would be like without the marriage, but it was a big reason that pushed me into thinking about maybe not living my life with a man.

After I got divorced I was by myself for a year or so, and then I decided that I would try having an affair with a woman, and I did. And from that time on I decided I could be comfortable with a man or a woman. Being raised with an Italian Catholic mother, sex was something that nobody talked about in our house. And homosexuality—forget about it—so I never was told that it was wrong.

After I lived as a single person for a few years, it became evident to me that if I were to choose to live with a man for the rest of my life, it wouldn't be very much different than what happened with my first husband. I spent much too much time dealing with people being prejudiced against women. It took a lot of energy to confront, and I wanted to do other things with my life than constantly have to remind people that they were treating me like a second class-citizen because I had a husband.

Molly Hermel

She is a housewife who lives in a small town in southern New Jersey and sometimes works for a temp agency. Until the birth of her first child, she worked as a secretary. She has three children; the youngest still lives at home.

"I was born here in New Jersey in 1943, and I've been married twenty-one years."

I've been in a lesbian relationship for close to ten years. It's still ongoing. She's in the same situation I'm in—married with children. My husband is not aware of it. When this happened I said, wow, maybe this is really what I am. I don't think it could be a sin because it feels so natural to me. If I was thirty years younger, I might have chosen not to be married and have artificial insemination—I wanted children very much. I've felt that I was a lesbian probably since I was playing doctor with a girlfriend when I was about twelve, and it just never went away.

I'm really very bisexual. I did find men attractive. I had a high school boyfriend, and in my twenties I dated men, but I also lived with women. I'm not saying that I don't like sex with my husband—that's what really confuses me. I enjoy it sometimes. I enjoy sex with my woman partner more. It does seem more natural, more gentle, more sensitive. The love is definitely deeper. When I first met my husband, he already knew—through a mutual friend—that I had been living with a woman in a relationship. I think it kind of excited him; it made me different. I was thirty when we got married.

If I were unhappy with my husband, I wouldn't be here. It's nice, it's comfortable. I don't chew my fingernails; he doesn't beat me. My husband is very faithful; I firmly believe that he is.

Marie Solerno

She was born in 1950 and is a social worker. She lives in the Midwest with her female partner.

When my mother gets nervous or thoughtful, she'll take her shirt, her blouse, or whatever she has on, and she takes her glasses off and she cleans the lenses of the glasses. This is her little personal habit, so I start telling her I'm a lesbian, and she takes off her glasses. I'm thinking, first, she's going to tell me that I'll go to hell, because I figured this would trip all her Catholic wires. Then I thought, well, maybe she'll just tell me that she doesn't want to see me for a while. It's going to be something! So she cleans her glasses for a while, and she puts them back on, and she looks at me, and I'm like figuring, well, here it comes, and she goes, "You know after being married to your father for forty-five years, I can understand it." And then we never talked about it again because she doesn't talk about sex of any kind.

Harder on the Marriage
Than on the Children

Martha Everett

She lives in Denver with her husband, is a partner in a large law firm, and has three children. She was born in 1939 in Seattle, Washington. Her ancestry is German, French, and English. "My father's family traces itself to somebody coming over on the Mayflower." (See also p. 492)

My father was a very good lawyer, and we didn't see him very much. He worked very hard. My mother was the archetypal traditional housewife, and it used to drive me crazy. She was always at home taking care of everything. There were a lot of things I liked about that, so part of my guilt toward my children is that I can remember, in some of my fondest memories, coming home in elementary school, for example, and walking in and smelling bread baking and some stew that had been simmering all day, and it was lovely. She was absolutely devoted to my father and to all of us. She did everything for us.

One time when I was in college I flew home and went on a boat trip with my mother and father up to Alaska. We'd gone into their state room. I was talking to my father, and my mother was racing around unpacking her things, and he was just sitting there, and he says, "Liliane, could you get my pajamas and this and that, and I blew up." I said, "How can you do this? It's like she's your slave." And he said, "Yes, but we like this. This is our relationship. Yours can be different, but we like it." And I talked to my mother about that, and she said, "Yes, it makes me happy. I enjoy doing these things for people." She wasn't servile. She always wanted to be a nurse. I think she associated this taking care of people with maybe what she thought of nursing, but she did not see it as restricting her from what she wanted to do.

I definitely did not want to marry early because I associated marriage with the end of opportunity. I decided to get a doctorate in English, so I went to graduate school and met Tyler. I married him when I was roughly twenty-nine. Same marriage. Amazing, isn't it? I won't say there haven't been rocky times—having two careers and children is difficult. When I first came here to Denver, I taught English at a community

296

college and did writing, got pregnant. I took about six years off from full-time work after Amanda was born. I did some freelance writing. In the course of doing that, I interviewed some people who influenced my decision to go into law. I began law school when our youngest, Michael, was two years old. The girls are just a year apart, so they were about six and seven at the time.

During law school I did a lot of my work at night. I would come home, do dinner, laundry, visit with the kids, read to them, put them to bed, and then I'd study till two or three in the morning. In fact, I had pneumonia at the end of law school just from exhaustion. During law school I averaged maybe four hours of sleep. I'm sure that's why I got pneumonia. But I just loved it; I also loved having children, and I didn't want to give up spending time with them. So that meant I had to use nights to study.

I hired a woman who was with Michael all day. She was very good in most ways, but she absolutely favored Michael because he was male. The girls would be working on their homework, and she'd say, "Girls, wouldn't it be nice if one of you would take some cookies up to your brother." It was creating a bad relationship between the girls and Michael. I fired her for that reason, and then I had a series of au pair girls from Switzerland, and that worked out quite well. I graduated from law school in '79. I have been at this law firm since then.

My husband believed somehow that once I started working, it would be more like his work. He teaches at the university and does research. He has very, very reasonable hours. But when you're a young associate in a major law firm, your time is not yours. Throughout the week I wouldn't get home until maybe nine or ten o'clock at night. Because I do international law, I'd also be gone a week or two at a time. And every weekend I would work at least one day and sometimes a day and a half. I lived on adrenaline. I would be very tired at night, but driving back to work the next morning, I'd be all gunned up again. It helped that I was able to turn off all the pressure when I was away.

It was the most difficult time in my marriage. I'd come home at eight-thirty, and the family is sitting there waiting for me to come in and cook dinner, and, of course, they're in a very bad humor. So my husband began doing TV dinners, and I thought that was terrible because it wasn't healthy. But, of course, I'm not the one doing it—it should be his choice. When he did cook, it was very often spaghetti. But he began branching out, and he's a superb cook now.

He was very supportive as a whole. He was an only child, and his mother doted on him and never asked him to do anything at home. He changed diapers, shopped for groceries, got up with them as much as I did. Tyler was the one man driving the carpools.

We did all of our own housecleaning. We should have hired somebody to help with that earlier than we did. He was very happy to do at least his share. We're not into a contract—how many hours have you spent and I spent. We just did it informally.

I loved the time I had with my children. I loved getting away from law and the intensity of it all to reading books with them. I would go to the school activities as often as I could, but if I couldn't, Tyler would. What was really draining was when you get up in the morning and a child has forgotten that they're supposed to take a costume, or that night we're to show up at something and bring a casserole. It's trying to work all of those things in. When that came up a lot, we would go to Kentucky Fried Chicken, and my husband would put the chicken in one of our dishes because he felt embarrassed that we weren't taking home-cooked things. But the Kentucky Fried Chicken always went first, and the kids were very pleased that people liked what their mom was bringing.

The most difficult thing to deal with was their being sick. Neither my husband nor I had any family in this area, but we had a number of close women friends who were home. So often I would bring the child over—but you don't want to take advantage of people who are home. Because my husband's schedule is more flexible, he could be home. Sometimes I could take work home. We were lucky. Our children were very rarely sick, but if they had been a lot, I don't know what I would have done.

If I could do it over, I would like to somehow have more time because I was more uptight than I would like to have been with my children. You want to go home and relax; you walk into the kitchen to fix dinner, and it's a shambles because they've come in after school with friends and made pizza and left everything out, and now they come rushing in when you're trying to get dinner, and they're saying, "Oh, I forgot to tell you, I need to have a chartreuse outfit" and "Can you take me now?" You get short, and it's too bad because that has to be part of life when you have kids that age. And maybe if you're relaxing all day, it's easy to laugh it off.

We had a lot of fun as a family, but I certainly went through the guilt people talk about. I still today have discussions with our children—"Let's look back and talk about your life. What did you like and what didn't you like?" And they say, "Is this going to be another guilt trip, Mom? We've told you we didn't mind at all. We were happy." But I still worry that there must have been times when they came home from school on a bad day, and I couldn't talk to them until four hours later, when it was too late. I compare it to when I went home, and I always had my mother, not a stranger, to be available. They all say that had they had a choice, they would not have chosen to do it any other way.

My daughters, especially, say that it helped them at an earlier age to be more independent. They tell me the story about when we lived in England and I was working,
and it was as busy as here, maybe busier. We'd get up in the morning in London—
most of the year it's dark—and we'd go down to the Underground, and all five of us
would leave in different directions. The children were riding the Underground on their
own: all three going to different schools. I would go last, and I would stand there and
see them go, and I'd have this wrenching feeling. They had their little book bags on,
and they loved it. Michael was in fifth grade, Claudia was in junior high, and Amanda
was in her first year of high school. There were a lot of adjustments going on there,
and it was a fragile time in their lives, but they said that they really loved that they
could be that independent. They compared it to friends who had mothers at home.
There was a lot more worrying about the kids. "Are you sure you can do this? Maybe
I should be there?"

Lawyers are workaholics, and it makes it particularly difficult for women with children. I think it had a real toll on our marriage. Our lives were wild, not unenjoyable,
just hectic. I had very few vacations for years, and when I did finally get time, I wanted
to have a chance to relax with the children and love them. For years and years we never
went on a vacation alone. And while we had a lot of fun with the children, it really
began to drive us apart. After a while, I only saw Tyler in the context of our taking
care of the family and the house and not ourselves, not our relationship. I had closer
relationships to men that I was working with intensely. The statistics on how many
women lawyers are divorced are simply horrible.

If we had taken time for ourselves, it would have been pretty hard on the children
because we almost never would have seen them and never when we were relaxed. The
happy medium would be that you would take at least one vacation yourself, but maybe
all the rest with the children. I don't know. In my case, I would say it was harder on the
marriage than on the children. It was very rocky for a while. We didn't actually separate, but for all practical purposes we did for a few years. It got to the point where Tyler
could no longer accept that this is what it was going to be for the rest of his life.

At the time that I came closest to divorce I was practically living in Europe doing
some major cable television deals there. Amanda had just gone to college. The kids
were very busy. Tyler had been so close to them growing up, and I think he was rather
lonely. He wasn't happy in his job. In my generation, it's still hard no matter how
liberated you may be for a man not to feel that he's become the woman—"She has
the job she loves; the kids are gone. What am I?" I think the next generation will have
this worked out.

I had to talk the client in to flying me home, to give me a break. Tyler said he just couldn't take it anymore. He thought we should separate. I had not realized it had come to that, and I went to the head of the firm and said, "I'm not going to go on like this. I don't want to lose my marriage and family." He said, "Just take off as long as you want." They sent somebody else back in my place to Europe. That's when we saw a therapist.

One of the things the therapist focused on was that Tyler was not happy in his career. I was doing very well and earning a great deal of money, and he wasn't. Faculty didn't receive raises for years and years at the university. I was paying for all of our trips and everything else, and I think there was something emasculating about that, even though Tyler is not a macho man, and neither of us get hung up about money.

My husband has gone to a lot of activities that I'm involved in where he's the spouse. In international law there are very few women, and so he's almost always the only male spouse. He doesn't usually go to them anymore. I once introduced him at a large formal legal party as my wife! I was just exhausted, and I actually said, "This is my wife." My partners have never let me forget it, and neither has my husband.

I went in at the end of about six months and talked to the firm and said, "I'm happy to continue as chair of international, but I am not going to work these kinds of hours, at least at this point in my life." Clients expect you to devote your life to them. I've had to tell them I've made some changes in my life, and these are my ground rules now. They all said, "That's wonderful—more people should do that. As long as you can get the work done for me, it's great." The firm was very good about it.

Ten years ago I was involved in trying to figure out how two women—although some men are interested, as well—could share one job. It's really tough in law. They rely on you. You come to know their company and how they want things negotiated. I get calls even at night. You're almost somewhere between a lawyer and a father confessor, and what I like most is having that sort of relationship with clients and feeling good when you get things to work for them. I could have shared a job if I did real estate closings—I'd rather work at McDonald's. So if you want to have this extremely challenging legal career, I don't know how you could do it.

What I'd like to see happen is law firms begin to convince the clients that lawyers also need to have lives. Clients will dump things on you Christmas Eve and say I need it two days after Christmas. If law firms took the approach that not just women, that men as well, should not routinely be expected to work these extraordinary hours, the lives of the men and the women would be better. You could handle the work by hiring more people; people would earn a little bit less. Within the structure of the firm, to have one person cut hours and earn less is not easy. This firm has been very good in its treatment of women compared to many others, but still you'll have a lot of males thinking that shows a lack of dedication. That's why I would like this to be presented not as a women's issue or even a family issue but a life issue. It's not lack of dedication. It's dedication to life with law as a part of it. Why do you have to give up all the rest?

My daughters definitely want careers, want to be independent, and they're very into women's lib, but they don't want as hectic a life. They don't know if they want children because they don't know if they can handle all that. I try not to say anything because I loved having children, and I hate to have that be the answer. To me, that would be very sad.

It Has to Be
a Shared Responsibility

Suzanne Havercamp

She was born in 1939 and lives in a small, upstate New York town with her husband, who is in business. (See also pp. 117 and 466)

I read about the need for shared parenting. We did that, and we never talked about it. If I came home late, dinner was ready. He was going to be late, dinner was ready. The laundry—we share that. The boys all know how to cook. They could press buttons on everything else, so they could learn how to do it on a washing machine. They were taught at a very young age to be self-sufficient and how to do those things. If we were going to do the fun things, well, we had to get through all the other stuff.

I would say my husband spent as much time with our sons as I did. What's unusual about it is that we never talked about it. We just did it. I'm glad they're starting to write about those things, so everybody can understand that it has to be a shared responsibility. How can you function if it isn't?

Nancy Douglas

She was born in Utah in 1934. She lives in the Midwest and is a political consultant. (See also pp. 103 and 270)

*A*fter getting married, I immediately got pregnant. Daniel was born in '57, Seth in '58, Gillian in 1960, and Ian in '64. I loved being a mother. What made it work was my energy and Florence Crittendon homes. You could get an unwed mother to come live with you. That was a society when to be in trouble meant being pregnant, so I had three unwed mothers who at different times helped with the babies. They were young. One was a farm girl. Her family sent her to the city, and she came to live with me, and we paid her maybe twenty dollars a month. She'd help with the dinner, make cookies, read to the kids, vacuum, she'd do all this stuff, and she became part of our family. Then after she had her baby, she put the baby up for adoption, and she went back to her little town. Then I had a WAC, probably one of the most wonderful women in the world. She was a bright, homely woman and the armed services would have been an unbelievable life for her, but—lo and behold, she got pregnant, and they drummed her out of the corps. She gave the baby up for adoption, but during her pregnancy she lived with me. There was a social worker who would come with these gals. She'd make a social work call every couple of weeks to be sure that the girl was happy, that she was getting to the doctors.

It made life for me easier; they were nice gals. The reason it worked so well is that these girls didn't have any place to go because they were ostracized in their own communities. They had no support structure except us. Putting their kids up for adoption was part of the deal. I'm not even sure they ever saw the babies. Now these mothers may be out looking for those children.

Frances Smith Foster

She is a professor of literature at the University of California at San Diego, has two adult children, and is divorced. She is African-American, and was born in Dayton, Ohio, in 1944.

"I have four siblings. My mom was a beautician. My father was a truck driver. Actually, he hauled stuff—dirt, coal—so he only worked when it wasn't raining and wasn't cold. I was brought up in the Pentecostal church." (See also p. 488)

Krishna was born on Christmas break. I was a teaching assistant, and I didn't miss a day of work, not one. It was the stupidest thing I ever did in my life, but I was determined that being a female and being pregnant, I wasn't going to give them the opportunity to say you can't do it. She was due the thirty-first, and I tried everything to have her during the break. I took castor oil—it was terrible, and she didn't come till January 7th. School started, I think, the 15th, so the first problem was finding somebody who would take care of a brand-new baby. Thanks to the exploitation of wives of foreign graduate students, I could drop her off at Student Housing and walk over to campus and then come back and feed her. Sometimes if I had a problem, my fellow TAs would watch her while I was in class. My husband did not do very much at all. We both thought he was being a good father. It wasn't him refusing, it just never occurred to us that it was fair to ask him to stay home from work or not to study because the baby was sick.

When we moved to San Diego, I put her in day care on campus, but she was two years old and she was coming home swearing. It was the seventies, the time of parent cooperatives and everything is free, and my little baby was saying, "Oh, shit" or "Fuck it," and we didn't use that language, and so we took her out of this university nursery school, and we put her with a woman who kept kids in her home. She took care of her until I had the second baby, Quint, about two years later. I worked up until the time he was born in April 1972. Then I stayed home with him until September, when school started. I had fun with the kids, but I was ready to go back to work. I really missed talking to people. I didn't mind having kids. I just didn't want to stay home with them.

We went through the whole thing. Day care, and different schools, and schools that had days off when you didn't. By the time they were three and five, I had gotten a young sixteen-year-old woman from Mexico, Lisa. I told her mother that in return for her living with me and helping me with the kids, I'd send her to school. (She graduated from high school, and she graduated from college, and she's now a manager in an insurance firm. I have two grandchildren by her.) So we were juggling her classes with my classes.

When I was teaching and administering, I would get home about five. Lisa would have dinner ready. I played with the kids or read stories. We talked about our day. After I put them to bed, I went back to school, and I'd work till probably eleven. The next morning I'd get up around six. I usually got them breakfast, and I had fun. Sometimes I'd make oatmeal and I'd dye the milk different colors. We made smiley faces with raisins on the oatmeal, or we made pancakes, and we made them in the shape of animals and things. They would help me fix breakfast, so it was really fun. It was quick.

I don't believe my kids ever suffered any feelings of being abandoned. I worked really hard to see that they had wonderful care. I paid more than I could afford. I tried to get them into schools that I thought were best for them—sometimes driving them across town to school. We used the La Mesa Cab Service for almost a year. I had a standing order for them to pick my kids up at school at three o'clock and drop them off at my house. They knew all the cab drivers. Lisa didn't drive but would be there and give them their snack.

Lisa lived with us until she got married. Quint didn't realize she wasn't his sister until he was about seven and some kid told him. They were nine and eleven when she left. At that time, I couldn't find a student who could do everything, so I hired two.

Basically, I was tired most of the time, but so what else was new? I still got most of it done. When I was getting my Ph.D. and I had the two kids, I used to get headaches and stuff. I was on Valium for probably a year. I began to read about the side effects and stopped. I was clinically depressed twice, at different times. I had to do counseling and for a while they put me on anti-depressant drugs. I didn't like that so I went off them. I think I got depressed because I was trying to be a superperson. I thought that I should be able to handle all those things, and I should not have. When everybody is telling you you're such a good mother, you're such a good scholar, and you're thinking, "Is something wrong with me that I don't feel good about it?" it takes its toll, and it was not all that easy, but it wasn't awful.

Yolanda Casarez

She was born in 1950, and lives in Los Angeles with her husband and fifteen-year-old daughter. (See also pp. 108 and 477)

*M*y daughter, she wants to start dressing like they're dressing now—what we call *cellos,* like a gang member, the long baggy pants, long shirts. I told her, I said, "You go out there dressed like that, and you're not going to last out on the streets very long." So she has to come back inside and change. She says that's the style. That's how they're all dressing, and I said, "You're such a pretty girl, why do you dress like that? You're just making yourself look cheap, like a gang member." "I'm not a gang member." I thank God for that. I don't let her out—like right now she's in the bedroom—because I feel like she's not responsible enough to be out on the streets. She's just going to get into trouble. She goes to the movies with her friends, or she'll go to her friend's house once in a while. I don't let her sleep over at anybody's house. It wasn't that bad when we moved here, but now it's getting so you can't even go stand outside in front because you know somebody will drive by and shoot or yell something at you. The way she gets dressed, they'll look at her, they'll stop her and say, "What gang do you belong to?" They'll beat you up first and ask questions later, so that's why I don't let her out. So many drugs and shootings, all these gangs.

My mother tells me you have to let her out sometime. When I think she's responsible, when she's able to take care of herself, I'll say okay. She gets upset quite a bit, but like I told her, "As long as you're under my roof, you do what I say."

When I was her age, you could be out ten, eleven o'clock, and you wouldn't be getting into any trouble. Now that's all it is out there, nothing but trouble.

Ruth Mandel

She was forty-two years old when interviewed. For a while, as a young woman, she lived in San Francisco and was a hippie. She now lives with her lesbian partner and their son in a small town in the Northeast. (See also p. 132)

I really wanted to have a baby for many years. But I always wanted to have my own kid and I thought that I couldn't do it, and it always made me sad. Then about ten years into my lesbianism, I met a lesbian who was pregnant. I figured she slept with a man, and then I found out that she'd been artificially inseminated. I watched to see how that baby looked when it came out—if it was all right, if it was healthy. It was, and I decided right then and there that someday I was going to have a baby. Melissa wanted to have a kid, too, but she wanted to wait. Our relationship wasn't in the best of places, and she didn't want to have a kid in New York City. So we waited and waited and waited, and I was very frustrated, and I used to really yearn to have a baby. So when I finally got pregnant, I was 37, and I was happier than could be.

At first we used frozen sperm from a sperm bank. There's a doctor in this area that is not homophobic, and he helped us buy the sperm. It was really weird, though, and Melissa and I didn't like it. We kind of felt uncomfortable with an unknown donor. When the baby would ask us, "Who's my father?" we wouldn't know what to say.

But then we talked to some friends one day about how we were trying this. The woman is a very close friend of mine who used to be a lesbian and was now in a straight relationship. She asked us to ask her husband, and we did, and he agreed. He donated his sperm, and I got pregnant, and so my kid is a half sibling of his kids. My son knows it. It's a little bit of an extended family.

We wrote a contract with a lawyer saying that we hired him. We paid him one hundred dollars and when we had the baby, we all went out to eat—We went by our gut feeling, which was a trusting one, since they are very nice people. It was very loving; she's the greatest, like a sister. She's a feminist and wants women to have babies when they want to have them, however they want to have them. It's worked out very nicely. Michael's five—he's a great kid.

After he was born, all I wanted to do was nurse my baby and hang out with him for a few years. I had friends, when I told them I was going to work part-time, they absolutely thought I had lost my mind and I really resented that attitude. They're career mothers, heavy feminists who gotta get to work—very important high-powered jobs. They put their kids heavy in child care. I put mine in child care for a couple of hours a day, and I ran home. I wanted to be with him not the child-care worker.

I'm very much a part of the feminist movement, but I don't like a lot of the attitudes of the feminist movement towards raising a child. There's so much stuff about women should get out there and get to work that we're losing something because you also have to be happy. And if what makes you happy sometimes is cleaning your house and taking care of your kid, then you want your friends to encourage you. I feel that feminists sometimes are a little removed from the child-mother relationship, and that's not good. If we go to work and have a strenuous schedule, we're not going to have the patience when we come home that children need. I don't know what the answer is, but I do know that I didn't get too much support on the way I'm raising my kid.

My son's biological father is not particularly interested in Michael—he's got his hands full with two other children—and Michael's not particularly interested in him. But I think that maybe at a later stage Michael will need something from a father image, and he will rise to the occasion, so it makes me feel very good. I don't want him to feel too different. I want him to have some male role model. He's always socialized with them. We call him a donor father. He's really not his father; the word *father* holds a lot of emotions that have to do with getting love from this person, and Michael already has two parents.

We volunteer a lot of information to him, plus he's been around other lesbians with kids, so he knows that we're not the only family with two mommies. He knows that it's not that common, but he doesn't think that we're so different. I know he will. That's one of the reasons I want to keep him in private school. They're very cool about it.

He came with us in the gay pride march, where there's a lot of men in dresses, so to Michael a man can wear a dress if he wants to. He can't wear it all the time. He's never asked me for a dress. I'm not buying him dresses. If my kid was a cross-dresser at four years old, I would be hearing about it from relatives. I'm kind of glad that he's not.

But we take him to the gay pride march, and I would say to him, "That's a man," and he'd say, "No it's not," and I'd say, "It is; it is." So I always say to Melissa, "Let's just keep him as confused as he can be. If he doesn't know what's a man, what's a woman, and like what are the rules, then it's just up for grabs." Keeping him really confused, however, sometimes I feel sorry for him, and I start giving him more information because I feel like he does have to exist in this world.

I definitely encourage Michael to play with girls a lot. The main thing is gearing him to not hate women, which is not easy because there'll be at some point this huge education that comes at boys to hate women. I keep the TV off; we have a VCR.

Melissa's a great coparent, but I was very shocked at one point. I breast-fed, and I was home for four months, and she was working most of that time. Then she started to have an opinion on every little thing, and I started realizing that my mother didn't have to ask my father's opinion with ninety percent of raising us. She was in charge. But Melissa was raised to be the mother of a child, too, so here are these two very dynamic women with opinions on every single thing about this kid. So two mothers gets very intense. That's certainly a new generation of mothering.

Elana Wiseman

She is a physician who was born in 1940 and lives on the East Coast with her husband and youngest daughter. Her older daughter, Sharon Wiseman, is also a physician and appears in the book. (See also pp. 88 and 491)

Mel and I got married when we were second-year students, and Sharon was born while I was a resident. I was the resident in charge one night when a patient was dying in the coronary care unit. I remember running down the hall being seven and a half months pregnant, holding my belly, to resuscitate this man, thinking, "Oh, my god, what's going to happen to my baby?" I had to do it, and we resuscitated him. We saved his life, but I didn't know if I was going to lose my child or not. I was exposed to German measles when I was pregnant with Sharon, and there was no way to know if she was going to have German measles. We decided not to abort, and she was fine.

I wanted to try to nurse her, and so I asked the chief resident to extend my time at home. I felt guilty because scheduling was so tight that if anybody left, somebody else would have to fill in. I don't think that I was much beloved by my resident companions that year. I think they felt like I had "taken advantage." I was changing. Medicine was important to me, but the baby was more important.

I was doing well until I had my second child. Sharon and Josh are fourteen months apart, so they were both in diapers for many months, and there were a lot of demands. I felt that the children were primarily my responsibility, but I'm not sure that Mel would have seen it that way. He was very much engaged with the kids and maintaining our household. We used to clean the house together. We did everything together.

I think that part of the reason that my marriage didn't work was that I just got exhausted. I couldn't do the work and take care of the kids and feel like I had any life. I started finding fault with Mel. If you're immature, you don't know how to nurture a marriage, and neither of us knew how to do that. Both of us got to feeling fairly isolated. We were doing it all but not really sharing it in terms of what our experiences were. When Josh was not quite two, I had a very bad auto accident and nearly died. And so that took a toll on me. About six months after that I sort of crumped. I think I had an agitated depression. It eventuated in the end of my marriage, and I just didn't understand what was going on. Until then I was playing by other people's rules—that one should be able to run a family, be a wife, have children, and be a professional, and I couldn't anymore, and I didn't know what to do. I was very disappointed in myself. That's life—you grow up with your kids.

I met Lewis after I'd been separated about three and a half years, and we got married in '75. We have a daughter who is sixteen now. After Rebecca was born, I was so much calmer than I had been after Sharon and Josh's births, even though my life was more complicated—we had three children, two of whom were going into adolescence. What a difference ten years and a lot of therapy made!

Julia Parker

She was born in 1951 in the Deep South, where she lives with her husband and children. She is an attorney and works for an environmental protection agency. (See also p. 449)

As the president of the PTA, I was talking to the principal and said, "I'm really interested in trying to get the legislature to pass some kind of latchkey program so that all the schools have an after-school program." His comment was, "Well, what we really need is for mamas to be back at home with their children." I almost dropped the phone. I couldn't believe that he was saying this, knowing that he was talking to a woman who worked full-time. I said that he could dream on but that those days were not going to come back, and that for the most part it was not economically feasible for women to stay home even if they wanted to, and that we had to look at the world the way it was and try to deal with it instead of wishing for the olden days. I'm just astonished that people are still in the dark ages.

It's Called Survival

Susan Willard

She lives in a small town in the Deep South. She is divorced, works in administration, and lives with her two daughters. Her son is in college.

"I was born here in 1953, the second of four children. On my mother's side, my grandmother was raised in New Orleans and was queen of the Mardi Gras parade back in the 1920s, and my grandfather was from the Midwest. My father's parents were from this area, but when the depression came, they moved up north. So Dad was raised there and went to an Ivy League college. I went to a boarding school for four years.

"I've ended up going back to the Episcopal church and becoming part of a renewal movement called Cursio—it is a more positive, loving, upbeat approach."

*M*y parents' main thrust was for me to find a nice man and marry him and belong to the garden club and have a family and live happily ever after. The college degree was not important. Now that I'm raising my children, I've tried to implant that they have to get their degree.

My sisters and brothers and I, we were raised to be polite, make small talk to older people, never say anything rude, negative, or ugly, socialize with the right people, dress conservatively, always look neat, have your hair combed, hands washed. We were never really allowed to develop our own sense of self.

Most women of my mother's generation were housewives. We had a full-time maid, and Mother belonged to the garden club. In the early 1930s, the garden clubs started house tours of the beautiful antebellum homes located in town and organized an annual spring pageant of the antebellum period to entertain tourists. It's a big production, so she would be very busy helping with the Confederate pageant. In the fall, she'd play bridge. They had a little sewing club. And she'd take care of us. She was home in the afternoons, carpooling, and would take us to dancing class. Dad ended up being a stockbroker for about twenty or thirty years.

I was queen of the Confederate pageant sophomore year. I dropped out of college for that. Being queen is like a debut. There's a court, and you have six maids and six generals. Parties are given for the king and queen every night. The local dealership gives you a convertible to drive. The king loved being in the limelight and was really rude. He thought I was supposed to be in love with him and tried to kiss me good night, but I wasn't about to kiss him. I was dating my future husband at the time. The last night, the king said something to me that just tipped me off, and I bopped him on the head with the scepter in front of a large audience which included many tourists, then burst into tears and ran off the stage. Thirteen years later I ran into him. He came up and apologized to me for being such a jerk. He had matured.

I was majoring in fine arts at the university when I met my husband sophomore year. While I was queen of the Confederate pageant, he asked me to marry him. So I got married the following fall, and I wore my queen's dress. He went back to school and finished his degree. I got a job selling men's cologne at a department store. I never did get to finish school. At the time I thought it was more important for him to get his degree, and everyone else did, too, and I didn't have enough self-confidence to say, hey, I'm important, I count, I'm going to do it.

He got a job upstate, and we moved. I got a job working as a bank teller up there, and then after we were married about two and a half years, I had my first child. I never really was happy in my marriage. My husband had a drinking problem, and he was verbally abusive. He would break pieces of furniture around me or punch a hole in a wall, which I knew was meant for my face, but he never actually physically abused me. During the divorce, we shoved each other around at one point, but that was twelve years later.

We stayed together twelve years and three children, and I was pretty much what he wanted—someone barefoot and pregnant to stay home. I had no sense of self, no self-esteem.

I would try going back to school, but then something would happen with him, and I would get so depressed that I would have to drop out. I had the babies, and I pretty much felt tied in to the relationship and didn't see any options. I was twenty-two and a half when I had my son, and then two and a half years later I had Julie. Then two years after that I had Lisa. Julie was the only child that was planned. When I got pregnant with Lisa, I ended up in some counseling, and Walter did go for a couple of years with me. That is when I really started to grow up, and I realized that I had options. I ended up in group therapy. Walter still had a terrible temper. He would come home, and if he had a bad day at work, he would yell and cuss and scream. My sense of self was getting stronger. By the time I chose to leave him, I had to feel like I had tried everything to make it work. It was a real bad divorce. He filed for custody, so we went through a year-long court battle during which he was never paying child support and I was making $750 a month at the bank. I had complete custody of the children, and he had visitation rights about every other weekend. He wanted the children, but he was not supporting them and was inconsistent with the time of seeing them. He was angry and was using the children as a pawn. It's been that way ever since.

I came back here around 1987, '88, and I lived with Mother for about three months. I found a house and got set up, and by the fall, I started to look for a job. I got a job as an administrator at a foundation and ended up working there for four years. It was a real interesting job, and it helped my self-esteem and my self-image.

I knew I had maxed out financially there, and so I ended up quitting about two years ago in July. I can't work in a dead-end job. A lot of women are fools to settle for low pay without any future, and you see a lot of that in the South, and it infuriates me. I'm out here supporting three children, and I'm not willing to settle for that.

I've been able to support my family, but I'm used to being poor, and I've learned how to do it. I was on food stamps at one point. It really is a demeaning experience. A year after I moved here, Walter was not sending child support, and I was working, but I still qualified because my salary was low, so I would get the food stamps and go across the river where nobody knew me and shop, because it was real embarrassing. It's a horrible experience. It's called survival.

Child support has been very inconsistent. He would go for a year or so and not send any, and I tried filing through the civil courts, and they would garnish his wages. He ended up moving out of the state. He's unemployed, but in his line of work he can take cash and not report it. So I ended up going through the Department of Human Services, and he was taken to court. He's supposed to pay one hundred dollars a month per child. A couple of years ago he went for nine months without paying, and so finally I went to court. He'd been to court four or five times already so the judge put him in jail for a week for nonpayment and said, "You've got to come up with twenty-five hundred dollars before I'll let you out." Ever since then he has paid, but he still doesn't pay the total amount, but I do get maybe one hundred or two hundred dollars a month. I'm finally to a point where I don't depend on it for food or shelter.

He hasn't remarried. The children don't see him much at all. The girls saw him Christmas before last for about a week. His main interest has been his son—the male child. When we first moved back here, the kids were all confused and had been through that horrible year of the court battle, and Walter worked on Jeffrey. When Jeffrey was going into the ninth grade, he chose to go live with his dad for a year. I didn't fight him on that and it was real hard, but it was probably the best thing I ever did. Jeffrey had so much anger towards me, but when he went down there and lived with his dad, he understood why I had done what I had done. He has never been back since then. He's a fine young man; I'm real proud of him.

My son has a lot of disappointment and sadness about his dad, and probably there's some anger too. But he understands where I'm coming from, whereas the girls still have this unrealistic picture of the whole situation. To them, it's always been my fault. It's hard.

A lot of women my age here did get their college degree. But a good majority of my peers don't work. They do the garden club thing, but I'd go crazy. I'm much happier working, and I like to be where I'm actively using my mind. Even if I had a lot of money, I'd be working. I work eight to five and some Saturdays. This job's been fun. I've loved it.

The children usually call me when they get in from school and tell me how their day's gone. Lisa right now is working for me—I'm paying her to do the laundry and the dishes—and Julie has gotten an afternoon job working for a dentist's office. One big plus for me has been living downtown. In this town you don't have to worry about crime, so the children can walk to church, to the library; they can walk downtown to buy a birthday present. My mother lives right around the corner, and that's taken a lot of pressure off of me as far as being a single parent and trying to juggle all of this.

I'm not depressed at all now. I've had a lot of therapy. I like myself. I like what I'm doing. I've got an inner strength I didn't know I had before. I don't date that much, but then I'm real picky. But right now it's not bothering me too much. I did have a relationship that went on and off for about three years with a nice man, but it just didn't work out. It was healthier, but I was still afraid to really be myself around him. Too afraid if I said the wrong thing, or was too assertive, he might get angry. Afraid that if he really knew what I was thinking, he might not like me. I think men are still threatened by women being their own selves and being intelligent and vibrant. They just as soon they were barefoot and pregnant. I've had to mentally grow to where I'm not going to settle for being subservient.

I'm pretty content, and I'm excited about my art work and my son going off to college. I'm so jealous I can't stand it. My goal in life is to be a dorm mother and go take fine art courses. I'm seeing the light at the end of the tunnel. My daughter's in the eighth grade, so I might be able to.

Therapy has been an important part in my life. When Jeffrey went to live with his father, I got real depressed, so I ended up going to one of those codependent twelve-step groups, and that was real helpful. I went to that for a year or so, and I ended up seeing a therapist. I still see him because I like to have some healthy input. With raising the children and being a single parent, I've learned that you can get a lot of bad advice from your friends. He told me I didn't need to see him anymore. I said, "I know that, but to me having someone that's healthy to talk to is real important as far as juggling all of this." I'm introspective, and I'm always going to be trying to improve myself.

I want my daughters to get a college degree and be self-supporting in a field that they enjoy. I want them to be completely independent and to know and have that inner knowledge that they can take care of themselves the way they want to live rather than just struggling to survive.

I Could Not Live
in a Traditional Setting

Hettie Jones

She was born in Brooklyn in 1934 and is the author of How I Became Hettie Jones. *(See also p. 119)*

*T*he men in my Bohemian circle shared many of the traits of the men of the fifties. They hadn't even thought about whether they were male chauvinists or not—it never occurred to them to welcome women into their "boys' club." The beats were a very boy-directed scene.

Those of us who somehow innocently got hooked up with these guys—because we fell in love and suddenly found ourselves pregnant and then having these children to take care of—didn't realize that the life of a woman was going to be a series of interruptions of the ambitions that we all harbored. And we hadn't studied our lives as women, so it is only in retrospect that we are able to see how innocent we were.

I think it was the women's movement that came after us that focused on these issues, and I know it helped me a lot, so I could have some perspective on my life. I was twenty-five when I had my first child, twenty-seven when I had my second. I never stopped working, but my life as an artist didn't begin until later, and I didn't realize that was going to happen. I just sort of sailed right into it and thought, "This'll be fun—sure, I'll have a a baby, why not?" But none of us ever regretted having our children. We love them so much.

I was in an interracial marriage, which was totally out of order at that time. My family disowned me for a while. Later, it was sort of a halfway rapprochement. It never really happened the way you think of—a family inviting you to dinner—it just didn't happen. When you walked down the street, people stared. They were either hostile or curious but mostly hostile. Even in the Village, people would stare. There were laws on the books at this time in, I think, thirty-one states that prohibited interracial marriages. There were places where we were an absolute threat because that was "against nature." When I walked out with my babies in my baby carriage, people would gawk—but then again, if you were wearing a short skirt, people would gawk.

Melinda Stratton

She is a social worker and lives near San Francisco with her husband and two children.

"When my mother graduated from college, she got a job teaching at an Indian reservation, and that's where she met my father, who is a member of the tribe. They were married, and then they left the reservation in the early 1940s. I was born in 1944, and in 1953, we moved back to the reservation, and that's where I was raised."

I can remember when I was getting my first divorce, my mother and I were standing out in the vegetable garden, and I was telling her that I was leaving my husband, and she didn't want that, mainly for the kids, and she told me that one time she and Daddy almost separated, but that they didn't, and that they were glad later that they didn't. I'm sure it was the era that you just didn't do that kind of thing, and that played a part in it. Well, they were married fifty years; they had their rocky times. People might think, "Three husbands, what's the matter with you?" I don't feel badly about that. They've all been different experiences, and they've all been good experiences.

This is my third life, I say. I had one life living on a reservation raising my children, being the homemaker, the mother; and then the life without children here in the Bay area doing all the things that people do when they don't have children at home and are both working. We had two poodles and tickets for the Warriors and trips to Mexico. We had a Porsche and all those kinds of things.

Then I got pregnant. Rob, my third husband, had no children. I had grandchildren—I have two adult children from my first marriage. I was forty-one when Seth was born and forty-four when William was born. It has been interesting raising children in the early sixties—I was a senior in high school when I got pregnant with my first child—and then again in the late eighties. With the younger children, I worked till the day they were born. I went back to work six weeks after they were born because that is all the disability allows you. At six weeks they went to child-care programs.

In my first marriage, my husband worked and provided me and the children with the monetary support so that I didn't have to work. I was the traditional wife. I stayed home until my younger daughter went to kindergarten and then worked part-time. My first husband loved the children as much as the current father loves these children, but in those days fathers didn't take care of kids. He would play with them. We would do family things together, but he never changed their diapers or did housework or cook or anything like that. Now, even though I'm the primary housekeeper person, my husband helps out. He'll sometimes stay home with them if they are sick. He used to pick them up from child care. Tomorrow, I need to be at work all day, so he will take care of the kids. He's even gotten to where he'll bring clothes off the line without being asked!

My three lives have been very different, and I don't see one as any better than any other.

Janet Moore

She was born in 1951 in the Deep South, where she lives with her husband and daughters and works as a nurse. She is a born-again Christian.

"We were pretty wild, my husband and I, when we were younger. I think I was sixteen, I met him through my boyfriend at the time. My husband owned a bar that we went to. But we didn't start dating till I was eighteen, maybe nineteen. I married when I was twenty. We're six years apart."

We were partiers for a long time. There were drugs, alcohol, the whole scene. There was like no morality involved in our lives. We didn't have a good marriage. There were other women. He was coming home late or not coming home at all. When our daughter was six months old, he was going to leave. He didn't.

We both had very dramatic conversions to Christ. My brother who plays rugby came home and told me about the Lord. I went to bed one night and said, "God, is this really true?" I hadn't really thought about the Lord in a long time, I guess since early high school. Our daughter was about two when that happened. I really felt the responsibility for her. In a sense she was the salvation for both of us. He got out of the bar business.

It's been a journey, growth. You're just not drawn to the things that you were drawn to before, parties or the types of people that stay out all night. We stopped being in that group because we changed. And it wasn't so much shunning them, it was more that we were weak and maybe would have gone back. You're on a different path. The focus is God, family, and your community.

We both get up at five, and we walk together, fast-walking, and then we come home and talk and pray. We listen to a lot of motivational tapes. There is a lot more affection, more I love you, faithfulness. It was definitely much more of a sexual thing when we were younger, all involved with partying. Now we both believe that life emanates from God, so that has changed everything. Why are we here? The meaning of life. It answers a lot of questions that we have. And purpose, purpose for our kids. It's not a live-for-the-moment life anymore. We plan and we set goals—financial goals, spiritual goals—and teach our children what we believe.

When Rich and I got married, no one thought that we would ever make it. We were the least likely to succeed in marriage. And it's funny, because all of my friends, they're all divorced, and right now I have so many friends whose husbands are going through midlife crisis. My brother-in-law split after about twenty-five years. They have four children. It's just horrible. It's a craziness. There's been a tremendous amount of growth in our marriage. I'm happy that we stayed and that things worked.

Divorce really stems from the man not being the spiritual head of his house. We think of the head of the house as domineering or controlling, and it's not like that at all. It's more a loving man to be with his family and teaching them at the same time. Husbands should instruct their children in spiritual things as well as the wife. That's a mutual thing. But there should be a lot of communication with fathers and children.

There's so much out there for kids to deal with. If they don't have strong beliefs and morals, I mean now you're talking death, which we didn't have to deal with. Yeah, AIDS, and there are all kinds of nasty sexually transmitted diseases. The drugs increased and the rap music! I'm horrified. So many standards have been so lowered and lowered and lowered.

Beverly Butler Lavergneau

She was born in 1940 and lives in New Paltz, New York, with her husband. She is an administrator at the state university. Her daughter Mara Lavergneau was also interviewed. (See also pp. 86, 102 and 109)

I saw my father as being a very, very traditional man, and I wanted someone who was not very traditional. I had a very long-term relationship with my high school sweetheart that stretched into college, and one of the things that very clearly destroyed the relationship was that he wanted a stage wife. He was very ambitious, had a lot of career goals, and I felt that he wanted somebody that was going to complement all of that. I felt that I could not live in a traditional situation. My generation was starting to change. I wasn't looking to marry somebody to support me for the rest of my life. I was being raised to be an independent person. My mother felt that was very important.

My husband is Panamanian born, immigrated here when he was six. He's a reha-bilitation placement counselor. My mother was really afraid when Armando and I got together because she felt that he had come out of a very traditional Latino background, and she said at one point, "I didn't raise my daughter to be a doormat." But almost from the very beginning, we had a partnership. I knew he was a very laid-back kind of guy and that we were a good match. Right after Mara was born, I had to have gall bladder surgery. She was nine days old—and he had a toddler and a brand-new baby. I was in the hospital for ten days, and then I was out of commission close to a month, and luck-ily he was on summer vacation, but he did everything. He was a very involved father. The only thing he never figured out was how to do hair. He was never very good at that.

I was a working mother. There's just nothing that needed to be done for their welfare, ours as a family, that he didn't do. If we needed diapers from the supermarket or the kids had to be fed or whatever, we had a partnership. He's done roughly half the childrearing and housework. The delineation came when they hit the preteen years. When they moved into the arena of interpersonal relationship and sexual tension, he kind of withdrew. I think that probably in most families it's the same-sex parent that's really involved in that time.

I make more money than Armando does, but that's never been an issue. My hus-band feels that because he has a wife who is very independent, that has been liberating to him. He's been a very aware person, very unusual. His parents divorced when he was nine. Then when he was about thirteen, this man became his stepfather. Armando saw his stepfather as being a very big, strong, macho kind of guy. He was a blue-collar worker. My mother-in-law went out to work every day, and his stepfather always helped out. He really was a role model and showed him that you could be a strong man and still be somebody who was helpful and sensitive and cared about what was happening.

It would have been impossible to have worked the way I worked in the kinds of positions that I had if he had not been a full partner in the enterprise. There would have been no way.

Amanda Johnson

She was born in 1952 and is a partner in a large western law firm. (See also pp. 79, 490 and 493)

My parents' divorcing affected me deeply in a number of ways, but my suspicion of the institution of marriage had already had quite a life. I said when I was twelve years old that I was never going to get married. Probably I didn't mean it then, but I never stopped saying it. I said it in college, and I said it in law school, and I sit here and say it today. People say, "What do you mean you are not married?" And I say, "I have a job—what do I need a husband for?" It isn't an institution that has ever really appealed to me, so my own parents' divorce may have confirmed that feeling.

My parents' marriage was not abusive or emotionally charged. There was nothing in the way that I was brought up to look at my parents' marriage and say I would rather die than be in a relationship like that. I think it's a marvelous institution for other people. I just never felt it would work for me. I never felt like I could make my plans and have to include someone else in them. That seemed too hard.

I don't think anyone lives to see her fortieth birthday and not have doubts about her life's choices. I rarely wonder what it would be like to be married because I think I have a pretty good idea. I occasionally wonder what it would be like to have kids. Spending time with my nephews more than anything has made me wonder what kind of parent I would have been and made me suspect that I would truly enjoy it. They sure are fun in short shifts. It's not so much a regret as a wondering what it might be like because I'm not unhappy with the choices I've made. I don't feel my biological clock ticking. I don't think you can have it all. So in my next life, I'd like to try motherhood. I have friends who aren't married and have arranged being impregnated to have children. I never felt that strongly.

I don't regret not having children because my life would be so different if I had had them. I don't think with kids you can work fourteen hours a day. My priorities would be different. I'm not a superwoman. I couldn't do it all. I couldn't put the energy I put into my career and have anything close to enough energy to be a good parent, so something would have to give. I would hope if I were responsible enough to bring children into the world that I would start with giving them the attention they need. I would always have to have a career, but it wouldn't be exactly what I'm doing now. It would have to be something different.

Family:
The Third Generation

I've taken a few women's studies classes, feminism makes a thousand degrees of sense, but it's not anything that was a battle for me. It's kind of like I'm an American because I was born in America, I'm not going to fight for the country, I just live here. This is my reality. This is where I was brought up. It's not like I came over here from some boat and wanted to get my green papers because this is such a great country.

—Sarah Wells, born 1972

You wonder how much things have changed when you have kids. This is a very conservative area in a lot of ways. In spite of all the changes there's still a lot of stuff that basically remains the same. In terms of the roles that people play in their family, it's like 99% of the stuff that has to do with the kids is the woman's responsibility and their husbands are sure more involved than their fathers were, but it's still not anywhere near 50-50.

—Sarah Miller, born 1955

I Do Things Out of the Norm

Gina Rotundo

She lives in the Northeast with her second husband and teaches at a culinary institute. She has two children from her first marriage.

"I was born in the Midwest in a small town in 1954. My father is Italian; my mother is from northern Europe. I went to a strict Catholic school for eight years. I have two sisters and one younger brother; I'm the third child. My father was adamant about having a son. He was bowling the night my mother went into labor; after he got to the hospital and I was born, he looked at me and went, 'Oh, another girl,' but I was dark like him so that made a difference. I graduated from high school and went on to college. I was from an all-white community and married a black man at twenty and was basically disowned by my father's side of the family." (See also p. 517)

He was the star basketball player at the university, and I was a cheerleader, so it was like a Cinderella-type of thing, very, very fun. I brought him home, and my father wouldn't even meet him. My mother's reaction was, "You're happy? You love him? Whatever you want to do." She would say to my father, "You're ridiculous. How can you tell your daughter she can't come in this house?"

My mother was a housewife, and my father had his own hardware store. It was a very small town where everybody knew everyone. My father felt I disgraced him by marrying this man, because he was black. His theory was that black men are no good, they'll beat you and they'll run around on you—that's all he knew from his father. My Italian Catholic grandfather was very, very prejudiced. Jews were no good, and neither were blacks.

I was a tomboy. I dressed like a little boy. My father would take me hunting, and I clung to him. But when I did this, I just crushed him. I understood it was hard for him, but I wanted him to accept it. My father loved basketball, and I was marrying the star basketball player. I would say, "Daddy, you know he's going to go and play in the NBA," and he would say, "But he's black." It took about a year and a half, until he saw my daughter. I'd plan my visits to my mother so my father wouldn't be there. One day when I was visiting he walked in. Well, my heart dropped. He looked at my child—she was about eighteen months old—and he said, "Who's that?" I said, "This is your granddaughter, Christina." He picked her up, took her into the other room, and I was welcome into the house again. We talked a little bit, but my father had a very hard time talking and showing emotion. He would ask my mother suddenly, "Is Gina bringing the baby to visit?" He would never say, "I'm sorry; I forgive you." He just said, "Do you need anything?"

My daughter looks like myself and my mother. She looks Hispanic, and maybe that was reassuring to my father, that he wasn't holding a black child, I don't know.

I had Christina in college, and she was our little mascot. We used to take her to games, dress her up like a little mini cheerleader. We were living a wonderful life. I stayed in school until she was born (when I got into about my fourth month, I stopped cheering) and stayed off a semester after she was born. When Christina was eight months old, I'd bundle her up, take her to the sitter, go waitress from six to two in the afternoon. I would take a couple of night classes. I was young and had lots of stamina, but I couldn't do it for a long time. I probably did it a good year, and then I stopped, and I was just working and being a mother. It was very hard.

My mother would send me a care package every week. My husband was getting a scholarship, but it wasn't enough to feed a wife and a child. He was a very good father, always kind, caring, loving. He was going to school and then had basketball practice. I was with her most of the time, but when he was there, he made time for her. I could go and do things. I would come home and they were playing tent. He would pin blankets up and let her walk underneath and play jungle and Tarzan. He was an artist, and he would draw for her. It was only after the basketball didn't work that things started changing.

Basketball was his life, and we had such hopes of him being in the NBA someday. In 1976 it came time to leave college, and then the NBA draft was coming up. It was like everyone knew—"Well, Lenny, you're probably going to get drafted in the third round, maybe even the first." His parents wanted to see their grandchild, and they have this huge house in another part of the state, and we thought from there we'll go wherever he gets picked up.

So we went down there, and his parents were very, very open because they lived in a diverse community. She was a schoolteacher; he worked for a construction company, but their heritage is very mixed. They would have a family reunion, you would see women of your features and your skin. His father's grandmother was an Afro-American slave; his grandfather was an Irishman, so this is part of their culture, and I got along great with the family. So we were down there, and he was drafted in the sixth round by a major team, so it looked like we'd go to live there. I was not working because I was pregnant with our son, and he went for a couple of months to the camp, and he got released. So he came back home devastated—everyone was. All our dreams crumbled. His father said, "Someone else will pick him up," but months went by, and we basically lived off of his parents. It was devastating for both of us.

There were lots of children in their family. When we were there, there were four girls still at home plus us, and I was pregnant, and I had my daughter. So I was like the domestic person. Everyone would go to school, go to work, and I would clean the house. I felt it was an obligation. I couldn't just sit there and live. My husband would go out during the latter part of my pregnancy; there were times when I wouldn't even see him for a day or two. He told me later that he was doing drugs, womanizing. At the time he'd tell me, "No, no, I'd never do that." In my eighth month of pregnancy, I packed up and tried to leave and go back to my mother. He chased me, and he found me, and his mother calmed me down.

Then I had a boy, so he started changing—"I'm going to take care of him, I'm going to find a job." He loves both his children dearly—even to this day there's always been that wonderful bond between them. Being young and in love, I didn't want to leave him. I wanted it to work, but I wanted him to change and be the better person that he was when we met. How could somebody fall so low so fast? But I said, "If you don't change, I will take these children, and I will go back to live with my mother." The thought of me leaving him and taking his son crushed him.

Another roller coaster—after I got home from the hospital, he got a call from another big team. He's on the top of the mountain. They flew him out there and I'm at home with the new baby thinking, "Maybe there is a God, and we won't be struggling blue-collar workers for the rest of our lives." Everyone said, "Oh, he'll make it this time." Well, he didn't, and he went down low, even worse.

He could've done a lot of things. That was the disappointing thing for myself and his parents. He was a handsome, charming man, but he didn't know what to do besides play basketball. He had gone through four years of college, but he was like twelve credits short of a BA. He didn't like to work.

When Jake was about three months old, we moved out of town and got a small apartment, and I started my first really successful waitressing job in a gourmet restaurant. I would go do the lunch shift, go back home, nurse my baby, go back and do the dinner shift. He was not working at all, and he was basically Mr. Mom, taking care of both children. He cooked and cleaned and enjoyed it, and I said, "If this is going to work, I don't mind it; I've got a good job." He did odd jobs. Then in '80 he got into a

fabulous company—the benefits are great—and things starting clicking. We moved
into a brand-new government apartment complex. We could pay rent according to
our income; we were in a three-bedroom condominium. I was the lead waitress at
this restaurant; I was training everyone. I was basically loving it. He was working; he
liked it. He's okay. Well, he gets a phone call from his friend in the Southwest, who
says there's a semipro team starting here and for him to come down. I said, "Why
would we want to move?" He told me he would have a salary of fifteen hundred dollars
a week. It turned out to be fifty dollars a week. I went against my better judgment,
and we moved there in 1981. We got there, he didn't have a contract, the team folded.
We were in a fabulous five-hundred-dollar apartment he picked out, and we can't
pay rent. There's a day care on the premises and a pool, so I brought them to the day
care and we start job hunting.

I went all over looking for a job in a good restaurant, and nobody would hire me—
I was a woman. I went to this four-star hotel and restaurant, and he said, "I have a breakfast waiter position open." I said, "I don't want breakfast. I have more qualifications
than that. I want to work in the main dining room." He said, "Do you know accounting?" I wanted to get my foot in the door. I had seen the waiters dressed up and looked
at the banquet room. I was determined to get in. I knew nothing about accounting, but
I said, "I kept books for my father in his store," so they hired me. I went down to the
maitre d' and said, "I can waitress, if you ever need me. I'm in accounting during the
day, but I'd be more than happy to help on the floor at night." I was there six months,
and one day the maitre d' was desperate, and he came to me. Soon I was working eight
or nine to five in the accounting office; then I changed and got on the floor and worked
until maybe ten or eleven. After eight months I transferred over to banquets full-time.
This was in 1982, and success started building. I was a waiter at the best hotel restaurant in the city. My husband was the assistant manager in a manufacturing company.
We started saving money. We bought a house. I became a captain. I did captain for a
couple of years and then the assistant maitre d' was let go. I became assistant maitre d',
and then the maitre d' left, and I ended up as the maitre d', and I changed my department name to Private Dining. So this took seven years.

Lenny had this great job, but he walked into the company one day, and the owner
said, "I'm going bankrupt." The company went chapter 11. He tried to look for another
job, but then he was going in that pattern again. I wouldn't see him for a couple of days.
He would get a job, and they'd ask him to leave or he'd quit because he couldn't get
along with people.

I bought him suits. I got him set up—briefcase, coats—and then he wouldn't put forth the energy. There were times when he would drop me off at eight, put the kids at the day care, and then go look for a job. Some days he didn't pick them up. They would call me at five o'clock to come and get my children out of the day care. I was on the other side of town without a vehicle. It could've been drugs. He could've been sitting high with someone and forgot to pick them up.

I wouldn't see him for three or four days, and I said, "This is it. My life for the last ten years has been a roller coaster with you. I have filed for divorce, and I'm going through with it this time. No more begging, no more 'I'll change.' Every time I get to a plateau in my life, you bring me down, and you're not going to do it again. You wanted to move to here, I did that for you. I quit my job. Well, I'm successful. I love my job, and I'm not giving it up for you, and you're not taking these children." (He wanted to go back to the Midwest.) And then I started with the tax returns. I pulled them out of the file for the last ten years—1981, 1982, 1984, 1985—and I kept throwing them at him. "Look what I made. Where are yours? Some years you didn't even have one. I have supported you and these children." I was furious. My income was always more than his, and he did not like that. I was always like a power. He never physically battered us. One swing, I would have had a moving company at the house and be gone.

I had always thought there were other women. He never really reassured me there weren't, and then when we got a divorce, it all came out. He was so angry with me, he told me that he cheated on me all the time. He made it all real—"When I went to basketball camp, I had a girlfriend." And I had been faithful to that man for ten years. I never violated our marriage. I suspected he was cheating from the beginning, but I didn't know. In college I was carrying Christina across campus, and a girl came up to me and said, "Are you Lenny's wife?" and I said, "Yes," and she said, "I met him at a party last night, and he didn't tell me he was married and had a child, and I just wanted to let you know I won't see him anymore." Well, she didn't say she slept with him, but she was with him the night before, and he didn't come home until six in the morning.

I wanted my marriage to work like my sisters' marriages, and I wanted to have the American dream. Meet someone, have children, have a home, have good jobs.

When we separated, he did go back home, and I stayed with the children. My son was about eight years old and went through a very, very bad emotional thing for about a year—not being able to sleep, wanting to sleep with me, wanting me to be in his room and hold him until he fell asleep, bed-wetting. I let Jake go and visit with his father. I was working, and I thought that it would be better for Jake to be around his grandparents and his other cousins rather than just be with me in an empty house. My daughter wanted to go visit my mother and father, so she went up there for the summer. I always had a bond with his parents. They respected me and admired what I did for their grandchildren, and whenever I needed them, I could call on them. They'd go to his family one summer; they'd go up to see my mother another summer. These were all decisions that we would sit down and make as a family. I'd never say to my children, "I can't take care of you. I've got to send you away."

For a while, their father would leave for months at a time, and the family wouldn't know where he was. He was tracking across the U.S. and trying to find himself in religion. He went deep, deep into some sort of religion. I think it was Muslim. After a while, he started surfacing more. I have not received one child support check. He has a child by another girl, and it looks like the woman he's living with now is trying to get pregnant.

There was one year that both children went to school near their grandparents, and that was my most successful year because I didn't have to plan meals. I used to prepare food, and my daughter would put it in the microwave, and they'd eat. They were latch-key children. My daughter was in charge. I would leave them lots of notes—"This is for dinner. Do your homework. Love, Mommy." I asked Christina to help her brother with his homework. Homework was easy for her but difficult for him. Jake gets distracted easily. He doesn't like school. Christina liked it. He's fifteen, and he still doesn't have good study habits. It's probably my fault for working so much. I wouldn't get home till twelve or one at night. I saw them in the morning. I was in an industry where you get a half-hour break, and that's it; I couldn't say, "I have to go get my kids." They'd say, "Do you want a job?" I did what I had to do to survive. I love my children, but I like to work. I don't think I'd be happy if I was at home and not working. I had one day off a week, and it fluctuated. My day off was always for my children. We'd either cook or go to the movies or go to Wet 'n' Wild or Action Park.

Now they say I was a workaholic. I can see that it affected my son in a way. But looking at both of them right now, I think they're remarkable children. Jake was here for a month this summer. He decided he wants to go back to the Midwest for high school. He had a rough time in school here last year. He's like me. I hated going to school. I wanted to have fun—like cheerleading. His grandmother's a teacher. She wants to work with him.

My children live black culture. My daughter's never had a white boyfriend. If their friends ask, they say they're Italian and black. My daughter graduated from high school a year ago and was an honor roll student. She's a bright, beautiful young girl, but she makes bad choices in men, and we talk about it a great deal—"I don't want you to go through the pain that I went through." The men she's been involved with, a couple of them have been arrested for drugs. One stole from her, one used her for money.

After the divorce I had a couple of episodes with men. I went through the emotional yo-yo with them. One was real supportive, and he loved me, but he couldn't deal with my having interracial children. The kids did not relate well to my boyfriends. They always wanted Mommy and Daddy back. Then I met my husband at the restaurant; he was working the grill. When he came into my life, I was thirty-five and he was twenty-two.

Paul is also black. I'm attracted to black men, I don't know why. As a very young child when I heard my grandfather say derogatory things about Jews and blacks, I was mad. When I was in high school, I would be listening to black music, and I would watch *Soul Train*. My mother-in-law and my sisters-in-laws would always say, teasingly, "Well, you're a black woman in a white woman's body" because of the music that I liked. I wouldn't want to do things differently because culturally I've been blessed. I've been exposed to black culture, going into a family at such a young age and going, wow, this is really neat. I do things out of the norm that my sisters would never do; they have this very controlled life. I go to the ashram, and I meditate. I expose myself to a lot.

When the culinary institute recruited me for a teaching job, I came back home and said to Paul, "I'm moving east." He'd never left home. I said, "Are you coming?" He said, "I don't think so," and I said, "I love you very much, it's been wonderful, but I'm going." The closer I got to the date, the more emotional I was getting about leaving him. So we had this big, long evening of crying, and then the next day he woke up and he came with flowers and said, "I want to go with you." So Christmas of '89 we moved here. He got a job very quickly. He's got two jobs right now, and he goes to school. We were up here a year, he gave me a diamond in a balloon and asked me to marry him.

We both were very, very excited about having a child, but we also went into it that if we couldn't, we wouldn't dwell on it. At forty-two, I probably can't have another child. We'll see what the success rate of different operations are within the next couple of years. I told him, "I like to work, so I may leave you with the baby for six months and go back to work, and you can cook at home and do catering," and he goes, "Okay, I'll do that." He's a wonderful person; we're soul mates. His relationship with my son and daughter is very good. When my first husband would not come home, I would be worried about what he was doing. Paul leaves a note, "Honey, I'm going to go change my tires. I'll be back in a while." He's at work, he's going to stay late with the guys, he calls me. It's caring; it's respect. Before we got into it, I told him that I need that in a relationship—"I can't live with you staying out till three or four in the morning, and I don't know where you are." He said, "Why would I do that?"

He's very quiet. With my first husband, there were times we were out when he would ask me not to talk because he wanted the attention. I was too aggressive, too dominating. He didn't like that. Paul says, "She's the loud one; I'm the quiet one." He feels very comfortable with it. I don't know how I would deal with a man that made more money than I did and was more domineering and controlling. I like to dominate and control, but Paul calms me down. If I'm out of control, and I'm all excited about a decision, and I'll say, "Well, I'm going to do this." He'll just look at me, and he'll go, "No, you aren't." He'll stay very, very calm. I'm an impulse shopper; I'm horrible. He made me cut up all my credit cards. Now I have my American Express, and I pay for it every month, and that's it. If I had to rewrite it, I wish I would have met someone like Paul from the beginning. I know it would've worked.

I Didn't Know Normal
Would Be So Tiring

Marianne Pages

She was thirty-three years old when interviewed. She lives in upstate New York with her husband, who is a car mechanic, and her three children. She works the night shift at postal services. (See also p. 505)

I think every girl wants to get married and live happily ever after. I wanted a family and the little house with the white picket fence and the whole ball of wax. Now we've been married for fifteen years, and we have our own home, three kids ages fourteen, eight, and seven, and a dog. Our single friends call us the Waltons. So we're just trying to be very normal, if there is such a thing as normal. I didn't know normal would be so tiring.

I work nights. We were in an apartment, and the only way we were going to get in a house is to have two salaries. There was a time when the kids were younger where I was working part-time and taking three or four classes. I had a Brownie troop. I'm not happy unless I'm working. I like to live a hectic lifestyle. If I'm not doing something, I'm bored. I can't go to the beach and sit all day. That makes me absolutely insane.

A typical day for me is I come home from work at eight o'clock in the morning. I get the two younger kids moving and on the school bus, spend about an hour doing housework, laundry. I jump into bed about ten, ten-thirty. I'm up at three because I have to get my shower before they get home. I like to lay down for an hour or so before I go to work. I usually don't really sleep, but I just want to be still. I'm not getting much sleep at all. Four and a half hours on a good day. My children also have many after-school activities, so I spend a lot of my time driving them back and forth, setting up carpools. My older son goes to soccer three days a week, basketball two days a week. My daughter has Cub Scouts once a week. She and my younger son are taking swimming lessons. My younger son takes guitar lessons once a week and is in Little League. My daughter is going to be taking piano lessons in September. Right now the boys are taking tennis lessons over the summer. I wanted them to have something to do. All their friends are going to camp. I couldn't afford it, so I said, "Well, we'll do tennis lessons."

A lot of times I spend two to three hours in the car. There's no way I'm going to come home at seven o'clock and start cooking dinner. I cook a couple days a week, then we get pizza one night, Chinese food another night. We have a bowl of cereal, have a sandwich, open a can of soup. Summer, it's nice—you just throw things on the grill—it's easier. If we're at a ball game, we'll stop at Burger King and get dinner.

We'll have dinner together, have barbecues, or visit friends on the weekends. A lot of times, when I cook, I get very upset. By the time I'm done everyone's like, "Oh, I just had ice cream at Bobby's house," or "I'm not really hungry." So it's like you do all this work for nothing.

My husband helps occasionally with the wash, housecleaning, but not on a regular basis. He works eight to four, but he doesn't drive the kids around. He calls me a martyr. I always say, "You need to help me more." I'll nag him, and he'll drive the kids once in a while, but once I let up, then he doesn't do it anymore. It's probably my own fault because I say, "Okay, kids, let's go," and I drive them. I don't say, "Go ask your father to do it."

He takes care of the outside of the house. I take care of the inside. He'll mow the lawn and do the trim work and plant the shrubs, and he likes to do that stuff. I've gotten smarter over the years. He tried to teach me how to use the lawn mower, and I was like, "No, no, no, I don't want to do it." He says, "If something happens to me, you should know how to use the lawn mower," so I said all right. So when I used this lawn mower, I just went like all over the yard. He does it where you have to go up and down in straight lines, so he got annoyed with me. He never asked me to mow the lawn again.

I don't really ask the kids to do their own individual wash. I'll usually throw a load of laundry in before I go to bed in the morning, and if there's more down there, I'll ask them to put the load in the dryer. If you don't tell them specifically what to do, they don't. You have to say, "Take the load out of the washing machine and put it in the dryer, turn the dryer on for sixty minutes, take the clothes pile and put that in the washing machine and turn the washer on." If you don't tell them to turn the washer on, they don't turn it on. If you don't tell them to put soap in, they don't put soap in. So I have to write everything out. I can't just say, "Pick up around the house, do the laundry," because it doesn't work that way. They just don't get it.

Sometimes I lose it. Maybe they've been slacking off on the chores, they keep coming to me, "Mom, I need ten dollars; Mom, I need twenty dollars," and I just keep handing out money, and I'm not getting anything in return. Instead of me saying something right away, I let it go until it gets out of control, and then I blow up. They call them my episodes. I run around the house stomping and screaming and throwing people's laundry around. I go on strike for a week. I don't clean, I don't cook, I don't do laundry, I don't drive, and then everybody gets back into what they're supposed to be doing again. And then we start all over again. But for the most part, I think it's all right; it's typical. Everybody I know is like that. I don't know too many husbands that do fifty percent of the work. They just don't make them like that. So maybe my expectations shouldn't be so high. I'm a perfectionist. I can't stand clutter. I have to try to back off a little bit. I'm trying to be understanding.

Robin Vaccai-Yess

She was born in 1964 and lives in Highland, New York, with her husband and two daughters. She has been involved in starting several small businesses and is now finishing her bachelor's degree in business administration. (See also p. 339)

*A*t my HMO you can either see doctors or midwives or both. I opted for the midwives. All their obstetricians are male, and I have a real problem with a man trying to help me through childbirth.

I had just turned thirty when Cassidy was born and thirty-two when Elena was born, so I didn't have amniocentesis. They don't do it if you're under thirty-five unless you're in an at-risk pregnancy. I did have sonograms. I saw a doctor once during each pregnancy because I had some spotting, and he sent me for a sonogram.

They put this goopy gel all over your belly, and there's this little electronic thing— a little ball with a smooth surface and with the sound waves—that makes these pictures on the screen. When the attendant moves the ball around on your belly, you see all different angles. You can see where the little head is, and sometimes you can see the bend of their leg or their arm. I have the pictures of both my daughters in utero. It's interesting, exciting, but you wonder. They say it has no effect. How could that be? Sound waves going through the uterus?

Louie and I did Lamaze both times, but I had stadol with Cassidy. I asked for it. The pain was absolutely terrible. Nothing prepared me for childbirth. The second time the only thing that saved me was the baby came way faster. I don't know how women did it when they used to take your husband away—nobody helping you.

The principle of Lamaze is to be in touch with what's happening with your body, try to relax. And then you go to the hospital, and the first thing they do is strap these two belts around you—one is for monitoring the baby's heartbeat and the other for contractions. They're like seat belts, and they go around your stomach—one up and one down. So there's a tape that's printing out with two lines on it now—the baby's heartbeat and the level of your contractions and how close they are together. Every now and then, the monitor beeps and makes noise. Once the machine was hooked up, all Louie did when I was having Cassidy was stare at this tape, and he'd be like, "Oh, here comes another one"—like the pregnant woman doesn't know when the contraction is coming. It's so stupid. Once they hook you up to this thing, it's not like you can be up and walking around and moving to work with your labor. You're immobilized in bed watching the printout.

When you go to Lamaze class, they tell you to bring your camera if you want to take pictures or if you want to film it. Film it? Get out of here! So we can show home movies of the baby's birth? I'm like, "Oh, that'll be great. Let's invite the whole family over. We'll have popcorn and soda." Some women are like, "Bring the family, bring the camcorder." I would probably kick Louie in the head if he stood down there with a damn video camera. I definitely would. I can't believe that people do that. I think we take this technology thing a little bit too far.

Elena was born at 5:53 A.M. on Wednesday morning, and I went home around lunchtime on Thursday. They said they were going to sign me out. I was really weak and tired. If I didn't know that my mother was going to be around, I wouldn't have wanted to come home.

June Wood

She lives in Virginia with her three-year-old daughter and works in an administrative position for a nonprofit organization in Washington, D.C. She is African-American.

"I was born here in Washington, D.C., in 1968. My mom and dad are from South Carolina. My mother has been a psychiatric nurse forever, it seems like. My father didn't work. He and my mom divorced when I was about six or seven, and we don't hardly see each other. I dropped out of college very early. I plan on going back once my daughter gets to a certain age."

She was definitely an accident. The year that my daughter was conceived, earlier that year I had had an abortion, and then it happened to me again, and I didn't get an abortion.

The first abortion, I had a girlfriend, and I was ashamed to tell her, she was ashamed to tell me. She and I had gone to our boss separately to ask for a day off. The next morning, I walked in to Planned Parenthood and I sat down, and then she came in and sat down, and she and I looked at each other, and we couldn't believe it because we were so close and we talked all the time. We sat in the clinic, and we roared. We told some jokes; we had the place laughing. It was something we had to do, or else we would have cried or had a nervous breakdown. She and I consoled each other that way.

Before I was pregnant with my daughter, when someone in the neighborhood became pregnant, I'd go, "Oh, look, another fool." Never would I have a baby and not have a job and a place of my own, and not be married—but the married part wasn't a big deal. You don't need to be married to have a family. And I'm not saying that I don't want to be, cause I do want to be married one day, with the house and a white picket fence and a Volkswagen and a dog and stuff like that.

But I was in love with her father for a year, and one night I was without any protection, and I refused to pass up the intimacy. I honestly don't know why I was so careless. What could I have been possibly thinking? He didn't pressure me at all. It wasn't until after a couple of months of dating him that I found out that he had a girlfriend. He'd lie to me. He would say that this wasn't so and that he was really in love with me, and I was somewhat still in love with him, and so sometimes if he would call and he'd beg me to go out, I'd be a stupid fool and I'd go out, but this didn't last long.

When I became pregnant the second time, he got on his hands and knees and begged me to keep this baby. He said he would be a father to her. Now he sees her maybe once a month, buys her birthday and Christmas presents, sometimes offers more.

I ended up keeping this child because I didn't have a dime to go to the clinic, and he wasn't going to give it to me. I just could not bring myself to tell my mother that I was pregnant a second time and needed money for an abortion. It was my pride. One day, finally, my cousin said to me, "June, you are almost five months pregnant—you are far gone past an abortion. You need to go to the clinic. You're not getting vitamins, you're not getting checked out." And that kind of rung a bell, and that was the day that in my mind and in my heart I became pregnant. It was the saddest and then the happiest day of my life, too, because I knew then that everything was going to change, and it was going to change for the better because I was going to do what I was supposed to for my child. It was almost like somebody had died. I called the doctor, went on public assistance. They gave me food, WIC, and a check. They gave me Medicaid, so that paid for the hospital and for everything.

I was losing myself until I had my daughter. It's wonderful. It's stressful—it's a lot of work, but it's a good thing for any woman that would love her child to the ends of the earth. It makes you stronger, makes you work harder, makes you more concerned about a little bit of everything. It opens your eyes.

I went back to work when she was three and a half months old. I had a cousin that babysat her while I worked, and she'd give her junk food—candy, bubble gum, sodas, fried chicken. This was when Samantha was close to one year old. It was a nightmare. She wasn't taking the baby out at all. She sat around and watched TV and ate. It's hard to find a good babysitter. Samantha had my cousin, my girlfriend, her father's niece, and her grandmother—her father's mother—until she could go to day care when she was two.

At my mother's house there was so much tension. She and I don't get along. I saved up for a year and moved into an apartment that's got a swimming pool, and the day care is on-site. I decided I wanted to live in Fairfax or Montgomery county because they've got the best schools, and I decided I'd find the day care first and then a place to live close by—I don't drive. I called this day care, and they were, "Well, we're on an apartment complex," and I'm like, "Get out of here," and I said, "Well, I'll be right over." I came and looked at the school and checked out the apartment complex, and it was really good. I went back out there twice. I peeked in one morning and said hello to the teachers, and I went back again one day in the afternoon and just sat and observed for about an hour, and I got a chance to talk to one of the parents coming out of the school. Except for the bills, it is like heaven now.

I take my daughter out just about every weekend. I take her to different muppet shows, to visit relatives, shopping, everywhere. I made it a point from a young age to spend serious quality time with her on the weekend. It was killing me then, and it's killing me now, but I'm still doing it. I'm tired.

Sunday I cook a nice big dinner, and I don't know why. It's just the two of us. I have just about no social life. I'm so tired I don't even want a social life.

I do want to get married one day. I'm not going to rush into it. A lot of guys are like, "Oh, can I come over?" "No. You can't." You've got to be careful who you're dealing with nowadays. I've got to know you for a really long, long time before you could start to come into my house and spend time around me and my daughter.

I'm hoping someday to meet the man of my dreams. First of all, I want a real man, because a lot of the guys that I have dealt with in the past, including her father, they're not real men. A real man would do anything for his kids and wouldn't let anybody stand in the way. I want a man that can stand on his own two feet. I want somebody to open the door for me, to call me, and check on me and my daughter and be concerned about us and just be a gentleman, and tell the truth, and not always be about all these games. Somebody that's hard working, that thinks I'm beautiful. I want what any good woman would want in a man.

Robin Vaccai-Yess

She was born in 1964 and lives in Highland, New York, with her husband and two daughters, ages two years and three months. (See also p. 335)

I go to the supermarket probably every other day. With two little kids, you're always running out of something. If I'm going in the morning, it's a half-day project. First, I've got to get Cassidy ready, give her her cereal. Then after I've nursed Elena, I'll bring her upstairs with me while I get dressed. Since I've had kids, taking a shower, doing my hair, putting on very little makeup, and getting my clothes on—I don't think takes me longer than six minutes, I swear to God.

So I come downstairs to get Cassidy ready. I'm prepared, with diaper in hand and the clothes that she's going to wear. As soon as she sees me coming, she grabs her toys and runs. I chase her around while she fights me. I'm, "Cass, it's disgusting—you're sitting in pee, you're sitting in poop, come on, change your diaper." "No, no, no." By the time I get her over to the table and lay her down on the blanket, it could take twenty minutes, and hopefully Elena didn't wake back up yet, ready for another nursing. I say, "All right, Cass, we're going, get your blanket—God forbid, you leave and go anyplace without anything of any importance for security purposes!" So I fill up Cassidy's milk bottle and make sure there are diapers in the diaper bag. I leave Elena sitting in her little seat on the table—inevitably, she's starting to fuss around by this time—and I carry Cassidy out to the car. I have to carry her because if I put her down, she takes off off the back porch and runs for the swing set, and then I have to chase her around the yard. So I put Cassidy in her seat, and I come back inside to get Elena. I grab my bag, grab the diaper bag, and get Elena set up—now we're all in the car.

Luckily, Elena falls asleep in the car. Cassidy never did. All she did was scream and cry until she was about eighteen months old. She doesn't like being confined. She's better about it now. So we're off to the market, and, luckily, we don't have that far to ride, not even ten minutes. I like to park near those big metal things that you push the shopping carts into. I'm really in trouble if the shopping carts are all gone. I have to carry Elena in her seat by the handle. Inside that carrier, she probably weighs twenty-five or thirty pounds. Cassidy weighs about 25 pounds, so I have to hold her hand and make her walk in the parking lot and hope that none of the lunatics speeding by runs us over.

Today I lucked out, there were shopping carts out there, and I parked right next to them. The Grand Union has huge shopping carts, so I can set Elena's car seat inside the basket.

People see me with Elena in the shopping cart and Cassidy on the seat, and they say, "Where do you put all your groceries?" And I say, "Well, it really cuts down on your shopping." I'm wedging loaves of bread in around the carrier, and, luckily, underneath they have those racks for bags of dog food and stuff like that, but I put all the stuff down there.

Most of the time when you go to the grocery store with kids, you have to give them something to eat. Luckily, Cassidy eats a lot of fruit, so I just clean off as much of the pesticide as I can, and then we have half-eaten nectarines back in the bag. Another thing Cassidy likes to do is go look at the live lobsters in the seafood department—that's a real thrill. We stop by and talk to the fish.

One time around the holidays—I always do a lot of baking then—Cassidy was eighteen months old, and she's sitting in the cart seat and grabbing stuff out of the shopping cart. I say, "No, no, no," and I try to put the groceries way at the end of the cart where she can't reach, but she's turning around and reaching out, even with the seat belt on her. I had put three or four dozen eggs in the cart, and I turned around to get something off the shelf, and sure enough she had stretched way over to grab those eggs. She couldn't reach them, but she touched enough stuff that one of the egg cartons tipped over, Suddenly, the eggs are breaking all over the floor. And I'm like, "What did I tell you? Don't do that"—and everybody's like, "That poor woman." So this man comes over with the mop, and he's like, "Don't worry about it. I'll get it." And meanwhile I know he's cursing me out under his breath, like, "These women with these bratty kids coming in here."

When I get to the checkout counter, people always have these annoyed looks on their faces. "Why is her cart so far from the counter?" Well, I can't push the cart up to the counter because Cassidy is sitting in the cart ready to lean and grab everything off the candy and gum rack next to the cash register. So the cart is sticking way out, and I'm standing between the front of the cart and the conveyor belt and I'm pulling everything out from underneath the cart. When the person ahead of me leaves, I zoom the cart right through to the end so Cassidy doesn't even get a chance to look at those brightly colored packages of candy.

Margaret White

She was born in 1968 and raised in the rural Northeast. She has been married four years and had her first child—now a three-year-old boy—at twenty-two. Her daughter is one year old. (See also p. 383)

My kids wake me up in the morning, and they're like, "It's morning time!" I make them their breakfast, and I do housework, and then I try to do something with them every day. We'll go to the pool or the mall. Sometimes we have lunch out somewhere or go to a friend's house. Then we'll go home, and I try to get them down for naps at about one o'clock. I take an hour every day and watch one soap opera! And I love it.

Then it seems like they wake up from their nap and we're getting ready for dinner, and Dad comes home around five. It's nice when he comes home, because I get a break. He's playing with them, and then he gives them their bath at night. Then we all just play around for a while, and they go to bed around eight-thirty or nine.

I always pictured that I would stay home with my kids. I wouldn't miss it. I wouldn't send them to day care. I want to be in the PTA and do all that stuff. I have some friends my age who have taken the same path as I did, but a lot graduated from college and got jobs, and now they want to get married and have kids. I think there's a shortage of men or something, because they're all searching and crying on the phone to me. I think deep down we all want kids, it's just whether you do it or not. But the grass is always greener on the other side. My single friends think my life looks so perfect, and I think, "Gosh, your life looks so nice to me. You're just working, you come home to your quiet house, it's the way you left it, and maybe you can take a bath and read." And they say, "Well, you come home to your husband and kids, and they're all waiting for you at the door!" No one seems happy with what they have.

In the last few years, sex has become a problem in my marriage. My husband wants it more than I do, and it wasn't like that until we had kids. I'm just so tired all the time. I've spent the whole day with the kids, and I would just like to read a book and go to sleep. He's been working, and sex is his release. He takes it personally when I turn him down, and it's not personal at all. He's so insecure, and I just can't make him see it my way. We try to make compromises. Last night was Monday night, and we had sex Sunday night, so I thought I was okay for a couple days, and then he says, "Are you just going to read your book?" and I said, "Yeah, I really want to finish it," and he said, "All right, when you come upstairs, wake me up." So I went upstairs, and he says, "How was your book?" and I said, "It was fine, but I'm really tired." So I figure tonight I'll have to give him some!

Before we had the kids you had afternoons, and your time was your own. Now there have been times where I've wanted to, maybe like a Sunday morning, and then they wake up. It's really different. I don't think it's a problem within our marriage, I think it's a time problem. For me sleep is a priority, and for him sex is a priority.

I think sex is so different for men and women. I do have orgasms almost every time, but my husband gets upset if I don't! It's fine for me if I don't—I don't care—but it's nice when it happens. And I feel like he thinks he didn't do a good job or something. I told him, "You don't understand. I have to concentrate, and I just don't have the energy right now to be that into it." Orgasm is the final goal for my husband, and then he just conks out. For me the closeness is just as important, and sometimes I would be just as happy to cuddle as I would to have an orgasm.

When I first started having sex, I didn't really know what an orgasm was. I think it was through masturbation that you finally realize what it is. At least for me and some of my friends, you just can't have it through straight intercourse. You have to work at it. I had a girlfriend just the same age as me, and she said, "I think I had an orgasm." She described it, and I said, "Yeah, I think you did!" So now she knows. Before she thought if she got really excited and started breathing heavily, that was it! She said, "He had to touch me while we were having sex." She felt a little guilty. I said, "Well, that's normal." So now she's happy and she knows that she can get pleasure.

Our Marriage Is Too Important to Fight over It

Jo Ann Jansen

*She was thirty-eight years old when interviewed. She lives in Kingston, New York, with her hus-
band and two daughters and works for an oil heating company.*

*"I'm lucky for having gotten married at thirty-four, for having children at thirty-six and thirty-
eight. Up until four years ago, it was mostly my work. I lived with my mom. My father had passed
away, so I stayed on with my mother. When I got married, that's the first time I ever moved in my
entire life."*

We got married in the bowling alley, and the reception afterwards was at the VFW,
but our wedding ceremony was out on the bowling lanes. They closed the place for us,
and we had 175 guests. We had the white carpet go down to the bowling lane and an
archway of flowers, and we stood under it and were married. We had to bowl afterwards for everybody, and with the dress, I couldn't; it went in the gutter every time.
Everybody, for their favors, got little wooden bowling pins. We were on the front page
of the local paper the day after.

It just seemed to fit. My husband had known my brother for some time. They bowled
together. My husband had to go out of town for a month, and I took his place in the
bowling league until he came back. The bowling banquet was in June, and because I
had bowled also, we went together, and that was the first time we went out. And it just
kind of clicked. Every night, we were out bowling.

When I was a senior in high school, my father became very ill, so my plans for
college came to a stop. He didn't pass away until three years later, but he wasn't able to
work. Mother had stopped working when she was waiting for my older brother. I needed
to work. I was offered a temporary position at this company. That was eighteen years
ago. Very steady person: one home till thirty-four years old, one job. When I started
here, all I did was answer the phones, file. I did a little typing. Eventually, I went to a
community college and took accounting courses. It was paid for by the company, and
I ran straight As the whole time. I now control a staff of ten people and answer directly

to the owners. My job is to prepare the financial statements, to handle all the tax returns, to make decisions regarding our computer system, our customer service group; anything clerical or computer in nature is under me. We have a CPA that does the final tax returns and audits the statement, but everything else is mine.

Probably less than a year from the point we got married, we decided that kids would be nice, and nothing happened, nothing happened, and nothing happened. So we bought a boat, and we bought a home, and we bought. We're not going to have kids, we might as well enjoy life. And finally kids started coming along. Two girls. I told him, "God knows I need the help. That's why I have girls."

For my first pregnancy, my husband was going to be in the delivery room, and then he wasn't going to, and his father didn't think he should—"It's no place for a man to be"—and finally he was in the room. He had come in to see me, and the doctor said to him, "This is going to happen right now—grab her leg," so he didn't have a choice. He was so happy, and he cried, and it was great. The second daughter, he was into it this time. He was in the room, and the nurse said, "Blow, don't push." She's calling for the doctor because next push that baby was coming out. My husband's like, he'd do it—the doctor doesn't have to come back. I'm like, "Get the doctor!" He says, "I would have just taken her head and pulled," and I said, "You didn't read the material. You didn't listen at Lamaze. They take the head out and turn the baby. You don't just pull."

Both times I stopped at the office on the way home from the hospital. With my first child, it was a Thursday, and everybody pretty much left me alone on Friday, but Monday morning the phone was ringing. I would bring a computer home. It was like I never left. First time I worked better since I didn't have another child in the house, just a baby. I worked on some projects and answered questions for the people who worked for me. I got a pile of work done. My mom was there and could help. I don't know if I would've enjoyed just six straight weeks of doing nothing. I would have gone nuts.

Leslie and I were the first women who worked here who came back after we had our children. Every woman before us stayed home.

My first child, Rosanne, within four weeks she was sleeping a good five, six hours every night, so I was getting some sleep at night, and I could relax and maybe take a nap if I wanted to during the day. I used to need a lot of sleep. I don't get it, so I'm getting used to not getting. Especially with this one. When I brought Victoria home, her and her sister made a pact never to sleep at the same time if I'm home!

My husband leaves for work at about a quarter to six in the morning. A lot of the time the baby wakes up like four, four-thirty—he'll feed her and put her back down. I'm usually up a quarter of six. My mother comes in, gets a cup of coffee, settles in. I get to work about quarter to seven. I leave about five-thirty, and that's the end of the quietness.

My husband comes home usually by three in the afternoon. He does roofing, and if it was ninety-some degrees out and he was on top of a roof all day, he's bushed. He takes his shower, and he may be doing something out in the yard, so Mom is still there, pretty much taking care of the kids. If it rains and he doesn't work, my mother still comes, and he truly has a day off. When I don't work, I take care of the kids all day; I'll let my mother have off.

In the evening, my husband may still be outside; he may be watching television. He loves Rosanne desperately, but he doesn't play with her. If she was a boy, they'd probably play boys' things, but he doesn't know how to play dolls or things like that, so he's usually sitting and relaxing.

I get home, my oldest daughter is looking out the window, going, "Mom, mom, mom," and I go in the house, and she runs right to me, wants me to play. So at least for a half an hour or so we play. My mom is still there to mind the baby. Then I try to get Rosanne occupied playing by herself, and I usually head in the kitchen and start organizing for dinner, pick up anything that's been left during the day.

I have a child gate going into my kitchen, so if she's annoyed because I'm on one side and she's on another, I'll get the little ball and we'll play catch. Dinner is usually something in the microwave defrosted—I use the freezers a lot. I like to be able to go shopping maybe every six months. I have almost everything I need but bread and milk and things like that. I try to make meat, potatoes, and a vegetable unless it's very hot. As long as I just keep right on going, I'm fine. Usually my mom is there for dinner. We don't eat out much. We usually bring pizza home—it's easier with two young children.

We rarely sit at the table to eat dinner. I want to, but he'd rather not. I told him as the kids get older, I want that. We're usually at tray tables in the living room watching news or something, and my daughter is in the high chair.

I just think it's very important for young children to have that one time of the day where you can talk to your father or your mother, and you don't have to wait for a commercial, and I want that for my children. Right now it's so hard for all of us to eat at the same time, anyway. There are nights when one of us just has to put the plate down and take care of the baby. But eventually.

Rosanne doesn't go to sleep until nine-thirty. Often, he'll go to sleep before she does. So it's tough right now. I've been doing just five hours sleep—it really doesn't hit me until seven, eight o'clock, and then I'm tired. I'm pushing myself. I will get four to five hours of sleep for maybe seven, eight days, and I won't get up. The kids cry—whatever, I just don't get up. Before children, I probably got a good nine hours.

Since the second child came along, I don't think we've gone out by ourselves twice. Last week was our anniversary, and I came home from work, and both kids were crying. My husband and I made a reservation for dinner. At one point we cancelled it, but then the kids settled down, so we went anyway. I think we were two hours with dinner.

I make more money. Even if we both have a full week, I do, and roofing is seasonal. If it rains and he doesn't work, he doesn't get paid. He probably wishes he made more than I did, being the man, but it's never caused any problems. He'd like to have his own business, but with the children, we don't want to take that gamble right now. We couldn't make it without any income from him. If we knew children were going to come along, I doubt we would have spent the money on a house, a boat, a car, so he probably would have tried going out on his own, but now we've got to pay some of our debts down.

We have a twenty-one-foot, cutty cabin boat. He's the only one that's used it lately. He'll sometimes take a couple of friends out. He likes to water-ski. You can't take an infant because when you're hitting waves, it's bouncing too hard, and if we're going to take Rosanne, it's a lot of work because you need to hold on to her all the time, and she's got to wear a life jacket, and she doesn't like the life jacket. I don't feel right asking my mom to watch them too often other than when I'm at work, and I don't feel right not seeing them on the weekends. So he'll go out on the boat.

We probably have a very old-fashioned-style marriage in that I do all the housework. He mows the lawn, and he takes care of the cars, and he takes out the garbage when I say, "Will you please? Will you please?" But we started out that way. Thirty-four years I cleaned the way my mother wanted it done. So when we first got married, and we got our house, it was my first time, and I wanted to do everything. I made a big mistake. But most of the time it works out well. It's ninety-some degrees out and he's been all day working, he needs to relax, and he goes outside and he might putter in the yard or whatever.

Most of the couples I talk to today who both work share the laundry and cooking. We're still working on that. I try to get across to him that I do need some help between now and when the kids are old enough to help. I do get frustrated. Sunday night I stayed up till one-thirty doing laundry. I was exhausted yesterday because I only got four hours' sleep. My husband would say, "Sit down, take it easy. Why don't you take a break?" He doesn't care if the house falls apart or if the laundry gets behind. I have to get it done—it is important. My daughter loves to help me with the laundry. It takes at least half an hour to take the clothes from the washer and put them in the dryer with her helping. She recognizes that something is mine, and she says, "Mama." "Yes, that's mommy's—now put it in the dryer." And her Barney shirt comes out, and, "Look, Barney, Barney," and she doesn't want to put it back, so she's helping, and it's fun. Fixing the brake line on his blazer took him the entire weekend. He'd run out for a part, and then somebody next door would come and they'd sit and talk about it for a couple hours. Meanwhile, I watched the two children by myself. I didn't get anything else done.

When I complain, he says, "Yeah, I know I have to start helping," but it hasn't happened yet. It's the same kind of situation as his parents. My father-in-law did not help around the house, but my mother-in-law only worked part-time occasionally. He was the only boy; he had four sisters plus his mother. Between them, the housework was done. He did live on his own for a while, and my mother-in-law tells me he was Suzy Homemaker. His apartment was spotless.

Our marriage is too important to fight over it. I love him. My husband's a really good person. He can't say no when somebody wants something. There's too many good things. With the couple of things that annoy me, we'll work on it. We had a talk about it this weekend again, and then I'll have a couple of good days, and the garbage will go out without my even saying anything. We'll pick our clothes up instead of leaving them where we take them off.

If I could have any situation I wanted, I probably wouldn't change anything. I have to let some things go at work, and I'd like to play outside with the kids more than I do; I'd like to have a spotless house. I enjoy my job too much to not work. I enjoy my kids— I would never want not to have them—and I like it when I finish that laundry. Even one-thirty at night, I felt good my laundry was done. I would never want to hire someone. My aunt once said she was going to give me a gift—she was going to come down every week and clean my house. It bothered me. I want to do my cleaning.

And if my husband said, "Okay, I'm going to give you a break. I'm going to take Rosanne, and we're gonna go to the park," I'd almost feel bad because I don't get to watch her play in the park. He's done that a couple of times, and I was, "Well, why can't I go?" There are times when I would like his help, and there are times when I don't want him anywhere near what I'm doing. All the guys, our neighbors are outside and hanging around their cars—and I want him to go outside and hang around with them. I don't want him thinking he can't be a part of that. But if it's like last weekend, and since Friday night I haven't set foot out of the house . . . and then finally Sunday night I did go out for a little while. I brought the baby out, and I went outside on the lawn, and all the women are outside, too. I start hearing about they diddled the weekend going to Grand Union. They were giving out free this and free that, and I'm like, "I never left my house all weekend." Then I get frustrated. It's hard to do all of it. But I wouldn't give any of it away.

Day by Day

Roberta Flaherty

She was born to a large Irish Catholic family in a small town in the South in the mid-1950s. "There wasn't ever enough money to go around." She has a master's degree in French history.

*W*hen I was a freshman in college, at the suggestion of my English comp professor, I read *The Feminine Mystique* by Betty Friedan. It opened my eyes to what my mother's life had been like and to what I was doing. I was at a teacher's college, and I was not challenged. I was spending a lot of time cooking in the dorm kitchen, raising house plants, and becoming a vegetarian. My professor said, "That's not really why you're in college. Read this book and see what you think." And so I decided to switch out of teacher's college into a university. I really wanted a career, and I wanted to share things fifty-fifty with whoever my husband would be. It sounds good in a book, but just because you decide, "I'm going to have a husband who's this way," that's not necessarily the person you fall in love with.

There was just no way to make it a fifty-fifty relationship. I didn't know what I was getting into when I married a doctor. He tried to tell me, to warn me off. He said, "It's going to be hard and long. You'll never see me during all these years of school and training." The first inkling I had of how tough it would be was my senior year of college. We were engaged, and I had only met his family at Thanksgiving. Christmas Day we were at his house. Everybody got up and opened presents, and then at eight o'clock his father said, "Well, I'm going to rounds. See y'all later." I thought, "It's Christmas!!!" and then I thought, "I have a lot to learn," and I did.

I thought I would have a career, but I don't know where I changed my mind along the line. I guess once I had kids I enjoyed being a mother so much that I didn't want to leave them. And my husband really wasn't ever there. His hours were horrendous. When he was an intern, a number of rotations still had every-other-night call, which meant that he would get up in the morning, go to work at seven o'clock, work all day, spend the night in the hospital, work all the next day, come home at seven P.M., sleep, go back to work for another two days and then come home. And that went on for nine weeks at a time, and some services it was every third night. And that went on for several years.

I had a real crisis somewhere along the way. My daughter was really difficult to raise at first. She had a lot of allergies, she developed asthma early on, and I breast-fed her for a while, but it didn't work, although I had done it very successfully with my son. My daughter screamed from the moment she came out, and she kept screaming. She only slept when I was swinging her. She was colicky with a capital C, and every time we'd try a new food on her, she'd break out or have diarrhea or have cramps, and I thought I was going to lose my mind.

Most of the women I met were through the medical auxiliary. A lot of them were working; a lot of them were also in training. I had a period where I felt sort of like an underachiever, like I wasn't realizing my potential and I had to have a career. I sort of had my turning-thirty crisis when I was about twenty-seven, twenty-eight, and thought, "You know, I'm wasting away, and I love being with my children, but I'm missing out. Here I am in a big city and there are all of these opportunities. I need to get a job." I felt like being a mother didn't have any status and wasn't valued with the people I was around. And so I started looking for a job, and I put my children in a day care. I didn't like it, but I wanted to get a job as a copy editor. I couldn't get a job because I had no experience. But you can't get experience unless you get a job—it was awful.

Once I got that anxiety about not having a career out of my system, I decided I was pretty content doing what I was doing—volunteer work, raising the kids, gardening, exploring my interests—and I really did not want to work full-time and leave the children with no parent, because I felt kind of like a single parent, and since I had the option of being there, I thought it better to do that.

I try to stay open to different possibilities, and maybe when my kids are grown, I'll do something full-time. But I'm happy at this point in my life with what I've chosen to do and with who I am. I've taught English as a second language, I've helped sponsor refugee families through my church, I've done a lot of campaigning for pro-environment referendums, and I feel like I contribute to the community a lot even though I don't have a job, and I feel like the family does well as a result. And I don't need the money—my husband's not one to clutch the checkbook. If I need to get something for myself or the kids, I do, so it's not a problem. But he wouldn't be opposed to my working, so I might do that in the future.

Chrissy Robinson

She works as a receptionist, is a single mother, and was born in 1969 in a small town in the Deep South.

    "Little jobs, secretarial and mechanic, was what my mom and stepdad did. I'm white. People say, 'Oh, you are Italian or maybe a little Spanish.' I don't know what I am—Heinz 57, a mixed breed." (See also p. 161)

I told my ex-boyfriend that I was pregnant, and he was like, "I'll give you the money for an abortion. I'm too young to have a family. I don't want my child being brought up in poverty." Now, I'm nineteen, and he is twenty-seven telling me this. I said, "You think my child will be brought up in poverty? My parents are going to help me. At least you've got a good job. I'm not asking for marriage; I just want your help." He said "Well, I don't want to have anything to do with it."

It was really rough at first. I decided to breast-feed, and she cried all the time. I was going through the blues. I just felt like, "Why did I keep her, why?" I didn't have that instant mother-daughter bond that a lot of people say they have. I found out later that a lot of people don't have that. It was just so weird and new for me. I never intended on having children. I felt resentful that my body was all screwed up. I gained ninety pounds when I was pregnant—stretch marks all over my stomach. I had moved back in with my parents, and I always felt like I wanted to go out and do something. At first my mom was good about babysitting, and then she got fed up with it. I was going out and having a really good time, and then after a while I met this guy, and he moved in with me for a whole week. We moved out the same time.

My little girl was about a year. My mom was paying for her day care, and I was working at a bank. A woman there owned this trailer, so I got a really good deal on it. In the town where I live there are no apartments. If there are apartments, it's in a very bad neighborhood. Everybody has a trailer, and it is cheap.

Last night I called this man I'm dating to talk to him, and he is like, "Well, if you are bored, you can just come on over. Me and my sister are going to rent a movie." I said, "No, I have my little girl tonight." I'd never give her up, but there are times when I would love to just not have her for a little while. That is when I get mad at the father. I want a weekend to myself. There are things I need to do. I've got to get on the roof of my house. It is leaking everywhere, and I can't fix it because I'm by myself. I have to leave her in the house while I mow the yard, and I don't like doing that. What if she turns on something. So I mow a run, and I go check on her. She has horrible allergies, so I can't put her outside. She was always sick when she was little. I couldn't go to work all the time. They were always calling me from the daycare saying, "She has another ear infection. She is sick. She is swelling up. She is broken out in hives. You need to take her to the emergency room."

There are times when I really feel locked in because I can't go out like I like to, but down here guys really could care less that you have children. Everybody has got a kid down here now. It is the thing to have. My little girl is a trip. She is highly intelligent. Her school thinks we need to have her IQ tested. I love her to death. Every day she does something else that just amazes me. It's hard, and it's neat. I always say about Regina, "She was an accident, but she is not a mistake."

Katherine Millard

She was thirty-two years old when interviewed. She lives in a small town in upstate New York with her husband and two children, and has a clerical job at the Department of Motor Vehicles.

I had absolutely no idea what I was getting into. The foster care people ask you what sex, what age group, and I told them I would like a boy between the ages of three and eight because I have room in my son's room. I didn't want anybody too old. If there was any kind of problem, I wanted somebody that I could control physically.

Three kids scared me a little bit. I said, "It's only for a week, how bad can it be?" It was the absolute worst. The brother and sister have been so badly sexually abused that all the counseling in the world is not going to save these kids. The little girl is eight years old—she's very sexually active. They said you have to watch her at night, she'll sneak into the boy's room. I'm thinking, "My husband's at work all night. I've got to get up in the morning for work. What am I going to do? Sit up all night and watch these kids?" So in the morning, I'm telling all the kids, "Come on, get ready for school. Come on, you got to eat breakfast, let's go, let's go." I smell this terrible stench. I go into my son's room, and this kid is standing there covered. This little boy, he takes feces and rubs it all over his body. (From what I'm told, this is a sign of sexual abuse.) He wiped it all over the walls, all over the furniture, all over the carpeting. I didn't know what to say. I just stood there with my mouth hanging open, I couldn't believe it.

"All right, you've got to get in the bathtub, wash yourself off." I'll deal with the bedroom later. I've got to get these kids to school—I've got to go to work. As I'm getting him in the bathtub and taking care of him, the older boy, who was, I think, ten or eleven, is beating up my daughter. I had to physically pull him off of her. The kids were all screaming. I'm like, "This is insane. This is a madhouse." In the middle of the week the case was turned over to another social worker. I called her, and I said, "Listen, this is not working. You told me these kids were well adjusted. These kids are not well adjusted. These kids are animals." They stole money out of my pocketbook. They lied about everything. If you asked them what color the sky was, they would lie to you about it. "You've got to come out here and talk to these kids." She came to the house, and she talked to them, and I told her the different things that had been going on, and she talked to me like I had been doing this for years, and I said, "I'm sorry, but this is the first experience that we've had." And she looked at me, and she said, "And they gave you these children?" And I said, "Yeah, why?" They were like the worst possible cases that anybody could get. She couldn't believe that they gave them to us.

These children had been in foster care for years. The older boy had been adopted two times, and the people had given him up. He wet the bed. I tried to be very discreet and not embarrass him, and I said, "I know this happens, but you have to either let me know or you have to take the sheets down to wash." He would continually cover it up. Then my son started wetting the bed. He said, "Well, he does it, and it's all right, so I can do it." So now I had two bed wetters. I had a daughter who was beaten up. The kids were all traumatized. It was just terrible. It was six days of hell. My husband was a basket case; I was a basket case. We would try to take them out and do things to keep them occupied, and it was just impossible. Finally, we sent them outside to play. It was a Saturday morning, and we had just had the pool put in, and all three of them were out there beating the sides of the pool. These kids must have been so angry. And I was thinking, "Oh, my god, there goes my two-thousand-dollar pool." Finally, my husband said, "That's it. I can't take it anymore." He got on the phone and called the social services and said, "You've got to come and get these kids." And they said, "Well, you have to give us time to find a place for them." He's like, "No, you come and get them now. I don't care if they come and stay at your house for the weekend." He says, "I cannot do this anymore."

Never again. We did it because we finally got on our feet and we were doing okay, and we wanted to help out somebody else less fortunate. We both agreed. I was the one that suggested it. Now I look back, and I say I must have been crazy. They gave me children that I specifically said I didn't want. And then they tried to turn it around and make it look like my husband and I were bad guys.

Jill Ladaine

She is the oldest of five siblings and was born in the Midwest in 1973. Her parents were married a year after she was born. "My dad's on disability because he got hurt when he used to work at a car plant."

I wasn't really into birth control. I made sure they wore the condoms until I met my ex-husband. After I had my little boy, I was on the pill, but I was always forgetting to take them, so I ended up having one again. Now I got a thing called Norplant. You can't get pregnant, it lasts for up to five years. I would never have an abortion. I don't know how somebody could do that. I think it shouldn't be legal.

I was seventeen when I first got pregnant. I was staying with my parents until I was old enough to move out. We ended up staying with his parents, too, for a little bit, until I got an apartment. I didn't get married till I was pregnant with my second one. It never worked out real good.

He was ten years older than me, but he never worked. I had welfare. He's one of them guys that are into drugs and alcohol, and I got into it because I was with him. He was already doing it for years when I met him. Crack and stuff like that. People were always coming over to buy some or to do some. It was always in and out, in and out, in and out. They were his friends, not mine. After I met him I didn't have no more friends because I was never going nowhere. I was always stuck at home with my children or with him. I would ask him to go do something for the children, and he wouldn't do it. I was always the one giving them the bath, getting them dressed, changing their diapers, feeding them, giving them their rattle. We always got into it about this or that. I wouldn't let him beat me up bad. I would defend myself and fight back.

I was twenty when I started doing crack. Just trying to be like them. I felt like I had to do it because they were doing it. I felt left out. I hated him when I first met him, and I didn't really want to be with him when I was married. It was just—that's how people are— you kick them out and then you take them in. It was a boring life. That's why I'm glad I'm doing better.

I got my kids removed from the home. One or two cops and—I don't know what they're called—some other guy came and got them and took them to a home. They said they had people calling about us. They had a warrant. It was hard for me when they first left. I couldn't eat or sleep or nothing. I had been doing a lot of crack. All day, all night. It wasn't good. I stopped the day the kids left.

My ex-husband still wanted to be doing crack. It made me mad. We was going through the courts. I told him, "I can't deal with you no more." I wasn't gonna lose my kids for good because of him. I had to let him go. He still does crack. Now that he's gone, I'm staying away from all that. Trying to get my kids home. It's been nine or ten months since they've been gone. I see them every Wednesday. The foster mother is named Ellen, and we get along. Her and her daughter drop the kids off at a Family and Child Services thing, I see them for an hour, and then they pick them back up. But it's hard for me because I live way over here, and I have to go all the way over there. My ex-husband goes to see the kids at the same time I do. I don't associate with him. I just pay attention to the kids.

The judge told me, he said, "They're too little to be out of their home. They need to be with their mom." They want me to have my kids back. I'm the one that's doing everything, not their dad. They got me working, going to see counselors, and going to parenting classes. I still go through drug tests. I call the lady, and she'll tell me, "Yes, you gotta go today," "No, you don't gotta go today." Probably every Monday, Wednesday, Friday. I just go pee in a cup and leave.

I'm looking for a job right now. Trying to look for one that's close to here so I could walk there and back. I'm trying to get my GED, but there ain't no school around here. It's hard for me to get anywhere. After the kids got taken away I moved in with my parents. I've been here in this new apartment for only three weeks. I have a cousin that lives in the other building over there. I came to talk to the landlord. He let me look at the apartment, and I was telling him about my kids. So he said, "Okay, we'll work out a deal," so I could be able to pay my rent.

It's been hard for me not to see my kids every day. Before they come home, they're gonna be doing home visits. I can't wait. My cousin works at night, and I watch her kids sometimes, so if I get a job during the day, she'll be watching my kids while I go to work, and like that. I want to be a cosmetologist. I've been wanting to do that since I was little. It stuck with me. I have aunts and uncles that were into that. It seems fun, perming people's hair and doing their nails. I'll just wait till my kids get old enough to go to school.

I don't really want to be in a relationship no more. I'd just rather go out and have fun and come home and be with my children. They got a new thing here, it's the Discovery Zone. They've got those tunnels and the stuff they jump in—it's fun for the kids. I used to take my little sister. That's where I'm gonna take my kids when they come.

I had an all right life and a boring life, and it got messed up. I never really thought about the future. I was always in the moment. I just go day by day. Do what I gotta do.

Whatever goes goes. I never thought about ten years from now. Now I'm doing good, I'm getting my kids back. It's not really boring no more. I can't wait till they come home. I'm gonna have a party, a welcome home party!

Julie Harris

She was born in 1957 in Illinois and has been horseback riding since the age of six. She works with horses and teaches riding. She says that it's very difficult to make a living, but "us horse-crazy people will do anything to stay with the animals." She now lives in a rural area in Ulster County, New York.

I married my high school sweetheart back in '79; Leslie was born in '82. Before she was a year old, we had split up due to his alcoholism, so I've been a single mother. My daughter's come to work with me from the time she was an infant. My pediatrician must have thought I was awful because when she was two weeks old, I sunburned her when I was managing a horse show. She was in the shade all day, she had a little hat on, a little blanket over her seat. I didn't know she'd sunburn in the shade. We went in for our monthly checkup, and she was beet red.

Then two months later I had a sick horse. It was the end of September, and I slept in the barn with the horse, and I brought her with me in her bassinet. About three o'clock in the morning, she was kind of blue, so I called the pediatrician the next day, and I said, "Look, I have to sleep in the barn again tonight—I've got a really sick horse. How do I keep my daughter warm enough so she doesn't turn blue?" What he must have thought of me! But when you think back, in pioneer days, it was the same thing. We ended up getting a kerosene heater and putting it in the barn, keeping the temperature above fifty.

I made the decision not to breast-feed, thinking it would be much easier to leave her with a babysitter. I was a cow! They gave me injections at the hospital to dry me up, and it was so uncomfortable. She started getting very colicky. So at a month old, I nursed her every twenty minutes for two days; the milk came back, and she nursed until she was two and a half. Her little Gerry pack had a zipper inside that opened up, and she nursed right when she was in the pack, and it made it so much easier.

I taught with her in one of the little Gerry pack pouches on my front. When she was two and a half, I put her into a nursery school so that she would see other children and learn to socialize, because she was a very loud child from being outside all the time. I wasn't the type of mother who at five years old is crying, "Oh, my baby's going to kindergarten." I said, "Break out the champagne—she's on the bus. I've got four hours to myself."

Melinda Steinberg

She was born in Queens in 1964. Her father worked for a frozen food company and her mother quit her job as a secretary to raise the children. "I ran away from being Jewish for a long time. I didn't want to be like my parents, so I didn't want to have much to do with it." (See also p. 506)

I'm in a relationship with a man right now, and he is the person in my life for as long as it lasts. I've been living with him for nine years, and we are still trying to figure out what to call each other. He is my boyfriend, he is my lover, he is my partner. We are not married, and that is something that is sort of in the background.

My sister is a lesbian, and I had a relationship with a woman when I was eighteen or nineteen that lasted awhile. I was terrified. I didn't know what was going on. I hadn't had that much experience with men. The first thing I did when our relationship was over was go out and get a boyfriend really fast. It was a dumb thing to do. I got involved with this guy who had been with a good friend of mine. They had just broken up, and I knew I should have left him alone. But instead I needed to grab on to someone just to say, "well, I'm not a lesbian, I'm heterosexual."

Of people in my age group and people that I know, women getting together with women is pretty common. It just seems like something that is a normal part of growing up, of existing. At this point, it's not a scary thing or something that I'm embarrassed about. It happened, and I think it was really important in my life. I don't really think of anyone as heterosexual or homosexual or bisexual anymore. I don't feel too strongly about making those divisions.

Greg really is not my "type" in terms of physical appearance. He is losing his hair rapidly, and I think what attracted me to him was just that he was very kind, sweet, and interesting. I guess I like men who just seem different. He was an artist, and I am definitely attracted to artists.

At this point, I would have a child tomorrow if I had the financial ability to do that and still work. I love children, and I feel like I would be a perfectly natural mother. I'm a teacher, and I've worked with toddlers, and it was the best job I've ever had. It was wonderful just to play with kids all day.

I'm thirty now, so I'm starting to get a little worried whether or not I should do it now, cause if I wait five years, will I be tired? Also, we talked about getting married, and I think I would like to do it. What I hear in my head is that the world is so complicated, why bring up a child trying to explain that you are not married, but I don't know if that is my grandmother or my mother talking. It just seems like—in terms of my allotted amount of rebellion—can I go so far as to actually have a child and still not be married? I don't know.

Greg wants to have children, too, but he is not as hot to do it as I am. He is thirty-six, and I'm more scared of his timetable sometimes than I am of mine because he tends to think he has forever. I think a lot of men feel that way. It is true to some extent. Older men have the physical means to father the child, but do they have the energy to bring it up? I get worried about his patience level dwindling. We just had our niece over for a weekend, and the things that drove him crazy took about twenty minutes longer to drive me crazy.

He Had to Have Total Control

Wendy Gardner

She is divorced and lives with her five-year-old son in a small town in the Northeast. She was thirty-five years old when interviewed.

"My father was part Indian. I haven't seen him in many years. They divorced when I was young. He kind of just disappeared. My stepfather worked for a concrete company, kind of like a foreman. I went to a community college for about a year and a half, but I didn't finish."

I had been working at a large company as a secretary for about eight years when I met my husband. I was twenty-eight when I got married, and we were together for about four years. I had known him for a couple years before that. We had lived together, and he wanted to be with me every minute, complimented me nonstop, bought me presents. I had never had that before. He would offer to drive me to work and come down and have lunch and bring flowers, and then he'd pick me up and take me out to dinner. We went out for like two weeks, and he said, "Oh, I love you. I want to marry you," and he wanted to have children. Most guys that I had met didn't ever want to get married. It felt good. He wanted to take care of me. "Let me fix your car, let me wash your car." I took that as, wow, he must really love me. But after that wore off and I wanted some independence, a little bit of my own life, that was not acceptable. He had to have total control in every area. He became very, very verbally and physically abusive. Little by little it was, "I love you, but if you just lost a couple pounds, you'd be perfect," and "Maybe you should get a nose job," and "My old girlfriend was a lot prettier than you, but you have a better personality." Little things like that to kind of keep you in your place.

He had a really bizarre childhood. If somebody told me now that their childhood was like that, I would really stop and look—How is this affecting them and are they going to be repeating this pattern? Because that's exactly what happened, especially when Michael was born. He was thrilled that he was born, and I think he loves him in his own way, but it reminded him too much of his own situation, and everything he said he wouldn't do, he started to do. He got more abusive verbally. He's big, about six-five, 270 pounds, and he'd have his finger in my face screaming, and he'd rip apart everything about me—my family, what I've done as a wife, as a mother. In five seconds flat he would just stomp all over me, and then he'd push me against the wall and take his hands and squeeze on the bones, squeezing my wrists, and it was very painful. I almost left several times. There was always an excuse, "Oh, I'm so sorry. My father's sick, my father's dying, I'm under so much pressure, I'm worried about money." Of course, he spent it like there was no tomorrow. When it came to my spending, he'd give me a check or cash to go grocery shopping, and there were a couple of times where he took the receipt out of the garbage and would go through the cabinets and make sure that I didn't spend any extra money or pocket it. He didn't want to give me cash; he'd say, "Well, a couple of times you wrote the check for twenty-five dollars over and you pocketed the money." I said, "I'm your wife."

He hurt me, and he hurt Michael. I took Michael to the doctor, and I filed charges, and we were all set to leave. Then he agreed to go to counseling, but he got in a fight with three counselors. It was awful. It was destroying my son. I said, "I gotta get out of this," and finally he ended up leaving. I didn't want him to come back unless he really got involved with counseling. But he came back about a week later to take Michael overnight and started screaming and yelling, and I tried to get away, and he dragged both of us out of the car and hurt me very badly. The neighbors called the police, and I had to get an order of protection. If his actions hurt his son, that was just the way it had to be, because he had to see me destroyed. "I won't stop until you're in the gutter"—those were his words. I didn't give him the satisfaction of ever getting to that point.

He started seeing this woman—they had this affair for a couple months—and he would tell me, "She's everything you're not." She was married; she kicked her husband out, and Bruce moved in the very next day. He'd only been out of the house three months, tops. She got involved in his fight. She didn't even know me, and she was going around telling people that I was abusing my son, that I was crazy. She'd come with him when he did pick Michael up and make faces, and he'd laugh at me. She helped him break into the house and take the TV and the VCR and a couple items of my clothing. It was very nasty.

He took every penny. He gave us a little bit the first couple of weeks, and then he got angry and cut off our money, and I had to get food stamps. He shut our electric off, and he took our car away. I came out of family court one day, the car was gone. I lived on a mountain and had to call friends to come get me. Thank goodness, I had friends that had a car they let me borrow. About a month after he took it, I went over with my mother—he had the club on the car—and I sawed through the steering wheel and pulled the club off and drove it home. Then he had me followed and got the plates off it and took it off the road, so for four months we were without a vehicle. When he bought the cars, he had them registered just in his name. There was nothing I could do. Legally, I owned it, too, because it was marital property, but they could not charge him with stealing.

The last year that we were together, he had changed the bank accounts so that they were just in his name. All the statements went to his office. When Michael was born, my husband needed somebody to run his office—he was working out of the home—so I quit my job and worked for him.

We had a home that we lost because he stopped paying for it. I couldn't afford the mortgage, so now we rent. We did finally start getting support—they garnished his wages. He makes a lot of money, so he doesn't have a choice. We came to a settlement, and the lawyer knows that he's making way more than he's claiming to, but it's just difficult to prove it because he's best friends with the partner. Now he's buying a new house and he's got a new 300E Mercedes, but he has no money! I'm very fortunate that he does have a good income. He recently started to take Michael on a more regular basis, every other weekend.

Now I can look back, and I'm glad to be away from him. I have a life again, I have confidence, but back then I don't know if I wanted it to end. I didn't want it to be the way it was. There's fear of the unknown. And when you live with somebody that tells you constantly that you're worthless and you're no good and that you're nothing without them, there's a part of you that does at least at that time, believe it. Now I can look back, and I think, "Oh, how could I stand it—even for five minutes—let alone the years that I did."

I've always had close women friends—I have one friend, since we were in junior high school, barely a day has gone by that we don't talk—and we support each other through ups and downs. In the last couple of years going through the divorce, just to know that I could pick up the phone and have friends that I could talk to, that really helped me get through it.

Through counseling I learned a lot about myself, why I would even get involved with a man like that in the first place and what made him the way he is. Ten years ago if somebody said they had an awful childhood and they hated their mother, I'd feel sorry for them and ignore a lot of what should have been warning signals.

He's been gone almost two years, and I'm pretty proud of myself, because the few men that I have dated, if there have been potential problems that I could see down the road, I recognized it and got away.

I rented this place, and every time I turn the key and walk in, I get these little goose bumps. I love living here by myself with my son. Maybe eventually I'd like to, if I found the right person, share it with somebody, but right now I just like it.

It was a hard marriage and what happened after the divorce was absolutely horrendous, and it really hit my son hard. He was having some problems. He's five now. Things have relaxed, and he's happy and making remarkable progress—I worked it out so I'm doing some freelance secretarial work at home. I get criticism sometimes because I love being with my son. Since he was born, I always wanted to at least spend part of my time at home with him. Pretty soon in a few years I won't be the most important person to him, and he'll have his friends. I like to be home, and I love to sew and make clothes and quilts, and I like to decorate. I don't think I'm a feminist. Friends that are more career oriented have told me that I should be pursuing some corporate type of position. Their children are in full-time day care. Maybe they're just envious because I am home for the summer.

In many cases, it's really necessary that both people work full-time jobs. But I've also seen people where it's a necessity because they have to maintain the lifestyle that they've chosen—a couple of fancy cars, a fancy house, and the best of everything. I know I could be farther ahead financially if I worked full-time, but somebody or something has to suffer, and I don't want it to be him. I see these kids getting tossed in day care from birth. I feel bad for them. I know when I'm working nine to five that by the time I pick him up and drive home, I'm tired. I don't have time to do anything with him, and he suffers, and I can see the difference now that I'm working part-time out of the house. We've been swimming, and we went to the circus, to the movies. He's so happy. He wakes up when he wants. We take a walk out to the pond, and he throws the stick, and the dog jumps in.

He gets a couple of dinosaurs and reptiles and goes out in his little pool, and his imagination gets going, and he'll play for hours. When I was little, we were home with my mother in the summer. We got up when we felt like it, we played outside, we rode our bikes. I don't think it's the same when you're in somebody else's care. You might be in good care, but they don't love you. I don't know what the answer is.

I feel sorry for a lot of these kids. From the time they're born every day they're on a schedule. They've got to wake up at six o'clock—and rush 'em through breakfast, rush 'em to get dressed. I don't think they get to just be kids.

Slapping Force

Pat Jamison

Born in 1962, she has lived all her life in a small town in New England. She has been divorced for seven years, has two daughters ages eight and ten, and works as an auto mechanic. (See also p. 201)

I ended up having an abusive marriage. When it got real bad, we went to a marriage counselor, who made me see that I was really worth something and could do anything I wanted, and so now I have a whole different outlook on men and life and wish I had this outlook way back then. My ex-husband was verbally abusive always, but towards the end he got worse and worse to the point where I was afraid to go to sleep. I was afraid for my kids.

The first sign of abuse was when I was six months pregnant with my daughter. He came home at four o'clock in the morning screaming and hollering. I got up out of bed, and he started pushing me around and slapping me, and he shoved me backwards in the tub. I thought I lost the baby. It scared the hell out of me. I never saw him like that. He had gotten in a fight with his girlfriend's husband. He had a girlfriend, and I knew nothing of her, and that night he told me all about her. He was terrible, awful, but he promised me he would stop, and I was six months pregnant and so I said okay, and it never got any better.

He liked his drugs. I smoked pot, I did some coke—it's something you just do as a kid, but you outgrow it. He just got into it more and more—a lot of pot, hash, speed. In the morning he would smoke a joint as soon as he woke up. It just went on all day long.

He was horrible. The house could never be clean enough. Nothing was ever done right. You would make dinner, and if you didn't serve the right vegetable with the right meat, you were in trouble. He would do weird, weird things, like rip the phone out of the wall and throw it across the room because I was talking to a friend. I enjoyed having friends, taking my kids to visit my parents, and he hated that.

We went out for three years before we got married. If I wanted to go off with my friends, it was no problem. But after we got married, only he could go out with his friends. He felt that I should stay in the house all the time with the kids and never talk to anyone other than him.

One time he put my daughter in the washing machine. It wasn't on, but he put her in there. I was on the telephone with a friend, and he yelled at me, "Pat, that's it, you're on the phone again—look at where your daughter is." I hung up the phone, and I went flying down the hall, and my heart went in my throat. He opened the lid of this washer, and my little girl pops up. "See, I told you to stay off that telephone—this is what happens." She was only two years old, and I believed him that she climbed in. But then like half an hour later I'm thinking, "How did she do that? No way!" When he wasn't around, I asked her, "How did you get in the washer?" And then she started to cry. "Well, Daddy picked me up by here" and she's holding her ankles. And she said, "Feel my bump on my head, but don't say anything, because Daddy made me promise not to tell you." I didn't think that he would ever do anything to hurt the kids.

Another time he was mad at me—it was probably something like I didn't wash a dish—and he took the kids and put them in the van and took off. It was around seven o'clock at night. I was yelling at him, and he backs out of the driveway and just takes off, and it was about three hours later before he came home. In the meantime, I didn't know where to look for him, and I was scared to death. Finally, he came home and sat in the driveway with those kids in the van. He locked them in and pointed towards a tree and told me how he was gonna kill them and himself. I just stood in front of the van, and I said, "You are not moving this van." I thought for sure that was it, we were all dead that night, cause he kept lurching the van like he was going to run over me. I said, "You're going to have to kill me, but I'm not moving, and you let my kids out now." It was ten o'clock at night, and the baby was standing up, crying. Claudia was just sitting there with her eyes this big. She didn't know what to think. It took about an hour to talk him into unlocking the doors, and I grabbed those kids.

I was in my car with the two kids the next morning, and he was mad at me, and he was trying to run the car off the road, banging into it with his car. That's when I called the lawyer and said I can no longer live this way. He was wonderful. Told me to hide in a hotel. "Just get your kids, diapers, bottles, whatever you need and go, and we'll have him taken out of there." It was scary, and it was the biggest step I've ever taken in my life, and I had no idea what would happen to us, but I knew it had to be better than the way we were living. I had to hide for a week till I got these papers in motion and got the police to literally take him out of there.

I had him arrested seven, eight times. He would scare me, come after me with the car. I was at work one day, and he pulled up in front and just sat there and stared at me and stared at me, so I would call the police and say, "He's here, come get him quickly," and I'd lock the door, and then he'd laugh and drive off—just real sick stuff. Once the divorce was final, he let off because he knew that he could not see the kids if he remained that way. The judge would not allow him to see the kids for a good seven, eight months.

He hasn't bugged me since. I was scared to death, but the only way he was allowed visitation was his parents have to be with him when the kids are there. But now it's so many years later, and he's wonderful with the kids, and they are big enough where if he would do something to them, they would tell me immediately. So I'm not afraid anymore. He's never, ever missed a child support payment. He's very good that way. It's not enough to buy the groceries every two weeks, but it's nice to get it. It's our fun money, and in the summer it goes towards their babysitter.

The only thing I regret is not continuing my education, and I've tried to go back to school. I went for three semesters. Between work, kids, and school, maybe I slept four hours a night. By the third semester, I ended up with pneumonia, and my doctor told me, "You have to stop." He was very right. I said, "Okay, I'll go back to school when the kids get older." But now with 4-H and Cub Scouts and Girl Scouts and all that, I have no time left, so school will have to wait, but that's fine.

My social life is my kids. I socialize with the parents while I'm at Scouts or 4-H. I don't have time for dating. I go out with very good friends every other weekend when my kids are with their father. We get together and we have dinner, and sometimes I stay out quite late and have too good of a time, but that's about it.

I have no interest in being married now. My kids take up my time. My older daughter is ten, and I figure in another eight years she's going to be off to college somewhere. By the time my younger daughter is sixteen, she's not going to want anything to do with me, and I'll still be young, and then I'll maybe be interested in men, in a companion. Right now I don't have time, and I don't want the headache. I will not take away from my children to give attention to somebody else.

Kim Faggins

She was thirty-two years old when interviewed. She has three children and over the years has held a variety of jobs, including several working with emotionally disturbed and retarded children and adults. She is African-American.

"I was born in Brooklyn and lived there all my life, in east New York right off the Belt Parkway. Except about three years ago I moved to upstate New York.

"I have a daughter sixteen years old, a nine-year-old, and a seven-year-old. The two youngest ones are from the second marriage; the oldest one is from the first marriage." (See also p. 519)

My daughter was born in June, and in July I turned sixteen. She was an accident, but me and her father loved each other, and we got married. Married at sixteen, playing house, liked it and hated it and knew not to have any more—I waited years.

I think I was married seven years. That was an abusive relationship. No black eyes, but he wanted me to sit there, listen, shut up. "If you don't, I'm going to slap you." His slapping force was so heavy that I would fall on the floor. Soon after we was married, it started. That's when they always start, when they know that they have some type of legal papers on you, like you're a piece of property.

He didn't want to split up with me. The hitting had stopped. I left him because he was messing around with a woman; he found jobs but wasn't staying on them too long, and I just got tired. When he went away for like a year and a half in jail, I got to spend more time with my sisters and go out, things that I wasn't able to do as a wife because he was very, very possessive. I liked that better, and we grew apart. Soon after we split up, I met my younger children's father.

My second husband was a good man but started to wrestle with drugs. The drugs just overpowered him. He's a truck driver, so he made pretty good money. He was never out of a job. He started hanging out, spending the money on crack. But he was a mechanic, also, so if he lost his job or he wasn't able to make it to work—if you're out messing with drugs all day and all night, sometimes you can't get to work—he wasn't out of money because he would fix people's cars.

One night I was over at my sister's house, and he was at the door, and I didn't answer him. I was fed up. We'd been married maybe about five years. So he slashed the gas line to the car, and he lit it on fire. Well, I ran downstairs, and I smothered it and put it out. He knew that attacking the car would get to me because I had to go to work all the way in Queens. "You're not working, you're messing with drugs. Don't you have the consideration? I'm working, I'm not bothering you for any money. I'm taking your kids to day care, picking them up. Why would you do something like that to a car that transports your kids? You really don't care, do you?" It was cause I was finished with him. I'd been finished with him for a while, but once you start ignoring them, it's like, "She's really finished with me."

We stayed away from each other for about ten months. Then he called us up. He was trying to straighten his life out because he didn't want to lose his family. He went to a drug program, and then he came here and couldn't find a job. I don't know whether it's a man thing or a black man thing, but he just couldn't take me working and making money and him not working. It made him angry. I really didn't understand it. He would do odd jobs, but it wasn't good enough for him. He left and found a job in Brooklyn driving a truck, and that's when he got arrested. He's locked up now. I don't know him for robbing people, even when he was messing with drugs. He's always worked. He said he didn't do it. He had a Legal Aid lawyer. You can't really get anywhere with a Legal Aid lawyer, so they convicted him. I think it's two and a half to four, or five, something like that. I figure maybe that's for the best because he was messing with drugs off and on. He's been in there—October will be two years. He's never been locked up before in his life.

When I lived in Brooklyn, I went to college a year, just liberal arts. I had my nine-year-old daughter, and I stopped. I was thinking about going back to community college this year. I have an appointment to go there next week. Even if I could just take two classes a week. Now the children are a little older, so I think I could do it.

I was recently working an overnight job with retarded adults. My daughter would watch the younger children. She'd get them up in the morning and send them to school. I don't know what I would do without her.

I haven't worked in a month. I couldn't do it anymore. My son has asthma real bad. It was a rough winter—sometimes I couldn't get to work because I couldn't drive to the bus. Most of the time, it took me about two hours to get to work by car and bus. I'd get off work at seven o'clock in the morning, and sometimes I'd fall asleep driving on the highway, and I'd catch myself. I'd get home around nine and wash clothes, set something out for dinner. I would lay down at maybe twelve o'clock, sleep until three. They would come in, have a snack, talk. It would be four o'clock, and I'd start cooking, while I'm doing homework with one, helping with words, sentences, spelling.

Sometimes I would get four hours of sleep, sometimes I would get six hours. I would never, ever get eight hours of sleep—never, ever, ever. I was really tired. I don't mind working, I like getting out of the house. It didn't last, though. You have a breakdown. I mean your body can go but for so long. I was tired all the time.

I stopped working in June, and Aid to Dependent Children wouldn't give me any money for July. I do have some money in the bank. (My grandfather was a supervisor at Con Edison. He always saved and taught us to save.) They gave me food stamps.

It took me about six weeks to be accepted for public assistance. They really give you a hard time. I haven't been on there for years, and they should appreciate that, and I tell them I'm going to look for another job. I have to call a job back—working with retarded children, daytime.

I wouldn't get married again. I've been married twice, and sharing—I don't feel like sharing, no, uh uh. I don't want to share my bed, I don't want to share my private things, I don't want to find stubbles of hair in the sink, toothpaste on the floor. I don't want to pick up clothes and belts. If you have to go through all of the aggravation that men put you through, you would rather raise their child by yourself and not even be bothered. It's a lot of aggravation.

Lizette Arsuega

She was born in New York City in 1976. She has eleven brothers and sisters. (See also p. 163)

I was thirteen when I got pregnant, and I was fourteen when I had my son. I always wanted to be around my friends. Now that I'm older I see that there's nothing to do but to go and hang out with your friends and wind up getting all stupid. If you've got two kids, you've got a big responsibility. And I understand that because I'm nineteen now. It's not like I'm a little girl anymore.

When I found out I was pregnant with my first child, I felt happy because I thought that me and the father were going to stay together forever. I left my mother's house. She didn't want me to see my boyfriend, so I ran away and I went to Florida with him, and we lived with his sister and brother-in-law. My boyfriend was nineteen, twenty at the time. He was a very generous, beautiful person, but to have a relationship with him, he was very possessive and jealous. He wouldn't want me to go outside, he wouldn't want me to wear skirts, he wouldn't want me to wear tight pants.

He and his brother-in-law were working together, and I would be the only person in his sister's house during the day. She was going to school. One day my boyfriend's brother-in-law didn't go to work, and when my boyfriend came home, he started blaming me for messing with his brother-in-law and supposedly sleeping with him, and we got into a big argument, and he started hitting me, and from there he tried to put lighter fluid on me. And that's when his sister came out onto the patio where we were, and she hit him with a broomstick and told him to get off me.

Three weeks later I left. I'd been down south for two months. My mother took me right back. She understood everything because I guess she went through it, too, and I have a very understanding mother. She had her first child at sixteen.

My mother told me when I got pregnant that it's a big responsibility, I had a lot of things to think about and the baby's father had a lot of things to think about, but other than that she would just tell me, "You know, I wouldn't want you to take it out because I don't believe in abortion. You'd be killing a child." And I wouldn't want to go through abortion because I'd be really scared. I wanted my son very much.

A few months before I had the baby my boyfriend came back to New York and stayed at my mother's house. He was in the hospital with me when I had my son. He was standing right by my side. He really helped me out with the baby, and he bought the baby's clothes and the carriage and things like that. He was always working.

He left after my son was two months old because I told him to. He kept hitting me, and I couldn't deal with it, and I was like, "Just pack your clothes and get out of here, I don't want to see you." He was like, "I'm taking my son with me." I said, "No, you're not. If you feel like taking me to court, you can take me to court. Other than that, my son is not going nowhere." After that I never got back together with him.

For my son's first birthday I invited all of his family. And nobody showed up but my family. My little brothers and sisters, my cousins. And I spent three hundred and something dollars on my son's birthday—I bought a piñata and a cake and a little costume for him and balloons, candy, cookies, everything—I was still in touch with my son's father then, but he never showed up to the birthday party, so I was like, forget it.

My son is really attached to my mother because I've been in her house ever since he was born. When he and I go out, he'll tell me, "Call Grandma—we've got to talk to her." On a typical day I'll stay home, I'll read to my son. I want him to learn his ABCs and 1,2,3s and his name and address. So I write it on the back of a notebook that I have in the house, and I do the little dots, and he traces over them. He'll say, "Mommy, look, I finished!" and then I'll do more of them. And we just have fun all day long. He hasn't gone to school or day care yet. He just got done with his shots, and I called in for his school. He's going on five years old. Next year he'll start kindergarten, but I want to put him in Head Start before he goes so that he'll know a little bit before he gets there.

I was going to think about getting an abortion for this baby that I'm carrying now. But this baby's father didn't want me to get an abortion. He was crying and telling me he might kill himself if I was to do that. We used to talk about everything. I told him I wasn't ready to have another baby because my son is still young, and I wasn't too excited about the baby. From there he was always telling me, "I want you to have my baby," so I told him, "Okay, I'll have the baby if you're going to stand by me." And he stood by me but not for long. He's only nineteen, like me, and he was really too much into his friends, not his relationship. His friends would tell him that I was just telling him I was pregnant, just to keep him, which wasn't true. And he believed it. From there we broke up. He said we were arguing too much. We were together eight months. We didn't use birth control. At the beginning I used it, but in the end, I don't know. I just didn't use it. I didn't feel like using it.

My whole life I had a lot of boyfriends but sex with only four of them. Because I really don't trust it now that everything is going around, STDs and AIDS and all of that. My dream is to become a nurse. I went up to the tenth grade in school, and then I just didn't get to go. I'm trying to get on welfare because right now I need to get my own apartment, and I want to start going to school to get my GED, and then from there I'm going to nursing classes to become a nurse.

My son is going on five years old and he's really the type that when he sees something, like any little child, he wants it. Sometimes times is hard, and you can't get it. It's very hard for me, but I see that I'll work things out.

I would only get married if I felt that it will last. But in society today it's not really known to get married and really stay with anybody. There's a lot of young guys that just like to hang out, and they don't like to stay locked down. It's up to them, really, because the girls is always willing.

His Family Is One Way
and Mine Is Another

Dana Coroff

She was born in New York in 1961. She has two older sisters and a younger brother.

"My father passed away about seventeen years ago. My mother never remarried. She never even dated anyone. My father was a union printer, and my mother never worked until my father died. She had no education. She went to work in a school lunchroom. A couple of years later her cousin was opening up a bridal shop, which is a business that my mother knew about because her grandfather and her father had businesses down on Canal Street. So she went to work for her cousin, and about six years later she saved enough money, and she opened her own business. She's had it since 1983, and she's successful. Our background is Italian. Our traditions are Italian. I went to Catholic grammar school, Catholic high school, Catholic college, and I swear I'll never send my daughter to Catholic school. I hated it."

When my father was alive, we went to church every Sunday. My father was religious, my mother wasn't. After my father died I sort of pulled away from the church. I questioned a lot of things. When I went to church, it was because I had to be there, not because I really wanted to. My husband's Greek Orthodox, so we got married in a Greek church. I believe that there's a god up above, but I don't believe in the Catholic ways and what they stand for. They're very hypocritical.

I just started going back to church. I was trying to get pregnant for a long time, and I was having a problem. I went to this prayer meeting with a friend of mine—"Pray to God, and you'll get pregnant." I was there for all of ten minutes, and then I was like, "I'm leaving. I can't stay here. I can't deal with this." She was like, "No, come on, stay." The nuns were supposed to pray over your head, and it was my turn. The nun was like, "Pray to whoever you want. It doesn't have to be a saint; it can be a person." I always prayed to the blessed mother—I believe in the blessed mother. So, I'm sitting there and I'm praying to the blessed mother, and after it was finished the woman turned around and said, "You prayed to the blessed mother." I was in shock. So I said, "Yes, I did," and she said, "Keep praying to her because she'll answer your prayers."

It was March or April, and I had started taking fertility drugs. My mother-in-law had called me, and she was like, "Go to church and bring a white flower for the blessed mother because this is the month that the blessed mother got pregnant." So I went, and I brought the flower, and I got pregnant that month. And I gave birth to my daughter right before midnight on Christmas Eve. It was weird. I'll go to church now, and I'll light a candle and say a prayer. But I refuse to go to mass, and I don't sit there and listen to the priest go on about things. You're sitting next to people who go every Sunday, and meanwhile outside of church they're not Christians.

I was fourteen when my father died, and my brother was nine. My two sisters were already married. Me and my brother were spoiled. Maybe my mother tried to compensate for my father not being there. I got a new car when I graduated high school, and so did my brother, whereas my sisters never got a new car. My sisters never went to college. They went to work, and they got married young.

I went to college in Dobbs Ferry. I lived home. I wanted to go away to school, but my mother laid on the guilt. I studied fashion merchandising and management. I worked for one year in Lord & Taylor's, and I hated it. And then I wound up working for a district senator. I became a legislative aide, which I loved. It was crazy. You were busy from the minute you went in to the minute you left.

As soon as I walked in, I'd get my cup of coffee, I would do the senator's schedule for the day on the computer, and then start with constituent work. People were constantly calling you with problems. They were really calling him, but you were doing all the legwork. So it was phone calls, research, writing letters to certain people and certain commissioners, and then also all that work had to be put into the computer. If there were fund-raisers, we'd work on the fund-raisers.

There were other women there, but I didn't get along with them too much because when I first started working for the senator, I started out at a lower position. Then I got hit with all this work, and I was like, "Well, if I'm going to do all this work, I want more money, and I want a higher position." When I went in to him, he had given me a promotion and more money, and about six months later he made me supervisor of the office. The older women who had been there a long time—I guess they felt they deserved the position.

Women can be so catty. They made life there miserable for me. I really didn't bother with them. I went in, I did my job, and I left. I had my own office. I had about six girls under me that I had to distribute work to, which was hard because all of them were much older than me. And then they used to think—I mean, he's a senator, for god's sake—they thought he was a god. "Oh, the senator's here, the senator's here!" I would be like, "He's a human being, just like everybody else is." I think half of them were secretly in love with him. They would get called in the office and put on their lipstick. These women were like forty-five years old. Most of them were sexually frustrated, if you ask my opinion. There were three men, and I was in charge of one of them. I got along great with all of them. There was never any sexual harassment. And I got along great with the senator.

My husband and I met in his restaurant. I went in to eat. I didn't fall in love with him right away, but it was just something about him that kept me going with him. My whole family was like, "Why are you doing this? He's nothing like you." And I was like, "I don't know, I enjoy myself when I'm with him." We both enjoy traveling, so we were always taking off. We went to Australia, we went to Hawaii. We were more like best friends, which is something I think we lost after we got married. I don't know, I just fell in love with him. Now that I think about it, he's a lot like my father in ways of helping people. He has a heart of gold. And he lives from day to day, and he loves life.

We knew each other for a while before we got married. I met him in December of '83 and we really didn't start dating until the latter part of '84. We got married in '87. But you don't know a person until you live with them, and that's why I believe two people should live together first. The little things that they do. The nights—Greeks love to play cards. When we were dating, my husband probably took me out and took me home and then went to play cards. When we got married and he was just going to play cards, he couldn't understand why I was so upset over it. And I was like, "Well, you never did this when we went out." He was like, "Yes, I did," and I was like, "Well, I didn't know about it."

I wanted to live with him first, but my mother went nuts. And he didn't want to, either—he wanted to get married. We went through a lot in our marriage, and we still go through a lot—it's very hard. His family is one way, and mine is another. It's a lot of stress on both of us, but we love each other enough to get through it.

My husband doesn't question me if I say I'm going out with my friends. He's like, "Fine, have a good time." I don't have to have the food on the table at a certain hour every day—I don't have to cook every day. But when I first married my husband, my family was in shock because I made like a 360. I mean, I never did wash, I never did dishes, I wasn't a home person, and here I am married, and I'm doing wash and doing dishes and learning how to cook and ironing my sheets. I guess when you first get married, you want everything to be so perfect. My family couldn't believe it, especially my brother. He was like, "What the hell happened to you?"

But then after a while what happened was I think I was doing it more to make my husband happy, and I was losing me, my identity, in the long run. And I was like, "Oh, wait a minute." And that's where a lot of the fighting came in. Because I couldn't take on everything plus hold down a job. My job was a lot of hours. And if I would say to my husband, "Could you get me a glass of water?" he would turn around and say, "Why, are you crippled?" I couldn't believe it. He would never—now he'll vacuum, he'll fold the clothes, but he would have never done that before.

He didn't realize he was doing anything wrong because this is what he saw all his life growing up. I'll go to one of his uncle's houses for dinner, or his cousin, and the way they talk to their wives, I can't believe it. It's a pity. I don't know how they could live that way, but I guess the women are used to it, too, because they see that their fathers spoke to their mothers that way, and that's how they feel life should be.

Marriage is hard enough, but marrying somebody from a different background is even harder. You have different ways. You believe in different things. My husband's family, their friends are Greek, they go to a Greek doctor, a Greek dentist, a Greek—it's unbelievable. For my husband to marry me, he went through hell, he really did. You would have thought that he was marrying a black person the way that his family was carrying on.

I'd always seen my father help my mother. I'd seen my father do dishes and do wash. I felt that my husband should help. He was constantly going out all the time. We were leading two separate lives, until I was going to get a divorce, and he agreed to go to marriage counseling. It really did help a lot. No matter who was talking to him and telling him, "Look, this is America, and we do things differently," it wasn't until we went to counseling that he changed a lot.

I stayed with my job in the senator's office until I was trying to get pregnant. And I still keep in touch; I still go to the political functions, and I work on campaigns. But I really want to go back to work. I miss it. That's something my mother and my two sisters can't understand. Both my sisters each have one child, and they stayed home until the boys were about thirteen. I'm itching now. I know it's terrible to say, but I just—it's not me to stay home.

It's hard for my husband to understand why I would be miserable staying home with my child, but I am. I'm not saying that I want to dump her, but I had wanted to put her in school, in day care, and he's against it. I'm trying to get into the Board of Ed, because the hours would be great. He could stay home with the baby during the day, and I could go back to work. He feels that she's too young for me to go back to work, even if he's there with her. He wants me to wait until she's about three, but I feel that going back to work would make me a better mother. If I had something going, something I enjoyed doing, I would have more patience for my daughter. I try to explain that to my mother, and she's like, "I was home for you kids every day! You never had to put the key in the door and nobody was home!" My mother and I fight about that constantly.

My mother didn't have that need—she didn't feel like she was missing something. Probably because she never knew what it was to have it. She got married at eighteen. So you're going from your parents' house and getting married. You never traveled, you never worked. Now that she has a great career, I say to her sometimes, "If you had the opportunity to do this when you were younger, would you do it or would you let it all pass you by?" and she can't answer me because I think deep down inside she would probably want to have had the store and us, too. I guess it's being selfish, but that's how I feel.

My husband puts in a lot of hours. He's had the business about nine years now. It's only in the past couple of weeks where they've hired somebody, and they have two days off, and they have decent hours. Otherwise, he would be working sometimes seven days a week. He would go in at eleven sometimes, and he wouldn't be home till eleven at night. Then he goes on night shifts, where he's in at five, and he closes, and he's home by two in the morning. If I went back to work and I got the hours that I wanted—eight-thirty to two-thirty or nine to three—he could just go on steady nights.

He's very old-fashioned, but he's changed a lot since we've been married. In the beginning, when I go back to work, I know exactly what would happen. We'd have to go through a lot of arguing, and then he'd straighten up. That's usually how it goes with him. It isn't easy for him because he's caught between two worlds. The men in his family, you would never catch them doing half of what he does.

I had two miscarriages before my daughter, and once I did get pregnant with her I was going to a high-risk doctor, and I had to be on certain medications and stay in bed for the first three months. It wasn't until the fourth month I started premature labor. I was in bed a lot; I was in and out of the hospital. I always wanted to have a lot of children. I don't know if it's because of what I went through and seeing how much it takes out of you, but now I would be happy with just my one daughter. But I don't think that I could do that to her. I want her to have somebody. But then I'm afraid—I got pregnant after her, and I lost it. I went back to the doctor, and in order to have another baby, I would probably have to go back on the fertility drugs again, which is something I really didn't want to do. So it's iffy. I grew up in a large family, and it helped. I know when my father died, having my sisters and my brother, we were always there for one and another, and we're still really close. On Sundays everybody is together and having dinner, and it's a good feeling.

Before I had my daughter, I never had fears. I used to get in the car, I used to drive, I never had a fear of dying. After I had my daughter, forget it! All of a sudden we were getting on a plane to go to Saint Martin, and I'm telling my husband, "We didn't write out a will. We didn't decide who the baby would go to." And he's like, "What's wrong with you? Just get on the plane and relax, and we'll go away." But when you have a child, that all changes. You never relax one hundred percent. You could sleep twelve hours, but you're not really sleeping.

My husband doesn't worry, and that's how I was when I was younger. If I would have married somebody that was more of a worrier, I probably wouldn't be. I handle the bills— I take care of everything. He doesn't. If I owe somebody five dollars, I get like crazy. Whereas my husband's like, "Don't worry about it! I'll put the money in the bank." He's very lax. Maybe I'm too organized, and I should just let go a little bit, but I guess I don't let go because I know if I do, he won't pick up the slack and take hold of things.

And he doesn't worry about the baby the way I do. I don't think men on the whole do. I remember pushing myself out the door a week after my daughter was born. I was like, "I'm going out. I'm going to have a good time." And I didn't. I was worried that my mother-in-law wasn't going to take care of the baby right, my mother-in-law wasn't going to change her, a million things. It takes a long time before you can actually go out and enjoy yourself, whereas men can just pick up and say, "Let's go!"

It would be different if he took care of her more. After she was born, he would come home, and I would want to talk for hours, and he would be like, "I'm watching TV," and I would be like, "You don't know what it's like to be in a house all day with a child." All my friends are working. They all got married before I did, so their children are grown, and they're back at work. To be in all day, and when somebody walks through that door that you can have a normal conversation with, you're going like ninety. If he was home and he could see what I have to do, it would help.

On Christmas, my sister came here with a kitchen. My mother came here with a broom, a mop. And I'm like, "Why are you buying my daughter a kitchen and a broom and a mop?" I guess it's a long time since my family had a little girl. My sister's like, "You never dress her in pink dresses with pink bows." Christmas, I bought her books. I bought her a cash register, blocks. I didn't buy her a doll. I don't want to give her too much girly stuff.

I would probably give a boy the same things I gave my daughter—the cash register, the books, and the blocks. I see so many boys that are raised—they don't want to do anything, they don't help, and they get married, and they don't want to help their wives. I would never want to be that way with my son. I would want my son to help his wife, to know what it is to do a load of wash or to do dishes.

I try to explain to my mother, "Why are you showing my daughter how to clean and cook? Why should she need to know? That shouldn't be the most important thing. You're doing this because she's a girl." And that's what it is from generation to generation. It's changing little by little but not fast enough. Responsibilities should be shared, give and take. I think women are always the givers, and that's how we're brought up to think in a lot of ways, and it shouldn't be that way. It should be one person helping another.

I remember my older sister burning her bra. I'll never forget—my father was having a fit. He was going crazy. And I remember her not wearing a bra, and she was huge. I must have been about nine, ten. It was around 1970, '71. But then she went on to lead a very traditional life. I think my mother held my sisters back a lot; I think she still does. That's one of my mom's faults. I would never listen to her, and it wasn't because I was trying to be a rebel; it was just because I felt there were things I had to do.

I admire my mother a lot. She struggled. When my father passed away, he didn't leave much. For someone who had no high school diploma, she came a long way, and we always had the best of everything. I see a lot of women, their husbands pass away, and they right away take up with someone else, just for the security. My mother's never done that. She's never relied on anybody. She has a lot of respect from her kids, and she deserves it.

Not the Kind of Life
My Mother Had

Sarah Miller

She was thirty-nine years old at the time of our interview and living in a rural area in the North-east with her husband and three children, ages three through eleven. She has a BA in psychology and works part-time. She was born in New England. Her mother was a housewife and her father a chemist.

I grew up on *Bride* magazines. My sister—she's much older—was always in the process of planning a wedding, and I was always picking out the dresses that I was going to wear. She was always engaged. First, I was going to be a flower girl, and then I was going to be a junior bride, and then I was going to be . . . dammit, I'm not getting that dress. She used to joke about it, that she would make these socks for the boyfriends, and as soon as she would get, like, almost to the end of the socks, they would split up. My father would get the socks.

What was important for the girls was to find a nice man to marry who would provide a good income. For me and my sister an education was nice but not essential. My brothers got a lot more financial support, encouragement. My mother was always proud of me, but it wasn't as important. I rebelled against that. The advice was flatter the boys, make them feel good; they're supposed to win. Boys don't like girls who are too smart. It was the girls' job to help their mother with the household tasks. And my mother's attitude was you need to iron your brothers' shirts, and that didn't fly with me. So my brothers learned to iron, eventually.

I think my mother really loved my father, and they had a pretty good relationship, but I don't know how much they had in common. My mother put him up on a pedestal and put herself down a lot. I watched what she went through and said I never want to be in that position, being so dependent on my father and so insecure about her own abilities and really not having any life other than being a mother.

I was influenced by the women's movement, probably in every way. It affected my expectations about what I could do. I saw that I didn't necessarily have to be the kind of mother that my mother was. I could take the parts that I thought were good. I could still have a life aside from just being a mother. Those other parts of myself were valid, added to what I could bring to parenthood. So I've always worked since I graduated in psychology, human-service–related jobs. I work three or four days a week at a residential facility for physically handicapped children. When I first had kids, I worked full-time, but basically over the last ten years it's been part-time.

My husband and I have always really shared. When I first had Jonathan, Greg was home more than I was because he was trying to get a freelance graphic design thing going, so it was really essential that I had a job outside the home just to have benefits, health insurance. He used to drag Jonathan along when he was little to the libraries to do research.

It's not that kind of situation I see with a lot of couples, where there's no understanding about what it's like to care for kids. Sometimes Greg gets sick of them; I think it's made us closer.

My kids have gone to babysitters since before they were school age so that Greg can work—he works at home. It's nice because he has that flexibility, and I have flexibility in my job, too. If somebody's sick, it's not a big deal for me to take off from work—I just have to rearrange things.

We share housecleaning and laundry, and nobody likes to do it. As a family, we fight a lot about cleaning the house; it usually doesn't get done very much. The kids don't willingly participate. The household-chore war is ongoing, and usually it's the adults that do most of the work. We were forced into sharing in a way, because of the type of work that Greg does; otherwise, I might have gotten into more of a rut where it's my job taking care of the kids. A lot of people don't have those options. Sometimes it's almost like they fall into traditional roles because the husband is the one who's making more money because women's work isn't as highly paid. I hear women complain a lot about that. Their husbands are more involved than their fathers were, but it's not anywhere near fifty-fifty.

I love being a mother—ninety-nine percent of the time I enjoy the kids. We sometimes have a break from them, which is great. We went on our first vacation without the kids for like six days. It was wonderful, and I wish we could do that more often. A couple times a year would be great, but hopefully it's not going to be another twelve years. But I really enjoy living with them and how they changed my life.

Joanna Katz

She is a rabbi living in Woodstock, New York. She was born in New York City in 1959 and received her degree from the Reconstructionist Rabbinical College in Philadelphia. She and her partner, also a rabbi, have three children.

"We're the cofounders of a spiritual retreat center. We both freelance as rabbis—weddings, bar and bat mitzvahs, funerals. Before we moved here about three years ago, I was a hospital chaplain primarily."

Jeff and I started living together when I was twenty-four. I lived in a community that was very gay and lesbian identified, and I didn't want to step into marriage as an institution that was not an option for my gay and lesbian friends. (I think most people are bisexual and fit in somewhere on the continuum. I haven't had lots of women lovers; by and large, I'm more heterosexually oriented.) The other thing was that the institution of marriage in lots of ways comes from very, very patriarchal roots and from a very misogynist sexist framework. Now, marriage like anything else can be transformed. We don't believe that the traditional Jewish wedding ceremony works well without being transformed. So from a liturgical, spiritual point of view, what we've developed is a commitment ceremony.

After two years of living together, we did a ceremony that sanctified our relationship in the public eye. We used rituals, but we didn't call it a wedding ceremony, we didn't call it a marriage, we didn't have a marriage document. We didn't use a chupah; we didn't use rings. Jeff and I didn't want to use any of the traditional symbols, and so we used other traditional symbols. There's a Jewish mystical system that looks at reality as fourfold, and it's a paradigm for seeing the world. It has four levels of being in the world—action, knowing, feeling, being. So our commitment took place on those four levels. We had like a hundred and fifty people that we took to Vermont for the weekend, so we did the Sabbath together—we did services. On Saturday night we talked about our commitments on these four different levels, and we did havdalah together—the ceremony for ending the Sabbath.

As part of the ceremony we said that our children would be known as Roth-Katz, we would be known as the Roth-Katz family, but we don't use Roth-Katz. I use Katz, he uses Roth, and the kids are Roth-Katz.

Our families were very supportive. They thought it was pretty weird, in some ways. They wouldn't have minded if we had had a chupah, a ring ceremony, one rabbi instead of fifteen. Inevitably, they translated it into their own language; Jeff's mother certainly went back home saying her kid was married, and my parents, while my father says married, my mother makes a point of trying not to say that.

We got a lot of flack. Our gay friends—not all of them but a lot of them—said, "You're getting married, anyway—you're just using different language." Our straight friends said, "You're getting married anyway, so what's the point of all this?" Some people were very, very moved by it and felt like it was very appropriate. It was one of the first ceremonies of its kind. Now oftentimes, people within our community do alternative ceremonies. I create ceremonies with people who want to get married.

For me, what needs to happen in a Jewish wedding is that two people come together and figure out what it is they're committing to, and their communities affirm that they think this is good. Do they envision that they're going to live together every day of the year? Do they envision that they're going to have shared bank accounts? Some people choose to have children, and some don't. Some people choose to bring Judaism into their homes; some don't. When I work with people, I encourage them to write up their own marriage contracts, to develop their own wedding ceremonies.

I had my eldest child, Esther, when I was twenty-eight. Jeff and I went into our partnership saying that we were going to split our child care fifty-fifty. When Esther was born, Jeff worked half-time, was in school half-time, and was with Esther half-time. Jeff is a full parent, and he's very significantly involved as a father. But in terms of the day-to-day burden of getting the laundry done and figuring out the shopping and getting children to where they need to go, since we've had our third child, he does less of that than I do. It is partly because I really wanted to have a third child, and he was ambivalent, and partly because for him it creates a lot more internal conflicts than it does for me.

Intellectually, Jeff and I are both very committed that we should be equal parents timewise. But Jeff gets very depressed if he has to spend twelve hours a day with his kids, if he doesn't get five or six hours a day to work on his passion. Whereas for me if I can go out and work in a hospital for three hours two or three times a week, that gives me a lot of nourishment. He actually works in the basement, so he's home all day. He has lunch with the kids when they're home. Jeff is up with the kids from whenever they get up at six in the morning until nine o'clock. So over the past five years trying to figure out what makes our family work, we've had to divide along gender stereotypical roles.

Lauren Morgan Stern

She lives in the Deep South. She was twenty-nine years old at the time of the interview. Her mother, Rachel Morgan, also appears in the book. (See also p. 165)

Until I married my husband, I never imagined that I would have the luxury of taking time off. I'm a child-care advocate. I'm referring parents with eight-week-old babies to child care every day. But I do believe for myself that I would love to spend at least a year and a half before putting a child into full-time child care. That is a luxury that my husband has brought to me that we agreed will happen, and it will be my time. He didn't fight me for it. He agreed that it was a good thing to do. My sister and her husband are going to switch, however. She does not have any interest in spending time with an infant, so if they have kids, he will be the one to stay home.

I want my husband to make it clear in his workplace that he is an operating father. If there is someplace I need to be, for instance, maybe he does need to get off early or come in late; maybe he needs to leave to get his child a ride somewhere. It will be important to him to have a real obvious role. That is part of what brings us together and makes it exciting to have kids together. There is nothing about it that scares him. Diapers don't bother him; waking up in the middle of the night doesn't bother him. He is as cranky as the next person, but he will do it all, and he is really looking forward to it as much as I am.

Cindy Aspromonte

She lives in Denver with her husband and two young children. She was born in 1954, works part-time as a nurse practitioner, and does holistic nursing and teaching.

"My father's a clinical psychologist. My mother is an artist and art teacher. My parents divorced the year I got married. I was twenty-seven. I have a six-year-old daughter and a two-and-a-half-year-old son." (See also p. 519)

My first baby, I worked until two days before she was born and I only took eight weeks off. I hated going back to work. It was terrible. My second child, I worked until a month before he was born and I took three months off, but that still was not enough.

Nine months to a year off is really important. In European countries, women have a year off.

My husband loves being with the children and is extremely involved. He was an economist and a banker and quit his job several years ago. He's doing some consulting work and trying to determine what career path he wants to take. He didn't want this traditional setting where you'd be at work ten hours a day. He wanted to be around a little bit.

The financial status has been real difficult because I've been mostly bringing in the money the last couple years, but he's getting back on track, and it's got other blessings like being able to enjoy the children while they're growing up. I work part-time. Both children go to a cooperative school where the parents have participation in the teaching and the school, and so he's on all these parent committees, and he likes to help out in the classroom. So the days that I work, John is home with the kids. There are at least three or four conferences a year where I'm gone for a weekend, and then he'll be with the children the whole time. He enjoys it, and if he needs a break, he'll get a babysitter for an hour or two.

I made it clear early on—"The household responsibility is not you have to help me, it's we help each other. This is our joint venture."

Abby Soong

She lives in the Northwest with her husband and works for a company that develops games for children and adults. (See also p. 189)

I've been married to Trevor going on my seventh year. I made sure I never got together with any guy that had any violence in him because I don't ever want to be beaten again. I was very careful.

I'm still scared to have children. I'm afraid I would repeat the cycle of child abuse. If I do have children, I'd probably adopt. I figure I can treat them a little better, and there's too many children out there who need a good home. My husband wants to have a natural child as well as adopt one.

If I had children, I think I would definitely stay on the job. I could eventually move away from a full-time job and be at home and work on children's books and painting. Trevor loves kids. He says, "Abby, if you can make enough money, I would rather have you out there and I'd be home taking care of the kids." I think it's a wonderful idea. I'm more ambitious than Trevor is.

Margaret White

She was born in 1968 and raised in the rural Northeast. She was twenty-five years old at the time of the interview. (See also p. 341)

*W*ith my kids, we talk about body parts and everything. We're really open, and it embarrasses my mom. I tell my son, "That's a vagina and this is a penis." They were changing into their swimming suits, and Roger and Suzy: "There's your vagina!" And my mother's going, "Oh, my god, these kids—what are you, a bunch of nudists?" I'm like, "Mom, I'm raising sexually healthy kids. Leave me alone."

My son's always touching himself, and if my mom sees, she says, "Put some clothes on him!" and I'm like, "He's just a kid." I know he's going to do it. And when he's a little older if he's still doing it a lot, I'll just tell him that he can do it in his room and not in front of people. It's fine. I've never felt guilty about it. It just felt really natural.

There's a really big difference in how I was raised and how my husband and I are raising our kids. With AIDS and everything I want to be as open as I can be, and the minute my son has a question, I just answer it without batting an eye. I hope that they'll always trust me and not have to ask some stranger. So, they can shock their grandparents!

Marquita Anderson

She was born in New Jersey in 1975 and is now a college student in Lansing, Michigan. "I'm black, and I grew up in a Baptist house." (See also p. 184)

I'm in a committed monogamous relationship with another woman now, and she just started law school in Washington, D.C. I'm planning on moving there in May. My mother doesn't want me to move. As long as I was queer and here in East Lansing, not too far from home, it was okay. Now she's just putting in this whole God thing. "God doesn't let you be gay—it's against *His* will." "Well, then, why did *He* make me attracted to my second grade teacher?" I'm not my mother's little girl anymore. I'm not really even her daughter anymore because being her daughter was about doing what she said. Be straight. Don't move. Stay at Michigan State.

What my partner and I want is really simple. We want close friends, a good community of women around us, cars that run, two cats, an iguana, a full refrigerator, and to be satisfied and fulfilled in the work that we do every day. I want to write feminist theory. I don't think either of us are ever going to produce any children from our bodies, but there are so many kids out there that I figure maybe one day we'll adopt someone's teenager or a child. Many years from now, if I have the energy.

I don't see managing work and children as being that difficult. I see myself having a community of friends that would be willing to take a natural part in the child's life. If I had a class to teach, I'm sure one of my friends could watch the child. Maybe I'm being idealistic about the lesbian community, but from what I've seen so far, it's very supportive.

I have straight and lesbian friends. Since I'm coming to a point where I really don't have any biological family, they are my family. We get together and play a card game, have coffee, talk. We're pretty laid-back folks, nothing loud and crazy. We're planning to go to a Michigan Women's Festival together in August, and we're all going to camp together, and from now on we're all going to have Thanksgiving together. Of course, we're not going to call it Thanksgiving—we're against the stealing, corrupt—celebrating that kind of shit. We just want to be together and be a family and have a great time.

Katrina Thomas

Her background is German and Swiss. She was born in 1964 and lives in Southern California with her husband of three years. She is a Christian. "God is the center of my life." (See also p. 520)

I think my parents' roles were more set than my husband's and mine. I am trying to think if I ever saw my dad vacuum. I don't think I did. Dad took care of the yard. My husband and I share a little bit more. I do more yard work than my mom used to do, and he probably does more cleaning than my dad.

I don't think my parents treated my brother and me different. Going to college was always stressed for both of us. There were certain things, now that I look back. I see it more now because I am thinking of having kids. I would have to say I always had dolls and he always had trucks.

I know I'd end up doing a lot of the same things. I've noticed that because my sister-in-law has twins, and one is a boy and one is a girl. My husband and I were like, "We don't treat them differently; we treat them the same." But we found ourselves, when we go for a walk with them, she would say, "I'm tired," and we would go, "All right" and pick her up. If he would say he was tired, we would say, "Come on, we only have a little ways to go," and we would make him walk. We really thought we were impartial, and there were several things that were similar to that. It made us think. I would be a little more conscious than my parents of not expecting my son to be the man of the house, or my daughter to always be dependent on us. I would try to encourage them both, where the boy could cry and girls can climb the hill themselves.

Elizabeth Ives

She was born in 1970 in a small, black, working-class neighborhood in the Northeast. She came out as bisexual after doing a study-abroad in Africa. (See also p. 186)

I don't believe I'm going to getting married. I'm not Christian, so I don't see the point. It's also kind of a political thing because being married, becoming a part of the proletariat, all that crazy madness—not that I'm one person among myself and I believe I'm such an individual, but it's just not important. If I had to sit down and write why I would get married, I wouldn't come up with a word. If I can tell someone that I'm going to stay with them for the rest of my life, then I'm going to do that, and I don't need a judge or a preacher to tell me that I should.

I am leaving the door open for a change. If to my partner, the natural state of "staying together forever" is getting married, if that is the only natural step or we'd have to end the relationship as far as they were concerned, then, well, okay—I'm not going to be stupid about this. I'd try to make it short and sweet, but I'd do it.

I don't see myself having children, but I worked at an adoption agency, and I worked for the city, and I feel it's really important to adopt, so I probably will. Older children, because past the age of eight it's almost as if they're just not going to get adopted. Nobody wants them, and I feel like it's just something I should do. I kind of think that now, bringing a child into this world seems a really silly, wasteful thing and an ego trip. I don't mean that for anyone else who wants to do it, and I always say maybe later on in life I'll want to experience giving birth, but for right now it doesn't hold any interest for me.

So maybe in my mid to late thirties, I'll think about adopting children. It's really hard to be an artist and have children because a lot of times you're doing art during the hours that you grab away from what you have to do to make money. So you lead a double life already. It's a very nontraditional upbringing that children of artists get. But I think I'd make a great mom, so I'll be looking forward to it. And I do not see bringing the child up alone, but if I have to, I will. I don't really want to. If I'm in a monogamous relationship with a woman or a man, I'd like them to be a part of it.

I've had friends who've had the exact same feelings I've had about not wanting to give birth to a child, and then they get all sentimental somewhere around thirty-two. They get all goofy about it—"I have to experience it, it's a womanly thing." I think, "Well, a perfectly lucid individual is totally going AWOL because they want to have somebody growing inside of them," and I don't think I'm so exceptional that I might not totally get mother-earthlike. Never say never.

If I did give birth to a child, I'm trying to think, "Who the hell would the biological father be?" God! What kind of person would this be? I would definitely want them to play a major role. I don't know what kind of role. I mean, we're not talking 1950s father, not the sentimental 1980s father, either. You know, the guy who cries and he changes the diapers, and everybody applauds while he does it. It bugs me because it seems like such a farce. Men definitely do have a different socialization, you can't deny that. So let's not make them step out of their socialization. I'd like for him to do it in his own way, to nurture the child in a way that reflects his personality. I want him to be very involved.

I don't want the father to be a name with no face attached to it or anything like that. I would hope that he'd be in the home, but I don't know because, how I feel about relationships, it may be that I decide I'm gonna have a child, and it might be a friend I decide to have the child with. But I might also be married, in which case he's damn sure going to be in the home. And I would expect that if I'm going to have to take time off from work to have the baby, he's going to have to take some time off, too.

Even though I make fun of the guy who changes the diapers, he'll be getting the diapers, he'll be changing the diapers, he'll be watching the kid. I think he'll be doing the exact same thing that goes into the maintenance of bringing up the child as I will. But as far as our ideas about how the child should be brought up, I expect that they will be different. He might be more nurturing than I am. He might take the kid, make him cut school, go buy concert tickets and make up excuses to tell your mother so she doesn't have a fit. I may have tighter rules, and he may have looser rules. I don't want a script written for us. I don't want motherly or fatherly to mean certain things.

How Did Someone Like
You Get Elected?

A LIFE STORY

Dorothy Gonzales

She has been divorced for many years and lives in East Lansing, Michigan, with her two adult sons. She runs the state Office of Multi-Cultural Services and serves on the Board of Trustees of Michigan State University.

"I was born in San Antonio, Texas, in July of 1943 and raised in the barrios, one of the more impoverished neighborhoods. My mother and father are both from San Antonio. My grandfather on my father's side migrated to Texas from Mexico, but my mother's family are all Native American. I have two brothers and two sisters.

"My grandparents were migrant farm workers. In the winter they would work in San Antonio at odd jobs, then migrate north during the April–May spring season and pick crops around Michigan, Ohio, Indiana. They did this for most of their adult life until my dad and his brothers and sisters were old enough to move out of the house. My father went into the air force."

*W*hen I was about eight years old, we came to Michigan to look for a better life. After my dad had been discharged from the air force, he was told by my grandfather that the factory jobs were in great quantity here because of the automobile industry, and so we settled in Adrian, Michigan, in 1953 and have been here ever since. My father worked in an auto parts factory and was not making enough money at that point for all of us. The factories used to pay well, but our whole lifestyle changed because we had to deal with cold weather. We all had to have winter coats and boots. We needed a different car because in the winter too many times the old car didn't start. So when we first came up here, we had to do farm work.

As soon as we were out of school we would go up north and pick cherries or tomatoes. We would do potatoes, clean onions. You follow a pattern in Michigan with the crops. You move around. We would go and do the cherries, and we'd come back and we'd pick potatoes, and then we'd work our way down and end up picking tomatoes because that's the last crop of the season. My father was working in Adrian in the factory, and he would come up with groceries and see us sometimes on the weekends. We worked all summer, and then we'd go back home to start school in September, but on the weekends we would still go out and pick tomatoes or apples or whatever. So we did this starting at about age eight. I did it up until I was about fifteen or sixteen.

I think at that time they paid you five cents a box of cherries. We would start at probably five o'clock in the morning, and we wouldn't finish till six or seven at night. There was no such thing as by the hour, still isn't, and, of course, no fringe benefits. It was some of the shabbiest housing imaginable. Some of the rooms had mattresses, and some didn't. We made do with what was there, and usually you brought all your blankets, linens, pots and pans, or whatever you needed because they didn't furnish that.

No indoor plumbing whatsoever. It wasn't even a house. The room we all slept in was maybe nine by ten. There was no refrigerator. You had a two-burner stove and maybe a little washbasin, and there were two beds. No running water except in the barn. The night before, we would go and pump the water and bring it back in a bucket and put it in the wash-basin so when you got up in the morning you could wash up before you ate. Since you only had one little washbasin, everyone took a turn. You would pour the water from the bucket into the washbasin, brush your teeth or whatever and throw out the water, and then somebody else would go through the same ritual. Then we all stood up or sat around the beds and had a sandwich, and off we went. It isn't like you get to sit down and eat this great joyous breakfast before you go out and do hard work for the day. We would pack our lunch and make sure that we took our jugs with drinking water because they didn't supply drinking water, either; there were no sanitary facilities, so if people had to go to the bathroom, you just went wherever. At the camps you had outdoor bathrooms. You showered in the barn.

My mother would cook very simple meals. By the time you got back you were too tired to think of sitting down and having a full-course meal. Sometimes you would just have a sandwich or two and something to drink, and you'd want to hit the bed. When you're picking cherries, you're climbing up and down the ladders to get to the trees, and when the picking bucket is full, it must weigh ten or twelve pounds and you have to bring it down, dump it in the box, climb up the ladder again, and move the ladder around until you get the tree all cleaned. You do this forty or fifty times for eight or ten hours, and it isn't going to leave you in the spirit of wanting to come home and have a steak.

It was six days a week—Monday through Saturday—and sometimes if the grower was a nice guy, he'd let us finish at noon or two on Saturday, but then if it was a day when he needed to meet the quotas for the cherries, we might have to work all day. On Sunday we rested, or the farmer would take us into town. The majority of the time we didn't have a car to get around in.

In some of the camps, the majority were Hispanics, but you also had whites and African-Americans. We would find ways to entertain each other. There was always someone that could play guitar or had a stereo, and you would listen to music. You would sit around and talk. Sometimes you would have a community cookout, just sharing food and some quiet time. Because we were so close to Lake Michigan, many times we would go down as a group to the beach and go swimming or cook by the water.

When we would be out in the burning sun picking cherries, my mom would always say to us, "This is why it's so important for you to go to college—you don't want to be doing this when you're sixty or seventy years old." My parents wanted all of us to go to college. It was never a question of if; it was a question of how, because we didn't have the financial resources. All of us got a college education.

My maternal grandmother would always stress, you don't get married at a young age because that doesn't give you the opportunities to find out who you are and what your potential is. She always encouraged her children to seek educational avenues as a way to give them a better life. She is a very nontraditional woman, very much ahead of her time. She, not my grandfather, was the dominant figure in that family. I'm very grateful that I had that kind of a role model. So my mother pretty much picked up a lot of those values.

We never owned our own home when we were growing up. When we moved to Michigan and were able to rent a house, it was way out in the boondocks; it was an old,

old house and didn't have indoor plumbing. We had to pump the water and bring it in for my mom when she had to wash, even when it was zero degrees. She had a washing machine, but she didn't have a dryer. The house was huge. It had maybe ten rooms, upstairs, downstairs, and a basement so my dad would close it off during the winter time and we would more or less stay downstairs in two rooms. It had an old, coal furnace for heating. It was all outdoor plumbing—terrible during the winter. You would have to put on your coat and shoes and run out there to the bathroom when you had to go. And it wasn't very close to the house; it had to be so many feet away. I didn't get to live in a house that had any indoor plumbing until I was eighteen.

We all had our responsibilities. The girls and boys had to clean and cook. My brothers still iron their shirts and do their own laundry. We didn't have a television set until we were in high school. My brother had graduated, and he sent money home for a TV. I think that was around 1960. We learned to play all kinds of games—checkers, cards, bingo—and mainly we would just play with each other. We would read. Since my two sisters were younger, we spent a lot of time entertaining them. I think we had one bike between all of us, and we took turns.

We would go outside and play ball, and there was a little creek running by our house, so we would pretend we were fishing. Once in the summer, we built a raft and we floated around. Out in back there was a big pond that froze over in winter, so we would ice skate. We had pigs, rabbits, chickens, so we always had chores to do, and we would entertain ourselves by watching after our pets.

We always had a good time when we sat down at the table to eat. We would share our experiences of the day at school. My mother always instilled in us the sense of family. She would say if anything ever happened to us, you only have each other and be good to each other, and we're very, very close, all five of us. We have scattered—California, San Antonio, Chicago, Flint. We got together this summer; my mom came up for about three weeks, and everybody met at my house.

I was just a month shy of my twentieth birthday when I got married. My husband was Hispanic, but Gonzales is my name. I never wanted to change my name; it means a lot to me. It represents my family. So I figured, Why can't men change their names if they want to. My husband wasn't very happy. But I just said, "Hey, that's the way I feel about it. I wouldn't ask you to give up your name. Why would you ask me to give up my name?" And my dad wanted me to keep my name, too. I didn't grow up in a very traditional family. I was never taught to be subordinate or that a man should be dominant or any of that.

My husband was drafted and was in the army for three years during Vietnam. I wanted to go to college, but I was real concerned during the war, what would happen if I didn't see him again. Those kinds of feelings tend to get in the way of your better judgment. He was stationed in San Antonio and then Fort Riley, Kansas. During that time I worked at a grocery store as a clerk and then as a salesperson. I have two sons, twenty-four and twenty-two. I was around twenty-six when I had them. I started going back to school shortly before I got divorced—the children were five and three. He wanted me to spend most of the time at home with them, and I kept trying to say the children benefit if the mother is educated. He thought that I should wait until they were older. I would say, "How much older? When is a good time to finally go back to school?" I figured if I keep waiting, that just puts me further behind, and I started taking some classes.

The conflict with the scheduling and stuff was probably more than he wanted to deal with. When I was taking classes at night, I told him that the children were definitely his responsibility, too, to cook for them or do whatever they needed. He thought that they could be better taken care of by their mother. My class usually started at six, and so sometimes I would leave them with a babysitter until he got home, and he wasn't happy about that. When we finally separated, I didn't have a job, I didn't have a car, but I was just determined.

The Ford Motor Company in Saline was hiring, so I applied, and they hired me to work on the midnight shift. That was my preference, because if I was working nights, I could go to school during the day. So when I started going back to school, I was working from twelve midnight to eight in the morning. I would have someone come in and stay with them overnight while I was at work. I would go home and get my kids ready to drop off to the babysitter—my older one was going to kindergarten—and then I would run off to class. I would pick them up and come back home. I would try to study in between. Things got easier as I progressed. Sometimes we would work on Saturdays because of the overtime, and so I would take my books with me, and I would try to study when I was at work. I did that for four years. I kept going. It was an overwhelming desire of wanting something so badly that nothing else mattered. Once I got in the swing of things, it was like I was on a roll, and there was no stopping me. When I first went to enroll for my classes, some of the instructors were shocked that I wanted to do this on a full-time basis, and I said, "Well, the only one who can determine what I can handle is myself, so you at least have to give me the opportunity to fail. Then I'll know that I can't handle it."

I even took classes on Saturday when I didn't have to work. I know I was nuts. I was a lot skinnier than I am now. I must have weighed about ninety pounds. When I got my breaks at work, I would try to take a nap or study or write some of my papers. The people at Ford were real supportive. When I needed time off to take a test or whatever, they would say, "Take half the day off. From my supervisor on up everybody knew what I was doing. The sisters at Siena Heights College could see how determined I was—Siena Heights is a private liberal arts college in Lenawee County, where I grew up. They had a Montessori school next door and gave my kids a scholarship so I could bring them to school while I was at school.

Everything just seemed to fall into place. I was done by three, would pick them up, and we would all come home. Usually I would try to get them to eat early. I would do laundry and then lay down for a while to try to rest. When I went to lay down, they would either play in their room, or I'd put them down for a short nap. I would go to bed about seven-thirty or eight and get up right around ten-thirty and then get ready to go back to work. I would try to get three or four hours' sleep. I probably averaged about four hours. It hasn't gotten any better. Even now, I usually don't sleep more than four hours. By Sundays I usually collapse, and I sleep at least until ten.

On the weekends, it was time to clean the house, get groceries, and try to do my homework. Mainly, it was trying to do things with my children. We lived in this small village, and there was a park in back of our house where you could go and you wouldn't have to worry. You didn't even have to lock your doors where I lived. So most of the things we did were centered around them. The playground, maybe going to the movies, sharing time with the little friends they had across the street, doing things with other kids.

One of the best things that happened to me was having to raise my kids differently. They've always known how to take out the trash, clean up their room, and that everybody had to help because Mom was working and going to school. They always had chores, and things just got done. Both of my boys had dolls. That was another big fight that my husband and I had. He was more concerned about what others would say versus would it be good for my kids. Sometimes we would get comments about them having a doll or not doing the traditional thing with boys. His family thought that was strange.

In the beginning there were numerous times when I couldn't find a babysitter, so I would take them with me to class and put them in the back someplace. I would take their toys and some books and tell them they had to wait until after the class was over, and everybody was utterly amazed that you could have two kids and not hear a peep out of them. I used to spend a lot of time explaining how they had to behave in certain situations and that you couldn't be disruptive in class because that disrupted everybody else.

They were really good about things like that, and they still are. Throughout our life together, we've been at events, and people would be utterly amazed that my kids would sit there all the way through and listen and not be disruptive, and I don't know what you attribute that to, other than if you start at a very early age, then they kind of understand. I'm really proud of my kids, because even now they run the house. They wash, cook, clean, do the laundry, and make up the grocery list. The joke with them is Mom only sleeps here. My one son is away at school, but he comes home every week, and the younger one is still at home. He goes to school part-time and works part-time.

I chose never to get married again. The kids and I managed. I had a pretty decent job that had fringe benefits and insurance. The less I needed from my ex-husband, the better I felt about it. If he wanted to see the children, that was his responsibility. He would see them sporadically. He probably had a lot of growing up to do himself. I didn't spend a whole lot of time focusing on that. I just figured that I had enough to do with my two children and myself. I didn't have family around, but I had a real good group of supportive friends that would help if I needed it.

When we moved up to East Lansing, I would send them on the bus when they wanted to see him or he would come and pick them up, and I told them when they got old enough to drive that that was no longer my responsibility. When they wanted to see him, they knew how to call him. They understood from a young age that you can't make somebody want to do something they don't want to do.

I don't think they suffered any great damage from that. I always tried to be very no-nonsense about the realities of life. There's no guarantees about anything. You have moms and dads who supposedly have everything, and it still doesn't work. It doesn't necessarily mean that people are happy, either, just because they're still married. I tell them that it's up to themselves to be the kind of person that they want to be and to take charge of their life, that nobody can do it for you. And so far so good.

My social life was kind of sporadic because basically I couldn't understand what a man had to offer me that I hadn't already done for myself. If anything, it probably would have been the finances. Money is what I don't have. The majority of the time I find that I've done a whole lot more with my life than most men have with theirs. I felt like

I really didn't need the hassle because it was hard enough for me to try to keep pursuing my career and taking care of my children and doing those things that I enjoy doing and being involved with social issues and community organizations and things like that. I just wasn't interested in a full-time serious relationship. Most of the time men didn't meet my expectations.

I did date. It was not so much dating as having friendships, but I didn't see them on a long-term basis. My grandmother says maybe when you're seventy years old, you'll see things differently, but I don't think so. She's never gotten married again after my grandfather died, so it's just one of those things that hasn't really been a priority in my life. If you want to have sex, hey, you can have it, but it doesn't mean that it's going to turn into any kind of a serious relationship. It's too hard to balance a life like that right now.

Just before I graduated college, I quit Ford Motor Company and went to work for the Community Action Agency in Adrian, for eighty dollars a week. I did that for about a year. I like being involved with different groups and trying to address economic, social, educational, health issues. After I graduated, I was contacted by Michigan State University to apply for a position here, and they offered me the job, so we moved to East Lansing, and I worked in their office of supportive services for incoming students. I thoroughly enjoyed the job. It involved making sure that my students were doing well, that they had tutorial help if they needed it. We set up activities to make them feel welcome and that they could achieve. They were Hispanic, Native Americans, whatever. There was a cross representation. They did not necessarily come from a grade A school where they had top grades, but they all had potential, and so it was a way of enhancing that potential for them to eventually graduate from Michigan State.

I did that for a year and a half, and then I was asked to apply for a position with the House of Representatives, working for the Speaker of the House. I got hired, and I did that for almost four years. I was a research analyst, and we were the ones behind the scene that put all the information together, the speeches, all the committee work for the Speaker of the House, and that was a fascinating job. I loved it. You would have a lot of contact with the policy makers. You got to see firsthand how decisions were made and how policy was developed and how some issues came to the forefront and others didn't and why. It was one of the best opportunities to make contacts with individuals all over Michigan. I did that until 1982, when the new governor, Jim Blanchard, came in, and I was asked to join his staff. I worked in the governor's office for four years before coming here, and I've been here since '86. Along the way,

I finished my master's in psychology–social work, and then my master's in business and personnel administration.

Here I run the Office of Multi-Cultural Services. Our services are specifically tailored to meet the needs of bilingual and bicultural staff, patients, and clients that traditionally do not fit into the typical mainstream mental health system that we offer in Michigan. We have a very sizable population of Arabs, Arab-Americans, Chaldeans, Hispanics, Native Americans, a lot of refugees. Many times when people come from war-torn Bosnia-Herzogovina or Haiti, if the services are not provided in their language and are not culturally based, it's hard to provide adequately for them.

This office is the only one that focuses on this. People will call from the Department of Social Services because they can't find someone to do an assessment for someone that's Vietnamese. It's my responsibility to look after the twenty programs that we have around the state and make sure that they're meeting their obligations and objectives.

Two years ago, I got elected to serve on the Board of Trustees of Michigan State University. I was real fortunate, but now I have no time to do any of the things that I planned on doing other than getting a long weekend vacation. But it's been a great experience for a woman to get elected to a public office and have input into one of the big ten universities, and it's never happened before to a Hispanic woman in Michigan.

In Michigan these are elected positions. Two years ago, I was approached by the Democratic Party to become a candidate. With the help of individuals that believed in me, I put a campaign effort together and ran around all over the state for three months and had to raise almost ten thousand dollars to do that. I felt really proud because I was the top vote getter on the ticket in 1992. The other part of me says, "That'll show people that if you're a woman, it's a plus, and if you happen to be Hispanic, it is not a minus."

Nevertheless, stereotypes and ignorance still prevail. Several months ago I was at a gathering at the university and we were talking about the historical perspectives on Michigan and agriculture, and I asked these two experts where the farm worker fit into that, and the reaction was "What is she talking about?" They said, "Give us some examples," and I was sharing with them some of the history that I knew, and I said, "My grandparents used to come to Michigan to work, and then my family picked cherries." And then one of the Ph.D.s says to me, "That's so interesting, and when did you and your family become citizens?" And I said, "Probably while you and your ancestors were coming over here on the *Mayflower*." They thought that farm workers were not American. It happens all the time. People will say, "What country is your family from?" Right away the color and the racial characteristics set you apart. And people will assume that because you're Hispanic, that maybe you're not educated, or all kinds of assumptions and stereotypes. It's very frightening. Or people will say, "How did someone like you get elected?"

Work

Work:

The First Generation

I got a factory job. It was an ammunition factory that made bullets for the war. The assembly work was all done by women. Men ran everything. Women could not be high level administrators. Women could not be foremen. There were no women machinists. They were not even considered. Nobody thought about it. It was just accepted.

Hazel Akeroyd, born 1911

When I started teaching substantive law courses to this predominantly male student body—at the beginning it was almost totally male—they were really shocked. They did not come to law school expecting to be taught by a woman. It was difficult for them at first. Their attitude was folding their arms and looking at me like "I dare you to teach me something."

Janet Mary Reilly, born 1915

I Found It Very Difficult
to Be Heard

Janet Mary Riley

Born in 1915 in New Orleans, she is a retired law professor who played an instrumental role in the Louisiana state legislature's 1979 enactment of a law giving married women equal rights in the management of community property. Previously, property earned by either spouse was controlled by the husband. She was also a key figure in the legal fight against racial segregation.

She is Catholic and a member of a secular institute for working women, the Society of Our Lady of the Way. "We take vows of poverty, chastity, and obedience, but we don't live like nuns. We don't live in community; we don't have a common apostolate. It's an important part of my life."

*E*verybody thought I would be a public school teacher. So did I. I didn't feel cut out for either social work or nursing. What else was there? I could be a stenographer; my older sister was a stenographer. I was not cut out to handle little children, but I didn't see anywhere to go except to be a teacher. Being a lawyer was something that I liked the idea of, but I considered it utterly impossible.

I wouldn't have gone to college except for getting a scholarship. I finished four years at Ursuline College, then the women's college of Loyola University, New Orleans, and then I went to normal school (teachers' college). I got a position as a public school teacher, and I hated it from the first day. I was miserable. I took a leave of absence without pay so that I could go to library school at LSU.

My first position was working at the information desk at the New Orleans Public Library. I loved it, but it was practically poverty, so I went to Loyola University as an assistant librarian in November 1941. The next month was Pearl Harbor, and all of a sudden the university almost emptied out. Students and faculty all were being drafted, or volunteering, for World War II. I think it was June '43 when I went to work for the army. I was post librarian at Camp Plauche, transferred to LaGarde General Hospital, which was also in New Orleans. In those days army librarians had a uniform. It was not required that we wear it, but I bought it because it was good-looking. It looked very much like a flight attendant's blue suit, with the rainbow shoulder patch and a patch on the pretty little hat.

In December 1945, I went back to Loyola but to the law library. I decided to take a few law courses in order to learn the literature and the language, better to serve the students and faculty. I got credit for each course I took, but I was not planning to get a law degree. Because it was to their advantage to have me have some law, the law school not only let me register and take courses, they also didn't charge me. The first semester I took legal bibliography and contracts, and the second semester I taught legal bibliography. You don't have to be a lawyer to teach people how to do legal research. So in the ten years that I was law librarian, I taught legal bibliography for nine of those.

I kept on taking law courses, one or two every year, with no intention of getting a law degree. But when I had reached the halfway point, I had to make a decision. So I finally did decide to finish the law degree, thinking I would stay in the library job. But then I began to realize that I was enjoying the work primarily because I had been studying.

There were very, very few women. Sometimes there'd be none in the class but me. A typical law school class is one where the professor encourages discussion, and I found it very difficult to be heard. When I'd speak up, my voice would be that one feminine voice in the room, and it was easily drowned out by two or three other people who were trying to say something at the same time. When I was called on, everybody would turn around, "Oh, she's gonna speak." I felt like, if only I could talk in a deeper voice. I knew that the very femininity of the sound of my voice was so out of place in this room where everybody was talking with a masculine voice.

The summer of 1950, I went to law school at LSU, and I took a course called "Relational Interests." The classes were very early in the morning, and one time I had a date the night before. We stayed out late enough that when I came home, I thought, "Oh, I'm not prepared for tomorrow morning's class. I'd better open the book and see what's tomorrow's subject matter." I discovered that the first case coming up was one of these very explicit cases about sex. I was the only woman in the class, and I knew the professor's reputation was to save embarrassing cases for the girl in the class. So when I saw what the case was, I said, "Oh, no, I can't go unprepared. He's going to call on me, surely." So I settled down to read this very lengthy case at about midnight. The next morning when the alarm clock went off, I slept right through it. I woke up frantic. This was a two-hour class with a ten-minute break. The class began at seven-thirty in the morning. So I showed up at eight-thirty during the break. There he was, standing at the door of the class, and he saw me rushing down the hall. He grinned and said,

"We waited for you." So sure enough he had jumped over to the rest of the cases and told the class he was doing it. He said, "She's trying to avoid that embarrassing case. Let's wait for her." And they all giggled before I ever got there, and so we started the second hour of the class. "Well, Miss Riley, it's your opportunity to tell us all about the case of So-and-So." So I told him all about it as explicitly as necessary. They were all waiting for my voice to crack, for me to get embarrassed. I told myself, "You've taught legal bibliography for years. You know how to make your voice project in a large class-room." I put on my professorial voice.

I finished the law degree in 1952, and I didn't leave the library job and start teaching until 1956. It must have been around 1954 that I began to think I wanted to use this new knowledge in a different way. Though I had been teaching legal bibliography for nine years, I hadn't thought I would be able to stay there as a law teacher because all the professors were men. I hadn't even dreamed of that possibility. I had given them a full year's notice that I was going to start looking for a job, and it was during that time that the dean came in and offered me the teaching job. I was law librarian from December 1945 till August 1956, when I became an assistant professor of law.

As a student and as law librarian the faculty were perfectly all right in the way that they treated me. When I became one of them, I think that there was some resentment on the part of some of the faculty members, that the dean alone had made that decision, to employ a woman as a law professor.

I always wondered whether or not I was going to be included at lunchtime. If I was there while they were making their decision—"Are we going to go to this place or that place for lunch"—I would be included. But if I was in my office with the door closed, the chances are they would not come knock on the door and say, "Come with us." I didn't want to be too pushy. If the boys want to talk boy talk for a while, that's their prerogative. I didn't mind. But I found that I would probably not have been included at all if I weren't a little pushy. So sometimes I just managed to be around the lounge or the entrance or wherever they happened to be at the time that they were going to lunch. Later on, that did change, but it took a long time. I was certainly included when it was a social function for the entire faculty.

The students were another question. When I was teaching nothing but legal bibliography, the students were a little surprised that a woman was teaching, but they would know that I was the librarian, so that was not so difficult. But when I started teaching substantive law courses, this predominantly male student body—at the beginning it was almost totally male—were really shocked. They did not come to law school expecting to be taught by a woman. It was difficult for them at first. The attitude was folding their arms and looking at me like, "I dare you to teach me something." Some of them had a hard look on their faces; some had an amused look, like, "Who does she think she is?" They were fairly respectful anyhow, because they still knew that I was faculty. When I reached the point where I had been teaching the same course several times and was much more confident of my own expertise, I probably spoke with more confidence, and they accepted it more. They soon found out that I had something to teach, and that they'd better learn it. I also had the power of the grading. Finally, some of that resistance wore down.

I found it very difficult at first to express my own opinion in a class. Because there wasn't that much respect for a woman's point of view. I would feel that they didn't want to know what I think, they want me to teach them the law, but, of course, the law is so much a matter of opinion. Finally, I got very interested in presenting both sides as well as my own opinion. Gradually, all that changed. I'm talking about the earlier years.

There are some male law students today who still have the attitude they would rather be taught by men teachers. Now that there are quite a number of women professors, they're more likely to make cracks about the femininity of the various women professors—their clothing or squeaky voices. We still are a minority, but it is certainly changing. Now women are almost fifty percent of the student body but still a small percent of the law faculty.

Over the years, among other courses, I taught insurance law and constitutional law. My first articles were in that area. I was also teaching Louisiana community property law, family law, juvenile law, and child advocacy. These fields are commonly thought of as women's fields. But when there were no women law professors, or almost none, and the men taught them, there was not that distinction. In order to get tenure you're supposed to do some publishing, and women had a tendency, all over the country, to write in those fields. Some schools didn't give much value to writings in what they call women's fields. "Oh, she only wrote about community property," or "she only wrote about divorce," or "she only wrote about children's problems." Those were not very important fields of law, they felt. But they had been important when there were no women law professors, or very, very few. So that we had to fight not only to be recognized as women law professors, but also to be recognized as able to write in a field of our interest and expertise and have it rated just as important as though we had been writing about corporations law, or admiralty, or patent law.

I slid into tenure. I had been there a long time—the first ten years as law librarian and teaching. I had enough years for tenure. But in the case of some of the women on the faculty, there was a tendency on the part of tenure committees to act as though their writings were insignificant. Now I think they've gotten over that, finally. But it was a problem for a long time.

Years later, when we were in need of more women on the faculty to satisfy governmental standards and accrediting associations, they said, "This is hopeless, we'll never be able to get a woman in those fields" (we were in need of a teacher in corporations and taxation). And, of course, we did find a woman with the right credentials. They couldn't believe it. There was an attitude of, this is such pure luck.

None of us women on the faculty have been particularly masculine in attitudes or approach or language, and I don't know whether that's just been luck or whether they selected us on that basis. I don't think so. I was probably more conservative in dress than the others, because I came to the regular faculty older, almost forty. They dress professionally but prettily. Many of the younger ones coming in wore mini-skirts when they were in. Not too terribly mini. I think we've been fortunate in that we've had decent women. They have not felt it necessary to act crudely or tell nasty jokes. They do laugh when a nasty joke is told, but they're not comfortable with it for the most part.

They're not overly aggressive, but they certainly speak their piece. That's another point. At faculty meetings, for a long time I had the feeling that I was tolerated, but my opinion was not sought. Sometimes when I expressed my opinion, they shut up long enough to let me finish the sentence and then picked up the conversation where it had been and practically paid no attention to what I had said. Very often I'd hear my opinion expressed fifteen minutes later by another faculty member, as though it was a brand-new idea, and adopted with enthusiasm. And I'd be telling myself, "Shall I say, 'I said that fifteen minutes ago,' or shall I not be strident and just go ahead and vote for it." Usually, I'd mutter, "I said that fifteen minutes ago." That was irritating, aggravating.

Over the years, I have been quite involved in civil rights and women's rights work. In my early days in the Catholic churches of New Orleans, black people sat in the back. Archbishop Rummel issued a proclamation that there should not be segregation in the churches, and most people ignored it. My dean at the law school was on the Catholic Committee of the South and had been given the assignment to do something about race relations in the church. He invited thirty or forty people, half of them men, half women, half of them black, half white, to a meeting, and we organized the Commission on Human Rights. Once a month on a Sunday morning we would go to mass together and sit up front together, bravely, and receive communion together and then have breakfast and a meeting.

The reaction was shock, absolute shock. If some people happened to be sitting in the front seats, they'd probably move back a little bit because they didn't want to be sitting close to us—that is, a minority. A great majority of the people were shocked in the sense of surprise more than objecting, recognizing that this was appropriate. After all, it was the house of God. It should be for all people. They stayed put. There were many, many people who were just horrible about it, who stopped being Catholics because of integration.

Back in the early fifties, some black students staged a sit-in at the lunch counter at McCrory's, a five-and-ten-cent store. First, they had done it at Woolworth's. Jack Nelson, now a retired member of our faculty, had always been very, very much involved in interracial activities in the city. When they were charged with malicious mischief, they asked Jack to represent them. He phoned our dean and said, "I would like a faculty member or a senior student to help me draft a memorandum in support of my motion to quash the indictment." I had finished the law degree and volunteered. It was very little pay. He wasn't paid at all. Months passed, and I heard nothing about it, except what I read in the newspaper, that he had lost in the criminal district court and lost again in the Louisiana Supreme Court. I happened to run into him downtown one day, and he said, "Janet, I need you again. I'm now applying for writs to the U.S. Supreme Court in that same case. Will you help me? But there's no money." And I said, "Yeah, I'd be glad to." And then I found out he had used my memorandum with very few changes before the Louisiana Supreme Court, and now was going to the U.S. Supreme Court, still using my memorandum almost as it was. Writs were granted, and he argued the case before the U.S. Supreme Court and won in the landmark case of *Lombard vs. Louisiana*. I couldn't go with him because we had no money.

When you argue a case before the U.S. Supreme Court, when you finally reach the ready desk—that is, you're the next case to come up—there are crossed quill pens on the table as a souvenir. This has been traditional since the days they actually used them. As a consolation prize to me for having worked so hard on his brief and helped him by throwing questions at him when he was preparing his argument, he gave one to me. So that's my souvenir, my reward.

I Have Done a Lot
of Volunteer Work

Betsy Miller

She was born in Oakland in 1929, and she lives with her husband in La Jolla, California. (See also pp. 35, 52 and 258)

I didn't graduate from college. I left six months early because my husband graduated and was going to be drafted and asked me to marry him. I still have saved this indefinite leave of absence—I've got it in my desk. I was going to be a lawyer.

I loved having children. It was grand fun. But the household chores were not distributed evenly at all. That's the part of being a housewife that I resented. Nobody did anything around the house. They were all the laziest bums. My husband is so messy that I have spent forty years cleaning up after him. All of my children's wives and husbands have complained vividly about how they've had to train them. They always left everything to me. I got so tired of watching them do it wrong that I did the age-old thing—I stepped in and did it myself. I'm a perfectionist. To this day my husband cannot make a cup of coffee without my having to go over with a sponge and clean up around the coffeepot. My daughter wouldn't pick up anything, and the boys, too. They were terrible. Eventually, I would go in and clean their room.

I have done a lot of volunteer work because I was brought up doing volunteer work. My mother, even when she worked, did volunteer work, and my grandmother also did a lot. I belonged to the Junior League after I was married and had children. I did fun things. I helped with opera for the children and painted scenery, and I worked for the retarded children's workshop one year. When we were living in Riverside, I taught Head Start as a volunteer when it first started. I was very interested in that. It was really worthwhile. I was a little resented cause I was whitey. I stayed there until we moved.

The Junior League's a good thing because it acquaints you with communities. I belonged to four different Junior Leagues because we moved four times—Omaha, Pasadena, Riverside, and San Diego. At times I thought, "What am I doing being dragged around the country like this?" I always felt sad about moving because I had made friends.

If I'd been an attorney, I could've said, "Well, you stay here and find another job because I have this fine job, and I like it here." But we always had to go where he had to go, and I felt that since we started in this path, and we had three children to feed, we had to continue it. At times I fought against it, but I realized I'd lost my options by not becoming a full breadwinner in my own right. I knew I'd made a mistake, but I didn't see how to go back. I had potential, and I did well, but I chose the route that we were given in the fifties of being a homemaker, and it was definitely society that put this upon us. Maybe it was a reaction to the war. The magazines of the time had articles that promoted baking cakes, having that little hour with your husband when he comes home from work where you keep the children in some other place so he can relax from his hard day.

Well, of course, I tried to substitute by going out and doing my charitable work. There were very interesting things that I got to do. But I felt frustrated, and at one time I started to take some courses at the university at Riverside, and I tried to apply to Claremont and several other places. The universities were not receptive to women going back to school in the late sixties or whenever it was. They said, "Well, you're a little too old, and you have three children, and what are you going to do with it? So I was discouraged and sort of put it out of my mind. I was grateful for the security of the family. We were managing, and this seemed pretty nice to me. There were lots of bumpy parts, but it was better than what I'd come from, which was extremely insecure.

When my children were grown up, I felt it was too late to go to school. I guess I thought I'd done a lot. I still have this enthusiasm. I think you're born with that—if you just love to open a new book or learn a new concept. It's hard to go back to school, really stick with these classes seriously for grades. I took cooking classes and art classes and stuff like that at night school. When the children were all still in grammar school and I was taking my little courses and trying to do work, I'd be sitting in my bedroom writing a paper and there'd be three people pounding on the door. "What are we going to eat?" and "so-and-so just hit me, " and "so-and-so won't play games." Or, "They're cheating." I didn't feel that I could hire a babysitter. Maybe there wasn't enough money. Money was a great consideration. My husband wouldn't have cared about my going back to school. He's a very secure person in that respect.

I don't do anything right now, just sort of sitting here. I took up contracting a little bit. My husband inherited a house down on the ocean, so I remodeled that, and I have a cottage here, and I finally redid that, so I rent it out. I contracted and designed and did the kitchen, so I thought, "Gee, I should have been an architect or a contractor." It's lovely. I have several other friends who have discovered that they are builders and architects, realizing that they had this talent. People didn't explore girls' ambitions.

I took these tests at the university, but I took the ones that were for men. You answer all these questions, and then it tells you more or less where your ambitions and skills lie. It told me that I could have made a wonderful architect or forest ranger. I didn't see the female test, but I imagine it would have steered you into you should be vacuuming the floor! I can't imagine anybody scoring very high in vacuuming. My friends and I have all discussed the fact that we were shortchanged as far as what we were allowed to do. They educated us at the college level, and then they said, "Now go home and turn on the stove." How did we get so brainwashed?

I felt vindicated by the women's movement. I always wondered why I had rebelled quietly against my fate. The thing that concerns me is when I hear these young women who don't realize the battle that was fought. They just accept it, and so they're not protective of their privileges—not privileges—rights.

Rosa Keller

She was born in 1911 in New Orleans, where she still lives, to a wealthy and prominent family. She got married, raised a family, and as a volunteer eventually became a leader of the antisegregationist movement in New Orleans.

I fell in love with a Jewish man, and he said, "We can't do this because I'm Jewish." I told my father that he was Jewish, and he said, "Have you thought what this might mean to you?" And, of course, I hadn't. Being married to someone Jewish sensitized me. For example, my father was a member of the Boston Club, the best club for men; he invited me to go to a party there with him, and I found out that people like my husband couldn't go. I didn't like it. It changed my whole life. The carnival was also like that—antisemitic. Jews were not allowed to be part of Mardi Gras organizations. When you find out that your father can be the king of the carnival and your husband can't even ride in a float, that sure changes your thinking.

It was World War II that made me think about segregation. I used to take long walks, and I would do a lot of thinking while I was walking, and it occurred to me that those black soldiers were going to come home and ride in the back of the streetcar. It made me mad. Until then I hadn't thought about segregation; that's the way things were.

I had been very active in the Presbyterian church, but I left it in the fifties. The church was so segregated. They didn't want me to talk about black people, about race relations. The YWCA did better work on race relations than anyone else; I think when I joined, they already had black women on the board. The cafeteria was integrated. It was very out of the ordinary.

I was a member of the Urban League, and around 1957 I got the chairperson to come and talk to a meeting at the church about race relations. The crowd was very large, and when the meeting was ending, he and I walked by a deacon in the church, and he said to Mac, the black man, "What are you doing here?" and Mac said, "Why, I'm an invited guest," and the deacon said, "You get the hell out of here. We don't like our white women marrying niggers." It wasn't very polite—it was very impolite—it wasn't nice at all. I was terribly hurt, and I still hurt every time I think of it. Mac was used to it. It had a real effect on the people who had come to our meeting; they couldn't believe that the deacon had behaved that way. The congregation was polite, but I felt that the church itself was very racist. That ended my relationship with the church. Leaving was a major thing for me. I had been raised in that church.

My family didn't understand anything about what I was doing. I told my husband, "You fought your war"—he was an engineer and colonel in the army—"fighting segregation is my war." He tried to make it a little difficult, but I just wouldn't put up with it. I felt so strongly about it. My father was very traditional. He couldn't understand it. I had a sister and a brother. My brother eventually said, "I have to agree with what you're doing," but he was very uncomfortable. It was terribly untraditional. I started socializing with black people. Most of my white friends stayed friends but tried hard to change me, to get me to stop doing this. A couple of white people stopped seeing me altogether—they were not people I cared about anyway, so it didn't matter.

People called on the telephone. They raised hell—it wasn't very nice. I was a little sorry later that I didn't keep all the hate mail. It was real hate mail—they were furious. I was at risk, very much so.

Nadine Williams

She was born in the Midwest in 1928. She lives in New York City, is widowed, and has two sons.

From the time I was born—I mean from the time I was conscious—I knew I wanted to be an actress. I wanted to explore other people's lives and be other people. And I was encouraged very much by all the special teachers that I had. Everybody always said, "You can make it."

When I was around eighteen, I wanted to come to New York to be an actress. I got married because my husband wanted to come to New York, too, and it seemed to me that it was a lot better for two people to come to New York together than one. That's how innocent and naive I was. I got married a month after I was twenty. We went to a midwestern university, and I got my MA in theater there. It was a very good program, and it kind of solidified what I was interested in.

While finishing graduate work, I worked as a researcher for a newspaper, and I got pregnant. As soon as the man who owned the paper found out that I was pregnant, I was fired. "I understand you're going to have a baby. We'll have your last paycheck next week." I was just a researcher—nobody saw me—and I didn't think to fight it. I accepted it because that was just common. I can't believe now that I accepted it, but I did. You were a wife and now you're a mother, and you have a different life, and that's that. I didn't feel that way. I still had my MA thesis to finish, so I did that, and I took my oral exams very, very pregnant. It was all men examining me and talking about my thesis, and they sort of got a kick out of my being pregnant. It didn't bother them.

We really had it planned out. He was going to go to art school and be an illustrator. I'd be an actress. It was a lovely daydream. His life was affected as much as mine from having two pregnancies that we hadn't planned.

I used a diaphragm all the time but got pregnant anyway. With just one baby, I planned to put him in some kind of a nursery and work. Eric could go to art school in New York, and I figured I'd get a chance to do some acting. Five months after we got to New York, I had my second baby. My husband worked for a radio station. We lived in Brooklyn in a small apartment, and then we moved to Long Island. Then I was really going crazy because I had these two little babies, and I wanted to study with an acting teacher that I had been hearing about for years. We took a little loan so that I could take lessons from him, but because we didn't live in the city—I let my husband talk me into living out there—I couldn't do anything about my acting. I could have if I'd really wanted to—I realize that now.

I was taking care of the children and occasionally doing an acting role in a theater on Long Island. I did not have a full-time job until my youngest son was in the third grade. I got a job as a student counselor at a private school. I directed some of the school plays. Every year I thought was going to be my last. I worked there fifteen years.

I always moved or arranged my life around my husband. It wasn't that I consciously thought, "Well, he's the main breadwinner." We had a very equal relationship. We were very good friends. He was in no way overpowering, except in my way of thinking he and his job came first. I was a good mother, and my children and I are very close. I loved them, but I always resented the fact that having two children at the time I did, before I wanted them, changed my whole life.

If I hadn't had unplanned children, I would have gone ahead with my career and then had children. I would have tried. I had enough energy and drive. I wanted to be the one to raise my kids. I know that some people who had nannies for their children had been successful both professionally and with their children. I feel very lucky my children didn't get involved with drugs. They're sensitive, caring human beings, and I think I had something to do with that. But I did not feel fulfilled at home, and I tried to pretend that everything was fine, but I was very, very unhappy. I wanted to be working as an actress. The student counseling seemed the most stable thing for me to be doing; for my family it was a good choice.

To want something in the arts, you have to want it so much that you're willing to give up everything else, and I wasn't. I didn't waste my time during my thirties. I was a good mother. I did a lot of things in the community, and I worked. There was absolutely no reason for me to be so unhappy, but I was.

I did one play in New York during that time. I would have the kids all ready for bed. My husband would come home from work. I would get in the car and drive to the city, do my theater thing, drive home. And, of course, on Saturdays there were two shows and one show every Sunday. And after six weeks—the show ran six weeks on Broadway—my husband said, "I'm sorry—I just can't stand it." We couldn't do things together because I was in New York. He said, "I just can't stand it." And I just said, "Okay, I won't do it anymore."

Caroline Hodges

She was born in the Deep South in 1927. She is Catholic and has five children. (See also pp. 46, 54 and 246)

*B*efore the women's movement, we all felt that volunteer work was very fulfilling. You didn't need to be paid for something that you did well and was a needed service. But the women's movement emphasized that if what you did was worthy, then you should be paid for it.

I had one or two children when I was asked to join the Junior League. We were a service league, and it was very social. It was women who were fortunate enough to have leisure time. It was a good introduction to the community. You had to go to a school board meeting, to a city council meeting. You found out how government worked, what were the cultural facilities in your community, and then you were required to do a certain number of hours of volunteer work, either on a league project or a community project.

When you're first in, you do whatever needs to be done. And I primarily worked at what we call Nearly New. League members or others would donate their unused, outgrown, out-of-season, or out-of-style clothes, and they were sold at very, very low cost to people who couldn't afford to buy things in stores. So you did the pricing and sales. I was always primarily more interested in the cultural programs. We had children's theater, puppets. My first committee chairmanship was public relations. I would do news releases. I ended up being president of the league here. I've served on a number of boards. I like to go to meetings. It's much easier than cleaning closets. I don't like to clean closets.

The Junior League is quite different now because forty-five percent of the members in the local league work. They can only do placement at night or on weekends, and if you're a full-time professional person and mother, you don't really have the enthusiasm or the time or the incentive to give the creativity to projects.

The women's movement has really hurt volunteerism. While there are a lot of families where both need to work, there are also a lot of families where both work in order to feel fulfilled and to have luxuries. If you don't believe in the family as the basic necessary unit for society, then it's all right to be a feminist. But if you think that the family is really essential, then a woman needs to realize that there are some things you can do as a mother in your home and in your community that you can't do if you pursue a career. That is not to say that you can't be a successful career person and a good parent, but it certainly strains. It's more difficult, and something has to give. And very often it's community work.

A Hundred and Thirty-One Women
and One Toilet

Lucille Thornburgh

She lives in Knoxville, Tennessee. She was a young woman working in a textile mill in Knoxville in the early 1930s when she became heavily involved in the unionization of her plant and in the General Textile Strike—one of the largest strikes in the United States—that swept through the South in 1934. She eventually became a union organizer for the American Federation of Labor.

"I was born at Strawberry Plains in Tennessee in 1908. That makes me eighty-seven now— oooh!! My father had a small grocery store. Twice a year he would come to Knoxville to buy supplies for the store, and at that time, even though it's only twenty-two miles out of Knoxville, it was a day's journey, because he would go by horse and wagon and wouldn't get back until in the night. Now the people living up there come to Knoxville for a movie. I went to grade school in a one-room school that just taught up to the eighth grade."

"When I was about fourteen, we moved to Dayton. We moved away before the Scopes trial was held there, but I graduated from Ray County High School. We moved to Knoxville around 1926, and that was the beginning of the depression days." (See also pp. 62 and 64)

*M*y father opened a small store here in Knoxville. Had it not been the depression, he probably would have gone out of business anyway because he tried to run a store in the city just like he did in the country, by giving credit to everybody. When he went out of that business, we were a family of six children, and nobody was earning any money. My parents had no skills and no way of making a living. The kids that were old enough—my two oldest sisters and my brother and I—started working in factories or wherever we could find a job. We lived at home and supported the family.

When I was seventeen, I started working at the Cherokee Bennett textile mill. I worked there for a while, and then my older sister, who had found a job in Detroit, sent for me to come up there. So I went up there and did clerical work for $15 a week until the depression really hit. I came back home in 1929 and started working back at Cherokee Bennett. I got $8.40 a week for ten hours on the night shift, five nights a week. I went in to work at five o'clock and worked until four the next morning. We had a thirty-minute lunch break. Eight dollars and forty cents could certainly buy more than it does now, but you didn't do any high living on that. You could not live on it unless you were living at home and pooling family money, which is what most people did.

I was a winding-machine operator. My machine was called a universal winder—it wound thread from a cone to a spool. There were twelve spindles, and I had to keep twelve cones and spools going all the time. I stood for ten hours—and I wonder why my knees hurt today! I'll never forget my first night going to work there in that winding room. I went in at five o'clock, and a woman trained me, showed me how to use the winding machine. I stood there and watched her and picked up the thread and tried to do what she did. After a while I got so tired and sleepy, and I thought, "Oh, I know it's time to go home. I know it is." So I walked over to the water fountain that had a clock over it, and it was nine o'clock! I didn't think I could make it, but I did. At first, all the lint flying around interfered with your doing the work, but you got used to it.

We went into work at five o'clock. You brought your own lunch, but I never cared too much about lunch, because we had to eat in the same room where we worked. They brought our work in an old, great big cart, and we'd sit up on the edge of those and eat, or we'd sit on the floor. But the air was filled with so much lint you couldn't see your hand in front of you. They couldn't even open the windows because the lint would fly into the machine if they were open. Your head would perspire, and the lint would stick in our hair, and we'd come out of the mills with snow-white heads. That's where the phrase or expression "lint head" came from. In the winter, we'd all put on our caps when we came out. A lot of the women wore dust caps to keep the lint out of their hair, but I just didn't like them on my head. They even had fancy dust caps to match your dress. You could comb the lint out very easily, but sometimes in the summer when your head had been so wet with perspiration, it was hard. I was dripping sweat all the time. I had to keep going—I wanted to eat, I had to work.

We did have a Coke machine. In the summertime we could go out the back door and sit on the steps and eat. People used to ask me, "Did they check up on how long you took for lunch?" They didn't have to. I took my lunch hour for fifteen or twenty minutes because we were on piece work. The more spools I made, the more money I could make. In the winter we had some kind of heat, but during the summer, it was hot, hellish. With the machines that close together and generating heat, it was never, ever under ninety. There was no air-conditioning.

As a young girl, I was very, very slender. I was so sorry for the heavy-set women, standing on their feet all night, and, boy, would they ever sweat! I wore gingham and calico—that's a cheap grade of gingham—dresses to work. Women didn't wear slacks then. You couldn't go to work without your stockings, winter or summer. Of course, nobody else was going bare-legged at that time. You never even thought about it.

When we went on strike, the contract we wanted provided that we have some kind of a place outside of that lint to eat our lunch in the winter. Another thing we put in our contract was more toilets. We were a hundred and thirty-one women, and there was one toilet, and if you stayed in the toilet too long, there was one of the straw bosses out there beating on the door for you to come out. The straw boss was under the main boss, who was under the superintendent. The straw boss walked around all the time looking to see if everybody was working.

There were far more women than men working in my factory. We had women who were as old as sixty-five and some so young that they had lied about their age to get in there. I was the only single person at the winding machines that I worked. The women were all married, and most of them had children. Most of their husbands were working in another mill or at the marble mill or as a laborer in construction or something like that. In depression days—and maybe today—it took both of them to make a living where there were children. I don't remember any day-care centers at the time. It was either grandmas or a relative keeping the children while they worked their ten hours.

Knoxville had three big marble mills at the time. We used to say that all the cotton mill girls married marble workers. Now, a marble worker could make as much as eighteen dollars a week, so the mill girls all liked to have a boyfriend in the marble mill. In fact, I had one. He wasn't worth much, but he had a car—big deal!

There was a sharp division of labor between the men and women. From the outside Cherokee looked like one large room, but it was actually three big rooms—the card room, the spinning room, and the weave room. It was all women in the spinning room. Weaving was the best-paid job in the mill. A weaver could make up to sixteen dollars a week, but only men could be weavers. Nobody ever heard of a woman being a weaver until after the strike. That was one of our demands—that women be weavers, too. Why not? It wasn't any harder than any of the other work. Women couldn't work in the card room, either, which also paid a little more. The bosses said that weaving was a man's job, and that's the way it was. The women were just accustomed to that. We had two hosiery mills here, and they had the same kind of discrimination. Knitting paid the most, and women took it for granted that they could get everything ready for the knitting, but when it came to operating the knitting machine, a man had to do it.

Once the strike started, the women started thinking about it. We had union representatives from Washington coming here to talk to us, and even though they were men, they talked about how there was to be no discrimination between the men and women, and women did pick up on that a lot. In the 1934 strike our major demands were the hours, wages, and working conditions. We wanted a decent toilet and a place to eat. We wanted more money—five cents on the spool instead of three cents. We never thought of demanding to stop working by piece work. (Black people were not allowed to work at the factory—never thought about that, either.) Of course, there were absolutely no benefits or vacations. It never crossed our minds. Nobody ever heard of such a thing as annual leave, sick leave, health insurance, paid holidays. We hated holidays because on holidays—Thanksgiving, Christmas—you didn't make any money. If someone got sick and had to go home, that was just their bad luck, because they were on piece work.

We did ask for an eight-hour day. Some people worked twelve hours; we worked ten hours, but you never got paid overtime, even if you worked fourteen hours. The railroad workers were the exception. They got the eight-hour day in 1912 by striking.

Until the National Recovery Administration came in under Roosevelt, there were absolutely no laws that I ever heard of limiting working hours. The eight-hour work-day—Roosevelt, bless him, he was the old boy that did that. Oh, I remember it well, when we found out that Roosevelt got elected. Everybody was singing "Happy Days Are Here Again," and they were. Democrat or Republican, they all loved Roosevelt. The major thing was that people could go back to work. We didn't have welfare at that time, like we have it today. When you were out of work, all you got was free flour from the Red Cross.

The unionization at our plant got started by a railroad boilermaker who lived in town. He called a bunch of us together—we got about eight or ten people, all women—and told us how we could get better wages and working conditions if we joined the union. We all decided, "Well, we've got nothing to lose anyway," so we joined and signed up all the others. We had a hard time organizing because we couldn't talk while we were working—you couldn't hear over the machines running. Even the person that was working two machines away from me, I would have to see her outside of work. The people that worked daytime had to work half a day on Saturday, so we met every Saturday afternoon.

Everyone at Cherokee—603 employees—signed up in the union. That was in 1934. We were working on a new contract when we joined in with the largest strike all over the South. I was a leader in it, but our plant wasn't really ready for it. We had been organized less than a year and had little leadership. People were called out on strike in the middle of the depression with no strike benefits. I think the strike should have been called all right, but two or three years later. We needed to educate our own members better.

The women were very active in the '34 strike, about the same as the men. Some of those women were mean as can be, too. They got mad at one woman because she wanted to break the strike and go back to work, and they stripped her naked on the street right in front of the men. They were a radical bunch. She was scared to death, begged them to let her have her clothes back. They made her go naked for a little while and then gave her her clothes back. She got on the picket line then, and she was all right.

We were blacklisted not only from finding a job but by our neighbors. The South is full of these fundamentalist churches. We'd talk union all week long, and those damn preachers would tear it down on Sunday—"it was sinful" and all that kind of stuff. Of course, the mill owners were paying the churches. The two religious groups that stayed with us and helped us were the Catholics and the Jews. A Jewish merchant let us meet up over his store on Main Street, and a priest brought us food down on the picket line. They were carrying out their religious beliefs better than these fundamentalists, who'd stand up there and say everybody's going to hell. One of the terrible things that happened to us—we had been on strike about three weeks, and darned if the president of Cherokee didn't have a heart attack and up and dies one night. Now, you talk about something to overcome, with these preachers telling their people, "Now, look, they've killed that man." Here, I'm supposed to be one of the leaders. I didn't know what to do, so I got a real radical organizer from the Amalgamated Clothing Workers to come in and speak to them. I said, "Tell them something. I don't know what to tell them," and he did. He told them, "Don't you let what that old man's conscience has done to him bother you." I thought that was pretty good.

After I got blacklisted, I got a file clerk job at Tennessee Valley Authority. They hired me and a lot of the other blacklisted workers. If it hadn't been for the TVA, I'd still be looking for a job. While I was working there, I got to meet Mrs. Roosevelt when she came here to Knoxville. She wanted to visit the coal mines. It was 1936, and we all went out to the airport to meet her. I was part of the greeting committee—I made myself pushy—and I got to ride in the car with her. That was a big deal. She was such a friendly, wonderful woman you didn't feel awed by her at all. She talked mostly about the mines. (They had bad conditions in the coal mines until John Lewis and the United Mine Workers of America did something about it.) Well, Mrs. Roosevelt went down in a mine out at La Follette, and the miners would not go to work the next day because they believed it's bad luck for a woman to go in a mine. They were scared to death. It was all in the papers. But Mrs. Roosevelt went in, and nothing happened.

All the time I was working at TVA, I was working for the union on the side as a volunteer. Eventually, I became a full-time union organizer for the American Federation of Labor. That's what I've done most of my life. I never did marry. I thought about it a few times, but something else would come up. The closest I ever came to getting married was when I worked for the labor movement in New York City. (I just love New York.) It was 1942, during the war years, and I was courting a Polish guy there, and he had a good job as an electrician. I was a little tired of traveling and thought, "Well, maybe I ought to marry him" because I liked him. He was all right—good-looking and everything. The AFL—at that time it was AF of L, not AFL-CIO—offered me a scholarship to Ruskin College at Oxford, England. I had to decide whether I was going to marry him or take the scholarship, and I decided on the scholarship. I thought, "There's other men, but this is probably the only scholarship I'll ever be offered." He got married while I was over there. I was there eighteen months.

I'd never had any college education before that. I worked at Cherokee about a year on the day shift, and I went to night school and learned to type and some shorthand, not a whole lot, and then I took correspondence courses.

When I came back from Oxford, I went right back into the labor movement. I lived here in Knoxville, but they sent me all over the South. I was so persistent that I made some inroads, but when I started out as a full-time organizer, they would only let me organize the women in factories—like a woman couldn't organize men. In 1934, in the AF of L there was one woman on the executive board, God bless her. She was with the Hatmaker's Union, and she said it took her years to get on there, but she was determined to do it. Now I think we have several women on the executive board. When I came back from England in late 1948, I was full of ideas that I'd picked up. Ooh, I talked about running for president of the Central Labor Council here in Knoxville, and they said, "Are you crazy? A woman president of the council?" They still haven't had a woman president.

The War Brought Women
Out of Their Homes

Hazel Akeroyd

*She was born in Canova, South Dakota, in 1911. She has been widowed several times and lives in
Lubbock, Texas.*

"*Just before World War II I was a housewife living on a farm in Iowa with my husband. The
attack on Pearl Harbor was in December of 1941, and in October, we had found out that my husband had an inoperable brain tumor, which left him paralyzed on one side. He never spoke again.
So we left the farm and moved to Des Moines, and I got a factory job right outside of town with U.S.
Rubber. It was an ammunition factory that made bullets for the war. We manufactured thirty- and
fifty-caliber bullets—tracer bullets.*" (See also p. 36)

I'd never been in a factory before. I was more educated than most of the women there.
I could have worked in the office—I had been through college and taught school, and
then I went back to business college. I was working in an insurance office in Billings,
Montana, when I met my husband. But you could get thirty dollars a week working in
the factory. It was big money, and I was very hard up financially. We worked six days
a week, eight-hour shifts and if you worked seven days, your seventh day was double
overtime. If you worked in an insurance agency in town, you could get as low as fifteen dollars a week.

The assembly work was all done by women. They were mostly housewives from
Des Moines. It was such a change, an awful shock. You had to clock in. Most of us had
never been regimented like this. As a teacher or an office worker, you dressed up, you
were very professional. At the factory we wore a blue jumpsuit uniform. There were
some black women working in the factory; I'd never been around blacks in my life.

The men there were either in administrative positions and considered "essential
for the war effort," so they were not called into the war, or they were what we called
4-Fers—men who were turned down by the military for medical reasons. We didn't
have a very high opinion of 4-Fers—the flat feet that suddenly developed and the
asthma. It was sort of an iffy time as far as a man's status if he did not go to war.

420

The factory consisted of five big buildings. It was a huge enterprise, acres and acres. It was isolated for security reasons. We had threats. The factory ran twenty-four hours a day, seven days a week. There were three shifts—seven to three, three to eleven, eleven to seven. We changed shifts every seven weeks.

You clocked in and went to your machine. The noise level was tremendous—hundreds and hundreds of machines working on brass, and then they would haul the cases from place to place. I worked on the cases into which the gunpowder was placed. The machine I operated was maybe about 6½ feet high and 10 feet wide. You sat on a stool facing a glass partition, and you turned your machine on and watched as the cases came through on a conveyor. We made sure that they went along okay because they could turn over, and that could stop the machine. When they came out, you took them and checked them with your finger for any kind of scratch or defect. That was what they called the first draw. At another time I worked on the third draw. On the first draw the cases were small—it was the beginning. After you checked them, they picked them up and took them to the second draw, and they were drawn out a little farther, and then they went to the third draw, and they were drawn out until they were finished, and then they went to another building, where they put the bullets into them. I was probably in the safest area. Nothing could blow up—there were accidents.

We had a half-hour lunch hour; we'd file in to the cafeteria, eat our meal, and go back to our work. We also had a ten-minute break, but most of the time you could not leave the floor. They watched people very carefully. It was tight security. You had to ask permission to go to the bathroom.

Men ran everything. Women could be supervisors to an extent, but not high-level administrators. Women could not be foremen, either. If anything went wrong, the men fixed it. There were no women machinists. They were not even considered. Nobody thought about it. It was just accepted. I mean, it just wasn't done. Women were not what they are today.

The women's reactions to their husbands being gone were varied. There were women who couldn't stand being away from their husbands and were so worried about them, and there were some women who felt like they were free. For some, it was a free-wheeling, fast-moving social life during the war. Kind of like there's no tomorrow. Some of the women would get off at midnight and go to a nightclub.

Most of the women went back to their husbands and homes after the war, but some of the women lost their husbands in the war, some of the men had changed—they were bitter—well, look what they had to go through. There were marriages that went by the way. I don't think the war made a marked change in the women wanting to have a career, but women were never the same. They had had a taste of independence, freedom, surviving on their own. The war brought the women out of their homes out into the work world, and some of them never went back home. That was the beginning—they found out they could live socially, economically, outside the home and survive by themselves.

After the war ended, my husband died, and I went back to Huron and worked in an office as the secretary to the president of a college.

Dorothy Sommer

She was born in 1912 in the Midwest, and lives in New York City. She never married. (See also pp. 27, 60, 228 and 249)

The depression came along just as I was about to graduate from high school. I was able to take two years of college. I was an English major and was trying to go with journalism or something like that, but then the money ran out. My father had just about lost everything.

I read the *New York Times,* I looked through the want ads, and I saw all these jobs. I'd taken enough business courses, shorthand and typing, so I saved up enough money and came to New York. I found a job in advertising. It paid thirty-five dollars a week. I started as a receptionist and worked up to copywriting and sent money home to my father. I had a lovely room right off Fifth Avenue, just across from the museum. It was on the third floor and cost fifty dollars a month. It was a private house which they'd broken up into rooms. It had a beautiful Carrara marble entrance and a wrought-iron door.

I'd take the bus across from the museum. Wendell Willkie lived in the building across from me. Nobody remembers him, but he used to be a candidate for the presidency. I said good morning to him every day, and he said good morning to me. That's as far as we got. I think the bus fare was ten or fifteen cents, and I went down Fifth Avenue to work and back. At that time, everything was cheap. I'd have my lunch hour at Schrafft's—beautiful, wonderful Schrafft's. On my way home, I'd pick up from the wonderful Horn and Hardart. They used to make baked beans and macaroni and cheese—and oh, you name it. I'd bring it home with a little coleslaw and have it in my room. I was poor but happy.

I could have climbed higher at work if I had wanted to, that's for sure, but responsibility frightens me. I turned down opportunities many times. They were always calling me in the office, and they would say, "Take another course, and then you'll be ready," and I would take another course. But then I'd get to the point where they'd say, "Well, now you can be an account executive," and I was off like a shot. I couldn't bear the burden of all the responsibility. Maybe it's because I didn't have enough faith in myself. I don't know.

I worked at that job until I went to California, where I worked for Jack Warner as a social secretary. I was trying to put my brother through Ohio State University, so I always continued sending money for education cause my father never recouped his losses. My apartment was owned by Fred Astaire's mother, and it was lovely. Pola Negri used to live in our house. She was the vamp of the times, like the Madonna of this era. It was the golden era of big stars.

I met a lot of people through their secretaries. Bing Crosby's secretary was a good friend of mine—also Joan Bennett's, Danny Kaye's. I knew Joan Crawford's secretary, Mary, very well, and I used to go visit. Mary and I would sit by the pool and talk. They had pool houses where the hairdressers used to come to fix their hair, and Joan Crawford would be dashing from the house to the pool house with a turban around her head. And she'd say, "Excuse me, excuse me—I'm on my way to get my hair done."

I never was very awed by them, and other people I knew out there weren't, either. You knew them too well, I guess, but they were generous people to work for. They were lavish with presents. They remembered your birthdays. Many of them had beach houses at Laguna or Palm Springs, and if they weren't using them, they would let you use the house for your vacation. Oh, this was a wonderful life. It got a little tedious, though, if you're used to living in New York. There is no cultural life there whatsoever. Everything is built around the weekend and the patio parties, and then it's just shop talk. Who was reading for a part, who was losing out, who won the part, and also a lot of gossip, terrible lot of gossip.

I worked mostly at Jack Warner's house. They had a big mansion in Beverly Hills, and he had an office in the house, and I did the correspondence. A lot of the executives would be at home in the morning. They would meet somebody at Chasen's for lunch, and then they'd go to the studio. They gave large dinners; they owned a big yacht. You had to send invitations to the guests. They entertained constantly in Beverly Hills. It was the era of Elsa Maxwell. A lot of up-and-coming movie actors would engage her services and become known, and she kind of steered them around. I lived in that house, and Jack was wonderful. Everybody liked Jack Warner. There's nothing you could say against him. He would just be finished with his masseur and he'd have his terrycloth robe on, and he'd come into the office, and I'd be briefing him about when he had to be home and who was coming and all that sort of stuff.

He was a very generous man—beautiful presents. I drove a car from his garage, and I could fill her up at the studio—never had to pay for my gas—and if I had a birthday or any celebration and I'd get in the car, there'd be a bottle of champagne.

I moved back to NYC because I missed the culture. I loved going to the opera and theater. I did a lot of copywriting until I retired.

Laurine Warren

She was born in 1912 and grew up in Mississippi.

"I have been on the vestry, and I was the first female senior warden of Trinity Church in Natchez." (See also pp. 25, 52, 63 and 225)

*F*rom age nine I decided I would be a registered nurse. My mother and father thought I should go to college, but when I graduated from high school, I told them I still wanted to be a nurse. Well, they talked to me about staying at home one year, and so I did. I took a music and a business course, and at the end of the year, I said, "I am now ready to go in training," so my mother saw my mind was really made up. We came to Natchez in 1931, and we went to the Natchez sanitorium, which was a small hospital three stories high. Very antique.

The doctors taught us out of books what we were to learn so that we would know how to pass state boards to be a registered nurse. Our hours were twelve hours long, from seven in the morning to seven at night or from seven at night to seven the next morning. I finished training in three years. If we were going to do private-duty nursing, we were paid five dollars a day for twelve hours. I loved every minute of being in training, and in my days that followed, I loved being a nurse.

We would get up in time to be in the nursing dining room about a quarter of seven, and we ate our breakfast. Then we went on up on the floors and got a report from the nurses who were on the previous shift. We were assigned either to the second floor or the third floor. The delivery room was room 19. We did not really have nurseries for the babies. One time we had a little preemie who got down to a pound and a half. We put cotton around him and put him in a little container. One of the nurses just took such wonderful care of that little baby. Today he is a priest in the Episcopal church. He really made it.

The nurses in the sanitorium were a very close group; I still have some friends who were in training with me that I see, and they are good, good friends of mine. We had a matron over us. She lived in the nursing home with us, but she was also over the kitchen, and she was a wonderful cook, and she had the cook and the maid just doing a great job with the food.

At that time there was a pleasure boat called *The President* that would come down the river. Miss Bauer would let student nurses go out on the boat. We had the colored man that drove the ambulance take us. We would all get in the ambulance and ride down to the river and get on the boat and dance and have a good time. At midnight when the boat would dock back, Roy would be down there in the ambulance for us and would bring us back to the nurses' home.

We would also have one afternoon a week off. We would go to town and look at shoes and look at dresses like girls like to do. We listened to the radio a little bit, and we had a piano in the nurses' living room. One of the girls really played well, and we and the boys would come to see. Everybody had a boyfriend. And, for the most part, those girls, just like I did, they married the boys that they went with while they were in training. Some didn't finish training because they were married before they got out. But, for the most part, my friends stayed in training and married after they got through.

If I had married before I finished training, I couldn't have gotten my degree. Now you can go and train whether you are married or not, but that was one of the rules of the sanitorium, that you could not be married. That is the reason I wasn't married before I got out of training. Being a nurse was something that I wanted to do and that I intended to do. I never once thought of not finishing training.

If you were working the daytime shift in the surgical section and we had someone come in for surgery during the night, the telephone rang, and you had to get up and go over there and help with the surgery. Then you would go back and get up at seven to work all day. So we worked hard. But we learned a lot. We learned how to take care of patients and to show them love, and we made good friends while we were there.

When I was in training, there was a little girl who was about twelve years old, and she had leukemia. She lived in Louisiana with her mother and her father. Every time she would get real sick, they would bring her to the hospital. That little girl loved me, and so every time they would bring her over, they would ask Miss Bauer, our superintendent, if I could nurse her. So I would be moved from one floor to the other to take care of this little girl. One day I was sitting by her bed, and she looked at me and she said, "Miss Guice, I am dying." I said, "Oh, honey, you are all right," and she gave a little gasp and died.

Her mother and father were out on the screen porch, and oh—well, I called the doctor immediately, and we had to tell them that their little girl was gone. They were just brokenhearted, of course, but they asked me if I would bathe her and dress her and put her in her casket, and they asked Miss Bauer if they could bring the casket up there. They didn't want her embalmed. So I did, and I was just so broken up over that, and I cried, and the superintendent came in, and she said, "Miss Guice, if you are going to get upset over things that happen in the hospital, you'll never make a nurse." Well, I knew that I was going to make a nurse, and I did stop crying at the moment, but I cried most of the night over that sweet little girl.

Marguerite Rucker

She was born in 1926 and lives in New Orleans. She is a retired professor of nursing. (See also p. 42)

I remember being told that I was supposed to stand when the doctor came into the nursing station. After a while I just decided that I wasn't going to stand anymore. And some of the doctors were very, very annoyed by that. On more than one occasion a physician asked me to get up and give him my seat. I just got up and gave him my seat. I felt better by having done that, because I think it made him feel kinda crummy. He wanted to sit where I was sitting. There was another empty seat there—he could've sat down. I didn't sit in the other seat—I just stood there. One time this man asked me to get up as if to say, how dare you? It made me very angry, but I did not say anything. He may have been more adamant because I was black, but he expected the white nurses to give him that same respect.

Once things started changing, I remember how I enjoyed sitting down and talking with the physicians. The status of the nurse has improved tremendously. The relationship with doctors is more on an equal basis. There's still a lot of racism but nothing like it was. Everything started being integrated in the sixties, after the school desegregation. We know that things happen. Patients are kept out of certain areas; black nurses may not be hired. But it could be questioned if it's really obvious.

Rose Kramer

She was born in 1900 and lives by herself in Manhattan. Her younger sister lives in the Bronx. "We talk on the phone at least three times a day. I call her in the morning. She calls me to give me the weather report before I go out, and after Jeopardy, *we discuss it.*

"I was born in Russia. and I came here when I was a year and a half old. If I was born sixty years later, I certainly would have studied medicine. No question. I made an attempt to go to City College. I went for about four months, and then it became too much for me. It was too difficult— there was no time to study. I was working." (See also p. 236)

After high school, I went to work at a famous clothes-trimming establishment. I was secretarial. It was in Manhattan, next to the Twenty-third Street library, and they used to get letters from France, and on my lunch hour I would translate the letters. I got five cents for each word. I was the only Jewish girl there, and after a while I asked for a raise, and when they refused the raise, they called me a Bolshevik, and I left. Was that discrimination?

I became an x-ray technician. I did that for ten years. I was at the job a very short time, and my boss went off to Europe to a conference, and I was left in charge of the office. I took the films and x-rayed the patients, and a doctor came in to read the reports. I made five thousand dollars for my boss in that month. I got eighty dollars a week, which was a lot of money in the 1930s. He had a home out in Westchester. I was always called back for an emergency; he didn't come down, he depended on me. In the midst of my dinner or whatever, I went downtown to the office and took the x-ray.

I used to go to the Academy of Medicine and look up things that my boss had to know. I was everything. I used to treat people with cobalt. It was a very depressing job because so many women had breast cancer, and we treated them in the hope of preventing recurrences. We had very important patients because he was head of the department at one of the big hospitals. Most patients were very nice to me; I got some very fabulous gifts.

After ten years I got tired and got a leave. I went on a six-week vacation to California. My husband planned it for me, very generously. I went through the Panama Canal up to San Francisco, and he was going to meet me coming back, but that never happened. He just couldn't do it. When I came back, I just sort of got fed up with all the horror. I quit and went to work for an opthalmologist at Mount Sinai.

I Don't Know Why
I Wanted to Be a Doctor

Margaret Veller

"I was born in southwestern Kentucky in Beaver Dam, a small town of about a thousand people near the Ohio River. My father was an electrician for a mining company. I was born in 1925, and along came the depression a few years later, and the mining company he was working for shut down operations. Eventually, when I was twelve years old, we moved to Harlan County in Appalachia for three years, and we lived in a mining camp where the company owned the store and everything around it. When I was fifteen, my father got a job with the same tire company my uncle worked for in Natchez, and we moved down here. This was 1941. I loved the school here. I had no idea that high school would be so wonderful."

I had wanted to be a doctor ever since I can remember, and I don't know why. Even if I walked by a doctor's office, I was so frightened I nearly fainted till I was about eleven or twelve. But by the age of fourteen that was the only thing I wanted to do. I really wanted to know how people worked. My parents had had a hard time because of the depression. They both lost their fathers quite young, so they had to go to work to support the rest of the family, and this may be one reason that my father felt it was exceedingly important to educate women, too. I was singularly fortunate in my parents. I was an only child, and they sacrificed way too much for me.

My mother was an executive secretary and helped support her little brothers and sisters. When she met my father, he thought wives shouldn't have to work. He felt it was up to him to support her, but she said she could not stop helping her family till her brothers and sisters got older, so he was willing for her to work and send her salary to her family. Then when I was born, she stopped working and devoted all her time to taking care of my father and me. We were not at all well to do, but I had a very happy childhood. My father said he would be delighted to do everything he could to send me to medical school.

The superintendent of schools here insisted that my parents send me to Vanderbilt for college and medical school. I think I made one B in college; I was Phi

Beta Kappa. I stayed at Vanderbilt through college, medical school, and four years of residency.

In college, you could go out at night, but you had to be back at the dorm by 11 or you got a demerit. I was a very law-abiding person; I never came in late. I can hardly believe I did this, but after eleven o'clock at night, you couldn't get into the dorm without waking up the housemother, and so my very close friends would tie a string—a piece of twine—to my toe and put a clothespin on the end. We'd drop it down the window, and they'd pull on it when they got in, and I'd sneak down and let them in. I was on the second floor right above the housemother. Nobody except them ever pulled it. It wasn't very obvious, and it wasn't like we were doing it all the time. We had a delightful housemother, and later I thought, I bet she knew what was going on.

I applied to only one medical school, partly because it cost money to apply, and we were really broke. I think I was just lucky—there were twelve hundred applications—but I was accepted at Vanderbilt right away; they didn't even ask me to come for an interview. This was during the war years. The men were disappearing; they would be drafted.

In medical school, I made AOA, which is the Phi Beta Kappa of medical school, and so I realized I had to be in the upper ten percent of my class.

We had lots of premed women, maybe partly because of the war. Usually, there were only one or two women per class. The year I got to medical school there were seven out of fifty-two. That was the most they ever had, and six of them graduated. We had an honor system at Vanderbilt. The girl who didn't make it cheated on an exam, and one of the other girls saw her. They both went to the bathroom, and Emily had finished her exam, and the girl who was dismissed told her that she had finished hers, too. She said, "What did you put for so and so and so?" Emily told her. Then when they went back, Emily noticed the girl had gone into the room where the exam was going on, and she was writing away. She came and said, "What am I going to do?" This was one of our friends, but it didn't occur to us at that stage of life that there was any alternative. An honor system was an honor system, and we had signed the thing, and she had to report it. We were really distressed that she had cheated. We encouraged Emily to report it. What sort of doctor is she going to be if she's dishonest? And so Emily reported her, and she was dismissed from school.

When we first got to medical school, they were giving the men a lecture on how they didn't want them to look too sloppy—times have changed a lot—that they expected them to wear a shirt and a tie to classes. They didn't say anything about the women, but we all showed up in a shirtwaist blouse with a ribbon bow the next morning. We just thought it would be funny. After that, we usually did wear a skirt and a blouse. You were expected to be dressed appropriately. You didn't wear shorts or slacks.

After you graduated college there was no place on campus for women to live. Later, they let you live in the nursing school dorm, but when we first started medical school, most of us lived in professors' houses. They were right across the street from the medical school. One of the women there had been a bacteriologist, and she came back to medical school. She was two years ahead of us and sort of a mentor, and she said the men will accept you, but don't go into their lounges and bother them—they had a lounge for the men—they didn't have one for the women, of course. She said, "They want this as men's territory. Just let it be that way, and you'll get along better. Do your talking to them outside of that."

It really didn't bother me. There was no law that said you couldn't go there, but we just didn't, and most of the time the men were pretty nice to me, and protective. I thought we women were pretty well accepted. At first they might tell you some jokes you thought were a little off color, but if you ignored them, they quit doing it, and I became very close with a lot of them.

Our professors did not embarrass women. And if they found any of the students doing it, they were corrected. Sometimes the students could be real protective. I remember going to this dermatology clinic, and they passed out the chart—you were supposed to present the patient to the class—and I had one that was a male patient with a carcinoma genitalia, and one of my male friends walked over and just swapped charts and let me have one that would not embarrass me.

We had an ophthalmology professor, and several times he said to me, "When I see a girl in medical school, I think she's taking the place of some fine young man." I don't know why it didn't bother me more, but it really didn't. One of the pediatric professors called me aside and told me that women had a hard time getting internships and so I better apply to a number of places, but I had already been told by the head of the ob-gyn department that they would like very much for me to be an intern. I had worked there a couple of summers. The other women got internships quite easily.

About ten years before I got to Vanderbilt, they had had a woman resident from Detroit, and they were still talking about her—oh, she was terrible. When things didn't go right, she burst into tears. She would sit down in the operating room and cry. Well, no wonder, the way they treated her! She was a legend around there, and they did not have another woman intern for ten years, and then they got Emily and me.

When they would have national medical meetings—for example, the American College of Obstetricians and Gynecologists meeting was once a year—frequently, they would select two or three male residents and take them with them, but the women didn't get to go. They kept saying it was cheaper to take men. They said they could put the men in one room at the hotel, but if they took the women along, they'd have to get other rooms for them. We never had that many women on staff. Most of the time it was just one woman on the house staff. We accepted it. I would have given anything to have gone, but I could see the logic; now I think it was discriminatory.

I didn't have the money to pay for it myself, so I never got to go to one. When I was an intern, they gave us a place to stay and some uniforms and they fed us, but you didn't make anything. After the first year I got thirty-five dollars a month for the next three years. It's different from the way it is now. You didn't marry without asking the chief of service permission. You were practically owned body and soul.

The most discriminatory thing that ever happened to me—and, again, I don't know why it didn't really bother me very much—was my fourth year of residency the chief of staff called me in and said, "Margaret, I want you to stay next year." He wanted me to stay after I finished and do research in the lab. "But I do have to tell you I can't call you chief resident. I'll give you the same training, but I can't ask my boys to work under a woman." As chief resident you would be in charge of the GYN ward or the obstetrical ward, and the interns and junior residents would work under you. It was mostly the prestige. It looked good to say you were the chief resident, but I was not allowed to say it. It didn't bother me; I accepted it. I was just interested in learning. It was only two or three years later that I thought that really was discriminatory. These days people get sued for it.

Vanderbilt was not air-conditioned at the time I got there. Even the operating rooms weren't air-conditioned until I was an intern. You just burned up. When I was an intern, the women doctors' living quarters weren't air-conditioned, and they were never under eighty-four degrees. The psychiatrists were on a hall in front of our quarters, and their offices were air-conditioned. They, bless their hearts, realized how miserable we were. So they said, "After we make our rounds at night and leave, you all can come over and sleep in our air-conditioned office," and we thought that was the most wonderful thing; we could hardly wait. One night three of us looked both ways, their cars were gone, we went in and we bedded down on the floor, and all of a sudden we realized that they were still in the corridor, and we had to get up and go back to our rooms.

Even though all our patients were women, they were not used to having women doctors, and some of them couldn't quite accept me. They felt men doctors knew more. Women should be nurses. They wouldn't necessarily say that, but it would be pretty apparent. They were very reluctant to accept what I would tell them. I learned right off, if they didn't accept me, to go to one of my male friend residents or interns and ask them to tell them what I wanted them to know, and then it would work out fine. But this was not really very common.

I experienced it more when I came back to Natchez and joined a group practice. When I first came down here, people frequently did not want me. "Are you going to deliver the baby? Are you going to operate on me?" I had a wonderful situation—I had a male associate, and so if he was there, that was fine. I had a few patients who said, "I'd really like you to do my hysterectomy, but my husband's not comfortable with that." It wasn't all that often, and I never felt that bad. There was plenty to do, and I would frequently say, "Look, if you're more comfortable with Dr. Bennett doing this, let's have him do it." I didn't feel diminished by it. In fact, sometimes it bothered my men associates more than it bothered me. I remember one schoolteacher I had, and she had carcinoma endometrium, and she wanted one of the male surgeons to operate on her, and he did, and I helped him, and the surgeons in my group were, "That's just terrible, that's not right." I don't know whether I have a very strong ego or a very weak one, but those things don't bother me much. I thought she was mistaken, but that was okay. But now the last ten years of my practice people ask me to refer them to a woman doctor. I don't think I had anything to do with that. It's the change—there are more women doctors now. Many women seem to think that we're more compassionate. I don't think that's true; maybe we're a little more understanding. I have known some women doctors that I didn't think were very kind and some men doctors that I thought were wonderfully compassionate.

One of my friends who moved up to Memphis mailed me this little brochure from her ob-gyn group. They are five women in her group, and the brochure told about all the nice things they did and how they had hand-knitted booties on the stirrups. They had everything I'd ever wanted for my office and never could afford or couldn't persuade my partners.

Not so long ago a young lady, a pharmaceutical representative, came in and said, "May I ask you a personal question?" and I said, "Surely," and she said, "I've been thinking about going to medical school, but looking back on your career with all the malpractice problems and the fees and the changes in medical care, would you do it again?" I was surprised, and I said, "Certainly. Even more so." I think I've been the luckiest person in the world. I got to do what I wanted to do. It's had its nightmarish moments, and it hasn't always turned out well, but I have been grateful, and I have enjoyed it. It was so much fun to wake up and go to work every day. I just couldn't get enough of it.

My obstetrical practice just ballooned. I've never been very interested in the business part. I just wanted to practice medicine.

I've practiced here since 1954, but I retired in 1991. I didn't want to, but malpractice premiums had come up to $52,000, and there was no way I could make enough money to pay them. I was out of practice for eight months, and then three internists who are friends said, "How would you like to come back?" If you only work twenty hours a week and don't do any hospital work or surgery, you can get a much reduced malpractice premium. I thought, a half a loaf is better than none.

I just don't have the stamina I once had, and I will retire completely at the end of this year, and I will miss it very much. There is a life outside of medicine even though I think it's a poor second choice. One of the things I treasure the most is that I'm the only obstetrician I know working for a doctor she delivered. He's a pulmonary specialist. When he first came back, I said, "I got you into the world. I expect you to get me out of it."

What a Rigamarole

Winifred Williams

She grew up in Brooklyn, moved to Long Island with her family, and then moved to the small up-state town of High Falls, New York. She was widowed a few years ago and has two daughters.

"I find my life very exciting, even at age seventy-seven. I'm into projects all the time day. I never have a spare moment. I sleep roughly four or five hours a night always. When I retired, I started to go to auctions and yard sales and found junk. I restore it and sell it, and it's fun. I wish I had gone into that earlier." (See also p. 240)

My daughter often says that I was way ahead of my time. I was never a housewife. I was bored with it. I always worked. I was in the real estate business in Malverne, Long Island, during the war. I had a kiddy shop with my sister called Tiny Togs, and the children were in a playpen in the back of the store. I was about thirty-eight when I went to Abraham & Straus, and I retired from there.

It was lucrative and exciting. I was doing executive sales—we're talking big sales—and worked on commission. I worked with twenty-two men. At that time there was no such thing as a female selling major appliances. I thought I could do it. I applied for the position. I was interviewed by somebody from RCA and Admiral and the president of A&S, and they decided to go along with me. Oh, what a rigamarole I had to go through. I still remember Bill Smith, who later became president of Admiral Corporation. The interview was ridiculous, and finally he said, "She could sell snow to the Eskimos."

I got the job, and I held it a long time. They weren't willing to pay me the same as they paid the men. They offered me $90 a week draw, and the men were getting $250 draw—you would get paid your draw, and at the end of the month you got what was over the draw. At thirty-eight years of age, I was kind of brassy and sure of myself, and I told them that I wasn't going to be paid less than the men. I said I would work for nothing to begin with, and if in ninety days I didn't exceed everything that the men did, I would quit. If I exceeded the men, then they would have to give me equal pay. I wound up with $250, same as the men, but I had to prove myself first.

To my knowledge, I was the first woman to sell major appliances except for Betty Furness, who was selling them on television. I sold air conditioners, refrigerators, stoves. I had a briefcase; I went out estimating. I was a pioneer. The clients were receptive. Microwaves had just come in. I used to go out to demonstrate at the hotels in New York City and different places, and I think they were warmer to having a woman sell them an appliance than a man. I had a little more difficulty selling televisions. I was in what they called white goods—stoves, refrigerators, air-conditioning—and the department kept growing from seven men to twenty-two. I was considered a male. We were making so much money that they decided to split the departments and gave us a choice whether we wanted to stay with the white goods or go with the TV and stereo, and I stayed with the white goods. Prior to that I sold both. It was very exciting. I've never enjoyed spending money. I enjoy earning it. It's always been a big challenge. I love picking up something and working on it and making a profit.

My boss and the executives approved of me because they always like an achiever in business. The men hardly talked to me; they never accepted me. It was difficult working with them. They never honored my CUs—a CU is somebody who comes back to see you—they may have forgotten your name. They wouldn't give me the sale. Little petty things. The company gave me a desk, which they didn't have, with my own little cards. They resented that. We started an "up" system, where you signed your name when a customer got off the elevator or the escalator. It would be your up—that way we all had an equal chance, and I still left them far behind. They were lazy, spoiled. They used to watch all the World Series games on the TVs, and there I was running around covering everything. I was hired as a pace setter. I liked it, it was lucrative, but I had to work hard. It was just part of my makeup. Had women sold cars, I would have been selling cars.

When I went to work at A&S, my daughters were ten and twelve. My friends all thought I was crazy. My husband was a good Catholic at the time and didn't approve of me going to work and leaving two teenage girls running around in high school, so we sent them to boarding school. They went up to Ladycliffe at West Point. We would pick them up weekends on our way up to High Falls. I did manage to take the summers off to be with my children.

After a while, my salary far exceeded my husband's. He didn't mind it. He took a little pride in it. I was aggressive; he was very quiet. If he wasn't so quiet, loving, and understanding, I could've never had the free rein that I had. He gave me lots of leeway even with the children. He was the one that read the children the nursery rhymes at night, not me. He tucked them into bed. He was remarkable—a very gentle, sensitive man. He was not a macho man. I do not like macho men. He liked poetry, literature. He liked to dance, loved the theater. We took the girls to Broadway shows. They had a wonderful background, thanks to their father. George would cook, and he did the laundry. About the only thing he never liked to do was to food shop. I always did that. I worked late two nights a week, Monday and Friday. I worked till nine-thirty, and I always managed to pick up the last customer at night, so I always got home late. He was there. He found excitement in what I did. I was loquacious and talkative and bubbly, and he was a good listener.

We had our ups and downs. He broke away once later in life and rebelled. He came back. He loved me, but there was something missing in his life. I failed him in some way. I'm not being guilty about it. I have no guilt at all. What happened with us was within him.

Jean Hughes

She was born and raised in Butte, Montana. She is a retired medical technologist and lives with her husband in La Jolla, California. She has four children and three grandchildren. (See also pp. 48 and 255)

My work as a medical technologist was interesting. My unhappiness was with my salary. I was in a woman's field, and the salary range was very low. I had taken difficult courses—all the chemistries and math—and after I graduated I had to serve one whole year as an intern without pay. So that was five years of training, and my salary was almost always about half of what my husband earned, who only had four years of training. He is a mechanical engineer.

Anne Plettinger

She was born in St. Francisville, Louisiana, in 1917, one of six children. She got her BA degree in physics from Sophie Newcombe College in New Orleans, at that time the women's college connected with Tulane University. During World War II she moved to Chicago to work on the Manhattan

Project. She was for many years an assistant to one of the professors working on the project to develop the atom bomb. When she took early retirement at age fifty-five, she moved back to Baton Rouge, Louisiana.

*I*n Chicago, I ran the laboratory for the Manhattan Project and Professor Zachariasen liked having someone that thought ahead and thought of things to do. I always consulted with him, but I would think, "Can't we try this? Can't we try that?" He really appreciated that, and we really turned out the research; both of us worked long hours. Toward the end he did include me as a coauthor of his papers. I didn't appreciate that; I felt a little bit uneasy being listed as the coauthor. I felt that I didn't know enough about the field that I could argue the results.

Right after I came back to Louisiana in 1975, I became concerned about the construction of a nuclear power plant in my home parish, Westville. I was worried about its safety and the impact it would have on the environment. I began attending hearings and meetings at the Louisiana Public Service Commission. I was not a member of any organization; I just saw the need for somebody to be looking and asking questions, and I am still doing this. I call myself a self-appointed watchdog. At the first set of hearings they said to me, "Miss Plettinger, you don't have to worry your head about your beloved west Louisiana parish. We're just country boys from northern Louisiana and Texas, and we wouldn't do a thing to harm your beautiful parish." I was so floored. I couldn't believe it. I felt that was such an insult to my intelligence. "Don't you worry, just leave it to us. We know what's best for you, and we think we have to have this nuclear power."

Lillian Roth

She was born in 1918 and worked as a legal secretary most of her life. She lives in Brooklyn. (See also p. 40)

I was probably in my late forties, some years after my husband died, and my boss was really badgering me to have an affair, and I have to admit that I did. I wasn't raped. I simply had an affair with him. I didn't have enough courage to say, "Look, get lost."

I went out with him for years. In a way, it suited me because I didn't have to actually live with him and put up with his idiosyncrasies—he was married—and yet I could tell myself that I had a boyfriend. A lot of it was very pleasurable, but this relationship started out because he was harassing me and I was afraid of losing my job, and I didn't want to. I had a very good job at this office. He was a real estate attorney, and I became so good at what I was doing that he thought nothing of going away for six weeks and leaving me in charge of the office. I didn't go to court. I wasn't a lawyer, but I was able to take care of people who called and needed all kinds of information about real estate law. Of course, I wasn't appreciated. He would come back and give me the same present as he gave the other young women, who sat at the switchboard.

I liked a lot of my jobs. I didn't like that I wasn't appreciated as a professional person, that I wasn't treated with respect, that I was treated like an inferior person because I was a woman. I worked overtime many times and never got paid for it. Women were exploited. They were treating women like this for so many years that I guess they are finding it very hard to change. Look how recently this thing happened with this man Clarence Thomas, who's on the Supreme Court. So this is still going on.

The last job that I had, we were moving to a new building. When I first looked at my new office, I saw this nice little room with a window where the sun was going to come in and there was a little park outside, and I thought, "Oh, this is much nicer than where we were." By the time I moved into the office, the window was blocked off. My boss decided that there wasn't enough wall space in my office, although this didn't really concern him. He blocked the window off. I never forgave him for that.

It was part of his power-mad image. His office was big, bright, colorful, beautiful, but to get there you had to walk through this little cell I was locked into—my office led into his office.

I don't remember that I ever did anything about the window because by that time he had files on that wall, but he also wanted the door to my office closed. So at that point I did speak up because at least when the door was open, I saw people going back and forth. I said to him, "I'm very claustrophobic," which was an exaggeration—I had to have a medical reason or he would not open that door—"and it's impossible for me to work like this." I moved the desk around, and I made him open that door. Every once in a while I think about all of these things, and I think, "Why did I tolerate all this stuff?"

I was once on the phone in a law office. I had a break, and I was talking to my daughter, and some lawyer came along and started to shout at me, "Get off that phone—I need you." I was so humiliated for my daughter to hear someone talking to me like that. Lawyers are a special breed. Some of them are terrible monsters. I shouldn't say that because I can remember jobs before I worked in law offices where the men were obnoxious, too.

I had a lot of resentment. All these years I really buried it. I've always been big on wanting to be treated with respect. And I was not treated respectfully in many of these places. I was seething. I resented things that a lot of women accepted.

Work:

The Second Generation

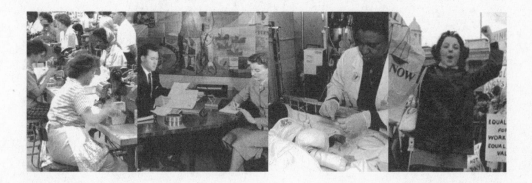

I love to see the strides women are making. I love seeing a woman on a telephone pole. But I'm a little old fashioned. I still like to have a door opened for me.

—Pricilla Lynch, born 1942

I've always felt sort of detached from the women's movement even though I was one of the founders of the Women's Studies department. The women's movement was a white middle-class thing and we had to fight very hard to remind them that we were here. My background was working class black segregated; my mother and all my friends' mothers worked. It wasn't something to be hoped for. You had to. So a lot of what they were talking about was very much "what is their problem?" Whoever said that a man was supposed to support you? But it would be very stupid of me not to recognize that a very significant part of my being able to function as a professor has come from the women's movement. If the women's movement had not applied that pressure, I couldn't be doing what I am doing now. Who would publish my work if they still thought that women were unimportant. Here I come with Black Women of the 18th Century.

—Frances Smith Foster, born 1945

You Are Like a Little Wife at Work

Leslie Hampton

She is divorced, has three adult sons, and lives in Michigan, where she works for the Department of Mental Health. She was born in 1940. (See also p. 101 and 286)

I never did anything very glamorous for the airlines. I worked for them about a year and a half as a secretary, and it was a lot of fun. I did not have enough confidence at that time to even dream that I could be a stewardess. I was so sure that I was not pretty enough and not thin enough, and now looking back at the pictures, I don't believe that anymore.

To be a stewardess you had to be all-American wholesome. You had to have a clear complexion, a certain weight, height, and you couldn't be married. They really made it sound like it was the cream of the crop of women's jobs to be a flying waitress. And many of us bought into the idea that it was the most wonderful, glamorous thing to be. They used to make you retire at thirty-five—you had to be young and pretty to fly the skies. I would have thought that I had reached heaven if I had been able to do that. It was just crazy.

I worked as a secretary for twenty-five years. A great part of that time I enjoyed it. If you're good and if you're smart, there's a lot that you can do as a secretary to help someone else, but you are the helper, you are boosting someone else.

When I worked for the airlines, the engineers were all men, and they could smoke at their desks, while the secretaries, who were all women, could not. I just took that for granted. It never occurred to me that we had a class distinction as well as a sexist thing going on. I accepted those things for quite a long time before there was a dawning of awareness. It was in the seventies that I finally began to question. People were starting to do things and say things out loud. The feminist movement totally changed my attitude.

In my first secretarial job at Northwest Airlines I would go in in the morning and dust my boss's office and sharpen his pencils and get everything set up. You're like a little wife at work. And then every morning, like nine-thirty, he would do dictation. Sometimes he would dictate to me, but he also had a Dictaphone. I think they made a little miniature record, and then you listened to it. We also had a fax machine. It looked like a cylinder standing upright. The letter would be put around that cylinder, and it would spin around. It would take about fifteen minutes to send one page. You could send it to whoever you were hooked up with. It had to have been either hooked up to the phone or to whatever the teletype was hooked up to. The teletype machines were another way of sending information. You typed into this, and it punched out a thin tape that had a code in it, and then that tape was put on another machine that read that code and sent the message out to a receiver. It is somewhat similar to a telegraph.

I had a telephone that had three lines on it, and you knew which line was ringing by their different sounds. You didn't have lights like you have now.

If we were going to make a few copies, we'd usually use carbon paper, but if we needed more than a few, then we would type either a stencil or dittomaster. It had this kind of goopy messy stuff on the back of a page, and as you typed, it made a master impression. You typed out that master and then fed the paper into a hand-operated machine that would spit out your copies. The stencil looked better than the ditto. They both took a lot of time.

I had a manual typewriter. To make carbon copies you would type on your original piece of paper. When the carbon paper was hit upon with enough force, it would leave an impression on the next piece of paper, and you could set up a stack of those. You could do probably seven or eight at the max. But your last couple of copies might not be very good, so if you needed more than that, you were in trouble. Sometimes you might end up typing something over twice in order to have enough carbon copies of it.

It is an amazing difference. Nobody uses that anymore. In the beginning it was a little bit more expensive to run copies on a Xerox machine than to use carbon paper, so that was a gradual transition. Probably by the mid-seventies I was using Xerox.

The first thing that I can remember being air-conditioned was this huge computer room, about 1965 or '66. The computer probably had the capacity of what one of our personal computers does now. The machines had to be air-conditioned because they could not function in the heat where people could. People would find excuses to go into the computer room to get cooled off.

It was a major thing, trying to figure out what to wear to work on hot days so that you would remain somewhat presentable by the end of the day. You still had to wear your nylons and your girdle and all your clothes, and you'd swelter in it. Gosh, I'd forgotten how horrible that was. What a moment of freedom that was when we decided not to do that anymore—no more girdles! It must have been the time that panty hose were invented. That would have been during the major revolution times, late six-ties, early seventies. Everything happened then.

It was a long time before you could wear slacks at work. You had to be professional looking, and that meant you dressed in a very nice dress or in a suit and wore nylons—perfect little office woman. If somebody came in who did not use makeup, they probably wouldn't get hired. You didn't see very many people that didn't have some makeup on and their hair done nicely and nice clothes.

Sometime around the early seventies, while I was working at Diamond Reo Trucks, we got permission to wear pantsuits. It did not take too much time before women pretty much started wearing what they wanted to wear, whether it was a pantsuit or not. The guys sort of lost control of that one.

I worked for one boss for many years at Diamond Reo. I paid all his home bills. I did a few other personal things for him, but by the time I went to work there in '67, the idea of not doing that stuff was beginning. I stayed for eight years, so by '70, making and taking coffee had become a big issue. I still did it, but I bitched about it a lot. I worked for that same man later in a law office for about a year, probably about '77, and I wouldn't bring him coffee by that point. It was like, "You want coffee, get your own coffee." He would wait until he had a client in his office, and then he'd say, "Could you get us some coffee?" Because the client was there, you could not say, "No, I won't," but he and I knew each other very well and had worked together a long time, so it was partially just his way of being a smart-ass, too.

All the managers and professionals were men. The clerical people were mostly women unless it was something that was considered kind of technical, then it probably would have been a guy. When I got to Diamond Reo in the late sixties, a few women were beginning to break into some managerial jobs.

I can remember maybe in the late seventies beginning to read articles about how secretaries at different companies had made this major leap into management. Before the women's movement, it was just pretty much accepted: You knew that when you trained to be a secretary, it was this lifelong thing. It was being realistic. You could not usually work your way up. I don't remember anybody even commenting on it, saying, "Isn't this awful?" Being a secretary was one of those things you fell back on when you didn't have a man to support you. If you were in a big company, then your goal would be to be one of the executive secretaries, which is what I became.

Salary scales were just terrible. At Diamond Reo Trucks I made pretty good money, comparatively speaking. In most companies, though the salaries were very bad in comparison to what the person that you were working for might be making, or other jobs of comparable responsibility that some guy was doing. Of course, I don't remember ever hearing anybody even talk about that until the comparable-worth work movement was started.

I never worked so hard in my life, as I did as a secretary in a law office. You worked all day long, as fast as you could, and you did a great deal of the prep work for the attorney. The guy I worked for did a lot of divorce work. Once he interviewed the client, I would be given a sheet with all the facts, and then I would do all the legal paperwork. It was pretty standard, so you plugged stuff in. You did all of the work, other than when he went into court, and at that time I was making maybe six dollars an hour, and he was probably making seventy dollars an hour. That year for me was like a major final awakening of the disparity between salaries and between what people were expected to do. When I left there, it was like I would never work in a law office again unless I were a lawyer. I was doing what would be considered paralegal.

In addition to being underpaid, there was always the possibility of sexual harassment. At one point I went to work for this company, and my boss expected me to provide him with favors for having gotten the job, and I finally had to quit. That was very difficult because I knew his family. It wasn't that great a job. I wasn't losing anything that wonderful, but he made it very uncomfortable for me. He talked about having sex, and then a couple of times when I was working late and nobody was around, he tried to kiss me and to get me to have sex with him on the davenport in his office. I was careful to not be caught there after everybody else was gone, and I started looking for another job. He probably would not have fired me. He would have just continued to make life very miserable for me.

The women's movement changed the way I viewed the work I did as a secretary. I began to think of doing something different. At forty I went back to college and completed my education. Now I work for the Michigan Department of Mental Health in our licensing, monitoring, and accreditation division. We go out and inspect group homes for the developmentally disabled. We make sure the clients are receiving active treatment, as defined by the feds. I just moved into that. Before that I was in the affirmative action office for about twelve years and was the assistant of the affirmative action officer.

I Never Planned a Career

Lois Mayer

"She was born in 1941 and grew up on Long Island, New York. She has been married for thirty years, has three children, lives in a suburb of Baltimore, and works as a business consultant. Her mother, Helen Schiffrin, also appears in the book.

When we were kids, my mother was always there when you came home from school, and even if you just ran in and ran right out, that was important. It's stability, security—she's there, and then you go out and do whatever you want. I did that for my kids. As they got older and I went to work, obviously that wasn't the case. My mother's expectations were when she married my father, she would never work a day in her life. She would be taking care of a family. I think my expectations were not much different. You get married, you have kids, and your husband takes care of you. My father encouraged exploring in college, expanding your mind, but, in retrospect, he probably felt I'd never use a degree, anyway, so it didn't matter what I got it in. From my mother it was, "Be a teacher so you'll always have something to fall back on."

When I was in college, I went to work for TWA—I was a ground hostess—and at that time they didn't hire Jews. The person who got me the interview said, "Do not tell them that you're Jewish." And when I went for the interview, the woman said, "Boy, you look Irish." I had long, blond hair. I just smiled, and I got the job. Then when I was training, TWA had a flight that went from New York to Tel Aviv to Cairo, and it was our responsibility that no one that was Jewish went beyond Tel Aviv—they didn't have diplomatic relations—and somebody said, "Well, how can you tell if a person is Jewish?" And the guy said, "You can tell by their name on the passport." And what if they don't have a Jewish name? "Well, you can always tell by looking at them." I didn't say anything cause I wanted the job, and I swore after that that I would never not say anything again.

I graduated in August, and I got married in December '63. Amanda was born October of '64. It just happened. I didn't work until my children were grown. Enjoyed it. Became very active in the kids' schools, including being the president of the PTA for many years. Worked for a few political candidates—donations, funding, having groups over where the candidate could come and speak, campaigning, literature dropping. I worked the polls. I was very busy. I had to carpool for nursery school. My kids all went to Hebrew school three times a week, after-school activities, sports, art, dance. Jessica must have been around eleven, I went back to work part-time; my main concern was being here for the kids.

I never planned a career. I didn't go to college so that I could work afterwards. It was getting a degree because everybody got a degree. I went back to work because it was fulfilling. Now I find myself in a very different situation, where we need the money I make. It's a responsibility. When my mother went to work many years after my father died, it was something to keep her busy. My daughter Amanda, on the other hand, has always known that she's going to have to support herself and that she can. This is not, "I'm going to find some guy who's a millionaire, and he's going to take care of me for the rest of my life." Her career, as a college professor, is very important to her, and she will always pursue it.

The idea that you can do something you like to do and earn a living at it enough to support yourself for the rest of your life, that's absolutely great. Women in my daughters' generation don't drop their career for some guy that has to move to California. I think it may put strains on relationships, but I don't think that's wrong, because you don't know what's down the road for you ten years from now. If you gave up all of this to get married and move where this guy had to move, and then the marriage ended, you're in deep trouble.

Sharon Goldberg

She was born in the Midwest in 1940 and lives with her husband in Southern California. (See also p. 75)

I went to Berkeley, and after two years, I got married. I had a baby, and we moved to Southern California. Right before my third child was born, I got my college degree. I went to work when she was only six months old. This wonderful woman, Bettina, came to live with us.

I built up an interior design business. I'm also a contractor. I've had the same business partner for twenty-four years. I'll do all the interior stuff. I just gutted a whole area, knocked down walls, hired structural engineers, figured out what to do.

The men are so nice and respectful to me, but I'm very respectful to them. If they do good work and we get along, it's not a one-time job. I have a team now—a guy who is pretty much my foreman, an electrician, a painter, a plumber. When I introduce them to my clients, I say, "This is my team. We work together." I don't want them to ever feel lesser than.

Because it was my business, when my children were little, I was able to say to a client, "I can't work from two to four—I drive carpool." I still tried to be Brownie leader and Girl Scout leader and all that stuff. It was not difficult for my older children; my younger child was very resentful. Now she's okay with it, but we've had a lot of problems because she feels that I would schlepp her to different clients in the afternoon after school. She used to say, "Why can't you be like Mrs. Brown," who lived up the street, who would always be there for her four children with cookies and milk, and I said, "Because I'm not Mrs. Brown, I'm Mrs. Goldberg. I'm really sorry. I can't do it. Though you'd be sorrier if I was home every single minute. But I still drive carpools, and I still take you places, and I love you."

My husband was not involved. He worked seven days a week trying to build up a law practice, and in those days you didn't even know to be resentful. My daughter would be really pissed if her husband didn't participate, but Jack didn't. He was a great dad when they got older. He didn't know what to do with little kids. And, you know what, I didn't care. It was fine with me. I loved babies, loved little children.

Julia Parker

She lives with her husband and children in the Deep South, where she was born in 1951. When her children were fourteen, twelve, and six, she decided to go to law school. Since there was no law school nearby, she had to move out of town. While she was away, her husband took care of the children part of the year, and they spent part of the year with her. She is now an attorney working for an environmental protection agency. (See also p. 309)

I got into law school, and then a friend of mine who's a lawyer said, "You really ought to start in the summer because it makes life so much easier. By the fall you'll understand how to write a brief, and you will have been reading along all summer." So I called the law school and said, "Can I get in for the summer?" They said, "You're four hours away, and you've got three children, and school starts in two weeks. We'll let you in, but can you really do this?" And I thought, "How long does it take to pack a suitcase?" It didn't seem like that big a deal. It was a big deal to leave my children four hours away and go down there, but they found me a room in an elderly widower's house, with a separate entrance, and I survived the summer fine, and my grades were fine, and I enjoyed it.

I just have too much energy, and my metabolism is spinning all the time. If I don't do a lot all day, keep going at that fast pace, I can't sleep well at night. We have a huge vegetable garden behind our house, and I canned a hundred quarts of tomatoes the summer before I went to law school. In my second pregnancy, early on I started some spotting, and I called the doctor, and he said, "What have you done today?" and I said, "Not a lot." He said, "Describe to me what you have done," and I said, "Well, I planted so many rows of flowers, so many rows of vegetables; I painted the baby's room, swam so many laps in the pool," and he said, "This is not a normal day for somebody who is pregnant. This is not even a normal day for somebody's who's not pregnant. You need to cut back." I've always been manic somehow or other. People say, "How did you do it? It's such a jump to go from being just a full-time mother to being a lawyer," and it didn't seem like a strange transition to me at all.

I Don't Believe in Being a Crutch;
I Believe in Assisting

Rosalind Cropper

She is a physician who started and runs a nonprofit clinic in New Orleans. She is African-American.

"I was born here in New Orleans in 1952 and raised in the projects. I have two brothers and four sisters. My mother died when I was eleven, my father died when I was about seventeen. I have a twenty-two year old, a six year old, and a foster child that's seven months. She is the baby of one of my patients. She was a crack baby, and no one else would take her. I took her when she was two weeks. My specialty is primarily geriatrics internal medicine, but I am now involved with a large group of substance abusers who are HIV positive, and I have approximately twelve hundred of those listed in my practice."

*W*e took care of ourselves. We could've been anything from prostitutes on the street to drug addicts, drug dealers, to what we are now. And the three of us girls that stayed together, one is a schoolteacher, and the other works for me here as personnel director. We all finished college. We didn't have anybody to wake us up and say, "Go to school," but we got up and went.

When I was in eleventh grade, I dropped out of school because it seemed like it would be so much easier to get a job. I got into selling magazines from door to door. But I wasn't getting anywhere, so I decided to try to get back in school. They told me that I needed to repeat the eleventh grade, and I figured this was so unfair because I was an A student. So I refused to do it, and I kept trying to find somebody to help me. Jim Duffy, who was a guidance counselor at Manderville High, allowed me to take a correspondence course at LSU; I got into an honors course for the twelfth grade and graduated on time. Because my father was a disabled veteran, I was able to go to college on the GI bill.

I just happened to be endowed with a good brain. I was always an A student. And I always had someone who was there to push me along. I don't forget. In elementary school there was Ms. Prejean; when I was in college, it was Dr. Jackson and his wife. It was like I had to do this stuff, or I would let them down. People believing in me helped me believe in myself. Before, I never could've even imagined I could be a doctor. I wasn't exposed to that. But people exposed me and made me believe that I could. So that's the same way I practice and live my life.

I don't believe in handouts, in being a crutch; I believe in assisting. If somebody gives you something, then when they get mad or tired of you, they can drop you from their grace. But if you've earned it step by step, if you ever have to backtrack, then you're on solid ground. If you took leaps and bounds, and you had to backtrack, you may fall in a hole. So I believe in taking little steps and making every step count, and being sure of what you're about. Because if you know what you're about, then everything else will fall in line. And that doesn't go well with a lot of people.

Except for Jim Duffy and Florence Haines, my mentors were all black people. I'll never forget Jim Duffy. He introduced me to James Baldwin's writings, and that was the first time I really started reading. Florence Haines was my eleventh grade teacher, who had me start reading Ayn Rand's *The Fountainhead*, *Five Smooth Stones*, and those kind of books. So it allowed me to vicariously live some of the things I had never been exposed to. When I dropped out of school in eleventh grade, Ms. Haines was relocating either to Boston or Maryland, and she wanted me to go with her because I was homeless. I had run away, quit school. I have lost contact with her, so I would like her to know that I did get back into the mainstream. Dr. Jackson said in order to change the system, you first must become a part of that system. And so that made me buckle down, do what I had to do.

I was a 3.89-average student at Southern University when Dr. Jackson filled out the application for me to go to medical school. Medical school had already started two weeks earlier, but they accepted me. I had a nine-month-old baby, and I told them I didn't have any money. They said that they'd send me a ticket. I had one suitcase, and me and the baby went to medical school. After I had the baby, just before I went to medical school, her father went to jail. She was fifteen when he got out and she saw him for the first time.

They allowed me to stay in the dorm with the baby, and my roommate helped me with her. I was very active in politics and became the president of the class and after the first semester was able to move out of the dorm into an apartment. During that time I needed to put the baby in day care, and I didn't have any money so I asked for welfare. They assisted me as long as I volunteered to be on one of their boards. So I received eighty-one dollars in welfare in medical school and was able to get the child care. You do what you have to do.

I took the baby to the library. When I slept, she slept; when I got up, she got up. It wasn't a big deal because all the other students pitched in. I had an aunt in New Orleans that kept her for me during the third year because going from the basic science to the clinicals was a little hard, and then the fourth year, she moved back with me.

She was somebody for me to read to and examine. We studied in groups, so there was always somebody there to play with the baby. It really wasn't a big ordeal. She was a very easygoing baby, and that helped.

I came back to New Orleans to practice. I could have gone anywhere, but this is where I wanted to be. My practice is with geriatric patients and terminally ill AIDS patients—primarily the HIV-infected population that's secondary to substance abuse. This population is very difficult to get to, because most people don't understand them. I understand because I lived there. I've got hardened criminals that were murderers that are now doing arts and crafts, and they come here every day. A lot of doctors just don't want to do that. It's too difficult. I used to get through making rounds at three o'clock in the morning. It's better now. For the last couple of months, I've been triaging my inpatients to another physician because I need a rest.

In this clinic, we have social services and medicine. We teach by example. Living our lives in a style that will let people know you don't need a million dollars to be successful and happy, that you need to define your own standards and live by them. You need to look at failure as competition and not defeat because if you fail, it lets you know what you gotta do next time to be a little bit better. The challenge, the excitement is going against the odds and believing in something, having that tenacity, that endurance.

I made my clinic nonprofit so that we could get grant money to work with these patients and do some social services. But for two whole years we had to function with just me working and paying for all of this. I worked. I worked. My own bills were never over $1,000 a month, and they're still not. Light, gas, and water and a small house. If there's something I want, I can moonlight and make enough money on the weekends to buy me a car. I'm just not that interested.

Medicaid pays $14.28 a visit, and it doesn't pay for any social services. At least 50 percent of drug addicts come in with no insurance. Now we have so many homeless people. While everybody is getting rich, I got stuck with the other population. Right now I only see patients three days a week. Each day we see about forty people. Monday and Friday I work on grants. I developed a system to make this more cost effective. We have a nonprofit component, and we have a hospice. At least you get paid for service. If we've got thirty Medicare patients that are terminal, you'll get $89 a day per patient.

A female doctor has a tendency to deal with the total person, to get more involved. I don't care what I do in detoxing these people. Unless we change their lifestyle and give them something else to be about, then we are not doing anything. I have people that have been shooting drugs for twenty years that are now living normal lives. I'd trust them to come in and clean up my house.

I've heard from a lot of the younger females that I counsel or talk with that they feel like they're trapped, that the system is set up so that you're not allowed to out migrate. I believe that a lot of them are not equipped with the tools that they need to out migrate. Even though I lived in the projects and my mother was on welfare, my father was from an upper-middle-class family, and so his thing was education. He spoke about thirteen languages. He was a chef-cook, had finished college at nineteen. And so even though we were around everybody else, and did everything everybody else did, I knew I had to keep my grades up, and I did. It was that background that allowed me to use the only tool that I had, which was education, to escape. My parents had separated, but they never divorced, and my father would come around. He was a career military veteran and had been shell shocked —he was in Europe and in the Pacific. I think he stayed fourteen days on a raft after he was shot, so he really had a hard time, and they gave him his disability. My father was so good at his cooking profession that when he felt like working, he could. They would beg him to come cook at Commander's Palace, one of the big restaurants here in New Orleans.

You've got to see that there are ways out. These young women see that if you have more children, you get more money on welfare. I hate that. They've got to see something different. Here we teach them how to sew. I learned how to sew when I was young so that I always had nice clothes because I could make them myself. Set some standards for yourself, be in a position to do things for yourself, or do without. If you learn to do that, then you can make it.

There are a lot of young blacks in the ghetto that are talented, and if you don't get molded in one direction, you'll go into the other, so these are your drug dealers and your pimps. Look at Malcolm X.

It's all in your attitude. People take you the way you present yourself. We start them. If you have one pair of underclothes and one top clothes, wash that, keep it clean. It's better to go to the secondhand store and buy five outfits than to go to Krauss and buy one outfit. TV and advertisement are traps. If you're on welfare and you're buying your child a one-hundred-dollar pair of tennis shoes, that's a trap.

At this clinic we have a GED program and a training program. We train them to be certified nursing assistants so that they can work in the hospice program. Two have gone on to be LPNs. When they feel hopeless or helpless with their children, we get involved. We go to school with the children. Before we let them lose their children, we go to court and take the children home with us. All we're doing is getting back to basics. This is what has allowed the black families to survive. We got away from that, and we're just going back. A lot of the families can't do it because you have Grandmother, Mother, and baby—we have some where the grandmother's thirty.

I have four sisters, and they all pitched in when I came back to New Orleans. My daughter's twenty-two now. She's in Nashville. She was going to the university but decided she wanted to rest awhile. I'd say, "What do you want to be?" She'd say, "I want to be a mother." She wants to be able to stay at home with her children. The life that I had as a medical student and the rigors of all of that maybe affected her in some way. And sometimes when she was growing up, especially after she became an adult, she would throw that at my face, that I never had time for her. So that's one of the flaws of a single parent doing all of these things—how it's gonna affect the child. In retrospect, I don't see how I could have done it any differently.

My daughter was almost eighteen when I had another baby, and I had more time. I could see that resentment. Before she knew nothing else, she accepted her life as all-in-all okay, but now she's saying, "Look at the time you have with this baby. You can go to school with her, take her to the zoo." She has not said it to me, but she's said it to my sisters.

The father of my second child is in health administration. We've been together since '78. He's very much involved with her. Her birthday was on the fifteenth, and he planned the whole party. He works in Memphis. It's just a five-hour drive, a one-hour flight. We see each other every weekend or every other weekend. It stays good like that.

I've slowed down a lot since I had my younger daughter. I'll get up about seven, get her ready for school. At two-thirty, one of the employees or my sister usually will pick her up and bring her to the day care, which is right next door to my house, or she will stay at after care at the school. Sometimes she'll be in one of those moods where she wants to come here. We have a social area upstairs where the patients are doing arts and crafts, so she'll go up there. She'll play or listen to tapes. We have *Hooked on Phonics* and a whole lot of things. She knows all the patients. Let's say I'm having a late day, then I'll go home, pick her up, take her to the hospital, and make hospital rounds. If it's somebody she knows, she'll go into the rooms, or she'll stay at the nursing station. All the nurses know her. Then we'll come home, take a bath. She's in bed by nine o'clock. She loves to look at tapes. She has every Barney tape there is. Sometimes we'll read. We usually eat out at Shoney's, that's a quick restaurant, where you can get a four-course meal. If I'm having an early day, I cook. On a Saturday, I'll cook a whole lot of things, and then take it out of the freezer and put it in a microwave. The weekend is usually no different for my schedule except that I have to make hospital rounds, so usually somebody will come pick my daughter up—take her to dancing school or a basketball game or the movies. She has a schedule. And then on Sundays we get up and go to Mount Sinai Baptist Church. We get out by two o'clock, and we're either going to visit my other sister or back home and relaxing.

Church helps make things easier. When things look bad, I stand on faith. I've always been optimistic. When things look bad, then I got this saying, "A setback is a setup to get up and get started again." I sleep about two or three hours on the average. I'm fine after that. Sometimes I'll sleep three, four, or five hours. I look at the news all night if I'm home, so I know everything that's happening. Sometimes I decide I'm gonna stay in the whole weekend and sleep. I did that this past weekend. But then I wake up tired. If I don't have anything to do, I'm bored. I enjoy sewing. I made all the drapes in the house. I go to family groupings. I write poetry.

My foster child goes to day care, too. I had a nurse's aide that came to the house to help with Sara because she was crying so much and had seizures, and then we weaned her to day care and the nurse's aide would be there with her. But in the last two weeks, we're trying her at day care on her own. She's slow in development, but she is developing. She's not having as many seizures as she was, and she's doing fine. Initially, it was like twenty-four hours of crying, but then I stayed home with her one weekend, and I realized that she wasn't really crying, she was having seizures. I took her to the hospital and told them. They put her in the hospital and got her on medication. Her mother was on crack cocaine and the state was taking all six of her children. We figured that the young lady had not had a fair chance to rehabilitation. So my sister, who's a substance abuse counselor here and a social worker, went to court with her and asked the judge to let us keep the children, to give her time to go through a structured rehab before he took the children.

I See Horrible Callousness

Alice Dumont

She was born in 1933 and lives with her second husband in a large city in the Deep South. (See also pp. 102 and 271)

There were three things that girls could do. You could be a nurse, secretary, or teacher. I became a registered nurse. In my case, it was a calling. From the youngest age, I wanted to be a nurse. If I had come from a different background, been told that I was intelligent and capable, been encouraged to go to college, I might have gone to medical school, I can see myself doing it.

Now we are getting more women physicians, and mostly they are wonderful. I'm treated as a very special person by the women doctors and their staff. I've heard patients say that women doctors treat you with more dignity. You're listened to a lot more. You're not rushed.

Most of the time I've worked in the recovery room. Now I'm working in a surgical holding area. I'm rotated. Doctors are notorious for sexual harassment. There's a lot of nasty jokes, a lot of talk about your breasts—"What size?" And, "Great boobs," things like that. One instance, this guy had done breast augmentation on one woman. He came out and called me over and said he did a real good job but they weren't as nice as mine. In the last five years they haven't been doing this because some of the doctors who have made remarks to the nurses have been written up. It's turned in—the doctor is called on the carpet.

Most of the younger male doctors are very, very different. They don't feel like they're gods; they're human beings who have a degree in medicine. They're in it because they care. I think they're better trained in the psychological part of their job.

The hospital I work at is a women's hospital. I see a lot of black women who are raped time and time again because they're living in a horrible section. Not only that, these poor women have no phone. They know that they can rape them and get away with it. They don't have air-conditioning. It's hot. They leave the windows up. If they put them down, they smother. The doors don't lock properly. Some of them have been raped two or three times, probably by the same guy.

Kate Merrill

She was born in 1945 and lives in Southern California. She is a registered nurse and runs a clinic at a large urban hospital. (See also p. 280)

When I first went to nursing school, if the doctor came to the nurse's station, the nurse got up and let the doctor sit down so he could chart. This was in 1980. There are a lot of older doctors who are still, "I'm the doctor, you're the nurse." But the younger guys are, "I'm Michael, you're Kate." They look at you as an integral part of the team. They discuss treatment plans with you. Forty is on the cusp, but the guys who are about thirty-five, thirty-six are really pretty together. It's very encouraging to me, and they make up for the other guys.

When I first became a nurse, some of the hardest people on the nurses were the women doctors. They were terrified that they would be mistaken for nurses and wanted to distance themselves. Patients would still call them nurses sometimes. It's classic. If you break out of a group, you don't want to be identified with that group. That's changed now pretty much.

Another thing that has changed is the kids coming into the clinic. Thirteen-, fourteen-year-old girls are sexually active. I see a lot of young pregnant girls. I see more children and babies as young as a year old who are abused, with broken bones, fractures. A lot of women come in all smashed up, black eye, something broken. Some of the older doctors never say, "How did this happen to you?" cause they don't want to know. They don't want to report it. The younger doctors all ask, and then we report it.

When I first started working here, I saw maybe one gunshot wound every three months, and now I get two or three a day. I see horrible callousness in some of these young people, a disregard for human life and a hopelessness. These gang kids don't think they're going to live past twenty or twenty-five, so they don't care, and they have no skills and no education. A lot of gang kids have a working parent, or a working mother. There are many single-parent households—five-feet-tall mothers with big, six-feet-tall, fourteen-year-old kids that they can't control. I think a lot of these mothers are scared of these boys, and they don't know what to do. They just come in and beg us, "Tell them to get out of the gang, tell them this, tell them that, he won't listen to me."

The future looks dismal. How do you tell a kid to go to work at McDonald's for minimum wage when he can make two hundred dollars in a couple of hours dealing drugs? I don't know what the answer is.

Kathleen Ryan

She was born in Poughkeepsie, New York, in 1948 and is the director of a human services agency. (See also pp. 130, 281 and 479)

For the last twenty years, I've worked with young people in group homes, schools, institutions, directed street programs. If there were more men in the human service field, salaries would go up. As long as women are continuing to do the work, it doesn't seem to have as much importance.

Most of the youngsters that I've worked with have been male, yet the staff has been predominantly female. Most of the programs I've worked in, you get the kids that are truant in school, they've run away, they're abusing drugs, alcohol. They're really sexually active. Most of the girls have had problems around sex. That's how girls act out—prostitution or promiscuity—especially girls that are coming from alcoholic or abusive homes. Boys act out by being violent. Yet that's shifted over the years. There's a lot more aggression by young women than there ever was.

Twenty years ago kids were being brought in for stealing a car, or burglarizing the neighborhood candy store or maybe acts of vandalism. Now they're coming in for beatings and mutilations and maybe killing family members, really sadistic, violent crimes. The age has dropped. Willy Boskett in the seventies murdered two people. I think that was the beginning of fourteen-year-olds committing murder. Well, it's down to ten-year-olds now. Kids are becoming younger and younger in facilities for treatment. We're also seeing an increase in the number of three- to five-year-olds that need placement because of their acting-out behavior. It's come up at several meetings that they are showing suicidal tendencies; they are setting fires. Seven seems to be the age that you get them into the mental health system, and that age is dropping. There are a couple of facilities now that are targeting their programs for five-year-olds, and that's really sad. Years ago there were specific problems—teen pregnancy, a runaway kid, an alcoholic kid. You get kids today, and it's not like their homes were just alcoholic. There's battering, there's sexual abuse; the problems are multifaceted.

Today there's rarely a true alcoholic. There's dual, drugs and alcohol. I think economic situations add, too. These kids are coming from homes where the problems are just so much more than what they used to be. It's all levels, white, black, low-income, middle-income, upper-income. The programs I've worked in have tended to be in lower-income programs. It's hidden more in middle class and upper class. People go to private treatment, private psychiatrists. There's certainly enough battering and abuse in upper-class households, too.

I'm a real strong believer that the violence on TV and movies is really desensitizing people. The teenage boys I work with don't flinch—you chop somebody's head off and pull out their tongue, and this is like okay, fine. I have seen kids—it's, "You won't give me your five dollars, I'll kill you." The value of human life seems nonexistent. I believe that the media does play into that. We're bombarded with it, and it has a real strong influence on the behavior, particularly of young men. I watch a group of teenagers after some particularly violent movie, the way they play it out, beating one another up; it's no big deal. Kids are disposable now. They get to an age, can't handle them, you throw them out. There's a lot of throwaway kids on the street. It tends to be around the fourteen-, fifteen-year-old age group.

There's a huge difference between a ten-year-old today and twenty years ago. A ten-year-old today is fifteen, twenty. They know as much, and they're out on their own. I don't know if we've made much of a difference in the programs that we've offered. We need to take a holistic approach; you can't do this piecemeal, band-aid shit anymore. It's like cancer, and we say, "Okay, we'll patch you up," and then we pull the money. You put a kid away for three years and they're not rehabilitated. The system isn't designed to do it. It's a sin when you get a ten-year-old that goes into placement and comes out at thirteen and still can't read or write. What did you do to this kid for three years? We have to start to really look earlier. Child abuse is far more prevalent than we care to look at, and we don't deal with that. I think the intentions are good and we try like hell, but we're not doing anything. It's frustrating, and for me it's always been very sad to see the kids' lives, to see a ten-year-old and think what his future is going to be like without some intervention.

I've Never, Never Worn Pants
to Teach

Elizabeth Russell

She was in her early sixties when interviewed and living with her husband in a rural area in the Deep South. She was a high school teacher for many years, went back to school to get her Ph.D., and is now a school administrator.

When I taught high school in the sixties, it was the golden age. We weren't paid a lot, but we worked hard, and we were respected. People appreciated what you did. The students worked, and they did well. You felt good, and they felt good. We didn't have this complaining, antagonism, and hostility that we have today, and we didn't have all the social problems.

In the sixties the students were neat and tidy—skirts and blouses for the girls and trousers and shirts for the boys, and now they wear anything and everything. There is a movement to go to uniforms. I don't like it. I think we need a dress code and that the dress code should start with teachers. We wouldn't have thought of going to school like these people do today—cut-off blue jeans, jogging suits, awful. They do not look professional.

I still dress the same way as when I started teaching or even more so. We wore skirts and blouses and dresses and blazers. I used to have a platform in my classroom for my desk and I had four-inch heels, and I jumped up and down off that platform every day. High heels definitely imparted more authority. We need that decorum and civility and that dignity, and that's what we've lost. It reflects society. In 1960, when I was in the city and I went downtown, I wore heels and gloves to the department store.

I've never, never worn pants to teach, ever. I always wear hose and no sandals, even in hot weather. We didn't used to have air-conditioning. It was awful in August and September. The perspiration would just drip down. You couldn't go anywhere after school. You had to come home and take a bath. If the teaching profession were male, there'd have been air-conditioning many years ago in these schools. The offices are always air-conditioned. Most administrators are men. Now the classrooms are air-conditioned here, but in a lot of places no. It's inhumane.

In those days I was naive in a lot of ways. In the mid-sixties I had a female student who was an A student, and we had a college scholarship offer and this fellow got it and he was a C student, and I could not understand. It was just out-and-out sex discrimination, and I didn't realize it at the time. As time goes on, you reflect on these things, but I was just blind to it all.

You didn't realize at the time that you did not have the opportunities you thought you had. I had taught history for years, and I had chaired the department for close to ten years. I did very well. The school principal had his daughter moved into my class, so that tells you something. They decided that they would hire someone to be a history supervisor part of the day and a teacher the rest of the day. I felt certainly I would be in line for that. Well, they brought a man in as supervisor who was not even in the system, and he had been fired, I was told, from another school. I figured that there was no future for me there, so I moved to another school district.

I taught, and then in the early seventies they approached me about doing public relations and working on curriculum. It was a federally funded job. When the grant ran out, they put me back in the classroom because they said they didn't have enough money, but the man working on the project stayed. I objected, and they rehired me for another year, and then I was back in the classroom again. I hired a lawyer and said "sex discrimination," but I didn't win. I filed with the Equal Employment Opportunity Commission. I went down and talked to the fella there, and he said, "You should have been a lawyer," but nothing ever happened. "We're under court order for integration," they told me, "but that does not apply to gender."

Even now in this district we have thirteen schools and only three female principals. A lot of women don't have the self-confidence, but more are becoming interested and are applying. There are no males entering the teaching profession to speak of because of the salaries, so it's going to be a matter of supply and demand eventually. Teaching does not appeal to a lot of people. It's not just the salaries but all the problems—the dysfunctional families, all the paperwork, the federal and state mandates.

We have parents who are fighting over children. One of them has custody, and the other comes to get the child at school and threatens the office help. You could have a child kidnapped. You have to be very careful to find out who the guardians are and who you may release the child to. Academic time is eroded taking care of all the social problems. Drug education, sex education, AIDS education, safety education, violence in the schools.

I'm a central office instructional supervisor. Anyone who has a complaint at the elementary level can come to me if they can't get satisfaction at the school, so I listen to parents a whole lot. I also am dealing with a lot of federal regulations. If there is anything that interferes with learning for a child, you have to make special accommodations within the classroom. If a child qualifies for special ed—physically handicapped, emotionally disturbed, regardless of what it is, if the parents want them "mainstreamed," then they are put in the regular classroom part of the day. The normal, regular kids are neglected nowadays. Everybody has rights, and you've got to cater to them. Anybody who has anything that substantially interferes with learning, whether it be diabetes, overweight, trouble breathing, dyslexia, ADHD (attention deficit disorder with hyperactivity—that's what we've been seeing the most of lately), you have to make accommodations within the classroom for these students. If you have a child who weighs two hundred pounds, then we have to get a desk to accommodate him. It's gotten to the point of ridiculous. And I'm just trying to keep us out of hot water. All this has to go through a process. The paperwork is horrendous.

It's very difficult to accommodate all these individuals within a classroom setting. Some of it may be good in the long run in that it maybe forces teachers to use some different methods to get across to the students, but on the other hand it is burdening teachers. We have more and more to contend with. If you are in the classroom and you think a child is being abused, you are bound by law to report that.

We had a case of a child last year, his mother couldn't understand why he wasn't performing, and then the teachers found out that he was spending the night out in the car. His mother had a boyfriend; she wouldn't let him in the house sometimes. These are things that you spend your time on. And then divorces and remarriages and fighting with their stepbrother or stepsister. Children not fed properly sometimes. All of this affects teachers profoundly.

We have parent conferences, and we have good response, but the very ones that need to be there often are the ones that don't show up. A lot of the parents now are uneducated. Seventy-five percent of the children are on free lunches. This is a pretty poverty-stricken area. Everybody didn't used to go to school. People would drop out and go to work on the farm, and now we keep everybody in school or try to.

We went through school integration in 1970. It was very difficult. We were not prepared for the hostility, the boycotts. The white parents would keep the students at home. People kept thinking, "We're going to be able to stop this," and one year we started school late because they were going to court. During integration there were more teachers on tranquilizers than probably at any other time in their lives, and some quit, and many just weathered the storm. I had a back problem at the time. The stress and strain took its toll physically. We had one white teacher who was threatened, but for the most part we accomplished this peacefully.

We were not prepared for the different culture. This is a classic experience: We integrated mid-year, 1970, and we had books that were transferred to us from the students at the black school that came to the white school. I had one student, and she didn't have any books. I said, "Well, why don't you have any books?" She grinned and said, "Well, I wasn't in school last semester; I was having a baby." We never had that. If our kids were out, they were out a whole year. They never came semester by semester. Before if they got pregnant, we didn't even know a lot of times because they just dropped out. It's become an open kind of thing. Some of the teachers have feared having to deliver a baby at school cause they come right up until they give birth. It's bound to affect their concentration and their academics.

People who can afford it send their kids to private school, and it skims the cream off the top. We've still got some good students, but it does take a lot of them away. Even hard-working people like teachers will work to send theirs to private school. I don't think it's so much racial as they want their children to have the best education possible. The public schools were excellent, and they have gone downhill. You have stabbings and that sort of thing. You want your children in a safe atmosphere. In many cases, the public schools are mainly black. Our population for the whole district is probably about fifty–fifty. And the sad thing is that they throw money at poor performance. If your test scores are low, then you qualify for more federal funding. We are a poverty area. About seventy percent of our students are on Free Lunch. Many of our students are from second- and third-generation welfare families. So it's a cycle that's hard to break. The public school teachers in a lot of ways are missionaries now.

The black and white students go their separate ways; that may change. We haven't had a whole lot of friction that I've seen lately. There's resentment on the part of the blacks; they think they're not getting what they should—they have been enslaved, and there needs to be reparation. And then there is resentment on the part of the whites that we are paying the price for a lot of this. We're paying taxes. We pay health insurance. We go to the doctor, to the hospital, and we've got to pay. If they're on Medicaid, they just go. They get scholarships. The National Merit Scholarships—they don't have to do as well. They don't have to pay tuition in college. There's a lot of resentment.

We have a lady in our office who went to work so she could send her daughter to college, but the blacks in her category, they get a free ride. Teachers want their children to go to college, and they're working hard and there's no help for them, and our wages are at poverty level now. I think we start about fifteen thousand dollars.

And then the other problem is the teachers. Under court order we must have so much racial balance, and a lot of people think that they're substandard. We have white ones that are substandard, but not as many as the blacks.

When I started teaching, I had good friends in the teaching profession from the same social background. A lot of it was second income and insurance because if you have a teaching credential, then you have something to fall back on. Most of us thought we would get married and not work all of our lives. And all that's changed. Now a lot of them are more working-class. I think of the students I taught, and many of them are in law, banking, accounting, doctors, all kinds of fields that we never would have dreamed of. There are many, many more opportunities for women.

I don't recommend teaching to a lot of these young women now. I try to point out what all they're going to have to face. You're burned out now in a short time. Even though it may seem grim, we have lots of dedicated, good people, and we have managed in spite of it all.

My Mother Said You Should Be
Equipped to Do Something

Suzanne Havercamp

She was born in 1939 and lives in a small, upstate New York town with her husband. (See also pp. 117 and 302)

I majored in elementary education. I really didn't know what I wanted to do. I wasn't very career oriented. My mother said you should be equipped to do something. She looked at it as an insurance policy. I decided on elementary education because it was one of the things that was offered at my college, and I didn't want to switch schools. I don't think I was ready at nineteen, when you had to declare your major, to know what I wanted, what my life work was going to be. There are some people today and even then who probably knew from the day they were born that they wanted to be a physician or an attorney. I was not that directed an individual.

I taught two years before I was married, and then I continued to substitute teach. I have three sons, twenty-eight, twenty-five, and twenty-two, and I had my name in a couple of school systems, so I worked quite regularly as my children went to school, which was very nice. When they were very young, I'd go in two, three times a week, and then I took some permanent positions.

It was out of choice that I taught part-time—there were days I couldn't teach because I was very heavily committed to the volunteer sector. I felt I had a duty to pay back. Life's been good to me; I'd like to be able to do something to enrich this community, to make it better. I was involved in a lot of different organizations. In my younger days, the Junior League took a lot of my time. I was a board member. Later, I was president of the garden club.

When we started to have a family there was no nursery school in this area, and we needed one desperately. So myself and two of my dear friends had a serious discussion about this, and we decided that we had to do something about it, so we started a nursery school. We established it, and we hired a teacher-director, and we found a space for it, and we got the furniture and the supplies. That took a lot of time.

I've often felt I've had the best of all worlds because if I wanted to work, I worked. I didn't have to ask my husband for money to go out and buy his birthday present. I could be financially independent to a certain degree. That was very nice. I could be heavily involved in the volunteer sector; I could be home if a child was sick. I could say, "No, I'm not going to teach today."

Josie Gilchrist Anderson

She lives in Mississippi, where she was born in 1946. She has been separated from her husband for many years. (See also p. 207)

My first job was in 1969 at a junior high school in Detroit. I remember that vividly. I had seventh graders that first year, and I think the next year I had eighth and ninth. I enjoyed it, but it was really traumatic for a while. That's one of the reasons I decided to go back and get a master's. I said, if I'm going to stay in a school setting, maybe the one-on-one would be better. Students don't particularly like grammar, and they don't want to do writing or research. One of the kids said to me the first year, "You better go on back to Mississippi because we don't do homework up here. I don't know where you come from giving all this homework."

The socioeconomics of the neighborhood was low. It was an all-black school, probably 99.9 percent. The only integration was faculty and staff. It was probably de facto segregation, in that you went to school in the neighborhood that you lived in. The majority of the kids wanted to learn, and you'd get a few bad ones who are disruptive and create the problems. Even then we had security guards in the Detroit schools. They would try to station a security guard or a school community relations person near the fire alarms. If the kids decided they didn't want to have class today, they'd try to get to a fire alarm and pull it and then everybody had to go out of the building. Some of them would be bold enough to start a fire. Some would throw entire bookcases of books out of the third-floor window if they had a substitute teacher. They would take the teacher's purse, throw it out the window, whatever.

One day a student in my class came to the door and said to me, "Please don't come out here in the hallway because that girl that you took the candy from yesterday is mad with you, and she has a knife, and she's been saying that she's going to get you." So I told the principal. He asked her, "Did you bring that knife to use on Miss Gilchrist?"

"No sir, I didn't bring it for her, but I will use it on her if I have to." I couldn't believe my ears!

What led to this was we were giving the California achievement test the day before, and she had a bag of candy. As I was passing out the tests, I asked her to put it away, and she did for the moment but then continued to give candy to students. Finally, I took the bag and told her she could get it at the end of the day. Instead, when the test was over, she kept coming to my room asking for the candy, and I said no. Then she would kick the door and use profane language. I told her if she did that anymore, I was going to throw all of it in the trash. She continued kicking the door and cursing, and I just threw the candy in the wastebasket, and I told her, "Don't bother about coming back at the end of the day." So then the next day is when she had the knife.

I would stand at my door. If you did not have textbook, pencil, pen, tablet, you couldn't come in. I saw no point in letting people in my room empty-handed because I knew they were coming to play, so they had to go back to their locker and get their supplies. Of course, the assistant principal told me I couldn't do that. He said, "When you grew up, kids were told to do something, and they did it, but these children aren't like that." And I said, "Well, it's because we allow them to be like that, and I have no intention of allowing them to be that way in my room. They can either conform, or I can go home." He said, "I just hate for you to be so young and get your work record messed up, so I'm going to try to work with you, and you just gotta learn that these kids aren't like you were."

There's so much leniency and taking the discipline out of the school, and there's the lack of community. When I was growing up, anybody in the neighborhood could make you mind. Miss Lucy down the street could say, "Josie, you need to do so and so." She better not tell my mama that she had spoken to me about something and that I didn't obey—then I was going to get it again. My mother would also go to school trying to check on us.

After I moved back here in 1975, I taught at North Natchez High. The student body was not integrated. The kids here seemed to be a bit more intact in terms of following rules and regulations. We had our problems, but they were not as far-fetched. Not that all the kids were bad in Detroit; it was just a very few. And then, too, I may not have gotten the brunt of the problems here in Natchez because I was the drug education teacher-counselor.

Three years later I started to teach English, speech, and literature at Natchez Junior College. I taught there for six years, and I've been here at Copiah-Lincoln Community College since 1984. I'm a counselor. I do academic advisement, testing, recruiting, job placement assistance.

Mimi Miller

She was born in 1945 in North Carolina and now lives in Natchez, Mississippi. (See also pp. 79, 130 and 272)

I was teaching eighth-grade English and social studies in Mount Holly, North Carolina, the first year they integrated, in 1968–69. I don't remember any particular horrible difficulties between those white and African-American children. There were funny things, like catching on to cultural nuances. I would be teaching, and I would hear an African-American child say something like, "He called my mama name." And I would turn around and say, "Huh? What?" One of the worst, degrading things you could do to somebody was to call their mother's first name. It probably was related to the fact that many of their mothers were domestic servants and were called by their first names at work. This would go on all day long; if you turned your back to the classroom, five women's first names would come out, and then the other child would get really upset, "Miss Miller, Miss Miller, he call my mama name." And then you'd have to calm that down. I think I was in school three weeks before I could figure out what in the world this mama's name thing was.

The second year I taught school, my husband went back to college at Chapel Hill, and I taught at an all-black school in Durham, North Carolina. There were two of us, and we were the first white teachers at the school. That was probably the most fascinating experience of my whole life. It was a great year. I have to be honest, I had difficulties at first telling them apart. I had five classes, and this stream of black faces came through all day, and I didn't have blond hair, red hair, brown hair, blue eyes or brown eyes or green eyes. It just looked like a sea of black to me, and I thought I will never know their names. Within three weeks each was an individual to me. Then I would go out in the hall between classes, and I couldn't understand what was being said because the dialect was so strong, but eventually I understood. And then the children were so fascinated by me. I couldn't go down the lunchroom line without them all wanting to feel my hair, which was a funny experience at first. They would call me Pin Nose. I have a short nose, and I would go into my classroom and they would have taken the chalk and drawn a long nose across three black boards and turned back around its side for pin nose. And once again I had a whole classroom of mama names going from eight o'clock in the morning until three o'clock in the afternoon. They were typical eighth graders. It's just that instead of doing things that Anglo-Saxon eighth graders might have done, that mama name was a big thing.

I realized very early on that standardized tests were very prejudiced against not just African-Americans but poor people. They might show a picture of a refrigerator, and you had to identify what room it went into, and a lot of African-Americans and poor whites may have had their refrigerators on the back porch. I would look at their test scores from the first grade on up, and I could see that something wasn't right because I had those kids every day and I knew they were brighter than those tests were indicating. They've made improvements in the tests, and I don't believe in getting rid of them.

At that African-American school in Durham the principal, James Schooler, was brilliant, a great administrator. When he finished high school in 1930 or so, there were no professions other than teaching open to African-American men if they went to college in the South. It was a ghetto school with some affluent children whose parents taught at an African-American university in Durham. He had such standards; he was such a stickler on things. He had a practice that would stop a child in his tracks. If a child was doing something wrong down at the end of the hall, he could toss his gigantic key ring down to the end of the hall and it would land at the child's feet, and that child knew to pick up that key ring and return it to him.

If a child wrote on one of the desks in your classroom, it was your responsibility to get it off that desk, to sand it and refinish it. He would walk into a classroom with coat hangers and rake behind closets looking for trash. When we left school every day, every window shade in the whole school had to be exactly the same length on the window. At first I thought, "This is the strangest person I have ever worked for," and then one afternoon he said, "Mrs. Miller, some of the things I'm doing may seem strange to you, but a lot of our students come from very disorderly households, and I want my school to stand for order and precision in this neighborhood. Children need this."

He believed that teachers were to teach, and if a child was a problem, the child came to him. We had some violence but not as much as in other schools that I'm familiar with. I taught in a private school one year, and Shepherd Junior High was far better administered in terms of what was expected of students, what behavior was not permitted. He ran a very tight ship, and if children were a problem, parents were called to come to school before the children were allowed back in classrooms. Oh, yes, the parents came.

They Don't Care
about the Little Guy

Anna Davis

"I was born in Poughkeepsie in 1941, the youngest of six children; I had five brothers. My mother was Irish Catholic and very, very staunch in the church. I graduated from high school, and my father wanted me to go to college. I got married at eighteen instead, which was a big mistake. I had that fairy tale idea. I wanted to be married and have four children, stay home and raise my kids." (See also pp. 78 and 103)

My son was sixteen months old and my daughter was about six when my husband said he didn't want to be married anymore. We hadn't gotten along for a long time, so it wasn't any big heartbreak. We were living in Colorado, so I came back east with my two kids, and he stayed out there. I stayed at my mother's until I got on my feet, got an apartment. I basically raised the kids by myself because twenty-five dollars a week is all I got from him.

I worked at Western Printing in the bindery. I used to drop my daughter off at my mother's house at six in the morning—I got up at five—and she would see that she got to school. I then dropped my son off at my mother-in-law's and got to work by seven.

My first paycheck was forty-nine dollars clear for the week. That was 1966. I had to pay my mother-in-law to babysit. I had rent, lights, telephone, food, toys for the kids. I managed, but I did work as much overtime as I could. When my kids were about 3 and 8 years old, I used to work seven days a week a lot of times.

When I first went to work at Western Printing, I enjoyed getting up in the morning and going to work. I fed the covers into the machine, and I checked the books, did quality control. It was hard work, but we were like a big family. We kidded around and we laughed and we joked and we enjoyed our day, and we still did the work. It was family owned, and if you had a problem at home, you could go to your boss and say, "Look, I can't come in until eight o'clock tomorrow morning, I have such and such I've got to take care of."

In the early years a man automatically started with more than a woman. They would tell you that. I started with $1.91 an hour, and the men started with $2.25. We were programmed at that time that that's the way it was. We didn't think about it. It didn't matter I was supporting a family; because I was a woman, I got less.

There was one woman who was upset because she had worked there five years, and her son came to work, and he was making more than her right off the bat. She's got the experience and the time, but he was a man so he got more money coming in the door. For doing nothing, just walking in the door. Maybe ten years after I started working there, they did change. It went by the type of job.

The women would grumble because all the men, like the operators, made good money, and all they did was push buttons. The men stood around and they'd start the machine up and turn the machine off, and maybe if something broke, they'd fix it, but basically that's all they did. They drove the trucks and the forklifts, while we were packing and lugging boxes and sweating to death. And they got paid more.

Those guys were crude. If young girls would come into work, they would stare at them and whistle and hoot and holler and act like idiots. Now we're going back to 1966 when men were still acting like animals. They weren't doing it to be malicious. They thought it was cute. I think the men in today's workplace know better because you can get them on sexual harassment. If anybody did anything to you at IBM, where I worked later on, and you reported it, they were out the door. No problem.

Eventually Western Printing was taken over by Mattel, and it started to go downhill. Even though we had a union contract, the management would always try to overstep its bounds. Nobody likes to be treated like you're a slave. You'd get out at three o'clock, and at quarter to three, they would say, "Well, you're staying till seven tonight," and I'd say, "No, not me, I'm outta here at three." They'd say, "Well, I'm telling you to stay," and I said, "Well, I'm telling you I'm leaving," and I'd leave. They gave me three days off because I wouldn't stay one night and work overtime. I said, "Fine. Well, now you don't have me for three days," and I left. It's like they cut off their nose to spite their face, but I'm just too stubborn. I won't work under those conditions. I don't care how it affects me. But if you asked me like a human being, I'll do whatever I can to help you. Of course, a lot of people reacted the same way, and so it really got bad towards the end. But it's like that now in all companies. They know that you need them more than they need you, and they treat you that way.

Mattel got rid of all the key people in charge and brought in all of their own people who didn't have the first clue how to make a book, but they were in charge. I had a guy pick up a book that had a blade mark on it; once that blade mark's on that book, there's no way you can get it off, but he said to me, "You have to send this through again and get that mark off of there." They would say stupid things like that because they had no idea. Another time, a book is already trimmed and in a box. He picks it up and he breaks it, the pages fly out, and he says to me, "You're going to have to send this through the binder again." I said, "You can't send that through the binder again." So he says, "Well, what do we do with it?" I said, "You see that garbage can over there? That's where you put it." They didn't have a clue. And yet they walked in there, "You, you, you, you, we don't need you. You can leave now." That's how crude they were. There was no "Gee, I'm sorry, we have to let you go." One man had thirty-five years in there, and they walked up to him and said, "Clean out your desk. You're no longer needed." The man was in shock. Thirty-five years, and that was what he got! Every week, they would go to different areas and just clean out all the people. So after Mattel had it for a couple years, it started going down the tubes. They sold it at a loss, and then they wrote it off. Companies do this all the time so that they have a write-off, a tax loss. They don't care about the little guy that's in there working his butt off all day long. They're just trying to make an extra buck for themselves, and look how many people's lives they ruin in the process.

I had worked at Western Printing for sixteen years when they closed the plant. So I went to IBM and worked there for ten years. We did everything concerning the chips for computers—exposing, developing, aligning, inspecting them. You know the problems with IBM, so I took the buyout because five years down the road, I collect my retirement, plus I got a buyout, plus I keep my benefits for life. I wouldn't be surprised if they close the plants around here. So now I'm working third shift at the post office. It's temporary, but hopefully I can take civil service tests and eventually get in full-time.

Even at IBM—and they do a lot of good things for their people—nobody cares. IBM is very good at lying to you. They will tell you for months and months and months, "Oh, you don't have to worry, nothing's going to change, your job is secure," and then turn right around and say, "Well, sorry, we gotta let you go." You find out that everything they told you was a fairy tale, so nobody believes them anymore. But I have to say that they have been more fair than a lot of other companies as far as severance money and things like that. They didn't have to do a lot of that. But again a lot of that stuff is a write-off for them. It looks good in print and everybody thinks, "Oh, what a great company."

Right now they're hiring temps to do the jobs that they let all these other people go for because they don't have to pay them benefits, they don't have to pay them as much, and they can let them go anytime they want without any notice. They kept people with two years seniority and let people with twenty years go. Somebody with twenty years, they're paying them much more, but they've gotten rid of talent. They could save money in other ways besides getting rid of their help, because you never saw a company waste more money than IBM. Everybody used to say, how did they ever get this big? They must have been okay in the beginning. They'll pay you double time to go in there on Sunday. They would just say there's overtime. If you want to go in, you go in. They might have thirty people sitting around making double time, but there's only one job to run. I said to my manager, "Why would you ask people to come in if you don't have any work?" He said, "Well, because if a job does come in, we want the people here to do it so it can get out the door." I said, "But why would you bring in twenty people when you only need five." "Well, " he says, "that's the way it's done." That may not be logical, but they did it all the time.

They have people in management that shouldn't be in management. They don't know how to deal with, talk to, or motivate people, and how they get that job and stay there is beyond me.

Then they went to this thing where they wanted everybody to have a two-year degree. I didn't have the energy to go to school and work and go home and do homework for four or five hours. And I said, "No, I'm not going," and they said, "Well, you won't be promoted." All these people would go to school half a day and work half a day. It's hard to come in after lunch and start to set up a machine. A lot of them would come back and not do anything. And I said to my second-line manager, "Look, you got people like me in there that are running everything, and then when they come back from school, they get the promotions. It's not right. I was brought up if you work hard, you move up. I don't want you to promote me into anything that I haven't earned and I don't deserve." But that's exactly what they do.

And how about Akers? He was chairman of the board. He gets himself a thirty-six percent salary increase. Now, that's a pretty good chunk of change when you're making about two million a year. But when you read a piece in the paper, it said, "Oh, Akers gave a chunk of his pay back." Yes, he did, but people don't realize that he already got himself thirty-six percent in the first place. But now he's a big shot because out of the goodness of his heart he's gonna give some back. He's still making $1.5 million a year. That's not bad on two million dollars. I'll take that. But me, I'm working every day, I'm making it possible for him to get that kind of money—I get five percent. They told everybody times were tough: "You're only gonna get a five percent raise this year." And you wonder why people say the hell with it. It's not just IBM, it's all over.

Now I'm at the post office. I hate it, but I have no choice because where am I going to get another job? It's like a big warehouse, and all the mail comes in, and it gets sorted and then shipped back out to wherever it's supposed to go. You've got crude people—the language, the swearing—you have to turn your ears off to it. You've got people that are in supervisory positions, I don't think some of them have the intelligence past the fifth grade. Anybody with intelligence wouldn't take the job. Thank God, they have a union, or they would be burying people. They would work them into the ground.

I could wear the same clothes for a week if I wanted to at IBM. Down there, you come home, you're dirty. It's just a big, huge room. It's open, the ceilings are high, and you've got the docks, and the trucks back in, and you smell the exhaust. Right now I sort the letters manually because I broke a bone in my foot, so I have a sit-down job. I am training for working on a machine where you just key in the zip codes. It's cleaner, but it's all boring. You don't really need a brain to do anything down there. They could have a robot come in and throw mail and they do have some people in there that don't have a brain. Working at IBM, it's high tech—you have to think, make decisions. At this job, you just need two hands.

Why Are You Doing
That Kind of Work?

Maria Rodriguez

She lives in Los Angeles where she was born in 1935. She is twice divorced and now works for an animal rights group. (See also pp. 91 and 284)

I worked at two different banks. I started out in bookkeeping. I did some teller work, some safe deposit work, and then I went into an officer position. I also worked in loans and as an operations officer. I was working at this one branch in Brentwood, and they used to bring a lot of college graduates into a management program, and I trained them. They were going to move into management positions and make a lot more money than I was, and here I am training them and I'm not in a management position. It used to bother me. They were all men, and I resented it.

I did a good job—in my working career I've always gotten excellent reviews—and at first I didn't say anything. Then I started saying things to my boss, and she—it was a woman—said, "Well, that's your job. You have to train them. There's not too much I can do about it." And I said, "Well, then this job should be reclassified or have a different title, and different pay should be given to this position." She didn't say much. She probably felt if I really didn't like it, I could always find another job.

It was not like I could just walk out of a job, because I was raising a child. So I always had to think twice, and I'd have to back down, and I really hated it because I never back down from things.

I remember one case in particular. I trained this person, and he stayed on in our branch, and we kind of became friends. There were certain aspects of his job that I helped him with, and because he was a man, he was making more money than me. They really, really used to discriminate a lot against women in banking. I was very unhappy and spoke up about it. I said, "I found out he's making more than I am. He's been here a few months, and I don't think that's fair." They didn't care. They didn't want to hear about it. Nowadays people wouldn't hesitate to file some kind of a discrimination claim, but at that time people didn't do that. I didn't even think about it. This was previous to 1970, before the women's movement.

There's still some discrimination out there as far as how high a level women can go in some areas, but I definitely think things have gotten better. You see a lot more women doctors now; there are women astronauts.

Isadora Damon

She was born in 1936 and grew up in Virginia. She lives in Brooklyn, does housework, and is African-American.

"I came to New York when I was twenty-three because there wasn't no work in the segregated South. I always wanted to be a nurse, but being the oldest, I only got to go to school on the days I didn't have to stay home and help Mother with the children." (See also p. 285)

The first time I came to New York, I slept in for about a half a year. I think it was in 1958. That was the worstest time, oh, my god! I got every Thursday and every other Sunday off. I was making about a hundred dollars a month. The people was nice, but two kids to take care of, clean, cook—oh, boy! In that time when you did housework, you had everything to do, windows, whatever—you had to do it at a dollar and a quarter an hour. It was rough, it really was. The days were much longer. You would maybe get in by eight in the morning and out by five-thirty or six in the evening. That's right. And then long in that time, I don't know why, but people didn't trust the black people; somebody always behind you. Now I'm at people's homes all day by myself and I got everybody's keys. Work has improved, oh, yes. I think that people changed; they changed a whole lot.

Yolanda Casarez

She was born in El Paso, Texas, in 1950 and lives in Los Angeles with her husband and fifteen-year-old daughter. She works in a factory. (See also pp. 108 and 305)

Mostly, I'm an electronic assembler. Sometimes it's enjoyable, like right now I'm prepping the parts. That's okay because it seems to make the day go faster, but when I'm doing just one type of job like soldering, it makes the day drag. I've been doing that for about seventeen, eighteen years. I work for Teledyne. Fifteen years for the same company. Before this job, the company I was working for merged with another company, and they moved to Orange County. They just laid off everybody except whoever wanted to move with the company. The people that went with the company were kept for about a year, and then when they merged with a company from Ohio, they just laid off everybody that was there because they brought their people from Ohio. That's around the time my daughter was going to be born; I took the layoff. Then I got this job.

Right now, it's very stressful at Teledyne because we're just sitting there waiting to see are we going to get laid off. Today we had a meeting with our boss, and we got a new contract. At least we have a job for one more year. The atmosphere at work has changed very much. There's been a lot of friction, conflict. Everybody wants to do what you're doing just to be sure that they have a job. Everybody wants to be boss. Some of the girls want to tell me what to do instead of my supervisor telling me.

Teddy Rod

She was born in a small, predominantly Hispanic farm town in Colorado and lives in Denver with her husband, who is retired from the post office.

"I was born in 1936 at home, delivered by a midwife. My father's family comes from Spain, and my mother's, I think they come from New Mexico. My father was a farmer. We are very very strong Catholics. I graduated from twelfth grade, and it was very hard because elementary school in our little farm town went to the eighth grade. We had a little group of kids, and we would drive back and forth to high school in Alamosa, and it was like thirty miles round trip. Then I came to Denver to babysit for my aunt one summer, and so I finally graduated here at Westminster High School. I've been here since then. I was twenty-one years old when I married, and I have four children."

My husband has always liked to see me home when he would come home from work, and so I thought, "Well, what work could I do and still be home when my children and my husband would be home." I talked to a friend of mine who was doing housework, and so I decided that maybe that's what I would want to do.

My family has always come first, and I thought if I would get a job from eight to five, I would probably be awfully tired and wouldn't be able to take care of my family the way I should, and this way I only work five to six hours a day. It has not been bad.

I kind of felt bad at first. I thought, "Why do this when I could get an office job?" but it has worked out for me. I don't mind anymore. Before, I just felt it was a really low-class job, that I was lowering myself to go and clean somebody's house. And then slowly I got to meet a lot of women that were doing this type of work because it's good pay, and a lot of them were even teachers that had quit teaching—they would rather do that than to be out in the classroom. Here you're your own boss. There's no one to tell you that you're not doing something right. I have worked probably with about ten families, and I finally picked three families that I was really comfortable in working with. Monday, Wednesday, and Friday I work five hours. Tuesday and Thursday I work six hours.

Even when I was growing up on the farm, I was a housebody. I liked baking, I liked to clean. But a lot of my friends would say, "Well, gosh, why are you doing that kind of work?" They made me feel, "Well, maybe they are right. Maybe I shouldn't be doing it." I wasn't a dummy. I knew how to do other things besides this.

I did think about going to college. I kind of wish that I had. All three of my brothers graduated college, and my sister graduated from beauty school, but it was hard with my children. I wanted to be home with them. Other times I'd say, "I think I'll go to school," and my husband would say, "Well, what are you going to do with the kids?" My mother was working at the time. I didn't want to pay anybody to babysit for my children. My oldest is thirty-four, and then my baby's twenty, so it was like having two families. I just never felt like I wanted to have a babysitter take care of them. I had heard so many things about what went on, and I did try once with my son, and it didn't work out. My cousin was babysitting, and one time I came home early, and my son was there eating by himself in the kitchen—she was in the living room eating—and I felt so bad for him, and so I thought, "No, that's not going to be the thing for me to do," and so that's how come I didn't do it.

Kathleen Ryan

She was born in Poughkeepsie in 1948 and is the director of a human services agency. (See also pp. 130, 281 and 459)

I drove a cab in New York City—that's how I supported myself through college. It made more money than the traditional women's jobs. My roommate and I saw her boyfriend make a lot of money driving a cab. It gave us a lot of flexibility; we could pick a cab up at five in the morning and go to classes. You got half of whatever you booked for the day, so if you hustled, you made a lot of money. There were very few women driving cabs at the time. We went to the company that he worked for, and they couldn't not hire us.

Both the cab drivers and managers were very nasty. They made it as difficult as possible. We were nineteen, twenty years old; most of the men were forty, fifty. It started with the really off-color jokes, anything to scare us away. They isolated us. They filled the cabs up with gas for one another, or the attendants would fill your cab up. We would go to the pumps, and the men would leave. We would go to get our sheet for the day, and they would leave and come back twenty minutes later and keep us waiting. Or it would be the sexually gross comments, jokes to see whether we would flinch.

They made remarks to us about being a piece of ass, or we had a cute ass, or those kinds of comments. And how are we going to handle it when some guy comes on to us in the city. Today it'd be termed sexual harassment. My roommate and I were determined not to let it get to us. You could tell us off-color jokes as long as it didn't get abusive, and it didn't. There weren't any advances, and I didn't feel in danger.

We did this together, so that helped. It felt like a challenge to see how much we could take. After a few months, they were wonderful. We kept coming back, we waited our twenty minutes when they ignored us, we pumped our own gas, so they decided that we were there to stay, and their behavior changed. I guess we became like one of the guys. At that time, some more women started coming into the company. The off-color jokes and the comments stopped. They were pleasant, and they pumped the gas, and we didn't wait. You had to prove yourself: "You want to stay here—are you as tough as the men?"

People in the cabs thought it was great that women were driving. We were tipped better than our male counterparts. I guess it was a novelty. We didn't drive at night. There was no sense in taking a tremendous risk to prove a point. I never had any trouble with male passengers. It was a great experience.

I'm a Fourth-Generation Priest

Katrina Martha Swanson

She was one of the first women in the United States to become an Episcopalian priest. She lives in New Jersey with her husband and is the rector of a church in Jersey City. She has two adult sons.

"I was born in Boston in 1935. My father was an Episcopal cleric, and my mother was a registered nurse. I was one of four children, the oldest daughter. At the age of seventeen I felt God would've called me to be a priest if I were a boy. I graduated from Radcliffe College, Harvard University, in 1956. My major was social relations. I used to say, "If I were a boy, I would go into the priesthood, but since I'm not a boy, I'll have to be a social worker instead.""

*P*robably most of my life I have wished I were a man. It's much more convenient. When you go on a camping trip, it's so much easier to go to the bathroom with a penis than to stoop down. Call it penis envy or whatever you want. It's everything, job opportunities, respect. Men get a lot of the goodies, and that's really why it's much handier to be a man.

I was the oldest child in the family. My father really cared about women and wanted women to have justice and equality, but I think he would have loved to have had his oldest child be an heir and a son. I really was close to him, but I think it would have been more fun for him if I had been a boy, but he never displaced me when the boys came along.

I had an aunt who had been a journalist that worked her way around the world. She was a wonderful role model to me, and so I planned when I got through college to work my way around the world. I started my first job in Oslo, and then a young man that I had dated during college came over to visit me and said, "Don't you think it's time for you to come home and marry me?" I did get one more job in Italy, but then I went home. We were married in 1958, and I became a homemaker. I am still married to the same person. We met at Harvard, and he is also an Episcopal priest. His first assignment was in Menlo Park, California, and so that's where we moved after we were married.

I used to say a lot that I was sent to wonderful schools that taught me to be a leader, but when I grew up, nobody really wanted my leadership. That probably happened to a lot of energetic young women. My parents always expected and encouraged me to do the best no matter what I decided to do. For quite a while I was planning to be a spinster social worker. This role-model aunt of mine never did marry. I felt that I didn't really need to be married to have a fulfilling life. I decided to marry because I fell in love with a certain person. I wasn't out looking for the MRS degree, as we used to say.

All of my life I've had a love-hate relationship with the church. My father was my closest friend, and during my early years the church took him away from me a lot, and I often resented that. Fortunately, he took two-month vacations in the summer, and we spent a lot of time together building things, doing errands, walking in the woods—sometimes we'd be bellowing hymns at the top of our voices. I would be at church for hours on end on Sundays, and I loved it. Out of that came this feeling of wanting to be a priest, and yet the church didn't have women priests. But when it became an issue in the sixties, I was totally against women priests. At that time, Bishop Pike confirmed the ordination of a woman named Phyllis Edwards. That raised the issue within the Episcopal church, and I can remember being against the ordination and talking about it with a Catholic priest I respected very deeply. He said the Episcopal church will have women priests within the next twenty years, and so I thought about it. I didn't change my mind right away. I was a loyal church person.

In the mid-sixties my husband and I and our two children went to Africa, to Botswana, for a year. My husband's parish there was about the size of the state of California, and many of the congregations had women leaders. But the church didn't allow them to lead the services. They could gather people, and they could be the political leaders of a congregation, but a man had to read the prayers.

Most of the congregations were indigenous, and in two cases the women had to hire men who had very little interest in the church to come in and lead their services for them. George could only visit these congregations sometimes four times a year, sometimes once a month. In two cases the men were known adulterers and drunkards. One of the men had even been flogged in tribal court for adultery, and there were these wonderful women who were not allowed to lead the prayers. That just made no sense whatsoever, and it really changed my mind. Justice and fairness have always been very, very important to me. When I saw this injustice—and lack of practicality—in these villages, it seemed ridiculous, and so I began questioning. My husband's reaction was total agreement. All of this led me to think that women should be priests.

By 1970 we were living in Kansas City, Missouri. George had started a program to train deacons informally within their congregation. He asked the congregation to suggest people, and my name surfaced, which really shocked me. I was just a preacher's wife, and I poo-pooed the whole idea. But the same year the church legislatively decided that women could be within the diaconate. I then got the strong, definite feeling that God was calling me to be a priest, not a deacon—while a deacon is ordained and has orders to serve, priests have sacramental ministries to bless marriages, to absolve sins, and to consecrate holy communion. I was lucky in a way that I didn't hear God calling me before, because I think it is complicated to work outside the home and raise a family. At least for me, because I really like to focus on things one at a time.

After talking to George and our two sons about my becoming a priest, I called up my father, who happened to be the bishop of that diocese, and I went out and talked to him. He was amazed that I felt that God was calling me to be a priest. He said, "As you know, I have been for the ordination of women for many, many years." I didn't know that. He had actually spoken in favor of the ordination of women to the priesthood in 1968. He had been in Oxford in the twenties and thirties and had bought a book published in 1928 by Canton Charles Raven for the ordination of women. There was a British women's organization founded about 1925 called the Anglican Group for the Ordination of Women. I didn't hear about any of this until 1971.

The next morning, my father said, "It suddenly hit me. All my life I'd wished that one of my sons would be a priest, and I never had any realization that it was my daughter that was being called to the priesthood all this time." My brothers were relieved, thrilled. They said, "No more pressure on us." I'm a fourth-generation priest in the family.

There had been some new canons passed that people could study informally to be deacons and didn't have to go to seminary. I was assigned to a local priest and took a few courses in a local deacon's school. I started in September of 1970 and was ordained to the diaconate in September of 1971. I really roared through the process and started working as a deacon. My children were about seven and ten at the time, and they were really behind the program, and luckily the priesthood is a fairly flexible job. We both felt we had equal responsibilities for our children, and George would arrange his schedule so that he could be home when the kids got home from school. It was tough; there were plenty of stresses, but we managed it.

The church still would not allow women to be priests. Sometime that month I got an invitation to go to a conference on women in the ministry taking place in Alexandria, Virginia. There were seventy women at that conference. Six of us, I believe, were deacons. There were only about seven or eight new women deacons in the church at that time. There were probably abut fifty women deaconesses. Some of them did not believe that they were real deacons in the ordination and ministerial sense, that men were deacons. Some of them did not want to be anything other than deaconesses.

Two men who had been to a meeting of the House of Bishops came to the conference and told us that the issue of the ordination of women had come up at that meeting—the bishops had had a hot debate about it and then had decided to study the matter.
The women in our meeting who had been talking and thinking about ordination for a
longer time than I were totally outraged by that news and said, "We've been studied
long enough. We need to be ordained now." We really were radicalized by the bishops' action, and we formed the Episcopal Women's Caucus. We began working towards
influencing the next general convention in 1973 to open up the priesthood to women,
and we were very, very disappointed because the majority of people in the House of
Deputies were for the ordination of women, but we lost on a technicality. You can
believe we were radicalized again when that failed.

In the spring of '74 at the ordination to the priesthood of some men, the preacher
said, "It's time to stop talking about if women can be priests and talk about when, how,
and where we're going to do it." After that service three people—a priest, a woman
deacon, and a bishop—started planning an ordination. The three of them contacted
others, including my father and me, to help them. The ordination took place on the
29th of July in Philadelphia. I was one of those eleven ordained. There was a huge
uproar. A lot of people had been working very hard to have women priests, and we
invited them to come. About two thousand people showed up. It was in a black church
in Philadelphia. It was the only place that wanted us—priests might be deposed for
having anything to do with us. My husband was advised not to participate because he
might lose his job. He decided he was going to be there in spite of that. My father took
the risk.

The place was cleared for blocks around the church, and there was a plan for escape if anybody tried throwing any bombs, because there had been some threats. We
were going to have the ordination at a motel if we had to. Fortunately, nothing happened. There were protesters at the service, and they were given a chance to speak.
Three of them spoke and said how awful we were and that this was a terrible thing and
that you could just as easily ordain stones as ordain women to the priesthood. Two if
not three of them were priests. But other than that the service was wonderful—a lot of
prayers, promises, questioning. The crux of the service is when the person kneels down
in front of the bishop, who puts his hands on the person's head and asks God to come
into this person and make this person a priest, and any priest in the congregation may
come up and put their hands on the person as well. There was a feeling that the holy
spirit was really there.

Many priests were told they might be deposed for participating in this ceremony. There is a picture of my ordination with my father in the middle and my husband on the left. Priests put their hands on my head, and then other priests would put their hands on their shoulders, maybe seventy priests. So that it was an electric chain of everybody participating in this, and this happened for eleven different women. There were three ordaining bishops, and so they each took a certain number of women.

Most of the experiences I have had since have been very positive. When we left Philadelphia, at the airport two nuns came up to me saying, "Are you one of the new priests?" and "How wonderful it is that you've been ordained, and we're so supportive, and we hope it's going to happen in our church, too." And one of them looked at me very steadily and said, "It's going to be very rough. Don't get bitter." And that's really been the talisman for me, because it would be so easy to get bitter. I got a lot of mail after the ordination—a few nasty letters, but most of it was really positive. We were invited to be on talk shows, to be interviewed on television, we were invited to college campuses.

I had been working as a deacon without pay—I felt that I didn't need to be paid; my husband made enough money for us to live on—and I planned to do the same thing as a priest. But there was enough uproar in our parish about my working as a priest that it looked as if George would lose his job in Kansas City. One or two people resigned from the board of directors of the parish because they felt what I had done was so wrong and that George had cooperated.

My bishop punished me, and I was not allowed to wear a clerical collar or function in any ecclesiastical matter for three months. George and I both agreed that he had to fire me from working in the parish as a priest. Luckily, somebody decided to hire me for a dollar a year at a parish in St. Louis, so I would go over there by bus one day a month. It was an interracial parish, which had dubbed itself the church of the liberation. They were proud to have a woman priest, to be integrating, to be a place of justice and fairness. It was in a very poor, downtrodden inner-city part of St. Louis. I was also an associate chaplain at Stephen's women's college in Columbia, Missouri, halfway across the state.

One of George's parishioners believed that I was her priest, and when she died, I decided to celebrate a requiem mass for her in the funeral home. Some outraged parishioners reported it to the bishop, and he sent out a nasty letter throughout the diocese that I'd done this terrible thing. I was never accepted in Kansas City. My father's funeral was in Kansas City a few years ago, and they wouldn't even invite me to participate in the service as a priest.

Finally, in 1976 at a convention with a lot of battling, it was accepted that women could be ordained to the priesthood. They decided to finally accept the fifteen of us— four other women were ordained after us, before it was officially acknowledged.

I've been here in Jersey City for sixteen years. When I first came here, they couldn't afford to pay me full-time. It is full-time now. I should be getting a minimum of twenty-five thousand dollars a year plus benefits, but I'm paid less at my own decision. This congregation can't afford to pay me much more than they are. The church is in an inner-city factory and residential neighborhood.

We were invited to this area by Bishop John Spong, who knew that we needed to get away from Kansas City. Ascension Church decided to call my husband as its rector. I was asked to take a service here in New Jersey when the rector was away. The roof didn't fall in. When the rector resigned from the parish, within the next year the bishop gave them three choices. They could have me, they could have me and George working as a team, or they could have an older priest who was just about to retire. They said, "We'll take that one," meaning me, and so they called me to be their rector, and I have loved it here. I was the first woman rector in the whole New York Metropolitan area.

The parish has a strong core of older people, many of whom grew up here; they are Italian, German, English, Greek. Union City has the second-largest Cuban population outside of Havana, second only to Miami. We now have younger people coming in from countries like Ecuador, Peru, Puerto Rico, Cuba, Guatemala, Dominican Republic. There are more women parishioners here and were when I came. It might be as high as seventy-five percent women, and they do the most work and raise the most money.

There was one family that left the church when I came because they weren't sure they wanted a woman priest. There is one man now who is Egyptian and comes to church occasionally. His wife is fairly active here, and I think he has a very uncomfortable time having a woman priest. But as far as everybody else is concerned, they judge me for who I am rather than my just being a woman. I care about the community, and I've stayed with the church and worked hard. I think I've become a symbol of somebody who cares and who has kept this place open for them.

Many of the Hispanics have come because I've learned Spanish, and I'm very approachable. We run an after-school program for kids. They know that was due to my work. Our services are in both English and Spanish. We have these little booklets which have the mass in them; Spanish is on the left-hand page, and English is on the right-hand page. When we come to places like lessons from the Bible or my sermon, we do them in both languages. When it's in the book and they can be reading along, we don't repeat. It makes the service a little longer.

I think the non-Hispanic parishioners are uncomfortable about it. It's something we wish that we didn't have to do, but we feel that it's very important that we work together rather than have separate services and not know each other. There are Spanish-speaking people who could have Spanish masses with no English, but I think they like the opportunity to meet people who don't speak Spanish. It's really hard work, but it's rewarding. There are other churches that are doing it now.

Second-Class Citizen

Frances Smith Foster

She was born in 1944 and is a professor of literature at the University of California at San Diego. (See also p. 303)

*T*he students would invariably say, "Mrs. Foster, Dr. Baker said." It's an unconscious thing that students, staff, and faculty have, that it's not normal for them to address a female professor as "Doctor" or "Professor."

I've looked at lots of women's evaluations. Students will write—"She is cold, she's not nurturing, she's impatient, she speaks above our head." The men are "challenging, professional." They expect certain kinds of behavior and relationships. They will come in and tell you all their problems, and you have done nothing to invite this. They want to know if you're married, how many children you have—especially women students, because they want to know can they have it all.

At San Diego State, I was the only black person in my department of about sixty. There was one woman full professor. She and I were the only two women who had ever made full professor. The department was very old-boy and saw nothing wrong with using the women to teach composition and keeping the important stuff for the men, and that didn't really change until five, six years before I left, when we began to hire more women and get women chairs.

The Women's Studies Department and two terrific deans led the change. Those guys would say, "I want to see why you have no women in the pool, why you put her number twelve out of twelve for merit. I want to see the documentation." The department was forced to come along.

There were some who told me that although I was smart, attractive, all these kinds of things, I was a gift, that I was not there because they sought me out, but because somebody placed me in that department—and that was after my being there, like, sixteen years. I remember that because I was one of the last hired before we had the retrenchment, and we were in a department meeting once with the deans, and they were complaining; they said we haven't had a hire since 1970, and I said, "No, I came in '72," and he said, "You were a gift." And people went, "ugh."

When I was at San Diego State, I came in in English and switched over to Afro studies because we were founding that department. Then after about five years I wanted to switch back to English. You put in your application, you get interviewed, the whole bit. So I'm in the finals now, and a colleague from the English department invited me to lunch, and he said, "You know, it's really very selfish of you to want this job. You already have a good job, and you have a husband who is a good provider. By your candidacy, you're keeping another person who deserves a job from getting it."

Theoretically, everybody gets the same salary, but people with the same or equivalent credentials are often brought in at different steps, and once you're brought in at that step you're forever behind, so women traditionally have been brought in as assistant ones, and men somehow came in as two or threes.

Now I know more about how it's played and have more undeniable credentials. I'm among the best paid in this department. This department has a lot of women. I came in as a full professor, a senior scholar—a little big shot. So people have perused my work and listened very carefully to what I said. Other times, you say something and they look at you and go on, and five minutes later he says what you said and they say, "Good idea, Joe." That still happens on committees. The whole university is not like the literature department, it's mostly male.

There are two kinds of assignments they give you. The female assignments—affirmative action, status of women—are usually very labor intensive, idealistic, and low-power committees. Lately, I've been put on power committees, and last year I was put on one that has to do with hiring, promotions, tenure, medical school—it's the final level. Except for the administrative aide, I was the only woman, only black person, and only one from humanities in that room of doctors, physicists, chemists. They live in a different world from humanities and social science. The whole world was "he." Someone would come in and say, "Gentlemen," and I'd say, "And me, too?" Here I am big as day, there's no missing me, and the man comes asking this committee for something and is not even going to address me. They would talk the language of men, full of sports and sex metaphors, and sometimes I didn't know what they were talking about. I'd say, "Excuse me, what's umm...." After a while, a new person was put on, and she was from theater, which was wonderful.

My feeling is that literature is rapidly becoming a woman's field, more marginalized, with less serious attention being paid to it. The majors command fewer jobs, smaller salaries.

My specialty, in the jargon of the day, is marginalized and dispossessed literatures. I did my dissertation on slave narratives. When I came up, I had never heard of them and they were not very available, but they had been best-sellers in the 1850s. Black male slave literature had been studied but primarily by historians, sociologists, and anthropologists. Now people are hot on them as literature, as cultural studies. I started looking for published literature by slave women, and that led me into black women generally before the Civil War, and I did a book on the early literature by black women from 1746 to 1892, and then I started doing children's literature—I think because I had two kids. Children's literature was all European, and I wanted to know, Was there a tradition for black children, Chicano children? San Diego State is a big teacher-education place, so they were beginning to do a lot of children's literature in the English department. It's only in the last twenty years that it's had any academic legitimacy at the university.

Amanda Johnson

She was born in 1952 and is a partner in a large western law firm. (See also pp. 79, 321 and 493)

I was a young associate working with a client, and after we closed this deal, all of the people from the client's shop and from our shop that worked on it had this wonderful dinner, and the client was sitting next to me. Well, at the end of the dinner, he put his hand on my thigh and starts to rub my thigh. I looked at him, and I said, "Please take your hand off my thigh," and he kind of laughed and starting rubbing me some more, and he says, "Oh, you like it." I said, "If you don't take your hand off my thigh, I'm going to rip your arm off and beat you to death with it." I did not raise my voice. I'm just telling him very matter-of-factly. He gets the point. Six months later I get my reviews where they tell us how we're doing and give us our raises, and I am told that everything was great, wonderful, except there was one client who had some concerns about my ability to get the deal done and to work as a team. You guessed it. The guy with the roving hand. One of the people delivering this message was a mentor of mine. I looked at him, and I just started laughing.

I said, "Let me guess who said this," and I gave him the guy's name and told him what happened, and he absolutely believed me. But this is the sad part: that was a very important client, and it didn't make any sense for me to do any of their work anymore. So I lost an opportunity because this son of a bitch couldn't keep his hands to himself, and, as far as I was concerned, once he took his hand off my thigh, it was over. I would not have dreamed of tattling on him, but he couldn't wait for the chance to try and torpedo my career.

Elana Wiseman

She was born in 1940 and lives in an urban area on the East Coast with her husband and youngest daughter. Her older daughter, Sharon Wiseman, also appears in the book. (See also pp. 88 and 308)

*T*he medical school was very unusual. We had a lot of women—twelve out of seventy-two. Usually, there were one or two. Nine of us graduated. We were anxious and extremely competitive with each other. Everybody kept saying, "You're using up a slot for a man; this is not a profession for women." I felt confused about my gender because people would say, "You're so aggressive to be able to do this," and I thought, "Well, are real women supposed to be aggressive?" I felt very anxious about the quality of my performance. You had to do really well, because, after all, a man should have this slot. It messes up your head.

They showed *Playboy* nudes in anatomy. They would do it to get everybody alert. In a histology or a physiology class showing a partially clad woman was a wake-up call. It was salacious, but it wasn't vengeful or vindictive. Now I find it offensive, and if somebody did that, I'd ask, "Where's your male Chippendale model?" At the time, it was no more offensive or discomforting than hundreds of things that happened that were equivalently so—like always feeling like a second-class citizen. There was an abiding sense of not quite being as okay as the men. We were interlopers. It took a long time, until I was a mature woman, for me to feel like the day of women in medicine had arrived. Now patients come to me and say they really like having a woman physician. Some male patients, in particular, say, "I'm really glad I came to you because I can talk to you better than I've ever been able to talk to a male physician."

Martha Everett

She was born in 1939 and lives with her husband in Denver, where she is a partner in a large law firm. (See also p. 296)

*E*arly eighties, around there, I was about to begin doing a lot of projects with this one executive. He called me aside. He said, "I'd like to be very candid about this. I've never worked with a woman lawyer, and I don't know if I'm going to like it." And I said, "Why? Is it me personally? Do I bother you?" He said, "No, no, but it's just so awkward," and I said, "Why is it awkward?" and he said, "The idea we would be traveling, going all these places. There are all these little things, like if we're in the airport, am I expected to carry your suitcase? If I offer to carry it, are you going to be angry or are you going to be angry if I don't offer?" I said, "Okay, I'm glad you brought this up. Let me tell you where I'm coming from. I like to have my cake and eat it, too. I'd love to have you carry my suitcase, open doors at all times, but treat me like an equal. Why not?" And so then he laughed, and it was easy.

If you do international law as a woman, what comes up is that in certain cultures— the Middle East, Japan, Mexico—they would never accept you in that country as somebody advising them. It's a loss of face for them. I've not found it ultimately to be a problem, and I've done a lot of work with Middle Eastern clients.

I practiced in London when we lived there for a year. There weren't a lot of people with my expertise in international law and tax, and so I got involved in a workout of a big construction deal, and I spent much of a month as the lead negotiator for the Saudis. When you have these big negotiations, with the intensity and the emotions, you get to know people very well. I remember late one night two-thirds of the way through, relaxing with the key Saudi executive, and I asked him, "Is this a problem for you, having a woman speaking for you at these meetings?" and he said, "No, because you have the expertise and the skills. I could never allow you to do it for me in Saudi Arabia, but in London it's different. It's not a loss of face because it's part of your culture here."

I've gone to Japan and worked for Japanese clients. They've told me they would not hire me if I was Japanese. I've said, "What if I was a Japanese-American woman?" They said, "Well, maybe."

Beginning of the eighties I spent a lot of time doing deals in Mexico, usually representing U.S. companies but on joint ventures, so the principals and all the counsel on the other side were Mexican, and usually I'm in charge of all negotiations. After a particularly difficult one, I met with the lead Mexican counsel for our client, and I asked him how he had felt about having a woman lawyer being the lead negotiator. He said, "You can do it, so I accept it." He said, "We discussed this in the beginning, with my other partners in the firm. We thought you were very aggressive, and it was strange for a woman, but it wasn't offensive. It worked, and so we accepted you." And I said, "But you don't have any women lawyers in your firm"—it's the largest firm in Mexico City—and he said, "No, but some day we will." He's become a terribly close friend over the years. We've had many discussions. I've met his wife, who's never been allowed to work, but, you see, they have two standards—"Just don't talk to my wife!" Now I do a lot of work in Russia, and, believe me, they are very sexist. It has not been a problem. I think maybe it's because American women are expected to be aggressive.

Amanda Johnson

She was born in 1952 and is a law partner in a large western law firm. (See also pp. 79, 321 and 490)

My area of practice is in natural resources, oil and gas, that kind of thing, and between '80 and '86 that area of the economy went from a boom industry to almost total collapse. People are not as tolerant, not as nice, when they're not making as much money, when they see every dollar going into your pocket as a dollar that's not going into theirs. Who bears the brunt of a contraction? The bottom of the pile. The bottom of the pile is where firms really started hiring significant numbers of women and minorities. They are the first that get squeezed out or told they have to bring in more clients. Women are already at a disadvantage. The world out there is predominantly male. When men choose their lawyer and they've got two very smart people, and one's a man and one's a woman, they're going to choose that man. They just feel more comfortable, especially in the business context, in the company of men. Women have to work extra hard to produce the same client base and the same numbers as their male counterparts. And that has nothing to do with men trying to hold you back in any conscious way—there's that, too. There are still people out there who presume that if you're a woman, you're not competent until you prove you are, and a man is competent until proven incompetent, so it's an uphill battle. I think minorities have the same experience.

So, in addition to this, women and minorities are now held to standards that the old guys were never held to. Firms are asking different things than what has been asked historically. There's a lot of pressure to work harder, and the more hours they require, the less likely it is that a woman who is trying to raise a family could feel successful here. The typical law firm is not a family-friendly place. You put in probably sixty or more hours a week. I don't know when the women with children sleep. A lot of women with children, when they have to cut back, cut back on the bar activities, and the wining and dining of clients. It puts them at a distinct disadvantage because they can't spend time shmoozing, building a client base. And good work is only part of what gets you recognized.

The ideal situation would be for men to take real responsibility for family, so that that change in their values would reflect itself in the institutions that they participate in and dominate. I don't think that I would be working sixty-hour weeks if men in any significant number took true responsibility for their families. The work ethic would change. There might even be on-site day care. If you want to make it equal, I would rather men take fathering more seriously than women take mothering more lightly. I would rather see women's choices influence how men think, as opposed to women buying into how men think. There will always be men and women (like myself) who would choose not to have families, and they would have a leg up in the competition, but that's life. What upsets me is when women who want a career have to choose that in addition to family and then be judged and penalized or even have their commitment questioned because the family is still their number-one priority.

Another problem for women is that legal work is increasingly adversarial and stressful. It's becoming more of a business and less of a profession. I find law absolutely fascinating, but I do not like this direction it has taken. Genderwise, you're playing by rules that are not yours. I hate to get into this nature-nurture kind of thing, but I do think that generally women are much more interested in a workable solution than a victory. Women are uncomfortable with direct confrontation. Women can learn to play the game by the same rules, and we can do it every bit as well as they can. I don't know what the emotional cost is. I think it's there. Or you can work on changing the rules, or you can kind of mush 'em up and just muddle through life and get on to the next day, which is probably what ninety-eight percent of the people do.

The last fifteen years have been a tremendous disappointment. When I was eighteen, I believed that my generation would change things, that the women's movement and the civil rights movement would be unnecessary when I was forty years old. It never dawned on me that we would actually lose ground. It was inconceivable that the children of the sixties could allow that kind of unfairness to continue. I didn't understand how deeply rooted in our culture, in our institutions, it was. I'm much more of a realist now, but even now I think we should be so much farther along than we are.

Work:
The Third Generation

Not only do I buy in to the women's movement, but I'm appalled at these youngsters. I had to talk to these young women yesterday. About fifty of them were chosen to come to this leadership seminar and I was a presenter—"oh no no I'm not a feminist." "What do you mean you're not a feminist? How can you say that you want to go on to law school and marry and share raising children and housekeeping with a husband and tell me that you're not a feminist."

—Nancy Douglas, born 1934

You can believe whatever you want but until you really understand that institutionally the country is still run by white men and what is moral, right, and good is still coming only from that perspective, things will not get better for women, minorities, or children because none of us are really involved in the power structure. The heart of feminism is shaking that power structure. We have so much farther to go. I hope that there will be women in seats of power for my granddaughters to see as models. I also hope that women stay in the seats that they are in—teachers and mothers—and that those seats become seats of power so that we don't need to desert important areas of life in order to get power or money.

—Lauren Morgan Stern, born 1965

I Run the Paver;
I Spread the Blacktop

Cynthia Rhodes

She is divorced and lives with her two children in a rural area near Binghamton, New York. She is project manager for a utility contracting company and supervises the construction of water mains, sewers, filter beds. She was thirty-two years old when interviewed.

"I was always a tomboy, hung out with my brothers. We played baseball and football and mini-bikes and bicycle jumps. We climbed the trees, built tree forts. My mother went out and bought this beautiful doll for me and sat there and cried because within five minutes I took the doll apart to see how it worked and what it was made of."

*A*round the time my marriage was going downhill, I was working in this little hardware store. The people that owned this utility contracting company used to come in. They watched me work—I pretty much took the store over. And they approached me one day and said, "Would you be interested in learning this business?" They were going to change the business to a woman-owned, woman-run business enterprise. (For personal reasons, they never did do it.) In the state of New York, any state or federally funded contract has to give a percentage of work to women- and minority-owned businesses, so that would give that company a little more of an edge. I said, "I'll do it," and I've worked for them ever since. It's been eight years.

I'm a project manager. I go out and make sure everything goes right. We do utility contracting. Water mains, sewers, filter beds, manholes, anything where you dig in the ground. We've built bridges, water tower tanks. I do the books, I manage. I go out to a job site every day. I check out what's going on. If need be, I do the physical work. I basically run the company.

This one town, we were putting in a fourteen-inch water main and were down a couple of men, so I was down in the trench right with the men putting the pipe together. You get a lot of looks. It's not easy at first if you go into a new town cause most of the towns are still run by all-men crews, and they don't like women around. They'll say things, make snide remarks.

One time, I was in a backhoe, a big excavator, and I was digging up the sides of a bank. We had just put a bridge in, and the town crew showed up. They're putting in guard rails and stuff, and they needed the post pounded down with the backhoe. And John, the man that owns the company, was on the bulldozer, and he called me over to drive down these posts for these men, and they refused to hold them because I was running the machine. They would drop them and say, "No way." They were afraid I was going to hurt them because it is a big machine, but I knew what I was doing.

We work for towns, basically, and if it's a town we haven't worked in, and I walk into a town meeting, you can feel the tension just by looking around the table. I'm introduced as the person to deal with, and the looks! They totally doubt me. In a lot of cases in the beginning of a job, they'll call for something and refuse to speak with me. They want to speak with Rich or Pete. Fortunately, the men understand this problem, and they will not talk to them. They say, "We're sorry. You have to talk to Cynthia. We can't help you." They break down, "Okay, well, give her to me." I get on the phone, and they start in, very matter-of-fact, on the verge of being nasty, like they're expecting me not to be able to answer them or help them. You can hear it in their voice, and I just remain calm. One time I did lose my temper, but it's rare. Next thing you know, we're getting along fine, and nine times out of ten I get, "I can't believe it. You really do know your job." I've heard that a hundred times, and it irritates me to no end. Inspectors are the same way. I worked with an inspector and he's a wonderful man—we ended up the best of friends—but at that time he was sixty-five maybe, semiretired, and I went on a job, and we went head to head. I just yelled at him. I said, "I can't take it anymore. You have to listen to what I'm saying to you. You cannot keep doing this to me." And then he just looked at me because I yelled and he had never heard me yell, and so I explained what the problem was, how we can correct it versus what they were trying to propose. He thought about it a minute, and he said, "You're good. You're right." I said, "See if you would just listen for a minute, we wouldn't have gone through this."

Once you have their respect, it's always there. I can go back to that town again, and they'll remember me. It's absolutely fine, but it's the initial getting over that hump. Younger guys, they're the same; it doesn't matter how old they are. They don't know how to react because there's not a lot of women in this field. "Women are secretaries," I was told the other day by this man. He said it laughing. When he walked away, I said, "If he says that to me again, he'll be pushed in the trench," but he turned around, and he looked at me, and he said something about if I screwed up, I'd be back in the kitchen, where I belong, and he's laughing. That's another thing, you have to be able to determine whether they're fooling around or not cause there's a lot of fooling around. So I just looked at him; I couldn't figure him out. He'll be out on the site a lot more so I'll have to watch this one. Cause if he's serious—I don't yell, I just have a way of saying things, and it gets across that I do not appreciate it.

I get along with our crew. They had a problem when I first came to work and the decision was made that I would be pretty much the project manager running the jobs. If I would ask them something, they would just look at me and laugh and walk the other way, and I finally had a talk with my boss, and I said, "They're not listening to me." And he said, "Well, you have to make them listen," and then he turned around, and he told them, "If she says something to you, she means it. Don't give her a hard time. Just do it." And they all just kind of turned and looked at me like, What is this? But I think they would have done it if I were a man, too, because at that point—it was seven years ago—I was twenty-five years old. And one man was forty-five, the other was in his fifties, and then here comes me out of nowhere, this young girl, and they're being told, "This is your boss."

When I first started managing, I was in a job site, and we had the job trailer set up. The engineers hired an inspector. He came in, and he was half-crocked and started to say nasty, crude, sexual things and come on to me. He was in his late forties, early fifties. He kept stepping towards me, and I just kept backing up, and he kept getting closer and closer and calling me, "Hey, honey, come here, and I know why you're here, and let's have some fun." And I kept saying, "Excuse me, please leave, I am not here for this," and I had a file cabinet—I pulled the drawers open, and I stood behind them because I figure, "Well, he's drunk, he'll trip over the drawers before he gets to me." Finally, some of our men pulled up, and they stepped in and could see that something was wrong, and I gave a look like, "Don't leave me," and they stayed right there. I asked the man to leave again, and he finally left. The man that owns the company came along, and we told him what happened, and I said, "I can't work if this guy is going to be on the job. That's not fair to me." I was very angry, and he was very angry. The next day we called the engineers, and we told them we wouldn't do the job unless he was gone. So he was fired. I was thrilled. That was my first real bad experience in this business. He was the worst.

I will not put up with anybody's mouth. If I even think something's going to start, I stop it before it does. From the very first comment, I say something. Example: This one man made reference to something disgusting—tits and asses—to do with women, and he's looking at me smiling, and I just turned around and said, "Do you eat with that mouth?" It stunned him. He looked at me and said, "Well, yeah, ha, ha," and I said, "Well, I wouldn't if I were you" and walked away. I was not working with him. He just came on a job site, walking by, stopped and said something. I will not tolerate bad language from men. I don't use it. I don't feel I should be subjected to it. The men I work with know that. They respect it. If anything does come out—they forget I'm there, or I happen to walk up and nobody saw me—they turn around and they apologize. Men are terrible. I have walked up on conversations that were unbelievable. They're talking about their dates or their wives or their girlfriends, and they're saying what they did with them sexually and they get graphic, and it's disgusting. A lot of times I'm not there, and I'll come walking in, and they're all standing there ha ha joking, and I'll clear my throat, and they all turn around and turn bright red because they're caught saying these things.

I don't care where I go, this is how men are. They are really disgusting pigs. Maybe that's another reason why I don't make a point of going out that often. If a man that went out with me turned around and talked like these guys talk, I'd kill him. They'll go into every detail, what they did, they ask each other, they joke about it.

I would never get involved with anybody I work around. He might talk about me. I find that with all men. The laborer right on up to the supervisor of the town. The age or anything, it doesn't matter. It's male ego. Probably showing off who's better. Who could get the most women in one weekend. I find it humorous because they don't realize how disgusting they really are. I just laugh at them. This is their life, this is what they live for.

I continue to work for this company, but then, in 1989, I started my own. What I began with was utility work, a small version of what my old company does. I've done a couple of sewer systems for hotels, homes where they have halfway houses and retarded people. I did a system for a restaurant, and then I paved a road one time, and I loved it so much that that is all I've done ever since. I run the paver; I spread the blacktop. It's great. I haven't done any in a year because the economy in this area went down; it's terrible. I do have a few jobs this year, not big, but it'll be a little bit of money, and it'll be nice. I don't advertise. The jobs I get are people who know me. They've seen my work.

I got what I wanted out of my company. We were living in a mobile home and growing out of it. The kids are getting bigger; the rooms are too small. I needed a house, and I couldn't afford one. The child support my ex-husband pays is enough for entertainment, movies, extra clothes for the kids. I'm the breadwinner. So I started that company, and I started making money and putting it away, and finally I had enough money to build my house. I needed a mortgage for fifty thousand dollars—I did a lot of the work myself. When I went for the mortgage, it ended up my lawyer had to threaten the bank. I was a single mom with two kids, and they did not want to give me a mortgage, but they had no real grounds not to give it to me—I was more than qualified—and it was a big fight. It was absolutely horrible, but I did it. I got my house.

What's Happening

Sally Carroll

She was born in the Midwest in 1974.

I work at Condoms 101 on one of the largest campuses in America. We get a lot of people shoplifting. I don't usually catch it, but then I'll realize, "Hey, that's missing." It's mellow. You have to talk about safe sex, which is no big deal for me. I get harassed, sometimes I get scary phone calls. None of it fazes me.

White males are usually the people who harass me more than anyone, and they'll come in asking for the dressing room. All I'll do is look at them, roll my eyes, and look away. We're open until midnight on Friday and Saturday, so about that time you're getting a lot of drunk people and especially from football games. On some of our condom packages we have women scantily clad in these little pornographic outfits. I think that enforces it inside of their heads, "Oh, yes, this is a woman. She's an object. Let me utilize this object to my benefit."

We've got every kind of condom you can imagine, American and Japanese. Glow-in-the-dark, flavored. We have pecker mugs, and mugs where the handle is a penis. When we initially started, we were simply there for the prevention of pregnancy and disease. It was not kinky at all. But during that time we realized we weren't gonna make any money this way, so we got a bunch of novelty items, and we've got catalogs. We sell incense, doodle pads, and a lot of stupid books like *Why Beer Is Better Than Women* and *Why Cucumbers Are Better Than Men*. But it's kind of cool because there is as much degradation towards men as there is towards women.

Some things offend me in the store, but it's a great job. It's five bucks an hour. Four thirty-five is minimum wage in this state. I don't have a boss looking over my neck. I walk in, I open the store, I'm there by myself for six hours. We're not that busy, so I can write in my journal, listen to the stereo, read, or just think. I can have people come in and visit me, bring me lunch.

I'm helping save lives because condoms, you know—there's so many different kinds, it's really confusing for people. They don't know what kind of contraception protects against what. It's kind of cool because you're like, "Hey, did you know this is necessary?" "Oh, wow, really? Thanks." So it's helping to educate people, and I love educating people.

Nichelle Ellison

She was born in a small town in Georgia in 1968, and raised along with cousins by a single mother. (See also pp. 162 and 184)

Religion is an important part of my life, and in every city that I go to or move to I try to find the church home. It is making its way into my dissertation topic for my Ph.D. in dealing with spiritual autobiography about black women writers in the nineteenth century. I'm a teaching assistant here at the university. I want to be a college professor, and this is giving me experience about students, teacher direction, working for an administration, and things like that.

My responsibilities are to teach the course material, which is emphasizing multiculturalism and different religions and cultures and also at the same time teaching the students how to write critically and analytically. I think that my responsibility as a TA increases with me being black because a lot of times, at a white university, I find I have to prove myself before I even give the lesson. There is this distrust in my capabilities because of my race and my gender. As a black woman, I have to prove myself twice. Some people think I'm here to fill a quota, so I have to prove to them that I'm here on my merit. I found myself in that kind of predicament a lot. In fact, tomorrow I'm going out of town to a conference, and I'm presenting a paper on my predicament as a black TA in a predominantly white university and some of the encounters that I've had.

A lot of the distrust seems to be around the students, and it probably is with some of my fellow TAs and even some of the administrators, but because they are in the system, they know not to say anything, and they know how to be more subtle with it. But students, especially freshmen, just say what they think, and they make it obvious. They haven't yet been in college long enough to learn what is politically correct in how to approach things like race and gender.

I haven't dealt with sexual harassment in the sense that the harassment comes from someone who is in a position of power over you. I've been harassed—I guess you can call it harassed—by one of my students, who would write notes to me on the end of his papers, and he felt like he could invite me out and call me at home to let me know he had an interest in me even though I told him that it was inappropriate—and even outside of it being inappropriate, I'm just not interested in you. But they don't define that as sexual harassment.

Someone who is in a position to provide me with a scholarship has made sexual advances towards me and used the fact that he could give me the scholarship to do that. It was very awkward. He even told me that I could basically have whatever I wanted by "lending my pussy." That was a letdown for me because I thought that this person had a genuine concern for my academic advancement. I thought he was impressed with the fact that I was trying to do school and I was basically on my own, without any financial assistance. He is not affiliated with the university directly, he is not on the campus, but he does all their fellowships and scholarships, and I was interested in getting one . . . but not that interested!

Louise Tang

She is fifth-generation Chinese-American and a native of San Francisco. She was forty years old and single when interviewed.

I'm sort of atypical for Asian women. I'm a marketing specialist for computer software. I've been with this company—one of the largest in the country—for fourteen years, and I've been enjoying it. It took me a long time to get to this point. We Asian women are not used to talking about ourselves, promoting the good work that we do, trying to encourage other people to buy our products.

Thirty percent of my company's staff has been cut recently, and another thirty percent will go at the end of this month. Where there's a lot of fat, people can afford to be less mindful of the business and more mindful of themselves and their careers, and that's not going to be the case anymore. In the first two go-arounds, politics played a major part in who stayed and who didn't, so those who were not correctly aligned politically didn't make it, but now the emphasis is on performance. Many Asian people feel that these changes are good for us, and I feel that way.

When I came into the work situation, my gut feeling was I do what's right for the team that I work with and for my boss, and I don't draw as much attention to my accomplishments. In this environment this doesn't get me promoted, and you would often see Asians wondering why we do such great work and everyone says so, but we don't get the big promotion. There are two sayings that symbolize the difference between the Asian and Western way of thinking. Western way of thinking is Squeaky wheel gets the oil. The Asian saying is The nail sticking its head up gets hammered down. And that symbolizes the way we were raised: If you draw attention to yourself, that's a bad thing cause you're forgetting the family and the rest of the people you work with and live with.

We have been putting our energies into the work all along, as opposed to promoting our careers. What the downsizing has done is pulled out those who got along by shmoozing, by hanging around the water cooler and making connections. In the past, people who generated results sometimes didn't get credit. Someone else cleverly stepped in and took credit. That happened a lot. It won't happen anymore, because there's no layers upon layers anymore—you're exposed. For instance, I'm now the only one who does what I do for all of Northern California. This used to be a game. If you knew that a customer was about to buy something, then you would jump on and attach your name so you got credit. You can't do it anymore. Everybody knows that if it's that type of product, that person was running it.

Marianne Pages

She lives in upstate New York with her husband and three children and was thirty-three years old when interviewed. (See also p. 333)

I go to work at ten-thirty at night. I do mail sorting, very tedious work. I don't enjoy it. The post office has a really bad reputation as far as the employees. It's a lot of nuts; I'm sure you must have heard of the shootings that occur. I think that might lead to a copycat here. I don't like to knock Vietnam veterans, but we do employ a lot of them, and I think that is where a lot of the problems come from. These people just are not right. You kind of know who they are. You know how to behave around them. I certainly don't want to upset them. It's difficult sometimes. They are on edge. We kind of joke about it. I don't think anybody's really scared to come to work. It's just something that is in the back of everybody's mind. They know it could happen, and they think it probably will. It is just a matter of who and when. I've seen some violent episodes. There's been fist fights. I'm also a union steward, and I've had to intervene between management and employees. A lot of times we'll have people that'll steal from the mail. They'll steal money out of birthday cards, they'll steal credit cards. You'll be sitting there doing your work, and all of a sudden the postal inspectors will charge in and grab this person and put him up against the wall, cuff him, and take him out. And everybody's like, wow. These things really do happen.

Melinda Steinberg

She is Jewish and was born in Queens in 1964. She has lived with the same man for nine years. (See also p. 356)

*E*ighty-five to eighty-nine I was doing textile design. It was a pretty good way to make a living. But I didn't feel like I was doing anything besides making these salesmen money. I was getting paid my salary, but what was I doing in this world? What was my purpose on earth? Was it to paint this pattern in another color combination for the fiftieth time? I had really always wanted to be an art teacher, so I started going back to school for a degree in art education. I would go to work during the day, go to school at night, and it was pretty hard. Then, eventually, I quit my job in the textile industry, and I became a playgroup teacher, which I just loved. I did it for a little over a year.

Then when I got my degree, I started subbing in the public school system. That completely changed my perspective on life! I was working with at-risk kids in East Harlem, and I was also working with very gifted kids in East Harlem in a magnet school.

When I was substituting at the school I wound up working at full-time, which was a very good magnet school, I would go in, and projects would be in process. I'd say, Hi, I'm here for whomever, and I know you are in the middle of this, so let's get going, and they'd go. Every now and then I had a few girls or boys that would really be obnoxious to me, but they stayed in their seats, they did their work, there was no threat of any rebellion, and it was a pretty pleasant day.

In contrast, when I worked at the school for at-risk kids, I would walk in, and immediately there would be some sort of crisis. These were all kids who, since kindergarten, had gotten Fs. They came from abusive or neglected homes, or some of them came from perfectly good homes but were not adjusted well for some reason. Or maybe they had been born to alcoholic or crack parents. If it wasn't environmental, it was biochemical. Every single one of these kids needed individual attention, and there were about thirty of them. Actually, there was a high absence rate, so maybe at any time there were like twenty-two, but two of them were more than you should have been able to handle.

So I'd walk in in the morning, and they would go, "All right!" and immediately kids would start throwing things. I tried to be really tough, and I would tell them, "Look, you're getting out of here if you can't obey my rules." The woman who was their teacher was very tough, and she was my mentor. She really taught me a lot about classroom management. I would walk in ready for battle. No matter how prepared I was, they threw things at me, sometimes literally, that I couldn't handle. Being a woman was a terrific liability because I was dealing with mostly very mature seventh- and eighth-grade boys. Being a woman, being a little woman, being a white woman—I felt like, "What am I doing here, and what can I give to these kids? Should I even be here?" I would tell a kid to sit down, and he'd get up and be like five foot ten, and I'm five feet tall, and he'd look down at me and say, "Are you starting with me?" No matter how tough I was at that moment I knew I had to say, "No, I'm not starting with you."

I had to know exactly when to pull back so that I didn't get punched out. Then I had to remember that these were kids at the same time. I couldn't go over the edge and totally obliterate them. They were making me feel really bad, and I knew I could have made them feel worse, but that was not what I was there for. But the impulse is to go one on one. When a kid is saying, "I'm going to jump you after school," what you want to say is, "Well, you're just a piece of shit." You really want to let them have it. But what you have to say is, "Sit down." You can't get personal. I would go home every day crying. At the same time I hated these kids, I really liked them. I was so ambivalent about it. I had this overriding feeling that I just didn't belong there. That I wasn't well trained enough or that I wasn't emotionally strong enough. They wanted to hire me for that school, and I knew I couldn't do it.

Sam Schwartz

She goes to college on the East Coast and works part-time at a graphics company. She is Jewish and was nineteen at the time of the interview.

"Work is very important to me. Number one right now, I'd say."

My boss amazes me because she's twenty-seven or twenty-eight, very good position in the company, and she manages to be really effective and strong and respected without either being a militant bitch persona or being sweet and cute. She's just really confident and competent, and I really respect her a lot, and I enjoy working with her. A couple of other people I work with are assistants to her and other managers, and I like them because they're women who are doing really well in the company.

Then there's the salespeople. It's a graphics company, so the salespeople handle the accounts. I can't stand any of them because they're just dumb and annoying. There are women in there who just make me shudder and who make me realize why women get treated so badly in the workplace sometimes. They're annoying and whiny and really inefficient.

It's almost archaic. I mean, the men are pigs. It's awful. Most of the men, they're boorish for the most part, sort of clannish with the other guys. I guess they're good at what they do, but they're not too bright. They treat the women really badly. I don't know if I'd really go so far as to call it sexual harassment. It seems so ingrained in them to assume that this is the way the women should be treated. And to their credit, I can see why because the women that they're working with are like that. This one woman I'm thinking of, she's very whiny, never takes responsibility for anything—everything is always someone else's fault.

And then you see these men come into contact with the woman I work for—she won't take any of that. She's very competent, and they know it, and they don't treat her like that. It's interesting to see. I don't really get regarded that much at all because I'm a lot younger and I'm not there that often. People see me, but they don't know too much of who I am. I see a lot of what's going on and what's happening.

Debbie Jones

She was born in 1969 and is the executive director of a state coalition against domestic violence in the Deep South. She has one younger sibling and both her parents are professionals. "I guess you would say I'm a WASP. My family heritage pretty much goes back to England, with some German." (See also p. 524)

Our office building is just two floors, so I get to see a lot of people from the other offices. I'm really fortunate in that all the people that work there are in nonprofit areas. We are all working to do something to help people. One group that has their office near mine, they do transplants, like organ donors. You know, when someone dies, the family might donate a part of their body for another individual that needs it, like a kidney or an eye. Those people are really neat to talk to, and they have great links to the hospitals, so they have been able to help me because right now I'm developing a policy for state hospitals on how to deal with domestic violence victims when they come to the ER.

The main people in the state working with domestic violence victims are women. I've been in the job for about eight months now, and I'm still learning a lot. I haven't really pinpointed why my board of directors is so keen on this all-women thing. To me, domestic violence is as much of a male problem as a female; we need to work together on this. For the most part, it is men who are the perpetrators of the violent behavior, and it seems to me that if we had men who we could educate and would become advocates, it would give a signal to the community that this isn't a behavior that will be tolerated anymore, and that we don't think this makes y'all macho, if you can beat up your woman and control her. My board is all women, and we are going to open up a membership drive this fall, and they keep talking about having the membership drive for women, and I'm thinking, "Well, why not men, too?"

You have to slowly get them warmed up to the idea, but I think they are coming on to it, because I've been able to back up what I say. There are plenty of law enforcement officers and judges who would love to get on to this. It is really frustrating when you have all these cases of domestic violence, and you can't get the guy prosecuted because of some red-tape bureaucracy in the system. The city police department here has this male officer who has shown a huge interest, and he has come to my office like two or three times and presented changes he would like to see in legislation. He would make a great advocate. I think it will come around.

My job is very busy with O. J. Simpson. I'm not kidding. The calls tripled when that whole thing with O. J. happened. I was getting crisis calls at work, which never, ever happens. It was mainly because they had seen my number on TV, I think, and then the stupid TV station flashed my beeper number on the screen, so that didn't help. I couldn't believe they did that. If they wanted a crisis line, I could have given them that, but they didn't ask me. My beeper was going off at four in the morning from women calling in need, and I'm like, "Hello, okay, just a minute, I'll get you the number." Oh, my god! If that was the only number they could show, I'm glad they showed it, but it was still kind of overwhelming. My roommate was like, "Great, we are not going to sleep tonight," and, sure enough, the phone rang and rang and rang all night.

I think that men would accept the responsibility of being involved in the movement against domestic violence, I really do, if we were to give them the opportunity to be involved. For a long time the issue with domestic violence has been labeled radical feminist, at least in this state, so a lot of my shelter directors try to be very careful about the way that they project their image out in public. They try to play it pretty even so they can still have Junior Leaguers come in and paint a room, because they are real dependent on that support, but they also like to have the NOW women come and cook or whatever they do. I respect that, to try to make the whole community feel like they can be involved and not push anybody away. If they are trying to be so careful so that a little lady church group won't feel kind of wary about the group, why don't they think about trying to get the men involved, too?

I've learned that in my job, depending on what group I'm with, I try to relate to them the best way I think that they could relate to me. So if I go talk to law enforcement officers, I try to relate to them—I'm from a small town, I'm from the South, I know where you are coming from kind of thing. Then if I go off to Chicago to a conference and it is all these women from NOW, I can relate to them, too. I can sit there and listen to someone talk about her victimization and really get into it. It is important to try to relate to all these different people because it is the only way that I know how to be effective in what I do. In my line of work you really have to keep your feet on the ground. You can't be on a soapbox all the time, or people will just tune you out. You've really got to stop and listen.

A Dream Job

Kim Moriki

She is Japanese-American, was born in 1963, and grew up in San Pablo, California. After years of temping, she landed a dream job in her field of illustration. She is ambivalent about marriage and children. Her mother, Miyako Moriki, also appears in the book.

San Pablo at the time we were growing up was rated one of the highest-crime areas in the United States for a city its size. There were like three murders in our neighborhood in the space of a month. There's a lot of drug dealing going on, a lot of welfare people. It's very bleak. I said, "I'm going to get an education. I'm outta here."

I graduated San Jose State in '89 with a BS in graphic design with an illustration concentration. I financed all my college. That was really tough, but I learned to live on almost nothing.

With a recession, it was extremely hard by the time I got out of college to find work. Nobody was hiring, and if they were, they'd hire for five, six, seven dollars an hour, which is an insult after you've been through college. They expect you to start real low and work up. It's a very, very competitive field. So I did temp work. I was doing a lot of secretarial, filing work for attorneys.

One time I was working at this really posh attorney place in San Jose in a nice high-rise. I noticed there were secretaries from other floors coming up to see the attorneys, and they all had high, high skirts and high heels. None of them was over thirty, and I go, "This is really strange." Then I got a call from one of the attorneys' sons, and he wanted to talk to me, and I go, "Well, I can't, I'm trying to learn these phones." (They had me try to work like a thirty-phone-system line, and I had never worked anything like that.) I was very nice, told him, "I just don't have the time right now." Later on that day, I was called in by one of the head attorneys, and he says, "Well, you don't have to return to work tomorrow," and I go, "What does that mean?" I can be very naive sometimes, and he goes, "You've been terminated." And I go, "Does that mean I've been fired?" And he looked really guilty, and he goes, "Well, yes," and I go, "Well, why?" And he would not give me a straight answer. I went back to the temp office. I said, "Don't you ever send me to any place like that." "What went wrong?" "I have no idea of what went wrong." And she goes, "Well, did you talk to the boss's son?" And I go, "Yes, very briefly." "Did you flirt with him?" And I go, "No." And she goes, "I think that's why you were fired." I go, "What??" She said, "I don't think your skirt was high enough," and I go, "What?"

One thing that really upsets me more than sexual harassment with men is when women pick on other women in an office. Why would you want to pick on somebody who's in the same boat as you? At one job, there was a woman who was about my age. I was doing ads, helping them do layouts, and she would only give me half the information that I needed, and I didn't find out it was wrong until the boss said, "What's going on here? This is not right." She didn't even know she was doing it, either. In meetings she would say very negative stuff about me to her boss. She was overweight, she watched a lot of TV, and I think she was very threatened by me because I don't have a problem meeting people. I don't sit home on Saturday nights. I'm very friendly, forward. I appear to be very confident, and that scares off a lot of women. I was very different when I was younger, very quiet, lacking in self-esteem, subservient. In the last couple years I finally began learning to establish better women relationships. I think I have grown up quite a bit, and I've met some women who are more like me, comfortable with themselves, at peace. They don't feel like I'm going to come by and take something.

I got a permanent job last May. Not even a year yet. I get paid to draw on a computer all day. It's a dream job. When we do games, we're given a lot of creative license and responsibility. Since it is competitive out there, a lot of people are after your job. Other jobs, you have to watch your back, you're always worrying, and that really affects the joy of your work and your performance. At this place there's none of that. It's amazing. We were hand picked. The interviews we went through, the shortest was four hours. They really want team players. We work very closely with each other. Sometimes when projects go on, we work weekends, weeknights. We do educational game software like "The Kid Detective" game. It's a logic game. You read stories, and you put clues together to figure out which person did the crime. It's never violent.

This company is just exceptional. The boss, from what I understand, taught school in L.A. in some really slummy areas for several years. He's very humanistic, and it takes that type of remarkable person to hand pick other remarkable people.

It's been a long road. There was a time when I thought, "God, I just went through eight years of education. Like, wow, did I waste time?" End of last year, I had broken up with somebody, I was in an apartment for three, four months without a job. It was awful. Now I have this incredible job, and I'm seeing somebody that I really like. Sometimes I feel so good when I get up. Just the sun coming up—wow, I'm so glad to be alive.

In the last two years I've gotten into Buddhism. The Buddhist people told me to write down fifteen things that I wanted in my life in the next couple of years, and they all worked out. We chant, and there's also a morning and an evening prayer, and people are very connected with each other. When I walked in the first time, I felt like I had come home. I have progressed so far in such a short time. It's a combination of chanting, having faith, going out there and making things happen.

I think I went through all the hard times to make me really appreciate what I have now. When I'm working, I feel such a rush of ecstasy. I'm doing exactly what I should be doing. With artwork it's like I have the potential of really being great, and, dammit, how many people have this chance to really fly, to show the world what you have? Maybe it's an ego trip, I don't know.

The last major relationship I had was probably four years ago. My boyfriend would say, "Why can't you forget about your career, about being a star? Marry me and have kids. Why can't you just be like everybody else?" He started resenting what I did because I spent more time with what I wanted to do as opposed to with him. It wasn't like that in the beginning. We had a really wonderful relationship for probably about two and a half years, and then he started getting very possessive because he knew that I was getting ready to move on, and he didn't want me to leave. I've had that fight in other relationships—"Don't you love me? Don't you want to spend more time with me?" Yes, I do, but when I get a great project, it just gives me such a rush, there's no competition. I always feel like if anyone ever made me feel the way I felt when I did artwork, then maybe I would think about staying with them.

As you get older, you begin to think more about the future, that you should have a home. You've done a lot of things by yourself, and it's like it would be nice to have somebody there. A lot of the problem is that I've met very few men who are like me, who want to keep educating and improving themselves. So many men, especially in college, they just settle for what they have—it dropped into my lap; okay, I'll go along with it.

It's really strange to meet people after they've been out of college for several years. It's like they've given up. They've gained weight, they're married to someone really strange. Like, why did you settle? A lot of people have the weirdest reasons for getting married, which is why there's a lot of divorces. I think you have to marry your best friend, someone that you have a lot in common with, someone who understands you, who is going to hopefully grow as you grow, and that's really hard to find because this world is very materialistic. A lot of people in San Jose, the Silicon Valley, it's money; it's flash. There's not a lot of heart left. When I was living in San Jose, it was the first question—"What do you drive? What kind of work do you do?" Who cares? It just astounded me the type of people who would ask me out. It's like, "What do you do for fun?" "I go skiing, I have this really new car, I go driving. What do you do?" "Oh, I like to read books, draw, run."

I've had a lot of opportunities to get married, and I've never felt I could live with that person. But it's really weird because my life has suddenly come together, and I've met someone who is so much like me. Sometimes I'll talk to him, and he'll finish my line of thought. We always have something to talk about. He is just about everything that I am. Very upbeat, expressive, emotional, and that's rare. I feel like he's one of my best friends right now. I've had so many bad relationships in the last four years that I'm kind of hesitant, and there's so many things going on in my life right now, I don't know if it would be fair to commit. We're not planning anything. We're just feeling it out for now.

I think I would like to have children. I can't say I've always wanted to. This day and age you don't have to have children. There are so many people in the world, and it scares me to think, "What is their future going to be like?" There's such a recession now. What is America going to be like? Is education going to be impossible to get to? I don't want to give birth to someone and say, "Well, the world was good when I was growing up. You're on your own." That's frightening. There's a very selfish part of me that does want to know what it's like to carry a life, to be a parent, but as I get older I think those chances become less and less simply because you're only fertile for so many years. And the financial responsibility is incredible. Who can afford to have a child and a house? It's a lot of work, a lot of sacrifice. I believe I can do it, but then again is my partner ready to do it? It's tough.

I am very ambivalent. I don't feel marriage is a must because I have my illustration work, something I can pour myself into and feel okay. I have a lot of really wonderful people to support me. If I do have children, I would want to be there for at least the first fifteen years. Because of financial necessity, a lot of parents are both working and somebody else raises the child—that's really terrible. You only get a certain amount of time to raise a child. It's usually just once in your life. I'd probably have to put artwork aside. That sounds really, really hard, but I also love watching people grow and learn. Mom said that she grew up with us kids, and that's a really neat thing. After children are raised, you can always go back and try to pick up where you left off. Art illustration is always there whether you practice it or not. So it would definitely be a big sacrifice, but if I really believed in it, if it was right, I think I would do it.

My father always told me, "Don't get married until you're ready. Do everything first that you want to do." My mother said that, also. They had always wanted to do things that they never got around to when they were young, and so they didn't want us to get married too young and to lose that independence and self-discovery.

The Girls Don't Stand for It

Mara Lavergneau

She was born in 1971 in upstate New York. She attends Lincoln University, which was the first traditionally all-black college in the United States. "Thurgood Marshall and Langston Hughes went there." (See also p. 146)

One night I was working at McDonald's and running the drive-thru, and I was calling the food in, I was doing everything. There were two cars in line. One at the window had two white males and a black male sitting in back, and then the car behind that was three white males. So I heard this horn beeping, and I looked in the window and I realized that the second car was tooting its horn. I said to the guys in the front car, "What's going on?" I heard some voices, but I couldn't make out what they were saying. And he went, "Oh nothing, they're just being jerks back there." And then I don't know if the black kid in the back stuck his middle finger out at the guy behind him or what, but they got out of their cars and one of the white guys said to the black guy, "You nigger!"

Whether the black guy did the hand gesture I don't know, I couldn't see, but I just know that all I heard was the white guy saying nigger, and my body literally went out of the window. I was like, "First of all, you're not going to say that word in front of me and feel comfortable about saying it, and, second of all, I'm not giving you your food, so you might as well go across the street to Burger King!"

So then he was like, "Well, I'm not moving, and I'm getting my food!" And I was like, "Well, you can think you're getting your food all you want to, but you're not getting it from me." And I was like, "Second of all, I'm calling the cops!" So I told my manager to call the cops. The cops didn't know if we'd been robbed or whatever, so in two minutes they had cops across the street, in the parking lot, five cop cars all over, surrounding the building. The guys had driven out of the parking lot, but when they saw the cop cars, they drove back in. I don't know why! The cop finally came inside, and he asked me what happened. The driver ended up being inebriated. They asked me if I wanted to press charges, and they asked the kid who he had called a nigger to testify, and then they got arrested for DWI and another charge for disrupting the peace.

Gina Rotundo

She was born in the Midwest in 1954 and now lives in the Northeast where she teaches at a culinary institute. (See also p. 325)

I was waitressing in a diner when I hit a trucker off the barstool for putting his hand up my skirt. I turned around and slammed him in the chest. I was a cute little twenty-year-old, curly black hair, real bubbly, friendly. After I knocked him off the barstool, he got back up and was embarrassed, so he started giving me these digs, making little innuendos, so my manager took me in the back, and I was really upset, crying. I said, "I quit," but he said, "If you quit, you're defeated. I'll go tell him he's not welcome back in the diner, but you go back up there and you tell him he's a son of a bitch." Thank god, I had this manager. He calmed me down. He walked out there with me, he had his arm around me, and he goes, "Tell him what you think." I said, "I think you're a son of a bitch. You need to leave and never come back. If you do, I'll knock you off your barstool again." It made me feel good. That was my first incident.

When I was working at a nightclub, I had a leotard on, and one young man made a comment that my breasts were really voluptuous, and I said, "Actually, I'm married to this big, huge basketball player. We just had a baby that I'm nursing, and my breasts are full of milk, and if you don't behave, I'll pop one out and squirt you." I found my mouth to help me a great deal. If somebody says something derogatory, I like to turn it around and go, "How would you feel if someone said to your sister or mother what you just said to me? What would you do?" He'd say, "I'd knock him out." I'd say, "Well, I have a brother and a husband. How do you think they would take it? Have a nice day." And then I walk away.

I've been in the restaurant business most of my life. It's getting better, but it's been a very hard struggle for women to get jobs at better restaurants. These European chefs came over here and made us believe that a woman's place is not in the kitchen and not in the dining room. There's probably not that many women who will go up to the door of a very expensive restaurant and go, boom, boom, boom, "I want to work in that dining room." I did. Women are making much less money by not working in those very fancy restaurants.

At the culinary school where I teach, they feel that because they are men, they are the domineering ones, and we're supposed to be submissive and say, "Yes, sir, I'll get that done right away." I don't take it. I get very aggressive.

I was setting up this beautiful display and dishes for the chef. Different types of food go in each chafing dish, and I mixed two up. Well, he blew up at me in the dining room in front of my class. He was screaming. He left, and I marched right behind him back into his kitchen and started screaming at him. "Don't you ever walk into my dining room and raise your voice in front of my class, like I'm raising my voice in front of your class now. Does this make you feel big? Do you think you're better than me? Do I make myself clear?" He looked at me and went, "Yes, ma'am." I walked out of that kitchen. We had that one horrible fallout, and ever since that day it's been wonderful. He and I are good friends.

I remember a long time ago being harassed by chefs, getting pinched. I'd turn around, and my mouth would get loose, so they stayed away from me. Years ago that was common. Things have gotten so much better because now the girls don't stand for it. They will go right upstairs and say this chef grabbed my ass or my breasts. The chef would be out of the school in a minute.

The older women are learning from the young women. They've got energy, self-confidence, support. They have organizations for women's rights they can call. I wish I had that support when I was twenty.

Loren Medway

She is Jewish and was born in the South in December of 1965. She lives and works in Southern California.

I work on the navy base downtown. I'm an operations research analyst. I'm the only female in my office down here. I feel like I'm having to work twice as hard just to gain respect because it's a man's world in the navy. It's uncomfortable.

There was one case where one of the guys took a project I had done and claimed it as his own. He felt threatened because we were at the same level, and we were competing for a higher position. I'm not sure exactly what he was thinking, but I know that the government definitely tries to get women up in its ranks. He saw me as a threat. I'd also been in the government longer than him, and a lot of what they do is on seniority.

I feel like the men I work with are trying to sabotage me somehow to make me leave. I keep fighting back to stay, but it's almost to the point where I'm just sick of dealing with it. A lot of them were in the navy, and they purposely try to tell old sea stories or talk about a football game that was on TV, things to make sure that I won't be included. When they go out to lunch, they never invite me. I just feel like an outsider at my own office. They don't want women on their turf.

Kim Faggins

She was thirty-two years old when interviewed.

"I was born in Brooklyn and lived there all my life until about three years ago I moved to upstate New York." (See also p. 365)

*T*hey had an ad in the paper that they had openings for an emergency medical technician at a local ambulance company. I got certified for EMT in New York City. I went to apply for the job. I brought in all my documentation. I showed them all of my credentials, and I was qualified for the job. It's not like I had never worked on a ambulance before, and I told them that I volunteered before in Brooklyn with the volunteer corps. Just how they looked at me, how they was talking to me. I was standing there speaking to, I guess, the lieutenant, and he was talking down to me. "Do you have all your credentials together? Have you ever did any volunteer work? Have you ever worked here before?" I thought something was wrong, and I didn't think I would get the job. They never called me, and they had the ad in the paper. I called them back, and they said all of the positions were filled. Well, maybe they are now. I didn't make a big issue out of it.

I feel racism more up here than I ever felt it before. Before, you knew it was going on, but it never really hit you in the face unless you're from down south, or you're older like my mother.

Cindy Aspromonte

She was born in 1954 and lives in Denver with her husband and two young children. (See also p. 381)

I'll never forget. I was in Boston, around '75—it was one of my first experiences as a student nurse. This doctor came in, and he yelled, "Nurse, nurse, come in here," and I walked in, and he goes, "Here, hold this chart for me," and all he wanted was for the nurse to hold this record while he read it and while he examined the patient, instead of just putting it down on the table. It was so absurd, and I was not able to say anything to him because I was a student nurse and I was young and I didn't have enough self-confidence.

In those years, in Boston, the doctors didn't usually consult with you very much or talk to you. I always thought the difference in pay was so unfair, so absurd, especially when I saw the nurses were there in the front lines, in the trenches. Nurses made $20,000, and the doctors made $200,000 or $300,000.

After I graduated from school, I hated working at hospitals, and I hated that sense of inequality. Your hands are always tied—if you thought the patient needed something, you had to get a doctor's orders. Even if it was a back rub or a heating pad, you had to get an order. I couldn't wait to get my nurse practitioner program under way and have more autonomy. Nurse practitioners are trained to do full primary care.

I work three days a week in a private ob-gyn office with a physician and another nurse practitioner. I do prenatal care and physical exams, pap smears, and breast exams. We usually have physician backup in case of complications or abnormalities. I also am a holistic nurse and health educator; I have a private practice where I see clients for holistic healing and teaching.

Katrina Thomas

"I was born on February 9, 1964, the night the Beatles had their first appearance on the Ed Sullivan show. My mom was bummed, but she got to watch a re-run the next week." (See also p. 384)

I always thought of myself as having a career or working. I've been a musician since I was a kid, but I wasn't sure if that was what I was going to do. When I went to college, it became really clear to me that music was it. I always wanted to be really successful in what I did, and I wanted to not necessarily make a lot of money or be famous but to make a difference. I wanted to touch people in some way with my gift of music. Now that I am almost thirty, I would have to say that I feel like my feet are more on the ground. My dreams are about the same, only I feel like my head isn't quite as in the clouds as it was.

I'm not quite as enthralled by the whole music lifestyle because I lived it for a while. I've been in a situation where I think I was hired because they wanted someone to be on stage in a short skirt. I didn't like that very well. It definitely is one way to get music jobs. The music business itself is really chauvinistic—obviously—you watch MTV for five minutes, and how many men do you see in string bikinis?

I've played for everything from Lion's Club installations to being in a top-forty band to being in an original band, playing for a zillion weddings. The top-forty band was the worst as far as the female thing. This was in L.A., the epitome of the whole music scene. I was really naive because I was just out of school. I remember when we auditioned singers. Four or five women would come in, some with the full bimbo look, and then they would leave. And I would be like, "Wait a minute, this girl can't even sing." "Yeah, but she has nice boobs."

These guys in my band, I'm looking at them like, "Excuse me, like you're really anything to look at!" It was different because musician men can be ugly. They can't be fat too often, but they can be fat once in a while! But the women pretty much can't be, if you think generally who makes the money. There were some bigger gigs that I had opportunities to do. I never did them. They were specifically because these guys wanted women keyboard players in the band. I guess there were a few times when I used that to my advantage, but I really don't like it.

I knew a lot more women that slept their way to the top than men. It is still pretty prevalent. To the men it is who you know or who you buddy up to, but for women it is more of a sexual thing, at least from my experience. Real close, tight circles of musicians.

I did reach a lot of my goals, although I had anticipated in my mind that I would go a lot further with them. When it came down to it, there were sacrifices that I don't think I wanted to make. I started seeing how phony the Hollywood thing was. I just don't value that, and I won't compromise what I think is right to make it. I'd rather be true to my music. I guess I'm a romanticist about it. My uncle was Rolf in *The Sound of Music,* so my musician stories go way back. I started singing with him when I was in junior high. He needed a pianist, and he basically pushed me into being able to accompany him. I learned so much, and I had some really positive experiences.

I'm at a changing point now because I met a lot of my dreams that I had when I was younger, so I'm like, wow! I made my dreams, and now I have a few more years left. I have a day job now, which is what I do to make money. I'm an office manager for a landscape architecture company, and I love it. I'm figuring out some new dreams and goals, like going further with my music, being better, and having children and being a really good mom.

Colleen McCarthy

She was born in the Midwest in 1970. She attended Catholic schools. (See also p. 195)

After I got out of high school I moved out west, and I was planning on starting school there. But there was this woman that had been pushing me to model. I didn't want to do it, but when I went west, she said, "Okay, here are the numbers. If you want to try it, call."

So after a couple of months I didn't have any money. I got this stupid job that I hated, working in a T-shirt shop with a horrible, mean boss. So I guess I just thought, "Well, maybe it's not such a bad idea. I could make some money." I called the places and made appointments. Right away I was offered to go to Paris. I think that's what got me interested. I was always anxious to travel.

You go over there, and you don't know a thing about anything. I knew a tiny bit of French from high school, but I couldn't really speak the language. They told you you've got to wear a short skirt to go to this appointment because they want to see your legs. You follow what the other girls do, dress how they dress. We all wore very tight, short, black, little skirts and shoes. They encourage you to dress like this, and then you go out and you're treated terribly by the men.

Some people argue that modeling is exploitation of the woman. For me it was just a way of earning money, it was just a job. I didn't ever think about anything. There are definitely some times when the pictures are really sleazy. There were also a lot of sleazy photographers that try very hard to get you to take your clothes off and tell you that you'd look really beautiful in a topless shot.

You have to learn that when a guy says this, he's not saying it because he's nice, he's saying it because he's a sleazeball and he wants to sleep with you. You have to learn how to dress so that people don't harass you. You just have to learn not to be so naive and not to think that people are nice all the time because they want to take you out to dinner or whatever. At first, you get over there and you don't have any money and somebody offers to get you dinner, and you're like, "Sure, I'm hungry," so you go. You don't realize what you're getting yourself into.

Photographers—some of them are nice and normal, but the majority just want something. They aren't necessarily going to ask you to sleep with them, but just the way they look at you, you can tell that they want to sleep with you. They're fine, they're nice, but they're all looking for a girlfriend, and you get tired of always being threatened. You have to change your clothes all the time, and you can just feel people looking at you. You want to run and hide, but you can't—you have to change your clothes right there, in front of everybody. You've gotta put another outfit on, and there's all these people that are helping, and you don't have a little bathroom that you can go and change in, you just change. When you're shooting outside, they have the clothes in the location van, and it's like, there's the van and there's the driver, and you get where you don't think about it. You get so used to just taking off your clothes. I don't mean your underwear, but your bra and all the rest of your clothes and putting them back on in front of these people. And you don't realize that some of these people are sleazy.

In the business, most girls, most models, they're like me, naturally skinny. I had a couple of friends that were always dieting. My one girlfriend ate nothing but Japanese noodles. She never lost—she even gained weight. She wasn't at all big, she was just not super skinny—she was just her normal weight. The girls that I was around that worked, most of them never had any problem. It was the girls that weren't getting the work.

There's one girl that I know of who had a nervous breakdown. We all thought that she was bulimic because she was super skinny, and she looked pale and sick almost, and she would go out and just buy boxes of cookies and sit there and eat like the whole box. Her roommate said that she was sure that she threw everything up. I'm sure that there were a lot of other girls like that, too.

I am now very conscious about things that I wear, because I've had so many bad experiences. Like people grabbing you up under your skirt in the subway. People masturbating in front of you. I almost never wear skirts anymore. It's like I don't even want to. If I do, I wear a big coat and only when I'm with my boyfriend.

Women models are paid at least as much as the male models. The market is more for women. I don't think that the men get paid less, but they have less of a chance of getting hired. I had, I guess, one boyfriend that was a male model. The majority of them are very stupid. I think they were treated fine. They're guys, they kinda just talk with the photographer, and, of course, the women aren't going to hit on them. They have to do the job like everyone else, and that's not always enjoyable, but as far as harassment, I don't think that they ever had problems.

When I went to Europe, I was just anxious to make some money and to travel a little bit. And I never liked modeling, I never enjoyed it. I tried hard to like it once I got more into it in Paris, but I never did. I always looked forward to going back to school eventually. My goal was just to save up enough money so I could go to school full-time.

Debbie Jones

She was born in the Deep South in 1969. She lives with a roommate and is the executive director of a state coalition against domestic violence. (See also p. 508)

*W*hen I graduated from college, I went to several job interviews with a major airline. It got to the point in my interview process where they started asking me really personal questions that I know they would never ask a man. They asked me if I was dating anybody, if I had sex or what kind of birth control did I use, whether I was planning to have a family.

The way they treat their flight attendants when you are going through training, it is like you are in a freshman dorm or sorority. They have all of these really ridiculous rules of what kind of jewelry, how you can wear your hair, your makeup. They had curfews, and you had to sign in and out. All this junk that is so backwards and stupid. I was like, this is not worth it for them to manipulate and control me. It turns out that most of the women that worked for the airline are not married or if they are married, do not have any children. It is basically because the airline has threatened them that they would lose their position or their moving up the ladder if they were to get married or have kids. If you want to make it, you are going to live by their rules.

A good friend of mine in college worked for a year in one of the vice presidents' offices, who happened to be a woman. According to my friend, she was very intelligent, a very attractive woman, but she was not married, she had no children, and it was basically because she had dedicated her life to the airline. That is fine if that is what she chose for herself, but I don't think it is right that the airline would push her to the point where they are limiting her choices. They don't do that to the men. So you can look at a situation like that and just automatically think, "Well, gosh, maybe we haven't made any progress." If there is still difference in pay between men and women and restrictions on moving up the ladder because of whether you have a family or not, that is depressing. Maybe we haven't made as much progress as we think. But then again, we have.

I Always Loved the Hospital

Sharon Wiseman

She was born on the West Coast in 1967.

"We're a very medical family—my mom, my father, my grandfather, and my uncle are all doctors. People were talking about medicine around me incessantly, and it felt like a club that I wanted to be a part of. It's really as long as I can remember that I wanted to be a doctor, although there was a period of time in about the second grade where I thought I might want to be a Supreme Court justice."

Her mother, Elana Wiseman, also appears in the book.

When my mom first got divorced, we used to go into work with her every once in a while. I enjoyed the intensity of the hospital and the machines. Then she decided to go back and retrain. She and my stepfather had been married for a year or so, and every fourth night she was on call. We used to go and visit her there quite a bit. More and more if she would go in for rounds, she would take me with her. It was an exciting place to be.

When I was about fifteen, I was talking to somebody, and I said, "I always loved the hospital," and they said, "Oh, I hate being in the hospital, it's terrible!" and it was the first time it ever really occurred to me that people didn't like to be in the hospital. I used to go in with my dad as well as my mom. It was just the place that my parents worked.

One day my mom and I were wandering around, and there were these little drops of blood on the floor. We decided to follow them, and we followed them all the way to the emergency room, where we walked in, and there was this room that was just covered with blood. Somebody had come in, and they had been shot. It was a bizarre thing to do, but we had a great time. And my mom would always introduce me to her patients. I'd look through the charts, and she'd teach me things. We had fun.

My brother and I were very fortunate because both of our parents were professionals and could always afford to have someone in the home. We were never latchkey kids. We never came home to an empty house. We did have quite a number of babysitters. I have this very vivid memory of my brother and a friend of his and I going up into the housekeeper's room and putting on her makeup. And she was absolutely devastated by it for some reason. It was the first and only time we had ever been grounded.

The person who was with us the longest was really the one who was there for my little sister, and she is a wonderful person who we loved to hang out with. She lived with us for many years and then continued to work with us after she moved out. The babysitters that took care of my brother and me were also live-in for the first little while. What my parents used to do, which is really nice, is they would sponsor people who wanted green cards. For the first ten years or so they were almost invariably people from Central America—El Salvadorans and then some Nicaraguans. And then as time went by, my stepfather became involved with the Ethiopian community, so people from Ethiopia worked for us, and a woman from Haiti. The woman from Haiti was really bizarre and towards the end really hated my stepfather, and she actually ended up getting fired, and in her room we found this voodoo doll of him with pins stuck in it! It was really weird.

My parents' custody agreement was that we would spend two months with our father in the summer and then two weeks with him at the winter holiday. He lived on the West Coast, and the rest of the time we'd be with our mother back east. It was especially hard for me to leave my dad because it was always such a long time until we were going to see him again. We were never around during the summer to be with our friends, and we never really went to overnight camp because that would defeat the purpose of being with our dad. I don't think there's a right way, though, to have divorced parents. The people who I've talked to with parents in the same city had a different variety of problems, but it was every bit as problematic.

As a child, I don't think I thought about my mother being a doctor much. Certainly, most of my friends had parents who both worked, and my mother just happened to be a doctor. I don't remember feeling like it was particularly unusual, but her medical school class was six or eight women out of a class of seventy or so. I ended up at the same medical school, and my class was about forty-five : fifty-five, although the year after was thirty : seventy, which is pretty appalling.

Recently at the hospital a male intern said to me, "Sharon, do you think that it's more difficult for you to get along with the nurses than it is for me?" He had not perceived that at all, but somebody had mentioned it to him the week before. It's really a complex issue. I was trying to think about what Deborah Tannen would have to say about it. If you want a patient to get a certain medication, if you want a patient to pee, you write an order, and it is given to the nurse to execute. It seems to me that there's a way in which men have an easier time giving the orders, and it's a little bit easier for the women nurses to hear that from the men. Most of the nurses are women, and the men and women have the addition of flirtation.

I remember once going to the hospital with my mom, and we were sitting there on a surgical floor, and the surgeon who had been on call the night before came up and was just standing around the nursing station, and all the nurses were fawning over him. We both kind of looked at each other and said that it was something that would never happen to us, going up to a nursing station full of male nurses and having them dote and flirt. It's not the sort of experience that women physicians have.

When I was a medical student, as part of my pediatrics rotation, I went down to juvenile hall. Any child who gets admitted to juvenile hall has to have a physical exam, and you have to ask them whether or not they're sexually active. If they say yes, they have to have a test for gonorrhea and chlamydia. Of course, if you ask a teenage boy whether or not they're sexually active, regardless of whether or not they are, they're going to say yes, which is their mistake because nobody really likes to have a cotton swab put into the tip of their penis! But in any event, I had to examine this kid—he was probably seventeen years old. As I put the cotton swab into the tip of his penis, he had an erection. We'd been taught that this is a normal reaction—it will happen whether it's a male physician or a female physician, and you should just tell the patient that. So I said this to him, and he said, "No it's not. It's because I think you're really cute." And I said, "It would happen whether I was a man or a woman," and he said, "No, you're really hot."

It was an odd situation, partly because here I was with admittedly only a seventeen-year-old but somebody who was in juvenile hall because he was a criminal, and I wasn't quite sure how to handle it. The funny thing about it was that I had remembered thinking when I first met him that he had been kind of an attractive seventeen-year-old. It was the first time I'd ever found one of my patients attractive. And then to have this happen, I thought, "Oh, god, what did I do!" It was uncomfortable, but then it was over and it was fine.

It's quite common and all of my women colleagues acknowledge openly that when we walk into a room, people automatically call us "nurse" or call us "girl," and it sort of depends on who the patient is and how they say it whether or not you get pissed off. We all deal with it. What happens with my mom is she goes into the hospital, and if she's not wearing a white coat, she picks up a chart and somebody says, "Who are you? Why are you looking at this chart?"

Just last week I found out that a patient of mine had come in as a walk-in to the clinic and saw a male colleague of mine and told him that she wanted to transfer to a male doctor. I e-mailed my colleague back and said, "Gee, I wonder what it was that I did that bothered her." He said, "No, she really just said that this was the first time she'd ever had a woman doctor, and she just would prefer to have a man." She thought it didn't work out. And I'm sorry that that happened, and I also wonder whether or not there was something specific about me that she didn't like, but I know that I wouldn't go to a male gynecologist, and it's absolutely her prerogative to pick whoever she wants. It bothers me when people feel like women shouldn't be doctors so the only acceptable doctor is a male doctor, but I don't think that's what she was saying. The issue that comes up more than my being a woman is how young I look, and that actually bothers people a bit.

My boyfriend is a professor at the medical school I went to, and we met each other as I was beginning there. I used to go to this home clinic, and he was basically the supervising person there. He was a great teacher, a nice person, and I felt like he was a faculty member who I'd really gotten to know. Then he started asking me out.

It took me a while to actually start to think about him in a role other than being my professor. And for a while I was upset with him because I thought, "I don't think there's going to be a way for me to not go out with you and still have us be able to be friends in the way that we have been, and I think our working relationship will really change." And then he was really perseverant. Over the course of six months we started to do more and more stuff together. We became good friends, and it developed into a relationship. So it did eventually work out. I was a student on the rotation that he was the attending of, so it was a little bit weird, and we had to keep it secret. It would have been very awkward if I hadn't ended up being interested in him.

Having a family is something I think about now. It's not something I just want in the abstract, I would really like it. I think the way my mom did it worked pretty well—actually, my mom and my stepfather—to be willing to spend the money to have somebody be with your kids. My boyfriend is quite a bit older than I am, and he actually feels like he's not all that far off from taking early retirement, so he jokes about being the househusband. I think equal responsibility is terrific, but I don't think I would want to ask somebody to take more responsibility than I was taking. But if he decides that's what he really wants to do, I would feel perfectly comfortable with it.

I hardly think I'm a perfect person, but I don't think any of my issues stem from the fact that my mother decided to go back to work right after having me. I just don't think it's reasonable to say that a woman shouldn't work. Maybe there are ways in which kids who had mothers who were home all the time had a more—I don't even know—well-adjusted growing experience, but it's sort of moot.

I remember feeling sort of odd about the fact that when my little sister was born, there was a while where she called one of the housekeepers mom. I don't know why, but it really bothered me. But I don't feel like that's had any significantly negative impact at all. And my mother got home in good time. She was almost always home at six-thirty. It wasn't like she was burning the midnight oil in the office.

As a woman, I don't feel like a second-rate citizen. It doesn't surprise me that someone of my mom's generation would. In some ways, she's a little hypersensitive about it; in other ways, she was made to feel that way. But I've gotten very positive feedback. It's nice that there would be that change. I certainly support the efforts to better women's rights and women's role in the workplace. It is something that I support on behalf of other people because I just don't feel like my life has been particularly adversely impacted by being female. I don't feel like I'm earning sixty-nine cents on the dollar or whatever it is these days relative to my male counterparts because it's just not true. And I did get into medical school and there were just as many women as men. I didn't have any personal experience that made feminism relevant to me. I must be very fortunate in that regard.

A Matter of Choosing

Lisa DiCiccio

She is Italian-American and was born and raised in the Bronx. At the time of the interview, she was seventeen years old.

"My father is a plumber, and my mother worked in a furniture company until I was born."

I don't want to have a man supporting me. I want to do it myself. I definitely want to go to college, and I want to be in the F.B.I., a cop or something. My mother doesn't want me to, but that's what I want to do. Have a career. That's the most important thing for me now. I like school. People call me a nerd.

In third grade I was like, "I want to be a cop," and my mother was like, "Why do you want to be cop for? It's dangerous," but if my brother were to say that, I know she'd be like, "Well, well well." And once I said I wanted to be a fireman—I said that a couple months ago—and my mother said, "You can't do that. All the guys in there, they'll be all mean to you, and you're a woman, you can't go into fires." I get very mad.

I want to get married, but sometimes I see like how it happened with my mother. Divorce. I want to make sure it's right. Marriage, it would be important to me but it wouldn't be the first thing on my mind. After I finish school and get everything started with my career, if I'm settled into it, if I'm making enough money, I would want to have kids. Probably not until I'm in my late twenties. Taking care of them and teaching them values and stuff, that's why I want to have a kid. Having someone to love. I think me and the father should have equal time with the kid; it shouldn't be all put on me. He's the father, he should contribute to that. I know it'll be hard to manage work and children, but I would just wait until I think the time is ripe.

I wouldn't want to stay home with my children and be financially supported by my husband. I just don't see the reason for somebody having to depend on someone else to get what you need. If you can do it yourself, you can do it. I wouldn't want to be stuck at home just taking care of the kids and that's all I'm going to be doing for the rest of my life. The kids are going to grow up and then what are you going to have? You're going to have nothing. If I'm making money for myself, I'd feel better about myself.

Annabelle Diaz

She was born to a Puerto Rican family in New York City in 1974.

I always wanted to be a lawyer. I'm not really good in math; I'm good in history and things like that, so something that I was good at, I figured I would go for. I have kind of a big mouth and I'm talkative, so I figured this might be the thing for me.

I applied to only one college and I went, but I was paying for my own college so it's hard. I wasn't getting enough financial aid because they say my mother makes too much, so I decided to take a semester off. I couldn't pay, and I didn't want to take a loan out. Next semester I'm going back.

I plan to get married. I don't want kids for maybe ten years. After we have a house and I'm a lawyer already, I might adopt. I don't even know if I want to have my own kids. My mother dropped out of junior high school, and my father had dropped out, too. My mother wasn't able to do a lot of things because she had kids early. Everything my mother didn't do is what I want to do!

Ilene Connolly

She is a graduate student in biology at a large university on the West Coast. She was born in the Midwest in 1965. "We lived in a working class town right on the lake. My father was a fourth grade teacher. I am basically Caucasian although my grandma was a quarter American Indian."

*M*y mom never worked, but I always thought that I would. I liked biology from a very early age. I can remember deciding I wanted to do something in science. I guess I always knew I would go to college, and I really wanted to leave the Midwest. So I went far away. I was the first kid in my family to leave the state to go to college. I really did a radical thing. My younger sister actually did, too; she followed me out.

I knew I wanted to get married. In my early twenties I decided that I would probably like to have kids. When you're younger you think, "Oh, I can do whatever, and it's not going to be a matter of choosing because women can have whatever they want." Then the older you get, the more you realize that not just with that issue but with everything, you've got to compromise, and you've got to decide what you want and what you are willing to do to get it.

So here I am starting my second year of grad school and trying to figure out if I want to keep doing it. It's a possibility that I won't. It's another four years, and I think academics isn't the greatest career for a woman who wants to have a family. The farther on you go, the more time you're expected to spend in the lab, and postdocs are even more work than graduate school, and the first three or four years of a tenure-track position are more work than postdoc. I took five years off between college and grad school, and I'm planning to have kids around thirty-four or thirty-five years old, so just when I want to have kids is when I'm going to start hitting the grind. And I don't know if it is the kind of life I want, you know.

I like to do a lot of things, and people who seem to be really successful have blinders on. They're just moving through the science career, and so the more I know of it, the less I think it might be for me. I think that science twenty years ago was great, and twenty years ago it was all men whose wives took care of the kids and the house. I know older guys whose wives edit their journals. If you want to be really good in science, a lot of the times you either have no other life or you've got an extremely supportive spouse who does everything else to keep the family together. So it is a two-person career with one person getting all the glory, I guess.

It's pretty old-boy, and it is not very amenable to a family lifestyle from the women's end. A lot of women drop out in postdoc, and I think it's because they're in their thirties and they are realizing that it is going to be difficult to have kids and get a job and spend time with your family. Some people do it and are very good at organizing their time. I just don't know if the sacrifices are ones I'm willing to make to work in the lab and to be a scientist. I guess I'll figure it out at some point.

I think that as students men are more believed and have more attention paid to them and are taken more seriously than women are. I think a lot of times science can seem kind of trivial or just sort of so self-contained. Men just get their problem and solve it. Women will do that, but they will also sometimes get frustrated with what is the point of what they're doing. I never hear men saying that, but women do.

Janice Borra

Her father is first generation Italian-American and her mother is of Irish origin. She was born in Massachusetts in 1964 and raised in the suburbs of Boston. She attended a prestigious business school and worked as a summer associate in municipal finance at a top-tier investment banking firm. After graduating, she returned to the firm for eighteen months. She lives in New York City with her husband and son.

Nine to nine was the standard day, six days a week, with a few all-nighters and late nights thrown in there. You get to be a bit of an automaton, really used to plugging away most of your day, saying no to all social engagements. Late at night it was kind of nice when everybody left because you couldn't get a darn thing done between nine and five. People would be bugging you, the phone would be ringing. You'd take a break at five, go get a coffee, come back, and kick into it for the long haul. And there was always one other guy who was there late nights with me, and he'd always have his boom box going, and you order out dinner, and it could almost be fun. The hours would pass quickly until you realized that you were so exhausted and didn't have a life and it's affecting your marriage because your husband never saw you anymore.

It was boot camp, and I think in a weird sort of way that women realize that more than men do, and women aren't as hungry as men are, either for money or for professional achievement, and that's why we do self-select out more and other things become more important to us—you just say, "I don't need this. The money isn't that important to me. I'd rather have a family. I'd rather keep my husband." I mean a lot of men there were divorced because it is just such a stress on your family life to work that hard and to travel that much. When you get to be an account officer, you're out soliciting business all the time.

When I was a summer associate, they had gatherings where we met with people from all the different departments—sales and trading, corporate finance—and except for maybe two people out of fifty, they were all white males. Banking is clearly a male-dominated world, and while there are more women in municipal finance, it's at the support level, and it really tapers off as you go up the food chain. It's partially the glass ceiling, and it's partially self-selection.

The men are both sexist and not sexist at the same time. A lot of times people say, "Oh, I need a skirt" because there's a woman client. It's a joke, and sometimes you're the one who says, "Oh, you're only bringing me because you need a skirt, not because you want me to go." And then the sales and trading side is notoriously bad in terms of verbal sexual discrimination, and yet you're perceived to be sort of a Goody Two-Shoes or too legit if you overreact to that. There's always something wrong with the personality of the woman—"Oh, she's too bitchy" or "she's too tough."

I don't think I knew any female associate who'd had a kid. At the top-tier firms you can't have a kid and be in that support position where you've got to kill yourself one hundred hours a week. I knew four guys who were associates and they had kids, but the one woman who did actually have one got laid off in the first round to go. And then the firm decided to get rid of its municipal finance department entirely, and after rounds of layoffs they finally wiped out the whole department. So I got laid off, got pregnant with my son almost simultaneously, and took the next sixteen months off from work. Frankly, I wasn't going to stay in the industry for a long time. I'd sort of done my bit, and I didn't find it that interesting, and I didn't think that the money was worth it in terms of the loss of lifestyle.

After my son was around six months old, I decided that as much as I loved spending time with him, I didn't want to define myself totally in terms of motherhood. I wanted to do something professional, but I didn't want to do it full-time, because I didn't want to make the sacrifice with him. And the one good thing about having been blown up with a whole department full of people is that I had colleagues who were in firms throughout Wall Street at this point, and one segment of these people started up their own investment banking firm to focus on municipal finance. They called me up one day and said, "We're really strapped. We need help, and you can work however many days a week. We'll set you up at home, you can come in, whatever you want." I said okay, and so I've been doing that now since May. I work Monday, Wednesday, and Thursday, and my husband works Tuesday through Saturday—he's a newspaper reporter, and he writes for the Sunday paper. So he takes care of our son on Mondays, and then I have a nanny who comes in two days a week.

I wouldn't trade my situation with either a full-time mother or a full-time working mother. I have a great husband, and I think you really need someone who is equally comfortable taking care of your child as you are, and my husband's almost more so, if that's possible. And he cooks dinner every night, does the laundry and the shopping. I actually think he does more than I do! So that works out well, and I really do think that I have the best of both worlds.

You Made *Law Review*

Jessica Tamler

*She was born in New Jersey in 1970 and raised in a modern Othodox Jewish family. She has re-
mained observant.*

*"My mom was pretty young when I was born; twenty-three I guess. She had been teaching for
a couple years, and she stopped. My dad worked for AT&T, and he still does. I was a twin. My
mom went back to work after three or four years. She taught high school. My house, I guess it wasn't
sexist; it was normal growing up in the seventies. To this day my mom's the one who does all the
housework, and my dad'll pay the bills. That's fine, but I guess I just decided that I didn't want that
role for myself. My twin is a brother, and we were brought up that we could do anything."*

I always wanted a powerful job. I wanted something that made a statement. I never
wanted to be a teacher. In college I worked as a law clerk during the summers, and I
thought it was interesting. I always wanted something that was intellectually challenging
but diverse. I just finished my second year of law school at New York University, so I
only have a year to go. Everything goes very fast. Your second summer job is generally
where you get an offer from and where you go back to after you graduate. I'm going to
clerk for a judge for a year, and then I'll go back to the firm that I'm with now. I've
taken out really large loans, and I have to pay them off. The firm works you really hard,
but they also pay you really well. Big firms basically only represent big companies.
They're the only ones who can afford them. So you're always on the defense unless it's
against another big company. They give you every luxury and expose you to all sorts
of things. But I don't want to stay there for long.

I wish I knew exactly what I wanted to do. I guess I want to work for what I consider the good guys. I always thought that I'd go into public interest straight out, and I
still think I probably will, but I've realized more and more that I have to do something
that's not quite grassroots or not quite individual client level because I found the quality of lawyering to be low. It's just not challenging enough. And that was really disappointing to me, that I couldn't be inspired by that, but I just couldn't, so I'm sure there's
a medium place out there. I just haven't found it yet.

You're called a summer associate when you work between your second and third year of law school. All firms wine you and dine you and show you a great time. Some show you a more practical side of the work experience, and some show you a less practical side. I'm at a firm that shows you the more practical side, and I've actually learned to appreciate it a lot because I might as well know what I'm getting myself into.

I get up early, and I go running. I eat breakfast on the way to work, or I eat there. I'm really productive between eight and ten o'clock. The quiet time is good. I'll either be in the library or doing research on the modem. Then at about ten the attorneys make it in, sit down, have their coffee. I'll get called with, "Oh, what about this?" "What about that?" I put off what I've been working on, which is generally a longer-term assignment and help them out with their one or two little questions. They're going to have a client meeting in a few minutes, or they're about to send out a document and they just thought of some issue and need research or a file on it that I have. If it's a client meeting, that would mean that I'm going to go, and since I'm the lowest person on the totem pole, I generally don't do much at the meeting. But it helps because then I have more of an understanding of the facts, so that when I go to research things, I can more easily apply them.

There are very few female partners. I've been in meetings where it's all male clients, all male attorneys, and me. I'm the youngest one in the room, and I'm female. They'll swear because the deal isn't working the way they want it to, and then they instantly turn to me, the girl in the room, and they say, "Oh, excuse me," and it's like, hello, I've used much worse language than that. It seems to be an age thing, also. The younger men know that they went to school with you and they swore in front of you there, and it didn't offend you, and they heard you swear.

It's interesting to see which women are the partners. I think that is changing. The first woman at the firm where I work to have made partner is incredibly male-like. She wears very masculine type suits, not much color, and she's terrible—everyone knows to stay away from this woman. She's very super aggressive and demanding, and she gives unreal deadlines that no one can make, and she wants her things to be in ship shape, and she wants to be in charge. She doesn't have a family. She's in her late fifties.

The younger female partners are your little wonder women who rush out at seven to see their kids playing softball and then rush back at nine to finish up some project, and they wear frilly things, and they're much more like, "We can be women, and we can be attorneys." The one definite trend is that just about all of them haven't had their children until later. If they didn't wait until they became partner, which is like eight years into their career, so they were in their mid-thirties, they had them just a couple years before. They have surreal lives. They have no idea what it is to cook a meal. They all have nannies. But their litigation style is very different from the men. In big firms, it's very rare that you go to trial. Generally, you do settle. I feel like women give a new tempo to that. They're much more into settling but not in a bad way; they can work together and do things, and it's a little quieter of a tone, as opposed to being so aggressive and hostile. There's definitely women who are aggressive and hostile, but in general, I think that women have added a different dimension to firms, and I think it's good.

Generally, the partner track in big firms is eight years, and by the fifth year a lot of the women have left. These firms start out with a class of forty or fifty, and they only make like three people partner by their eighth year, and although you can stay if you don't make it, there's no real advancement. So by your fifth year you want to know, What are my chances? and if they tell you fifty-fifty, you don't feel secure and you want to try something else, whereas men feel like, "Oh, I can do it. I'll be more aggressive, I'll put it out." It's definitely a time in your life where after working for five years you're considering a family and you just don't know if you want to put in those hours, especially if becoming a partner is not guaranteed. A lot of corporate counsel jobs pay not as well but well, and you have much better hours. I also think it's a time where a lot of women who want to go into public interest feel like now they have the chance to do that.

The male partners at the firm open the door for me, and I'm just like, you would never, ever do that for a male summer associate. If anything the male summer associate should hold the door open for you. They play tennis, and they probably ask the guys to play tennis, but they never ask me. No male partner would ever—or at least has not yet—approached me to say, "Let's go to a bar," but they have approached the guys. They'll take me to lunch, but they can't get beyond the idea that I could even have a beer. We were at this party the other night, and this partner was talking to us, and he was like, "Oh yeah, Craig—do you know how I hired him?" and we were like, "No." Our firm has offices in Japan, and he was the partner in Japan at the time, and he hired this guy there. "He was at the karaoke bar with me, and when I saw him lip-syncing those Japanese songs, I knew he could do it!" I just don't think he would be as impressed if he saw a woman kind of tipsy lip-syncing Japanese songs; I just don't think he would have wanted to hire her.

In my firm, people can now work three or four days a week. They have three months' paid maternity leave. They can have arrangements where they leave at five. The women who go to see their children in plays or baseball games, that's totally tolerated, but when the male goes, it's like, "Isn't he a great dad?" When the female goes, it's like, "Of course she has to go." And no one says, "Oh, she missed this meeting" or "he missed that meeting," but the male still looks better. And then there are jokes about the woman's name—what she wound up doing with it if she's married. If she kept her maiden name, it doesn't affect them, they wouldn't know. If she took on her husband's name, the men certainly don't discuss that, that's fine, also. But if she hyphenated her name, they have problems. They're like, "Oh, such a long name."

My parents encouraged my becoming a lawyer. It's a stable career, and it's something you can do on your own or in a firm. And although I always said that I wanted to go into the nonprofit sector, they saw it as a big money-making thing, and they think that's great. One college professor also encouraged me. Every other professor was totally against it. One professor in particular was completely patronizing. He was like, "You're so good with people. You should be a social worker." I was like, "Why would that be the role for me?" And it turned out that that was a very feminine thing to be and a lawyer wasn't, and he said to me, "Well, you won't be home with your family." I was just like, "Well, I can figure out when I'll be home with my family." It was very disturbing to me. Other people said, "Oh, that's so aggressive" or "Oh, that's so hostile" or "Oh, you wouldn't like that, you're fighting all the time." I'm not very aggressive, but I feel that I have a lot to offer as a lawyer anyway, and if anything it's more to offer because it's a whole other style of lawyering that I definitely believe in and that I think is possible. You can settle disputes without hating your adversary, and, if necessary, you can be mean to them.

My family was always supportive, and only recently, as they've learned the truth about how I'd be working such incredible hours, have they questioned the decision or said things like, "Well, maybe you do want to find something else. You're going to be working too hard." I think for my brother they would have said the same thing. Your first year of law school is very isolating. They call you by your last name, and some professors really try and grill you. It's an ugly experience, and they love to see women flounder.

There are big decisions in criminal law as to if rape will be taught and how it'll be addressed. We had a huge uproar because my professor wasn't very good at it. He always talked about hapless victims and is it possible that these women asked for it. He was terrible, but he's not getting tenure. My classes are generally fifty percent women, although constitutional law and a lot of theory classes are very male dominated. It's really frustrating to a lot of women. There's no way in. A lot of men start off learning it in college, a professor helped them, and it's an inside circle. And it is this very revered part of the law. A lot more women seem to go into practical and clinical areas.

New York University has a lot of female law professors, but I don't think there's a single con law/theory class taught by a woman.

Women rarely if ever raise their hand in class and rarely if ever volunteer the answers. Some teachers try to elicit responses so that they don't have to actually call on you, and even then it was very rare that women, even though they made up fifty percent of the class, participated. There were a few women who sat around and decided, "We are going to raise our hands," and they would do that, but I was not one of them. And I wound up doing very well in law school, and I think people were very surprised, like, "Oh, you made *Law Review?* I never heard you open your mouth." I would only open my mouth if I was called on, and I guess if I did it again, I would do it differently, but I was very insecure. *Law Review* is done by grades, a writing sample, and affirmative action—at N.Y.U. that doesn't include females; in the past few years it's only included minority status. Getting on *Law Review* is an honor, kind of like getting Phi Beta Kappa, but the *Law Review* is a journal. What's published is articles by outside professors and notes, which are articles by students. In the past two years no woman has gotten her note published. It's really lame.

I really don't have any ambition to make partner, and I know that now. At first I thought that if I made partner, my life would be easier. I could start going home at six o'clock. But the worst part is I'm watching people make partner, and they're still there until two in the morning, and I'm just like, "No way." The women who do that put their family second, and you have to, and so do the men. There's a sense that, "Oh, you made it to one of the top law schools in the country, you made it on to *Law Review,* and you're on the senior board, how could you not be completely devoted to this?" There are definitely times where you don't feel comfortable saying, "I totally want to be home more than is typical." I said something like that to people in my class, and they were like, "What are you thinking? That's what you have your nanny for." And I was like, "No, I won't have a nanny raise my children." They've decided that the way to deal with having children and having a career is to say that children are fine between five and seven P.M. on Saturday. When I say that that bothers me, they say, "It bothers all of us, but what are you going to do about it?" and I say, "Well, I am going to do something about it. I'm going to work a different type of day or find a place where I can still have a challenging career but not put in those kinds of hours," and they said, "Oh, good luck, you're not going to find it."

I try to explain that it's important to me to just actually be with my children, and they're like, "To do what?" and I just felt like, "Well, not everything has to be a zoo trip." I tried to explain that my mother was always there for me when the bus came home when I was little, and I don't necessarily want to be there every time to pick up my kids from school, but I just feel like that was a really important part of my development. I think it would be terrible if every day I'd come home to an empty house. And so they said, "Oh no, they won't come home to an empty house. They'll come home to a nanny." And I was just like, "Well, that's true, except that how much emotional support can a nanny give?" and they said, "Oh, she can give a lot," and I said, "Oh, well, then why bother being a mom?"

Creative Ways

Rachel Goldman

She was born in New York City in 1970. "My parents are still married, incredibly enough. They both always worked. They are Jewish, both reform." (See also p. 200)

Being right out of college is really a more complicated thing than anyone ever tells you it's going to be. All of life is on a pretty self-contained schedule up until the time you graduate, and then all of a sudden you say, "Hold on, all of a sudden this is life, and it's not just one more rung." So, the future looks a little fuzzy. I think something that's important for me in any career is looking at the context in which I'd be working. Is it a job where I'll be communicating with people? Where I can use the skills that I have? Is it maintaining my commitment to different political issues?

I just think that I owe it to myself, and I'm very particularly a person of my generation in saying this, to really try out a lot of different things before I commit myself to something. I think that in the past, women either weren't able to make any choices about their career because it wasn't an option for them or they would say, "Okay, I'm good at this. This has to take over my whole life because it's so hard for women to get into this field." They were right in thinking that, but I very much have benefited from a lot of women that have come before me in being able to say, "Well, maybe I'll do this for two years and find that I don't like it." So I'm definitely in flux careerwise.

I don't know about marriage. I just really have never thought about it. But I know that I'd want to have children at some point. I mean, zero population growth notwithstanding. I just think that, what a wonderful thing, to have children, to bring people into this world and see them happen. But I think that this whole supermom thing is so impossible and such a total way of keeping women crazy. I would want to either be in a career that was a little more flexible or be at a point in my career where I could feel comfortable about having kids. It's so heartbreaking to see women who are just totally crazed by the constraints of working and having children. It would be important to me to have a supportive partner if I did have children. So much of this supermom thing is based on the idea that women should be doing all the work and that men are totally let off the hook, and I'm not interested in living that in my life. Saying to women, "Well, you can go out and work and you can do all the work on the kids" is really not a great deal. Men have to be revolutionized to thinking it's not just cute if they pick up the kids one day a week—it's their kids. That's really the only equitable way of having a family with two people who work outside of their home.

I always thought I'd have a career. For as many problems as women face today, I think we are very fortunate in having the expectation that we have the right to do things that we want to do, and I think that that's a huge and tremendous thing that I would never underestimate in thinking about myself. I don't know if what's important is a career in a really rigid sense, like, "I'm going to go to law school. I'm going to be a lawyer for my whole life." I just think that what's important to me is looking at myself as having a lot of different parts and really trying to be attentive to everything that is a part of me. A hundred years ago a woman might be a genius, but that didn't matter if she couldn't bake bread.

I don't think I'd be happy just taking a few years off and primarily being a homemaker, but I don't think that any women really are only homemakers. I think that things that we put in the role of being homemakers could just as easily be put another way, but because they are roles ascribed to women, they get totally devalued. Women can be community organizers. They can be on the PTA. There are so many things that women do that we say, "Oh, she's just a housewife." Women who work full-time for the PTA—I mean, that's serious work.

I don't think I'd be happy being totally directed in the home. I do think it will always be important for me to have some kind of job outside of the enormous job of being a mother.

Janey Desroschers

At the time of the interview she was twenty-two years old and pregnant with her first child.
"My dad was born in Indonesia. I was born here in California in 1971. I am a Christian."

I've been married for almost two and a half years. I've always had it in my mind since I was little of being a mother, getting married and having a family. If financially it was possible, I would probably like to just stay home and do it the old-fashioned way and raise the kids. We'll see what happens.

I graduated from high school, and I took a few college courses. I work at a publishing company. My husband is a technician for Xerox, and he is a musician on the side.

My job is full-time. Right now it looks like I'll probably go back to work after the baby. The company I work for prints pricing manuals for contractors and sailors. We get price books in from manufacturers of heaters and air conditioners and things like that, and we have a big service book which we have all the products in, so we will update the prices as it changes. Basically, the day is just that; pricing comes in, and we stand at our computer and put in the new pricing, and on pages we paste the pictures. It goes slow sometimes, and sometimes it gets real busy.

My department has about fourteen people. The majority of them are women. We are getting more men in there now. There is a wide variety of people and attitudes. Often people clash. It can be interesting at work sometimes. Where I sit there are four of us, two women and two men. I get along fine with my coordinators, but the other two are kind of different.

It's going to be hard when the baby comes. My mother-in-law does day care, so the baby will probably go to her. But hopefully in a few years we'll have another one, and then maybe I'll get to stay home. My mother-in-law's day care makes me feel better than having to go out and look for a stranger. At least there is a little more comfort that the family will be there. We haven't really discussed the money issue with her. But even if she did not want us to pay her because she is family, I don't want to take advantage of her. If we took the baby anywhere else, we would have to pay. That is her time.

I hope my husband will be there for the kids more than my father was. It would be a nice change for me if it were financially possible, either for mothers or fathers, where there would be a parent at home. Or that desire maybe, too. People have lost that desire to be there for their kids and to know them. Not to just be there to put food on the table.

Crystal Romero

She is a twenty-seven-year-old career counselor living in Southern California. She was born in the Philippines but came to the United States when she was a baby.

When I was younger, the games that I used to play were very career oriented. My mom didn't work outside the home, so I didn't have a model for it, but I'm sure that I was always encouraged and pushed and told that I could do whatever. In eighth grade I would play public relations. I would have all my favorite stars, and I would be the one that would control when people could come in and talk to them. I remember I had a little basket with a little folder on what times everybody could come and see the stars. It was very organizational. I like to do things, I like to plan things, I like to organize things.

I always thought I wanted to be a psychologist. My father was a psychiatrist, and my mom has a master's in psychology. I guess I found I didn't like it. Going so far inside really didn't interest me. Sitting around and talking to someone about a really tough time that you are having, I know that is important, but I didn't want to be the one on the other side. What is interesting, though, is that I like that aspect of sitting down and talking to someone one-on-one. Someone enters the office, you close the door, you have the privacy and the opportunity to really work with someone that way. I'm really fortunate that in the past year and a half I've been able to get something that I've wanted for a very long time, and that is a job as a career counselor.

Most people in career counseling are women. I know a lot about the business world. I do a lot of research in it. I know that sometimes when I work with someone, they are kind of surprised because they think that counseling is a hand-holding experience, and it is not. The most success that I have with students, for some reason, is with male business students. Those are the ones that relate to me the most and that I relate to the most. I never thought that would be the case, but we speak the same language. I'm talking very direct and I'm being very assertive. They want that. And they didn't realize that they were going to get it from me. So it works.

I'm teaching a communications writing course to navy personnel at the end of this month. It is an eight-hour class, and I've never done it before, and I'm scared. These are sheet-metal workers in the aircraft industry. I'm talking with them about something that they could probably care less about because it is mandatory training for them. I'm young, I'm Asian, and I'm female. The whole thing on what do you wear and how you present yourself. I have to remember not to be too animated when I speak.

I'm very conscious of being an Asian woman. I remember meeting someone once a couple years ago who obviously didn't know what he was talking about, but he said something like, "Oh, I've never met any other Asian women with a master's degree in education." It was really odd. He thought he was trying to compliment me by saying, oh, you'll have it easy in the job market.

All of my mentors are women, actually, because I think being female is not something that tends to work in my favor, and I want to be with women because they know what it is like out there. Last year for part of the graduate program you actually had to put in hours out of site doing counseling in your field. Rather than go to a university, which would have been really easy for me to do, I chose to do military career counseling because I thought, if I can do that, I can do anything. They see women as seamstresses, behind cash registers, or as prostitutes out on the bases.

I remember one guy right off telling me, "I have a problem working with you because you are my kid's age." I'm sure all the other stuff applied, too, but he took it on the age. I said, "Thank you for telling me that right off, so that we wouldn't have to play a facade where you are not trusting me and I'm not helping you and then ten minutes later you say I can't do this." I knew I knew my stuff, but it was one of those things where I had to win him over. An hour and a half later he was telling me, "Oh, the military should hire you."

When I graduated from college six years ago, I was one of those people that said, "I don't want to work nine to five, Monday through Friday." Everyone said that. But I was really serious. It's a Thursday, and I don't go to work today because I didn't feel like it. I'm doing a presentation tomorrow in Los Angeles. I like having a day just to process or even just to have a day that's mine. A lot of people don't have that luxury. I don't have to answer to anyone. The fact that I can control my time is very important.

People are just like, "How could you do that?" but again it's been a few years in the planning. I put myself through graduate school, and that took two years. But it really paid off. I took a six-week vacation in Hawaii last year with my boyfriend. Not too many jobs give you that at twenty-seven, and it was a paid vacation. I feel like I'm very fortunate in the fact that I just realized, from here I can only go up. I felt like for so long I hustled to try to get through graduate school, to read all those papers and do everything at the same time that I'm working. Sometimes I stop and think, "Wow, I don't feel like I'm working as much." I'm doing more, but I don't feel like, "Oh, my gosh, I'm so exhausted."

I hope it becomes more than just a few people that work the way that I work, where you have a flexible schedule. Doing the sort of employment research that I do, I'll hear things every now and then about companies that will let you share a job. At my university we have four women that are doing that, where two women share the same job. One comes in from eight to twelve, the other one comes in from twelve to four. They both have young children at home. What is even better is one of the pairs of women actually take turns with the kids.

On-site day care is something that I'm very much an advocate of. I don't see myself doing career counseling for college students forever. I love to do it now because

I'm near their age. One of the things that I'd like to work towards in the future are human resource–type issues like on-site day care, job sharing for women, flexibility in schedules for women. Things like that really concern me.

I don't think that men in our generation just want to go off and be the work warriors. They never really got to know their own fathers. It would be nice to have a father where his work schedule is flexible. If I had to work from eight to twelve, he doesn't have to go in until one. Maybe that means he would work later that day, or maybe he works at home. I think there are creative ways to do it.

The hope and dream of getting married and having kids is not just up to me. If you want to be a career counselor, who has to do all the work? You do. But if you want to be a wife and mother, it's not just you who calls the shots. I think that is where I have to sit back and just kind of say, "Okay, I have to trust this man that I'm with and know that he is going to get to a place where he is ready for that." I have no idea when it is going to happen. At twenty-seven I just had dinner with two friends the other night for my friend's birthday. She turned twenty-six. The other friend of mine was twenty-eight. None of us are in any sort of mode where we can see ourselves having kids in the next three years. That was really interesting because by this age our moms had had their children already. It was sort of weird to think, "When does that happen?"

Didi Bowen

She was born in the Southwest in 1965. She is African-American.

"My parents were together. We had a comfortable life. My sister and I would excel. We were always encouraged, rewarded, and complimented."

When I realized I was pregnant, I went to the doctor and I had tests, and I was like, "Look, I know I'm early, I'll come back later, I'm not even late yet. I just thought maybe I should check it out." I was trying to run out the door. I was afraid. I knew I was pregnant. He came back with this plus sign. I couldn't breathe, and he was like, "But you knew that." And he took it real light, and I was like, whoa! All of a sudden I was just incredibly amazed at having life in me. I had the biggest smile on my face.

I did not plan it, I had no idea I was maternal, and I didn't want to marry this guy. It was relatively young in our relationship. But I've always felt very capable. So I was like, "Well, this is a beautiful thing, and I don't want to destroy this. I'm going to do this." I walked out of the doctor's office and immediately went down and registered for my master's in business. I figured, I need an MBA if I'm going to support this child. I finished my MBA in nine months. I had to appeal before the board every month and ask them to double up on course work, and I had to give them a reason why, and they had to vote on it. And I got it done in nine months, because I wanted to.

Emotionally, I separated from the child's father because he wanted me to have an abortion. He was like, "Well, let me just give you some money for child support," and I was like, "If you don't want to help me, you don't have to give me your money." He was like, "This is what I want to do, what's right, and what I need to do." He gave me money, and then seven months into my pregnancy he called and said he wanted to go to Lamaze. And we hadn't spoken for five months. Our relationship had ended over the disagreement about the pregnancy. He really wanted to talk to me. His ex-wife had wanted to move back with him, and they started living together. He said he wanted to be a part of our child's life.

He pays for her school, which is about $350 a month. We're really cooperative. We are committed to helping each other. We don't have a formal visitation, but my daughter spends about two days a week with him. He and his wife have a son now who's ten months younger than my daughter. We're all very friendly, and everybody loves everybody. I live with another single mother, and she's a real friend. She's a secretary. Most single parents seem to be secretaries. It's unfortunate how the work world treats single parents.

I used to be so macro-oriented, like I wanted to go and develop countries and help economies function more efficiently and work with women cooperatives and help them, but now my focus is so much more micro-oriented because I have a family, and that's my priority. All of my energies are going into my home, and that's why I chose the career I did, because it allows me the flexibility to be a mother. I take that more seriously now than my career. I think it's the biggest challenge. It's really hard.

I'm a financial planner. I deal with investment and insurance. I work with small businesses and families. I go to homes, do interviews, find out what their goals are, what current programs they're participating in, what levels they can afford, how to manage their resources. I have an office downtown, but I don't really need an office. I've got a fax machine and a car phone and a laptop computer—I'm pretty self-contained. One of the companies I work for provides me with a secretary and ongoing training. There's a lot of training involved.

I'm dealing with a lot of people who have traditional values, because those people have money. Why should they trust me? I'm a young black female. What reason in the world do they have to trust me? But I'm making a good living for myself and my daughter. It doesn't seem to be a problem. They have no real reason to trust me, but they do.

The work world should be ordered differently for women. Especially in home economics. When I'm working, I go out and I say, "Do you need life insurance?" and women will say, "Yeah, put some on my husband." "What do you mean, 'put some on your husband'? What do you do for a living?" "Well," she'll say, "I stay home with the kids. I don't bring home the bread." "Well, you don't bring home the bread, but he couldn't bring home the bread if he didn't have you staying home with the kids. You provide an economic benefit to this household, as well. So we need some insurance on you." I think the whole mentality should be different. And I'm a feminist, yes I am.

Other countries, like Sweden, are so much more ahead than we are in terms of the workplace accommodating parenthood—totally give you like six months off work and give you your job back and pay you. Granted, it's a socialist sort of situation, but, come on, we can at least go in that direction. We have to. We're not using our resources efficiently.

I think the movement where women had to do everything the men did, I hope that's dead, because that's stupid. That's like men are better, and we have to measure up. I don't like that attitude. A lot of women are still stuck there. And I think that sometimes the feminist movement in the way that we've expressed it here in this country is not necessarily appropriate in other countries, in other areas. Like Africa, for instance, where 80 percent of the workforce is female, and yet they don't make any of the decisions in their communities. That's a totally different feminist issue, a totally different scenario, so it needs to be explored differently.

People sometimes say to me, "How do you identify yourself? Are you a black Christian female, are you American, are you a Christian black female American, American female black"—and it's like, "Don't ask me to order it. I'm just all of that, but don't ask me to put it into words." My experience has been that I'll talk to someone who's not black, and their issue will be women's issues, and mine will be race issues. Because I've been more affected that way. So I'm a feminist but not necessarily first—that's not the biggest thing.

I think the women's movement was very important, totally important. I have so many more opportunities. Just as the civil rights movement has done so much for me in terms of access, the feminist movement has given me so much access, too. I mean, sure we had to start from that point where we were trying to do what the men did because we had to start from somewhere. That's where we were at, but we've come a long way.

Sometimes I'm scared that feminism is dying, like I called one of my insurance companies that I broker for, and the answering machine—I got a voice mail, and it was like, "Our service girls are not available right now." I was like, "'Our service girls'?" So the first thing I said was, "You know, I doubt very seriously that you have any girls working for you. Number one, you have a lot of women working for you, and, more importantly, I'm sure you've got some men there doing some service work, as well. You've got to do something about that message." That throws us back about two generations at least. Gosh, it scares me in the same way that the hatred surrounding all the prejudice out there scares me.

But I've made decisions, like having my child and feeling confident that I could support her. I had access to get a job and to provide enough to support her, at least that I could work toward it. And maybe I wouldn't be able to successfully accomplish it, but at least I had access, and I had a chance. I don't think that would have been the case in the past. The other thing is athletics. I always felt that I could excel, and that it was a girl thing, too—it was cool. I want my daughter to know that she can do whatever she aspires to do and I'm never going to raise her to depend on anyone.